THE DEFEAT OF THE DAMNED

The Destruction of the Dirlewanger Brigade at
the Battle of Ipolysag, December 1944

DOUGLAS E. NASH SR.

CASEMATE

Philadelphia & Oxford

Published in the United States of America and Great Britain in 2023 by
CASEMATE PUBLISHERS
1950 Lawrence Road, Havertown, PA 19083, USA
and
The Old Music Hall, 106–108 Cowley Road, Oxford OX4 1JE, UK

Copyright © 2023 Douglas E. Nash Sr.

Hardcover Edition: ISBN 978-1-63624-211-8
Digital Edition: ISBN 978-1-63624-212-5

A CIP record for this book is available from the British Library

Printed and bound in the United Kingdom by CPI Group (UK) Ltd, Croydon, CR0 4YY
Typeset in India by DiTech Publishing Services

For a complete list of Casemate titles, please contact:

CASEMATE PUBLISHERS (US)
Telephone (610) 853-9131
Fax (610) 853-9146
Email: casemate@casematepublishers.com
www.casematepublishers.com

CASEMATE PUBLISHERS (UK)
Telephone (0)1226 734350
Email: casemate-uk@casematepublishers.co.uk
www.casematepublishers.co.uk

Cover image: Oskar Dirlewanger (French L. MacLean); collar insignia (author's collection).

Contents

To my wife Jill DeForest Nash for inspiring me to pursue my dream of becoming an author and suggesting the title for this book

Foreword

With the publication of this book, Colonel Doug Nash, United States Army Retired, has become the finest author in the US concerning the *Waffen-SS*. That is a tough mountain to climb, because for years British and German authors owned the subject (although French authors are coming on strong). Dr. Charles W. Sydnor Jr. first showed that Americans could excel writing about the subject, when in 1977 he hit a home run with *Soldiers of Destruction* about the *3. SS-Panzer-Division Totenkopf*. Jay Hatheway wrote on the SS Officer Schools. Waitman Wade Beorn, from Virginia, has written numerous books on aspects of the *Waffen-SS*, as has Jeff Megargee. For years, Mark Yerger—from Pennsylvania—produced a dozen books, using close contacts with *SS* veterans, through whom he was able to access private archives. Many are biographies in nature, with interesting nuggets of information on every page.

However, Colonel Nash has now written seven books in which *Waffen-SS* troops were major combatants. That is quite a feat, but perhaps more importantly, his breadth of knowledge and presentation cover not only personalities, but also combat operations, equipment, and organizational subjects within each book.

What is most important about these works, in my opinion, is that they touch on several complex relationships involving the *Waffen-SS* in Nazi Germany that perhaps we should remind ourselves of—especially as we begin consuming this latest book about the *Waffen-SS* Dirlewanger Brigade during the battle of Ipolysag in Hungary in December 1944.

First, Nazi Germany was a labyrinth of organizational fiefdoms from 1933–45 that dwarfed Byzantine complexity. There may have only been one *Führer*, but there were thousands of "little Adolfs" out there—all carving out their own niches of power through bureaucracies of all shapes, sizes, and responsibilities. And despite the images of "Teutonic efficiency," Adolf Hitler wanted it that way—even though it would lead to immense inefficiency that contributed to Germany losing the war. This did not spawn from a lack of knowledge about how to run a complex military, political, economic, and security apparatus—which Germany certainly was—but was rather to cause a fragmentation of supremacy, so that no rival of Hitler could amass enough power to cause a tipping point in who actually ran the *Reich*.

When Hitler ferally sensed that such an imminent hazard was about to emerge, he struck without mercy. The clearest example was, of course, "The Night of the

Long Knives," a three-day terror in 1934 of political extrajudicial executions to consolidate his power and alleviate the concerns of the German military about the role of Ernst Röhm and his "Brownshirts." Hundreds died, including Röhm. Four years later, "The Blomberg–Fritsch Affair" effectively put the German Army in its place. First, War Minister (and Army Field Marshal) Werner von Blomberg—who had been "all-in" on the downfall of Ernst Röhm—had the misfortune to marry a younger woman after his first wife died. Not that a second marriage was frowned upon in Germany—but one by a field marshal to a prostitute certainly was. Hitler was informed of the situation by cheery subordinates and ultimately received Blomberg's resignation. To further neuter the German Army, a month after Blomberg's departure, Heinrich Himmler and Reinhard Heydrich of the *SS* dusted off an old file on the commander in chief of the German Army, Colonel-General Werner von Fritsch, that accused him of homosexual behavior. Von Fritsch soon resigned, protesting his innocence as he walked out the door.

What these dismissals caused, along with the rise in numbers of the *Waffen-SS*, beginning in 1940, was at least a whispered dislike by senior German Army officers of the *SS*, which included the *Waffen-SS*. To be sure, German Army personnel were glad in some respects to see *Waffen-SS* units roll into their sector, as many were well-armed (Dirlewanger being one of the exceptions.) But historically, Germany had one army and now the Fatherland had two—maybe more if you count the paratroop units and several high-powered mechanized units like the *Hermann Göring Division* that were *Luftwaffe* troops (another Byzantine fragmentation of effort).

In many cases, the German Army officer caste looked down on *Waffen-SS* officers, disparaging their experience, manner of selection, and whether they were of the appropriate officer caste. The *Waffen-SS*, while tactically subordinate to the Army, had its own command and control channels and effectively answered to Himmler. German Army officers were, in general, much better educated and had at least graduated from secondary school (what we would term high school). As for *Waffen-SS* troops, Army officers often felt that overall, most *SS* troops suffered from a combination of recklessness and lack of training. And these feelings were not only from a professional competence perspective.

Post-war, senior *Waffen-SS* generals went through tortuous explanations, separating those *SS* personnel who served in concentration camps or *Einsatzgruppen* from those who were truly combat soldiers and fought at the front. That was simply not accurate. Examining almost 1,000 *SS* officers that served at concentration camps, we find that six would go on to command *Waffen-SS* divisions; 14 would receive the Knight's Cross; and at least 419 have documentary proof of *Waffen-SS* service as well as in the camps. The murder of Jews in Germany and occupied Europe was not a total secret. Most German Army officers, in my opinion, had general knowledge of who was disappearing and who was doing the killing.

Having said that, the *SS* was not a monolithic organization, and rivalries within the *SS* adversely affected the *Waffen-SS*, especially the Dirlewanger Brigade, which had started as a battalion, and would end up as the *36. Waffen-SS-Division* of perhaps 7,000 men. Some of Dirlewanger's soldiers came from concentration camps, so he had to deal with camp administrations. Others came from the *Strafvollzugslager* (penitentiary camp) *der SS und Polizei* in Danzig-Matzkau, administered by the *Waffen-SS*. However, it appears that some of the commissioned officers (lieutenant and above) seem to have been assigned to Dirlewanger not because of their criminal past—but for six–twelve-month tours of duty from administrative jobs back at *SS* headquarters in Berlin and other parts of Germany. They could get some "combat" time, maybe pick up an Iron Cross and an Anti-Partisan Badge, and then return to their old job with some front-line stories.

Dirlewanger's "guardian angel," *SS-Obergruppenführer* Gottlob Berger, was the head of the *SS* Main Leadership Office in Berlin, which concerned itself with all administrative, recruitment and training for the whole *SS*. In Poland, Dirlewanger ran afoul of *SS-Obergruppenführer* Friedrich-Wilhelm Krüger, the Higher *SS* and Police Leader (HSSPF East) (*Höherer SS- und Polizeiführer*) in the part of German-occupied Poland called the General Government; Krüger reported directly to Heinrich Himmler. All the above can be summed up by the following single sentence, as I discovered after writing a 292-page book on Oskar Dirlewanger:

> It is an enduring lesson that a military unit, formed under an evil ideology, led by a social outcast and composed of vicious criminals, will sink to its lowest common denominator—hate.

COLONEL FRENCH MACLEAN, US ARMY (RET.),
FORMER INSPECTOR GENERAL FOR THE US ARMY IN EUROPE
AND COURSE DIRECTOR, NATIONAL WAR COLLEGE, WASHINGTON, DC

Author's Note

Until three years ago, I had no intention of writing this book. Having read all of the available history about the *Sondereinheit Dirlewanger* (the Dirlewanger Special Unit) written nearly 20 years ago, it seemed to me to be a subject unworthy of any further examination. After all, what could one learn further about this band of Nazi *Schutzstaffel* (*SS*) ne'er-do-wells than what had already been written? I was certain that it was nothing more and nothing less than a band of criminals paroled from concentration camps to hunt partisans and murder innocent civilians. I simply could not believe that a band of predatory *Landsknechts* (16th-century German mercenary bands) led by such a notorious criminal could have been a part of the *Waffen-SS*, a military organization I had once admired in my youth before I had begun to study it more critically as an adult.

What changed my mind were some documents I read while conducting research for Casemate's Volume II of my trilogy *From the Realm of a Dying Sun* concerning the attempts by the *IV. SS-Panzerkorps* to relieve the beleaguered garrison of Budapest during January 1945. As I read reports contained in the war diary of *Heeresgruppe Süd* (*H. Gr. Süd*, Army Group South) to get a sense of what had occurred in Hungary prior to the city's encirclement, to my surprise the title *Sturmbrigade Dirlewanger* kept turning up. Even more astonishing was the fact that this unit had been committed to fight in the front line, and not merely against partisans and innocent civilians in the rear areas as it once had, but against powerful elements of the Red Army.

In these same records, I next learned the name of a Hungarian town I had never heard of before either—Ipolysag, better known today by its Slovak name, Šahy. What was more, I read that this *SS* brigade, an enlarged version of the regiment that had murdered its way through Warsaw during August and September 1944, was alleged to have contributed to Budapest's predicament by its spectacular inability to hold its defensive positions, and was also involved in one of the largest mass desertions of German troops in World War II. What followed was the near-collapse of the German defensive line north of the Danube River and the diversion of no fewer than three *panzer* divisions to do what they could to set things right. Their absence at a critical moment ensured that the Third Ukrainian Front, attacking south of Budapest, was able to surround the Hungarian capital from that direction and link up with the Second Ukrainian Front attacking from the north.

I had also not expected to learn about the near destruction of Dirlewanger's brigade during the second half of December 1944. Although I did not have an opportunity at that moment to delve more deeply into the official records of *H.Gr. Süd*, it had aroused my curiosity and desire for later study. What was *this* unit doing there? Why was it in the front lines in the first place? How did it grow so quickly after sustaining grievous losses in Warsaw, merely two short months before its commitment to battle at Ipolysag? Did it actually commit, as alleged, more than its share of mistakes that led to the slow-motion disaster that ultimately resulted in the loss of Budapest?

Fully committed to completing the last two volumes of my trilogy, I mentally shelved these questions until I had completed my project. When this was done by the spring of 2021, I began gathering material in earnest from a variety of sources to answer these questions. I soon realized that there was a story here to tell—one that has never fully been told before. It is a story of how a *Strafeinheit* (punishment unit) composed of the damned, the demoralized, and the dregs of the *Wehrmacht*, *Waffen-SS*, and Hitler's concentration camps made a stand against a tank army of the Soviet Union and failed spectacularly, being very nearly annihilated in the process.

That this result should have been clearly foreseen by the *Wehrmacht* before the Dirlewanger Brigade was sent off to fight in Hungary is a black mark not only against the leadership and military judgement of *H.Gr. Süd*, but also against the *Oberkommando des Heeres* (*OKH*, German Army High Command) as well as Heinrich Himmler, who had himself authorized the creation of the *Sondereinheit Dirlewanger* four years earlier and approved its expansion into a brigade. All of these events and personalities, and more, have been critically examined in the book you hold in your hands. I hope that the need to create this kind of military unit will never occur again, just as I hope that a conflict on the scale of World War II will never happen again either; but with the conflict in Ukraine that began on 24 February 2022 continuing to claim its share of victims, and with large numbers of prison inmates being enrolled into Yevgeny Prigozhin's Wagner Group mercenary army to fight for Vladimir Putin's Russia, my hopes might be in vain.

Introduction

One of the most notorious yet least understood bodies of troops that fought on the side of the Third Reich during World War II was the infamous *Sondereinheit Dirlewanger*. Formed initially as a company-sized formation in June 1940 from convicted poachers under the command of *Obersturmführer* (*Ostuf.*, First Lieutenant) Oskar Dirlewanger, one of the most heinous criminals in military history, it was initially used to guard the Jewish ghetto in Lublin and support local security operations carried out in the *Generalgouvernement* (the Third Reich's official title of occupied Poland) by *SS* and Police forces. Here, Dirlewanger employed the purported hunting and marksmanship skills of his troops against the nascent Polish resistance in the forests surrounding the city of Lublin.[1]

After 16 months of increasingly brutal abuse of the local population in the Lublin area, punctuated by Dirlewanger's own questionable misconduct, complaints from local Nazi functionaries had grown so loud and insistent that Heinrich Himmler was compelled to transfer the unit to occupied Belarus at the end of January 1942 to maintain the peace. Adding weight to the case being made against him by *SS* judicial authorities were his highly questionable financial dealings and accusation of "race pollution," including allegedly sleeping with his Jewish servant and translator, the 16-year-old Sarah Bergmann.[2] After being compelled to leave occupied Poland, for the next two-and-a-half years his *Sondereinheit* would play an active role in the deadly war being waged by the forces of the Third Reich against the growing and increasingly effective Soviet partisan movement. Continuously bolstered by an influx of concentration camp inmates, including career criminals and sociopaths, Dirlewanger's troops committed some of the most horrendous atrocities ever recorded on the Eastern Front as they burned and looted their way through Belarus.

As the war progressed, the purported success of Dirlewanger's "scorched earth" anti-partisan tactics became widely known and copied throughout the various *Höherer SS und- Polizeiführer* (*HSSPF*, Higher *SS* and Police Leaders) controlling the occupied eastern and southeastern territories of Russia, Belarus, Ukraine, Poland, Greece, and Yugoslavia. Buoyed by his unit's deadly reputation and supported by influential backers in the *SS-Hauptamt* (*SS* Main Office) in Berlin, Dirlewanger's unit soon grew in size to a battalion in 1942, then into a regiment by the spring of 1944, swiftly followed by expansion into a brigade during the autumn of the same year, and finally ending the war as a fully fledged division of the *Waffen-SS* engaged in conventional warfare against the Red Army.[3]

It was in this latter capacity that the unit, officially titled by that time as the 2. *Sturmbrigade* (Assault Brigade) *Dirlewanger*, fought one of its most controversial actions near Ipolysag in northern Hungary (the modern-day town of Šahy in the Slovak Republic) between 13 and 18 December 1944. As a result of its overly hasty and piecemeal commitment to battle, lack of heavy armament, and a splintered chain of command, it was virtually destroyed by a Soviet mechanized corps. Consequently, the *Wehrmacht* leadership blamed its commander and the performance of his troops for the resulting encirclement of the Hungarian capital of Budapest during late December 1944 that led to the annihilation of its garrison in early February 1945. The brigade's reversal at Ipolysag also led to its compulsory removal from the front lines by its newly appointed field army commander, *General der Panzertruppe* (*Gen.d.Pz. Tr.*, Lieutenant General of Tank Troops) Hermann Balck, and its eventual shipment to a rest area where it would be completely rebuilt, so thorough was its destruction.

History yields few such examples of "punishment" units growing to such size and prominence. Various armies of the past had frequently resorted to the use of such measures for punishment or rehabilitative purposes of soldiers thought to be "redeemable" after proving themselves worthy of a pardon by service at the front, but usually not to such a scale. During World War II, both the *Wehrmacht* and Red Army routinely used them, but they generally did not grow larger than a battalion in size. Infantry divisions often created their own company-sized "in-house" punishment units for their troops who had committed relatively minor offenses, who could "redeem" themselves (often posthumously) after demonstrating bravery in often high-risk operations, such as clearing minefields while under enemy fire.

In late 1942, the *Wehrmacht* experimented with a division-sized unit composed primarily of *Bewährungs-Schützen* (probationary soldiers, not convicts) from German Army *Strafbataillone* (punishment battalions), led by hand-picked officers and non-commissioned officers. Known as *Afrika-Division 999*, after a relatively brief period of service in Tunisia, it went into captivity along with the rest of *Panzer-Armee Afrika* in May 1943, having insufficiently proven whether it was worth the expense to arm and equip it.[4] As far as is known, this unit did not engage in mass murder or predatory treatment of the civilian population in Tunisia.

The closest thing in modern European history matching the record of the *Dirlewanger Einheit* in terms of sheer criminality was a certain irregular *Pandur* regiment. An element of the Hapsburg Empire's army, this light infantry unit was composed of volunteers from the Kingdom of Slavonia and the Slavonian Military Frontier Guards. Raised under a charter issued by Empress Maria Theresa of Austria in 1741, its leader, Baron Franz von Trenck, a law unto himself, turned a blind eye whenever his men took whatever they wanted—be it property, women, or livestock—from the local population while on campaign, a common practice of many warring bands during this period. Wearing no formal uniform, the men of the regiment presented a wild, "Turkish" appearance and were preceded wherever they went by the regiment's colorful military band. Despite their unruly nature, Baron von Trenck and his men fought with distinction in the War of the Austrian Succession, as well as the First and Second Silesian Wars, where the regiment earned a reputation as being "brave, fearless, and audacious."[5]

The *Pandur* Regiment also became infamous for its extremes of looting, rape, and pillaging, epitomized by its sacking and burning of the Bavarian town of Cham in December 1742. "Prone to disobedience, breaches of military discipline, and stubbornness," his regiment had grown so unruly and so unreliable that Baron von Trenck was relieved of command in 1746 and put on trial for unspecified "acts of violence," as well as for selling officers' commissions without permission of the Crown. Sentenced to death, Empress Maria Theresa commuted this punishment to life imprisonment in Spielberg Castle, where he died three years later. With their leader and protector gone, the *Pandurs* were brought under firm disciplinary control and by 1756 had been reorganized as the 53rd Regiment of Foot. Although there are many similarities between the conduct of von Trenck's troops and that of the *Dirlewanger Einheit*, the chief difference between them was that the *Pandur* regiment was composed of actual volunteers, not convicts (technically, all of the *Dirlewanger Einheit* recruits were "volunteers" as well, but this will be discussed later in detail).

In the war in Ukraine that started in February 2022, it has been reported that a private military company titled the Wagner Group—financed by one of Russian President Vladimir Putin's cronies, Yevgeny Prigozhin—actively recruited tens of thousands of convicts from Russian prisons for service at the front line.[6] These convicts, promised full pardons for their crimes in exchange for six months of military service, quickly became notorious for their depredations against Ukrainian civilians and war crimes against captured Ukrainian military personnel. It was reported that they had suffered a significant number of casualties in the conflict (as many as 30,000 as of March 2023), and even if they survived the war, they were reportedly never to be allowed to return to Russia, but had to continue serving the Wagner Group until the conclusion of hostilities. Their performance in battle has yet to be formally evaluated, but initial reports were not favorable and any minimal gains they made had resulted in thousands of casualties.[7]

The story of the *Sondereinheit Dirlewanger* has been recounted in numerous works, ranging from French MacLean's excellent groundbreaking *The Cruel Hunters*, a comprehensive military history of the unit, to Christian Ingrao's *The History of the Black Hunters*, a popular account that falls within the social and political history category. Other authors have weighed in as well, including Rolf Michaelis with his trilogy (a two-volume unit history and a memoir by a survivor of the unit) and Hans-Peter Klausch's exhaustively researched *Antifaschisten in SS-Uniform*, a study of the "political" concentration camp inmates drafted into the unit in the autumn of 1944. There is also a history of the unit by Italian author Andrea Lombardi and a recent one by noted Polish author Soraya Kuklińska. A Russian history of the *Sondereinheit*, titled *Partisan Hunter: Dirlewanger Brigade* by Y. S. Zhukov and I. I. Kovtun, appeared in 2013 and features accounts of how this unit was perceived then and now by ordinary citizens of the former U.S.S.R., as well as the 1961 trial of 13 native collaborators who served under Dirlewanger from 1942–43.

The first magazine article covering Dirlewanger and his troops was serialized in *Der Spiegel* magazine in 1951. Titled "*Sie haben etwas gutzumachen: Ein Tatsachenbericht vom Einsatz der Strafsoldaten*" (They have something to make up for: A Factual Account of the Deployment of the Penal Soldiers), this six-part article introduced the public to a unit that up to that point had been obscured by the larger crimes of the Third Reich. It featured interviews with numerous survivors, including many of Dirlewanger's concentration camp draftees who had deserted to the Red Army during the battle of Ipolysag. There have also been numerous shorter articles written about the *Sondereinheit*, including a scholarly one by Hellmuth Auerbach that appeared in the pages of the prestigious *Vierteljahrshefte für Zeitgeschichte* in 1962 and another one by Richard Landwehr in a 1987 edition of the revisionist *Siegrunen* magazine.

Considering the unit and its founder's notoriety, as well as the Third Reich's penchant for destroying incriminating documents, there is a surprisingly large amount of official unit documents and correspondence that survived the war. Much of it can be found in the microfilmed records maintained by the U.S. National Archives and Records Administration (NARA), the originals of which are now kept by the German Federal and Military Archives (*Bundesarchiv-Militärarchiv* or *BA-MA*) within record groups RS 3-36 and RH 7/2455, 2456, and 2461. The NARA records fall into two categories—those of the *Reichsführer-SS* (*Reich* Leader of the *SS* and German Police), Record Grouping T-175 (Reels 140, 178, and 225), and those of the *Waffen-SS*, Record Grouping T-354 (Reels 161, 648, 649, and 650). These records allow the researcher to trace the growth and activities of the *Sondereinheit* from late 1940 until they end abruptly in June 1944, after which they are conspicuously absent. Of course, there are no mentions of the battle of Ipolysag in the thousands of pages included in these record groupings because that event occurred nearly six months later.

Published accounts of this battle are harder to come by. The only historical recounting of what happened at Ipolysag from an operational standpoint is Norbert Számvéber's heavily researched *Days of Battle*, a 2013 account of the various battles fought north of the Danube River by *H. Gr. Süd* and the Second Ukrainian Front between mid-December 1944 and March 1945, wherein the battle of Ipolysag merits a chapter. In postwar German and Russian studies, mentions of the battle are one or two pages at the most, if mentioned at all. The official U.S. Army history of the second phase of the War in the East, *Stalingrad to Berlin*, devotes a single paragraph, but gives a clue to where original German records might be found in a footnote.

With these scant leads, the author began to gather materials from both German and former Soviet sources.

Fortunately, the activities of the *Sondereinheit* that relate to its operations in the autumn of 1944 were recorded both by field commands of the *Wehrmacht-Heer* (German Army) and by the *HSSPF-Slowakei* (Higher *SS* and Police Leader for Slovakia). These microfilmed daily records—including *Kriegstagebücher* (war diaries), *Kampfstärke Meldungen* (combat strength reports), commander's assessments, radio messages, and office correspondence—were maintained by *H.Gr. Süd, 6. Armee/ Armeegruppe Fretter-Pico, 8. Armee/Armeegruppe Wöhler,* the *LXXII. Armeekorps* (army corps), and the *HSSPF-Slowakei.*

These records are fairly comprehensive and cover the activities of Dirlewanger and his troops from 9 December 1944 until the end of the month, with the battle of Ipolysag receiving prominent mention. The records of the *SS-Führungshauptamt* (*SS* Main Leadership Office) also contain organizational information concerning armament and equipment, unit structures, and reports of *Kriegsstärkenachweisungen* (*KStN*, wartime strength organization and equipment) as the regiment was transformed into a brigade during the autumn of 1944.

Actual documents from Dirlewanger and his brigade for the period October– December 1944 are scarce. How many of these were lost in May 1945 when the truck convoy evacuating the *Waffen-SS* historical archive from Sasmuk Castle outside of Prague were put to the torch is unknown. Undoubtedly, some of the unit's records were captured by the Red Army when the *Sondereinheit* was first overrun on 15 December 1944, and again when it was finally wiped out for good at the end of April 1945 in the Halbe Pocket. Luckily, a few of these official records turned up recently via the German-Russian consortium digitizing the hoard of "trophy" or captured documents maintained by the *Deutsch-Russisches Projekt zur Digitalisierung Deutscher Dokumente in Archiven der Russischen Föderation* (German-Russian Project to Digitize German Documents in Archives of the Russian Federation; for more information, go to Germandocsinrussia.org). Many of these records can be found online in Fund 500, Inventory 12493 (Documents of the *SS*, *SS* Troops, and Police), Cases 70 and 88–90. Dirlewanger's own post-battle report of how the events at Ipolysag unfolded can be found in Inventory 12472 (Field Armies), Case 380.[8]

The bulk of the official *SS* military service records of Dirlewanger and many of his officers maintained by the *SS-Personalamt* (personnel office) in Berlin from 1933–45 survived the war and found their way into the postwar Berlin Document Center (BDC) maintained by the victorious Allies as Records Group A3343, Series SSO. Here, they were used as evidence in the investigation and prosecution of war crimes committed by Nazi Party members and those belonging to its various sub-organizations, including the *SS* and Police. The records maintained by the BDC, however, were not complete in one respect because they did not contain all of the files of possible perpetrators.

For example, not every officer or enlisted man in the *Ordnungspolizei* (Order Police) joined the Nazi Party or the *SS*. To obtain the files of these men, a persistent researcher would have to contact the records departments of the various German *Länder* (states) where they had originally served as police officers before the Nazi Party's *Machtergreifung* (seizure of power). In many cases, the files of members who had served in the *Wehrmacht* before transfer to the *Dirlewanger Einheit* were obtained from the *Bundesarchiv-Militärarchiv* in Freiburg or from the former *Deutsche Dienststelle* or *WASt* (*Wehrmachtsauskunftstelle für Kriegerverluste und Kriegsgefangene*) in Berlin-Reinickendorf.[9]

Other documents used during the writing of this book include testimony and findings culled from the International Military Tribunal records of the Nuremberg Trials, particularly from the trials of the Nazi ministers, including that of Gottlob Berger, Dirlewanger's sponsor and chief patron. Correspondence between Himmler, Berger, Dirlewanger, and other *SS* luminaries such as Erich von dem Bach come from the files maintained by Himmler's own personal staff. Lastly, another useful source of information are the investigative files maintained by the office in Ludwigsburg, formerly known as the *Zentrale Stelle der Bundesarchiv Landesjustizverwaltungen zur Aufklärung nationalsozialistischer Verbrechen* (Central Office of the Land Judicial Authorities for Investigation of National Socialist Crimes), now under *Bundesarchiv* administration. Using these various sources, the author was able to piece together a chronology of events and what went wrong during the battle of Ipolysag, and whether or not the *Sondereinheit* was responsible for the loss of Budapest.

Sources from the Red Army's perspective were somewhat harder to come by. The English translation of the Soviet General Staff's study of their offensive into Hungary, *The Budapest Operation 1945: An Operational Strategic Study*, provides a good overview of the campaign from the army group level and describes in some detail the planning that went into the operation, as well as the overall course of events as the campaign unfolded. Much more relevant is the war diary of the IX Guards Mechanized Corps, which fought the Dirlewanger Brigade between 12 and 18 December 1944. Located on the website of Tsentral'nyy Arkhiv Ministerstva Oborony Rossiyskoy Federatsii (TsAMO, Central Archives of the Russian Federation Defense Ministry) in Podolsk, the corps' war diary details the day-to-day fighting against the various German and Hungarian formations it faced as it fought its way through the Ipolysag River valley and onto the Hungarian Plains during that critical week in December.[10]

Dirlewanger and his infamous unit continue to survive in popular culture, including mentions in video games, war games, novels, and films (in particular, a grisly scene from the 1985 Soviet classic, *Come and See*) that indicate a continuing fascination with the man and his terrible deeds. This was not always so; at one time, the horrible actions of Oskar Dirlewanger and his men inspired loathing and disgust. No reputable historian would have dared touch upon the subject. With the passing of time, however, the rough edges of history have been worn away and the facts buried under layers of myth and legend. Yet, for a brief moment in time, in the valley encompassing the town of Ipolysag, the "Cruel Hunters" of the *Sondereinheit* became the hunted. Subjected to a thrashing at the hands of the Red Army, Dirlewanger's brigade of misfits and criminals received their first real taste of defeat and a foretaste of what would soon become their collective fate.

A Word on Place Names

Readers may notice that the author frequently uses German place names for Slovak or Hungarian localities or terrain features. This is not a mistake, but a conscious decision to use the same place names as written in the original German military records referenced in this book. Because this entire area once fell under the control of the Austro-Hungarian Empire until 1918, it was common to find towns and villages with German, Hungarian, and Slovak place names simultaneously. When necessary, the author has written the proper Slovak or Hungarian place name in brackets immediately following the German name, using the modern-day names as found in Google Earth.

Acknowledgements

No successful work would be possible without the generous assistance of others, and this book is no exception. I would like to thank the following individuals for providing advice, additional research materials, and photographs that helped make this book possible. In particular, I would like to single out Stuart B. T. Emmett, Vladimir Krajčovič, Soroya Kuklińska, John P. Moore, Roland Pfeiffer, Albert Smetanin, Norbert Számvéber, and Stephen Tyas for generously sharing the contents of their archives and assisting me in making contact with a variety of research institutions. In the U.S.A., I would like to thank the Staff of the U.S. National Archives (NARA) in College Park, Maryland; Thomas Albright, Josh Baldwin, Frederick Clemens, Peter DeForest, Colonel (retired) French MacLean, Ray Merriam, Michael D. Miller, Marc Rikmenspoel, Barry Smith, and Remy Spezzano; in Canada William Hughes; in the United Kingdom Stephen Andrew, Stephen Ballantyne, Philip W. Blood, Alan Buet, Richard Deveau-Maxwell, Malcolm Hunt, Drew Maynard, James McLeod, Michael Melnyk, and Ian Michael Wood.

In Europe I especially want to thank the following: Christian Bauermeister, the staff of the *Bundesarchiv-Militärarchiv* in Freiburg in Breisgau, Carol Byrne, Erich Craciun, Flemming Daugaard, Uwe Enders, and Margit Bugner of the *Volksbund Deutsche Kriegsgräberfürsorge e.V.*, Daniel Feldman, Nikita Fialkov of the *DRK Suchdienst Standort München*, my mapmaker Ivo Férin, Tomáš Hofírek, Georges Jerome, Peter van Holsteijn, Petter Kjellander, Hubert Kuberski, Christina Kunkel of the *Institut für Zeitgeschichte* in Munich, Rolf Michaelis, Andreas Mix of the *Stiftung Topographie des Terrors* in Berlin-Kreuzberg, Albert Neumann and his living history organization Pomerania 1945, Daniel Popielas, Alexandra Ritchie, Chistoph Schulz, Mr. A. I. Stepanov, Rahel Thiel of the *Geschichtsort Villa ten Hompel* in Münster, Charles Trang, the B. Uhsemann Foto Archiv, Viktor Ukhov, Timo Worst, and Andrii Zubkhov. I would also like to thank Mr. Reuven Ben Ari of Ashqelon, Israel for his advice on where to find important source material. Thanks to you all. My apologies to anyone I might have inadvertently overlooked who also contributed material.

I would also like to thank the staff of Casemate Publishing, especially Ruth Sheppard, Isobel Fulton, Adam Jankiewicz, Declan Ingram and Daniel Yesilonis, whose interest in the subject and continued support made it possible for me to complete the manuscript without interference. The free hand they granted me, as well as their constant encouragement and support, allowed me to explore areas of this controversial unit's history not previously known.

CHAPTER ONE

Dirlewanger's Willing Executioners

Before understanding why and how such an unusual unit as the Dirlewanger Brigade was diverted from an ongoing anti-partisan operation in Slovakia on 11 December 1944 to plug a gap at a critical moment during *H.Gr. Süd's* defense of Hungary, a brief retelling of how it came into existence in 1940 and the brigade's subsequent employment until the end of September 1944 is in order. Shrouded in myth, obscured by lurid tales, and cloaked in factual errors from numerous retellings of its history, its origins are surprisingly rather banal in the bureaucratic yet typically idiosyncratic Third Reich manner.

The roots of Dirlewanger's infamous unit can be traced to one of Adolf Hitler's whimsical mealtime utterings translated into action through the machinations of one of his regime's greatest toadies, *Reichsführer-SS* Heinrich Himmler, who took one of the *Führer's* frequent dinner table topics and made it a reality. Himmler must have thought that if his efforts (and similarly outlandish ones that followed) succeeded, it would not only allow him to increase his influence with Hitler, but would also increase the power and influence of his rapidly growing *SS* empire within the Nazi hierarchy.

The action that led to the founding of the *Dirlewanger Einheit* can be traced back to two near-simultaneous triggering events: the first was one of Hitler's nightly "table talks" that took place shortly before the beginning of the 1940 Western Campaign; and the second was Hitler's receipt of a letter from the distraught wife of an "Old Party member" who had been caught shooting game on government property without a hunting license. The source for the first was Hitler himself, who frequently brought up the subject of poaching in his table talks as late as 1942. According to Hugh-Trevor Roper, these table talks "took place at meal-times ... more often at his last, most sociable meal ... [when] Hitler would expand. A passionate talker ... [Hitler] fascinated his hearers; for his informal talk was ... fresh, flexible, sometimes gay. Of course, it was often a monologue."[1] His table talks frequently revolved around the topic of hunting.

Hitler, a vegetarian, was against any illegal killing of wild game by poachers, who were acting in defiance of longstanding German hunting laws. However, though he strongly disapproved of poaching, he had grudging respect for the hunting abilities of those who tracked and killed wild game with a rifle, in contrast to those "cowards" who trapped and killed game using snares or nets. The latter he held in contempt; as for the former, he believed that "wild game marksmen" (*Wildschützen*) who hunted to feed their families constituted a form of unrealized military potential, having tracking and marksmanship skills that could be put to good use.

For example, at a table talk on 28 October 1941, Hitler stated: "I see no harm in shooting at game. I merely say that it's a dreary sport. The part of shooting I like best is the target—next to that, the poacher. He at least risks his life at the sport."[2] At another evening gathering after dinner a year later, he told his guests:

> I am no admirer of the poacher, particularly as I am a vegetarian; but in him I see the sole element of romance in the so-called sport of shooting. Incidentally, there is no doubt that we number quite a few poachers among the most stalwart adherents of the Party. When I say all this, do not imagine that I condone the wholesale depredations of poachers among the wildlife of the forests. On the contrary, my sympathies are entirely with the gamekeepers.[3]

The first statement may have been influenced by the letter he had received at roughly the same time in March 1940 from the aforementioned wife of an "Old Party member" (someone who had joined the Nazi Party before Hitler came to power in 1933) whose husband had just been sentenced to two years in prison when he was caught and convicted of poaching after shooting several stags in one of Germany's national forests without a permit.

Gottlob Berger, who later became the influential head of Himmler's *SS-Hauptamt* (*SS-HA*, Main Office), revealed during his interrogation while being prosecuted for war crimes by the International Military Tribunal (IMT) that this unnamed woman had written to Hitler to inform him that her husband, an early member of the *Nationalsozialistische Deutsche Arbeiterpartei* (*NSDAP*, German National Socialist Party), had been placed in prison. In her letter, she begged Hitler to release him and allow him to "prove" himself in battle in order to atone for his crime in a more honorable way.[4] "That," Berger later testified at Nuremberg, "was the basis of the unit's founding." Berger, who was to prove himself the Dirlewanger Brigade's creator and biggest supporter, remembered what happened next:

> The special Dirlewanger Brigade owes its existence to an order of Adolf Hitler given in 1940 while the campaign in the West was still going on. One day Himmler called me up and told me that Hitler had ordered all men convicted of poaching with firearms who were [currently] in prison were to be collected and formed into a special detachment. That Hitler should have such a somewhat unusual and far-fetched idea at all is due to the following reason: first of all, he himself didn't like hunting and had nothing but scorn for all hunters. Whenever he could ridicule them he did.[5]

The second reason Berger gave was the letter from the jailed Old Party member's wife, which he thought had been the catalyst for Hitler's seemingly nonsensical order.

Apparently, after mulling over the woman's letter, Hitler had seen the wisdom of her logic and—influenced by his own opinions about poaching in general—sought to put this thought into action. Naturally, the most suitable organization in his empire that could bring his idea quickly to fruition was Himmler's, who was responsible not only for internal security in Germany but also the nation's prison and concentration camp system, where most of the convicted poachers were conveniently confined.

Hitler concluded that allowing these poachers to serve in uniform made a great deal of sense; it could serve as a fair means of their rehabilitation, and putting their purported hunting skills to good use "at the front" (as the unnamed woman had written) would also benefit the war effort. That he believed this to be true can be attributed to a later statement he made on 20 August 1942, when he said: "As it is, a poacher kills a hare and goes to prison for three months! I myself should have taken the fellow and put him into one of the guerilla companies of the SS."[6] And putting them into a guerilla company of the SS is exactly what followed next, although in March 1940 even Hitler could not have foreseen how the Dirlewanger Brigade would eventually be put to use.

Having made up his mind, by the beginning of the third week of March 1940 Hitler spoke to Himmler and told him that he wanted all men subject to military service who had been convicted of poaching game with a rifle, and were currently serving terms in prisons or concentration camps, to be collected and formed into a military unit. Having received this verbal order, on 23 March 1940 Himmler started the bureaucratic wheels turning that would eventually send the Dirlewanger Brigade to Ipolysag four years later.

On this date, Himmler's adjutant, *Gruppenführer* (*Gruf.*, Major General) Karl Wolff, placed a telephone call to *Herr* Sommer, an advisor to the *Reich*'s Minister of Justice at the time, Franz Gürtner.[7] According to one witness involved in the action, "Wolff told the startled bureaucrat that it was Hitler's wish to send selected poachers to the Front for the purpose of granting them an amnesty after proving themselves." Six days later, Himmler himself sent a written request to Gürtner asking for the names of all men currently convicted of poaching and awaiting sentencing or already serving their terms.[8] Doctor Roland Frieser, later described as a "hard-core Nazi" who was at the time serving as the Ministry of Justice's secretary of state, enthusiastically supported the request and on behalf of Gürtner ordered that the names of all poachers being held in custody should be identified immediately and furnished to Himmler's Main Office.[9]

There was one possible obstacle to this action being carried through, however, and that was the *Reichsforstmeister* of the *Reich* Forestry Office, none other than Hermann Göring, whom Hitler had also appointed as the *Reichsjägermeister* (Master of the *Reich* Hunting Ministry). Göring, an avid huntsman himself, was known for jealously protecting his domain and was particularly adamant that poachers should be caught and given lengthy prison terms for daring to hunt in his jurisdiction without permission. Any request to release convicted poachers on probationary status, even to voluntarily serve in uniform, would have to be personally approved by him.

Berger later related that this was the most difficult part of the task that Himmler had given him. He testified at Nuremberg:

> I didn't enjoy this order one little bit for the simple reason that I had considerable difficulties with the *Reich* Marshal and *Reich* Master of the Hunt, Hermann Göring, and especially with the *Gauleiters*, who quite suddenly all turned out to be wild game huntsmen [sic] ... I saw all this trouble coming in advance so I told Himmler [that] without a clear-cut order I couldn't do anything, but I got the order ... Thereupon, in accordance with my orders, I got in touch with the Chief of the *Reich* Criminal Office (the *Kriminalpolizei* or *KriPo*), [Arthur] Nebe. We agreed that at the beginning of the summer all suitable men should be sent to the barracks at Oranienburg.[10]

To Berger's surprise, Göring had no opposition to the idea and gave the project his expressed approval. On 10 April 1940, the *SS-Reichssicherhauptamt* (*Reich's* Security Main Office) and the *Reich's* Minister of Justice established guidelines describing what kind of imprisoned poachers would be deemed acceptable. As an incentive, the prospective recruits were informed that service in this special unit would be voluntary and would fulfill their military obligation to the nation (this was formalized in a letter from the *SS-HA* on 1 December 1941).[11] The next step would be recruitment of enough men to form a company of such marksmen.

On that same day, Berger's office in the *SS-HA* sent a directive to all concentration camps establishing the criteria describing which kind of poachers might be induced to "volunteer." Only men convicted of using firearms to illegally kill their game would be accepted. Volunteers had to be no older than 45 years of age and no shorter than 1.65 meters (5ft 4in). They did not have to meet any of the other *SS* entry requirements (except the racial ones, of course) and would not be required to become a dues-paying member of the *SS*, though that was a possibility should they "prove" themselves and earn rehabilitation later.[12]

This search for suitable recruits throughout Himmler's concentration camp empire would continue over the next two months. By the end of this period, some 90 poachers serving time in the penal institutions of the *Reich* Justice Administration had been identified, collected, and were shortly afterwards transferred by the *KriPo* via *Eiltransport* (express rail transport) for reason of *besonderen Verwendung* (special employment) to the Sachsenhausen *Konzentrationslager* (*KL*, concentration camp) near Oranienburg in northern Germany, where they were assigned to a barracks isolated from the rest of the camp.[13]

While they waited for their barracks to fill up, the initial influx of recruits were issued with uniforms, settled into their new routines, and began receiving rudimentary training under the watchful eyes of four or five veteran NCOs from the guard detachment at the Sachsenhausen *KL* next door. Although the poachers had come from prisons and concentration camps, their trainers did not treat them as common criminals; rather, they seem to have held them in a certain amount of esteem due to their reputation as daring marksmen. While discipline was strict, the new recruits were not treated with undue harshness, nor were they abused. Except for confinement to their barracks when not outdoors training, they experienced the same treatment that any other *Waffen-SS* recruit received at this stage of the war; after all, these former poachers were volunteers too, just like everyone else in the *Waffen-SS* at the time.

After Germany's defeat in 1945, *Hauptsturmführer* (*Hstuf.*, Captain) Karl Radl, the former *Adjutant* to Hitler's infamous commando leader, *Obersturmbannführer* (*Ostubaf.*) Otto Skorzeny, admitted during an interrogation:

> The poacher is not a "character criminal," not a lawbreaker out of inferiority, but out of passion. He will be given a heavy burden, namely to be treated like a "criminal" [but] if given the chance to prove himself before the enemy for his homeland … [he] can exploit his passion for hunting in the vast forests of the East in the fight against partisans.[14]

After waiting several weeks for some sort of official designation, on 15 June 1940, the unit's first official title was decided upon by an official in the *SS-HA*, possibly Gottlob Berger himself—it was to be named *Wilddieb-Kommando* (Poacher Command) *Oranienburg,* after the name of the garrison town outside of the Sachsenhausen concentration camp.[15]

The missing ingredient needed to make *Wilddieb-Kommando Oranienburg* successful was the right sort of commanding officer; one who could whip these men into shape and train them to become soldiers, as well as a man who could deal with the disciplinary issues that would necessarily arise when dealing with former convicts. After all, few of the former poachers had served in Germany's armed forces before and the only discipline they had known was that of the harsh sort practiced in the concentration camps and prisons from whence they had come. Conveniently, Gottlob Berger had the right person in mind for the job, a hitherto obscure and somewhat disreputable former officer of the Kaiser's army named Dr. Oskar Dirlewanger.

Oskar Dirlewanger himself was a convicted criminal, soldier of fortune, rabid anti-Semite, drunkard, and sexual deviant. Born in Würzburg on 25 September 1895, the 6ft-tall (1.83 meter) Dirlewanger voluntarily enlisted in the Baden-Württemberg *Infanterie-Regiment 123* on 1 October 1913 at the age of 18. Without going into detail, he amassed a great deal of experience as an infantry officer during World War I, where he was awarded the Iron Cross, First and Second Classes, for bravery, and was wounded in action six times. After the ensuing general demobilization of the *Kaiserliche Heer* and his own discharge from active service on 31 December 1918, Dirlewanger served in several *Freikorps* units, including *Freikorps Haas, Epp*, and *Sprösser*. The *Freikorps* was a paramilitary organization authorized by the Weimar Republic, created to help suppress a number of communist-inspired revolts that had broken out in Berlin, Württemberg, Bavaria, the Ruhr, and Rhineland in 1919.[16]

Most *Freikorps* members were right-wing-leaning demobilized veterans or college students eager for adventure or desirous of avenging the "injustices" inflicted upon Germany by the harsh terms of the Versailles Treaty. During this period, Dirlewanger established and led his own company-sized *Freikorps* unit, putting his combat leadership experience to good use in street battles waged against communists and socialist revolutionaries. His most significant military achievement during this period of instability was the command of an armored train that helped put down the communist revolt in the city of Sangerhausen in 1921. With stability restored, Dirlewanger returned to school and earned his Doctorate in political science from the Frankfurt Goethe Institute in 1922. He then set out to make a living for himself, but peacetime tranquility was not for him.[17]

The 1930s were a turbulent time for Germany and Dr. Oskar Dirlewanger. A member of the Nazi Party since 1923, he capitalized on his status as a veteran and *Alter Kämpfer* (Old Fighter) member of the *NSDAP* to gain employment in a series of civil servant positions. He was well on his way to a successful career in Nazi politics until he was accused and convicted of statutory rape of an underage female in 1934. Sentenced to two years' imprisonment in the Ludwigsburg Prison, shortly after his release on 12 October 1936 he was arrested for recidivism by his archenemy, Wilhelm Murr, the powerful *Gauleiter* of Württemberg and sent to the Welzheim concentration camp on 14 March 1937, where he remained until his influential friend Gottlob Berger arranged for his release.[18]

Gottlob Berger, like Dirlewanger a former Reserve *Oberleutnant* in the *Kaiserheer* during World War I and a veteran of the *Freikorps*, had risen in the ranks of Heinrich Himmler's *SS* and by 1937 had become the head of the organization's sports and physical fitness bureau. The following year, Berger—nicknamed the Duke of Swabia for his outgoing and boisterous manner—was promoted and made the head of the *SS-Ergänzungsabteilung*, responsible for the recruitment and expansion of the *SS-Verfügungstruppe* (*SS* Contingency Troops). By 20 April 1941, Himmler would further promote Berger to the head of the *SS-Hauptamt*, where he would wield significant bureaucratic power and exert enormous influence on the growth of the *Waffen-SS*.[19]

After Berger arranged his release from Welzheim, Dirlewanger had to demonstrate atonement for his offenses and avoid further imprisonment by leaving Germany for a while, somewhere out of the public eye and where his skills as a soldier could be put to good use. To achieve this necessary rehabilitation, on Berger's advice Dirlewanger left Germany in 1937 and volunteered to serve with the German-led Condor Legion in Spain as an infantry tactics instructor for Francisco Franco's Nationalist forces, which were badly in need of a professional's touch. By this point, Dirlewanger had amassed nearly eight years of military experience, most of it in combat, and had proven himself an effective and efficient instructor of troops. He was perfectly suited for this position, and by all accounts during his 17 months in Spain, Dirlewanger had performed his duties in a superb manner, as attested in a letter of recommendation by his superior while in Spain, future *Wehrmacht panzer* commander *Oberst* Ritter von Thoma.[20]

Not wishing to be left out in the war that he saw coming, Dirlewanger wrote to Himmler for the first time on 4 Juy 1939, requesting entry into the *Waffen-SS* (then still known as the *SS-Verfügungstruppe*), but was turned down on 9 August because the appeal of his previous conviction was still being adjudicated. In his written response, Himmler stated that once his case had been favorably concluded, then he would reopen Dirlewanger's case and re-examine his application.[21] By the spring of 1940, Dirlewanger had won his appeal and cleared his name with the courts. Soon thereafter, he contacted Gottlob Berger again seeking gainful military employment. Dirlewanger told his old friend that he wished to serve as an officer, but not in the *Wehrmacht*.

Due to Berger's help, Dirlewanger had already been reinstated into the Nazi Party on 18 May 1940 (backdated to 1 March 1932). He had been thrown out of it in 1934 on account of his *Ehrenstraffe* (violation of honor) when he was first imprisoned, but ever since then, Dirlewanger had been involved in a lengthy court battle to clear his name and expunge his criminal record.[22] In addition to having his *NSDAP* membership reinstated, his doctoral degree was restored for the same reason after it had been revoked by Frankfurt Goethe University. He was quite determined to join the *SS*, but had to have a clean record if Himmler was ever to accept him as someone suitable to command *Wilddieb-Kommando Oranienburg*.

To help his old friend, Berger penned a letter to Hitler's *Reichskanzlei* (*Reichs* Chancellery) in March or April 1940 professing his belief in Dirlewanger's good political and soldierly character, and requested, in accordance with Dirlewanger's sincere wishes, that he be accepted into the *SS* immediately and be given an opportunity to serve on the front line as soon as possible. Surprisingly, Hitler's office approved the request in a letter dated 17 May addressed to Berger's office in the *SS-HA*. Armed with this letter, Berger wrote to Himmler and requested on 4 June that Dirlewanger be allowed to join the *Waffen-SS* as a Reserve *Obersturmführer*, the *SS* equivalent in rank to an *Oberleutnant* (first lieutenant).

Himmler's approval was not immediately forthcoming. It was at this point when Berger met personally with Himmler and convinced him of the necessity to consider selecting someone forthwith to train the new *Wilddieb-Kommando Oranienburg* then being set up at Sachsenhausen. Berger told Himmler that it would have to be someone with considerable experience as a leader and troop trainer. A commander for the unit had yet to be appointed, but of course Berger already had someone in mind. On the same day, Berger's *SS-HA*—in a bureaucratic sleight of hand—arranged for Dirlewanger to be informally made responsible for the basic and further training of this special unit, though he would remain as a member of the *Allgemeine-SS* and not the *Waffen-SS*. That step would require Himmler's approval.[23]

On 15 June 1940, Berger finally asked the dithering Himmler directly in a formal letter that Dirlewanger be officially transferred into the *Waffen-SS*. In the same letter, Berger also formally proposed that Dirlewanger be named as the chosen *Ausbilder* (trainer) and commander of the new *Wilddieb-Kommando*. Having already spoken to Berger of this proposal, Himmler finally gave in and agreed. Accordingly, Dirlewanger's official date for entry into the *Waffen-SS* was to be 1 July 1940, in the rank of *Obersturmführer der Reserve* and assigned to the *Inspektion der SS-Totenkopfverbände* (Office of the Inspectorate of SS Death's Head units). On that same day, *Wilddieb-Kommando Oranienburg* was officially activated in Sachsenhausen as an *SS* unit and attached to the reinforced *5. SS-Totenkopf Standarte* (Death's Head Regiment) for logistical and administrative purposes. *Wilddieb-Kommando Oranienburg* was not yet considered a part of the *Waffen-SS*, but rather as an element occupying a rather nebulous position within the *Allgemeine-SS* as part of Berger's *SS-Hauptamt*.[24]

Finally, with a commander to lead and train them after over a month of waiting, the company began a rigorous training regimen. Assisted by his small cadre of veteran *Unterführer* (NCOs), including four from the famous *Germania* Regiment's recruit depot, Dirlewanger put the ex-poachers through their paces throughout July and August, while simultaneously evaluating their fitness to serve.[25] By the end of the first month, six of the recruits were found unfit and sent back to the prison or concentration came from whence they had come to complete their sentences, while the remaining 84 men were deemed acceptable. On 1 August, after commanding *Wilddieb-Kommando Oranienburg* for only a month, Dirlewanger was promoted to *Hauptsturmführer* and formally transferred to the *5. SS-Totenkopf Standarte* from the Inspectorate of SS Death's Head Units.

One month later, the unit was retitled and was henceforth known by the name of its new commander, becoming the *Sonderkommando Dirlewanger*. Events thereafter would occur in rapid succession.[26] On 1 September 1940, the men of the newly designated *Sonderkommando* were informed that they would not be sent to the front lines to prove themselves as sharpshooters after all, but would go instead to the Lublin district of the *Generalgouvernement* to assist with security duties. At that time, Germany had not yet declared war against the Soviet Union, nor had it invaded the Balkans. Occupied Poland at that time was the closest thing to a "front" that existed, and with France and all of Western Europe except Great Britain more or less peacefully occupied, there was nowhere else for them to apply their "unique" skills.

Once in Poland, the unit was subordinated to the *HSSPF-Ost* (Higher SS and Police Leader-East), a key position filled at that time by the brutal *Obergruppenführer (Ogruf.) und General der Waffen-SS und Polizei* Friedrich Wilhelm Krüger. Besides this important development, the unit was reinforced with over a hundred additional "volunteers" from Sachsenhausen, though sources differ as to whether they were all convicted poachers, ordinary SS men, or a mixture of both.[27] Armed, equipped, and supplied from the stores of the *5. SS-Totenkopf Standarte*, the *Sonderkommando*—now approximately 280–300 men strong—began its move from Sachsenhausen to Lublin in early September 1940, a journey of 10–14 hours by rail.

Upon arrival in occupied Poland, the *Sonderkommando* was subordinated to the command of *Brigadeführer* (*Brig.Fhr.*, Brigadier General) Odilo Globocnik, who was the local *HSSPF-Ost* representative for the Lublin district. Here, Dirlewanger's men received additional training, but instead of being sent into combat were used instead to guard the Jewish ghetto in Lublin, where they routinely abused the impoverished and starving inmates. During this phase of the unit's history, 33 of the original poachers proved to be "unsuitable for the intended use" (perhaps due to the routine brutality they witnessed) and were sent back to Germany to complete their original prison sentences.[28] After three months of this dreary duty, at the end of December 1940, the now battalion-sized *Sonderkommando* was deployed to apprehend or kill a group of up to 500 "violent" Polish criminals who had escaped from the prison in Warsaw and were seeking refuge in the surrounding forest.[29]

In the spring of 1941, the Sonderkommando was sent to guard the Jewish labor camp at Stary Dzikow in the Lublin District. Here, among other security tasks, the men of the unit supervised the construction of fortifications and antitank ditches along the Bug River in the Belzec area. Later that year, it was occasionally engaged in small-scale combat operations against the growing Polish partisan movement. When not thus employed, it was frequently deployed to combat black market trafficking. Here, Dirlewanger's men committed "numerous aberrations" (including extortion and robbery) against the local Polish and Jewish populations, so much so that their depredations began to attract the notice of higher *SS* authorities, most notably Friedrich Wilhelm Krüger.[30]

As a result of the growing controversy and mountains of incriminating evidence, in the autumn of 1941 the *SS* and Police Court in Cracow initiated an investigation against members of the unit, with Dirlewanger's name at the top of the list. *Gruppenführer* Berger soon learned about the investigation, intervening yet again to protect his old friend. Using his authority as the head of the *SS-HA* and influence with Himmler, Berger was able to get the proceedings suspended temporarily, though the court's *SS* lawyer, *Ustuf.* Dr. Konrad Morgen, continued pressing onwards with his investigation until it was finally ordered to be shut down by Himmler in early 1945 before Dirlewanger could be brought to trial. Clearly, Dirlewanger's *Sonderbataillon* could not remain in Poland much longer, especially when Krüger threatened to have Dirlewanger arrested if he and his troops were not quickly removed from his territory.[31]

On the Eastern Front, where Germany had been locked in mortal combat with the Soviet Union since the beginning of Operation *Barbarossa* on 22 June 1941, more troops were needed to counter the increasingly powerful partisan movement metastasizing within the vast region of occupied Belarus. It was a good time to leave Poland, and Berger used the opportunity to arrange the *Sonderbataillon's* withdrawal from the *Generalgouvernement* on 29 January 1942 and subsequent transfer to Mogilev, where it fell under the command of the *HSSPF-Russland-Mitte* (Russia-Center). This organization was led by *Ogruf.* Erich von dem Bach, under whom the battalion would later serve in Warsaw in August 1944. Here, the unit would operate for the next two-and-a-half years, initially in Mogilev, then Lahojsk, and finally in the area surrounding Minsk.

Two days prior, Himmler's office (through Berger's machinations) had reclassified the unit as a *Freiwilligen* (volunteer) element of the *Waffen-SS*, which essentially placed it within the same category as the *SS* foreign legions then being recruited from Nordic countries such as Denmark, Norway, Finland, and Sweden.[32] Therefore, the *Sonderbataillon's* members were not considered to be fully fledged members of the *Waffen-SS*, but fell in a nebulous category under the rubric of *Sondertruppen* (Special Troops) of the *Reichsführer-SS*. Berger's bureaucratic maneuver did not go unnoticed by the head of the *SS-Führungshauptamt* (*SS-FHA*, *SS* Leadership Main Office), *Gruf.* Hans Jüttner.

Jüttner, who served as the de facto chief of staff of the *Waffen-SS*, was well aware of Dirlewanger's sordid reputation and the alleged criminal activities of his unit in Poland. A rival of Berger's, he wanted nothing at all to do with Dirlewanger and his gang of poachers. He feared that its association with the *Waffen-SS* would taint the organization's "elite" reputation, a reputation that he jealously protected. Jüttner complained bitterly to Himmler about this, telling him that "the classification is intolerable for the soldiers of the *Waffen-SS* and ideally suited to cause considerable unrest among [its members]."[33]

To allay Jüttner's concerns, a compromise was worked out between Himmler, Berger, and Jüttner; the battalion would become eligible to receive weapons, supplies, and equipment directly from the *SS-FHA* via the *Waffen-SS's* logistics department, but would continue to be administered by Berger's *SS-HA*, providing Dirlewanger the sort of administrative and disciplinary protection that he so often needed.[34] Nevertheless, his men were issued with *SS* pay books, drew regular *Waffen-SS* active duty pay, along with a family subsidy if married, and were eligible to establish life insurance accounts for their families like any other member of the *Waffen-SS*. In short, as of 27 January 1942 the unit was now officially a part of the *Waffen-SS*, whether or not Jüttner would publicly admit it.

Between February 1942 and June 1944, *SS-Sonderbataillon Dirlewanger*, along with numerous regiments and battalions of the *Ordnungspolizei*, ordinary *Waffen-SS* units, *SS-Einsatzgruppen*, *Wehrmacht* troops, and locally recruited *Askaris* (a derogatory German term for native troops such as Belarusians, Russians, or Ukrainians), waged merciless warfare against the partisan (officially referred to as "bandits" by the *SS* on 1 September 1942) movements in Belarus.[35] Dirlewanger's unit participated in as many as 37 local partisan sweeps and large-scale multi-unit operations during this period, including Operations *Kottbus* (Cottbus), *Hermann*, *Heinrich*, *Frühlingsfest* (Spring Festival), and *Kormoran* (Cormorant).

Operation *Kottbus* was one of its biggest actions, fought between 25 May and 23 June 1943. During this operation, the 17,000-man strong *Gruppe von Gottberg*, to which the *Sonderbataillon* was subordinated at the time, killed as many as 20,000 "bandits" and detained 6,053 civilians for forced labor in Germany. Dirlewanger's unit was allegedly responsible for killing 14,000 of these partisans alone, but most of the victims were merely unlucky civilians—or even unluckier Jews—caught in the dragnet. The battalion also reported the captured of 492 rifles, an indication that there were only a few genuine partisans among its victims.[36] One source claimed that between 1942 and 1944, the *Sonderbataillon* by itself murdered "around 30,000" Russian partisans, peasants, and Jews and burned approximately 100 villages, even before it arrived in Warsaw in August 1944.[37]

During this phase of the *Sonderbataillon's* existence, Dirlewanger had perfected his brutally effective method of "pacifying" the region surrounding Minsk. One of these methods involved marching innocent civilians ahead of his troop columns to detonate minefields laid by Soviet partisans. Another method, the unit's most notorious, consisted of surrounding a village during the early morning hours, sorting through the townsfolk, sending able-bodied men and women to Germany as forced labor, and herding the remaining women, children, and older residents deemed unfit for labor into the village's largest building, such as a barn or church. Dirlewanger's troops would then set the structure afire with flamethrowers, followed by hand grenades tossed through the windows. Machine guns would be set up outside to shoot anyone who managed to escape from the inferno.

In this manner, *Sonderbataillon Dirlewanger* and its imitators among the *Ordnungspolizei*, *Wehrmacht*, and *Waffen-SS* "pacified" vast swaths of Belarus by simply denuding whole regions of people and driving any survivors into the hands of the Soviet partisans. Dirlewanger's men would frequently take advantage of the resulting chaos by plundering what meagre belongings the villagers possessed or raping the women, many of whom were simply shot afterwards once his men had slaked their perverse appetites. Generally, Dirlewanger turned a blind eye to such excesses; after all, he was probably guilty of committing the same offenses himself, although more discreetly. The unit had thus come a long way from its whimsical origins: the romanticized sharpshooters and poachers of June 1940 had become a group of hardened, sadistic marauders by 1943—not unlike Baron von Trenck's *Pandurs* of 200 years earlier.

Losses suffered by Dirlewanger's men during their anti-partisan operations began to mount, a sign of the increasingly effective resistance of the partisans. During October and November 1943 alone, the battalion lost 41 men killed and 143 wounded in action, nearly half of its strength.[38] This figure was added to the number of men already lost between February and the end of August 1943, which amounted to a further 318 men killed, wounded, and missing. Although roughly more than half of these losses were suffered by the Russian and Ukrainian auxiliaries recruited by the unit, it was still a very high casualty rate.[39]

The *Sonderbataillon* experienced its first exposure to front-line combat on 14 November 1943, when it was ordered into the line as a reinforcement for *H.Gr. Mitte* (Army Group Center) near Kosari, a small town 20 kilometers southwest of the city of Polatsk. The army group was severely short of infantry after long and costly fighting that autumn, and even *Polizei* units were being called upon to help with the defense. At the end of December, Dirlewanger's battalion was committed to bolster the defenses in the vicinity of Lake Beresno in the neighboring *H.Gr. Nord* (Army Group North) defensive sector. During the heavy fighting that followed until it was relieved at the end of the month, the battalion was reduced in size to only 259 men, including six officers. During the six weeks the battalion spent at the front, it had lost 50 men killed and 130 wounded, but had gained valuable front combat experience.[40]

As its losses grew, the *Sonderbataillon* slowly increased in size. When it arrived in Belarus at the end of January 1942, it was actually only the size of an overstrength infantry company, numbering approximately 250 men. Convinced that this number was insufficient to carry out his mission, Dirlewanger—on his own authority—established two "volunteer" companies composed of the aforementioned Russians and Ukrainians, led by German officers and NCOs and armed with captured Soviet weapons. With these additions, by 15 October 1942 the *Sonderbataillon* had grown in size to over 700 men and consisted of a battalion staff, a headquarters company and two German *Bewährungs* (probationary) companies. This number also included 300 Eastern volunteers organized into two companies. To carry on processing new arrivals from the Sachsenhausen concentration camp who continued to trickle in, *SS-Grenadier Ersatz-Bataillon Ost* (*SS-Gren.Ers.Btl.Ost*) in Breslau was assigned as the replacement unit associated with the *Dirlewanger Einheit* (eventually this unit relocated to Zhitomir, then to Minsk).

By May 1943, the unit's size generally remained the same, but had undergone continuing evolution as Dirlewanger juggled the dwindling number of available German replacements to meet his mission requirements. During this month, mounting casualties had forced him to reduce the number of German companies to one, with three Russian companies, a Ukrainian platoon, a German motorcycle platoon, and an attached *Ordnungspolizei* light artillery battery; in all, some 720 men.[41] Throughout, Dirlewanger had been constantly badgering both *Gruf.* von Gottberg in Minsk and Berger in Berlin for more replacements, but at the same time had also been lobbying for permission (and the funding) from Himmler to expand his battalion into a regiment. Himmler, at Berger's urging, finally gave in to his demand—after all, Dirlewanger's battalion had been very successful from the point of view of the *Reichsführer-SS* in the fight against the partisans in Belarus and increasing its size would make it even more effective.

This led to an order being issued on 10 August 1943 by Hans Jüttner's *SS-FHA* authorizing the expansion of the battalion into a regiment. The order stated that the unit was to be set up along the lines of a conventional infantry regiment and was to consist of three infantry battalions of four companies each, a regimental staff, a regimental headquarters company, a heavy mortar company, a machine-gun company, and a supply company.[42] Had this action been followed through to completion at the time, it would have resulted in an infantry regiment of roughly 3,000 men, quite an ambitious goal even for Berger and Dirlewanger. However, this plan had to be put on hold, at least for the next eight months, due to shortages of manpower to fill its ranks as well as the lack of sufficient weapons required to equip it. By the late summer of 1943, shortages in almost every category of weapons were beginning to be felt by every *Wehrmacht* and *Waffen-SS* front-line unit, and there were none to be spared for second-line units primarily established to conduct rear area security.

Therefore, most of the weapons and ammunition needed to expand the battalion into a regiment would have to come from captured stocks, i.e., primarily from the rich booty acquired from the Soviet Union during the early victorious days of Operation *Barbarossa*. So although not considered a first-line unit, the *Sonderbataillon* was equipped adequately for the kinds of missions that Dirlewanger's troops were carrying out at that time. Actually, Dirlewanger had no further options; Hans Jüttner continued to vociferously object to Berger and Dirlewanger's designs, and opposed them both officially and unofficially by "slow-rolling" or delaying their requests for more weapons and equipment.

The first indication that this expansion into a regiment would finally take place occurred on 31 March 1944, when an order establishing new *Feldpostnummern* (Field Post Office Numbers) for the unit was issued by the *Armeefeldpostmeister Ost* (the Army Field Postal Minister, Eastern Front). This directive, addressed to *Sonderregiment Dirlewanger*, assigned separate Field Post numbers to the regiment's staff, staff company, and each of its three infantry battalions.[43] Worthy of note was that this order omitted any mention of a heavy weapons, mortar, or antitank companies, which did not yet exist.

The actual expansion of the battalion into a regiment did not begin until May 1944, when the *II. Bataillon* was formed out of its old *2. Kompanie*; its *1. Kompanie* would become the *I. Bataillon*. There were not enough men to form a *III. Battalion*; that would have to wait until August. The lack of heavy weapons was partially made good by the attachment of *1. Batterie, SS-Polizei-Artillerie Abteilung Weissruthenien* (*SS-Pol.Art.Abt.*, Police Artillery Battalion White Russia), which had formed a habitual relationship with Dirlewanger's unit since 30 April 1943. On 26 June 1944, this attachment was made permanent when the battery was officially made a part of the *Sonderregiment*.[44] Composed of German *Ordnungspolizei* artillerymen and led by *Hauptmann der Schutzpolizei* (*Hptm.d.Schu.Po.*) Josef Steinhauer, it was the first non-probationary unit assigned to Dirlewanger, but would not be the last.

At each step of the way since the unit's arrival in Belarus, both Berger and Dirlewanger had been tirelessly hounding the *SS-Personalamt* in Berlin for more manpower. Authorization to expand into a regiment meant little if no human materiel to fill its ranks were available. Increasingly heavy losses did not make Dirlewanger's job any easier. In 1942, he had already resorted to using turncoat Russians and Ukrainians to form two volunteer companies, but Dirlewanger still preferred German replacements. At first, he wanted to limit his replacements to convicted poachers from concentration camps, as the initial group had been at Sachsenhausen. In fact, a replacement draft of 115 convicted poachers was shipped to the *Sonderbataillon* on 20 September 1942, but these men were soon used up in battle.[45]

Despite his ambitions, circumstances beyond his control forced both Berger and Dirlewanger to lower their standards and begin accepting replacements from a variety of sources. In late March or April 1943, a small number of German citizens (less than 50, born in 1901 and later) illegally residing in the *Generalgouvernement* were rounded up and shipped to the *Sonderbataillon* via *SS-Gren.Ers.Btl.Ost*. These men were judged to have been avoiding military service (i.e., draft dodging), a criminal offense under German law. To expunge this crime from their records, they were assigned to Dirlewanger's unit for the purpose of "probation before the enemy," in accordance with an instruction issued by the *Reichsführer-SS* on 20 March 1943.[46] After that, the replacement pipeline began to send more *Bewährungs-Schützen* (*B-Schützen*, probationary troops) on a more or less regular basis.

Beginning in May 1943, more "volunteers" from concentration camps began to arrive. The first group consisted of 350 ordinary criminals recruited from the Sachsenhausen *KL*, including petty thieves, bank robbers, swindlers, gangsters, rapists, and those convicted of aggravated assault. These men had been categorized as "*Berufsverbrecher*" (*BVer*, career criminals) and considered irredeemable by the *Reich*'s criminal courts.[47] Shortly afterwards, 150 more convicted poachers arrived, representing nearly all of those that remained in the entire concentration camp system. This allowed the *Sonderbataillon* to grow in size to the aforementioned 720 men, but heavy casualties suffered during the fall and winter of 1943 soon reduced this number dramatically.

Another development that year took place on 10 August 1942, when Berger gained Himmler's permission to authorize the transfer of selected SS and Police prisoners convicted of criminal offenses to serve in Dirlewanger's battalion as *B-Schützen*. Most of them came from Himmler's own SS and Police disciplinary camp at Danzig-Matzkau as well as the SS prison in Prague, but initially this number was very small after each one was approved on a case-by-case basis. Many of these SS transfers had been officers or senior NCOs reduced in rank after being convicted of various crimes, such as former high-ranking *NSDAP* official Fritz Missmahl.

Missmahl, a highly decorated World War I veteran, had been dismissed from the Nazi Party's civil service and position as vice-president of the *Landes-Versicherungs-Anstalt* (National Insurance Institution) in June 1942 after he had been sentenced by an *SS* and Police court on suspicion of embezzlement of government funds and of having committed homosexual acts, a violation of Paragraph 175 of the *Strafgesetzbuch* (German Criminal Code) updated in 1935. Found guilty of the first charge (there was insufficient evidence but he was still suspected of the second), he was sentenced to three-and-a-half years' punishment. In July 1942, he was then shipped to the Sachsenhausen *KL* to await the outcome of an appeal for leniency. Instead of serving his entire prison sentence, due to the personal intervention by his friend Karl Florian, the powerful *Gauleiter* of Düsseldorf, and by Gottlob Berger—who was seeking officers for Dirlewanger's battalion—Missmahl's punishment was commuted in September 1943 to perform front-line probation in the *Sonderbataillon* as an *Obersturmführer*, where he initially served as a platoon leader, then as a company commander.[48]

These new replacements fell into two distinct categories, depending upon whether they were discharged from an *SS* and Police disciplinary camp or a *KL*. This distinction determined how they would be treated by Dirlewanger and his subordinates. The former poachers who had volunteered for the unit in 1940 received relatively preferential treatment; their time served in the *Sondereinheit* counted towards fulfilling their mandatory military service obligation.[49] They were allowed to wear *SS* insignia and were eligible for promotion to higher *SS* rank once they had proven themselves. They also were granted *Kriegsurlaub* (wartime home leave) as well as the same pay and benefits as any other volunteer in the *Waffen-SS*, especially after they had been considered rehabilitated by Dirlewanger himself.

This also applied to the *SS* and Police *B-Schützen* who had been sent from Danzig-Matzkau, whose prior membership in the *SS* or *Polizei* would be restored once they had completed their probationary period. Among this group were several former *SS* or *Polizei* officers who had been demoted or reduced to enlisted status for offenses they had committed. Dirlewanger used some of these men in key leadership positions, such as *Hauptmann der Schutzpolizei* (*SchuPo*, Captain of Protection Police) Herbert Meyer, who had been convicted of petty theft and embezzlement by an *SS* and Police court in November 1942. Sentenced to two-and-a-half years in prison to be served at Danzig-Matzkau, he volunteered for the *Dirlewanger Einheit* in March 1944 and was assigned as the *Kompanie-Führer* (acting Company Commander) of the *1. Kompanie*.[50]

These *SS* and Police *B-Schützen*, as well as the original remaining poachers, were given special recognition on 26 January 1943 when Himmler approved Dirlewanger's proposed design of special collar insignia for the battalion. It was to be worn on the right collar instead of the traditional *SS Siegrunen* or lightning bolts, and consisted of two silver embroidered crossed rifles on a black cloth background above a silver embroidered "potato masher" hand grenade.[51] This design signified the battalion's identity as a unit whose purpose was to close with and kill the enemy in close combat. While most of his non-probationary SS officers and NCOs continued to wear the standard SS runes, a few chose to have the new insignia; it stood out among all the other SS unit insignia and identified the wearer immediately as a member of the *Dirlewanger Einheit*. Veteran members of the unit at that time viewed it as a badge of honor.[52] It was not until after the war that the badge acquired its legendary and dreadful reputation.

The ordinary criminals from the concentration camps, in comparison, were not authorized to wear the new insignia. Rather, these so-called *BVer* were considered second-class soldiers and remained under prison-like discipline, unless they had held an officially recognized position within the camp, such as barracks-elder or *Kapo*. Convicts were usually issued worn-out uniforms and used boots. They were not awarded SS badges or rank; they wore only blank collar insignia and the *SS-Hoheitsadler* (the Nazi eagle) on the upper left sleeve of their uniform jacket. They were not eligible for promotion. Time spent in the *Sonderbataillon* was not considered as counting towards fulfilling their military service obligation. If they survived the war, at best they could expect to have their prison sentence declared fulfilled, or in certain cases have their criminal records expunged entirely, especially if they had demonstrated extreme valor (or were killed) in battle. Few ever survived long enough to claim this status. The first group of these *BVer* volunteers began arriving at the end of 1943 from the Neuengamme concentration camp.

Battalion discipline was strict, especially for the "ordinary" concentration camp *BVer* who had been induced to volunteer. While in Lublin, Dirlewanger's punishment for infractions fell within the acceptable range of what the SS service regulations allowed, but once the *Sondereinheit* moved into Belarus—where there was less supervision and oversight—Dirlewanger proved to be a very mercurial enforcer indeed. His punishments, which he often inflicted with his own hand, ranged from beatings and whippings to even arbitrary death sentences, depending on how much alcohol Dirlewanger had consumed that day or the night before. Other crimes or breaches of discipline were punished by forcing the offender to stand upright for hours or even days in a coffin-like wooden box that left them unable to sit or kneel. By the winter of 1943–44, the disciplinary situation had become so unacceptable and troop morale so negatively affected, that Himmler himself had to step in and issue an order on 20 February 1944 specifically tailored to the *Sonderbataillon* that placed limits on Dirlewanger's disciplinary authority.[53]

In a revealing speech given later to an assembly of *Gauleiters* in Posen on 3 August 1944, shortly before *Sonderregiment Dirlewanger* was committed to the battle of Warsaw, Himmler boasted about the harsh discipline prevailing in the unit:

> In 1941 [actually, June 1940], I had set up *Wilder-Regiment Dirlewanger*. Dirlewanger is a good Swabian, has been wounded ten times, is an original "type." I got permission from the *Führer* to take out of the prisons in Germany all the poachers who hunted with rifles, not those who

caught game with snares … I have replenished this regiment again and again with probationers from the *SS*, because in the *Waffen-SS* we have a terribly hard discipline. We give people years in prison for [going absent without leave] for even a few days, and it is good if the justice is tough, because then the troops stay healthy … I told Dirlewanger: "Watch out, pick out suitable ones from our concentration camp thugs, from among the professional criminals." The tone in the regiment is, of course, in many cases, I would like to say, a medieval one, with beatings and so forth … Or if someone looks questioningly [at someone who says] "we are winning the war," then he falls down dead from the table because the other one has shot him. There is no other way to deal with such people.[54]

With the disciplinary boundaries re-established, the manpower situation began to improve markedly after 19 February 1944, when Himmler granted Berger permission to withdraw even larger numbers of "volunteers" from concentration camps in order to fulfill the need to increase Dirlewanger's unit in size from a battalion to a regiment with an initial planned strength of 1,200 men (reduced shortly afterwards by Himmler to only 1,000).[55] As many as 800 of these men (some sources state 700) between the ages of 17 and 35, with exceptions for men as old as 40, signed up as volunteers (anything to escape the harsh regimen of the *KL*), but over half of them would not arrive until June 1944, once the *Sonderregiment*'s new replacement company was activated in Minsk. This large group would consist of not only ordinary criminals from the *KL*, but for the first time of *Asoziale* (asocials) too.

Asocials were German citizens deemed by the Third Reich courts as drifters, vagabonds, pimps, and other men who refused to work, as opposed to being career criminals (the *BVer*). They were deemed slackers and social leeches, and considered poor soldier material. Why these asocials had volunteered for the *Dirlewanger Einheit* can only be surmised; perhaps they also wanted to avoid the boring routine of the camps or they had been forced to volunteer. In all likelihood, they had no idea of what lay in store for them, particularly in light of what soon followed. At any rate, nearly all the former concentration camp inmates, except the former poachers, were treated harshly by Dirlewanger's veterans. Despite this, whenever an opportunity presented itself, many of these men soon reverted to their former criminal habits, especially when they were operating in the field under looser supervision. A few even attempted desertion.

The signs of the further evolution of the *Sonderregiment*'s personnel replacement policy became apparent on 22 March 1944, when Himmler received a proposal drafted by Dirlewanger and endorsed by Berger that suggested that all *SS* and Police convicts serving time at Danzig-Matzkau or any other *SS*-administered disciplinary camps be routinely transferred to the *Sonderregiment* to perform their probationary duty in the front lines and thus earn their full rehabilitation, instead of with other *SS* probationary units.[56] It would, the proposal agued, be a good way to put their military experience to positive use, despite their records of criminal offenses. This step would provide as an additional benefit the professional military expertise that the rapidly growing regiment needed.

Himmler at first demurred, since he had other ideas concerning what to do with his *SS* and Police convicts. After mulling over the idea, two months later Himmler issued an order on 6 June 1944 outlining his priorities for the "rehabilitation" and probationary service of these men. His order established three levels of *Waffen-SS* probationary units, ranked in order of priority of assignment. First priority was given to *SS-Fallschirmjäger* (Parachute) *Bataillon 500*, which was considered an elite unit. The second was *Sonderverband z.b.V. Friedenthal*, which eventually morphed into *SS-Jäger Bataillon 502*, part of *SS-Jagdverband* (an *SS* special forces unit) led by Oskar Skorzeny.

Third in order of priority was *Sonderregiment Dirlewanger*, which would receive personnel not deemed sufficiently qualified for the other two organizations. In practice, Dirlewanger would still be assigned the majority of the *SS* and Police *B-Schützen* because the other two listed organizations were relatively small in number and required fewer replacements. With this bureaucratic maneuver, Dirlewanger's regiment would become the largest of the official *Bewährungs-Einheiten* of the *Waffen-SS* and *Ordnungspolizei*.[57] This step would grant him access to a large and steady source of replacements, but this measure would not begin fully operating until 24 September 1944, when 1,500 *SS* and Police *B-Schützen* would be assigned to the *Sonderregiment* from the Danzig-Matzkau camp.

Between the middle of April and the end of June 1944, the newly established *Sonderregiment* was engaged in protecting supply convoys, carrying out anti-partisan sweep operations (including Operation *Frühlingsfest*), guarding supply depots, and training the first batch of 337 new recruits it had received on 18 March.[58] By the middle of June, both the *I.* and *II. Bataillon* were considered operational. On 30 June, the regiment reported a total *Iststärke* (its actual present for duty strength) of 17 officers, 87 NCOs, and 867 enlisted men, for a total of 971 personnel. This did not count 769 more who were on their way from several concentration camps to its dedicated replacement company in Minsk.[59] In addition, the unit continued to be supported by Steinhauer's *SS-Pol.Art.Abt. Weissruthenien*, composed of 105 men equipped with four captured 76.2mm Soviet divisional guns.

On 24 April 1944, the regiment acquired its own dedicated communications capability, when a 16-man radio platoon from the *SS*-administered *Postschutz* (Postal Protection Troops) station in Berlin was transferred *en masse* without going through the formality of asking its members to volunteer. These soldiers had no criminal record, nor were they undergoing any sort of probation. Until that point, the *Sonderregiment* had been dependent upon attached troops from the *Wehrmacht* for its communications.

During this same period, most of the regiment's Ukrainian volunteers were reassigned elsewhere, except for a few dozen native *Hilfswillige* or volunteer helpers, referred to as *Hiwis*, who preferred to remain with Dirlewanger as cooks, groomsmen, or supply troops. Ukrainian horsemen in the unit's reconnaissance platoon also remained with the regiment.[60] Most of its Russian contingent had already been transferred to *SS-Polizei-Regiment 24* the previous November, where many of them were assigned to *SS-Jäger-Abteilung Pannier*, another anti-partisan unit.[61]

Throughout this period, as his continuing success as a counter-guerilla fighter became generally recognized within the *SS* empire, Dirlewanger carried on his rise through the ranks. On 9 November 1941, he was promoted to *Sturmbannführer*, the equivalent rank of a *Wehrmacht* major. At this point, he was still being carried on the books as a member of *SS-TK Inf.Rgt. 5*, but since 1 November 1942, his home base unit or unit of permanent assignment had been changed to *HSSPF-Russland-Mitte* (formerly known as *HSSPF-Ost*) in Minsk. On 12 May 1943, he was promoted to *Obersturmbannführer*, the equivalent rank of *Oberstleutnant*, or lieutenant colonel. Once it became certain that his unit would be expanded in size to a regiment, he was promoted on 19 March 1944 to *Standartenführer*, a rank that loosely translates as a junior *Oberst* (colonel).

Awards also came his way in recognition of his leadership and bravery in battle, evidence of the same positive leadership traits that had manifested themselves during World War I. In addition to receiving both Clasps to the Iron Cross, Second and First Classes, he was awarded the Close Combat Badge in Bronze on 16 September 1942, the Gold Wound Badge on 9 July 1943, as well as several lesser "Eastern People's" awards. His highest award during this period was the German Cross in Gold, presented on 5 December 1943. This award, second only to the Knight's Cross in prestige, was given in recognition for his overall manner of performance during the period encompassing February 1942 to 1 August 1943, where he led his unit in nearly every major anti-partisan operation carried out by *HSSPF Russland-Mitte*, including the deadly Operations *Adler, Greif, Nordsee, Regatta, Karlsbad, Franz, Erntefest I* and *II, Hornung, Zauberflötte, Draufgänger I* and *II, Kottbus, Hermann,* and *Erntefest.*

His award recommendation did not, of course, mention the mistreatment of, or the crimes inflicted upon, the local population by the men of his unit. All of these operations carried out by his troops, as well as by *Polizei, Wehrmacht,* and other *SS* units, resulted in the impoverishment, deportation, or death of the local population, and not a few partisans who happened to be unlucky enough to be trapped in these areas. His own losses, as mentioned earlier, had meanwhile continued to escalate, an indication of the severity and risks entailed in fighting against increasingly skilled and well-equipped partisans. Dirlewanger himself was contemptuous of danger and was frequently seen in the front lines inspiring his troops. During one engagement, a sniper shot a cigarette out of his mouth; on another, he suffered a grazing wound when a bullet tore across his chest during one hotly contested anti-partisan operation.[62]

Characterized as a *Draufgänger* (daredevil) by his superiors, his German Cross award recommendation was submitted by *Gruf.* Kurt von Gottberg and approved by none other than *Ogruf.* Erich von dem Bach, who endorsed it with the statement:

"As a result of the extraordinary services and outstanding bravery which *Ostubaf.* Dr. Dirlewanger has repeatedly demonstrated in a large number of undertakings against [partisans], I support the award of the German Cross in Gold to this *SS* leader."[63] By this time, of course, Dirlewanger had become a fully vested member of the *Waffen-SS*, with an *SS* Membership Number of 357 267.

When Operation *Bagration*, the great Soviet summer offensive, began on 22 June 1944, his *Sonderregiment* was still in the process of absorbing new replacements and carrying out normal security duties. Shortly after the offensive started, but before they became involved in the fighting, Dirlewanger and his regiment were caught up in the maelstrom of the 250-kilometer-long retreat from Minsk that began on 7 July when *H.Gr. Mitte* collapsed under the Red Army's hammer blows. Somehow, Dirlewanger and his two battalions managed to extricate themselves from the various encircling nets being cast by advancing Soviet troops and successfully escaped to the west. At one point, the two battalions became separated, but each continued making their way westwards to safety. During the first week of the retreat, Dirlewanger's main column encountered the arriving *Marschbataillon* of approximately 700 new concentration camp recruits at the fork in the road east of the town of Lida. They had come from the direction of Molodechno along with the regiment's *Tross* (supply train) after both groups had hurriedly evacuated Minsk and its men had not yet been assigned to either of the two battalions.[64]

While operating under the control of *Kampfgruppe* (*K.Gr.*, battlegroup) *von Gottberg* between 7 and 20 July 1944, the *Sonderregiment* and its attached *Polizei* artillery battery fought in several delaying actions, including ones at Lomsha and Lida that bought time for the long retreating columns of *H.Gr. Mitte* to struggle towards safety. Dirlewanger's men even managed to make up equipment losses by appropriating *Wehrmacht* weapons, supplies, and vehicles abandoned along the way. After breaking out from encirclement at Grodno on 16 July, the regiment was detached from von Gottberg's command on 20 July and ordered to East Prussia.[65] Here, it was supposed to undergo *Auffrischung* (reconstitution) at the Arys *SS* troop training area west of the town of Lyck (the modern-day town of Ełk), where it arrived on or about 21 July.

One large infusion of troops that Dirlewanger had been counting on to bolster the strength of his regiment did not reach fruition. On 1 May 1944, Dirlewanger was notified by Berger's office that a Muslim unit, *Turkestanische Gren.Btl. 450* with 800 men, was to be attached to the *Sonderregiment* as an integral part. Composed of Turkoman POWs who had volunteered to fight for the liberation of their homeland from the U.S.S.R., this unit was to be based in Usda and would form the basis of the new *Ostmusselmanische* (Eastern Muslim) *SS-Regiment 1*, which would also include Uzbeks among its rank and file.

By 25 June, this regiment had grown in size to approximately 1,400 men after 600 additional Turkistanis arrived from a POW camp in Norway.[66] However, due to the collapse of *H.Gr. Mitte* its consolidation with Dirlewanger's unit was never completed; instead, this regiment of *Ostvolk* (*SS* term for "Eastern Peoples") would eventually be assigned to the *29. Waffen-Gren.Div. der SS* after fighting primarily with the *Waffen-Sturmbrigade der SS RONA* during the Warsaw Uprising. Here, *Ostmusselmanische SS-Rgt 1* would also occasionally fight under Dirlewanger's command, when not under that of Bronislav Kaminski, the commander of the renegade *RONA* Brigade.

Another asset that Dirlewanger was successfully able to pry from Jüttner's grip with the help of Gottlob Berger was a heavy weapons company, which the *Sonderregiment* had lacked since its inception. Although a *schwere Kompanie* had been authorized since 1943, the antitank guns and heavy mortars needed to support the regiment's infantry in battle were not available and had to be provided by temporarily attached *Polizei, Wehrmacht*, or *SS* heavy weapons companies. Fortuitously for Dirlewanger, a *schwere Kompanie* matching this description had already been established as an independent unit as early as 27 March 1944. Berger, ever on the lookout for ways to meet his friend's request, had it sent to the Eastern Front and began arranging its attachment to Dirlewanger's unit.

Based upon an order issued by Berger's office on that date authorizing contingency measures for an emergency, this heavy weapons company had been formed at Zeesen in Germany using excess personnel taken from the *Ersatzabteilung der Fronthilfe* (Replacement Detachment of the Front Assistance) of the *Deutsche Reichspost* (*DRP*, or German National Postal Service), the *Waffen-SS-Kraftfahrstaffel* (motor park) at Zeesen, and the *SS-Sicherungsbataillon der Deutschen Reichspost* (Security Battalion of the German Postal Service). The company consisted of two platoons equipped with 120mm mortars and a platoon of light antitank guns. Its first commander was *Ostuf.* Otto Rühs.[67]

It was originally intended to be used to support the chief of staff of the *SS-Fronthilfe DRP* and the *SS-Kraftfahrstaffel* for internal security duties, but by the late spring of 1944 Berger had it transferred to the Eastern Front.[68] At some point shortly thereafter, certainly by late June or early July 1944, this unit would be attached to *Sonderregiment Dirlewanger*, where it was incorporated into the regiment as its heavy weapons company. Again, this was not a probationary unit, but was composed of ordinary *Waffen-SS* troops who had committed no offenses, like the men in the newly incorporated communications platoon.

Upon its assignment to the *Sonderregiment*, the *Fronthilfe der Deutschen Reichspost der Waffen-SS* was designated as its *13. (schwere) Kompanie*, given that the numerical designations for *1.* to *12. Kompanien* were already being used by the *I. (1.* through *4. Kompanie*) and *II. Bataillone* (*5.* through *8. Kompanie*) and the new *III. Bataillon* (*9.* through *12. Kompanie*) then being established (the number of the *13. Kompanie* was the traditional title of German heavy weapons companies dating back to World War I).[69]

During its two-week stay at the Arys training area, *Sonderregiment Dirlewanger* used the time to reorganize its platoons, companies, and battalions and to train the flow of replacements coming in from its newly relocated replacement company in Cracow. Additionally, over 100 men who had been declared missing in action after the 14-day withdrawal from Minsk would continue trickling in until 25 August. Losses were tallied up; surprisingly, the regiment had come through its ordeal in relatively good condition, with nearly 1,000 men still in the ranks, including the survivors of the group of replacements it had picked up during the retreat. Not only had the number of casualties been less than anticipated, but with the extra weapons and equipment scavenged along the way from retreating *Wehrmacht* units, it had even more than the usual number of small arms and light mortars. With his regiment busily occupied with such administrative matters, during the last week of July Dirlewanger himself left the regiment in the care of his *Ia* (operations officer), *Stubaf.* Kurt Weisse, and flew to Berlin to lobby Gottlob Berger for more men and equipment.

While at Lyck, the future employment of the regiment remained a mystery to its men. Barracks rumors mentioned that the regiment was to be expanded into a brigade and that it might even be given "special missions" by the *Reichsführer-SS* himself. If fact, the regiment had been withdrawn from *K.Gr. von Gottberg* on Himmler's specific order for just such a purpose.[70] Thus, the men of the regiment must have not been too surprised when they were alerted on the afternoon of 3 August and informed that it was to immediately prepare one battalion-sized *Kampfgruppe* for movement the next day by truck to Warsaw, where fighting had broken out in the city on 1 August.[71] A second *Kampfgruppe* was to follow as soon as transportation was available. The rest of the *Sonderregiment*, including the regimental headquarters and the artillery battery, would follow as soon as possible.[72]

The first *Kampfgruppe* was formed from the *Sonderregiment's I. Bataillon*. It was named after its commander, the now-rehabilitated Herbert Meyer, who had been promoted to *Obersturmführer* in August after being assigned to the unit in March 1944 as a *B-Schütze*. *Kampfgruppe Meyer*, with a combat strength of 356 men not counting support troops, arrived in the western outskirts of Warsaw on the evening of 4 August. The other battlegroup, *K.Gr. Steinhauer*, with a *Kampfstärke* of approximately 350 men, would not arrive on the scene until two days later.[73] Upon arrival, both battalions would fall under the command of the notorious *Gruf.* Heinz Reinefarth, who led a combined *Waffen-SS*, *Polizei*, and *Wehrmacht* battlegroup of the same name. In turn, Reinefarth answered to *Ogruf.* Erich von dem Bach, who was tasked by Himmler on 4 August to take charge of the overall German response to the Uprising in his capacity as the Chief of Anti-Partisan Operations.[74] Placing this responsibility into the hands of von dem Bach freed the commander of the 9. *Armee*, *Gen.d.Pz.Tr.* Nikolaus von Vormann, to focus his efforts east of Warsaw towards the rapidly approaching forces of Marshal Rokossovsky's First Belorussian Front.

When the bulk of its component elements—including its headquarters, heavy machine-gun company, heavy mortar company, and antitank gun platoon—finally arrived in Warsaw, the *Sonderregiment's* first *Kampfstärke* report (combined combat strength, not including administrative and logistics troops) submitted on 8 August stated that it had 881 men present for duty, including 16 officers, three days after *K.Gr. Meyer* had begun fighting.[75] Although *K.Gr. Meyer* and *Steinhauer* had fought separately for the first three days, once the Brühl Palace had been retaken and the Warsaw *Kampfkommandant* (battle commander), *Gen.Lt.* (*Generalleutnant*, Major General) Reiner Stahel, had been rescued, the regiment would unite as *K.Gr. Dirlewanger* that evening when Dirlewanger returned from Berlin and took over from acting commander *Stubaf.* Weisse. Dirlewanger then led it until the Polish Home Army capitulated two months later.[76]

Losses throughout the battle were extremely high until nearly the end. *Kampfgruppe Meyer* alone, in three days of fighting from 5–7 August, was reduced from 356 to only 40 men after Meyer had fought his way through 5 kilometers of insurgent resistance to reach the Brühl Palace. When the initial phase of the battle ended on 8 August, the combined combat strength of Meyer and Steinhauer's battalions—not including the regimental headquarters, headquarters, supply, and heavy weapons companies—was only 120 men.[77] After two months of more or less continuous combat in Warsaw, the portion of the regiment engaged in the battle reported having a combat strength on 8 October of only 648 men. Hundreds of its original members and over a thousand replacements had been killed, wounded, or declared missing during this 65-day period. In addition to the *SS* and Police *B-Schützen* and concentration camp *Straffälige* (convicts) who were killed, several of Dirlewanger's officers also met their fate, including unit old-timers such as *Ustuf.* Max Schreiner and *Ostuf.* Adalbert Trattenschegg.[78]

Fighting Polish insurgents in a densely populated urban environment was not the same as fighting isolated bands of partisans in the forests and swamps of Belarus. Dirlewanger's officers and troops were slow to learn the basics of street fighting and often resorted to human wave attacks across open areas, where they were mowed down in their hundreds by Polish Home Army members manning prepared defensive positions. His men frequently resorted to using civilian captives as human shields, but without much success since the Poles shot at them anyway. Dirlewanger himself seemed to have not concerned himself with how many men he lost or how many they killed, only whether or not they had achieved his objectives for the day.

To bolster the sagging infantry strength of the regiment, at one point in mid-August both battalions of *Ostmusselmanisches SS-Rgt 1* were temporarily placed under Dirlewanger's control, along with portions of the Azeri *Inf.Btl. 111* of *Sonderverband Bergmann*. At one point, in addition to what his own unit possessed, Dirlewanger had two heavy antitank guns, 12 medium mortars, 10 assault guns (*Sturmgeschütz III, StuG III*), two self-propelled antitank guns, six 120mm heavy mortars, four 20mm *Flak*, and 17 flamethrowers attached to his *Kampfgruppe*.[79] Yet even this considerable amount of weaponry was not enough to compensate for the steady drain of manpower.

At the peak of the fighting, *K.Gr. Dirlewanger* attained a level of savagery and brutality during the Warsaw Uprising that was matched but not exceeded by the equally barbarous *Waffen-Sturmbrigade der SS RONA* led by the Russian renegade Bronislav Kaminski. Together, both units were responsible for the murder, rape, or injury of tens of thousands of innocent civilians in the city as well as Polish Home Army prisoners. Besides committing numerous instances of these crimes, both units were also guilty of looting and pillaging hundreds of Polish homes and businesses. In Warsaw, *K.Gr. Dirlewanger* alone was estimated to have been directly responsible for the deaths of between 12,500 and 30,000 people, most of them civilian non-combatants.[80]

When the commander of the *9. Armee, Gen.d.Pz.Tr.* von Vormann, learned of the atrocities being committed within his field army's *Kampfraum* (combat zone), which included the city of Warsaw, he was quick to inform the newly appointed Chief of Staff of the *OKH, Generaloberst (Gen.Obst.*, 4-star General) Hans Guderian. After verifying the accuracy of von Vormann's report with *Ogruf.* von dem Bach, an appalled Guderian voiced a request to Hitler that both Dirlewanger's and Kaminski's units should be removed from Warsaw immediately.

At first, Hitler refused to believe his legendary *panzer* general, and as Guderian stood watching, he turned to Himmler's liaison officer, *Brig.Fhr.* Hermann Fegelein, and asked him whether this was true. To Fegelein's credit, he replied: "It is true, *mein Führer.* Those men are real scoundrels!" As a result, Hitler relayed an order to Himmler directing him to sort it out; shortly thereafter, Himmler ordered von dem Bach to remove Kaminski and have him secretly executed, but Dirlewanger was left undisturbed, probably due to Berger's intervention.[81]

Except for a brief period from 11–23 September 1944 when it manned a security line along the western bank of the Vistula River to block river crossings by Soviet and Polish forces attempting to relieve the Polish Home Army, *K.Gr. Dirlewanger* was employed almost exclusively against the insurgents in the city. Whether fighting in the Ochota or Wola District, the Saxon Gardens, or against the defenders of the city's Old Town or Mokotów, Dirlewanger's tactic was nearly always the same—attack, attack, attack, directly into the most stubborn nests of resistance using hand grenades, flamethrowers, submachine guns, and bayonets. Occasionally, these attacks were supported by German armored vehicles, such as assault guns, or artillery. If these were unavailable or delayed, the men of *K.Gr. Dirlewanger* would attack without them anyway.

As a result, his regiment usually gained the most ground the quickest, but typically suffered the highest losses of any other unit in *K.Gr. Reinefarth.* Few Polish inhabitants were spared, whether resistance fighter or innocent civilian, until the Polish Home Army and civilian population began to surrender *en masse* at the end of September. Any of his own men who fell into the hands of the Poles were usually executed on the spot. After his men had finished with their gruesome work and moved on, the area where they had been operating had usually been reduced to little more than an open morgue, with thousands of bodies heaped upon one another. It went on like this until the Polish insurgents finally begged for a cease-fire and signed the capitulation agreement with *Ogruf.* von dem Bach on 2 October 1944.

Although unsurpassed in savagery and disregard for human life, a direct reflection of the personality of its commander, the *Sonderregiment* had done its part to help defeat the Warsaw Uprising. But the battle had also been a winnowing process, unlike anything the *Sondereinheit* had previously experienced. Most of the concentration camp "volunteers" who had joined the unit during 1943 and the first half of 1944 were killed or wounded between 5 August and 28 September 1944, leaving its original members—including the few remaining poachers who had joined in 1940 and 1941—as its hardened core. Most of these survivors were now NCOs and a few of them had even been promoted to officer rank. They were a tough, hard-bitten lot and would soon face their biggest challenge yet, that of transitioning their murderous partisan-hunting *Sonderregiment* into a conventionally armed infantry brigade.

But this would not happen until Dirlewanger had received his Knight's Cross, which was approved by Hitler on 30 September.[82] He had already been promoted to *Oberführer* (senior colonel) on 12 August 1944, the highest rank he would ever obtain. The award proposal was submitted on 10 September by none other than *Gruf.* Hans Reinefarth himself, with whom Dirlewanger had a contentious relationship throughout the battle. *Ogruf.* von dem Bach, overall commander of the forces responsible for putting down the Warsaw Uprising, endorsed Reinefarth's recommendation and forwarded it to Hitler's headquarters in Rastenburg with the statement: "I warmly support the proposal. The successes achieved [in Warsaw] are first and foremost [due to] the personal merit of *Oberführer* Dirlewanger, who is always a shining example to his men through personal courage and bravery. [He] has been wounded a total of 11 times."[83]

To mark the victory over the Polish Home Army, the *Wehrmacht* communique for 3 October announced: "The insurgency in Warsaw has collapsed. After weeks of fighting that almost led to the complete destruction of the city, the remnants of the insurgents, abandoned on all sides, stopped resisting and surrendered."[84] In a similar vein, the public announcement of Dirlewanger's award in *Das Schwarze Korps*, the in-house newspaper of the SS, reported the following on 16 November 1944:

> The 49-year-old's path ... has always been fighting destruction and Bolshevism ... In this war his unit fought Bolshevik gangs so successfully that the Soviets put a heavy price on his head. When the uprising broke out in Warsaw, *Oberführer* Dirlewanger and his men fought the battle

for the houses and streets of the city with unheard-of ferocity and doggedness. The Führer honored their fight and the personal commitment of their commander by awarding the Knight's Cross of the Iron Cross to *Oberführer* Dirlewanger.[85]

Having Germany's most prestigious medal hung around his neck would mark the highlight of his military career; the fact that it had been awarded despite the heavy losses his regiment had suffered and the thousands of innocent civilians killed and wounded was of no importance. The Third Reich needed victories and heroes, especially in the autumn of 1944 when everything seemed to be turning against it.

CHAPTER TWO

From Regiment to Brigade

On 26 September 1944, surrounded by his subordinate commanders and his staff, Dr. Oskar Dirlewanger celebrated his 49th birthday at his headquarters in Warsaw's St. Stanislaw Infectious Disease Hospital in the Wola District. Even *Gruf.* Heinz Reinefarth attended, though he left early after becoming embroiled in a heated argument with a drunken Dirlewanger. The commander of the *Sonderregiment* had much to celebrate, including the pending award of his Knight's Cross, as well as the inevitable victorious conclusion of the battle against the Polish Home Army a few days hence. In gratitude for the presentation of the award, Dirlewanger wrote to Hitler's *SS Adjutant, Hstuf.* Otto Günsche, three weeks later and told him:

> [Y]ou know as well as I do that I received this high award for the soldierly achievements of my regiment, among other things. With this, the last unwelcome voices from "higher places" about my unit should have faded away! My men have achieved superhuman things in this fight to the death and destruction and have earned themselves a place in the honor book of the German soldier by their sweat, blood, and heroic sacrificial commitment![1]

Another reason for Dirlewanger to celebrate was that his old friend Gottlob Berger had finally come through with a large number of replacements from the *SS* and Police prison at Danzig-Matzkau two days beforehand. His unit was in dire need of them. After committing *K.Gr. Meyer* to the suppression of the Warsaw Uprising on 5 August and *K.Gr. Steinhauer* two days later, by 8 August the now-united *K.Gr. Dirlewanger* had lost approximately 586 men fallen or wounded in the first three days of fighting and reported a *Kampfstärke* of 881 men.[2] Throughout the battle, Dirlewanger's losses did not diminish, but continued apace. Finally, after two months of more or less continuous combat in Warsaw, *K.Gr. Dirlewanger* reported having a combat strength on 1 October of only 648 men.[3]

These awful statistics tell only part of the story. Large numbers of replacements had begun to pour in as early as 8 August. Indeed, during the period 8 August–30 September, the *Sonderregiment* received between 2,870 and 3,370 replacements, including between 1,350 and 1,750 men from the *Wehrmacht* military prisons at Glatz, Torgau, and Anklam. It also received 120–200 common criminals from the Sachsenhausen concentration camp.[4] However, by far the largest number of replacements it received at one time were the 1,500 *SS* and Police *B-Schützen* from the aforementioned Danzig-Matzkau prison, who were supposed to have arrived in the Warsaw area as early as 24 September according to the transfer order but probably arrived much later.[5] Of this number, a portion were supposed to be used to reinforce the two-battalion *Kampfgruppen* fighting in the city; the rest were most likely intended to form the newly established *III. Bataillon* (and perhaps even the new *IV. Bataillon*). Taken in their totality, the regiment's losses (killed, wounded, and missing) can be estimated as being somewhere between 2,316 and 2,733 soldiers, an appallingly high number representing several times its combat strength of 881 men reported on 8 August.[6]

How Himmler had got his hands on so many *Wehrmacht* probationary troops deserves a book all by itself. Suffice to say, when the 20 July 1944 assassination plot to kill Hitler had failed, the leader of the *Ersatzheer* (Replacement Army), *Gen. Obst.* Friedrich Fromm, was suspected of being involved in the plot and removed from his post the following day (he was later executed). Himmler, sensing an opportunity, took over the position with Hitler's consent and began using the *Ersatzheer* to serve his own ends. One of the duties that fell under his jurisdiction was the administration of all *Wehrmacht* prisons, containing thousands of men serving sentences from the *Heer*, *Luftwaffe*, and *Kriegsmarine*.

One of Himmler's first orders was to direct the first shipment of 300–400 of these *B-Schützen* from the *Wehrmachtsgefängnis* (Armed Forces Prison) in Glatz, who arrived in Warsaw on 8 August to replace the grievous losses the *Sonderregiment* had suffered since 5 August, buttressed by an additional 400–500 men from the prison at Anklam two days later.[7] Even as the *Sonderkommando* was suffering heavy casualties during the battle of Warsaw at the hands of the Polish Home Army, plans were already in motion to expand it into a conventionally equipped assault brigade and bring it into the *Waffen-SS* as a front-line unit, while cementing its status as one of the three official *Bewährungseinheit* for the SS and Police, as laid out in Himmler's directive of 6 June 1944. The *Sonderregiment's* involvement in the battle against the Warsaw Uprising had put this plan temporarily on hold, but with the victory over the insurgents assured by late September, Berger and Dirlewanger—with Himmler's support—revived the idea and began to put their earlier plans into effect.

One week after the capitulation of the last surviving Polish resistance fighters on 2 October, the new commander of the *9. Armee, Gen. d. Pz. Tr.* Smilo von Lüttwitz, proposed sending Dirlewanger and his surviving troops to Volonov (modern-day Wolanów), a *Luftwaffe*-administered training area located west of Radom in Poland. It would also take his regiment out of Warsaw, scene of some of its most egregious war crimes. In Volonov, the *Sonderregiment* would undergo a lengthy reconstitution process while converting into a brigade, pending Himmler's approval of von Lüttwitz's proposal.[8] The *Sonderregiment* was certainly in dire need of rebuilding, and von

Lüttwitz would also have wanted Dirlewanger and his troops as far away from his *Kampfraum* as possible, being well aware of its criminal tendencies.[9]

The commander of the *9. Armee* was informed by the *SS-HA* on 9 October that more replacements were on the way to increase the number of men in the *Sonderregiment* to 6,000.[10] However, despite the preparations underway to host Dirlewanger and his troops, von Lüttwitz and the commander of the army's *Rückwärtiges Gebiet* (rear area) would not have to implement these instructions after all. Apparently, upon a request made by Gottlob Berger in mid-September 1944, Himmler had already made up his mind to send the regiment to the puppet Slovak Republic instead, where it would fall under the operational control of Dirlewanger's sponsor for the first time in its sordid history. Berger, who had chafed at being continually kept behind a desk in Berlin, had finally been granted his long-desired field command in Slovakia on 31 August and evidently wanted his old friend by his side.[11]

Once it arrived, Dirlewanger's unit was intended to take part in the suppression of the Slovak Mutiny (also called the Slovak Revolt), which had begun over a month earlier on 23 August. As a result, few, if any, of Dirlewanger's men arrived at the new camp being built for them at Volonov—most of his troops probably remained in Warsaw until they departed by rail for Slovakia or had been sent to Slovakia directly from Danzig-Matzkau or Chlum. The camp being built at Volonov was not wasted; it was used instead as the base for the formation of the newly authorized *Fallschirmpanzer-Korps Hermann Göring*.[12]

The first of eight troop trains carrying the *Sonderregiment*'s surviving veterans and some of its new replacements began departing Warsaw for Slovakia on 13 October. The last train left the following day. However, two weeks before the *Sonderregiment* had entrained and while fighting in Warsaw was still ongoing, Himmler had ordered Berger on 19 September to hand over control of the operation to *Ogruf.* Hermann Höfle the following day. The transfer of Berger had become painfully necessary due to his demonstrated unsuitability as a field commander, having failed completely in suppressing the Slovak mutineers. With Berger reassigned, the ruthless Höfle was simultaneously named as the new *HSSPF* for Slovakia as well as the *deutscher Befehlshaber in der Slowakei* (*dt.Befh.i.d.Slowakei*, German Commander in Slovakia).[13] Höfle was apparently not pleased with this dubious addition to his forces and described how it had transpired in his testimony after the war during his war crimes trial:

> When I was already in Slovakia and reported that the forces at my disposal would by no means be sufficient to fight the insurgent army, Himmler, when I met him in Vienna (in the first days of October), told me that he had decided that a brigade of Dirlewanger troops would be transported to Slovakia. After I realized that the Dirlewanger Brigade consisted for the most part of probationary personnel (mainly Army men and officers), I expressed to Himmler my misgivings about sending a probationary force to Slovakia, which was an allied

and sovereign state. I assume that this suggestion had been made by Berger to Himmler. Since Berger had left Slovakia only a few days before, I take this to mean that Berger may have intended his friend Dirlewanger for this assignment while he was still in Slovakia and may not yet have known that he was to be relieved. Himmler replied sharply that I could not express any reservations about this, since I did not know the brigade at all, and that, moreover, discipline was particularly strict in this brigade, because particularly strict disciplinary measures were laid down for this unit. In spite of my refusal, the brigade arrived in Slovakia by rail transport before the middle of October.[14]

After replacing Berger with Höfle, Himmler softened the blow by informing the former officer that his talents were in even greater demand in his previous position as Chief of the *SS-HA*, requiring him to return immediately to Berlin. Once back in his role as head of the *SS* Main Office, Berger was given the additional duty of organizing the *Volkssturm*, the *NSDAP*'s home guard formed from all males aged between 15 and 65 who had not yet been called up for active military service.[15]

Meanwhile, Höfle quickly realized that he would be unable to suppress the Slovak insurgents with the limited number of troops available, and requested reinforcements. One of the few available assets the *Waffen-SS* had in reserve at that moment was Dirlewanger's unit, which had ceased combat operations by 2 October. By that point, the *Sonderregiment* had been beefed up by the addition of several thousand replacements to a strength of between 4,000 and 4,500 men, although its structure was still fluid at this point.[16] Berger's mislaid plans to have Dirlewanger and his men transferred to Slovakia had borne fruit, after all. It must have been with some misgivings that Höfle finally accepted the brigade; he would probably have agreed with the old German saying "*In der Not frisst der Teufel Fliegen*," the equivalent of "beggars can't be choosers." He soon got his troops and quickly got them engaged in the fight against the Slovak insurgents.

With this new mission, the complete reconstitution of the unit would have to wait, although new men and equipment would continue to be funneled to its assembly area in Slovakia. Meanwhile, several more-or-less combat-ready battalions would take part in suppressing the Slovak Mutiny, at a point when the tide had already begun to turn against the rebels. In truth, the mutiny had peaked and was beginning to diminish just as the *Sonderregiment* was arriving. Slovakia was hardly a secure and peaceful area. The front line of the Eastern Front was less than 120 kilometers away, where elements of *General der Infanterie* (*Gen.d.Inf.*) Otto Wöhler's *8. Armee* were involved in heavy defensive fighting against the vanguards of the Second and Fourth Ukrainian Fronts.

Upon arrival, Dirlewanger's troops would initially be quartered in the Deviaky–Laskár–Mošovce area, where the new companies and battalions would be established and old ones reconstituted. His men quickly realized that even the skies were not under firm German control. On 16 October, one of the unit's veteran battalions, while detraining in the Slovak village of Deviaky after completing its 400-kilometer rail movement from Warsaw, was attacked by several LaGG-5 fighter-bombers of the Soviet-sponsored Slovak Air Force operating in support of the mutineers. Some of the battalion's men were killed and wounded after their train was repeatedly strafed with machine-gun and cannon fire.[17]

Most of the *Sondereinheit* had finished concentrating in its forward assembly area located between Ružomberok and Bialy Potak by 18 October. Except for the new subordinate elements being formed near Mošovce, the rest of the unit was ordered to attack south towards the center of Slovak resistance, the city of Neusohl (Banská Bystrica), located 112 kilometers (by road) to the south.[18] Dirlewanger's troops, operating in concert with several other German units—including the *271. Volks-Grenadier Division (V.G.D.), 178. Panzer-Division (Pz.Div.) Tatra, SS-K.Gr. Schill*, and the Ukrainians of the *14. Waffen-Grenadier Division (W.Gren.Div.) der SS Galizien*—slowly pushed the Slovak rebels into an ever-shrinking perimeter from which for most there would be no escape. By 30 October, Neusohl had been retaken and most of the remaining Slovak forces had been crushed or scattered, finally allowing Dirlewanger to continue with the formation of his brigade near the Slovak town of Revúca. Except for occasional forays to eliminate partisan groups that had escaped the German dragnet, the rebuilding of his unit continued apace.[19]

Exactly when Himmler made the decision to officially expand the *Sonderregiment* into a brigade is not clear; it had already been informally proposed as early as July 1944 by either Dirlewanger or Berger, but the Soviet summer offensive had put that plan on hold, just as the Warsaw Uprising had delayed it for two more months. In a periodic memorandum issued by the *SS-FHA* on 11 October 1944, titled *Bezeichnung der Feldeinheiten der Waffen-SS* (Designations of Field Units of the *Waffen-SS*), it was still officially titled as an *SS-Sonderregiment*, although it was already being unofficially referred to as a brigade in message traffic.[20]

The *SS* bureaucracy finally caught up with the unit's official title when the next *SS-FHA* memorandum appeared on 13 November and officially designated it as *SS-Sturmbrigade* (Assault Brigade) *Dirlewanger*.[21] This memorandum did not mention any corresponding list of *KStN* or organizational diagrams that specified how the unit was to be organized and what it would be equipped with; these documents would not be provided until 19 December 1944, by which point the brigade was already involved decisively in battle.

Although records are sketchy and no organizational diagrams of the draft structure of October or November 1944 are known to have survived, Dirlewanger most likely would have been given general guidance by Department II of the *SS-FHA*'s Organizational Bureau. While strong in terms of troop numbers, the brigade's weaknesses included the lack of heavy weapons to equip its men and insufficient logistical capability to keep them adequately fed, armed, and clothed. Regardless, formation of the brigade continued apace, possibly incorporating design modifications put forward by Berger, Dirlewanger, and his *Adjutant, Stubaf.* Kurt Weisse.

The month-long *Auffrischung* process resulted in a virtually new unit. The expansion of the *Sonderregiment* into the *SS-Sturmbrigade Dirlewanger* continued throughout November and into early December. It not only added to the unit's size, but changed its composition as well.[22] Instead of a single regiment of three battalions with relatively few regimental heavy weapons or support units, the new brigade—on paper at least—would consist of a brigade staff, a staff or headquarters company, two assault regiments of three battalions each, a *gemischte* (mixed) battalion, and a small artillery *Abteilung* (battalion) consisting of two 105mm light howitzer batteries and a 76.2mm divisional gun battery. The structure of the new second regiment, soon titled *SS-Sturmregiment 2* (*SS-St.Rgt. 2*), was most likely a mirror image of the original regiment activated in Minsk during May 1944.

Since there was not yet enough weaponry to equip each regiment with an antitank company and heavy mortar or infantry howitzer company, the available heavy weapons would be concentrated into a single *gemischte Bataillon*. This was to have a 120mm heavy mortar company, an antitank gun/antiaircraft (*Flak*) company, a mounted reconnaissance company, and a *Pionier* (combat engineer) *Kompanie*. This organization would continually evolve throughout November and December. The brigade would also include beefed-up medical, supply, and repair units. In addition to forming these units, many from scratch, there was also the additional challenge of equipping and training the new platoons, companies, and battalions to such a degree that the brigade would be able to function on the battlefield as a unified whole.[23] This was to prove a significant challenge, as will be seen.

All told, by the first week of December 1944, the *Sturmbrigade* had an *Iststärke* of approximately 6,500 men, making it virtually a miniature division.[24] Its official designation as a *Sturmbrigade* was another matter, because this implied that it would have a larger complement of heavy weapons than a normal *Wehrmacht* infantry brigade and could perform missions expected of an upgraded assault unit. Why it was awarded this impressive-sounding title is a mystery; at no point in its history was the brigade ever equipped as such, unlike the famous *5. SS-Freiwilligen-Sturmbrigade Wallonien*. This latter unit was formed from French-speaking Belgian collaborators in June 1943 and was lavishly equipped with everything an assault brigade needed to perform as such, including an 88mm *Flak* battery, *Sturmgeschütz* assault guns, and heavy *Panzerabwehrkanonen* (*PaK*, antitank guns).

The reason why the brigade was so poorly armed and equipped can be easily explained. During the autumn of 1944, the *Wehrmacht's* bureau of ordnance had given top priority to reconstituting *panzer* divisions and the equipping of the newly established *Volks-Grenadier* divisions in preparation for the upcoming Ardennes Offensive; second-line SS formations like the Dirlewanger Brigade had to wait their turn. Consequently, shortages of German-manufactured weapons would force

Dirlewanger to appropriate large amounts of surplus Soviet small arms and heavy weapons and mostly Czech-manufactured weapons captured during the suppression of the Slovak rebellion. Depending upon availability, other foreign-manufactured arms and equipment were used, whenever German arms were lacking

For example, one battalion in the brigade was issued Italian-made Type M38 Carcano rifles firing 7.35mm ammunition, which was unsuitable for German-designed Mauser 98-type rifles that used 7.92mm rounds. These Italian-made arms were issued to some of the men in the newly formed *III. Bataillon* of *SS-St.Rgt. 2*, which would later contribute to ammunition supply problems in December 1944. Chronic shortages of heavy infantry weapons would force Dirlewanger to form the aforementioned mixed battalion, which served as a centralized temporary expedient until adequate numbers of trained troops and supplies of German-made weapons could be acquired.

To facilitate delivery of recruits to the rapidly expanding brigade, its replacement company (*Ersatz-Kompanie*), *2. Sturmbrigade Dirlewanger*, was re-established on 1 October 1944 in a Catholic nunnery at Cracow after surviving the retreat from Minsk.[25] Here, new arrivals or returning convalescents were received and processed, including the issue of uniforms and equipment, and sent on their way to the brigade via rail under strict escort of responsible NCOs or junior officers. If time permitted, the new arrivals, especially those coming directly from concentration camps, would be given a week or two of rudimentary drill at Cracow to prepare them for service at the front. For many of these unfortunates, it would be all of the formal training they would ever receive, if that. If some of these men had passed through the *SS-Bewährungs-Abteilung* in Chlum near Prague, they would have received some form of training or fitness assessment, but the exact number is unknown.

However, even before the brigade left Warsaw, Dirlewanger and his sponsor Gottlob Berger realized that there were simply not enough candidates in all of the various *SS* prisons and *Wehrmacht* punishment installations to provide the number of men the brigade needed to reach full strength. The 1,500 *SS* and Police *B-Schützen* from the Danzig-Matzkau *SS* and Police prison that were supposed to be shipped to the *Sonderregiment* beginning as early as 24 September would be used to replace the heavy losses suffered in Warsaw by the *I.* and *II. Bataillone* and to form the new *III. Bataillon* (and possible the *IV.*). The exact date of their arrival is not known, but it is likely that they arrived too late to participate in the fighting, as previously mentioned.

Even taking control of the *Wehrmacht*'s probationary units and prisons was not enough to meet the requirements; before it departed Warsaw, the *Iststärke* of the *Sonderregiment* was between 4,000 and 4,500 men. This was after receiving nearly 2,000 *B-Schützen* sent from *Wehrmacht* prisons, detention facilities, and punishment cells, men who had been convicted of theft, fraud, assault, insubordination, and having political views contrary to the Nazi orthodoxy, as well as a host of other criminal offenses.[26] The quality of these former soldiers, sailors, and airmen varied substantially, from officers of the *Heer* suspected of disloyalty or involvement in the 20 July 1944 assassination plot to petty swindlers of the *Kriegsmarine*.

Like the *SS* and Police *B-Schützen*, these soldiers, sailors, and airmen had also received some sort of military training in their past, including a few highly experienced officers who had been cashiered and sent to the brigade for rehabilitation.[27] One of these men, former *Oberst* Walther Freiherr von Uckermann, was a 1937 graduate of the *Kriegsakademie* (general staff college) who was assigned as the *Adjutant* for *SS-St.Rgt. 2* with the lowly rank of *Grenadier* in a position that normally called for a *Major* or *Hauptmann*. Surprisingly, these men were not considered *SS* members, nor were they required to join it.[28] Most of the two dozen or so former officers chose to keep wearing their *Wehrmacht* uniforms, although a few of them—such as former *Oberst* Harald Momm—decided to wear the full kit of an *Hauptsturmführer* rather than accept demotion to a lowly *Grenadier*. Regardless, for all of them, serving in the brigade counted as fulfillment of a portion of their military obligation, even though they were still considered to be in a probationary status.[29]

Despite the infusion of these 3,000–3,500 *B-Schützen* from the *SS*, Police, and *Wehrmacht* between 8 August and 24 September 1944, it was still not enough to bring the new brigade up to its envisioned *Sollstärke* (target strength) of 6,500 men. While the *Dirlewanger Einheit* had been sent replacements from various *SS*-run concentration camps since its foundation, most of these men were *BVer* or career criminals incarcerated for various crimes, such as poaching, theft, attempted murder, and rape, but not for political offenses, which had heretofore been one of the few offenses disqualifying men from the camps as a manpower source. Of course, Jews imprisoned in the *KL* system were excluded from joining, it went without saying—that would have been going too far, even for Berger. By October 1944, the population of convicted poachers had been exhausted, yet there was one more source of manpower that had not yet been tapped.

Taking advantage of Berger's position as Himmler's right-hand man for personnel-related issues, Dirlewanger, through Berger, convinced the *Reichsführer-SS* to consider another source of replacements for his unit. He did not have to look very far. Incredibly, there was still one source remaining—from within the wellspring of the original *Dirlewanger Einheit*, the concentration camps, no less—where thousands of political prisoners were still being held in dozens of *KLs* scattered across the landscape of the Third Reich. These political *KL* detainees had been arrested in the 1930s and early 1940s and had remained under protective custody status ever since, mostly for demonstrating socialist, communist, or other anti-regime sentiments. That these men could be induced to volunteer to fight for Germany had been unofficially suggested to Dirlewanger during one of his inspection tours of the Flossenbürg concentration camp by its commandant, *Ostubaf.* Egon Zill.[30]

The National Socialist regime had previously considered these men unredeemable as early as 1933 from an ideological standpoint, and had been arresting them ever since coming to power and placing them in an indefinite protective custody status. That is, they had been considered unredeemable until 7 October 1944, when Dirlewanger himself convinced Gottlob Berger that these same men could be recruited for the unit, per Zill's earlier suggestion, on account of their "steadfast and loyal character" and dedication to their own cause, however ill-founded it may have been, at least in Dirlewanger's eyes. Men of such moral and steadfast character, Dirlewanger thought, ought to prove themselves to be excellent soldier material. Berger wholeheartedly agreed.[31]

After a considering the proposal for a week, Himmler approved it on 15 October. Consequently, with Himmler's blessing, on 3 November each of the primary concentration camps were given a quota of political prisoner volunteers to fill Dirlewanger's brigade up to its maximum strength of 6,500 men, which amounted to 1,910 new recruits. For example, the quota for the Auschwitz camp was 400 volunteers; Buchenwald, 150; Dachau, 300; Neuengamme, 130; Mauthausen, 10; Flossenbürg, 45; Gross-Rosen, 30; Ravensbrück, 80; Sachsenhausen, 750; and Stutthof, 15. Those who volunteered were to be forgiven their past crimes provided they proved themselves at the front in defense of Germany. Few of them were told that they would be signing up for the Dirlewanger Brigade.[32]

The recruitment process, once it got underway during the first two weeks of November, varied between camps, depending on the personality of each camp's commanding officer. For example, in Sachsenhausen on 17 November 1944, those deemed suitable for recruitment were given a choice by one of the camp's SS officers: either volunteer for the *Sonderkommando Dirlewanger* or receive a bullet in the back of the neck. According to one eyewitness, "Since we did not wish to die, we volunteered against our will."[33] Other camps resorted to appeals to their patriotism, their pride in their "Germanness," or the need to defend their families against the mortal danger posed by the approach of the Red Army.

While each of these camps had sufficient political prisoners that would have allowed them to exceed their quotas, the response was far less than anticipated. Eventually, a total of only 770 of them volunteered from all of the camps and were accepted as recruits. Undoubtedly, some *KL*s used this as an opportunity to rid themselves of some of their most unwanted or most troublesome prisoners. To address the resulting shortfall in numbers, 1,140 other career criminals or asocials—whether actual volunteers or not—were signed up, bringing the total number to the required quota of 1,910 men.

After being sent under guard to the Sachsenhausen *KL*, which functioned as the central receiving facility for the recruiting campaign, the men were issued second-hand uniforms without rank or collar insignia and used boots. They were then issued *SS Soldbücher* (pay books), given *Marschverpflegung* (march rations), and then transported by rail to Cracow. The first group departed Sachsenhausen on 10 November. With this addition of this badly needed manpower, Dirlewanger's unit finally attained its desired *Sollstärke* by the end of that month.

According to *SS-Richter* (Judge) Dr. Bruno Wille on temporary duty to review clemency cases, at the beginning of December 1944 the 6,500-man Dirlewanger Brigade consisted of 10–15 percent *Waffen-SS* personnel (including the original cadre of remaining poachers as well as SS and Police prisoners undergoing rehabilitation), 30 percent former *KL* inmates (including career criminals, asocials, and political prisoners), and the remainder were from the three branches of the *Wehrmacht*. Upon viewing the brigade's composition, Wille could only say: "Almost all of them were people who had been convicted of capital crimes and who, in human terms, represent the worst that a nation could assign to a body of troops."[34]

The only troops not considered criminals or *B-Schützen* were those who had been assigned to its artillery detachment, consisting of three *SS-Polizei* batteries transferred *en bloc* to the brigade, the postal protection heavy weapons company that had been incorporated into the *gemischte Bataillon* the previous July, and the signals platoon.[35] A handful of *unbestrafft* (unpunished) SS officers and NCOs who had volunteered to serve with Dirlewanger rounded out the picture, either as a career-enhancing move or out of loyalty.

The new brigade's complement was a colorful lot, to say the least. Many of the transfers from the various *Wehrmacht* prisons arrived wearing their ordinary *Luftwaffe*, *Kriegsmarine*, or *Heer* service uniforms, without rank or insignia, which they would continue to wear in combat. The former *KL* inmates wore second-hand SS uniforms without insignia in exchange for their prison stripes. Then there were the few old hands who wore normal SS uniforms, awards, rank, and SS insignia. Some of the former *Heer* officers placed in leadership positions either wore SS officer uniforms or standard army uniforms without rank insignia if they wished to evade the stigma of wearing the uniform of the SS.

Even some former high-ranking Nazis fell into the clutches of Dirlewanger's *Heldenklaukommando* ("hero drafting gangs"). One of these unfortunates was a former *Brigadeführer* in the *Allgemeine-SS*, Rudolf August Weiss, a decorated World War I veteran. Born in Berlin on 31 May 1899, Weiss became a member of the *Reichstag* and rose through the ranks of the Nazi Party hierarchy, serving in various high-level capacities in the Prussian Ministry of the Interior and then the *Polizei* until 1939, while continuing to serve as the *Reichstag* representative for his district in Pomerania. When war came, Weiss was appointed to a senior leadership position in the *Luftschutz* (the Air Defense League), until October 1943 when he took over the position of Deputy *HSSPF* in the Russian city of Nikolayev.

By March 1944, Weiss had returned to Germany to become the chief of police of Saarbrücken, followed by his posting to the city of Metz in the same capacity while simultaneously serving as *Generalluftschutzführer* for the region's air defenses. When the U.S. Army began its assault on Metz in late August, Weiss fled the city without permission on 1 September with a large personal baggage train. Apprehended by the *Wehrmacht Streifendienst* (Armed Forces Traffic Regulation unit) shortly thereafter, he was tried and convicted in an *SS* higher court for cowardice on 24 September. Rather than face execution, he was offered the opportunity of redeeming himself by volunteering for the Dirlewanger Brigade like so many others. Shortly thereafter, he found himself in Slovakia wearing the uniform of an ordinary *SS* private.[36]

With this enormous infusion of such a wide variety of recruits, the greatest challenge Dirlewanger faced at this point was how to successfully incorporate this disparate pool of unwilling manpower into something resembling an effective military unit while simultaneously carrying out low-level security operations. Unlike *Sonderkommando Dirlewanger's* previous practice for assigning personnel, which spread the various types of prisoners throughout the unit with the goal of leveling the degree of military experience throughout each platoon and company, Dirlewanger—for reasons difficult to understand—decided to concentrate more than 400 of the 770 *KL* politicals into one battalion—the new *III. Btl./SS-St.Rgt. 2*. Of the rest, many went to that regiment's *II. Bataillon* and the remainder were spread throughout the regiment, especially in the *Tross* (supply trains). A large proportion of the newly enlisted career criminals and asocials were assigned to this regiment as well.

Most of these 400 politicals were assigned to *III. Battalion's 9.* and *10. Kompanien*, while the remainder went to its *12. (schwere*, heavy weapons) *Kompanie*, which also included a number of demoted *Waffen-SS* and *Wehrmacht* personnel. An *11. Kompanie* was not yet raised at that time, since the inmates who were supposed to come from the Buchenwald concentration camp would not arrive until much later. The new battalion was commanded by a former *Luftwaffe* antiaircraft artillery *Oberstleutnant* named Nitzkowski, who had been demoted to *Oberleutnant* for an unspecified offense yet still wore his *Luftwaffe* combat awards on his uniform jacket.

Although the entire brigade itself had been designated as an *SS-Bewährungseinheit* (probationary unit) since 6 June 1944, at least most of its *SS* or *Wehrmacht B-Schützen* were permitted a certain amount of freedom while in Slovakia as long as they adhered rigidly to orders. Within the *II.* and *III. Btl./SS-St.Rgt. 2*, conditions were quite different. Except for the battalions' *SS* or *Wehrmacht* probationers, the politicals were treated like prisoners, kept under armed guard 24 hours a day, and confined to their living quarters by barbed wire except when outside training. Most of these men had been in the *KL* system for as long as 10 years and were not in good physical condition, having subsisted on near-starvation diets, and required additional time for strength training. Good and plentiful food helped redress this deficiency, one area where Dirlewanger's quartermaster excelled. In garrison, these men were not permitted to carry weapons and would only be issued ammunition while moving into the front line.[37]

The 770 politicals received at best two weeks of hasty military training either in Cracow or Mošovce, since few of them had the benefit of any prior military experience. This period of instruction, provided by a few SS NCOs who were mostly former *B-Schützen* themselves, was grossly inadequate to prepare them for what was to come. They even had to be taught how to give the proper *Hitlergrüss* (the Nazi salute), since as mostly former communists or socialists they had never learned it and showed little enthusiasm for doing so. Whenever training in the field, they were watched by armed guards, lest they attempt to desert. Their company and platoon leaders were mostly disgraced *Waffen-SS*, *Polizei*, or *Wehrmacht* officers themselves, many of whom wore no insignia of their own except between one and three narrow silver bands on the lower left sleeve of their jackets, depending on their duty positions.[38] Their officers were addressed as *Kompanie-Führer* (company commander) or *Zugführer* (platoon leader) rather than by their former rank, as was the normal custom in the *Wehrmacht* or *Waffen-SS*.[39]

When left alone in their barracks near Mošovce, the "politicals quickly reverted to their former cells of between eight and 10 men that they had habitually practiced while in the concentration camps and discussed how best to desert without being shot by either their hated SS overseers or by the Red Army.[40] They appointed informal ringleaders, usually men with whom they had been incarcerated while in the camps. Dachau inmates stayed together, as did those from Sachsenhausen, and so on. Should they desert, they decided they would do it *en masse* and not individually when the most suitable opportunity presented itself at the front line.

Consequently, the politicals were well-behaved and obedient in comparison to some of the other concentration camp inmates, who not surprisingly quickly resorted to their old criminal habits. Some of the SS officers and NCOs in the formal leadership chain of command thought that their compliant behavior was rather odd, considering that they had probably suffered far more under the heel of the Third Reich's criminal justice system than their career criminal and asocial comrades.[41] Dirlewanger's ill-founded decision to concentrate so many admitted enemies of the Nazi regime—so-called "Antifascists in SS Uniform"—into one battalion and part of another would soon have negative consequences.

Meanwhile, shortly after arriving in Slovakia, Dirlewanger had to begin the process of forming his brigade, which would include selecting his brigade staff and organizing his brigade staff company (similar to a U.S. Army headquarters and headquarters company), two regimental staffs and their staff companies, as well as three entirely new infantry battalions. In addition to senior officers needed to lead these two new regiments, the staffs at all levels required specialist personnel, such as clerks, radio operators, truck drivers, and logisticians. For the brigade staff, Dirlewanger simply upgraded his existing staff from his old *Sonderregiment*, but filling the key positions in the two regiments and six infantry battalions with qualified men was to prove a persistent challenge.

One way in which the Dirlewanger Brigade differed from the *Wehrmacht-Heer* sponsored *Bewährungseinheiten*, such as the former *Afrika-Division 999*, was the composition of its officer and NCO corps. As a matter of *Heer* personnel policy, only the best junior leaders were assigned to "999er" units, hand-picked to ensure that the rank and file of *B-Schützen* were not only well led, but provided the ideal specimen of the German soldier for them to emulate and hopefully achieve their complete rehabilitation by following their example. It is no surprise that in battle, these "999" units performed far better than expected, even though the rank and file were soldiers on probationary status.

Not so with the Dirlewanger Brigade, in which most of the leaders were convicts or former convicts themselves, ranging from those on probationary status to prisoners of conscience, convicted murderers, and rapists. It also had its share of psychopaths filling leadership positions, who, without the normal restraints imposed by society, allowed their inherently savage nature to manifest itself. When it was still a battalion-sized unit, Dirlewanger himself frequently supervised individual platoons and companies and knew each of his men by name; how this system would work in a 6,500-man brigade with nearly all of his junior leadership positions filled by men of low moral character who possessed few of the military virtues was another matter altogether. This insurmountable flaw in the composition of its leadership would soon manifest itself on the battlefield.

Dirlewanger, of course, would remain as the *Sondereinheit*'s commander. His Ia was *Stubaf.* Kurt Weisse, who also doubled as the brigade's deputy commander whenever Dirlewanger was absent. Weisse had been acting as his battalion, then regimental, *Adjutant* since November 1943 and had Dirlewanger's complete trust. When *Gen.Obst.* Friessner, the commander of *H.Gr. Süd*, visited Dirlewanger's headquarters in Hungary on 15 December 1944, Weisse impressed him with his military bearing and seeming comprehensive understanding of the situation; unlike Dirlewanger, whom Friessner wrote off as an "adventurer type." Appearances can be deceiving. If anyone in the *Dirlewanger Einheit* came close to matching its leader in brutality, cruelty, and outright sadism, it was Weisse. If there was anyone in the unit who matched the classic profile of a psychopath, it was he.

Kurt Weisse was a Nazi's Nazi, a sadist's sadist, a thug's thug, the epitome of all that was evil in the Third Reich. He was also a competent officer, but his route to the *Dirlewanger Einheit* was a circuitous one. Born on 11 October 1909 in Ehrenfriedersdorf, he went through the *Real-Gymnasium* and after finishing he worked as a foreign trade correspondent, having learned to speak French and English fluently. An early enlistee in the *Allgemeine-SS*, on 16 February 1935 Weisse was promoted to *Untersturmführer* while serving with the *17. Standarte* of the *Totenkopfverbände (T.V.)*, which was operating the Sachsenburg *KL* at the time.

A year later, he was elevated to the rank of *Obersturmführer*, and less than eight months later to *Hauptsturmführer* in command of a company. In July 1937, he was transferred to the *29. SS-Standarte* of the *T.V.*

After that, his star seemed to be on the rise and on November 1937 he was appointed as acting battalion commander in the same unit. In March 1939, he transferred to *SS-Standarte Ostmark* in Austria, where he commanded the *I. Bataillon* of the *4. SS-Standarte* of the *T.V.* His next assignment featured his appointment as commander of *I. Btl./SS-Totenkopf-Standarte Ostmark*. Seemingly on the fast track to promotion, Weisse married on 27 May 1939. He attained his pre-war career high point on 1 September 1939 when he became the first commander of the newly activated *III. Btl./SS-Inf.Rgt. 11*, which was stationed in Linz at that time.

However, things began to sour for him in late 1940. When *SS-Inf.Rgt. 11* was absorbed within the *SS-Division (mot.) Reich* in 1940, he was appointed commander of *9. Kp./SS-Standarte Deutschland*, a step down from his previous three years of service in the *SS-Totenkopfverbände* as a battalion commander. He had already been reprimanded and punished with room detention on 28 March 1939 for ignoring an order given by a superior officer. On 19 July 1940, he was brought to trial before the *SS* and Police Court in Den Haag on suspicion of sexually assaulting a 10-year old boy. Although the *SS* tribunal was convinced that Weisse had intended to assault the child, it accepted that he had failed to carry out his plan and instead judged him guilty of drunkenness in uniform, punishing him with 14 days' intensified detention. This was a serious offense, but it would not be his last.

Weisse's first taste of combat occurred during the invasion of the Soviet Union, where he led *3. Kp./SS-Inf.Rgt. Deutschland* from 22 June 1941 until 2 March 1942, until he was hospitalized after suffering a knee injury—his second combat wound—at the end of February 1942. After two months of convalescence, he was sent back to the Eastern Front in May 1942, where he worked as the *Adjutant* for *Nachschub Kommandantur* (Logistics Command) *der SS und Polizei Russland-Nord*. On 25 August that year, he was sent to France to serve with the staff coordinating the reconstitution of the *SS-Totenkopf Division* and its conversion into a *Panzergrenadier* (*Pz.Gren.*) *Division*, but was quickly appointed acting commander of the *9. Kp./ SS-Pz.Gren.Rgt. 3* of the division instead.[42]

His greatest character flaw was an uncontrollable temper. This became apparent on 19 December 1942 when he assaulted one of his own grenadiers with a rubber truncheon at the Sennelager troop training ground for a minor offense. During the same period, Weisse also beat at least two or three other men of his company in a similar fashion. As the facts of this criminal act became known, his wife divorced him by the end of the month. Letters of admonition had no effect. Less than a month later, an enraged Kurt Weisse beat *Grenadier* Barthel for 15 minutes on 17 January 1943 with a rubber truncheon. Barthel died in the Sennelager detention room the following day of a concussion resulting from the beating.

Weisse was brought before a court-martial convened by the commander of the *SS-Pz.Gren.Div. Totenkopf* on 23 January 1943 and was judged guilty of negligent homicide. His punishment was correspondingly harsh: the court sentenced him to serve a life sentence of hard labor for two cases of mishandling a subordinate, imposed an additional four years' prison sentence for assault and perjury, declared him unworthy to bear arms, stripped him of his rank, denied him his civil rights, and ordered his expulsion from the *SS* for violating the honor of that organization. The court's presiding judge, *Stubaf.* Dr. Rudolf Barth, also issued a warning to Weisse's superiors that "he should never again be entrusted with men's lives." Weisse was then transferred to the *Strafvollzugslager der SS und Polizei* at Danzig-Matzkau to begin serving his sentence.[43]

The story of Kurt Weisse should have ended there and he would have disappeared from the pages of history. However, after enduring only 17 weeks of punishment as an *SS* convict, his case came to the attention of Oskar Dirlewanger, who was looking for more officers to staff his growing battalion. Dirlewanger, who had established good contacts with the *SS* and Polizei higher leadership, especially regarding *SS* prisoners, had evidently become aware of Weisse's case during a visit to Danzig-Matzkau in April or May 1943. In Weisse, he must have found a kindred spirit, because Dirlewanger submitted a formal request to Himmler via the *SS-Gericht* (court) of the *SS-HA*, asking that Weisse be released to his *Sondereinheit* and reinstated in his previous rank of *Hauptsturmführer*. Surprisingly, Himmler agreed on 26 May and ordered him released on probationary status on 24 June.

Arriving at his *Sonderbataillon* on 1 July 1943, Dirlewanger appointed Weisse as acting commander of the *1. Kompanie*. He served in this capacity until November 1943, when the battalion's *Adjutant, Stubaf.* Erwin Walser, became the acting battalion commander when Dirlewanger was sent home to Germany on a prolonged leave of absence to recover from wounds received in battle with partisans that same month. Upon Dirlewanger's return in January 1944, Weisse was formally instated in the *Adjutant* position and continued to serve in that capacity until the end of the war, while Walser was appointed as the battalion's personnel officer. Weisse's legal status improved significantly during that same period when Himmler agreed to reduce his life with hard labor sentence to a lesser punishment and set aside his *Ehrenstrafe* on 2 September 1943, provided that he successfully completed his probation at the front.[44]

Surprisingly, Weisse was highly decorated, despite his deadly character flaws. He had been awarded the Iron Cross, Second Class on 12 August 1941 and the Eastern Front Medal the following year, followed by the award of the Infantry Assault Badge in Silver on 20 November 1943. On 13 December 1943, he was presented with the Iron Cross, First Class for valor and the coveted Close Combat Badge in Bronze the same week. He suffered his third wound during the winter of 1943–44, earning another Black Wound Badge. For his participation in numerous anti-partisan operations, he was awarded the rare Anti-Partisan Medal in Silver on 23 May 1944.

His highest award by far was that of the German Cross in Gold, approved on 15 August 1944 and presented on 25 August while the fighting in Warsaw was ongoing. This decoration, second only in ranking to the Knight's Cross of the Iron Cross, was presented in recognition of his leadership and continued work as Dirlewanger's *Adjutant* during multiple operations in the Minsk area and in Warsaw between the autumn of 1943 and August 1944. Finally restored to the same level of respectability he had been when the war started, he even exceeded that when he was promoted to *Sturmbannführer* on 1 August 1944.

While Dirlewanger had a well-earned reputation for brutality and harshness, ironically he had gained the loyalty if not the outright fondness of his *B-Schützen*, particularly the poachers who had formed the basis of the unit in July 1940. While many of his veteran troops considered Dirlewanger a caring, inspirational, and dynamic leader who looked after his men, they thought the opposite of Weisse. Former *Sonderkommando* troops recalled that he possessed "sadistic tendencies and a violent demeanor that knew no bounds."[45] According to eyewitnesses, Weisse enjoyed watching corporal punishment being inflicted upon troops for minor offenses, and even joined in when the mood suited him.

No other officer in the *Sondereinheit*, except perhaps Dirlewanger himself, did more to craft its image and dreadful reputation. It was Weisse, acting as regimental commander in Dirlewanger's absence between 5 and 8 August 1944, who had led the unit during its bloodiest fighting in the early days of the Warsaw Uprising, including playing an active role in the infamous Wola Massacre. One officer who came to know Weisse well during the performance of his duties was former *Oberst* Harald Momm, who had been demoted and assigned to the brigade as punishment (more about him later). After the war, when being questioned during the Ludwigsburg war crimes investigation of the Dirlewanger Brigade, Momm testified:

> During my affiliation with the Division, I came into contact with Dirlewanger and Weisse during operational briefings. Weisse was in charge of the tactical operations of the Brigade and later of the Division, which were always ordered in a particularly ruthless manner and with the most severe threats of punishment. The number of casualties during operations did not concern him in any way; on the contrary, this brutal characteristic made him very popular with his superiors. In the unit, corporal punishment was introduced as a disciplinary [measure], of which Weisse made extensive use. The corporal punishment was carried out by two or three *Scharführer* [NCOs] who were attached to the staff, and was executed with rubber truncheons. The delinquents usually fainted.[46]

Despite their insidious character traits, Dirlewanger and Weisse worked well together, and when not indulging in his sadistic tendencies, Weisse was a reliable, meticulous, and conscientious officer, despite his lack of a formal military education. It was most likely Weisse who designed and followed through on the implementation of the brigade's transitional structure, recommended who should lead the new regiments and battalions (with Dirlewanger's approval), and planned most of the brigade's operations against the Slovak mutineers between October and November 1944.

The brigade's staff and staff company were mostly filled with *Sondereinheit* old hands who had served Dirlewanger in various positions between 1940 and the spring of 1944. Most of them were merely elevated from the same position they had held with the *Sonderregiment*, since the duties were similar, only with a slightly larger scope of action. Most of the SS officers on his staff had either requested assignment to the *Einheit Dirlewanger* or had been sent there to undergo probation at the front. Of these, many had been declared as rehabilitated and could have returned to their previous unit, but chose to remain out of loyalty or because they enjoyed their duty position. Weisse, as discussed, had been moved up to the Brigade *Ia* position, performing more or less the same duties he had as battalion and regimental *Adjutant* since November 1943.

The brigade's first *Ib* (supply officer) was *Ostuf.* Adalbert Trattenschegg, who had served under Dirlewanger in Belarus. However, when he was killed in action on 21 September 1944 in Ołtarzewo, a suburb west of Warsaw, he was replaced by *Ostuf.* Otto Gast. Born on 6 July 1908 in Tangermünde, Gast had the SS number 177 886 and initially served in the *SS- Totenkopf Division*. Joining the unit in 1943 as an *unbestraft* officer, he first served as the *Stabs-Intendant*, responsible for the quality and quantity of meals prepared as well as arranging a steady supply of provisions for the field kitchens.

The brigade's *Ic* (staff intelligence/counterintelligence officer) has yet to be identified, but a possible candidate is *Standartenführer* Kurt Neifeind, the former head of the *SS-Sicherheitsdienst* (SS-SD, SS Security Service) office in Paris who was demoted in rank to *Grenadier* for 'cowardice' during the late summer of 1944 (possibly due to the inability of the Germans to defend, and then destroy, the French capital) and assigned to the Dirlewanger Brigade in the autumn of 1944. As a former high-ranking officer in the *SD*, he would have been well qualified to work in the *Ic* position. It could also have been another *unbestraft* officer from the *SD*, a support-supporting relationship that was frequently practiced in Belarus throughout 1943–44.

The brigade's *IIa* (staff *Adjutant* responsible for personnel matters) was *Ostuf.* Franz Bauser, born on 28 September 1906 in Wehingen, Baden-Württemberg. He joined the *NSDAP* in 1930 and the following year the *Allgemeine-SS*, and was given a very low SS number of 4657. He was promoted from *Sturmmann* to *Untersturmführer* in 1935 under an order that all senior members of the SS—meaning those with a membership number below 5000—should be given a higher rank as a reward for their early support of the Nazi movement. Shortly before the outbreak of World War II, he enlisted in the *Wehrmacht* as a volunteer. Bauser was promoted to *Leutnant* (second lieutenant) in 1943 and then voluntarily transferred to the *Waffen-SS*, where he was given the commensurate rank of *Untersturmführer*.

Instead of being sent to a combat leadership position, the *unbestraft* Bauser was assigned to the *Deutsche Reichspost der Waffen-SS* and sent to France, where he commanded a supply company. In May 1944, he was ordered to report to the SS

Main Office in Berlin, where he learned that he had been transferred to *Sonderregiment Dirlewanger*, which was in dire need of staff officers with specialist knowledge. Here, Bauser met *Hstuf.* Erwin Walser in June 1944, whom he replaced as the regiment's *IIa* when the latter was transferred to Berlin in August to serve as Gottlob Berger's *Adjutant zum besonderen Verwendung* (for special tasks).

The brigade's *IIb* Staff Officer (responsible for enlisted personnel matters and the acting *IIa* in the latter's absence) was *Hstuf.* Fritz Missmahl, the former disgraced *NSDAP* politician mentioned in Chapter 1. During the Warsaw Uprising, Missmahl had commanded one of the infantry companies in *K.Gr. Dirlewanger* but had returned to his *IIb* position when the brigade was transferred to Slovakia. According to one source, he did not remain in this position very long, but took command of *Artillerie-Abteilung Dirlewanger* when that unit's commander, *Hstuf.* Willy Schneier, was transferred at the end of November 1944 to the *SS-Ostturkische-Waffenverband*.[47]

Serving as the brigade's *IVa Stabsintendant* (assistant supply officer) was the *unbestrafft Ostuf.* Hans Schäftlmeier. Born on 18 June 1910 in Stuttgart, he was serving as a junior enlisted man when the war began, but by June 1943 had been promoted to *Untersturmführer* and was assigned as the supply officer of a training unit, *SS-Panzer- Aufklärungs-Ersatz Abteilung 2*, in Popervalen, Latvia. After service there, he was promoted to *Obersturmführer* in 1944 and assigned to the Dirlewanger Brigade in November 1944 shortly before it moved into Hungary.

The brigade's *III* Staff Officer (staff judge advocate) was *Hstuf.* Dr. Bruno Wille, who had been assigned to the *Dirlewanger Einheit* at the beginning of December 1944 from the *Hauptamt SS-Gericht*. His task was to begin instituting formal disciplinary practices within the organization to ensure that proper legal procedures were being followed for those undergoing probationary service at the front. He soon clashed with Oskar Dirlewanger, who felt that he—and only he—was the sole arbiter of what crimes would be prosecuted, what punishment would be meted out, and who would be considered rehabilitated. Wille's stay was a short one—approximately one month—but he left with some trenchant observations of the state of the unit, its leadership, and the composition of its rank and file.

There were several other officers serving in secondary staff positions, including the *IVb* (chief medical officer), *Stabsartzt* Dr. Heinz Hartlieb, and its *IVc* (veterinarian), *Ostuf.* Dr. Friedrich Turek. The latter had been one of the staff doctors at the Auschwitz II Camp and had been sentenced to the Dirlewanger Brigade as punishment for unauthorized testing of medications on some of the *KL* guard personnel. The commander of the brigade's *Stabskompanie* was *Hauptscharführer* (*Hascha.*, Senior Sergeant) Karl Staib, who was born on 12 January 1901 in Auenstein near Heilbronn. Joining the *Dirlewanger Einheit* as an early volunteer, Staib had commanded the staff company during most of his time with the unit, except for a brief period during the Warsaw Uprising when he commanded one of *K.Gr. Dirlewanger*'s infantry companies.

Two other officers must be mentioned—the assistant to the Brigade *Ia*, or *Ordonnanz Offizier* (*O1*), *Ostuf.* Helmut Lewandowski, and the commander of the brigade's *Ersatzkompanie* in Cracow, *Ostuf.* Paul Zimmermann. Lewandowski, born on 1 April 1906 in Liegnitz, made the transition from the *Allgemeine-SS* to the *Waffen-SS* in 1942 when he was assigned to the *SS-Hauptamt*. In 1943, he was convicted by an *SS-Gericht* for an unspecified crime and sentenced to the *SS* and Police prison in Danzig-Matzkau for punishment. On 5 July 1944, he was assigned to the *Sonderregiment Dirlewanger* on the eve of its retreat from Belarus. As the *O1*, Lewandowski served as Kurt Weisse's right-hand man, though he had little combat experience or any experience as a staff officer for that matter. Apparently, he and Weisse worked together well and he was able to perform the functions of the *Ia* whenever his superior was temporarily absent.

Zimmermann was a World War I veteran, born on 22 August 1888 in Landsberg, Wartheland. Discharged as a *Leutnant* in 1920, after enduring the turbulent 1920s and 1930s he enlisted in the *Waffen-SS* at the beginning of 1943 at the age of 54 after being repeatedly turned down by the *Wehrmacht* on account of his age. Promoted to *Hauptscharführer* shortly thereafter, he voluntarily joined the *Sonderbataillon Dirlewanger* in March 1943 and quickly rose to prominence. He commanded both German and Russian companies on several occasions during the next 18 months and fought in a number of close-combat engagements with Soviet partisans.

Known within the unit as a trustworthy NCO who could be completely relied upon, Zimmermann was promoted to *Untersturmführer* by Dirlewanger himself during the Warsaw Uprising, where he had been leading a company in *K.Gr. Steinhauer*. Sidelined due to a knee injury that required surgery, Dirlewanger assigned him to serve as the commander of the replacement company in Cracow, *SS-Gren. Ers.Btl. Dirlewanger*, where Zimmermann would carry out the task of equipping and training of thousands of new recruits assigned to the brigade during the autumn of 1944. A close confidant of Dirlewanger, he was also a friend of Kurt Weisse.

There were several other "old-timers" who had served with Dirlewanger for several years holding undetermined staff or junior leadership positions. Nearly all of these men had been *SS* or *Polizei* officers who had been court-martialed or jailed for a variety of offenses, ranging from petty embezzlement to moral offenses. Demoted to *SS B-Schützen*, most were restored to their former ranks upon agreeing to volunteer for *Sonderkommando Dirlewanger*. Included among this group were such stalwarts as the former engineer *Stubaf.* Ernst Heidelberg, former *Hptm.d.OrPo.* (*Ordnungspolizei*) Wolfgang Plaul, and a former *SD* officer assigned as the *Ia* of *SD-Abschnitt Nord*, *Hstuf.* Josef Grohmann.[48] These men served Dirlewanger at various times as platoon leaders, company commanders, and staff officers between 1943 and 1945, including their participation in the suppressing the Warsaw Uprising, though it is not yet known what positions they held during the battle of Ipolysag.

In addition to the brigade staff, the staff company included a field kitchen section led by former poacher *Uscha.* Gerhard Hellkamp, who fed the brigade; a mapping section, led by *Gren.* Walter Fentzahn; and a large transportation section that included a motorcycle platoon, populated mostly by former poachers, now considered fully rehabilitated. At some point in October or November 1944, the motorcycle platoon was assigned to the *gemischte Bataillon.* The brigade's *Stabskompanie* also included a *Nachrichtenstaffel* (signal platoon) of between 60 and 70 men. This element was responsible for operating radios, field telephones, and cable-laying for the brigade headquarters and battalions, but when the regiment expanded into a brigade, many of its members were parceled out to each of the new regiment's *Nachrichtenstaffel,* stretching an already limited capability even further.

Rounding out the *Stabskompanie* was its *Tross,* led by *Uscha.* Franz Panten, who was responsible for leading a team of 10 German *B-Schützen* and as many as 30 Russian *Hiwis* who had previously served in one of the *Sonderbataillon's* Russian rifle companies before these were disbanded in May 1944. Another element within the *Stabskompanie* before it was transferred to the *gemischte Bataillon* was a horse-mounted reconnaissance platoon, consisting of Ukrainians who had formerly been led by *Ustuf.* Zimmermann before his injury in Warsaw.

Lastly, the brigade's small medical platoon, which operated its field dressing station, was led by Dr. Med. Hugo Erbguth, who supervised a dozen or so *Sanitäter* (medics) who were mostly *B-Schützen* themselves. Dr. Erbguth, born in Hamburg in 1893, had been operating a private medical practice until he was arrested for performing an illegal abortion, a serious racial offense that landed him in a *KL*. In need of qualified medical personnel, Dirlewanger was able to secure his release from prison to lead his medical platoon, although Dr. Erbguth was not considered an *SS* officer. As for the rest, there were enough of the old hands remaining to fill most of the remaining positions in the brigade staff. With the two new regiments, however, it was an entirely different story.

SS-Sturm-Regiment 1 was formed using the old *I.* and *II. Bataillone* as its basis, joined by the new *III. Bataillon* that had been forming while the other two fought in Warsaw. The majority of the brigade's veterans from the pre-Warsaw period were concentrated in this regiment, although they constituted at most 15 percent of its total. Most of the rest were SS, *Polizei,* or *Wehrmacht B-Schützen,* with a sprinkling of former *KL* inmates. The regiment's staff and staff company had to be created from whole cloth—most of the leadership or staff positions were new at their job or recent arrivals. By 11 December 1944, the regiment had between 2,400 and 2,600 men assigned for duty. It still lacked its own regimental infantry howitzer and antitank gun companies, relying instead on the heavy weapons companies in the mixed battalion for antitank and indirect fire support.

The regiment at first did not have a commander assigned. At the end of October 1944, when *Stubaf.* Weisse was acting as brigade commander while Dirlewanger was in Germany scouring the various *KL* for new volunteers, recently-promoted Josef Steinhauer served as the regiment's acting commander until the end of November. Handing over temporary command of his *II. Bataillon* to another officer, Steinhauer was faced with the task of forming the regiment's staff and staff company, but shortages of men and equipment meant that the headquarters of *SS-St.Rgt. 1* would not be ready to deploy to the front line in Hungary until after the battle of Ipolysag had begun. At some point before the middle of December, Steinhauer returned to lead his battalion and passed nominal command of the regiment back to *Stubaf.* Weisse, who would exercise administrative command—though not tactical command—until a permanent commander could be found. By that point, Dirlewanger had returned and he needed Weisse back as his Brigade *Ia.*

The commander of the regiment's *I. Bataillon*, with *1.–4. Kompanien*, was former *Hptm.d.Schu.Po.* Herbert Meyer, now serving as a rehabilitated *Obersturmführer* after leading *K.Gr. Meyer* during the suppression of the Warsaw Uprising, which also earned him the clasp to his World War I Iron Cross, First Class on 22 August 1944. Still an enigma today, he was described by men who served under him as "an impeccable officer and decent person who was always accommodating, acted humanely and always tried to moderate [Dirlewanger's] behavior."[49]

His *4. Kompanie* served as the battalion's heavy weapons company, but its weapons were limited to obsolete 50mm German mortars, Czech heavy machine guns, and either Czech-manufactured 37mm KPUV vz.37mm antitank guns or Soviet 45mm antitank guns, both being too small and obsolete to be of much use against Soviet tanks. Its *1. Kompanie* was led by disgraced *Ustuf.* Johannes Hempel and the *4. (schwere) Kompanie* by *Ustuf.* Hermann Finnern, who was replaced on 20 December 1944 after being wounded by disgraced former *Hauptmann* Hinrich Pape. The names of the commanders of the *2.* and *3. Kompanien* remain unknown.

By 13 December 1944, the *II. Bataillon*, with *5.–8. Kompanien*, was led once again by the aforementioned 36-year-old Josef Steinhauer, who had been associated with the *Sondereinheit* for most of the past year-and-a-half, first as the commander of *1. Batterie, Schutzmannschaft Art.Abt. 56* in April 1943, then as commander of *SS-Art.Abt. Weissruthenien* by the end of the year. After being asked by Dirlewanger to transfer to his unit in early 1944, Steinhauer was first appointed as the commander of its *2. Kompanie* and finally as commander of the *II. Bataillon* in May 1944.

His veteran battalion had also fought in Warsaw as *K.Gr. Steinhauer*, where at one point (8 August) it had been reduced in size to only 80 men. *Bewährungs-Schützen* who served under Steinhauer described him as a "good, decent officer and as an 'orderly' man."[50] With his battalion now largely rebuilt with new *SS*, *Polizei*, and *Wehrmacht* probationary troops, his *5. Kompanie* was led by *Ustuf.* Erich Böttcher and the *6. Kompanie* by a degraded *Leutnant* from the *Heer.* The commanders of the other two companies are unknown.

The new *III. Bataillon* was commanded by *Ustuf.* Siegfried Polack, a World War I veteran who had risen to the rank of *Leutnant* in a *Füsilier* regiment before the war ended. An awardee of the Iron Cross, Second Class, and Wound Badge for the three wounds he suffered in that war, after a brief period of service in the post-war *Grenzschutz* (border guards) Polack joined the *NSDAP* in 1928 and was awarded the relatively low party membership number of 75 148. A year later, he was appointed as a District Leader for the Nazi Party in eastern Franconia, then on 12 November 1933, he was elected to a seat in the *Reichstag*. He entered the *Allgemeine-SS* in 1932 and over the next several years was promoted to higher positions in both the Party and the *SS*, attaining the rank of *Sturmbannführer* in the *Allegmeine-SS* on 31 May 1932. However, on account of a charge of falsifying official Nazi Party documents, Polack was thrown out of the *SS* on Himmler's orders on 30 November 1935, followed shortly thereafter by his expulsion from the *NSDAP*.

For the next several years, Polack worked as a minor office functionary in a civilian capacity, including working for *Staatsrat* (Counselor of State) Dr. Walther Schieber, who later became the head of the Armaments Supply Office under Albert Speer after attaining the rank of *Brigadeführer*. When war came, Polack attempted to volunteer for the *Wehrmacht* as an enlisted man with the intent of regaining his former lieutenancy, but was denied due to his age. By this point, he had not served in military uniform for nearly 20 years. After repeated requests to Himmler to approve his request to rejoin the *SS* in an active capacity, the *Reichsführer-SS* finally gave in. This was due in part thanks to Dr. Schieber and Gottlob Berger's intervention with Himmler on his behalf in July 1943; Himmler agreed that fighting at the front as a volunteer would allow Polack to regain his military honor and earn his reinstatement as an *SS* officer. Shortly afterwards, on 21 September that year, Polack was activated for service in the *Waffen-SS* and promoted to *Untersturmführer der Reserve* on the same day.

He was first assigned to *SS-Gren.Ers.Btl. Ost* in Breslau from September–November 1943 for refresher training, followed shortly thereafter by his transfer to the *Sonderkommando Dirlewanger* on 20 November, where he was made a platoon leader. Polack was a rarity in the Dirlewanger unit, being one of the few former officers not sent there to undergo front-line *Bewährung*, but seeking out the assignment on his own volition. Since his posting to the *Sonderkommando* in November 1943, he had served as a platoon leader, then company commander, and finally as a staff officer at the battalion and regiment until the Warsaw Uprising. By November 1944, Polack was an experienced company commander, who found himself now elevated to battalion command.

Shortly after arriving in Slovakia (or just before departing Warsaw), a *IV. Bataillon* was formed to temporarily accommodate the flood of new arrivals until the establishment of the second regiment could be carried out. At some point in late October or early November 1944, the *IV. Bataillon* was simply renumbered as the

II. Bataillon of the new *SS-St.Rgt. 2.* The commander of this battalion was *Hstuf.* Ewald Ehlers, who was to lead it during the fighting that soon followed.

The formation of the new brigade was a chaotic process, to say the least. According to one veteran of the brigade, one of the few remaining original poachers who had been assigned to *Sonderkommando Oranienburg* in June 1940:

> In Deviaky, we now began to set up a brigade. The companies and battalions were brought together, but it was an absolute catastrophe, because it was made up of criminals, social misfits, and other not-particularly-trustworthy contemporaries. Maybe we could have established a reasonably tight unit in three months, on a military training ground shielded from locals of the surrounding area. The really difficult cases would be sent back to concentration camps.[51]

Neither the brigade nor its regiments would get that time, because events would soon overtake Dirlewanger's carefully prepared plans. By this point, Weisse, Meyer, and Polack were veteran leaders and had been considered fully rehabilitated, but for reasons of their own, they chose to continue serving alongside Dirlewanger. Steinhauer had no need for rehabilitation, but opted to remain with Dirlewanger for personal reasons.

SS-Sturm-Regiment 1's three battalions were at nearly full strength and were probably the most combat-ready of the brigade by the beginning of December. Over a month of anti-partisan operations in Slovakia during October and November had given the men some measure of combat experience and had hardened them to withstand living and operating in the field. As previously mentioned, the headquarters of this regiment was not initially deployed for the upcoming action, most likely because there were insufficient staff and headquarters personnel as well as communications equipment needed to make the regimental headquarters fully operational. It also lacked its own regimental commander, as already described.

The brigade's other regiment, *SS-St.Rgt. 2*, had only been established in early November. Unlike the first regiment, it did have its own commander, *Ostubaf.* Erich Buchmann. Born on 23 May 1896 in Berlin, Buchmann had fought during World War I as a *Vizefeldwebel* (vice- or senior sergeant) with *Infanterie-Regiment 20*, where he earned both classes of the Iron Cross, as well as the Black Wound Badge. In 1919, he joined the *Gardeschützen-Division*, where he served until 1920. After his discharge from a *Freikorps* unit, he returned to his profession as a baker and owner of a *Conditorei* (pastry café). Buchmann had joined Nazi Party on 1 October 1930 with an *NSDAP* membership number of 334 035. Two weeks later he joined the *Allgemeine-SS*, with a membership number of 5118, a very low number indeed.

Following a series of pre-war leadership assignments in the *Allgemeine-SS*, where he rose to the rank of *Standartenführer*, he was reduced in rank in 1940 to *Sturmbannführer* for misuse of a military vehicle. Entering the *Waffen-SS* on 1 March 1940, he then served consecutively as a commander of two *Totenkopf* reserve infantry battalions between 1 March 1940 and 1 January 1941, where he saw no combat. He was then posted to desk jobs in southern Germany and Berlin

until 1 December 1944, when he was assigned as the commander of *SS-St.Rgt. 2*.
He apparently suffered from a heart ailment, as mentioned by Gottlob Berger in
an efficiency report from December 1944:

> For some time Buchmann has been engaged as leader of an auxiliary position and has always
> garnered great successes in the auxiliary field through his diligence and experience. Physically
> severely handicapped by a heart defect, Buchmann volunteered for duty at the Front and is
> taking over a regiment of the *SS-Sturmbrigade Dirlewanger*.[52]

This glowing efficiency report was perhaps meant to cover up the fact that he had
no combat experience since 1920, when he had last fought with the *Freikorps*, and
no combat leadership experience since September 1939 at all. Therefore, it is curious
that Dirlewanger accepted the volunteer Buchmann as one of his new regimental
commanders. Perhaps Himmler or Berger insisted upon it, or there were no other
experienced senior officers available.

Whatever the case, his suitability would soon be put to the test. Buchmann,
whose combat experience, knowledge of battlefield leadership, and skills needed
to successfully command and control a regiment in combat were minimal at best,
was aided in his new position by a senior officer from the *Heer* who had been
degraded and sent to the brigade as a *B-Schütze* for punishment for his peripheral
involvement in the 20 July assassination plot. This former officer, one-time *Oberst*
Walter Freiherr von Uckermann, was a 1937 graduate of the *Kriegsakademie* and a
fully fledged member of the *Generalstab*, and would serve in the role of regimental
Adjutant until the end of the war.

Born on 3 March 1904 in Zerbst, Saxony, *Freiherr* von Uckermann was mobilized
as the *Ic* of the *XIII. Armee-Korps* (*A.K.*, Corps) in August 1939. After serving as *Ia*
of the *XII. A.K.* from 1941–42, he was promoted to *Oberst* on 1 January 1943 before
being assigned in May 1943 as *Ia* of the *291. Infanterie-Division* (*Inf.Div.*), where
he served until 10 December 1943. He was then assigned as *Ia* of the *4. Luftwaffe-
Feld-Division*, which was in dire need of professional staff officers experienced in
ground combat. At some point after 20 July 1944, he was arrested by the *Gestapo*
and imprisoned in a concentration camp awaiting execution. Rather than die in front
of a firing squad, he opted to serve out his sentence as the *Ia Leiter* (operations staff
leader, without the formal title of *Adjutant*) for *SS-St.Rgt. 2*, which was in need of
an experienced staff officer. Although wearing the uniform of a lowly *Grenadier*, von
Uckermann provided the steady hand that Buchmann needed as well as someone
who knew what a properly run staff was supposed to look like.

The leader of his regiment's *I. Bataillon* was *Ostuf.* Wilhelm Stegmann, who
was born on 13 June 1899 in Munich. Stegmann, a highly decorated World War I
veteran, was an early member of the *NSDAP*, joining the organization in December
1925. His meteoric rise in Hitler's Brown Shirts culminated in 1932, when he was
elected to the *Reichstag* and was elevated to the position of *Gauleiter* in the Central

Franconia Gau. Becoming dissatisfied with the Nazi Party's failure to implement many of the societal reforms it had promised its members, Stegmann and 2,000 *SA* men from his *Gau* broke from the *NSDAP* in March 1933 and formed their own political party to represent "true National Socialism." Shortly afterwards, he was arrested for plotting to assassinate his arch rival, Julius Streicher, and was convicted of mutiny and treason by a Nazi court after a brief show trial.

Sentenced to 18 months in prison, Stegmann was transferred a few months later to the Buchenwald *KL* to complete his sentence. Due to Himmler's intervention, he was released on parole by 1938 and appointed as an administrator of an agricultural estate in Braunschweig, followed by a similar assignment in the eastern occupied territories after the invasion of the U.S.S.R. Drafted into the *SS* on 1 October 1944 in order to expunge his criminal record and "restore his honor" while serving at the *SS-Hauptamt,* he was promoted to *Obersturmführer* and transferred to the Dirlewanger Brigade one month later.[53] Stegmann's leadership of the *I. Bataillon* during the latter stages of the Slovak Munity was his sole experience as a battalion commander before it was committed to battle along the Hungarian–Slovakian border. Most of his men were recent arrivals from concentration camps and military prisons, although his battalion was assigned a number of politicals as well.

The commander of *II. Bataillon* was the previously mentioned *Hstuf.* Ewald Ehlers, born on 3 January 1910 in the town of Lelm in the Helmstedt district. After 10 years' combined service in the *Reichsheer* and *Luftwaffe,* where he had risen to the rank of *Hauptfeldwebel* (master sergeant), he began his *SS* career on 1 October 1938 when he joined *SS-Totenkopfverband Thüringen* as an *Untersturmführer.* A year later, he transferred to the *5. Standarte* of the *SS-T.V. Oranienburg,* where he served as a company commander in the Sachsenhausen *KL* guard force. In September 1940, he was moved again, this time to a staff position with *SS-Totenkopf Standarte Kirkenes* in northern Norway. Shortly afterwards, this unit was renamed *SS-Inf.Rgt. 9* and attached to *SS-K.Gr. Nord,* which was subordinated to the *2. Gebirgs-Divisio*n (*Geb. Div.,* Mountain Division) of the *Heer* for the invasion of the Soviet Union.

Ostuf. Ehlers's heretofore promising *SS* career was sidetracked when he was accused of cowardice before the enemy and relieved of company command in April 1942 after it had disintegrated during the battle of Salla in Finland almost a year before. He may have been chosen as a scapegoat in place of the actual officer responsible; the real circumstances may never be known. Ehlers was never brought to trial due to the *SS* Court's inability to make his accuser available to testify against him. Consequently, his trial was suspended and charges would be dropped completely provided he prove himself at the front. Thus, he remained unpunished, although the stigma of the accusation continued to haunt him for the rest of his brief service career. Despite the charges leveled against him, Ehlers was promoted to *SS-Hauptsturmführer* on 1 October 1943, a sign perhaps that someone in the *SS-Personalamt* thought he was valuable enough to keep within the ranks of the *SS.*[54]

Following his departure from Finland, he served in a variety of *SS* training units between April 1942 and May 1943, when he was transferred to the *SS-Division Polizei*. He remained with this division for only two months as a training instructor while the formation was undergoing reconfiguration as a *Panzergrenadier* division in Milowitz. Next, he was briefly assigned to the *3. SS-Pz.Gren.Div. Totenkopf* on 10 July 1943. He served as a company commander in combat with this division on the Eastern Front for three months until he was sent to *SS-Gren.Ers.Btl. Ost* in Minsk on 1 October, where he was assigned as its commander until July 1944. Here, he would certainly have had contact with Oskar Dirlewanger, who drew his replacements from Ehlers's unit.

Although Ehlers seemed unable to find a true home, by late summer 1944 he was a two-time veteran of the Eastern Front and had commanded troops at the company and battalion level in the *SS-Nord*, *SS-Totenkopf*, and *SS-Polizei Divisionen*. He had returned to the latter division on 9 July 1944, serving until his transfer to the *Dirlewanger Einheit*. By September 1944, Ehlers had earned the Infantry Assault Badge in Bronze, the Eastern Front Medal, and the War Service Cross Second Class. Despite his controversial past, Ehlers was rated by his superiors as possessing "good theoretical knowledge which he understands to put into practice." He was also evaluated as being a good trainer, someone who took care of his men, and was driven to achieve good results. Importantly, his efficiency report states that he was "well-liked by the men below him and the troops ... Ehlers fulfills his task well."[55]

When he was finally assigned to the *Sonderregiment* on 15 September 1944, he was initially posted to command of the new *IV. Bataillon* and may have led it during the fighting against the Slovak Uprising and afterwards when it was renumbered as *II. Bataillon, SS-St.Rgt. 2*. He also briefly commanded the *gemischte Bataillon*. The reasons for his transfer to the *Sondereinheit* are unclear; nothing in his record indicates that he had committed any offense since April 1942 warranting such a move, in fact he had performed adequately if not spectacularly. Ehlers had probably become acquainted with Oskar Dirlewanger during the early days of July 1940, when both were assigned to the *5. SS-T.V. Standarte* at Oranienburg, and most likely became reacquainted in Minsk while commanding *SS-Gren.Ers.Btl. Ost*.[56] In his assignment to the *Dirlewanger Einheit*, Ewald Ehlers had finally found a home.

In one respect, Ehlers was fortunate in the assignment of some of the men chosen to lead his *5.–8. Kompanien*, in that most of them were *bestrafft* German Army officers who had been caught up in the frenzied dragnet cast by the *Gestapo* in the wake of the 20 July plot, or had been sentenced for expressing defeatist attitudes. One of these officers was *Oberst* Harald Momm, who had been the leader of the equestrian showjumping team at the 1936 Olympics. Until the evening of 20 July 1944, he had been in command of the *Wehrmacht's* horse cavalry school in Potsdam. After uttering a remark in the officers' casino that night expressing his disappointment that Hitler had survived the assassination attempt at his headquarters in Rastenburg, Momm was arrested by the *Gestapo*. Sentenced to death, he was given a reprieve if he volunteered to serve in the Dirlewanger Brigade at a reduced rank of *Hauptsturmführer*. Momm agreed, and soon found himself in *SS* uniform commanding the *5. Kompanie* in Ewald Ehler's *II. Battalion*.

The commander of the *6. Kompanie* was another *bestrafft* officer from the *Heer*, a *Leutnant* Thelen. Very little is known about him. Similarly, the identity of the commander of the *7. Kompanie* is completely unknown, but he was also believed to have been a former army officer. In contrast, the commander of the *8. (schwere) Kompanie* responsible for leading the battalion's heavy weapons company was *Hptm.* Paul Ruhsam, who was born on 10 December 1898 in Ebensee. A salesman by profession, he lived in Mainz until 1939, when he was mobilized for the war. The nature of the offense that landed him in the Dirlewanger Brigade is unknown, but it was not so serious that it had resulted in his demotion to *Grenadier*. Instead, he was allowed to retain his previous *Heer* uniform, having evidently declined to join the *Waffen-SS* and wear that service's *Hauptsturmführer* rank.

The *III. Bataillon* was the last in the regiment to be formed, and as mentioned had the misfortune of being assigned the largest number of former concentration camp inmates, including some 400 politicals from the *KLs* at Sachsenhausen and Dachau. This battalion, composed of 500–600 men, was led by a former *Luftwaffe* officer, believed to have been a former *Oberstleutnant* named Nitzkowski, who had been degraded to the rank of *Oberleutnant* for an unspecified offense. After the war, some of the surviving members of his battalion described him as a "small, wiry officer" who "looked almost normal." He still wore his *Luftwaffe* uniform adorned with "all rank insignia and orders, including the Iron Cross," even, according to one eyewitness, the prestigious German Cross in Gold.[57]

It seems that Nitzkowski's battalion was assigned the dregs of the brigade's remaining unassigned officers, including the commanders of the *9.* and *10. Kompanien*. One of these, Georg Wild, was a *bestrafft* former *Untersturmführer* appointed as commander of the *9. Kompanie*. Wild, born on 7 April 1915 in Baden bei Wien, had joined the Austrian *Heer* in October 1937. A year later, he transferred to the *Wehrmacht*, where he served for two years before volunteering for the *Waffen-SS* on 7 April 1941. After completing basic training with *SS-Totenkopf Inf.Ers.Btl. II*, he graduated from the *SS-Junkerschule* at Bad Tölz in January 1942 and was given SS number 423 850.

In April 1942, Wild was assigned as an *Untersturmführer* to *SS-Pz.Gren.Rgt. 4 Der Führer* of the famous *SS-Division Das Reich*. After only three months, Wild was assigned to the *SS-HA* until February 1943, followed by a tour of duty with *SS-Polizei-Pz.Gren.Rgt. 1* of the re-formed *4. SS-Pz.Gren.Div. Polizei* until 14 July 1943, then another a year later with the newly formed *12. SS-Pz.Div. Hitlerjugend*. This assignment lasted until 13 June 1944, when he was sent to the Latvian *15. Waffen-Grenadier Division der SS*. His assignment there lasted only four months.

His final assignment before being sent to the Dirlewanger Brigade on 8 November 1944 was to serve as an instructor for the platoon leader course at the *SS-Pz.Gren. Schule* in Kienschlag. According to his official record, Wild was held in low esteem everywhere he was assigned. For example, during his assignment at Kienschlag (Prosečnice) in modern-day Czechia, the school's commandant expressed his dissatisfaction with Wild's performance, and after two instances of disobedience he was judged to be "unfit for further use in the *SS*."

On 7 November 1944, the *SS-Hauptgericht* agreed and without a trial remanded him to the Dirlewanger Brigade for rehabilitation, where the disgraced *Untersturmführer* arrived on 11 November.[58] For reasons unknown, possibly because he had not yet been subjected to a court-martial, he was chosen to command the new *9. Kompanie* of *SS-St.Rgt. 2* of the Dirlewanger Brigade. Nicknamed "Tom Mix" by his newly assigned *KL* convicts after the famous American cowboy actor, Wild was known for his penchant for frequently brandishing his Luger pistol and threatening his men. Dirlewanger's or Weisse's decision to have Wild serve as the *9. Kompanie* commander would soon prove to have been a mistake.[59]

The *10. Kompanie* was led by an Austrian, the 48-year-old former *Oberleutnant* Erich Langelotz, who had done "a number of shady things which he did not like to talk about," according to one of his men in an interview after the war.[60] He had been expelled from the *Wehrmacht* and sent to the Dachau *KL* on 9 July 1944, but after volunteering he was sent to Warsaw, where he fought with the *Sonderregiment* as a *B-Schütze*. After being wounded in that battle, he was sent back to the Dachau *KL* with several others to recuperate in its *SS* hospital, but when asked to volunteer again on 10 November 1944 during Dirlewanger's recruiting drive, Langelotz raised his hand, took the oath, and was made a company commander with the rank of *Untersturmführer*. Langelotz would also soon prove to have been a rather unfortunate choice to serve as a *Kompanie-Führer*.

The battalion's *11. Kompanie* was not formed prior to the battle, leaving Nitzkowski with only three infantry companies. The bulk of the men intended to fill its ranks were to come from the Buchenwald *KL*, but due to transportation difficulties did not arrive until weeks after the battle of Ipolysag was over. Both the *9.* and *10. Kompanien* were formed almost completely from political *KL* prisoners from either the Sachsenhausen or Dachau camps. Each company consisted of approximately 170–200 men, equipped solely with small arms and light machine guns. Dirlewanger's request to the *SS-FHA* for eight officers and 50 NCOs to lead this particular battalion went unanswered, due to the pressing need by the *Waffen-SS* for replacement personnel to bring its *panzer* divisions up to strength in time for the upcoming Ardennes offensive. Consequently, Dirlewanger was forced to recruit *Kapos* and block leaders from among the new *KL* arrivals to serve as squad and platoon leaders. In the *III. Bataillon*, most of these *Kapos* had already been elected as cell leaders while they were in the Sachsenhausen or Dachau *KLs* based on their status as long-standing members of the German Communist (*KPD*) or Socialist (*SPD*) Parties.[61]

The other company in the *III. Batallion* was the *12. (schwere) Kompanie*, equipped with three Czech 7.92mm heavy machine guns mounted on tripods, four or six 80mm mortars of German manufacture, and three 88mm *Raketenpanzerbüchse* (antitank rocket launchers), nicknamed the *Panzerschreck* (tank terror) by German troops.[62] The commander of *12. Kompanie* was a middle-aged white-haired former *Oberstleutnant* of the *Heer* named Stockhaus, who had begun the war as a *Hauptmann* serving in the *Wehrbezirkskommando* (Home Defense District Command) in Düsseldorf. According to *Gren.* Bruno Meyer, one of his company's *B-Schützen*, Stockhaus was not a "big Nazi" but was instead fed up with the war and the Nazi regime.

Although it was rumored that Stockhaus had been implicated in the 20 July plot, former *B-Schütze* Meyer refuted this allegation after the war:

> He [Stockhaus] said that he had last been on the Wolchow Front, had then been found guilty of irregularities with ration cards while on home leave, and had been sentenced to one and a half years in prison for this offense. After serving his sentence in the *Wehrmacht* prison in Potsdam, he was then sent to us on probation.[63]

Rather than be filled with early 100 percent political prisoners, unlike the other two companies in the battalion, Stockhaus's company was composed of a roughly equal mix of politicals, ordinary *KL* criminals, *SS B-Schützen*, and ex-*Wehrmacht* probationary troops, some of whom had previous experience with handling heavy weaponry. Stockhaus's second in command was a degraded former *Heer* staff officer named Hermann. Neither Wild, Stockhaus, nor Hermann wore rank insignia and were not to be addressed by their former rank, only by their position as *Bataillon-* or *Kompanie-Führer* (acting battalion or company commander).

The last ground combat battalion rounding out the new brigade was the aforementioned *gemischte Bataillon*. Lacking sufficient trained personnel, equipment, and weapons to assign dedicated heavy weapons companies (*Flak*, antitank, infantry howitzer, and engineer) for each of the new regiments, Dirlewanger and Weisse were forced to improvise for the time being, until these assets could be provided. To address the infantry battalions' need for heavy weapons support in combat, the brigade's leaders established a separate battalion in late October 1944 consisting of individual companies composed of elements of each of these supporting arms, hence the "mixed" title. The battalion's first commander was *Hstuf.* Ewald Ehlers, who soon moved on to take command of the new *II. Btl./SS-St.Rgt. 2*. He may have been replaced by another officer with the same surname, *Hstuf.* Walter Ehlers (no relation), who was born on 18 January 1907 in Bremen. Very little is known about Walter Ehlers, except that he had been a former officer of the *Heer* assigned to the brigade on probationary status on account of a disciplinary infraction or involvement in the 20 July plot.

The mixed battalion was composed of five companies—a staff and staff company and *1.* through *4. Kompanien.* The *1. schnelle* (fast) *Kompanie* consisted of the brigade's motorcycle platoon, a bicycle platoon, and the mounted Ukrainian platoon. The *2. Kompanie* was the battalion's heavy mortar company, equipped with six captured 120mm Soviet *Mörser* and their *Prötze* (limbers) towed by horse teams. Many of the men in this company were probably surviving *unbestrafft* veterans of the old Postschutz mortar company assigned to the *Sonderregiment* at the beginning of July 1944. *Hauptsturmführer* Otto Rühs, the company's original commander, continued in this position, making him one of the few *unbestrafft* officers commanding troops. At some point shortly before the battle at Ipolysag, this company was withdrawn from the battalion's organization and became an independent unit within the brigade tasked with providing general support to all of the other battalions.

The *3. Kompanie* served as the brigade's combat engineer or *Pionier* company, responsible for mine clearing, mine emplacement, construction of obstacle and barriers, and removing the same with explosives or hand tools, as well as other sundry tasks such as building reinforced earthen bunkers for commanders and troops. At the time of the battle, this company had a low *Kampfstärke*, not counting *Tross* or company headquarters personnel, of approximately 60 men. The *4. (schwere) Kompanie* was equipped with up to six captured Soviet 45mm or Czech 37mm antitank guns (the accounts differ) formed into two platoons of three guns each, plus a *Flak* platoon equipped with three or four 20mm antiaircraft guns of unspecified origin. All of the company's antitank and antiaircraft guns were horse-drawn.

SS-Artillerie-Abteilung Dirlewanger consisted of three firing batteries, ranging in size from captured Soviet 76.2mm divisional cannon to German-manufactured 105mm *leichte Feld-Haubitze 18* (*lei.F.H. 18*, light field howitzer). The *1.* and *2. Batterien* were equipped with this type, but neither were deployed when the brigade initially went into battle on 13 December 1944. The *Abteilung's 3. Batterie* was equipped with four 76.2mm cannon, also horse-drawn. To make up for this glaring shortage of artillery, two *Wehrmacht* or Hungarian 105mm batteries would be initially firing in support of the brigade while it was fighting in Hungary. The commander of the brigade's artillery detachment was initially *Hstuf.* Willy Schneier, who was possibly succeeded at the end of November 1944 by *Hstuf.* Fritz Missmahl when the former was transferred out of the brigade. The *Adjutant* of the *Abteilung* was *Ustuf.* Ludwig Bahrke.

Suffice to say, activation of many of the brigade's smaller elements was still ongoing when Dirlewanger got the call to deploy his brigade to Hungary. The most consequential activity not completed during this period was the expansion of the regiment's signal platoon into a much larger *Nachrichten-Kompanie.* At the beginning of December 1944, this signal platoon only possessed one 80-watt Fu. 12 set and a single 100-watt Fu. 11 radio transmitter/receiver, both truck-mounted, which were to be transferred to the new signal company. The signal company was also to be equipped with the authorized number of land-line field telephones, switchboards, and wire-laying teams, all of which would be expanded during the latter half of December 1944.

This new signal company would be drawn mostly from the communications platoon of the brigade's staff company, but was still undergoing formation and had not yet received all of its communications equipment when it was ordered to deploy. When it did, it was only able to send one signal platoon equipped with the 80-watt set, along with a few wire-laying troops and field telephone sets with operators. This contribution would soon be proven to be completely inadequate to provide the necessary command and control capability when put to the test. Neither of the two assault regiments of the brigade received their full complement of communications equipment either, the lack of which would soon be sorely felt when the brigade went into action.

The brigade would also deploy to Hungary with its newly activated *Sanitäts-Kompanie*, responsible for setting up a field dressing station to treat and evacuate the wounded to field hospitals, and a bare-bones *Verwaltungs* (supply) *Kompanie* to provide food and ammunition to the troops and fodder for the horses. What few trucks the brigade possessed would be assigned to this *Kompanie*, but most of the supplies being brought forward from a brigade supply point would still have to be carried aboard horse-drawn wagons. An *Aufklärungs* (reconnaissance) *Kompanie* was envisioned, but was not ready for combat (or had not yet been formed) when the brigade deployed in December.

The activation of the brigade and its constituent elements proceeded apace throughout November and into December, while simultaneously carrying out counterinsurgency operations. During the time between the brigade's arrival at Deviaky in mid-October 1944 and the beginning of its deployment to the front lines on 10 December from its assembly area near Neutra (Nitra) in Slovakia, Dirlewanger's troops did not, however, merely limit their activities to training their new troops and anti-partisan sweeps.

Rather, in the course of these operations, their worst traits once again came to the fore. Throughout their time in Slovakia, the Dirlewanger's *SS-Leute* (*SS* people) stole, appropriated, and looted whatever and wherever they went. Even the dreaded *SD* was appalled by what they were seeing, particularly in the village of Jastrabie. One *SD* officer complained to *Ogruf.* Hermann Höfle:

> The bad behavior of Dirlewanger members, e.g. in Jastrabie, has led to numerous complaints. Numerous *SS* members had behaved worse than partisans, had broken into shops, had served themselves without paying, had demanded food and drink from the population while they had taken the men away, had then wanted to sleep with the women and had also taken off the shoes of many an innocent farmer and robbed him of everything he had with him. If the severing of the last thread of connection with the local population is to be avoided, the removal of these troops, who have proved themselves very useful in front-line operations, needs to take place as soon as possible.[64]

Reports of depredations against the loyal Slovakian population began to pour into the headquarters of Höfle, the *HSSPF* charged with the security of the portion of Slovakia still under German control. Responsible for ensuring stability in the wake of the suppression of the Slovak Mutiny, the conduct of the brigade was making Höfle's region less stable and more insecure.

Accusations of rape, intimidation, and desertion, as well as selling their weapons to Slovak partisans, were also reported, some by commanders of other *SS* units involved in suppressing the partisan movement, such as the local *SD* commander who said that members of the brigade acted "worse than partisans."[65] Even the commander of the neighboring *14. Waffen-Grenadier Division der SS, (Galizien Nr. 1), SS-Brig.Fhr.* Fritz Freitag, refused to have anything to do with Dirlewanger or his brigade, after Dirlewanger ignored every order issued to him requiring his brigade's cooperation. Höfle himself complained directly to Himmler about the atrocious conduct of the brigade, but the head of the *SS* rebuked him sharply, stating: "You do not know the brigade at all … as a matter of fact, the discipline in this brigade is particularly strict, because particularly strict disciplinary measures have been established for this organization." With that, Höfle's hands were tied.[66]

With such a varied unit composition, constituted almost exclusively of criminals, probationary troops, disgraced officers, political prisoners, and *SS* outcasts, and armed with a hodgepodge of obsolete weapons from all over Central and Eastern Europe, many of *H.Gr. Süd's* senior leaders might have wondered how a unit of such a diverse background could ever have any chance in conventional combat? Most of the brigade's officers and NCOs had committed a criminal offense of some kind or another, and nearly all of its rank and file were convicts, guilty of a variety of petty and heinous crimes—how could this unit ever be knit together to become a cohesive, effective force?

In view of its composition, how was the Dirlewanger Brigade viewed by units of the *Wehrmacht*? While its existence had been widely acknowledged by members of the *Heer* and by 1944 the brigade had already gained an unsavory reputation that was to be even further amplified after the war, relatively few *Heer* or *Waffen-SS* troops had ever fought alongside it until this point. Even during the Warsaw Uprising, most of the troops that fought with or next to it were either *Polizei* or other *SS* units (such as the Kaminski Brigade) composed of foreign volunteers, or perhaps *Sicherungs* (security) battalions of the *Heer*. One prestigious unit that was soon to gain considerable familiarity with the *Dirlewanger Einheit* was the *24. Pz.Div.*, under which three battalions from the brigade would be later be subordinated during the second half of December 1944. The opinion expressed by one senior member of the *24. Pz.Div.* was not complementary. Its historian later wrote:

> All in all, this "brigade" was a bunch of delinquents, those politically disliked by the Third Reich or considered an inconvenience. It included demoted *SS* men, soldiers connected with the July 20 [assassination plot] and, for example, senior officers who had been demoted because

of correct but negative assessments of the situation, which were thus described as "defeatist." This brigade did not have any real fighting power; its leader wore a monkey on his shoulder as a constant companion and was usually very drunk.[67]

How true (or inaccurate) this portrayal would prove to be would soon be demonstrated during the second half of December 1944 in a spectacular manner.

However, as alluded to in the above extract, one last topic must be explored before moving on. While the regiment had been expanded into a brigade, consisting not of two battalions but of two regiments and six infantry battalions, was the brigade's senior leadership properly prepared or even qualified to lead a unit of such size? Until December 1944, Oskar Dirlewanger's style of command had stood him in good stead while in command of a single battalion and briefly as a regimental commander, where he had frequently fought in the front line alongside his troops. He knew his men and their abilities, and they knew his. But could his talent and experience as a battalion and regimental commander be sufficient preparation to enable him to serve as a brigade commander?

While leading *K. Gr. Dirlewanger* during the fighting against the Warsaw Uprising had given him some experience in commanding a force consisting of several battalion-sized battlegroups, Dirlewanger had still been able to continue practicing his style of hands-on leadership on a battlefield measured not by kilometers but by city blocks. However, command of a 6,500-man brigade in a conventional battle spread out along a wide frontage was an entirely different matter, requiring him to direct his units from a central position a few kilometers behind the front line. Instead of personally supervising his battalions as he had since his unit's inception, he would now have to exercise command and control as well as integrate the combat power of his forces (especially artillery) remotely by radio and tactical telephone, like most other battlefield commanders of the era.

Visits to the front lines would have to be limited to short duration due to the distances involved. To drive to the scene of the action from his brigade command post and back, usually 8–10 kilometers behind the *Hauptkampflinie* (*HKL*, Main Defense Line), including stops at each of his six battalion command posts, could take several hours. During this time, he would be out of contact with his *Gefechtsstand* (command post) because his Volkswagen *Kübelwagen* did not have a radio transmitter that would allow him to communicate with his own headquarters, much less that of a neighboring unit or a higher headquarters such as an *Armeekorps*.

Additionally, Dirlewanger's military education had been limited to company-level instruction, and what practical on-the-job experience he had gained as a battalion or regimental commander had been limited to counter-guerilla warfare. While this was all well and good for fighting partisans, in his capacity as a brigade commander he would by necessity have to exercise command while integrating his unit into a corps-level operation requiring cooperation with similar large (brigade and higher) combat formations on his right and left flanks. How he would accomplish this task, for which he had never received any formal military education, would have to be revealed in the crucible of combat. His limited record of having exercised brigade command during the latter stages of the Slovak Uprising, where his record of cooperating with other brigades and divisions had been less than stellar, did not bode well for the future.

Nor were his staff adequately prepared for their new or expanded duties. Most of these men—including Kurt Weisse, Helmut Lewandowski, Fritz Missmahl, and Otto Gast—had been hand-picked by Dirlewanger due to their loyalty and shared criminality, not their talent. While adequate as a battalion *Adjutant*, Weisse had not attended any general staff training, nor had he gained the necessary experience that would have made him minimally qualified to serve as the chief of staff or *Ia* of an assault brigade. The same reasoning applied to the remainder of Dirlewanger's close associates, many of whom traced their membership back to the original *Wilddieb-Kommando Oranienburg* days at Sachsenhausen in July 1940.

Had it not been for the infusion of a number of disgraced and degraded former officers of the *Heer* in October 1944—such as Harold Momm, Freiherr von Uckermann, and Paul Ruhsam—it is doubtful whether the brigade would have been able to function at all, even at a low level of efficiency. While three of his battalion commanders—Herbert Meyer, Josef Steinhauer, and Siegfried Pollack—had recent combat experience in that critical leadership position in Belarus and Warsaw, they were all concentrated in *SS-St.Rgt. 1*, while the battalion commanders of the second regiment were an entirely unknown quantity. Only combat would provide a true test of their ability.

True, the brigade's leaders had gained some degree of combat experience while mopping up the remnants of the Slovak Mutiny during late October and November 1944. However, these combat operations involved chasing down, trapping, and successfully liquidating small bands of poorly armed insurgents across the hills and valleys of rural Slovakia. How such a hodgepodge unit would perform against a numerically superior and conventionally armed opponent, such as the Red Army, was another question.

Indeed, how would it perform when put to the ultimate test? With so little time to incorporate thousands of new recruits, arm and equip them, and send them into battle with little to no training, against a foe who at the stage of the war was at his most lethal combat effectiveness, its unsuitability should have been obvious to anyone on the staffs of *HSSPF-Slowakei* or *H.Gr. Süd* paying attention. The answer is, it could not hope to succeed, and did not do so. How the *Wehrmacht* and SS leadership could possibly have thought this unit was capable of holding the line at such a critical time in the war is the subject of the next chapter.

CHAPTER THREE

Budapest Threatened, 5 October–8 December 1944

The historic town of Ipolysag (Slovak: Šahy) lies on the northern bank of the Ipoly River (Ipeľ), forming a portion of the northern border between Hungary and modern-day Slovakia. As a result of Nazi Germany's *Anschluss* with Austria and the resulting First Vienna Award of 2 November 1938, a large portion of Czechoslovakia (11,927 square kilometers), including Ipolysag and its environs, was ceded to the Kingdom of Hungary, which had entered into an alliance with the Third Reich. Although small in size (population 7,238, according to the 2018 census), the border crossroads town has played an important role since the time of the Hapsburg and Austro-Hungarian monarchies due to its strategic location. Although it boasted a majority Hungarian population (even today they comprise 70 percent of the population), it had been a multicultural and multilingual town for centuries. Tragically, as part of the Holocaust, the town's entire Jewish population, some 900 residents, were deported in 1944 and sent to extermination camps. Little survives today of that once-vibrant community.[1]

Positioned as it is on the southwestern exit of the southern tip of the Matra Mountains (themselves the southern extension of the Carpathians), Ipolysag lies astride the historic invasion route leading to Vienna used on several occasions during the 16th and 17th centuries by the Ottoman Turks. To gain control of this key position, Ottoman, Hapsburg, and Austro-Hungarian armies repeatedly fought for its possession, which led to the town changing hands numerous times during its 700-year history. To the west, beyond the narrows or "gap" at Ipolysag formed by the Ipoly River valley and the Hron (Garam or Gran) River, the terrain opens up into the Vienna Basin, a flat, relatively open expanse that forms the northern portion of the Little Hungarian *Puszta* (plains). Vienna itself lays 250 kilometers to the west, less than a four-hour drive by motorcar in 1938.

In order to understand how the transfer of the Dirlewanger Brigade to Ipolysag came to pass, and how Dirlewanger and his men found themselves almost immediately involved in heavy sustained combat upon arrival, a brief review of the events occurring during the three months leading up to the battle is in order. Its genesis was the aftermath of the 22 June 1944 attack against *Generalfeldmarschall* (*G.F.M.*) Ernst Busch's *H.Gr. Mitte* by the combined forces of the Red Army, an offensive codenamed Operation *Bagration* that led to his army group's catastrophic defeat by the end of first week of July 1944.

A month later, when Soviet forces had reached the outskirts of Warsaw and had pinned *H.Gr. Nord* against the Baltic, a series of similar cataclysms befell the German forces and their allies arrayed in southeastern Europe between mid-August and early October 1944, especially *H.Gr. Südukrain* (Army Group South Ukraine), *H.Gr. E*, and *H.Gr. F*, the latter two army groups defending the Balkans and Yugoslavia. Coupled with Allied victories during the Normandy and Italian campaigns during the summer and fall of 1944, it seemed as if the Third Reich and its dwindling number of allies were on the ropes, with certain defeat assured by Christmas.

Beginning on 25 August 1944 with the destruction of *Gen.Obst.* Johannes Friessner's *H.Gr. Südukrain* with its 6. and 8. *Armees* in Romania at the hands of the Second and Third Ukrainian Fronts, aided and abetted by the treachery of the Romanian government, the rest of Germany's southeastern front collapsed like a house of cards. Invaded by Colonel General (Col.Gen.) Fyodor I. Tolbukhin's Third Ukrainian Front on 8 September, Bulgaria immediately switched sides, thereby opening the door to the Balkans. Here, 900,000 German occupation troops and their auxiliaries in Greece, Albania, and Yugoslavia of *Gen.Obst.* Alexander Löhr's *H.Gr. E* were fighting to keep various resistance movements at bay, including Josip Broz Tito's formidable People's Liberation Army. The Germans had 300,000 men fighting in Greece alone, positioned at the end of a long and vulnerable supply line.[2]

While *Gen.Obst.* Löhr and *G.F.M.* Maximillian von Weichs, who served as both *Oberbefehlshaber Südost* (commander in chief, Southeast) and as commander of *H.Gr. F*, attempted to simultaneously reconstruct a coherent front line in the wake of Bulgaria's defection and evacuate as many German troops from Greece and Yugoslavia as possible, the main Soviet effort, spearheaded by General of the Army Rodion I. Malinovsky's Second Ukrainian Front, quickly closed up on the eastern slopes of the Carpathian mountain range by 5 September. These mountains marked the last natural barrier to the *Puszta*—the wide-open plains of eastern Hungary—where superior numbers of Soviet armored and mechanized forces could be employed to their full effect.

While Tolbukhin's army group was busily engaged in chasing von Weichs and Löhr's forces out of southern Romania, Bulgaria, and southeastern Yugoslavia, Malinovsky's forces were able to gain control of several critically important Carpathian Mountain passes and force their way through the mountains between Oradea and Arad between 28 September and 5 October 1944. By this point, *Gen.Obst.* Friessner's *H.Gr. Südukrain* (renamed *H.Gr. Süd* on 23 September), cobbled together from the remnants of 6. and 8. Armies and bolstered by a mishmash of German and Hungarian units of varying quality, was able to reassemble a coherent front of sorts.

While on paper it looked like his new line could be successfully defended, Friessner feared that it would shatter when struck hard by Malinovsky's forces.[3]

By this point, the Hungarian Regent, Admiral Miklós Horthy, and his supporters were also under no illusions as to which direction the wind was blowing, sensing that unless peace was quickly made with the Soviet Union, their country would be destroyed in the fighting that would soon follow. While Friessner was desperately attempting to reconstruct the front line and marshal as many German and Hungarian divisions as possible to defend it, Horthy, through his representatives, was just as desperately trying to secretly negotiate a separate peace agreement with one of Stalin's intermediaries that included the mass defection of the *Magyar Királyi Honvédség* (the *Honvéd*, or Royal Hungarian Army).

Although Horthy made every effort to keep the negotiations secret, these developments did not go unnoticed in Berlin by *Ogruf.* Ernst Kaltenbrunner's *SD* and his agents on the ground in Hungary. Informed of the plot, Hitler made it clear to his subordinates that he would not tolerate Hungary changing sides, like Romania and Bulgaria had done two months earlier.[4] The loss of Romania and its irreplaceable oil fields at Ploesti was an especially bitter blow to the Third Reich's war economy. Hitler, the supreme commander of Germany's armed forces, felt at this stage of the war that should Hungary—with its modest oil fields, other natural resources, and large population—fall into enemy hands or become allied with the Soviet Union, the war was as good as lost.

To prevent this from occurring, Hitler, in his capacity as head of the *Oberkommando der Wehrmacht* (*OKW*, German Armed Forces High Command), ordered a preemptive strike in Budapest to "decapitate" the Hungarian leadership, beginning on 15 October 1944 with two of his *SS* "specialists," *Ogruf.* Erich von dem Bach and *Ostubaf.* Otto Skorzeny. Codenamed *Unternehmen Panzerfaust*, this *SS*-led task force initiated a coup that began with the kidnapping of Horthy's youngest son, Miklós Jr., as ransom. This deed compelled the Regent to resign his office and be taken to Germany as a "guest" after the *SS* threatened to kill his son unless Horthy gave in. The political vacuum that immediately ensued allowed *Ogruf.* von dem Bach to quickly seize Budapest with a minimal amount of bloodshed.

German troops rapidly took over all the key points in the city, including the telephone exchange, radio station, and key bridges and road intersections, and confined the Hungarian Army to its installations in the city.[5] Before he was bundled away to Germany, Admiral Horthy, at Hitler's expressed order, dissolved his cabinet and installed a pro-German government, led by the notorious Arrow Cross Party's leader, Ferenc Szalási. A dedicated fascist, Szalási professed his guarantee to Hitler that Hungary would remain loyal until the bitter end, but he was little more than a puppet doing Hitler's bidding. To ensure that Szalási's loyalty did not waver, actual control of the Hungarian government was entrusted to *Brig.Fhr.* Edmund Veesenmeyer, whom Hitler appointed *Reich* plenipotentiary in Hungary after the German occupation.

With his political flank thus protected, Friessner could direct his undivided attention to the heavy fighting that awaited. His army group's situation had begun to improve by 15 October 1944 after several *panzer* divisions, under the control of the commander of the reconstituted *6. Armee, General der Artillerie (Gen.d.Art.)* Maximillian Fretter-Pico, encircled and nearly destroyed three Soviet corps during the tank battle of Debrecen. Sensing an opportunity, Malinovsky had sought to take advantage of the Hungarian government's disarray by incautiously splitting his forces and launching a daring drive towards Budapest on 6 October, despite the fact that he did not have the accustomed overwhelming superiority his front normally brought to bear. During the heavy fighting that took place between 10 and 15 October, German and Hungarian forces managed to inflict significant damage to the 6th Guards Tank Army, which suffered the loss of over 200 tanks on 12 October alone.[6]

Friessner's counterattack, while it stabilized the Hungarian front, proved to be only a temporary reprieve, but one that gave the leaders of *OKH* and *H.Gr. Süd* time to pause and re-evaluate the situation. Using this breathing space, *Gen.Obst.* Heinz Guderian, as *OKH* Chief of Staff, ordered Friessner to pull his forces back to the Tisza River, a more defensible line than the one *H.Gr. Süd* had previously tried to hold. Viewing his defeat at Debrecen as only a temporary setback, Malinovsky ordered the hastily re-equipped 6th Guards Tank Army and the powerful Cavalry-Mechanized Group Pliyev to closely pursue the withdrawing Axis divisions in hopes of encircling and destroying the bulk of their forces before they could cross the Danube to safety. Too closely, as it proved. Taking advantage of the headlong Soviet advance, Fretter-Pico's forces turned about on 23 October and conducted a pincer attack of their own, led by *Gen.d.Pz.Tr.* Hermann Breith's *III. Panzerkorps (Pz.Korps)* cutting off and nearly destroying three more Soviet corps by 26 October.

This German–Hungarian victory brought major operations by both sides in Hungary to a halt until 28 October, the first time since mid-August that Friessner's army group had been able to establish a cohesive, though thinly occupied, front line.[7] Taking advantage of this brief pause in operations, Friessner did everything he could to strengthen the new front along the Tisza. Much of his attention was focused on the reorganization of the Hungarian forces, which were in complete disarray by this point in the wake of the resignations or defections of so many of its senior officers after Horthy's failed peace attempt. Additional German units, deemed more capable and reliable, were hastily inserted into the line between Hungarian units to serve as *Korsettenstange* (corset stays) to buttress the defense and deter the defection of their ally, as well as to ensure that the Hungarians bore their share of the burden of defending their country.

Malinovsky resumed his advance towards Budapest on 29 October, an operation that the Soviet Supreme Command, or *Stavka*, had now codenamed the Budapest Operation. He had also used the pause in battle to concentrate his forces and replace the tanks he had lost the week before. The German front line along the Tisza was soon pierced at several points by Lt.Gen. Ivan Shlemin's 46th Army after the Hungarian *3. Armee* disintegrated under its hammer blows. With little remaining to slow his army down, Shlemin's spearheads, with their left flank demarcated by the line of the Danube, had pushed west and north to a point only 10 kilometers away from the southeast suburbs of Budapest by 2 November. On 3 November, his tanks broke through the city's outer defense line on the eastern side of the Danube, but a series of counterattacks on 4 and 5 November by the *8. SS* and *22. SS-Kavallerie* (Cavalry) *Divisionen* and the *13. Pz.Div.*, soon joined by two other *panzer* divisions, forced Shlemin's 46th Army to pull back from the city.

During this tank battle, fighting could clearly be heard in the distance by the city's population, who began to display signs of panic despite assurances from Arrow Cross members that the Red Army would never enter Budapest. Matters were made more complicated when a German engineer inadvertently ignited demolition charges emplaced on the Margarethe Bridge over the Danube that linked the two sides of the city (Buda on the western bank and Pest on the eastern side). The explosion heavily damaged the bridge and caused a portion of it to fall into the river, at a time when the German and Hungarian defenders needed this bridge more than ever. Nor did it engender much trust between the city's population and their German overseers—its residents began to fear that the Germans might sacrifice their beloved city to delay the Soviet advance, though the bridge's destruction was purely accidental.

Despite the nearness of the Soviet vanguards, very little had been done by the Germans or Hungarians at this point to fortify the city or to prepare it to withstand a long siege, especially against an attack from the western bank of the Danube should the Red Army seize a crossing site and attempt an envelopment from that direction. According to Friessner in his postwar account, on one of his visits to Budapest during this period the city still seemed to have a peacetime atmosphere. He later wrote: "While in Budapest, I realized that the population had no inkling about how serious the situation at the front was. Everywhere I was still seeing scenes of the deepest peace and, unfortunately, this poured some bitters drops into the festive cup for [my] victory at Debrecen."[8]

Between 11–22 November, Malinovsky, using four of his armies (the 7th Guards, 27th, 40th, and 53rd), fought and maneuvered against determined German resistance, advancing along a broad front from the Tisza to the Danube before finally closing up along the Danube south of Budapest by 25 November. On his right flank north of Budapest in the Carpathian foothills of eastern Slovakia, General Ivan Y. Petrov's Fourth Ukrainian Front struggled against a determined German defense staged by *Gen.d.Inf.* Otto Wöhler's *8. Armee* or *Armeekommando 8* (*AOK 8*), which carried the additional title of *Armeegruppe Wöhler* (*A. Gr. Wöhler*) due to the inclusion of the Hungarian *1. Armee* in its order of battle.

In the heavy fighting that ensued, the Fourth Ukrainian Front managed to penetrate German and Hungarian defenses in the eastern Matra Mountains, but barely managed to push the Germans back as far as the city of Miskolc after suffering heavy losses. On Malinovsky's left flank to the south of Budapest near Baja, Tolbukhin's Third Ukrainian Front had already initiated its own attacks as early as 22 November, breaking out of the bridgeheads his troops had established over the Drava River at Apatin and Batina. Blasting through thin German defenses arrayed in the Drava–Danube triangle, Tolbukhin's 4th Guards and 57th Armies had seized the key city of Mohacs by 26 November, ripping open the flank of *H. Gr. Süd's* neighbor to the south, *H. Gr. F*, thereby opening the way to the Lake Balaton region, the source of the Third Reich's last substantial oil reserves. Only the understrength *2. Pz. Armee* of *H. Gr. Süd* blocked its path.

On 29 November, the historic city of Pecs fell to Tolbukhin's spearheads, and two days later the 4th Guards Army, which had been transferred from Malinovsky to Tolbukhin's command, arrived along the Danube, linking up with the 46th Army of Malinovsky's Second Ukrainian Front on 1 December, thus creating a continuous front along the Danube from Mohacs to just a few kilometers short of Budapest.[9] Neither *H. Gr. Süd* nor *H. Gr. F* had been able to do much to stop Tolbukhin, with their few reserves being switched from one crisis point to the next before another one broke out elsewhere, much like the fabled Dutch boy frantically trying to plug rapidly appearing holes in an earthen dyke.

The next round of fighting would happen along the northern approaches to the city, where German and Hungarian defenses were less established. While Tolbukhin's forces inexorably approached the area southeast of Lake Balaton, Malinovsky's attention focused on Budapest and the German positions north of the city. As Shlemin's 46th Army aimed its attack westwards across the Danube towards Lake Balaton, the 7th Guards Army, 6th Guards Tank Army, and Cavalry-Mechanized Group Pliyev attacked north of the Danube and took the key city of Hatvan by 5 December, a move that threatened to crack the German main defense line north of Budapest established by the *III.* and *IV. Pz. Korps* of *6. Armee/A. Gr. Fretter-Pico*.[10]

By 8 December, despite fierce German resistance, the forces of these two armies and the cavalry-mechanized group had taken the town of Waitzen (Vác) and closed up along the eastern bank of the Danube on a 10-kilometer-wide front. Soviet spearheads were now less than 30 kilometers north of Budapest, a move that completed the isolation of the portion of Budapest east of the Danube. At the same time, the 4th Guards Army of Tolbukhin's Third Ukrainian Front had completely closed up along the southern length of the *Margarethestellung* (the "Margaret Position"), the German and Hungarian's newly occupied main defensive position that ran along the line Lake Balaton–Stuhlweissenburg (Székesfehérvár)–Lake Velencze, terminating at the southern outskirts of Budapest on the western bank of the Danube (see Map 1).

This was a natural defensive position southwest of Budapest manned by the troops and tanks of *6. Armee/A. Gr. Fretter-Pico*, now a mixture of German and Hungarian units.[11] The portion of the position in the gap between Lakes Balaton and Velencze was heavily defended, as was the northern shore of Lake Balaton, but the integrity of the positions east of Lake Velencze was an open question. Although *H.Gr. Süd's* commander had originally intended to incorporate Budapest into its *HKL* as the eastern anchor of the *Margarethestellung*, the defenders' lack of sufficient infantry to hold it from the northeastern corner of Lake Velencze and the southwestern corner of Budapest was a vulnerability that could not be adequately addressed. The unit tasked with defending this stretch of the position, the *153. Feldausbildungs-Division* (*Feldausb.Div.*, field training division), which was composed mostly of green recruits, was woefully underequipped and possessed few heavy antitank guns. This weakness was soon detected by Soviet reconnaissance, giving Tolbukhin a window of opportunity to complete the encirclement of Budapest from the south.

He would soon move to take advantage of it, although there were inherent risks to this course of action. One of the major risks that Tolbukhin faced was that his and Malinovsky's fronts were concentrated to the south and north respectively, and separated by Budapest in the center and by the Danube in the north. Hence, they would be unable to quickly come to the aid of one another should any of their armies find themselves under a concerted German counterattack. During the first week of December, both *Gen.Obst.* Guderian and Friessner realized this vulnerability too and believed that if *H.Gr. Süd* could be reinforced and strike at least one of the Soviet armor spearheads in the flank and destroy it, Friessner's army group could fortify its defensive lines around Budapest before winter arrived.

As the *OKH* chief of the general staff, Guderian ordered Friessner to concentrate three recently reconstituted *panzer* divisions (the *3.*, *6.*, and *8. Pz.Div.*) that he would send from the *OKH* Eastern Front operational reserve to carry out the attack. In addition to the *panzer* divisions, they would be reinforced by several newly refitted tank battalions equipped with *Pz.Kfw. V* Panthers and a battalion of heavy *Pz.Kfw. VI* Tiger tanks. This counteroffensive, to be codenamed *Unternehmen Spätlese* (Operation Late Harvest), would be carried out under the operational control of *Gen.d.Pz.Tr.* Hermann Breith's *III. Pz.Korps* of *6. Armee/A.Gr. Fretter-Pico*. The attack was initially supposed to occur within two or three days, by 11 December at the latest. When *Spätlese* had been completed, the same three *panzer* divisions would be returned to the Eastern Front's pool of divisions held in reserve. However, both Guderian and Friessner disagreed as to which Soviet concentration to attack—the one northeast of the Danube (Second Ukrainian Front) or west of the river (Third Ukrainian Front).

With both generals at loggerheads, Hitler intervened and chose the course of action favored by Friessner, who wished to launch the *Spätlese* counteroffensive towards the south in the gap between Lakes Balaton and Velencze. Once each spearhead had broken through the 4th Guards Army's front, both would race eastwards and encircle their opponent's forces southwest of Budapest. After several days' delay, due to bad weather and continual bickering among Friessner and Guderian's staffs, the final start date was set for 17 December, but even this was to prove overly optimistic.

While this counteroffensive southwest of Budapest was being planned and the forces to carry it out began assembling, the situation north of the Danube had taken a decided turn for the worst.

Even more dangerous than the vulnerable front-line positions of the *Margarethestellung* east of Lake Velencze in the *6. Armee/A.Gr. Fretter-Pico* area of operations was the disintegrating front line connecting the armies of Fretter-Pico and Wöhler north of the Danube. When the four German and two Hungarian divisions of Breith's *III. Pz.Korps* defending east of the city were forced to withdraw into Budapest's eastern suburbs in the wake of Malinovsky's bold advance to the Danube and seizure of Waitzen between 5 and 8 December, German and Hungarian defenses north of the city, led by the *IV. Pz.Korps* of *6. Armee/A.Gr. Fretter-Pico*, had been pushed away from the *III. Pz.Korps* to the northwest. This move had created a gap separating the two corps, leaving the forces defending the portion of Budapest east of the Danube isolated and reliant upon the remaining bridges across the river for supply and evacuation.

Friessner's greatest fear on 8 December was that Malinovsky would take advantage of the east–west movement corridor along the Ipoly River valley north of Budapest. The commander of the Second Ukrainian Front, who clearly held the initiative at this point, posed a two-fold threat, against which the Germans and Hungarians had few countering options. By thrusting around the northern bend of the Danube and continuing his advance towards the west-northwest, Malinovsky's two most powerful mobile units, the 6th Guards Tank Army and Cavalry-Mechanized Group Pliyev, could prevent the *III.* and *IV. Pz.Korps*, both of *6. Armee/A.Gr. Fretter-Pico*, from re-establishing a contiguous front line north of Budapest.

In addition to this threat, should Malinovsky choose to continue driving his armies northwards towards the Slovakian border instead, he could split *H.Gr. Süd* in two by punching a gap between *6. Armee/A.Gr. Fretter-Pico* and *8. Armee/A. Gr. Wöhler*. Should this occur, there would be little possibility of restoring any semblance of a defensible front line in Hungary, and the ability to establish a defensible position in Slovakia would also become problematic. Taken to its logical conclusion, Malinovsky's bold advance could completely separate *H.Gr. Süd* and *H.Gr. Mitte* from one another. Malinovsky could also pursue both courses of action simultaneously, which is exactly what he did.

After breaking through the German and Hungarian defensive line erected east of Budapest at Hatvan on 5 December, Malinovsky had refined his initial plan. Instead of attempting a crossing of the wide Danube at Waitzen north of Budapest, he decided that he would direct the bulk of his troops in a northwesterly direction along the northern bend of the river, while his 46th Army continued its envelopment of Budapest from the south. In the north, he would focus his main effort along the Ipoly River valley, seize Balassagyarmat at its eastern end, and push westwards through the Matra and Börszeny Mountains towards Ipolysag.[12]

The objective of Malinovsky's lead element, Col.Gen. Andrey Kravchenko's 6th Guards Tank Army, was the narrows in the Matra Mountains 3 kilometers west of Ipolysag, forming the Ipolysag Gap 5 kilometers west of Ipolysag. Should the gap and the surrounding hills fall into their hands, Kravchenko's tanks could then swing north and drive into southern Slovakia, or turn south and attack along the eastern bank of the Hron River until his troops reached the Danube at Esztergom, where they could establish a bridgehead and complete the encirclement of Budapest from the north. These were the immediate threats causing Friessner's greatest concern.[13]

An additional worry, should a Soviet tank army get beyond the Ipolysag Gap, was the knowledge that there was little remaining defensible terrain that the Germans or Hungarians could use to their advantage to stop or slow down a Soviet advance to Vienna once they crossed the Hron River. With few German or Hungarian reserves available to block the advance of the Second Ukrainian Front should its commander choose this course of action, by 8 December it appeared that the route to Malinovsky's objective lay wide open, as it had for the Ottoman Turks 263 years earlier when they last attempted to seize Vienna.[14] Fortunately for the Axis, this was not Malinovsky's intent, nor was he authorized to undertake such a bold course of action, but the German high command did not know this at the time.[15]

The few remaining German and Hungarian *Sperr* (blocking) units in his path from the *IV. Pz.Korps* had fallen back as quickly as they could to the portion of the *Margarethestellung* erected north of the Danube, but these hastily scraped-together *Alarm* (emergency) units and half-constructed fortifications, even if they could be manned by these troops, would not be enough to hold the portion of the line between Esztergom and Balassagyarmat against a concerted attack by armored and mechanized forces. Just as Tolbukhin was doing south of Budapest at the same moment, Malinovsky sensed an opportunity to exploit the situation and take advantage of the momentary German weakness.

Malinovsky's immediate challenge and the accompanying risk was to break through German and Hungarian positions before his opponent could fortify them. The *Wehrmacht* was not known for reacting slowly to a threat, as Malinovsky was well aware. To carry out his plan, he had to drive his forces as quickly as possible westwards along the Ipoly River valley. The advance towards Ipolysag itself would not be too difficult. For most of the 30-kilometer-long route between the towns of Szécsény and Dregelypalánk, the river valley was wide enough to enable armored and mechanized units to deploy and maneuver, but the closer they got to Ipolysag, the narrower it became.

The task then became a daunting one for the attackers. Only 1.5 kilometers wide at its narrowest point, the Ipolysag Gap was bounded in the north by the Carpathian foothills of the Matra Mountains, some of which exceeded 300 meters in height, and to the south by the Börszeny Mountains, with heights of 500 meters or more. To get there, Soviet units would have to cross the Ipoly River in full view of German defenses arrayed along the hills surrounding Ipolysag. As the staff of *H.Gr. Süd* had already noted, these terrain factors would severely limit the maneuver possibilities of enemy armored forces should the gap remain in German hands.

To punch through, the lead element of the 6th Guards Tank Army—the IX Guards Mechanized Corps, commanded by Lieutenant General of Tank Troops Mikhail V. Volkov—could not rely on armor alone; two or three well-positioned heavy antitank guns or a blown bridge over the Ipoly River could hold up the entire advance for hours or even days. In addition to pushing armor through the valley, Volkov's corps would need to maneuver through the heavily wooded mountains on both sides of the Ipoly to get around German and Hungarian defenses. To carry out this flanking maneuver, the 6th Guards Tank Army would have to be reinforced with additional infantry that would have to be supplied by the XXVII Guards Rifle Corps of Col. Gen. M.S. Shumilov's neighboring 7th Guards Army.

Due to its commanding location, possession of the town of Ipolysag, along with the gap to the west and the hills surrounding it, figured prominently in the future offensive plans of the Red Army. At that time, *Stavka* was planning to carry out its strategic Vienna Operation during the early spring of 1945 once Budapest had fallen and Hungary was "liberated." On the other hand, should the Germans and their Hungarian allies block this gap and prevent the rapid egress of Malinovsky's tanks, it might upset the timetable for seizing Budapest, investing Vienna, and ending the war by the spring of 1945 in conjunction with the strategic offensives planned against *H.Gr. Mitte* and *Nord*, with the ultimate objective of Berlin. Such a delay could upset the U.S.S.R.'s timetable, and its leader, Joseph Stalin, simply would not tolerate any delays, a character attribute of which his generals were well aware.

Generaloberst Friessner was determined to prevent Malinovsky from realizing his intentions at all costs, but all he had to send on 8 December to assist *6. Armee/A. Gr. Fretter-Pico*, responsible for defending the area north of the Danube as far as the southern outskirts of Ipolysag, was the understrength *Magyar Királyi 2. Páncéloshadosztály* (Royal Hungarian 2. Pz.Div.), which was being reconstituted at the time.[16] On that same day, its headquarters and all of its combat-ready elements were ordered out of its assembly area in the city of Esztergom on the southern bank of the Danube, where it would be subordinated to the *IV. Pz.Korps* when it arrived. Once deployed, the *2. Pz.Div.* would establish defensive positions along the portion of the *Margarethestellung* in the Börszeny Mountains. Its headquarters would be established in the large town of Vámosmikola on the eastern bank of the Ipoly River, 26 kilometers north of Esztergom and 19 kilometers southwest of Ipolysag.

Fretter-Pico had considered sending elements of the *357. Inf.Div.* as soon as it could be relieved from its position on the western bank of the Danube north of Budapest. But this unit, commanded by *Generalmajor (Gen.Maj.)* Josef Rintelen, was a division in name only. It had been shattered between 5 and 7 December by Cavalry-Mechanized Group Pliyev of the Sixth Guards Tank Army at Hatvan during the initial stages of the defense of Budapest, suffering heavy losses. As a result, it had been downgraded in status from a division to a *Divisions-Gruppe* (*Div.Gr.*, Division Group), with the combined strength of a reinforced infantry regiment. At the moment, most of Rintelen's 782 remaining infantrymen were positioned on the western bank of the Danube under the command of other divisions, leaving Fretter-Pico no option at that moment but to task the Hungarian *2. Pz.Div.* with the mission.[17]

North of the Danube, adjacent to the *IV. Pz.Korps* of Fretter-Pico's army, lay *8. Armee/A.Gr. Wöhler.* The bulk of Wöhler's forces were over 50 kilometers east of Ipolysag along the southeastern border of Slovakia and were embroiled in heavy fighting against the 53rd Army and Cavalry-Mechanized Group Pliyev of Malinovsky's Front as well as the southern wing of the neighboring Fourth Ukrainian Front. Lacking sufficient forces himself, Wöhler had nothing he could spare on 8 December to provide immediate help. The most that he could do at that moment was to order *Gen.Maj.* Gustav von Nostitz-Wallwitz, commander of the *24. Pz.Div.*, to extend his right flank even further to the west to incorporate Ipolysag in his 35-kilometer-wide defensive line. This he would do, beginning on 9 December.

This venerable division, although competently led, had been reduced in size to 30 percent of its normal combat strength, and currently fielded only eight operational *panzers* and assault guns.[18] To address this weakness, Wöhler would have to shift the *4. SS-Polizei-Pz.Gren.Div.* and the *18. SS-Freiwilligen-Pz.Gren.Div. Horst Wessel* to take over its positions as soon as von Nostitz-Wallwitz could reposition his division to the west to strengthen the *8. Armee* right flank. This process would take two days and would overextend the *24. Pz.Div.*, making it vulnerable to an enemy attack through Balassagyarmat. Unfortunately for Wöhler, Fretter-Pico, and Friessner, by 8 December the bulk of *H.Gr. Süd's* nine *panzer* or mobile divisions were either tied up in and around Budapest (including the *13. Pz.Div.*, *60. Pz.Gren.Div.*, and the *8.* and *22. SS-Kav.Div.*), where they would be completely encircled two weeks later, or were assembling between Lakes Balaton and Velencze preparing to launch Operation *Spätlese* (including the *1.*, *3.*, *6.*, *8.*, and *23. Pz.Div.*) once the ground hardened sufficiently for Fretter-Pico's *panzers*.

This aspect of German troop dispositions worked to the advantage of the attackers. The defenses north of the Ipoly River had been made the responsibility of *8. Armee/A. Gr. Wöhler*, whose right-flank corps, the *IV. Pz.Korps*, was tasked with the mission of blocking any attack in that direction. This corps, commanded by *Gen.d.Pz.Tr.* Ulrich Kleemann, had been released from Fretter-Pico's control and transferred to Wöhler's *Armeegruppe* on 9 December to simplify command north of the Danube.[19] The subunit of this corps that actually had to carry it out was the aforementioned *24. Pz.Div.*, a task that now included defending the town of Ipolysag, beginning at the northern bank of the Ipoly. Everything to the south of the Ipoly River remained under the control of *6. Armee/A.Gr. Fretter-Pico*.

It was the task of the *H.Gr. Süd* staff to coordinate the actions of these two armies, but in order for this arrangement to work, both armies had to take concrete steps to make sure that everything possible on the ground was being done to coordinate and integrate their defenses in this key area, especially antitank weapons. In such a fluid situation as existed on 8 and 9 December, this was a difficult task indeed. But there is not much proof that the troops on the ground actually saw much evidence of this, at least not from the perspective of the unit that had been given the mission of defending the area.

Remarking upon this situation 17 years later, the historian of the *24. Pz.Div.*, retired *Gen.Lt.* Dr. Fridolin von Senger und Etterlin, wrote:

> This was to be the right wing of the division sector, which extended from there [Ipolysag] along the edge of the heights on the north bank of the Ipoly for about 35km to the ridge north of Balassagyarmat. At first, the command situation at the narrows of Ipolysag was unfortunately completely unclear, because the border between [*6. Armee*] and [*8. Armee*] also ran there. The former subordinated the parts of the division deployed at the narrows, while its main section at Ipoly belonged to [*8. Armee*]. Both armies had seemingly greater concerns in their [defensive] sectors at the moment and therefore could not give full care to their extreme left and right wings, respectively. This dilemma was later to have a disastrous effect and [was] not addressed by the army group [i.e., *H.Gr. Süd*] by changing the army boundaries until the consequences were beyond repair.[20]

By 9 December, the key town of Ipolysag was initially defended by a single German battalion from that division—the *II. Bataillon* of *Panzergrenadier Regiment 26* (*II. Btl./Pz.GrenRgt. 26*). The rest of the division was fighting to the east along the *HKL* stretching between Ipolysag and Szécsény.

This mechanized infantry battalion, under the command of *Rittmeister* (Captain) Emil Zischler, had a reported *Kampfstärke* of only 175 men. However, his veteran *Schützenpanzerwagen* (*SPW*) mounted unit was still equipped with its complement of heavy weapons, including antitank guns, infantry howitzers, and 20mm antiaircraft guns, backed up by a light field howitzer battery from the division's artillery regiment. Although each of Zischler's *Panzergrenadier* companies had been reduced to a combat strength of 40–50 men, they were well-trained, experienced, and above all, well led. For its reduced size, his battalion still packed a powerful punch and could easily bloody the nose of an unsuspecting adversary.[21]

At 7.10pm on 10 December, one day after it had arrived in the Ipolysag area, Zischler's *Kampfgruppe* was placed under the temporary control of the Hungarian *2. Pz.Div.* (and by extension that of *6. Armee/A.Gr. Fretter-Pico*), though it continued to draw its supplies from its parent division. It was intended to be returned to the *24. Pz.Div.* (and control of the *IV. Pz.Korps*) once it was relieved by another unit.[22] For the commander of the *24. Pz.Div.*, this could not happen soon enough, because he and his outnumbered division needed all of the combat power they could muster to keep the approaching 6th Guards Tank Army from breaking into southern Slovakia. Thus, Wöhler and his staff needed no further incentive to divest themselves of the

Ipolysag mission and would continually urge *H.Gr. Süd* over the next several days to order the return of the *II. Btl./Pz.Gren.Rgt. 26* to its parent division.

To the east, the range of hills dominating the approaches to the town along the northern bank of the 40–50-meter-wide Ipoly River were defended by an engineer company attached to the newly arrived *Pionier-Regiment Stab* (*Pio.Rgt.Stab*, Engineer Regiment Staff) *36*, a formation designed to control engineer and road construction units, hardly suited to serve as a front-line headquarters. In addition to temporarily exercising control of Zischler's battalion, its two battalions—*Heeres-Bau-Pionier-Bataillone* (*Bau-Pio.Btl.*) *144* and *Heeres-Pionier-Bataillon 666* (both *Heerestruppen* or general headquarters troops)—had a combined *Kampfstärke* of 386 men, less than half of their authorized strength, but the German force had been augmented by two Hungarian scratch-built company-sized units, *Kompanie Gaal* and another unnamed unit.

An engineer company from *Bau-Pio.Btl. 144* occupied favorable defensive positions along Hills 283 and 323 overlooking the northern bank of the Ipoly River. This *Pionier* company was attached to Zischler's battalion, but the rest of *Bau-Pio.Btl. 144* and the other battalion (soon joined by a third) were ordered to occupy positions in the Börzeny Mountains south of the river under the control of *Oberstleutnant* (*Oberstltn.*) Grosse's *Pio.Rgt.Stab 36*. The German *Pioniere* under Zischler's control would dig in and give a good account of themselves in the coming battle, especially given their limitations (many of their men were middle-aged and deemed physically unsuited for combat) and lack of heavy weapons.

In summation, the successful defense of the Ipolysag Gap would be the mutual responsibility of two separate field armies, which had to work together in order to prevent a Soviet breakthrough. With so many different units being deployed in the front lines at the same time, a well-laid communications network would thus be crucial to a successful defense of the Ipoly River valley. This necessity placed great emphasis on the reliability of tactical land-line telephones, FM and short-wave radios, and teletype. If handled properly by an experienced commander, assuming dynamic leadership and employing the right kind of units in the most advantageous positions, this command-and-control arrangement should prove sufficient, as it had so often in the past in similar situations that arose on the Eastern Front.

If not done properly, establishing field army boundaries along such an important terrain feature (known as a "seam" in modern-day military parlance) could be a recipe for disaster and a vulnerability that the 6th Guards Tank Army would be quick to exploit once its reconnaissance troops detected it, as the scouts of the Red Army invariably did.[23] As noted, the *24. Pz.Div.* pointed out the weakness of this arrangement and was against subordinating Zischler's battalion to the neighboring Hungarian *2. Pz.Div.* of *6. Armee/A.Gr. Fretter-Pico*, but the division commander followed his orders and directed Zischler to set up a deliberate defense of the town.

Fortunately, he and his men would have three days to fortify their positions, plan artillery supporting fires, and lay minefields before the enemy approached.

On 8 December, the Hungarian *2. Pz.Div.* had been formally directed by *H.Gr. Süd* to assume command and control of the southern half of the Ipolysag Gap. It had been resting in *H.Gr. Süd* reserve in Esztergom since 2 December after being mauled during the withdrawal battles of October and November 1944, and had not yet completed its reconstitution. On 8 December, the division was led by its acting commander, *Ezredes* (*Oberst*) Endre Zádor, the former commander of the Hungarian *Pz.Rgt 30* and more recently the chief of tank gunnery at the Royal Hungarian Central Tank Gunnery School. The actual division commander, experienced veteran *Vezérörnagy* (*Generalmajor*) vitéz Zoltán Zsedényi, was serving detached duty elsewhere and would not return to assume the reins of command until the beginning of January 1945.[24]

The choice of the Hungarian *2. Pz.Div.* to defend the Ipolysag Gap was not an ideal one; it was an armored division in name only. Established on 1 October 1941, it had fought in Ukraine and Romania during the spring and summer of 1944, as well as the frontier battles in the Carpathian foothills and along the Tisza in October 1944. By the beginning of December 1944, it was much the worse for wear, a reflection of Hungary's fortunes by this point in the war. In addition to shortages of nearly every kind of equipment—especially tanks, antitank weapons, and trucks—Zádor's headquarters lacked the robust telecommunications equipment of a similarly sized German *panzer* division and was reliant upon a small German liaison unit, *Divisions-Verbindungs Kommando 149* (*D.V.K. 149*), led by *Maj.* von Gossla, to transmit radio and telex messages. There were no other German divisions available at that particular moment, so the Hungarian *2. Pz.Div.* would have to carry out the mission until reinforced or replaced by another unit.

This division, although it had been at Esztergom for over a week reconstituting its combat power, was still weak. On 9 December 1944, it reported having one strong, two above average, and one average strength infantry battalions (with a total of approximately 1,500 men), but many of its infantrymen were new recruits and not ready to deploy. It fielded five operational heavy antitank guns (75mm), five *Toldi IIa* light tanks, seven *Nimrod* self-propelled *Flak* vehicles, and two operational German *Pz.Kfw. IVs*. It had 18 additional German *panzers* of this type, but they were all undergoing repair. It also had six light artillery batteries (with approximately 20 105mm howitzers) but lacked enough prime movers to tow them all. Its motorized combat engineer battalion was currently serving elsewhere, but would return by 11 December. Overall, it reported a mobility percentage of only 30 percent, having had most of its rolling stock "borrowed" by the Germans earlier in the campaign. Because of all of the noted deficiencies in manpower and armored fighting vehicles, *H.Gr. Süd* awarded it a combat value rating of Category IV—meaning that it was suitable for limited defensive operations only.[25]

In the order directing its employment, the Hungarian *2. Pz.Div.* would first be subordinated to Kleemann's *IV. Pz.Korps*. This arrangement lasted for a single day; on 9 December, this corps was subordinated to *8. Armee/A.Gr. Wöhler*. Thus, on that same day, Zádor's *2. Pz.Div.* was subordinated to *6. Armee/A.Gr. Fretter-Pico*, reporting directly to the field army's headquarters without an intervening corps command to provide additional support. This was a decided disadvantage considering the seriousness of the situation, but Fretter-Pico had no other corps headquarters that he could spare at that moment to do the job.[26] This jury-rigged command and control arrangement would have to suffice for the time being in the hope that the Red Army's methodical advance would continue at a slower pace on account of the terrain factors already mentioned.

To make matters worse, the train carrying all of the Hungarian division's 20 *Pz.Kfw. IV* medium tanks (including the two operational ones) from Esztergom to the railroad yard in the town of Vámosmikola had been accidentally diverted to northern Germany and would not return for at least a week. This left the division at that moment with only five heavy antitank guns of its own, and little else, to hold back any Soviet armored assaults.[27] Although the division was able to bring up five *Toldi 32M IIa* light tanks with 40mm guns and seven *Nimrod* self-propelled 40mm antiaircraft guns, these light vehicles had proved themselves to be nearly useless in battle against Soviet T-34s and American Lend-Lease M4A2 Shermans equipped with 85mm and 76mm cannon, respectively. In regards to artillery, due to a lack of prime movers it could deploy only a single battery with seven 105mm *le.F.H. 18* field howitzers, later to be augmented by a German artillery battalion (its remaining gun batteries were still undergoing reconstitution and awaiting their towing vehicles).

After moving into its new defensive positions in the Ipolysag area on 8 and 9 December, the Hungarian *2. Pz.Div.* reported a total *Kampfstärke* of 1,627 men, of whom 731 were attached Germans troops serving under *Pio.Rgt.Stab 36*, which had been subordinated to it on 9 December.[28] Nearly a thousand untrained replacements had been left behind in Esztergom. In total, the Hungarian troop contribution amounted to an understrength motorized infantry regiment of three battalions (combined combat strength of 363 men), a reconnaissance battalion (231 men), and a *Pionier* battalion (302 men). To bolster the division's weak antitank and antiaircraft defenses, the *leichte-Flak-Abteilung 91* of the *Luftwaffe* would be attached to it on 11 December, bringing with it 18 light antiaircraft guns (20mm), to be followed several days later by a battalion from *II. Abt./Flak-Rgt. 24* with its nine 88mm cannon to serve in the antitank role.

Still, *H.Gr. Süd's* commander and his chief of staff continued to be concerned that even with this augmentation, it would not be enough to hold Ipolysag and the Ipoly River valley against a deliberate attack by the Red Army. German intelligence had reported that on 8 and 9 December, the advance elements of Kravchenko's 6th Guards Tank Army had crept inexorably closer, inching their way westwards along both banks of the Ipoly River valley. Town after town fell in rapid succession, as German and Hungarian rear guards from the *IV. Pz.Korps* struggled in vain to stem their methodical advance. When the 31st Guards Mechanized Brigade of the IX Guards Mechanized Corps seized the key town of Dregelypalánk during the evening of 9 December, the outline of the developing Soviet advance could clearly be seen.[29]

Dregelypalánk was located on the southern bank of the Ipoly River and only 9 kilometers southeast of Ipolysag, less than 10 minutes away by automobile. Fortunately, the German rear guard blew up the bridge over the Ipoly before pulling out, slowing down the Soviet advance by a day. To the south, the Danube riverside town of Kismaros, defended by *K.Gr. Lehnert*, was lost the same day. Local residents who had fled the town of Dregelypalánk during the night of 9/10 December and reached the safety of Hungarian lines at 7.10pm on 10 December reported that they had counted 80 Soviet tanks and large numbers of infantry positioned in and around the town as well as bridging equipment.[30] With this report confirming Friessner and his chief of staff's worst fears, the crisis that they had tried so hard to prepare for had now arrived.

CHAPTER FOUR

The Plan to Defend the Ipolysag Gap, 9 December 1944

To mount any sort of effective defense of the Ipolysag area, what the Germans and Hungarians needed above all were infantry and heavy antitank weapons. With Lt.Gen. Volkov's IX Guards Mechanized Corps bearing down on them, it was clearly evident to even the lowliest staff *Leutnant* that the Hungarian *2. Pz.Div.* was a weak reed, even though it had been reinforced by the engineers of *Pio.Rgt. Stab 36* and a *Panzergrenadier* battalion from the *24. Pz.Div.* Faced with this stark reality, the staffs of *H.Gr. Süd* and *6. Armee/A.Gr. Fretter-Pico* realized that despite these additions, the Honvéd's *2. Pz.Div.* still would not be strong enough to hold the Ipolysag Gap for very long.[1]

However, by 9 December, nearly everything else that *H.Gr. Süd* had, including Hungarian reserve units, was already manning the front line between Lake Balaton and Budapest, and could not be spared or was being withheld for Operation *Spätlese*, such as the elite Hungarian *Szent László* infantry division, *H.Gr. Süd's* sole infantry reserve commanded by *Gen.Maj.* Zoltán Szügyi. To the south, the neighboring *2. Pz.Armee* of *Gen.d.Art.* Maximillian de Angelis did not have anything to spare either. Hoping that perhaps Berlin might have more forces to send, *H.Gr. Süd's* chief of staff, *Gen.Lt.* Helmuth von Grolman, telephoned *Gen.d.Pz.Tr.* Walter Wenck of the *OKH Führungsabteilung* (*OKH* Command Staff Operations Section) at 12.30pm on 9 December. In the ensuing conversation, von Grolman requested an additional temporary "loan" from the *OKH* operational reserve be sent to Hungary to clear up the situation. Wenck, whose office had already authorized the deployment of three *panzer* divisions for Operation *Spätlese*, would not (or could not) immediately commit more forces, leaving von Grolman at a loss as what to do next.[2]

Shortly after his inconclusive conversation with Wenck, von Grolman contacted *Ostubaf.* Hans Greiner, the chief of staff of the neighboring *Deutsche Befehlshaber in der Slowakei* (*dt.Befh.i.d.Slowakei*, German Commander in Slovakia), in Pressburg (Bratislava) to inquire what sort of forces he might have available to help reinforce the Ipolysag Gap.[3] Von Grolman learned that within Slovakia, there were only two combat units that met *H.Gr. Süd's* requirement: the Dirlewanger Brigade, then wrapping up another anti-partisan drive, and an armored field training division, *Panzer-Feldausbildungs-Division (Pz.Feldausb.Div.) Tatra*. Greiner told him that the German commander in Slovakia, *Ogruf.* Hermann Höfle (also performing double duty as the *HSSPF-Slowakei*), could spare neither of them at the moment because Höfle was mobilizing his own forces to defend the southern border of Slovakia against the approaching Red Army.[4] *Generalleutnant* von Grolman immediately voiced his preference for the *Tatra* Division, at the time commanded by *Gen.Lt.* Friedrich-Wilhelm von Loeper, should it become available.

Although von Loeper's division was greatly understrength, it did have the equivalent of three *Panzergrenadier* battalions, a small artillery battalion, two operational *Sturmgeschütze*, and a complement of heavy weapons, though no tanks.[5] As for the Dirlewanger Brigade, it was an unknown quantity, but had recently gained considerable notoriety within the *Wehrmacht* due to its excesses during the suppression of the Warsaw Uprising. Whether its vaunted anti-partisan experience could translate into the sort of capability needed to defend the Ipolysag Gap was an open question, which probably influenced von Grolman's preference for the *Tatra* Division. The matter was settled, for the moment at least, when Greiner told von Grolman that *Ogruf.* Höfle had already earmarked the *Tatra* Division specifically for defending the Waag valley area east of Bratislava, and therefore it could not be spared.[6] If Höfle might consider the release of any of his forces to *H.Gr. Süd*, Greiner told him, it could only be the Dirlewanger Brigade.

In a subsequent telephone conversation about the same topic later that afternoon, Greiner told *Oberstltn.* Heinrich Schäfer, the *H.Gr. Süd* First General Staff Officer (or *Ia*), that he had already begun making contingency plans to send the Dirlewanger Brigade with its six "very strong" battalions to the Ipolysag-Balassagyarmat area, to be deployed along the Slovakian side of the border as follows: two battalions east of Ipolysag, two more north of Ipolysag as a reserve, and the remaining two battalions north of Balassagyarmat.[7] For his part, Schäfer recommended that sending both *Pz.Feldausb.Div.Tatra* and the Dirlewanger Brigade to block the gap would be even better, but Greiner would not commit to his proposal at that moment, stating that it was important to keep the *Tatra* Division where it was for "political reasons."

As will be seen, Greiner's personal assessment of the Dirlewanger Brigade's true strength was either unrealistically optimistic due to inadequate information, or he deliberately concealed its actual condition merely to be rid of it, a goal that he most likely shared with Höfle. This was understandable, given the headaches Dirlewanger's men had given Höfle and Greiner since the suppression of the Slovak Mutiny. While it may have been "strong" in terms of the number of men assigned (approximately 6,500), it could not objectively be considered combat-ready, given the huge influx of untrained personnel, especially political prisoners, that it had received during the past two months. As detailed in the previous chapter, it lacked competent leadership, especially at the battalion and regimental level, and had far too few qualified non-commissioned officers assigned who were not former convicts themselves. Discipline was lacking. Its lack of modern weaponry also made it a poor choice to fight enemy tanks. Without knowing the true state of affairs, there was no other option but for von Grolman and Schäfer to accept Greiner's offer at face value.

In the same conversation, Schäfer asked Greiner whether Dirlewanger himself could take over command of the Ipolysag defensive sector.[8] In this case, Greiner was more forthcoming. He replied that Dirlewanger's headquarters lacked an adequate command and control apparatus agile or flexible enough for combat. Even should Dirlewanger be able to fulfill the mission based on timely face-to-face cooperation with other units, Greiner told Schäfer that his superior, *Ogruf.* Höfle, personally believed that the two battalions of the brigade that could be made immediately available for deployment to Balassagyarmat would need to be placed under the direct command of *H.Gr. Süd* immediately upon arrival. Evidently, neither Höfle nor Dirlewanger possessed the means to exercise direct control of the brigade from Pressburg or Neusohl, respectively. This should have been a warning sign, but apparently did not attract any attention at the time.

In response, Schäfer agreed but made the point that in order to comply with Höfle's wishes, he would have to subordinate the first two available battalions to the Hungarian 2. *Pz.Div.*, the force representing *H.Gr. Süd* on the ground, which at the time was executing the mission of blocking advancing Soviet forces beyond the western outskirts of Balassagyarmat, a city on the southern bank of the Ipoly River that lay within the 8. *Armee/A.Gr. Wöhler* area of responsibility. Greiner, again, whether he lacked a true understanding of the situation or simply did not care, had no objections to this proposal. To finalize the necessary coordination for the employment of these two battalions, Schäfer, as Friessner's representative, asked Greiner to have Dirlewanger report in person to *H.Gr. Süd* headquarters, located at the mountaintop resort in Dobogókó, for a meeting with him and *Oberstltn.* Otto Marcks, the *Ia* of 6. *Armee/A.Gr. Fretter-Pico*, the following day, 10 December.[9]

Their attempt to obtain control of *Pz.Feldausb.Div. Tatra* stymied for the moment, the most that Friessner and von Grolman could put together in the meantime within *H.Gr. Süd's* own meagre resources to assist Fretter-Pico's *Armeegruppe*, besides the aforementioned Hungarian tank division, was to subordinate to it *Oberstltn.* Grosse's *Pio.Rgt.Stab 36*, which had taken up positions in the same area on 8 December. Grosse, whose headquarters were located in the town of Kémence, by this point controlled three subordinated German engineer battalions (*Pio.Btl. 112, 144*, and *666*) and over the past 24 hours had been augmented by the 165 men of *Feld-Strafgefangen Abteilung 18* (a *Heer* field punishment unit), a 51-man company from *Feld-Ersatz Bataillon 13* of the *13. Pz.Div.*, a 120-man company from *Maschinengewehr-Bataillon* (Machine-gun Battalion) *Sachsen*, an unspecified number of men from *Res.Inf.Btl.* (*Ohrkrank*) *284*, and some additional Hungarian emergency units of company size.[10] The fact that Grosse's headquarters was actually a regimental planning staff and not suitable for directing front-line combat operations was apparently not taken into account, nor was its lack of a logistical component. Despite its incompleteness, it was nevertheless subsequently referred to as *K.Gr. Grosse*.

To provide some measure of support to *K.Gr. Grosse*, von Grolman was sending a 105mm German artillery *Abteilung* of 17 guns to *Pio.Rgt.Stab 36* and four *Sturmgeschütze* from *H.Gr. Süd*'s dwindling pool of *Heerestruppen* (General Headquarters Troops) that would arrive late in the evening of 10 December. With the bulk of its men positioned in the Börzeny Mountains between the riverside village of Hont in the north and the mountain resort of Királyháza in the south, *K.Gr. Grosse* would be unable to spare anything for the defenses north of the Ipoly River except one company from *Bau-Pio.Btl. 144* and two small Hungarian *Alarm* infantry companies composed of stragglers and remnants of other units.

Kampfgruppe Lehnert from *Pz.Gren.Div. Feldherrnhalle* (*FHH*), already operating east of the city of Esztergom along the northern bank of the Danube where the Börzeny Mountains ended, was also temporarily subordinated to the Hungarian *2. Pz.Div.* on the same day. *Oberleutnant* (*Oberltn.*) Lehnert's 180 men were deployed west of Kismaros, where they blocked the Danube River highway emanating from the Soviet bridgehead at Waitzen with a pair of heavy antitank guns and an *SPW-*mounted *Panzer-Pionier* company. The *Luftwaffe*'s local headquarters responsible for providing air support to *H.Gr. Süd*, *Luftflotte 4*, offered to increase sorties against Soviet armored columns and supply depots with ground attack aircraft from its *I. Fliegerkorps* beginning on 11 December, following aerial reconnaissance of the Ipoly River valley and Ipolysag area, weather permitting.

While Friessner and Fretter-Pico and their staffs grappled with how to temporarily shore up the defenses in the Ipolysag Gap, *Gen.d.Pz.Tr.* Wenck, at his office in Zossen near Berlin, had not remained idle either. After all, the movement of units large enough to carry out this assignment had to be personally approved by Hitler, who was acting ever more frequently in his role as the supreme commander and habitually interposing himself in low-level tactical details. Since speaking to von Grolman earlier that day, Wenck had continued searching for a solution as to how best fulfill *H.Gr. Süd*'s request for additional forces. While the conversation between Friessner and Höfle's staff officers went back and forth on 9 December, at the same time Wenck—on his own authority—had contacted the Commander of German Forces in Slovakia separately and asked him whether he truly had any formations to spare. Wenck told Höfle: "The *Führer* himself had marked the importance of the narrows at Ipolysag with a black line in his map during the discussion of the situation."

During his telephone conversation with Wenck, Höfle received the following verbal orders that he later testified originated from Hitler himself:

1. The German commanders in Slovakia [Höfle] and *H.Gr. Süd* [Friessner] are dependent upon one another and must exercise the closest cooperation.
2. The defensive positions in the narrows east of Ipolysag must be strengthened to the greatest possible extent by forces of the German Commander in Slovakia [i.e., Höfle].

3. The German commander [in Slovakia] is given a *completely free hand* [author's emphasis] in the deployment of his forces. However, he is primarily responsible for securing the southern border [of Slovakia].[11]

This was in accord with a previous statement by Höfle to von Grolman that "the *Führer* has in principle forbidden the removal of German troops from Slovakia."[12] Whether he wished to do so or not, Höfle had been told by none other than the *Wehrmacht*'s Supreme Commander himself that he must do his part to strengthen the defenses in the Ipolysag Gap. In effect, his contributions to the effort were no longer voluntary, as they had been until that moment. Without hesitation, Höfle, as Greiner had told von Grolman earlier that day, immediately offered up two battalions from the Dirlewanger Brigade.[13] Wenck accepted Höfle's proposal on the spot, apparently in the belief that this brigade was as strong as advertised.

Based on this phone call from Wenck, Höfle felt that he now had the proper authority, at least from the *OKH*, to order the deployment of the brigade to the combat zone. As mentioned, he had not yet bothered to consult Himmler about this decision. He later stated in his response to a letter of reprimand from the leader of the *SS* that Dirlewanger's unit was:

> the most readily available [unit] for this mission and was also my only unit with artillery and heavy mortars of any significance … I … immediately ordered the Dirlewanger Brigade to continue its march [and] directed the bulk of its troops to the section of the [Hungarian–Slovak] border between Esztergom and the Starárieka [River] north of Balassagyarmat … [I] arranged for the motorized transport of two battalions to Ipolysag.[14]

This was patently false, of course, since *Pz.Feldausb.Div. Tatra* was also available at the same time, was already motorized (with armored vehicles, no less), and had more heavy weapons.

General der Panzertruppe Wenck was well aware of this unit's existence and its readiness status, but from the perspective of being Heinz Guderian's right-hand man at *OKH*, he felt that the *Tatra* Division should be left alone for the moment in order to continue its primary mission of training *panzer* troops. Agreeing with Wenck but for a different reason, Höfle—acting in his capacity as the German Commander in Slovakia and not as the *HSSPF* for Slovakia—had already decided that he needed *Gen.Lt.* von Loeper's armored division to defend the approaches to Bratislava, where his headquarters lay, much more than it was needed to defend the Ipolysag Gap. Given the seriousness of the situation north of Budapest, it is difficult to comprehend how such parochial concerns took a higher priority, but such was the nature of the Third Reich's leadership hierarchy that it permitted local political leaders to make decisions based on their own personal interest rather than the survival of their nation.

Wenck, like von Grolman, probably did not completely understand the brigade's composition or readiness status either, evidently believing that Höfle was going to send a full-strength and combat-ready *SS* assault brigade that would be sufficiently strong to defeat the Soviet attack and block the Ipolysag River valley.[15] In fact, it was anything but, as has already been described in the previous chapter. After advising Guderian, who concurred with his recommendation, Wenck then gained the *Führer's* official permission to order Höfle to deploy Dirlewanger's unit. Once Hitler's approval had been confirmed, the brigade was alerted for movement during the late evening of 9 December.

To speed the deployment and to get them into position as quickly as possible, the first two battalions to arrive, as agreed to with *H.Gr. Süd*, would be initially subordinated directly to the Hungarian *2. Pz.Div.* and not the headquarters of Dirlewanger or either of his two regiments. If needed, more of the brigade, including Dirlewanger and his headquarters, could be sent later, but there were several caveats governing its commitment. In the discussions with *H.Gr. Süd*, Höfle made it clear that his first priority was defending southern Slovakia, so sending more of Dirlewanger's troops would be dependent upon the situation there. Dirlewanger himself, as previously stated, was to report to the army group *Ia* at *H.Gr. Süd* headquarters the next morning (10 December) to coordinate the deployment of his two battalions to the *Kampfraum* of *6. Armee/A.Gr. Fretter-Pico*.[16]

The negotiations that took place between Höfle's and *H.Gr. Süd's* staffs on 9 December did not take into account the three stipulations that had been levied upon the brigade's deployment by Hitler as described earlier; nor is there any evidence that Höfle brought them to Friessner or his staff's attention. Nor was Hitler the only decision-maker that Höfle had to satisfy; he still needed to notify Himmler of the deployment of the Dirlewanger Brigade. Unaccountably, he did not do so until several days later when the troops had already been deployed, a decision that would eventually result in his letter of reprimand. At the time, however, Höfle's decision accomplished two things—it would position the brigade where it was most likely needed and would remove it as far away from his region as possible, where it once again had become a threat to peace and security due to the unregulated plundering and other depredations upon the local population by Dirlewanger's troops.

Shortly after the IX Guards Mechanized Corps had taken the town of Dregelypalánk in the early evening of 9 December, Höfle's staff sent out the alert order to the Dirlewanger Brigade. He had never seriously considered releasing *Gen.Lt.* von Loeper's *Pz.Feldausb.Div. Tatra* during the negotiations earlier that day, a ploy that had given the *H.Gr. Süd* leadership the false hope that they might later pry this unit from Höfle's grasp. Höfle and his chief of staff, *Ostubaf.* Hans Greiner, were evidently so eager to rid themselves once and for all of Dirlewanger and his troublesome band that they were willing to risk the outcome of the battle for the Ipolysag Gap at the expense of *H.Gr. Süd*. After all, in his capacity as the Commander of German Forces in Slovakia, Höfle answered directly to Adolf Hitler (and Himmler, indirectly, as *HSSPF-Slowakei*), and not Johannes Friessner, so he must have not feared any repercussions for his decision.

However, the brigade was not as ready to move to its new area of operations as Höfle and Greiner had led Wenck, Friessner, and von Grolman to believe. The bulk of Dirlewanger's combat-ready troops, consisting primarily of the three battalions wrapping up a major anti-partisan operation (Operation *Wolfsburg*), had begun assembling in the area 20 kilometers north of the town of Neutra, approximately 170 kilometers west of the Balassagyarmat area. Wilhelm Stegmann's *I. Btl./SS-St. Rgt. 1* had been attached to the *167. Volks-Gren.Div.* for the same operation and was located to the northwest in the vicinity of the village of Trenčianska Turná, and had the farthest to travel.[17] The brigade had no motorization of its own to speak of, which meant that the majority of its movement to its new area of operations would take place the old-fashioned way—by foot and by hoof, a process that would take several days to accomplish.

At this point, it might be worth asking why Himmler was not included in any of these deliberations at the time. The most likely answer is that Höfle thought they were local and tactical in nature, and besides, Hitler himself had given him a completely free hand in deciding how to deploy his troops in defense of southern Slovakia. This allowed Höfle considerably more leeway than Himmler would normally have granted. In addition, Himmler himself had recently moved out of Berlin and on Hitler's orders had taken command of *H.Gr. Oberrhein* (Army Group Upper Rhine) on 26 November in Alsace. In his new role as an *Oberbefehlshaber*, Himmler would have been preoccupied with the myriad of details that accompanied such a senior leadership position while continuing to serve as the head of the SS.

Due to his new duties and accompanying concerns, Himmler would have been unable to exercise the same degree of micromanagement over his minions as he was accustomed to when he was in his Berlin office. However, Himmler had given Höfle one standing directive—that given the overwhelmingly criminal composition of Dirlewanger Brigade and the fact that the strictest discipline was needed to keep its men under control, the brigade must not under any circumstances be broken up and employed separately outside of its usual chain of command.[18] Given the battlefield realities of the present situation, Höfle evidently decided to ignore this order, or at best to interpret it very loosely. It was to have near-fatal consequences.

At first, deployment of the entire brigade as a single unit to the Ipolysag area was not a given. As agreed, Höfle would send to *H.Gr. Süd* the Dirlewanger Brigade with his six "very strong" *Grenadier* battalions into the Ipolysag and Balassagyarmat area, but under one condition: all but two would remain in Slovakia. He intended to send the first two battalions available (*II. and III. Btl./SS-St.Rgt. 2*) to the area north or west of Balassagyarmat, where they would have to be temporarily subordinated to *K.Gr. Grosse* until a regimental headquarters to control them arrived. They were also the closest troops to the Ipolysag area, since neither battalion was involved in the anti-partisan *Wolfsburg* operation, unlike the remainder of the brigade.

Then, to secure the southern border of Slovakia, which Höfle saw as his primary mission according to Hitler's directive, he would retain control of the other four battalions for defending southern Slovakia—two battalions to be deployed to the mountains east of Ipolysag (*III. Btl./SS-St.Rgt. 1* and *I. Btl./Sturm-Rgt. 2*) and two (*I.* and *II. Btl./SS-St.Rgt. 1*) to the area northwest of Ipolysag as a reserve. Deployment of the *gemischte Bataillon* was not factored into this arithmetic, since it consisted of heavy weapons and other supporting troops and was normally parceled out among the six *Grenadier* battalions as needed. However, for its impending deployment to the Slovakian border, the mixed battalion would later form two small *Kampfgruppen* in combination with two companies (the *7.* and *8.*) from *II. Btl./SS-St.Rgt. 2.*

Armed with this knowledge about the imminent release of the two SS battalions, *H.Gr. Süd* chief of staff von Grolman then instructed his subordinate, *Oberstltn.* Schäfer, to prepare an operations order prescribing how these reinforcements would be employed within *H.Gr. Süd's* area of operations. One key planning factor that Schäfer had to take into account was the rate of movement of each of the Dirlewanger Brigade's elements. The average marching distance from the assembly area near Neutra to its forward assembly area at Terany in Slovakia was 85 kilometers (52 miles), and a further 22 kilometers to Ipolysag. This meant that these reinforcements would require at least two days to reach their new destination by foot, with the leading elements arriving by 12 December at the earliest, unless trucks were provided to move them instead. Lack of motorization, except for a handful of trucks, had forced Dirlewanger to rely predominately on horse-drawn transport to pull his artillery, heavy infantry weapons, and baggage train. Trucks were a scarce commodity, and Höfle's domain had few available. Unaccountably, neither *H.Gr. Süd* nor *6. Armee/A.Gr. Fretter-Pico* offered any of their own wheeled transport to expedite the brigade's movement.

As previously stated, the first elements of the brigade to deploy on the night of 9/10 December were its *II.* and *III. Btl./SS-St.Rgt. 2*, composed predominately of political prisoners, mostly communists. At the time it was alerted for movement on the evening of 9 December, *III. Batl./SS-St.Rgt. 2* was occupying quarters in the hamlet at Laskár near Nováky. Since it and its sister *II. Bataillon* billeted nearby were not involved in an anti-partisan operation at that moment, these two battalions were the closest to the scene of action. Because of this, they were immediately available for deployment. The fact that they were the newest battalions in the brigade and filled with large numbers of recently arrived politicals did not seem to have influenced the decision to send them first, and Dirlewanger would in fact try to persuade *H.Gr. Süd* and *6. Armee/A.Gr. Fretter-Pico* not to use them the following day. However, the situation in the Ipoly River valley was so dire that there was simply not enough time to substitute other battalions. There was none other immediately available, in any event (see Map 2).

In the meantime, *K.Gr. Grosse* was tasked by the Hungarian *2. Pz.Div.* to hold the 16-kilometer-long *Hauptkampflinie* using *Pio.Btl. 666* and several attached *Alarm* units. This battalion, 690 men strong including its attachments, was tasked with defending an extended frontage that arced eastwards from the southern outskirts of the village of Hont (which was held by the Hungarian *IV. Btl./Inf.Rgt. 3*) and ended at the forest ranger's settlement at Királyháza in the south, where it linked arms with a Hungarian unit. Between these two points lay the northern peaks of the Börszeny Mountains, dominated by the 284-meter-high (931 feet) Nagyszuha (Mt. Szuha). The area was cut by many deep ravines and mountain streams and traversed by few roads, these mostly unpaved logging tracks. Visibility was extremely limited, averaging less than 100 meters in any direction. Consequently, German engineers believed that the terrain was virtually impassable, especially for tanks.

As the staff officers of *H.Gr. Süd* and *6. Armee/A.Gr. Fretter-Pico* had assumed, these terrain features alone should have posed enough of an obstacle to discourage any probe by the Red Army through the mountains and thereby force its troops and tanks to confine their movements along the valley floor. Relying upon the dictates of conventional wisdom, as they must have reasoned, the deployment of two additional German battalions, regardless of their composition, should have been more than enough to deter any enemy advance, even if they had only enough troops to establish a thin outpost line. But then again, the same staff officers had not reckoned with the IX Guards Mechanized Corps and their commander, Mikhail V. Volkov.

One of the few senior German leaders to recognize the threat posed by the IX Guards Mechanized Corps' advance along the Ipoly River valley was *Gen.Obst.* Friessner, who wrote on the evening of 9 December:

> [Our] main concern—apart from the extremely weak infantry occupation of the *Margarethestellung* and the Budapest bridgehead—is the protection of the narrows of Ipolysag, the possession of which would open the way for the enemy to the Upper Hungarian Plain and the Budapest bridgehead. According to today's enemy picture, there is no doubt that the enemy will form a *Schwerpunkt* [point of main effort] against the Ipolysag Gap, [which poses an] especially [dangerous threat] against the rear [area] north of the bridgehead Budapest.[19]

Even at this early date, Friessner was already having doubts about the ability of the Hungarians to effectively coordinate and lead the defense of the Ipolysag Gap. He was also beginning to realize Budapest's vulnerability to an encirclement from the north, adding to the considerable danger posed by the Soviet advance south of the city. In the same evening report, he wrote: "The Hungarian *2. Pz.Div.*, which is responsible for the defense in [the] Börszeny Mountain range north of the Danube bend, will not be able to cope with this, in spite of the support by a German mixed anti-aircraft *Abteilung*, which is already deploying to Ipolysag." Although he could not have known this at the time, his thoughts were soon to prove prophetic.

CHAPTER FIVE

Initial Troop Dispositions, 10 December 1944

Lieutenant General of Tank Troops Mikhail Vasilevich Volkov had come a long way since enlisting in the Red Army in May 1919 in the aftermath of World War I, where he had fought as an enlisted man. Not only had he successfully risen through the ranks during and after the Russian Civil War, but he had survived the purges of the late 1930s that claimed the careers or lives of so many of his equally talented contemporaries. Born in the city of Nizhny Novgorod east of Moscow on 25 March 1895, the 49-year-old's career began its rapid rise in 1938, when he was promoted to the rank of colonel. By 5 November 1943, he was made Lieutenant General of Tank Troops in command of a mechanized corps.

Among his leadership accomplishments were his contribution to the successful defense of the Western Front from December 1941 until March 1942 while commanding the 77th Mountain Rifle Division, the victory at Stalingrad in 1943, and the battle of Korsun-Shevchenkovsky in February 1944 (otherwise known as the battle of the Cherkassy Pocket). After successfully leading the V Mechanized Corps during the second Iași-Chișinău (Jassy-Kishinev) offensive, resulting in the near-annihilation of the German 6. and 8. *Armees* in Romania during August and September 1944, his corps was upgraded to "Guards" status and renamed the IX Guards Mechanized Corps on 12 September. This renaming indicated that the Soviet Supreme Command expected even greater accomplishments by Volkov and his command.

Although he is more widely known as a dynamic leader of armored and mechanized forces, one overlooked aspect of Volkov's career was that from November 1938 until March 1942, he served exclusively in the Caucasus Mountains—first as a deputy chief of staff to a mountain rifle division, then chief of staff to another mountain division, then as the officer in charge of training for all mountain divisions stationed in the Caucasus, and finally as the commanding officer of the 77th Mountain Rifle Division on the Western Front. Following the last assignment, he was hand-picked to attend the Red Army's general staff academy until November 1942, where he received a well-rounded education in the Red Army's evolving doctrine for the employment of mechanized forces. After that, he took command of the V Mechanized Corps during the Battle of Stalingrad.

During his three years spent serving in the Caucasus, Volkov learned the peculiarities of mountain warfare, including how to employ every category of weapon, ranging from mortars to armored vehicles, in rugged, mountainous terrain. He learned that while mountains may seemingly pose an obstacle to maneuver, this disadvantage could be negated by good reconnaissance, imaginative maneuver, and bold action—thus, their seeming impassibility could work in one's favor, especially when the enemy was not expecting an attack from that direction. Although by December 1944 he had already proven himself as a successful leader of armored forces, Volkov's past experience as a mountain troop officer would soon prove very useful as his corps approached the mountain gap at the western end of the Ipolysag River valley on 8 December 1944.

The unit under Volkov's command, the IX Guards Mechanized Corps, was no ordinary armored formation of the Red Army. It was nothing less than one of the Red Army's most elite formations. Formed on 8 September 1942 as the V Mechanized Corps from the wreckage of the XXII Tank Corps smashed by the German *6. Armee* at Kalach during the initial stages of the Battle of Stalingrad, it was reorganized with three mechanized infantry brigades, a tank brigade, three self-propelled artillery regiments, a mortar regiment, an antiaircraft regiment, a motorcycle reconnaissance battalion, and supporting troops. Although designated as a mechanized corps, it was a corps in name only, having the approximate strength of a similarly organized German *Panzergrenadier* division, but with more armor.[1]

During World War II, the Red Army formed only 13 of these corps, compared to over 30 tank corps that were raised. In terms of sheer numbers, mechanized corps were a rare breed in themselves, but they played an oversized role during the campaign against Nazi Germany, especially during the last two years of the war. Each of the Red Army's six tank armies had at least one mechanized corps operating within its table of organization, where they provided the infantry support needed to seize and hold objectives, cross water obstacles, and defend in depth. According to one source, mechanized corps were by far the "largest, most expensive, lavishly equipped, divisional-sized units in the whole of the Red Army."[2] While ordinary rifle divisions were chronically understrength, the *Stavka* ensured that its mechanized corps were kept as near to full establishment as possible.

The fact that they were maintained at such a high level of readiness was due to their primary mission in accordance with the Red Army's latest doctrine for the conduct of mobile operations. Within this context, their mission was to serve as assault forces that would seize and hold key terrain, and defend it if need be in order to clear the way for one or more tank corps to penetrate the enemy's main defense line and begin their exploitation mission deep in the enemy's rear area. Performing this role often resulted in heavy losses in men and armored fighting vehicles, which partially explains why there were so few mechanized corps raised during the war, but experience showed that the results usually justified the cost. The IX Guards Mechanized Corps was a case in point where its value was repeatedly demonstrated.

When it was upgraded to Guards status due to its stellar performance during the summer campaigns of 1944, it would henceforth receive the best available equipment, the pick of the best manpower, and first priority for resupply. Fully motorized and organized along the lines of the January 1944 tables of authorization, the corps had an authorized strength of 16,369 men, 197 tanks, 51 self-propelled guns (SU-76, SU-85, and SU-152) filling out its three artillery regiments, and 36 heavy 120mm mortars. Thus constituted, at full strength a mechanized corps had more tanks and self-propelled guns than a Soviet tank corps and three times the number of infantrymen. The corps' three mechanized infantry brigades of 3,685 men each (the 18th, 30th, and 31st Guards Mechanized Brigade) had their own tank battalion, and the corps' single tank brigade (the 46th Guards Tank Brigade) had one motorized infantry battalion. Of course, the number of men and vehicles available for duty fluctuated constantly—due to losses in battle, sickness, or mechanical failure—but compared to conventional units, these losses were replaced more quickly.

After having been reduced to only 10 operational tanks and self-propelled guns of all types by 28 October 1944 in the aftermath of the disastrous battle of Debrecen, the corps had been substantially replenished with men and materiel throughout November when it lay in reserve.[3] When Volkov's corps began its attack toward the Ipoly River valley after the breakthrough at Hatvan on 7 December, it reported 154 operational tanks on hand (including a large number of Lend-Lease M4A2 Shermans, nicknamed *Emchas*), 11 self-propelled guns (SU-76 and SU-85), 52 antitank guns, seven 122mm multiple rocket-launchers, and 76 mortars of all types.[4] Just as important was that it was nearly at full strength in the number of infantrymen assigned to its mechanized battalions. However, the shortages of self-propelled guns in its artillery regiments had not yet been made good, leaving the corps reliant on lesser-caliber indirect fire weapons and a single battery equivalent of 122mm *Katyusha* ("Little Kate") rocket launchers from the 385th Guards Rocket-Propelled Mortar Battalion.

When the leading element of Volkov's corps, the 31st Guards Mechanized Brigade, had taken the town of Dregelypalánk, three days and 100 kilometers later, his corps was still nearly at full strength, except for the aforementioned lack of artillery that would be felt much later. The corps' primary objective was Ipolysag, the importance of which its commander was quick to recognize. In the corps' combat journal summary for 9 December, Volkov's operations officer, Lt.Col. Sobolev, wrote:

> By itself Šahy [Ipolysag] is not a large city. But from the point of view of the future progress of our offensive actions, it is of huge significance. Šahy is located between two mountain ranges and is a natural gateway to the Czechoslovak [the Danubian] plain. This has been made clear by the stubbornness of enemy in defense of Hont and Homok along the approaches to the

city and of Šahy itself. Should we take Šahy away from the enemy, it would open the way to Bratislava, Vienna, and Prague ... and for the fraternal people of Czechoslovakia ... who have long been awaiting the arrival of [the] Red Army as their liberator.[5]

Hence the need to accelerate the pace of the advance. Colonel Kuzma F. Seleznev's 31st Guards Mechanized Brigade had already taken Dregelypalánk by storm on the evening of 9 December against determined resistance by the Hungarian *IV. Btl./Inf. Rgt. 3 (mot.)*. As an illustration of the severity of the fighting during the struggle for the town, the Hungarian battalion suffered 30 percent casualties, as well as the loss of two heavy antitank guns, before it was forced to withdraw towards Hont.[6]

At the same time that Dregelypalánk was being contested, the 30th Guards Mechanized Brigade seized the towns of Vadkert and Tereske, securing the corps' right flank. To the corps' south, the XXV Guards Rifle Corps of the Seventh Guards Army was moving along the course of the northern bank of the Danube, protecting Volkov's left flank, with the XXVII Guards Rifle Corps not far behind. This movement would bring all three corps as far west as the eastern foothills of the Börszeny Mountains. More importantly, the rapid advance allowed the IX Guards Mechanized Corps access to the paved north–south highway connecting Dregelypalánk in the north with Waitzen on the Danube. Numerous unpaved mountain logging trails connected at numerous points along the length of this highway, offering tantalizing opportunities to outflank the Germans and Hungarians in the valley, should General Volkov decide to take advantage of them. Later that evening, he received reports that the enemy was reinforcing the villages of Hont and Homok, both located on the southern bank of the Ipoly River. Both would have to be taken before an assault on Ipolysag could be launched.

Hont, only 4.5 kilometers west of Dregelypalánk, would be the first objective for the IX Guards Mechanized Corps on 10 December (see Map 2). Volkov had deemed this the fastest and most direct approach that would avoid a slow and laborious attack through the mountains. The northern mass of the Börszeny Mountains loomed over Hont and neighboring Homok as his tanks and troops occupied their forward attack positions between Hont and Dregelypalánk. Interrogation of Hungarian and German prisoners captured on 8 and 9 December indicated that his opponent's forces were weak and in disarray (including the battered Hungarian *IV. Btl./Inf. Rgt. 3*), inviting bold action by the seasoned Red Army tank commander before his opponent could set up a cohesive defense line.[7] Indeed, it was his precipitous advance during the past three days that had brought about the frantic scramble to find something—anything—to block his advance and that would bring the Dirlewanger Brigade to the Ipoly River valley.

As the lead element of the 6th Guards Tank Army, Volkov intended to punch through quickly towards Hont with an armored assault after sunset to take advantage of the approaching darkness and minimize losses from enemy antitank guns. To maintain a rapid pace of operations, the *Emchas* of the 46th Guards Tank Brigade would lead the attack, followed by the 31st Guards Mechanized Brigade, which would reinforce the tank brigade with one of its infantry battalions. On the right, the 18th Guards Mechanized Brigade would cross the Ipoly River at Dregelypalánk and advance along the northern bank in a supporting attack; the 30th Guards Mechanized Brigade would be the corps reserve. The attack was timed to begin at 6pm on 10 December.[8]

As General Volkov had surmised, the Germans and Hungarians had yet to set up any sort of deliberate defense capable of stopping his corps' assault. While the *Panzergrenadier* battalion from the *24. Pz.Div.* was firmly establishing itself in Ipolysag, including the attached engineer company from *Pio.Btl. 144* atop Mt. Magas, south of the Ipoly River the Hungarians were still moving forces into the Hont area and along the hastily mapped-out *Margarethestellung* sketched through the Börszeny Mountains. Eight hundred meters east of Hont, *IV. Btl./Inf.Rgt. 3* of the Hungarian *2. Pz.Div.*, reinforced by the remaining two companies of *Pio.Btl. 144*, began setting up a new *Hauptkampflinie* during the early hours of 10 December. Aware of the near proximity of the Soviet spearhead, the approximately 500-man-strong force began digging fighting positions and laying antitank mines in earnest. This task force was strengthened by the addition of at least one heavy antitank gun and would be backed up by a battery of Hungarian 105mm howitzers.[9]

Meanwhile, the staff of *6. Armee/A.Gr. Fretter-Pico* continued their efforts to obtain more capable forces to defend the Ipolysag Gap. The chief of staff and his assistant had not given up their hopes of obtaining *Pz.Feldausb.Div.Tatra* to bolster the defense, but on 10 December they received the final decision from Höfle's staff that the German Commander in Slovakia could not spare it. That ended the matter. On the same day, Dr. Oskar Dirlewanger, as ordered, paid a visit to Fretter-Pico's headquarters in the morning to carry out the final coordination with the staffs.

During this meeting, Dirlewanger told *Oberstltn.* Schäfer of *H.Gr. Süd* and *Oberstltn.* Marcks of *6. Armee/A.Gr. Fretter-Pico* that two of his battalions had already begun moving towards the Balassagyarmat area that morning, the first having been partially motorized. But then Dirlewanger said something that should have raised warning flags—he told Schäfer and Marcks that "[we] cannot fight the Soviets with Communists," referring to the two battalions he was sending (*II.* and *III. Btl./ SS-St.Rgt. 2*) that were composed primarily of political prisoners recently recruited from concentration camps.[10] To minimize this risk, Dirlewanger proposed that he would "select the men suitable for combat duty from the other convict battalions," but at this late stage of the operation this would be impossible to carry out due to the urgent need to fortify the Ipolysag Gap; and in any event, both battalions were already in transit.

Instead, Dirlewanger, Schäfer, and Marcks worked out a compromise, in which the two above-named battalions would be assigned to the least-threatened sector of the front lines, where contact with the Red Army was deemed least likely.

Sending them to the Balassagyarmat area no longer made any sense, because the city had fallen (for the first but not the last time) the previous evening. Additional troops from the brigade could be brought into the Ipolysag area upon approval by the German Commander in Slovakia if the situation dictated their deployment. In the meantime, the battalion from the *24. Pz.Div.* would continue to hold Ipolysag under the operational control of the Hungarian *2. Pz.Div.*[11] Thus began the transfer of the hastily activated and only partially rebuilt brigade to a battlefield it was unprepared for, but the wheels were already in motion and could not be stopped, and nor could those of the IX Guards Mechanized Corps.

At the same time on 10 December that the combatants were preparing to battle for possession of Hont, the two battalions from *SS-St.Rgt. 2* began making their way towards the front. Before sunrise, the troops of both battalions (except for the *7.* and *8. Kompanien* of the *II. Bataillon*, which were with the rest of the brigade) had packed their equipment, moved out of their temporary billets, and began lining up on the road leading out of town. The *II.* and *III. Btl./SS-St.Rgt. 2* were ready to begin their march towards Balassagyarmat at dawn, but their objective lay over 143 kilometers (86 miles) to the southeast. The other three battalions from *SS-St.Rgt. 1*, the remaining battalion from *SS-St.Rgt. 2*, and the headquarters of both regiments would not begin marching to eastern Slovakia until the evening of 11 December at the earliest.

Before beginning their march, the former *Oberstltn.*, now *Oberleutnant* Nitzkowski, acting battalion commander of *III. Btl./SS-St.Rgt. 2*, gathered his men around him and tried to motivate them with an inspiring speech. According to one of his men, former concentration camp inmate but now *SS-Grenadier* Wilhelm Engelhardt:

> The battalion commander then made the following speech "The Russians have broken through, and you have the honorable task of throwing him back. You now have the opportunity to prove yourselves at the front and to show that as Germans you are inspired to defend your homeland. Your relatives expect this of you."[12]

What Nitzkowski left unsaid was the underlying threat of *Sippenhaft* should any of the men desert or shirk his duty. Under the Third Reich edict of *Sippenhaft*, any German soldier who deserted or disgraced himself before the enemy put the lives of his family members in jeopardy, subject to arrest and imprisonment for the treasonous conduct of their husband, brother, or father.[13]

As for the rest of the brigade's battalions, once they arrived at the front, both Polack's *III. Btl./SS-St.Rgt. 1* and Stegmann's *I. Btl./SS-St.Rgt. 2* would remain in Slovakia under the control of *SS-St.Rgt. 1* headquarters. These had been picked as the two battalions that would establish blocking positions between the village of Ipolyfödémes (modern-day Fedymeš) and the area south of the town of Blauenstein (Modrý Kameň), east of Ipolysag, yet still in Slovakia. Should conditions dictate, both battalions could be subordinated to the *IV. Pz.Korps* of *8. Armee/A.Gr. Wöhler*, where they could either operate under the control of *SS-St.Rgt. 1* or be parceled out individually to reinforce the *24. Pz.Div.* or the *18. SS-Freiw.Pz.Gren.Div. "Horst Wessel."*[14] In accordance with the order stated above, the brigade's last two battalions, *I.* and *II. Btl./SS-St.Rgt. 1*, would move into an assembly area in the town of Terany, a few hundred meters within Slovakia and 17 kilometers north of Ipolysag. Dirlewanger had designated them as the two reserve battalions that would have an "on order" mission to move into Hungary and reinforce both sides of the Ipolysag Gap if needed.[15]

The two battalions (*II.* and *III. Btl.*) from Buchmann's *SS-St.Rgt. 2* began marching towards their objective on foot on 10 December, but at such a rate of movement it would take at least three and possibly four days to arrive at the front lines, far too slow given the seriousness of the situation. Providentially, *Ogruf.* Höfle arranged to have a small fleet of *Feldpost* (post office) trucks that were under his control catch up with the leading column and convey its men to their staging area later that day, thus expediting their movement. *Oberleutnant* Nitzkowski's *III. Bataillon* arrived late that morning, followed shortly thereafter by *Hstuf.* Ehler's *II. Bataillon* (minus two companies), which arrived during the late afternoon in the same trucks that had conveyed the *III. Bataillon*. However, due to space limitations on the trucks, both battalions arrived without their baggage trains; their extra rations, ammunition, and field packs with their blankets and additional clothing had been left behind to be brought forward later by their horse-drawn supply wagons as soon as possible.[16]

While enroute, the two battalions learned that their intended destination, Balassagyarmat, had fallen to advancing Soviet forces the night before, resulting in the diversion of both battalions to an assembly area southwest of Ipolysag near the town of Bernecebaráti. Once they arrived, *Oberstltn.* Marcks of Fretter-Pico's staff, apparently following Dirlewanger's advice, sent a message to the acting commander of the Hungarian *2. Pz.Div.* instructing him to direct the two battalions into the Börzeny Mountains. Here, they would be sent several kilometers east of the town of Kémence to strengthen the main defense line in the mountains held by the understrength *Pio.Btl. 666* and other elements of *K.Gr. Grosse.*[17]

This diversion was in direct contravention of the original deployment order, which expressly forbade splitting up the brigade and removing elements from their normal chain of command. No one in *H.Gr. Süd* nor in the German Command in Slovakia asked any questions about this or expressed any objections to this decision at the time, most likely due to the enormous pressure being placed upon them to move foot soldiers into the Ipolysag Gap as quickly as possible.[18] With Zischler's battalion and its attachments exercising control of the area surrounding Ipolysag as far as Hill 312 (Mt. Vereb) 4 kilometers northwest of Ipolyhidvég, the greatest need at the time was to quickly reinforce the thinly spaced German and Hungarian defenses arrayed along the heavily forested Börszeny Mountains south of the Ipoly River, defended on paper by the aforementioned *K. Gr. Grosse.*[19]

Oberstleutnant Grosse had decided to position the two *SS* battalions in the mountains along a line beginning 200 meters south of the village of Homok, which was defended by Hungarian troops, and extending as far southeast to the woodsman's settlement at Csitari Puszta, a straight-line distance of over 3 kilometers. Between these two points lay the northern peaks of the Börszeny Mountains. South of the woodsman's settlement, *Pio. Btl. 666* and its attachments had taken up positions on the next ridgeline, after giving up a portion of its sector to the two incoming Dirlewanger battalions. On the left, the two remaining line companies of Ehler's *II. Bataillon* (the 5. and 6.) established themselves in the hills overlooking Homok, including *Hstuf.* Harald Momm's *5. Kompanie.* On the right, the three companies of Nitzkowski's *III. Bataillon* moved into the fighting positions vacated by *Pio. Btl. 666* that morning.

This was an inordinately wide sector to be defended by a force with a *Kampfstärke* totaling less than 700 men from the two battalions, averaging roughly 200–250 defenders for each kilometer of frontage.[20] To complicate matters, the zig-zag front line ran over or around mountain peaks, deep ravines, rapidly flowing streams, and steep hillsides. The entire area was heavily forested, limiting visual contact between squads, platoons, and companies. Numerous logging trails and footpaths crisscrossed the area, none of them paved. The distance from the *Tross* of both battalions, located in the town of Bernecebaráti, to the front line averaged between 7 and 10 kilometers. Any supplies going forward or evacuation of wounded along these trails could only be accomplished by horse-drawn wagon, a round trip that could take up to five hours.

Control of their men under these circumstances would have been a challenge for any commander, especially for anyone leading units composed exclusively of former concentration camp inmates and *B-Schützen.* To add to the scene, the weather during the second week of December 1944 had turned cold, wet, and foggy, with temperatures hovering around 40 degrees Fahrenheit during the day and dropping to below freezing at night. The men in Ehlers and Nitzkowski's battalions, lacking sufficient cold-weather clothing and warm food, could only huddle together in their hastily dug fighting positions to share their bodily warmth. Fires were forbidden, adding to their deprivation. These discomforts would have been nothing out of the ordinary for experienced Eastern Front veterans, but for these men, of whom most had been living in the relative shelter of concentration camps for the better part of the past 10 years, it was an altogether new and unpleasant experience.

Not all of the companies arrived in their positions at the same time. At least one unit arrived in the early morning hours of 11 December, former *Oberstltn.* Stockhaus's *12. (schwere) Kompanie.* It was led by guides to its initial positions in the front line east of Bernecebaráti, marking the first time most of its men had ever been that close to the enemy. Reflecting what must have been a typical first impression, one member of the *12. Kompanie, Gren.* Hans Grundig, later wrote:

In a forgotten valley bottom we left horses and wagons and formed a long column, which followed a narrow forest road for hours. Up to here the … [former *Oberstltn.* Stockhaus] led the company … We had no Russians ahead of us yet, he said, but they would be there by night at the latest. According to his reckoning, there were Hungarian troops to the right and left of our company and a *Waffen-SS* unit in our rear … Every thirty steps one dug into the frozen ground. We positioned ourselves in such a way that we could easily fend off [attacks]. But there was nothing to be seen of them.[21]

Another member of the battalion, Gren. Bernhard Behnke of the *9. Kompanie*, described his first impressions

The battalion moved … still at dawn onto a beech-wooded hill into a trench system dug by the Hungarian civilian population … The position was already occupied by *Wehrmacht* reservists of older age [men of *Pio.Btl. 666*] when we were deployed … The occupation of the trenches including the *Wehrmacht* [troops] was still much too dense. In fact, there was talk from the officers of a planned attack by the "Ivans," which we were there to defend against. How wide our attack sector was, we could not determine.[22]

The remaining hours of 10 December and the early morning of the following day passed relatively peacefully. Due to the foggy conditions and heavy rain that fell throughout most of the day, aerial activity on both sides was limited. German and Hungarian defenders continued to dig in and reinforce their positions along the approaches to Hont, while the opposing troops of the IX Guards Mechanized Corps used the time to conduct pre-combat operations, including taking on supplies, performing maintenance on their vehicles and weapons, and catching up on their sleep. Soviet commanders studied their maps and briefed plans for the assault to their subordinates, while they awaited the results of their reconnaissance patrols.

The *Heer* artillery *Abteilung* tasked to support the Hungarian *2. Pz.Div.* had also begun to arrive and some of its guns would be ready for action the following day. Additionally, two *Sturmgeschütze* (and possibly a third) from an unnamed German assault gun unit were scheduled to arrive at the same time to provide the Hungarians further reinforcement to the troops defending the Ipolyhidvég area.[23] But what was needed most of all was infantry, the kind of troops required to defend the *Margarethestellung* all along the line and keep the gap sealed off against further Soviet advances.

Meanwhile, on the morning of 10 December as the vanguard of the IX Guards Mechanized Corps continued its advance beyond Dregelypalánk, the acting commander of the Hungarian *2. Pz.Div.* radioed the chief of staff of *H.Gr. Süd* in desperation and asked him whether *Ogruf.* Höfle could release even more troops from Dirlewanger's brigade for commitment to the Ipolysag area. At 5.40pm, the operations officer for the German Commander in Slovakia replied, telling him that the German Command in Slovakia was already in the process of sending to the Ipolysag area two "strong" battalions of 800 men each (the *I.* and *II. Btl./SS-St. Rgt. 1*).[24] The addition of these two battalions from the Dirlewanger Brigade, in terms of sheer numbers at least, seemed to be a partial answer to the shortage of troops to hold what had been deemed the *Sperriegel* (blocking position) in the Ipolysag Gap.

While the Germans and Hungarians continued with their hurried defensive preparations, the IX Guards Mechanized Corps resumed its advance towards Hont. At 10.30am, it sent two reconnaissance patrols south of the town in an attempt to find a bypass through the eastern foothills of the Börszeny Mountains. After being discovered by German troops (possibly from *Bau-Pio.Btl. 144*) manning a screen line on the town's outskirts, the Soviet patrols were driven off. Undaunted, the lead element of the 46th Guards Tank Brigade, consisting of six T-34s with mounted infantry, carried out a reconnaissance in force later that afternoon along the main road connecting Dregelypalánk and Hont. Hoping to take the village by storm if they found light resistance, two tanks were quickly destroyed by the Hungarian heavy antitank gun, while another was knocked out by a soldier using a *Panzerfaust*. The remaining T-34s withdrew into Dregelypalánk and for the next several hours both sides traded artillery and mortar fire with one another.[25]

At the same time, the 18th Guards Mechanized Brigade in Dregelypalánk began its attempt to storm the town of Ipolyhidvég using the existing bridge. As the leading battalion approached the river, the bridge was blown up in their faces, leaving the brigade commander no choice but to order his sappers to construct a field expedient bridge while under heavy fire. A few men made it to the opposite bank, but were quickly driven back by the defenders, captured, or killed. Heavy and continuous German and Hungarian mortar and machine-gun fire on the bridging site quickly proved any daylight attempt to cross there to be a fruitless endeavor. The brigade lacked sufficient equipment and material of its own to build a bridge long enough to cross the Ipoly River, which was 300 meters wide at this point. Realizing that crossing at Ipolyhidvég stood little chance of success, the brigade commander, Col. Alexander M. Ovcharov, decided to move his forces upriver 5 kilometers to the east to construct an improvised bridge at the village of Ipolyvece, which was not occupied by the enemy. While this was to prove successful, it would delay his attack by at least 12 hours.[26]

Faced with this situation, Lt.Gen. Volkov decided to postpone his attack until the following day. Now that he knew the Germans and Hungarians were determined to defend Hont, he would need considerably more troops and tanks to take the town. The situation called for a deliberate attack, which would greatly increase the chances for success though it would require more time to prepare. It would begin with sappers and engineers from the 31st Sapper Battalion and 70th Engineer Battalion moving forward in darkness to clear the mines and other obstacles from the road leading into Hont. At the same time, 6 kilometers to the northeast, the 18th Guards Mechanized Brigade would carry out its attack across the river at Ipolyvece to take Ipolyhidvég from the rear.[27]

For its part, the Hungarian *2. Pz.Div.* duly reported that its troops had successfully defended Ipolyhidvég against the 18th Guards Mechanized Brigade's crossing attempt, but predicted that a stronger enemy effort would most likely take place the next day, 11 December.[28] Elsewhere, the Hungarian division had not been as successful as it had been along the Ipoly River; the key town of Kismaros on the north bank of the Danube had fallen that same day to elements from the 297th Rifle Division of the XXV Guards Rifle Corps, despite the efforts of *K.Gr. Lehnert* to hold it.[29] Soviet reconnaissance patrols had also been spotted northwest of that location approaching the outskirts of the villages of Kóspallag and Márianosztra. To counter this dangerous development, which left unattended could undermine the *2. Pz.Div.* right flank along the Danube, the division commander had no other choice but to commit his only significant offensive reserve, the Hungarian *2. Aufklärungs-Abteilung (Aufkl. Abt.,* reconnaissance battalion) to set up a series of blocking positions.[30]

Even with the addition of two battalions from the Dirlewanger Brigade and the possibility of receiving at least two more, the Hungarians and their German liaison team soon realized that the division still lacked sufficient troops to defend its overextended front line, especially since the size of the attacking enemy force was coming into focus. With such a collection of troops as it had, and with so many having dubious combat power, the *2. Pz.Div.* sent out a request to *6. Armee/A.Gr. Fretter-Pico* on the morning of 10 December for even more troops, in particular the transfer of the entire *M.G. Btl. Sachsen* and the rest of *Feld-Ers.Btl. 13.*

Both of these units except one company from each had been detached and sent to Budapest while the Hungarian *2. Pz.Div.* was still undergoing reconstitution at Esztergom. Recognizing the importance of keeping and maintaining the numerous bridges in its area of operations, the *2. Pz.Div.'s* commander also requested that *Brückenbau-Kompanie 255* (a German bridge construction engineer unit) be attached for this purpose. In addition to these extra troops, *Oberst* Zádor also reported the shortage of motor vehicle fuel, requesting 40 cubic meters (10,567 gallons) of *Otto-Kraftstoff* (gasoline) be sent immediately to address the shortfall.[31] While the results of the fighting on 10 December were a mixed bag, the Hungarians were under no illusion as to the ultimate outcome of a pitched battle against the IX Guards Mechanized Corps if they were not speedily reinforced.

In the Börszeny Mountains, the front line on Sunday 10 December 1944 (the first day of Hanukkah) was initially very quiet, eerily so; the only sound was the distant rumble of artillery fire from the east, where the Hungarian *IV. Btl./Inf.Rgt. 3* and the two German *Pionier* companies were involved in repelling the Soviet probing attack against Hont over 6 kilometers away. There were no other signs of the enemy, so perhaps assigning these two battalions from Dirlewanger's brigade to this defensive sector had not been such a gamble after all. Based on the actions of the IX Guards Mechanized Corps and its movements up to this point, it seemed any significant combat action would probably take place in the valley and not in the mountains.

By mid-morning of 11 December, the *II. Bataillon* (minus its 7 and 8 *Kompanien*) and the three companies of the *III. Bataillon* had completed their deployment into the mountains and were positioned on the far left of *K.Gr. Grosse*'s defensive sector abutting the southern bank of the Ipoly River a few hundred meters south of Hont. The command posts and *Tross* of both battalions positioned themselves in Bernecebaráti, 6 kilometers behind the front lines. Neither battalion had radios, relying instead on field telephones or messengers on horseback to communicate with their troops in the front line. Sporadic enemy shells began to impact at random locations, with the echoes of their blasts reverberating amongst the trees as the shelling increased.

Once the men from both battalions had fully arrived at their new positions in the mountains, the living conditions they found there were anything but encouraging. According to one of the original poachers from 1940 who was now an *Oberscharführer* (Senior NCO) with Harald Momm's *5. Kompanie, SS-St.Rgt. 2*:

> It was mainly trenches here, and in the rear were the artillery positions. The relief [of a *Wehrmacht* company from *Pio.Btl. 666*] took place in the evening and worked out quite well. At night, heavy artillery fire rained down on the positions and we suffered losses. The guys were really freezing outside. It was below zero [centigrade] and the men had not received any winter clothing, except for their greatcoats. They stood in the trenches or warmed up inside the wooden bunkers. They carried their Italian carbines [at the ready] on their breast—[but] there was practically no shooting. We did not see any Russians. Around dawn [on 11 December], our *III. Bataillon* moved into positions near us. Not only had the men all been political prisoners, but the fact that they had only been soldiers for eight weeks raised a lot of doubts for me. Even if they tried, they were no match for the Russians![32]

He was not the only member of *SS-St.Rgt. 2* to express his dismay at the conditions they found upon arriving in the Börzeny Mountains. One previously mentioned member of Nitzkowski's *III. Bataillon*, Wilhelm Engelhardt, later wrote:

> There was no question of a front line. We only passed a few bearded *Volkssturm* men [these were actually soldiers from *Pio.Btl. 666*] standing on the edge of the forest with their *Panzerfausts*, looking to us like *Rübezahls* [German folkloric mountain spirits]. We were in a hilly forest area, which made orientation very difficult. To the right and to the left we had no contact with other troops.[33]

Despite what Dirlewanger had requested, both battalions had not been sent to a quiet sector after all, but in fact were about to be drawn into the area where the fighting would soon be the heaviest. Here, their suitability as soldiers would be put to the test in the most severe manner imaginable. Ironically, the battalions' ex-concentration camp politicals would also soon find themselves face-to-face with their fellow communists from the Red Army, something Dirlewanger had strenuously sought to avoid despite his protestations to the staff of *6. Armee/A.Gr. Fretter-Pico* and *H.Gr. Süd*.

At the moment, however, the command and staff of the Hungarian *2. Pz.Div.* could not see how events would unfold. With the enemy threat still 6–10 kilometers away, it seemed that Ehlers's and Nitzkowski's battalions in their mountain fastness would be left alone for the moment and allowed to get settled into their new defensive positions. Here, it was assumed, they would be able to carry out their mission undisturbed without having to be put to the ultimate test. Whether this was an accurate assessment of the situation or not, the *Ia* of *H.Gr. Süd, Oberstltn.* Schäfer, was not so optimistic. Indeed, how would these two convict battalions perform under pressure? Would they fight their "fellow travelers" of the Red Army of Workers and Peasants?

After listening to Dirlewanger's arguments on the morning of 10 December about how he could not possibly fight communists with communists, Schäfer by this point most likely had a more realistic idea of what sort of troops were being sent to *6. Armee/A.Gr. Fretter-Pico* as reinforcements. What is unclear is whether his *Oberbefehlshaber, Gen.Obst.* Friessner, or the commander of *6. Armee/A.Gr. Fretter-Pico* shared the same assessment. A clue can be found in the army group's war diary, where that evening, with apparently some reluctance (and most likely with his Chief of Staff's silent concurrence), Schäfer wrote that within the army group's senior leadership, "there are no reservations about using the Dirlewanger Brigade in the front line."[34] Little did Friessner and Fretter-Pico know that they had placed their faith in an illusion, although after the war, Friessner wrote in his memoirs that he had immediate doubts about the brigade's capability, commenting that "[it consisted] of a great bunch of delinquents, communists and adventurers! I should have gotten to know them a little better."[35] Of course, by then it would be too late.

CHAPTER SIX

IX Guards Mechanized Corps Attacks, 11–12 December 1944

During the winter in northern Hungary, sunrise comes late. Like it had the previous day, 11 December dawned with similar weather conditions. Along the Ipoly River valley, frigid temperature, overcast skies, and fog greeted the several thousand half-frozen combatants. While the defenders had done what they could to prepare for the upcoming engagement, Volkov's troops had labored throughout the night to ensure that everything that could be done was completed before the main attack began. Shortly after midnight, sappers and engineers of the IX Guards Mechanized Corps had moved forward towards the Hungarian and German defensive barrier east of Hont and begun their dangerous work. Surprisingly, the defenders did not observe or report any Soviet activity until it was too late.

Once they had signaled that the mine and obstacle clearing had been completed by 3am, the 1st Battalion of Lt.Col. Nikolay Mikhno's 46th Guards Tank Brigade began its attack "at maximum speed" an hour later, straight down the Hont–Dregelypalánk road. The leading tank company was commanded by Senior Lieutenant Dimitri Loza, with as many as 10 M4A2 *Emchas* including 30 infantrymen (nicknamed "*tankodesantniki*") clinging aboard to provide close-in protection.[1] At the same time, motorized infantry from the 31st Guards Mechanized Brigade attacked on his left, bypassing Hont from the southeast with a flanking maneuver. Corps cannon and rocket artillery augmented by heavy mortar batteries fired in support of the attack, although the presence of the Red Air Force would be minimal due to the poor flying weather that morning.

Anticipating a tough fight, Loza had sent out two Shermans from Lieutenant Fedor Dankin's platoon ahead of his company to reconnoiter beyond the now-harmless Hungarian obstacle barrier. Dankin reported soon afterwards that he had made contact with the enemy 700 meters in front of the town: "There are Germans in Hont. They opened up on us with heavy fire." Loza ordered his subordinate to halt and observe any signs of enemy firing positions. Once he had this information, he intended to attack these targets with main gun and machine-gun fire and suppress them while the rest of his company steamrolled through the village.[2]

Outflanked from the south by Col. Seleznev's 31st Guards Mechanized Brigade, the Germans and Hungarians holding Hont immediately started to pull back once Loza had begun his attack. Surprisingly, the village fell to his tanks without much of a fight; none of them had been damaged or destroyed and in less than an hour it was all over. The defenders withdrew 1 kilometer west of the town and attempted to establish a new defensive line, but when the Soviet spearhead resumed its advance at 10am, the defenders withdrew, abandoning their position to Loza's battalion, and did not stop until they reached the enclave of Parassa Puszta, 2 kilometers northwest of Hont, at 11.35am. Here, the lead element of Mikhno's brigade occupied a forward assembly area and awaited further orders.

Some 3.5 kilometers to the south of Hont, Seleznev had pushed his own brigade's troops forward and quickly occupied Hill 496 (Mt. Kö-Kapu) on the eastern edge of the Börszeny Mountains after it was abandoned by troops from *Pio.Btl. 666*. While the fight for Hont was still in progress, Col. Ovcharov's 18th Guards Mechanized Brigade, operating to the northeast, crossed the Ipoly River using a hastily constructed bridge at Ipolyvece and quickly took the village against light German and Hungarian resistance. Having seized a bridgehead, Ovcharov decided to wait until nightfall to push the main body of his brigade across the river. Lieutenant General Volkov also directed him to make another attempt to cross the river at Ipolyhidvég that same evening.

The most important development of the day concerned the armored advance towards Homok that morning, which set off alarm bells as high up as *H.Gr. Süd* headquarters. The only unit available that the Hungarian *2. Pz.Div.* could send to reinforce the defenses at Homok was the division's own *Pz.Pio.Btl. 2*, which had a *Kampfstärke* of 302 men, including officers. Other than that, it had a few *Toldi* light tanks and Nimrod self-propelled light *Flak*, but little else. Two of the four attached German assault guns (the other two were with *K.Gr. Lehnert*) had been sent to the area north of Dregelypalánk and could not be quickly recalled. One of the few remaining sources of combat power was the division's organic and attached field artillery; its 23 105mm howitzers gave good service that day, being superior in quantity and quality to what the IX Guards Mechanized Corps had brought to the battlefield.

Luckily for the Hungarians, the *Luftwaffe's leichte-Flak-Abt. 91* was already marching towards the Ipolysag Gap, as well as two 88mm antiaircraft gun batteries from *II. Abt./Flak-Rgt. 24* with nine guns; both units would arrive during the afternoon of 11 December and be ready for action by early evening. These antiaircraft units were to be emplaced within the region encompassed by the towns of Pereszlény, Homok, and Bernecebaráti, a relatively flat, wide-open area where the heavy *Flak* could be put to good use in the antitank role.

But what was needed most of all at that moment was *Luftwaffe* ground attack aircraft, especially given that up to 80 Soviet tanks had been spotted in Dregelypalánk on the night of 9/10 December. The *I. Fliegerkorps* had promised that they would make sorties available on the afternoon of 11 December and the skies had finally cleared—so where were they? A request was transmitted by the German liaison cell with the Hungarian *2. Pz.Div.* headquarters to *6. Armee/A.Gr. Fretter-Pico* that was received at 12.12pm, urgently requesting close air support. Anticipating the request, the *Luftwaffe* was able to oblige relatively quickly.

Aware of the danger posed by remaining in the open on a relatively sunny afternoon, and their vulnerability if they stayed where they were, the 16 Soviet tanks from Loza's battalion that had momentarily stopped in Parassa Puszta were ordered to continue their attack towards Homok by mid-afternoon. Rather than expose his tanks' right flanks to German fire emanating from the *Panzergrenadier* battalion in Ipolysag, the battalion commander decided to funnel them through the narrow open ground between the east–west railroad line that ran through the town and the steep hillside of the mountain 200 meters to the south. But it was too late.

Amid the "growling howl of aircraft motors" that filled the air, as many as nine German ground attack aircraft, most likely Henschel Hs 129 tank busters from the *14. Staffel/ Schlachtgeschwader 9* (14th Squadron, 9th Ground Attack Wing), pounced on the tank column.[3] As they loitered over the area for 90 minutes, each aircraft took its turn and conducted a strafing run on the helpless *Emchas* of 1st Battalion, 46th Guards Tank Brigade. One after another, Soviet tanks were destroyed or damaged by bombs or the aircrafts' 37mm cannon, forcing the remainder to turn around and retreat to the relative safety of Hont, where they could find concealment among the houses.

Following several hundred meters behind the lead tank company, Senior Lieutenant Loza saw the approaching Henschels and hurriedly directed his company into a stone quarry on the southern side of the railway. Although his tanks could not maneuver inside its narrow, confined space, neither could the Germans accurately aim their bombs at their "easy" target. After the war, Loza related:

> Nine [aircraft] circled over the river and road, but they could not drop their bombs on the tanks with any precision. More than once the enemy pilots attempted to attack from the more desired northern direction. But to no avail. The bright winter sun blinded them. Fearing a collision with a high hill, they broke off. More often than not, their bombs detonated against the railroad embankment and did our company no harm. Multiple attempts to set up for dive-bombing from the south also failed. The elevation of the hill and the dense woods prevented the pilots from seeing the tanks. Consequently, they could not drop their cargo of death on the selected target with any precision. The winding road and especially the spur of the hill prevented the [enemy] from reaching the detachment from the east or west. Thanks to our fortunate choice of position, our *Emchas* were well protected. The depression in the northern hillside was a combination of nature and the hand of man.[4]

None of his *Emchas* were damaged during the attack. During the same engagement, Soviet gunners claimed to have shot down one German aircraft with a 37mm

Bofors gun from the 388th Guards Antiaircraft Artillery Regiment. For its part, the *Luftwaffe* claimed to have destroyed 10 tanks and damaged a further five.[5] For the moment at least, the all-too-rapid advance of the IX Guards Mechanized Corps and its penetration of the Ipolysag Gap had been delayed for another day.

To make matters more complicated for their enemy, Soviet troops had been able to occupy a hill mass named Nagy Hegy (Hill 271) 1 kilometer west of Hont. From the hill's peak, they could observe German and Hungarian preparations in Homok, Ipolysag, and the village of Tesmák (Tesmag). Within its woods, large numbers of troops could be hidden. How it had come into the hands of Lt.Gen. Volkov's troops was not explained in the surviving German or Hungarian records—most likely, the defenders of Hont had withdrawn so quickly that morning that no one at the time thought the hill important enough to occupy before the enemy did. Not only did it offer excellent observation, but it could also be used to direct artillery fire and help provide an outer bulwark for the defense of Hont, should that become necessary. The Hungarian *2. Pz.Div.* would have to retake it as soon as possible before any counterattack against Hont could be launched.

In addition to the loss of Hont and Hill 271, the counterattack by *K.Gr. Lehnert* to recapture the key town of Kismaros in the south had not gone as planned. Although *Oberltn.* Lehnert's battlegroup had been reinforced with the addition of the Hungarian *2. Aufkl.Abt.*, a light *Flak* battery, and the two remaining German assault guns, Soviet resistance was so fierce that Lehnert's attack got no nearer to Kismaros than a point 1 kilometer west of the town before it ground to a halt. Here, *K.Gr. Lehnert* took up defensive positions as its mission changed from counterattacking to once again establishing a blocking position to deny the enemy use of the paved highway along the northern bank of the Danube. Perhaps as a sign of dwindling confidence in *Oberst* Zádor's leadership of the division, or to provide more combat power to the neighboring *Korpsgruppe Breith* (the *III. Pz.Korps*), Lehnert's battlegroup was detached and placed under the latter's control on the night of 11 December.[6]

That same evening, the headquarters of *6. Armee/A.Gr. Fretter-Pico* provided additional guidance to *Oberst* Zádor describing what was expected of him and his division for the following day, 12 December. The order, sent out by teletype and received by Zádor's German liaison team at 4.30am, dealt with three separate topics. The first concerned the detachment of *K.Gr. Lehnert* to *Korpsgruppe Breith* as described in the previous paragraph. The second was the delineation of the new corps boundaries between the Hungarian armored division and *Korpsgruppe Breith* that became necessary after *K.Gr. Lehnert* was detached. The third, and most important, portion of Fretter-Pico's order read as follows:

> [The] Hungarian *2. Panzer Division* will block the Ipolysag Gap using all available forces … All means are to be exhausted to ensure the protection of the deployed *Flak* against being overrun by enemy troops to the north and south with [our] infantry forces already present as well as those on their way. The favorable terrain in the Ipolysag Gap is to be exploited to a large extent

for the employment of close combat antitank teams. The emplacement of obstacles in the gap and along its flanks is to be pushed forward with special emphasis.[7]

But something still had to be done about the large grouping of enemy troops occupying Hont, and that task could not wait another day. These had to be eliminated and the town reoccupied—the problem was that it was held by at least one and possibly two tank battalions and a motorized infantry battalion of the 46th Guards Tank Brigade. If left undisturbed, and with at least 60–70 tanks still remaining at its disposal, this Soviet formation continued to pose a clear and present threat to the integrity of German and Hungarian defenses in the Ipolysag Gap, regardless of the aspirations of Fretter-Pico in his order. The solution to the problem, to *H.Gr. Süd* at least, was obvious—Hont had to be retaken as quickly as possible by a counterattack. This meant that the Hungarians would have to plan it and see that it was carried out to completion.

The command and staff of the Hungarian *2. Pz.Div.* had been shaken by the Soviet attack that day. They must have realized that had the *Luftwaffe* not carried out its persistent attacks against the lead tanks of the 46th Guards Tank Brigade that afternoon, the enemy may very well have broken through the gap and forced their way into the little Hungarian Plain. The troops who had attempted to hold Hont had been scattered and driven back into Homok.[8] Shortages of ammunition for the attached German contingent had become critical, especially since Hungarian and German rifle and machine-gun ammunition were not compatible.[9] Fuel was insufficient to power the few armored fighting vehicles the division possessed. The Hungarian *Pionier* battalion that had just arrived would have to remain in Homok to organize the town's defense. This left only one other significant body of troops in the area that were not heavily committed—the two battalions from *SS-St.Rgt. 2* of the Dirlewanger Brigade occupying the fastness of the Börzeny Mountains.

While the Hungarians hastily formulated plans to retake Hont and Hill 271 with the assistance of their German liaison staff, other steps were being taken on 11 December to bring the remainder of the Dirlewanger Brigade into the fray. That morning, it had become obvious to the leaders of both *6. Armee/A.Gr. Fretter-Pico* and *H.Gr. Süd* that the Hungarian *2. Pz.Div.* lacked enough ground troops to carry out its mission to defend the Ipolysag Gap. While the possibility of deploying the entire brigade had been a topic of discussion between *H.Gr. Süd* and the German Commander in Slovakia since 9 December, the restrictions on its use imposed by *Ogruf.* Höfle had narrowly circumscribed any remaining options to employ it.

All that changed by mid-morning on 11 December when *Gen.Obst.* Friessner, fully realizing the seriousness of the situation once he received word that Hont had fallen, contacted the *OKH* Operations Staff and requested that the bulk of Dirlewanger's troops be immediately released from Höfle's control and subordinated to *H.Gr. Süd. General der Panzertruppe* Wenck promptly complied and issued the orders to the German Commander in Slovakia to provide the requested forces, though Höfle was still allowed to retain control of the headquarters of *SS-St.Rgt. 1* with two battalions within Slovakian territory. Thus instructed, at 11.50am Höfle released the two reserve battalions of Dirlewanger's brigade (*I.* and *II. Btl./SS-St. Rgt. 1*), setting them in motion towards the Ipolysag Gap, a move that brought the total number of battalions thus deployed to four.[10]

H.Gr. Süd's operations staff drafted the formal order outlining the intended employment of the incoming elements of the Dirlewanger Brigade. Until that point, all of the coordinating and issuing of orders between it and the German Commander in Slovakia had been verbal, but the *Wehrmacht* preferred to have its official orders issued in writing for an operation of this magnitude. The message containing the order was sent out via teletype at 3.00pm. Since the recipients had been warned in advance that it was on its way, Dirlewanger and his staff had time to begin their own planning process, and as mentioned had already moved two battalions from *SS-St. Rgt. 2* into the area the previous day. At first, the brigade would not be deployed directly into Ipolysag proper, but this was to change within 24 hours as the situation continued to evolve.

Addressed to *Armeegruppen Fretter-Pico* and *Wöhler*, as well as the German Commander in Chief, Slovakia (Höfle), the first paragraph of the order read:

> From the *SS Brigade Dirlewanger* one regiment (1 regiment staff, 2 reinforced battalions, 1 light battery and 1 mortar battery) will be transferred to the Ipolysag area and subordinated to *A.Gr. Fretter-Pico*. The regiment is to be deployed to reinforce the defense of the narrows on both sides of Ipolysag united under their commander [this order also pertained to the two battalions from *SS-St.Rgt. 2* that had already been attached to *Pio.Rgt.Stab 36*]. Due to the special personnel composition of the Brigade, the deployed formations or units *must not be broken up* under any circumstances [author's emphasis].[11]

Despite this injunction, the two battalions that had arrived on 10 December had already been broken up the moment they arrived in Bernecebaráti.

The regimental headquarters that Dirlewanger chose for this mission was that of *SS-St.Rgt. 2* under *Ostubaf.* Buchmann. As has been previously described, the two battalions that were initially supposed to be subordinated to him were the *II.* and *III. Bataillon* of his own regiment. The order retroactively applied to them even though they had already been in position since the early morning of 11 December.[12] Ironically, neither battalion would fall under his command at any point during the upcoming battle (except for the two companies from *II. Btl./SS-St.Rgt. 2*), but would remain under the control of *K.Gr. Grosse* for the next 10 days. The light battery described in the order was to be the artillery battalion's 76.2mm battery; the other two batteries, equipped with 105mm light field howitzers, would remain inside of Slovakia and would see no action at all.

Rittmeister Zischler's battalion from *Pz.Gren.Rgt. 26* defending Ipolysag had not been left out of the order, nor had the need to shift the boundaries between

Fretter-Pico's and Wöhler's armies brought about by the changing situation. The second paragraph of the order read:

> After the regiment has been deployed, the parts of the *24. Pz.Div.* still west of the new army border [Zischler's battalion] are to be detached at an accelerated pace and returned to *8. Armee/A. Gr. Wöhler* via Blauenstein to Zsely (northeast of Balassagyarmat). Deployment and arrival are to be reported by the *Armeegruppe*.[13]

The new boundary between the two field armies was drawn along the hill-mass running north–south roughly 10 kilometers east of Ipolysag towards the town of Ipolynyék. Everything to the east of that line continued to remain under the jurisdiction of Wöhler's *Armeegruppe*; to the west, Fretter-Pico's.

The third paragraph contained the sort of details needed to begin thorough planning by the units involved, including who was to go where. The portions of the brigade remaining in Slovakia would remain under Höfle's overall control, unless the situation dictated that they be sent in to reinforce Buchmann's regiment sooner. According to the order:

> 3. The remaining parts of Brigade Dirlewanger will be provided as follows: Brigade Staff and two battalions [*I.* and *II. Btl./SS-St.Rgt. 1*] in the area of Hor-Terany (12km north-northwest of Ipolysag), and two battalions [*III. Btl./SS-St.Rgt. 1* and *I. Btl./SS-St.Rgt. 2*] in the area south of Blauenstein [Modrý Kameň] to block the roads leading north from Balassagyarmat across the border. These parts will remain under the command of the German Commander in Slovakia. The German Commander in Slovakia is requested to explore possibilities of using the brigade:
>   a. to reinforce defenses on both sides of the narrows of Ipolysag,
>   b. to occupy a defensive front line along the course of the *Margarethestellung* running from west to east of Ipolysag as far as the area north of Balassagyarmat.

The order left it up to the regimental commander (i.e., Buchmann) to determine where to emplace his light artillery battery and heavy mortar company, as well as where to establish his regimental supply trains. Lastly, the order ended with a brief description of coordination requirements so all of the parties involved in the brigade's deployment would know who was reporting to whom:

> 4. *Armeegruppe Fretter-Pico* [the *6. Armee*] will report the subordination of the reinforced Dirlewanger Regiment [Buchmann's *SS-St.Rgt. 2*] as well as intended deployment and will ensure the establishment of rapid communications with the brigade staff of the Dirlewanger Brigade.

The last sentence was an important one. *Heeresgruppe Süd* had already been informed that Dirlewanger lacked sufficient communications capability to exercise "agile" control of his forces; hence, he would require additional radio and teletype equipment to effectively do this. This would become the responsibility of Fretter-Pico's *Armeenachrichtenführer* (*A.N.F.*, army signals officer) and implied that he was to ensure that sufficient communications means were provided. In this regard, time was certainly of the essence. Without suitable radio and teletype communications, Dirlewanger (and by extension, Buchmann) would have difficulty controlling any battle, especially against enemy mechanized forces. The ability to effectively direct artillery and mortar fire was also extremely important. This was to prove a major shortcoming in the German plan.

The deployment order issued by *6. Armee/A.Gr. Fretter-Pico* did not dictate the employment of the *gemischte Bataillon*, portions of which would be combined with two companies (*7.* and *8.*) of *II. Btl./SS-St.Rgt. 2* to form two small battlegroups, one of which (the *8. Kompanie*) would later be designated as *K.Gr. Ruhsam*. Exactly when the *gemischte Bataillon* and *7.* and *8. Kompanien* arrived is unknown, but by midnight on 12 December at the latest, both *Kampfgruppen* had established defensive positions 500 meters northeast of Ipolysag atop Hill 227. The records do not indicate why these troops were deployed there instead of with the rest of the *II. Btl./SS-St.Rgt. 2*; perhaps this had been arranged prior to their arrival between the headquarters of the Hungarian *2. Pz.Div.* and *Rittmeister* Zischler of the *24. Pz.Div.*

By positioning them on Hill 227, Ruhsam's and the other *Kampfgruppe* would be able to secure the eastern flank of the Ipolysag defenses erected by *K.Gr. Zischler* and the western flank of *Bau-Pio.Btl. 144*, entrenched along the mountains east of the town, including Mt. Magas (Hill 283) and Mt. Somos (Hill 323). Within a day or two, Ruhsam, who commanded the heavy weapons company of his own battalion, would not only have control of his own heavy weapons company, but would be augmented by a platoon from the antitank company and a heavy machine-gun company from the *gemischte Bataillon* once they arrived. These reinforcements would soon prove quite useful because Hill 227 would soon have to withstand a concerted attack. If the hill fell into the hands of the enemy, there would be nothing to stop them from outflanking Ipolysag or driving northwards along the road connecting Ipolysag with the large town of Palást (Plášťovce).

Dirlewanger intended to establish his *vorgeschobener Gefechtstand* (forward command post) in Palást, which lay 11 kilometers north of Ipolysag. Dirlewanger had been given specific guidance from Höfle as to how he was to control his brigade during the upcoming operation and had chosen Palást accordingly. As stated in Höfle's order, Dirlewanger was to be mindful of the following: "It is a special duty of the brigade commander to establish [your] command post near the command posts of the staffs tactically leading your two reinforced battalions, and from there to supervise the consideration of the requirements of the parts of your brigade [that are] tactically subordinated elsewhere."[14]

This location would later prove to have been a poor choice. From this seemingly convenient location, Dirlewanger would be positioned in the center of his brigade, equidistant from either of its flanks. There was a good road network that would allow him to drive quickly to Ipolysag or across the river to visit his troops near Bernecebaráti. A drive to the location of the two battalions on his left flank was

SS-Oberführer Otto Dirlewanger, *circa* spring 1944, shortly after the award of the German Cross in Gold in 1943 for his anti-partisan actions in Belarus. The Knight's Cross which was awarded at the end of September 1944) was edited into the photograph at a later date. (French MacLean)

SS-Obergruppenführer Gottlob Berger, sarcastically known as the Duke of Swabia, who was the originator of the *Dirlewanger Einheit* and Dirlewanger's chief friend and powerful sponsor in the *SS* hierarchy while head of the *SS-Hauptamt* or Main Office. (U.S. National Archives)

SS-Obergruppenführer Erich von dem Bach, who, as Chief of the *SS Bandenkampfverbände*, or Anti-Partisan Combatting Units, led the German effort to eradicate the Polish Home Army during the Warsaw Uprising from August–September 1944. (U.S. National Archives)

Dirlewanger's second-in-command and *Ia* (Operations Officer) was *SS-Sturmbannführer* Kurt Weisse (shown here in a prewar photograph as a *Hauptsturmführer*), an experienced front-line veteran of the *Das Reich* and *Totenkopf* Divisions with a reputation for sadism and brutality, traits that fitted in very well with the command climate fostered by Dirlewanger. (Stuart B. T. Emmett)

SS-Hauptsturmführer Fritz Missmahl, a highly decorated World War I veteran and high-ranking *Allegemeine-SS* official who was sentenced to serve a term in the Sachsenhausen *KL* for corruption in 1943. Recruited by Dirlewanger in September 1943, Missmahl was released to perform front-line probation and served in numerous capacities until the end of the war. (Berlin Document Center/ Bundesarchiv)

SS-Sturmbannführer Ernst Heidelberg, the architect and bureaucrat sentenced to serve a period of probation with Dirlewanger for "irregularities" concerning the use of construction-related funds earmarked for building the Dębica *SS* Training Camp in Poland. He served on the brigade staff at Ipolysag. (John P. Moore, digital enhancement by Ivo Ferin)

SS-Hauptsturmführer and former *Hauptmann der Schutzpolizei* Wolfgang Plaul, who had been sentenced to two years of imprisonment for corruption. Dirlewanger arranged his release from the *SS* prison in Danzig-Matzkau and assigned him as a company commander. (John P. Moore, digital enhancement by Ivo Ferin)

SS-Obersturmbannführer Erich Buchmann, Commander, *SS-St.Rgt. 2* of the Dirlewanger Brigade, who was made personally responsible for the defense of Ipolysag from 13–15 December 1944, shown here as a *Hauptsturmführer* in 1937. (John P. Moore)

SS-Obersturmführer Herbert Meye shown here as a *Hauptmann de Schutzpolizei*, who commanded *Btl./Sonderregiment Dirlewanger i* Belarus and Warsaw, as well as the *Btl./SS-St.Rgt. 1* at Ipolysag. (Berli Document Center/Bundesarchiv)

Major der Schutzpolizei Josef "Jupp" Steinhauer, who commanded *II. Btl./Sonderregiment Dirlewanger* in Belarus and Warsaw, as well as the *II. Btl./SS-St.Rgt. 1* during the battle of Ipolysag. He and his men were accused of committing some of the worst excesses during the suppression of the Warsaw Uprising. (Berlin Document Center, digital enhancement by Ivo Ferin)

SS-Untersturmführer Siegfried Polack, who commanded the *III. Btl./SS-St.Rgt. 2* during the battle of Ipolysag. A highly decorated veteran of World War I and former official in the Nazi Party before the war, he was assigned to *Sonderkommando Dirlewanger* in November 1943 as punishment for political offenses. (Berlin Document Center/ Bundesarchiv)

SS-Hauptsturmführer Wilhelm Ste mann, commander of *I. Btl./SS-S Rgt. 2* during the fighting on tl Slovakian border alongside the *2 Pz.Div*. He volunteered for front-li probation on 1 October 1944 to ser in the Dirlewanger Brigade in ord to atone for his pre-war crimes ar restore his honor. (German Red Crc Search Service)

Major der Schutzpolizei Franz Falter, who was sentenced to serve a three-year term of imprisonment for "cowardice in the face of the enemy". In September 1944, Dirlewanger had Falter transferred to the Dirlewanger Brigade, where he served as a the acting commander of *II. Btl./SS-St.Rgt. 2* during the second half of December 1944. (Privatarchiv Daniel Popielas, Welzow)

SS-Hauptsturmführer Harald Momm, Commander, *5. Kompanie, SS-St.Rgt. 2*, who rallied fleeing troops from the brigade and blocked the Soviet advance at the bridge of Kistompa on 15 December 1944. This prewar image depicts him as a member of the *Wehrmacht*'s prize-winning equestrian team. (Vladimir Krajčovič)

Erich Langelotz, former *Oberleutnant* and Commander, *10. Kompanie, SS-St.Rgt. 2*, who led the desertion of his entire company on 15 December 1944. He had been sentenced to serve a term at the Dachau *KL* for espionage in the summer of 1944 but volunteered for front-line probation with Dirlewanger. He died while in Soviet custody. (Archiv des KZ-Gedenkstätte Dachau, photo Courtesy of Roland Pfeiffer)

Prison photograph of *SS-Hauptsturmführer* Josef Grohmann, who served as the *Ia* of *SD-Abschnitt Nord* in Hannover before he ran afoul of the law and was sentenced to a prison term at Danzig-Matzkau for "failure." He was recruited for the *Sonderregiment* on 2 June 1944, where he served as a company commander. (Roland Pfeiffer)

Hauptmann Paul Ruhsam (former Army *Oberstleutnant*), Commander, *8. (schw.) Kp./ SS-St.Rgt. 2* and *Kampfgruppe Ruhsam*, was reported missing in action and presumed killed at Ipolysag on 15 December 1944. (German Red Cross Tracing Service)

SS-Obersturmbannführer Egon Zill, Commandant of the Flossenbürg *KL*, who suggested the idea of recruiting politicals for the Dirlewanger Brigade to Oskar Dirlewanger on or about 7 October 1944; shown here as an *SS-Hauptsturmführer*. (Gedenkstätte-Flossenbürg)

SS-Obergruppenführer Hermann Höfle, the Higher *SS* and Police Leader and Commander-in-Chief of German Forces in Slovakia. Dissatisfied with the performance of the *2. SS-Sturmbrigade Dirlewanger* during and after the suppression of the Slovak Mutiny, he drew the ire of Himmler when complaints about Dirlewanger's poor performance reached Berlin. (courtesy of John P. Moore)

Generaloberst Johannes Friessner, *Oberbefehlshaber, H.Gr. Süd* at the time of the battle of Ipolysag. His memoir left a colorful description of Oskar Dirlewanger and his monkey when he visited Dirlewanger at his command post in Palást on 15 December 1944. (George A. Petersen)

General der Artillerie Maximilian Fretter-Pico, Commander, *6. Armee/A.Gr. Fretter-Pico*, who was responsible for the overall command of the German-Hungarian defenses between Ipolysag and Lake Balaton until 24 December 1944. (George A. Petersen)

Generalmajor Josef Rintelen, Commander, *357. Inf.Div.* and *Divisions-Gruppe Rintelen*, under whom the Dirlewanger Brigade was subordinated after 13 December 1944, shown here as an *Oberst*. (Erich Craciun)

Generalleutnant August Schmidt, the hard-bitten commander of *LXXII. Armeekorps*, who ordered machine guns set up behind Dirlewanger troops to prevent their desertion in combat after the disaster at Ipolysag, shown here as an *Oberst*. (George A. Petersen)

Hauptmann Otto Hafner, Comm ander, *Feld-Ers.Btl. 357* and leade of *Kampfgruppe Hafner*, wh incorporated the remnant of *SS-S Rgt. 2* into his battlegroup after th battle of Ipolysag. (Erich Craciun

eneralmajor Gottfried Fröhlich, ommander, *8. Pz.Div.*, who was sked with the mission of retaking olysag on 18 December. (George . Petersen)

General der Panzertruppe Friedrich Kirschner, Commander, *LVII. Pz.Korps*, who unsuccessfully attempted to the stem the Soviet counteroffensive after the failure of *8. Pz.Div.* to retake Ipolysag. (George A. Petersen)

Colonel General Andrey Kravchenko, Commander, 6th Guards Tank Army, who commanded the powerful Soviet advance through the Ipolysag corridor. (warheroes.ru)

eutenant General of Tank Troops likhail V. Volkov, Commander, IX uards Mechanized Corps. He knew w to employ tanks in mountainous rrain, a skill that was put into practice 15 December 1944. (generals.dk/ neral/Volkov/html)

Colonel Alexander M. Ovcharov, Commander of the 18th Guards Mechanized Brigade. (warheroes.ru)

Colonel Mikhail V. Shutov, Commander of the 30th Guards Mechanized Brigade. (warheroes.ru)

Colonel Kuzma F. Seleznev, Commander of the 31st Guards Mechanized Brigade. (warheroes.ru)

Lieutenant Colonel Nikolay M. Mikhno, Commander of the 46th Guards Tank Brigade. (warheroes.ru)

Guards Major Grigori R. Nemchenko, Commander of the 83rd Guards Tank Regiment. (*Front illustration Magazine*, No. 20, July 1943, via Yandex.pics)

Captain of Tank Troops Dimitry Loza, 1st Battalion, 46th Guards Tank Brigade. (Wikipedia Fair Use; Loza and Gebhardt)

...oyal Hungarian Army *32M Toldi* light tank fitted with ...*hürzen* (skirt armor); tanks like this model were unsuccessfully ...ployed at Ipolysag. (Author)

Royal Hungarian Army *Nimrod* self-propelled 40mm antiaircraft gun, a number of which were easily destroyed by Soviet troops from 13–15 December 1944. (Author)

...aptured Soviet 76.2mm regimental cannon. Four of these ...ighly versatile weapons were used to equip the *3. Batterie*, ...S-Art.Abt. *Dirlewanger* that was overrun at Ipolysag on 15 ...ecember 1944 after expending all of their high-explosive ...nmunition. (Author)

A Hungarian 80mm Bofors Model 29M antiaircraft gun, similar to the single gun unsuccessfully employed by its Hungarian crew north of Ipolysag on 15 December 1944. (Author)

...Hungarian 100mm Skoda Model M14 howitzer used by ...Hungarian artillery batteries of their *2. Pz.Div.* at Ipolysag ...n 15 December 1944. (PK-Aufnahme, 18 April 1944 by ...*riegsberichter* Petraschk; courtesy of Klemen Kocjančič)

Czech 37mm KPUV antitank gun similar to tho[se] used by the Dirlewanger Brigade at Ipolysag; this ima[ge] depicts the same model being used by the *13. Waffe[n] Gebirgs Division der SS Handschar* in late 1943. (Pub[lic] Domain, Brushesandbayonets.blogspot.com)

M4A2 Sherman tanks of the 6th Guards Tank Army, Hungary, December 1944. (Sovfoto)

A typical crew of a Red Army M4A2 *Emcha* durin[g] autumn 1944. (Author)

T-34/85s of the 6th Guards Tank Army's V Guards Tank Corps, which punched through *Div. Gr. Rintelen*'s positions northwest of Ipolysag on 20 December 1944. (Sovfoto)

more problematic, given the terrain and the sparse road network. Palást would soon prove to be too close to the action, yet too far away to effectively control his brigade. The brigade's *Hauptquartier* (main command post) along with its *Tross* would be established in the town of Deménd (Demandice), 17 kilometers southwest of Ipolysag.

As far as the location of the regimental headquarters and the heavy weapons were concerned, Dirlewanger ordered Buchmann to establish his headquarters in Kistur (Dolné Turovce), a village 4 kilometers north of Ipolysag. Both the 120mm heavy mortar company from the *gemischte Bataillon* and the 76.2mm light artillery battery from *SS-Art.Abt. Dirlewanger* would establish firing positions in the neighboring village of Középtúr (Veľké Turovce), 1 kilometer north of Kistur. The location of the headquarters of *SS-St.Rgt. 1* cannot be determined exactly, although it most probably was a few kilometers northwest of Blauenstein inside of Slovakia, approximately 38 kilometers to the east.[15]

Altogether, nearly 6,000 men of the Dirlewanger Brigade would eventually deploy to Hungary for the impending battle, including support personnel.[16] The brigade would be later augmented by Hungarian units, particularly light and heavy *Flak* as well as light tanks, the best that the *2. Pz.Div.* could send from its limited resources. Thus, a heavy responsibility had been laid upon the shoulders of Dirlewanger and his troops. *A.Gr. Fretter-Pico* and *H.Gr. Süd* were counting on the brigade to stand and fight, like all good German soldiers should, but whether Dirlewanger and the men of the newly expanded, hastily equipped, and only partially trained brigade would be up to the challenge was another matter.

Having sorted out the deployment of the Dirlewanger Brigade to their satisfaction, the command and staff of *H.Gr. Süd*, and by extension 6. *Armee/A.Gr. Fretter-Pico*, focused their attentions on the other crisis points along their extensive *Hauptkampflinie*, including the fighting between Miskolc and Szécsény by troops of *8. Armee/A.Gr. Wöhler*, the impending siege of Budapest, and the ongoing planning needed to carry out Operation *Spätlese* between Lakes Balaton and Velencze. The only portion of the front lines not in crisis at that moment was the region defended by the *2. Pz.Armee* southwest of Lake Balaton, whose primary mission was defending the oil fields in the Nagykanizsa area. It was now up to *Oberst* Zádor's armored division to carry out its orders.

While the orders directing the deployment of the rest of the Dirlewanger Brigade were being implemented during the late afternoon, the counterattack to retake Nagy Hegy (encompassing Hills 271 and 294) and the village of Hont was scheduled to take place at 6pm that same day, even while the Soviet tank column was still being bombed and strafed by the *Luftwaffe*. At that point, the two battalions from the Dirlewanger Brigade (minus two companies from the *II. Bataillon*) reported a combined infantry *Kampfstärke* of two officers and 470 men. There were other officers leading companies of course, but under the peculiarities of Dirlewanger's system, they were all on probationary status and not entitled to be addressed or referred to by their former ranks.[17]

Oberstleutnant Grosse, commander of *Pio.Rgt.Stab 36*, initially decided to position *Hstuf.* Ehlers's *II. Bataillon* in the center, while *Oberltn.* Nitzkowski's *III. Bataillon* would be on the right with the Hungarians on the left. On the left, the strength of the Hungarian *IV. Btl./Inf.Rgt. 3* was reported as only 175 men, half of what it had the previous day before Hont was overrun. Positioned on the left flank of the attacking force, the reformed Hungarian battalion would continue to fortify its position in Parassa Puszta, a hamlet straddling the main road 2 kilometers west of Hont, and if conditions permitted, would advance to a point where it could provide supporting fire for the attack by the two Dirlewanger battalions. Coordination with *K.Gr. Grosse*'s artillery liaison officer was carried out to ensure that fire support would be provided during the initial phase of the attack.

The operation began several hours behind schedule. In the darkness, the advance towards Hont proceeded very slowly, as the troops moved in single file through the heavily wooded and hilly terrain between the front lines and Nagy Hegy. Occasionally, the columns would halt so the company commanders could reorient themselves whenever they strayed off the path. The advancing columns of the *II.* and *III. Bataillone* soon became separated and lost contact with one another. In the dark, each *Kompanieführer* had to keep their troops as close together as possible to ensure they would not stray or desert at the first opportunity. Somewhere in the distance, German and Hungarian artillery fire hammered Hont and its environs in preparation of the attack.

Initially, the former political prisoners in *III. Bataillon* had planned to desert *en masse* before they were forced to fight against their comrades in the Red Army, but since the unofficial leaders of their groups did not know where they were, much less where the front line was, they unanimously decided to postpone their mass action until the moment was more favorable. What they feared the most was becoming embroiled in a firefight with their own ideological brethren. Had this transpired, the politicals swore that they would never fire their weapons rather than support the hated SS and the Nazi regime. Fortunately for Ehlers and Nitzkowski (as well as the politicals), Soviet reconnaissance patrols did not make an appearance, so the approach by the Dirlewanger troops—though slow, noisy, and hesitant—went undetected. On account of this delay, the assault on Nagy Hegy and Hont did not actually get underway until it grew light the next morning.

When it did begin shortly before sunrise on 12 December, the attack by the two SS battalions initially made good headway as the troops approached their initial objective, Hill 271, which had been pounded by artillery shortly beforehand. The hill was the objective of *Hstuf.* Ehler's *II. Bataillon*, while Nitzkowski's *III. Bataillon* would go around it on the right to approach Hont from the southwest. Surprisingly, the motorized infantry battalion from the 46th Guards Tank Brigade withdrew from the heights before the German attack, either because its commander did not want to engage in close combat or he feared being cut off from the rest of the brigade. On the left, the Hungarian battalion remained behind its positions in Parassa Puszta and made no effort to push forward towards Hont.

To provide the counterattacking force with more firepower, the division commander had tasked six *Toldi IIa* light tanks or *Nimrod* armored self-propelled antiaircraft guns from the *panzer* regiment (the records are not clear which type was used) to attack Hont along the east–west paved road parallel to the Ipoly.[18] How the commander of *K. Gr. Grosse* planned to control the attack was not described, though neither *SS* battalion had adequate tactical radios should *Oberstltn*. Grosse wish to communicate with them. There is also no evidence that shows whether Grosse ever left his regimental headquarters in Kémence to more closely supervise the attack. In essence, both *SS* battalions would be on their own once they crossed the line of departure at approximately 7am.

Upon reaching the eastern side of Hill 271, both battalions assembled to begin their attack against Hont, which lay approximately 500 meters away. It was not yet 7am and still dark. Both battalions, five companies in all, began to advance slowly towards their objective. Evidence indicates that both battalions became intermingled at some point early during the assault. There was no sign of the Hungarian battalion. On the left, Stockhaus's heavy weapons *12. Kompanie* reached the town's railroad station on the town's western outskirts. Apparently, some troops from another company even penetrated into the village proper. But that was as far as they got. To their surprise, the leaders of the two *SS* battalions discovered that during the night the village had been reinforced by additional Soviet infantry, whose heavy defensive fire pinned down both battalions before they could make any further headway. According to one survivor of the action, former political prisoner *Gren.* Georg Müller:

> We were brought forward and then got into a very bad firefight with the Russians. We were pinned down by heavy tank and artillery fire and suffered many casualties. We ourselves did not do any firing, not at all. I left my mortar base plate at the Hont [railroad] station. Then it was time to retreat—even for us … At the water tower next to the station, which the Russians had shot up pretty badly, I found Willi Raeder from Osterholz-Scharmbeck. He was lying there and had been shot through the thigh. I carried him back to the village and delivered him to the first aid station.[19]

Behind the *SS* attack, the Hungarian armor had finally made its appearance along the main road west of Hont. But before they reached the Hont railroad station, all six light armored fighting vehicles were knocked out in rapid succession by the 37mm antiaircraft guns of the 388th Guards Antiaircraft Artillery Regiment. With this threat removed, the 46th Guards Tank Brigade began to launch its own counterattack to retake the ground it had just given up and continue its attack towards Homok begun the previous day.

Sensing an opportunity, a number of politicals from the *12. Kompanie* pinned down on the slope between the railway line and the Ipoly River decided then and there to desert. Led by Richard Doering and Willi Fänger, both old communists, a dozen or so men crossed over to the Soviets. According to one participant, Hermann Schulze:

> Our group was briefed by the company commander [Stockhaus] far forward in a system of [field] emplacements to await further orders. I was lying with comrade Ketzinger at the heavy machine gun at a valley bottom. It was a wooded area, not far from us a mortar platoon. An *SS* man from the other MG fired blindly at it. Machine pistol fire could be heard passing overhead; it hit the treetops … We remained silent, and suddenly the order came. Retreat! We said to Helmut (an *SS B-Schütze* in their squad) Scram! He went back without a word.

With the *SS* man, who may have interfered with their desertion plans, having departed from the scene, the stage was set for what happened next. Schulze continued:

> Richard Doering then passed by and pointed with his hand upwards and said: "When I go uphill it's time. Now don't wait any longer, whatever may come." I ran over together with Hans Stocker … [our] machine gun was tossed into the ditch before we went … We heard overhead the whistling of machine-gun fire; there was nothing to see but we had been spotted. We probably shouted "Tovarich, Tovarich!" (comrade, comrade!) but the firing continued above us. Our intention seemed to have been recognized then. A Red Army soldier from above pointed downward with his hands; we understood that meant: throw everything away … We were the first from the *12. Kompanie* to desert.[20]

The *SS* attack quickly collapsed in the face of the heavy enemy fire. In the resulting confusion and without any firm platoon or company leadership, both battalions retreated to the wood line west of Hont. No attempt was made to rally the survivors and make another attempt. After taking into account the number of casualties their units had already suffered and still being subjected to heavy enemy fire, both battalion commanders decided to withdraw to their starting point in the mountains in the vicinity of Csitari-Puszta.

Meanwhile, radio and telephone messages flew back and forth between the various headquarters at a dizzying speed. At the headquarters of the Hungarian *2. Pz.Div.* in Vámosmikola, the initial report that *Oberst* Zádor received at 9.30am indicated that the counterattack at Hont was proceeding satisfactorily. Shortly thereafter, *Oberstltn.* Grosse reported that he had received a message at 10.15am informing him that Hills 271 and 294 west of Hont had been retaken by the two *SS* Dirlewanger battalions. However, the information must have been at least two hours old because by that time the attack by both battalions had already been repulsed and their troops forced to withdraw into the mountains.

Another report, sent by *D.V.K. 149* at 9.50am and received at *6. Armee/A.Gr. Fretter-Pico* headquarters at 10.08am, confirmed this unfavorable development. It also passed along the news that the artillery officer attached to *K.Gr. Grosse* had reported that 15 Soviet Shermans with mounted infantry had attacked out of Hont along the main road at 8.30am and had approached the outskirts of Parassa-Puszta before being turned back after a *Luftwaffe*-manned 88mm *Flak* gun had knocked out one tank.[21] In the blink of an eye, the situation had taken a quite unexpected turn for the worse.

Hills 271 and 294, recently taken by Ehlers's and Nitzkowski's men, were quickly reoccupied by Soviet troops by 12.15pm after the Germans withdrew. Although its tanks had been forced to pull back by the lone 88mm *Flak* and its brave crew, the 46th Guards Tank Brigade's motorized infantry battalion continued its advance, attacking Homok from the south after passing over Hills 271 and 294. According to the official Red Army records, the battalion "burst into Homok" and began fighting house-to-house, finally seizing the village from the Hungarian *Pionier* battalion late that afternoon.[22] Thus secured, at least one battalion of *Emchas* moved into Homok after the 88mm *Flak* had been hurriedly withdrawn. *Oberst* Zádor's only reserve, the engineer company from his *2. Pz.Div.*, was hurriedly thrown into a counterattack to restore the situation at Homok, but such a small force stood no chance at all against the better part of an enemy tank battalion and a motorized infantry battalion, and was forced to fall back towards Bernecebaráti, though some of its men were left behind in the town.

The news seemed to grow worse by the hour. While the two Dirlewanger battalions made their way back to their starting points from the night before after their failed counterattack, the commander of the IX Guards Mechanized Corps kept urging his brigades forward with all possible speed. While the 46th Guards Tank Brigade's attack to seize Homok was underway, at 9am elements of Col. Seleznev's 31st Guards Mechanized Brigade pushed into the Börszeny Mountains, 5 kilometers south of Hont, along the unpaved logging road running through the narrow valley of Bernece Creek. German observation posts reported Soviet infantry advancing into the hills along that route in overwhelming numbers. The defense mounted by troops from *Pio.Btl. 666* was too weak to stop them. The hamlet of Deszkás Puszta fell shortly thereafter when German troops manning a roadblock positioned east of the village fled in haste.

Continuing their westwards movement, the brigade's 1st Motorized Infantry Battalion advanced along the valley floor for nearly 6 kilometers, shoving aside feeble efforts by overmatched elements of *Pio.Rgt.Stab 36* to block its approach. Within hours, the Soviet infantrymen had scaled the southern slope of Hill 397 and seized the settlement of Csitari-Puszta by 4pm, effectively splitting *Oberstltn.* Grosse's force in two. By this point in the fighting, they were a mere 3 kilometers east of Bernecebaráti and Grosse's headquarters. At the last minute, an emergency company hastily formed from Hungarian tank crews without tanks was thrown into a counterattack and brought the enemy's advance to a halt, but this was a temporary measure at best.[23] Unless something was done to retake the lost ground, not only would the two Dirlewanger battalions soon be cut off, but the defense of the Ipolysag Gap would also be outflanked from the south.

That was not the only German-Hungarian setback that morning. At the same time that the 46th Guards Tank and 31st Guards Mechanized Brigades were preparing their attacks, on the night of 11/12 December one infantry battalion of the 18th Guards Mechanized Brigade began to cross the Ipoly River at Ipolyvece at 9.30am using a field expedient brigade and at Ipolyhidvég with a rudimentary ferry constructed the day before. The river crossing in the Ipolyhidvég area was supported by the artillery battery of Guards Lieutenant Kozyrev, which suppressed three German or Hungarian self-propelled guns that were contesting the crossing from the opposite bank. The infantry's river crossing was also supported with direct fire from the 83rd Guards Tank Regiment, which had moved into Dregelypalánk to wait its turn to cross once a suitable bridge was constructed.[24]

The brigade's other two infantry battalions crossed the river upstream at Ipolyvece at the same time and immediately launched an attack to overcome the German and Hungarian defenses manned by two weak infantry companies before they could be reinforced. First, the village of Balog fell to their attack, followed shortly thereafter by the village of Nagyfalu (Vel'ká Ves) that lay 2 kilometers to the west, and Hill 151 several hundred meters to the north. The battalion that had crossed at Ipolyhidvég joined with the other two battalions and quickly consolidated their control of the area. Colonel Ovcharov, the brigade commander, left one battalion to construct a defensive barrier at Hill 151, and with the two remaining battalions prepared to carry out an attack along the northern bank of the Ipoly directed at Ipolysag once it had grown dark. The tank brigade would follow as soon as a suitable bridge capable of bearing the weight of its vehicles was constructed.

The defenders had fallen back to the town of Tesmag (Tešmák), a mere 3.5 kilometers east of Ipolysag. Here, the terrain was more favorable to defense. At this point, the maneuver space available to the 18th Guards Mechanized Brigade was reduced to less than a kilometer in width, with the river on their left and front, and Hills 283 (Mt. Magas) and 323 (Mt. Somos) on their right where the course of the Ipoly River lay at the base of the hills. Here, an unpaved road ran along the northern bank of the river, connecting Ipolyhidvég to Tesmag. The hills were defended by a German company from *Bau-Pio.Btl. 144*, while the two Hungarian companies that withdrew from Ipolyhidvég would defend Tesmag proper. By pulling back, the defenders once again fell within range of German-Hungarian supporting artillery fire, which had been lacking during their attempt to keep hold of Ipolyhidvég. Although they had lost or abandoned their self-propelled guns at Ipolyhidvég, they could still direct artillery fire and aim their remaining antitank gun and heavy infantry weapons upon the Soviet forces approaching from the east, as well as those occupying Hont to its immediate south on the opposite bank of the river.[25]

There is no evidence that either Dirlewanger or Buchmann knew anything about this attack or what was happening to their two battalions in the mountains, because they had no means to communicate directly with Grosse or with the German liaison team at the Hungarian's division headquarters. Efforts by the *6. Armee Armeenachrichtenführer* to establish communications with the brigade had not yet been carried out, forcing the Hungarian *2. Pz.Div.* to communicate with Dirlewanger during the brigade's movement using dispatch riders. A Hungarian liaison officer with a radio would not arrive until the following day.

During the morning of 12 December, both Dirlewanger and Buchmann were understandably focused on moving the rest of the brigade from its previous area of operations near Neutra towards the Ipolysag area along the route Neutra—Golden-Morawetz (Goldmorawitza)—Slovak border north of Leva (Levice), where it was intended to occupy a temporary assembly area at Szántó, 20 kilometers northwest of Ipolysag. However, the German liaison team at the Hungarian *2. Pz.Div.* headquarters knew what had happened, and so did *Oberst* Zádor and his staff—they were watching a catastrophe unfolding before their very eyes.

It had become painfully obvious that more troops were needed to defend the Ipolysag Gap, especially in the mountains north and south of the river, which up to this point had been merely secured by a thin line of troops. While the *Luftwaffe's Flak* batteries with their 88mm guns could prevent tanks from breaking through the gap, they were virtually useless against infantry. And that is what the Hungarian *2. Pz.Div.* needed the most and what spurred its request for two more of Dirlewanger's battalions to be deployed into the area. The division sent a radio message at 12.15pm that day, stating: "Heavily outnumbered by enemy infantry. Our last reserves have been committed … [an] accelerated reinforcement by infantry forces urgently necessary especially for the [coming] night."[26]

Later that same evening, the Hungarian commander, through his German liaison team, sent another message, informing *A. Gr. Fretter-Pico* headquarters that his forces were too weak to prevent Soviet troops, which were advancing into the mountains on either side, from bypassing his defenses in the Ipolysag Gap. In the same message, *Oberst* Zádor requested reinforcement by Hungarian *Fallschirmjäger-Einheiten* (paratroop units) as well as additional sorties by *Luftwaffe* ground attack aircraft no later than the following day.[27] An air of desperation hung about the *2. Pz.Div.* headquarters as the reality of the situation, and its inability to do anything to stop it, began to sink in.

This need for decisive action would accelerate the deployment of additional elements of the Dirlewanger Brigade into the Ipolysag area. Kept abreast of the serious nature of the day's fighting, that afternoon the commander of *H. Gr. Süd* had authorized *A. Gr. Fretter-Pico* to request the release of two additional battalions of the brigade from the German Commander in Slovakia. According to the message sent out that afternoon to the Hungarian *2. Pz. Div.* by Fretter-Pico:

> By order of *H.Gr. Süd*, two battalions of the Dirlewanger Brigade are to be brought from the area around Szántó to the narrows of Ipolysag by Divisional Liaison Command 149. They will be subordinated to the Hungarian *2. Panzer Division* ... The battalions are to be deployed northeast of Ipolysag in order to free up forces for the fight south of the narrows.[28]

This order did not specifically mean that the brigade would become responsible for defending Ipolysag itself, only that its presence would enable "other" forces to be freed up for the mission. What these "other" forces were was not specified in the order.

Reviewing the available documentation, the only forces that could be freed up, were this to occur, would be the two *SS* battalions from Buchmann's regiment that were already fighting in the mountains east of Bernecebaráti, as well as the three mixed German and Hungarian companies defending east of the Ipolysag near Tesmag, hardly sufficient to hold the gap and the surrounding mountains. The town of Ipolysag itself was still being defended by Zischler's *II. Btl./Pz.Gren.Rgt. 26*, but it was subject to recall at any moment to return to its parent division. The remaining two reserve battalions of the Dirlewanger Brigade (*I.* and *II. Btl./SS-St. Rgt. 2*) had not yet been ordered forward and were still at the disposal of the German Commander in Slovakia, but their commitment was now only a matter of time.

The failure of *Oberst* Zádor and his division to hold their ground, when his German overlords had initially believed he had sufficient forces to do so, caused a great deal of consternation within the leadership of *H.Gr. Süd* and *6. Armee/A.Gr. Fretter-Pico* that evening. It was becoming evident that Zádor and his staff, even with the assistance of *D.V.K. 149*, did not have the skill or experience to orchestrate a defensive operation of such magnitude with his available infantry, artillery, and armored forces. It had also become obvious that the terrain on either side of the gap was proving to be no obstacle for the advance by the IX Guards Mechanized Corps, which seemed to have more than enough infantry to envelop Ipolysag through the mountains on either side while simultaneously pushing through the valley floor with armor.

Concerned with how the battle was playing out throughout that day, the key staff officers of *H.Gr. Süd* and *6. Armee/A.Gr. Fretter-Pico* grew increasingly worried, to the point that they knew that something had to be done immediately to turn the situation around to their favor. One conversation between *Gen.Maj.* Heinz Gaedke, Fretter-Pico's chief of staff, and *Oberstltn.* Schäfer, the *Ia* of *H.Gr. Süd*, was recorded in the latter's war diary that evening, as follows:

> At 12:10 p.m. the Chief of the General Staff of *A.Gr. Fretter-Pico* notified the *Heeresgruppe Ia* of his concern about the command in the Börszeny Mountains, especially near Ipolysag. He said that the Hungarian 2. *Pz.Div. was hardly up to the task of leading at this focal point of the action* [author's emphasis] ... [Gaedke] asked that a German command staff be deployed there. After the easing of tension in the morning, the situation at Ipolysag has considerably worsened in the evening due to [the] enemy attack.[29]

Clearly, something had to be done quickly to prevent a major breakthrough by the vanguard of the Sixth Guards Tank Army. Another headquarters staff and a new leader had to be found from somewhere within the extended combat zone of *H.Gr. Süd* to take over from *Oberst* Zádor and his staff. The search did not take long. In the war diary later that night, the army group's *Ia* wrote:

> The command by a German staff in this area [of Ipolysag] has been arranged by the *Heeresgruppe* on its own initiative by deploying the staff of the *357. Inf.Div.* The army group *Ia* was given the order to contact *SS-Oberführer* Dirlewanger in order to lead the two battalions into the area northwest of Ipolysag for action … The enemy seems to be inserting a tank unit [into the Ipolysag sector]. If we [suffer] a complete failure there, the overall situation would change completely and new decisions would become urgently necessary.[30]

Generaloberst Friessner, preoccupied at that moment with the final stages of preparation for Operation *Spätlese* and the defense of Budapest, agreed that the solution was not only to insert a German staff to control all of the forces deployed in the Ipolysag Gap, but also to pick a capable officer to be in charge of the battle. That officer was a junior *Generalmajor*, Josef Rintelen, commander of the *357. Inf.Div.*[31]

Selecting the commander and staff of this division for the mission was a logical choice. Charged with defending a portion of the front line north of Budapest on Szentendre Island along the western branch of the Danube, the division headquarters controlled hardly any troops from its own regiments and had been divested of half of its artillery. Its meager front-line strength consisted of five weak Hungarian battalions and 14 Hungarian antitank guns. Its only battalion with any combat value, *Feldersatz-Bataillon* (*Feld-Ers.Btl.*, field replacement battalion) *357*, was undergoing reconstitution behind the front lines at Neuhäusel and would not be available for employment for several more days. The division's primary mission, since nearly being wiped out at Hatvan on 5 December, was to secure the western bank of the Danube along Szentendre Island, with its headquarters in the town of Leányfalu.[32] Its troops were not in direct contact with Soviet forces across the Danube and most of its combat activity was limited to exchanges of artillery fire and patrolling the riverbank for infiltrators.

The command group of *A.Gr. Fretter-Pico*, after being given additional guidance that evening from the *Ia* of *H.Gr. Süd*, issued an order in the evening describing the division's new mission. The order laid out the following:

1. The staff of the *357. Inf.Div.* is be withdrawn as quickly as possible from its current employment on the Szentendre Island. It will assume the command and control of the defensive sector currently exercised by the Hungarian *2. Pz.Div.* north of the Danube.

2. The division will appoint a regimental staff to take control of the remaining forces operating on the Szentendre Island, which will report directly to the *IX. SS-Gebirgs-Korps.*[33]

3. The Hungarian *2. Pz.Div.* with all Hungarian and German forces deployed in its sector will be subordinated to the staff of the *357. Inf.Div.* upon its arrival. After taking command, the staff will bear the designation "*Divisions-Gruppe Rintelen*" [*Div.Gr. Rintelen*].

4. The staff of the *357. Inf.Div.* will report no later than noon on 13 December 1944 its assumption of command to the headquarters of the *Armeegruppe*, to which it will be directly subordinated.[34]

This order also extended to the portions of the Dirlewanger Brigade that had already been subordinated to the Hungarian *2. Pz.Div.* and would apply to any additional elements of the brigade once they arrived in the Ipolysag Gap, having passed into Fretter-Pico's *Kampfraum*.

In the meantime, however, the Hungarian *2. Pz.Div.* would have to do the best it could to prevent a complete breakthrough by the troops of Volkov's IX Guards Mechanized Corps. Until noon the following day, the time when the staff of *Div.Gr. Rintelen* was officially scheduled to take over, there were still several measures that could be taken to stabilize the *Hauptkampflinie* between Tesmag and Bernecebaráti during the next 12–16 hours. The most urgent were the need to prevent a penetration beyond Homok and to retake Csitari-Puszta, as well as to re-establish a main defense line east of Bernecebaráti. The only forces available for this operation included the two somewhat-battered *SS* battalions, *Bau-Pio.Btle. 112* and *666, Feld-Strafgef.Abt.18*, and several smaller Hungarian emergency units. A total of 27 artillery pieces were available to fire in support.

During the late afternoon of 12 December, the counterattack began. By midnight, the elements of *K.Gr. Grosse* mentioned above had advanced far enough that they were able to liberate Csitari-Puszta without great loss.[35] At least one of the *SS* battalions that had abandoned the settlement during their precipitous retreat earlier that day played a role in the counterattack, Nitzkowski's *III. Btl./SS-St.Rgt. 2*. During the counterattack, the *10. Kompanie*—under former *Hptm.* Langelotz—overshot the objective and became lost in the forest, but eventually made its way back to German lines the following day. Langelotz had originally intended to desert to the Red Army with his entire company, but as the day passed into night, he became disoriented and could not tell which direction the German lines or the Soviet lines were.

Because of lack of familiarity with the terrain, he was convinced that going much further in the darkness would have had tragic consequences for himself and his men. During the early morning, he and his company stumbled quite accidently back into his battalion's defensive position. Surprisingly, he was hailed as a returning hero because he and his company had already been given up for lost. To cover his tracks, Langelotz concocted a fanciful story about his men's heroics. One of the men who returned with him, Wilhelm Engelhardt, later wrote:

We reached the lines manned by [other] Dirlewanger units, were hustled through, and marched to a village [Bernecebaráti] where our battalion commander had taken up quarters. In the end, he must have been glad to have found his *10. Kompanie* again. Our company commander [Langelotz] was an avid teller of tales, telling of tremendous battles and casualty-filled clashes with the enemy. In the end, after a few rounds of schnapps, [he and Nitzkowski] are said to have embraced each other as friends.[36]

Nitzkowski was convinced that the tale was true and wrote up a glowing report. He had no idea at the time that Langelotz would soon try again once conditions were more favorable for him and his company to desert *en masse*.[37] A small number of Dirlewanger's politicals used the opportunity to desert, though most remained in the ranks out of fear of being shot by their *SS* overseers. Official Soviet records do state, however, that the 1st Motorized Infantry Battalion of the 31st Guards Mechanized Brigade was forced to withdraw from the area to avoid encirclement after "fighting a hard battle."[38]

South of Csitari-Puszta, Hungarian troops and *Pioniere* from *Pio.Btle. 112* and *666* were able to re-establish the front line 3 kilometers east of Bernecebaráti. The front west of Homok held firm, thanks to the *Luftwaffe's* heavy *Flak* battery positioned there, but without infantry to protect them, the guns were vulnerable to attack by Red Army ground troops. The Hungarian *2. Pz.Div.* made no further effort to retake Homok, since there were simply not enough men to spare for such an attempt. The additional troops of the Dirlewanger Brigade that had been promised would not arrive until the following day at the earliest. For the next several hours at least, a front line had been cobbled together, but whether it would hold for another day until the arrival of *Gen.Maj.* Rintelen and his staff was an open question. The situation had truly devolved into a race against time, as well as with the IX Guards Mechanized Corps.

CHAPTER SEVEN

Rintelen Takes Command, 13 December 1944

Except for the two battalions deployed in the Börzeny Mountains, for the majority of Dirlewanger's troops the daylight hours between 12 and 14 December 1944 were mostly spent moving from Neutra to the brigade's new staging area north of Ipolysag between the towns of Szántó and Dudince. A good portion of this movement was being carried out on foot; with an average distance 63 kilometers to Szántó and 75 to Dudince, it would require at least 12–15 hours a day to cover on foot with a light load, not counting rest halts. But the men were not carrying the minimum amount of equipment; most were in full marching order, including weapons, packs, ammunition, and a day's ration. Altogether, that amounted to 70lb (or nearly 32kg) of kit to carry, which would have affected how quickly each soldier could march the entire distance to reach his destination.

While the brigade had a few trucks and automobiles to transport its equipment and supplies, most of its men would have to travel on foot, horseback, or aboard horse-drawn wagons, unlike the men of *II.* and *III. Btl./SS-St.Rgt. 2* who had been transported by Höfle's *Feldpost* truck convoy on 10 December. Suffice to say, many of these men were from older age groups and not in great physical condition, having been recently discharged from concentration camps or military prisons, so the actual distance they were able to march in a single day was probably no greater than 25–30 kilometers at best. Straggling would have been commonplace and many men would have dropped out from exhaustion, blisters, or other maladies, leaving the few motorized vehicles to drive back and forth picking them up and delivering them to their drop-off point. Thus, it would take over two days for the brigade, strung out along the entire route, to reach the Ipolysag battle area. It would not be until the afternoon of 14 December that the last soldiers would arrive.

The first significant portion of the brigade to reach its destination on 13 December was *Ostuf.* Herbert Meyer's *I. Btl./SS-St.Rgt. 1*, which began to close on its assembly areas north of Ipolysag at 2pm that afternoon. Along with this battalion, the brigade's 120mm heavy mortar company with six tubes and the four 76.2mm regimental guns of *3.Bttr./SS-Art.Abt. Dirlewanger* also arrived at roughly the same time. The rest of Ehlers's *II. Btl./SS-St.Rgt. 2*, its *7.* and *8. Kompanien*, also reached Ipolysag on the same day, but they did not join the rest of their battalion south of the Ipoly. *Obersturmführer* Meyer's *I. Btl./SS-St.Rgt. 1* was then ordered to take up positions along the high ground 2 kilometers northeast of Ipolysag, encompassing the area north of Hill 227 as far as Hill 291, a front line stretching nearly 8 kilometers in width.

The arrival of the *7.* and *8. Kompanien* of *II. Btl./SS-St.Rgt. 2* enabled the thickening of the German defenses north of the Ipoly River. Both companies would be temporarily attached to *II. Btl./Pz.Gren.Rgt. 26* and were ordered to occupy Hill 227, thus allowing all of Zischler's *Panzergrenadiere* to concentrate upon the defense of Ipolysag itself. Why the two aforementioned infantry companies were not sent on their way to join the rest of Ehler's *II. Bataillon* in the mountains remains a mystery; perhaps Dirlewanger or Buchmann thought they were needed more for the defense of Ipolysag than with the rest of Ehlers's battalion. The arrival of these two companies also permitted the platoon from *1. Kp./Bau-Pio.Btl. 144* to hand over its positions on Hill 227 and rejoin the rest of their company positioned to the east atop the ridgeline encompassing Mt. Magas and Mt. Somos.

As planned, Dirlewanger's heavy mortar company and light artillery battery both took up firing positions in the village of Közeptúr. The regimental command post was established in the village of Kistur, located 3.8 kilometers north of Ipolysag. One of the later battalions to arrive on 13 December was *Ustuf.* Siegfried Polack's *III. Btl./SS-St.Rgt. 1*, which did not depart the Neutra area until 5pm that day. It was lucky in the sense that it did not have to march entirely on foot; after beginning its journey on 12 December, it was picked up the next day by Hungarian trucks in the village of Vámosmikola and transported to the brigade's *Hauptquartier* (main command post) at Deménd, a distance of 20 kilometers northwest of Ipolysag and only 4 kilometers southeast of Szántó.

From there, his battalion was further trucked through the towns of Szalatnya (Slatina) and Palást before reaching their final destination of Ipoly-Födemes (Ipolyské Úľany) at 1.50am on 14 December. Polack's battalion, as well as Stegman's *I. Btl./SS-St.Rgt. 2*, would be placed under the control of the headquarters of *SS-St.Rgt. 1*, which was located somewhere between Blauenstein and the Slovak town of Karpfen (Krupina). Both battalions would remain under the control of the German Commander in Slovakia for the time being until notified otherwise. The same should have applied to the two 105mm artillery batteries of *SS-Art.Abt. Dirlewanger*, but these would not leave their cantonment area near Deviaky at all during the entire battle, for reasons which are still not entirely clear.

East of Palást, the two infantry battalions under the control of *SS-St.Rgt. 1* would establish a thin defensive line to block or at least warn against any attempt by the 6th Guards Tank Army or Cavalry-Mechanized Group Pliyev to penetrate into the far-right flank of the *24. Pz.Div.* north of the town of Balassagyarmat. This *panzer* division itself had begun pulling out of the Ipolysag area on 9 December in order to carry out counterattacks against Pliyev's advance in the eastern portion of the *IV. Pz.Korps'* sector at Szécsény. The only unit of the *24. Pz.Div.* still defending the Ipoly River valley was the aforementioned *II. Btl./Pz.Gren.Rgt. 26* in Ipolysag, with a single artillery battery from the division's *Pz.Art.Rgt. 89* in support. According to the original plan, Zischler's battalion was supposed to remain behind in Ipolysag for at least 24 more hours to ensure that a thorough relief in place was conducted with the incoming Dirlewanger Brigade, originally scheduled to be completed during the early hours of 15 December at the latest.

The 60-man combat engineer platoon attached to Buchmann's regiment arrived in Kistur at midnight on 12 December, after having marched 60 kilometers on foot during the past two days. Footsore and exhausted, the platoon would ideally need one or two days to recuperate before it would be ready for action as the regiment's reserve force. With two of his three battalions fighting south of the Ipoly River under *K.Gr. Grosse* and his other battalion moved to the Blauenstein–Karpfen area, Buchmann had little of his own regiment under his direct control except the two companies from Ehlers's *II. Bataillon* beginning their occupation of Hill 227. Instead, Meyers's *I. Btl./SS-St.Rgt. 1* would be temporarily subordinated to his regiment.

The *Panzerjäger Kompanie* of the Dirlewanger Brigade, equipped with either 37mm or 47mm antitank guns (or both types—the records are unclear), would be sited in Gyerk in order to block the defile west of Ipolysag. These small-caliber weapons would be nearly useless against T-34s and Shermans, lacking both in size and penetrating power. *Oberst* Zádor's staff had already realized that Dirlewanger's forces would need to be augmented by more powerful antitank weapons if they were to stand any chance of holding their positions. At some point on 13 December, Dirlewanger would be told that he would be augmented by four Hungarian *Nimrod* self-propelled *Flak* and a towed 80mm antiaircraft gun by 15 December. If employed properly, the powerful 80mm *Flak* could prove to be a significant augmentation to the brigade's antitank defenses, but Dirlewanger had never faced the possibility of having to confront Soviet armored forces until this moment.[1] His *Ia, Stubaf.* Weisse, certainly had some combat experience fighting enemy armor while serving with the *SS-Division Das Reich* from 1941–42, but there was little either of them could do until the weapon and its crew arrived except issue a few *Panzerfaust* antitank weapons to the units concerned.

While Dirlewanger's own forward command post would be sited in the town of Palást itself, the brigade's *Hauptquartier*, consisting of its administrative and logistics staff elements, as well as the brigade's and both regiments' *Tross*, would continue to operate in the town of Deménd some 18 kilometers to the southwest. Dirlewanger and Weisse would spend most of this period in Palást with a signals team, a few motorcycle dispatch riders, and a small security element from the brigade headquarters. To visit his scattered battalions before the battle actually began, Dirlewanger and Weisse used a Volkswagen *Kübelwagen* driven by *Gren.* Arno Böhm—once the battle began on 14 December, such visits became far too hazardous.

By 4pm on 13 December, Dirlewanger informed the Hungarian *2. Pz.Div.* that he had assumed control of his defensive sector. At that point, he had approximately 1,400 of his own men (two-and-a-half infantry battalions) from his brigade on the ground, not including the two battalions fighting under *K.Gr. Grosse.* He also exercised temporary control of the *Panzergrenadier* battalion from the *24. Pz.Div.*, *1. Kp./Bau-Pio.Btl. 144*, and the Hungarian *Kompanie Gaal.*[2] Only one key element was missing—the brigade's newly raised communications company, which had been misrouted and would not arrive until noon on 15 December, nearly two days after the rest of the brigade.[3] This error deprived the brigade of its powerful 100-watt and 80-watt radio transmitters, each mounted on trucks, which the brigade and its regiments relied upon for rapid transmission and receipt of orders and reports.

Without this equipment, Dirlewanger and his regimental commanders would have to communicate with each other (and higher headquarters) using landline telephones and motorcycle messengers until augmented by assets from the *6. Armee Nachrichtenführer, Oberst* Köpcke. This officer had already been directed by his army's chief of staff to ensure that solid communications were established between the brigade and the Hungarian *2. Pz.Div.* Evidence indicates that a Hungarian liaison officer with a radio did finally arrive before the evening of 13 December to at least guarantee communications between Dirlewanger and the *2. Pz.Div.*[4] Normally, it would take the brigade's *Nachrichtenkompanie* at least 24 hours to lay in all of the field telephone cable need to connect Dirlewanger's command post with his *Hauptquartier* and the headquarters of both regiments. Whether this task was accomplished in time is unknown, but it is unlikely.

This oversight would soon have serious consequences. By midnight on 13 December, Dirlewanger had no direct radio or landline contact with the two battalions from *SS-St.Rgt.2* attached to *K.Gr. Grosse* fighting in the mountains east of Bernecebaráti, despite the orders from *H.Gr. Süd* and the *HSSPF* for Slovakia prohibiting the brigade's dispersion. Dirlewanger had only tenuous contact with Siegfried Polack's *III. Btl./SS-St.Rgt. 1* that had taken up positions near Ipoly-Födemes and was cooperating with but not attached to the *24. Pz.Div.* Dirlewanger had no contact at all with Wilhelm Stegmann's *I. Btl./SS-St.Rgt. 2*, which was somewhere near the Slovakian town of Blauenstein, 38 kilometers to the east of Dirlewanger's headquarters in Palást. It might as well have been in China.

As mentioned earlier, the final major component of the brigade, *Maj.d.Schu.Po.* Steinhauer's hard-marching *II. Btl./SS-St.Rgt. 1*—until now held in reserve—would be the last to close on the assembly area near Szántó. That same day, *Oberst* Zádor had already requested that this battalion be deployed immediately to the Ipolysag area due to the developing situation.[5] Aware of the critical nature of the timing, at 5.30pm on 13 December Dirlewanger told the staff of *D.V.K. 149* that this battalion would be late in arriving unless trucks were sent to transport it. Because this battalion had been designated to relieve the *Panzergrenadier* battalion holding Ipolysag, Buchmann, the commander of *SS-St.Rgt. 2*, personally asked *Rittmeister* Zischler to keep his troops in place for the time being to ensure that a proper relief in place could be carried out.[6] It was a request that Zischler did not have the power to fulfill—while he most likely sympathized with Buchmann, Zischler ultimately answered to the commander of the *24. Pz.Div.*, not Dirlewanger or Buchmann.

While *Ustuf.* Polack's *III. Btl./SS-St.Rgt. 2* theoretically operated under control of Dirlewanger, there was no physical connection on the ground between Polack and his nearest neighbor, Meyer's *I. Bataillon* of his regiment. Meyer's leftmost company, occupying defensive positions near Hill 291, was located approximately 5 kilometers to the west and would not be able to provide any kind of support should Polack need it. Furthermore, neither Dirlewanger's nor Buchmann's regimental headquarters had any radio or telephone contact with Polack's battalion. Except for sending messages via dispatch riders, he and his men were practically on their own. If anything, it made more sense to attach the battalion to the *24. Pz.Div.*, which happened several days later though not in the way intended. One bit of good news arriving later that day was that the German Commander in Slovakia had rounded up enough trucks to fetch up Steinhauer's *II. Btl./SS-St.Rgt. 1* the next morning. After hastening to reach the front, his footsore battalion was not expected to arrive at its staging area at Kistompa (Tupá), a town 7 kilometers northwest of Ipolysag, any earlier than 10am on 14 December.

While the main body of the Dirlewanger Brigade marched or rode towards the Ipolysag area on 13 December, the fighting continued between Homok and Ipolyhidvég. Having made inroads into the German and Hungarian defenses the previous day, Lt.Gen. Volkov redoubled his corps' efforts that day to break through the mountains on either side of Ipolysag. After occupying Homok, the 46th Guards Tank Brigade and elements of the 31st Guards Mechanized Brigade still had to contend with small detachments of German and Hungarian defenders who had stayed behind to delay the invaders. Once Homok was completely secured after eliminating this nuisance, Volkov's troops had to endure shelling from enemy artillery fire from the battery in support of *II. Btl./Pz.Gren.Rgt. 26* in Ipolysag as well as mortar fire originating from the small force holding Tesmag. The next step for his two brigades in Homok was to seize a crossing over the Ipoly River lying 400 meters north of the village, but this was to prove a challenging task after the Germans blew up the bridge that same morning, forcing them to face the reality that they would have to construct their own, most likely while being shot at.

To the south, at least two battalions of the 31st Guards Mechanized Brigade continued their efforts to reach Bernecebaráti through the mountains. Undeterred by the German and Hungarian counterattack of the previous evening that had restored their previously held positions along the *HKL*, the Soviet troops maintained the pressure all along their enemy's main defense line and launched an unsuccessful effort to retake the key position of Csitari-Puszta at the top of Hill 337. However, two rifle companies of the 31st Guards Mechanized Brigade pushed past Homok, changed direction to the south, entered the mountains, and captured the Kinszky Manor farm against light resistance that evening. This position would enable them to observe and interdict traffic along the Homok–Bernecebaráti highway with small-arms fire.[7] It also afforded an ideal jump-off position for the next day's operations, should the brigade commander decide to take advantage of it. The occupation of Kinszky Manor was not detected by the Germans and Hungarians until 8am the following day.[8] Creeping incursions such as this forced *Oberstltn.* Grosse to move his regimental headquarters from the now-threatened Bernecebaráti to a safer location in Kémence, a town 1 kilometer further to the southwest.

Soviet artillery and mortar fire fell upon German and Hungarian positions at irregular intervals, and although not accurate, further stretched the defenders' already taut nerves. Having spent three nights in the open without shelter and adequate clothing or warm food, the two *SS* battalions of Ehlers and Nitzkowski could do little but endure their hardships as best they could. Troop morale, already low, fell even lower. Defecting during such conditions was out of the question—any political attempting to do so in broad daylight would be shot down by their own *SS* leaders or by Soviet troops who would not immediately recognize their "comrades in the struggle" but would rather shoot first and ask questions later. Any attempt to do so at night invariably resulted in getting lost in the forest. All of the conditions needed for a successful defection had to be present in order for their gambit to succeed.

Meanwhile, the task that lay before the 18th Guards Mechanized Brigade on the morning 13 December was more straightforward—continue pushing along the northern bank of the Ipoly and get as close to Ipolysag and seize it, if possible. Rather than risk his infantry being exposed to German artillery during daylight, the brigade commander, Col. Ovcharov, decided to infiltrate the enemy's thinly manned positions on foot before sunrise. Following the road leading out of Ipolyhidvég to the northwest, the brigade's leading elements rapidly bypassed the undefended village of Hidvežska Puszta as well as the settlement of Wollnerova that lay at the base of Mt. Magas.

Avoiding detection, the brigade's spearhead used the terrain to its advantage and bypassed Tesmag and its garrison from the north, crossed the Berinesen Creek 500 meters to the north of the village, and reached Hill 241 1 kilometer northeast of Ipolysag before daylight. Finally alerted to the threat and suddenly aware that they had been bypassed and were now in danger of being cut off, the Hungarian unit defending Tesmag, *Kompanie Gaal*, and another unnamed unit, as well as its artillery forward observer team, hastily pulled back towards Ipolysag.

This withdrawal effectively ended enemy flanking fire being directed against their units moving along the river road between Hont and Homok, and eliminated the need for Col. Ovcharov's troops to fight to gain control of Tesmag. The company from *Bau-Pio.Btl. 144* positioned atop Mt. Magas was virtually powerless to prevent any of this from happening—only 80 men strong to begin with, the company could do very little but man a string of outposts arrayed along the ridgeline between Mt. Magas and Mt. Somos, a distance of nearly a kilometer, and report whatever they observed.

Instructed by Lt.Gen. Volkov to continue his advance, at 11am Col. Ovcharov ordered his troops to feel out German defenses in Ipolysag by conducting a large-scale reconnaissance in force, including tanks. Some of his troops attacked uphill towards Mounts Magas and Somos, forcing the troops from *1. Kp./Bau-Pio.Btl. 144* to withdraw. With the threat to their rear removed, Ovcharov's two battalions proceeded to push the Germans back along the line delineated by Hills 227, 254, and 245 northeast of Ipolysag.[9] This marked the first time that any of Dirlewanger's newly arriving troops experienced combat, though it is unclear whether this involved the two companies from Ehlers's *SS-St.Rgt. 2* or Meyer's *I. Btl./SS-St.Rgt. 1*. Evidently, these *SS* troops were only lightly engaged and probably arrived at their positions just as the engineers were falling back from Mt. Magas.

When it attempted to enter Ipolysag from the east, Ovcharov's troops were driven back by Zischler's battalion after suffering heavy losses in the process. Later, the intelligence staff of *6. Armee/A.Gr. Fretter-Pico* estimated that at least 1,000 Soviet infantrymen (two battalions) and 17 tanks were involved in this failed attempt.[10] As an indication of the severity of the fighting that day, the men of *II. Btl./Pz.Gren.Rgt. 26* claimed to have knocked out nine Soviet tanks, seven of them using hand-held infantry weapons (*Panzerfausts*), and counted 180–200 enemy dead afterwards. One of Zischler's men, *Wachtmeister* and platoon leader Julius Poeppel of *5. Kompanie*, personally accounted for four tanks destroyed and was awarded the Knight's Cross for his deed two weeks later.[11]

The steadfast resistance to the Soviet advance on the outskirts of Ipolysag was not the only setback that Lt.Gen. Volkov had to contend with that day. At noon, after an urgent request from the Hungarian *2. Pz.Div.*, a resurgent *Luftwaffe* carried out another air raid on Ipolyhidvég, bombing and strafing the town with unknown results. This raid was a reflection of the priority for air support assigned that day to buttress the far-left flank of Fretter-Pico's army, where not only the Hungarians were having difficulty, but the *24. Pz.Div.* was as well. In that small sector of frontage on 13 December alone, the *Luftwaffe* flew no fewer than 60 ground attack sorties against Soviet assembly areas and artillery positions in the Ipolysag–Szécsény area; three artillery batteries were reportedly destroyed and rail activity was temporarily disrupted, but no enemy tanks were reported as knocked out.[12] Yet these losses amounted to mere pinpricks that hardly impacted the operations of the 6th Guards Tank Army.

Throughout the evening of 13/14 December, the troops of the IX Guards Mechanized Corps seemed to satisfy themselves with launching random artillery and mortar fire, directed primarily at the town of Kistur. No infantry attacks were reported, but Soviet reconnaissance patrols were especially active that night all along the *HKL*. To the Hungarians at least, the tactical situation appeared to be well in hand, although throughout the night Soviet troops south of Ipolysag could be heard singing while they were engaged in some sort of construction activity.[13] However, Lt.Gen. Volkov had not given up, but had determined that "a maneuver was necessary." Ipolysag appeared to be well defended, as the 18th Guards Mechanized Brigade could attest after it had attempted to feel out its defenses earlier that day. A further tank attack out of Homok also appeared to stand little chance of success, now that the Germans had emplaced at least two batteries of heavy 88mm *Flak* on the flatlands west of the town. The only direction of attack that seemed to offer much promise was one that led through the mountains in the south, which meant that once again, the 31st Guards Mechanized Brigade would become the main effort for the following day.[14]

While the fighting was still ongoing, by noon on 13 December, *Div.Gr. Rintelen* had assumed overall control of the Ipolysag defensive sector from Zádor's *2. Pz.Div.*, which was then immediately subordinated to the incoming German commander. The field replacement battalion from the *357. Inf.Div.*, intended as *Gen.Maj.* Rintelen's reserve under the leadership of a *Hptm.* Otto Hafner, was marching up from its rest area at Neuhäusel and was expected to arrive by the morning of 15 December at the latest. This battalion was the only remaining infantry element of his division under his control, and Rintelen intended to use it to reinforce the defenses at Ipolysag if needed.[15]

The Dirlewanger Brigade, less its two battalions in the south fighting under *K.Gr. Grosse*, was immediately switched from Hungarian control and directly subordinated to Rintelen's command. The remnant of Rintelen's division positioned along the Danube (artillery, engineers, support troops etc.) and its attached Hungarian troops would remain where they were and continue to operate under the title *Div.Gr. 357* to distinguish it from *Div.Gr. Rintelen*.[16] Nearly all of its remaining infantry, some 332 men in all (not including the headquarters of its two infantry regiments and *Feld-Ers.Btl. 357*), had already been incorporated into the defensive lines north of Budapest commanded by the *IX. SS-Gebirgs Korps* (*Geb.Korps*) and few of them would survive the ensuing siege if left behind.

Of all of the available general officers within *6. Armee/A.Gr. Fretter-Pico, Gen. Maj.* Josef "Jupp" Rintelen was a logical choice to take command of the Ipolysag defensive effort. Not only was he effectively out of a job at the moment, but he possessed the skills, knowledge, and ability to lead and coordinate the efforts of a hastily organized, polyglot force consisting of Hungarian forces and German *Heer*, *Luftwaffe*, and *Waffen-SS* units. In comparing the two men, Rintelen and Dirlewanger could not have been more different from one another. The only similarity they shared in common was their mutual service in the Kaiser's army during World War I, where both had distinguished themselves in action. After the war, both had forged radically different career paths.

Born on 7 March 1897 in the town of Esch-Elsdorf to middle-class parents, Rintelen volunteered for service in 1915 and by 1918 had been promoted to *Leutnant* in the *Pionier Korps*. After a brief two-year period of service in the *Reichswehr*, he transferred to the *Polizei* in 1920, where he was to serve for the next 15 years, attaining the rank of *Hauptmann der Polizei*. In July 1935, he was seconded to the new *Wehrmacht-Heer* as a *Hauptmann* and within three months had been given command of an infantry company. During the invasion of Poland, the now-*Major* Rintelen commanded *I. Btl./Inf.Rgt. 478*, where he earned the Clasp to his World War I-era Iron Cross, Second Class. From that point onward, a rapid succession of promotions, awards, and leadership positions followed.[17]

By June 1941, he had been promoted to *Oberst* and appointed as commander of *Inf.Rgt. 222* in time to lead it during the opening stages of Operation *Barbarossa*. Medically sidelined in May 1942 due to an inflammation of the sciatic nerve, he returned to the Eastern Front in September 1942 to lead *Inf.Rgt. 931*. Two months later, after a relapse of his sciatica, he was transferred to Denmark, where he took command of *Gren.Rgt. 713*, a unit that he was to lead for the next year-and-a-half. Fully recovered by the spring of 1944, he attended the division commander's course at the Hirschberg training area in Silesia. After successfully completing this course, he was transferred to the Eastern Front, where he was temporarily assigned as the deputy commander of the *131. Inf.Div.*, then holding a defensive sector in *H.Gr. Mitte*. After three months in this billet, he was appointed acting commander of the *253. Inf.Div.* for three weeks during the critical month of July 1944. This experience prepared him for his formal assignment as commander of the *357. Inf. Div.* on 12 September 1944.

Between that point and 13 December 1944, he had ably led his division during the retreat to the Beskids Mountains in Slovakia, the suppression of the Slovak Uprising from September–October 1944, and the battle of Dukla Pass, where his division played a key role in stemming the Soviet offensive. On 18 November 1944, his division, having disbanded its *Gren.Rgt. 944* in Slovakia and distributed its remaining men among the other two infantry regiments, was transferred to Hungary to provide badly needed infantry strength to *H.Gr. Süd*. Occupying a key defensive position at Hatvan while serving under the *IV. Pz.Korps*, his division, outnumbered by 10 to one, was smashed by Cavalry-Mechanized Group Pliyev on 5 December. It was then forced to withdraw across the Danube at Waitzen, where his much-depleted force was assigned the mission of securing Szentendre Island on 7 December.

Throughout this challenging period as division commander, Rintelen had remained steadfast and calm, leading his battered formation through one crisis after another. His efficiency reports bore out these personality traits and were consistently positive. A typical example was the one written by *Gen.d.Pz.Tr.* Ulrich Kleemann, the commander of the *IV. Pz.Korps*, in March 1945. Kleeman wrote: "[Rintelen is an] agile, energetic personality … [and an] experienced troop practitioner. [He is a] proven division commander who leads his division well and safely. He fills his position very satisfactorily." He concluded with a very positive final recommendation, in which he stated that Rintelen had "Unrestricted suitability for division commander. Leave in [his] current position."[18]

Rintelen's bravery was never in question, as borne out by his numerous decorations. By 12 December 1944, he had already been awarded the Knight's Cross for the leadership of his regiment during the Western campaign in 1940, and was recommended for the German Cross in Gold for his leadership in Hungary (which was awarded in February 1945). He also received the Clasps to both classes of the Iron Cross, the Gold Wound Badge for serious injuries sustained in combat in Russia, and the Eastern Front Medal. A better officer with the right qualities could not have been found to defend the Ipolysag Gap—one who was personally brave, tactically proficient, loyal, and optimistic.

From the remnant of his division, all he would be bringing with him would be his divisional staff and headquarters company (approximately 100 men), one or two artillery batteries, most of the division's signal battalion, his division *Tross* (medical, supply, and transportation units), and two or three heavy antitank guns from *Pz.Jäg. Abt. 357*. The only appreciable infantry force that would accompany *Div.Gr. Rintelen* to its new assignment would be the aforementioned *Feld-Ers.Btl. 357* once it had completed its brief *Auffrischung* process.[19] To rebuild the division itself, over 6,000 replacements would be needed, but this would not occur until mid-January 1945.[20]

Still, this represented a considerable augmentation of the strength of German and Hungarian defenses in Ipolysag area, especially given Rintelen's leadership ability. Due to the confusion that ensued over the next several days, the portion of *Div.Gr. 357* occupying Szentendre Island was soon disbanded entirely and its troops, mostly Hungarians by this point, were parceled out among other units of the *IX. SS-Geb. Korps*. Any remaining elements of the division, including the framework of one of its remaining regimental headquarters, were to rejoin the division within the next two weeks.[21] Shortly thereafter, the terms *Div.Gr. Rintelen* and *Div.Gr. 357* were used interchangeably, both meaning the same tactical entity.

Rintelen's challenge, as a newly appointed commander over a diverse grouping of forces, was to forge a cohesive, effective defense in a very short amount of time. His first task was to gain situational awareness. Within the next 24 hours, he had to obtain an immediate understanding of a number of essential elements of information. For instance, where was the main defense line? Where were his units located? What was the *Kampfstärke* of all of his units? How many antitank guns did his force possess? Did it have any armor? What was the *Stimmung* (morale) of his troops? Where was the enemy? Who were his subordinate commanders? For starters, he needed to quickly become acquainted with *Oberst* Zádor, *Oberstltn.* Grosse, and

Oberführer Dirlewanger. The first two officers at least would have had an idea of the situation, but Dirlewanger most likely was just as unaware of the situation as Rintelen, having just arrived in the area himself. These questions, as well as many others, would have been in the forefront of Rintelen's mind as he grappled with the magnitude of what he was expected to accomplish.

His headquarters troops wasted no time in establishing Rintelen's new command post alongside that of the Hungarian *2. Pz.Div.* in Vámosmikola, but it would take a day at least to move all of its equipment from Szentendre Island across the Szentendre Danube (the western branch of the Danube) to the new location. Until his *Nachrichten* battalion could wire in his headquarters, he would temporarily have to use the communications suite operated by *Maj.* von Gossla's *D.V.K. 149.*

Shortly after he arrived, Rintelen set about having a first-hand look at the subordinate elements of his new command by traveling by staff car to their various positions along the front line, ranging from the towns of Kismaros along the Danube in the south to Palást in the north. During his first or second day in command, Rintelen would most likely have met with Dirlewanger in his headquarters in Palást at least once, though there is no record of him having done so.[22]

It was not long before Rintelen's superior, *Gen.d.Art.* Fretter-Pico, began issuing detailed tactical guidance. The first message from him, relayed at 7.43pm through von Gossla's liaison team, stated: "For General Rintelen: Reinforce your antitank defenses on the eastern edge of Ipolysag and the area around Kelénye using heavy *Flak.* Get some infantry in there too."[23] This was probably the first time that Rintelen had ever heard about the latter location; situated on the far-left flank of his new area of operations, the only German force located anywhere near Kelénye was the incoming *III. Btl./SS-St.Rgt. 1* of the Dirlewanger Brigade, which had nothing more than *Panzerfausts* to defend against tanks.

How he was to get heavy *Flak* assets there quickly or where he was to get them from was left unstated, but implied in the order was the need to quickly establish liaison with the *IV. Pz.Korps* of *8. Armee/A.Gr. Wöhler,* under which the neighboring *24. Pz.Div.* was fighting. Clearly, Rintelen's new assignment would require a maximum amount of determination, patience, and improvisation, qualities which he had repeatedly proven in the past as a division commander. For his upcoming mission, Josef Rintelen would need to bring all of these qualities to bear, and more.

CHAPTER EIGHT

IX Guards Mechanized Corps Occupies Ipolysag, 14 December 1944

After the heavy fighting of the past three days, for most of the troops of the newly named *Div.Gr. Rintelen* the night of 13/14 December passed relatively quietly. But not for everyone. At 12.30am, the displacement of *Ustuf.* Polack's *III. Btl./SS-St.Rgt. 1* from its forward position at Ipoly-Szecsenke in order to occupy *Margarethestellung* positions to its rear south and west of Kelénye took place without a hitch; Dirlewanger, or perhaps Rintelen himself, had determined that without any antitank weapons, the battalion was too exposed in this forward position and could not be supported if attacked. Rather, a safer, more defensible position on the southern outskirts of Kelénye was deemed more appropriate by the high command, although the troops would be occupying partially dug positions running through open terrain. After finding habitable dwellings to occupy in Ipoly-Szecsenke that provided shelter from the cold and rain, the state of troop morale within Siegfried Polack's *III. Bataillon* must have sunk to a new low when they received the order to move.

Undoubtedly, *H.Gr. Süd* would be satisfied by the news of this move because it would mark the first time that this previously unmanned portion of the *Margarethestellung* north of the Ipoly River would be occupied by German troops before the Red Army arrived. The move of Polack's battalion may have also been prompted by the headquarters of the neighboring *24. Pz.Div.*, which was understandably interested in what was occurring on its far-right flank, where it was supposed to maintain physical contact with the Dirlewanger Brigade, *6. Armee/A.Gr. Fretter-Pico*'s northernmost unit. This division had expressed its concerns the previous day, when it sent a radio message via its higher headquarters, the *IV. Pz.Korps*, to Fretter-Pico's staff, stating: "Our own security line was pushed back towards the western edge of [the villages of] Inam and Ipoly-Nyep. Along the road [between] Ipoly-Nagyfalu and Palást there are no security [forces] to be seen. What [unit] is employed southwest of Palást?"[1]

Perhaps the battalion's movement had been influenced by this message, or it could have also been ordered to pull back because Dirlewanger (or Polack) realized that establishing a security line at Ipoly-Szecsenke was too impractical or dangerous since it placed the battalion in an exposed and unsupportable position. Regardless of the reason, Polack's *III. Bataillon* pulled back to the north and occupied Kelénye and the adjacent section of the *Margarethestellung*. Presumably, the *SS* commander would have established contact with Nostitz-Wallwitz's *panzer* division. In the hours since their move, Polack's troops reported no contact or sighting of the enemy, but news travelled slowly when it was being carried by runner or even by motorcycle messengers.

On 14 December, temperatures in the Ipoly River valley hovered consistently around 40 degrees Fahrenheit (5 degrees Celsius) and were below freezing in the Börszeny Mountains, where the inadequately clothed troops from the two *SS* battalions shivered in their soggy uniforms. The *H.Gr. Süd* meteorologist recorded the skies as being partially overcast, with low-lying fog expected in the afternoon. The intermittent rain of the past week had caused the Ipoly River to rise to near flood-levels, overtopping its banks at several locations. The soggy ground inhibited cross-country movement by wheeled vehicles, and even tracked vehicles were mostly confined to the roads. It was a miserable place to fight a battle. But for the army that held the initiative, its troops at least could be comforted by the fact that they were winning—for the opposite side, there was no such succor, only the prospect of more death and suffering. Unless, of course, one could surrender before the fighting started—which is exactly what the politicals of *III. Btl./SS-St.Rgt. 2* intended to do at the first opportunity.

One event that was to shortly have unintended consequences was the planned relief-in-place of *Rittmeister* Zischler's *II. Btl./Pz.Gr.Rgt. 26* by the Dirlewanger Brigade. In the original plan, this was to have taken place on the afternoon of 14 December at the earliest and no later than noon on 15 December at the latest, which would have provided ample time for the incoming battalion from the Dirlewanger Brigade to carry out a thorough assumption of responsibility for the defense of Ipolysag, including tasks such as familiarizing with the terrain, knowing the location of the enemy, emplacement of obstacles, fields of fire, and so forth. To put it succinctly, this crucial operation did not happen as intended, the failure to carry it out successfully setting in motion a series of cascading effects that was to influence the outcome of the ensuing battle (see Map 3).

The first leader who realized that the original plan was beginning to go off the rails was Oskar Dirlewanger himself; when the rest of the Dirlewanger Brigade began to deploy on 13 December, he had designated Steinhauer's *II. Btl./SS-St.Rgt. 1* as the unit to replace the *Panzergrenadier* battalion defending Ipolysag. He had already notified *6. Armee/A.Gr. Fretter-Pico* that unless provided with motor transport, this battalion could not possibly arrive until some point on 15 December. As mentioned in the previous chapter, at the last minute enough trucks had been found to pick up Steinhauer and his troops while they were halfway to their destination and deliver them to the designated assembly area at Kistompa by 10am on 14 December.

From there, they would have to march to Ipolysag on foot, a further distance of 7.5 kilometers, which would take two hours. Realistically speaking, the earliest the battalion could reach Ipolysag would be noon on 14 December, and then five or six more hours at a minimum would be needed to carry out a relief-in-place of the departing battalion. Steinhauer would need at least that amount of time to position his four companies, lay field telephone cable, and integrate his defenses with that of the two companies (*7. and 8. Kp./SS-St.Rgt. 2*) of *K.Gr. Ruhsam* occupying Hill 227. *Obersturmbannführer* Buchmann, who had assumed responsibility for defending the area north of the Ipoly River on 13 December with his regiment and attached troops, had estimated that a proper relief-in-place could be completed at some point during the evening of 14/15 December. Once this was completed, *K.Gr. Ruhsam* atop Hill 227 would become the regiment's reserve force, after being relieved themselves by one of Steinhauer's companies.

But neither Buchmann nor Steinhauer would get that much time. Ever since Zischler's battalion had been tasked to defend Ipolysag on 9 December, the commander of its parent unit had been agitating for its release so it could reinforce the rest of *Pz.Gren.Rgt. 26* fighting at Szécsény. Until 13 December, *Oberst* Zádor, with the backing of *6. Armee/A.Gr. Fretter-Pico*, had successfully been able to resist *Gen. Maj.* von Nostitz-Wallwitz's entreaties, mainly because there was nothing available to replace it with. That all changed at 2am on 14 December, when an order relayed by the Hungarian *2. Pz.Div.* arrived at Buchmann's command post in Kistur stating that *II. Btl./Pz.Gren.Rgt 26* was to be released to its parent division immediately.

Buchmann, realizing the impossibility of conducting any sort of comprehensive relief-in-place at that moment because Steinhauer's battalion had not yet arrived, responded via the Hungarian liaison officer at Dirlewanger's headquarters. In his reply, he listed his reasons why releasing the battalion at this time was impractical:

1. An enemy attack was imminent, and only a body of troops already familiar with the defensive sector would be able to fend off this attack with a chance of success, not a unit that was newly arriving.
2. A suitable body of troops to defend against an enemy attack would only become available the next night (with the arrival of the *II. Btl./SS-St.Rgt. 1*) [the night of 14/15 December].
3. A temporary occupation of Ipolysag was only possible if he employed insufficient forces [the Regiment's *Pionier* Platoon] but this could not be justified due to the enemy situation, since neither a suitable command staff nor signal equipment, nor sufficiently heavy weapons, nor sufficient infantry fighting force were available for this platoon to cover the defensive sector.
4. It was already so late that it was no longer possible to conduct a relief in place in the dark.[2]

The Hungarian liaison officer agreed with his reasoning, and seconded Buchmann's message by informing *K.Gr. Rintelen* via the Hungarian *2. Pz.Div.* that a relief would not be possible before the evening of 14 December.[3] Shortly thereafter, Dirlewanger received an unambiguous direct order to replace Zischler's battalion during the night of 13/14 December, regardless of the reasons for not doing so, following an order from the next higher command level (*Div. Gr. Rintelen*). Passing on the order to Buchmann without comment, Dirlewanger probably was not fully aware of the gravity of the situation.

Obersturmbannführer Buchmann therefore had no choice but to carry out the order. Acting quickly, he ordered that the Ipolysag sector be taken over by the commander of the *8. Kp./SS-St.Rgt. 2, Hptm.* Ruhsam, who would move some of his heavy weapons into the town, and that the infantry forces of *II. Btl./Pz. Gren. Rgt. 26* be temporarily replaced by the *Pionierzug* attached to his regiment until the arrival of Steinhauer's battalion. Thus, the relief-in-place had to be carried out hastily in the darkness and under extreme time pressure. With this action, the defense of Ipolysag was temporarily entrusted to a single combat engineer platoon of 60 men with three light machine guns but no heavy weapons, whereas a heavily armed *panzergrenadier* battalion had defended the town only a few hours before.[4] With only 60 men, the most that the platoon leader could do was to set up a thin outpost line outside of the town to warn of any approaching enemy.[5]

Buchmann (and by extension, Dirlewanger) must have taken comfort in the belief that the danger of such a risky move was minimal, since Zischler's troops had driven back a large Soviet force on 13 December after inflicting heavy losses, and the Soviets therefore should not have been eager for a repeat assault. Buchmann must also had evidently believed that once the *Pionierzug* had been augmented by some of Ruhsam's infantry heavy weapons (heavy machine guns, mortars, and antitank *Panzerschreck*), it would be enough to control the situation until Steinhauer arrived with his 800 men by noon. Although *Ostuf.* Meyer's *I. Btl./SS-St.Rgt. 1* was only a few kilometers away, the Soviet incursion of the previous day must have been enough to convince Buchmann to keep them in place, as well as the bulk of *K. Gr. Ruhsam* atop Hill 227. It is unknown whether Dirlewanger visited Buchmann at all on 14 December; the available evidence indicates that he probably had only a vague understanding of the overall situation.

Other than the previously mentioned "singing and conspicuously loud manner" displayed by Soviet troops at the bridging site at Homok "indicating the issue of alcohol" that night, German observers atop Hill 227 reported that the enemy "seemed more industrious than usual." In addition to these indicators, the sound of tank engines being turned over could be heard in the distance, but there were other indications that the Soviets were preparing to attack.

Several kilometers to the east, *K. Gr. Ruhsam*'s observers could hear the sounds of "very heavy traffic by tracked vehicles and trucks" along the road from Ipolyhidvég to Ipolysag, evidently moving along the north bank of the river.[6] Apparently, they had removed all of the land mines left behind by *1. Kp./Bau-Pio.Btl. 144* that were supposed to render the road impassable. As these reports began to filter in to his command post in Kistur, *Ostubaf.* Buchmann and *Hptm.* Ruhsam atop Hill 227 must have felt more than a little amount of trepidation; understandably, they both probably began to fear that Steinhauer and his battalion might not arrive in time.

So, as *II. Btl./Pz.Gren.Rgt 26* began to pull out, the combat engineer platoon of Buchmann's *SS-St.Rgt. 2* took over from them, position by position. Over the period of several hours in complete darkness, *Rittmeister* Zischler's troops loaded up their equipment, hitched their infantry howitzers and antitank guns to their prime movers, and drove away as quietly and surreptitiously as they could. Still, they could not conceal the sounds of their half-tracks and trucks driving away—it would have been impossible for anyone not to hear it. Shortly before the sun rose, the 60 *Pioniere* must have contemplated the silence in the now nearly empty town and wondered how long it would take for the promised heavy weapons to be hauled down from Hill 227 a kilometer away and put into position. They had no direct telephone connection with the headquarters of *SS-St.Rgt. 2* or *K.Gr. Ruhsam*, only runners. As far as they were concerned, the arrival of Ruhsam's heavy weapons could not happen quickly enough.

Unlike that experienced by most of the German and Hungarian troops (with the exception of the troops occupying Ipolysag), the night had not been a quiet one for the Red Army's IX Guards Mechanized Corps—rain or shine, the corps commander had decided to exercise his maneuver option, and wasted no time in devising a plan to overcome his enemies' defenses and take Ipolysag. Lieutenant General Volkov's plan was as simple as it was straightforward. North of the river, the 18th Guards Mechanized Brigade, having been repulsed the previous day, would renew its assault against Ipolysag from the east. The 30th Guards Mechanized Brigade, previously kept in reserve, would launch an attack through the woods in the south, orienting on Bernecebaráti and Kémence.

The main effort of the attack would be made by Col. Seleznev's 31st Guards Mechanized Brigade, which would move the bulk of its forces through Homok and into the mountains via Kinszky Manor, then attack towards the northwest, cross the Ipoly River, and hook around Ipolysag, attacking it from the west and north while avoiding the antitank gun barrier around Pereszlény (Preselány). This brigade had begun moving into its attack positions since midnight. The 46th Guards Tank Brigade would now become the corps reserve. It was given a "be prepared to" mission to exploit any breakthrough once it occurred, but would initially be positioned behind the 18th Guards Mechanized Brigade in the valley.[7]

The men of Lt.Gen. Volkov's four brigades had been preparing all night for the early morning attack. It had been the engineers attached to the 31st Guards Mechanized Brigade whose singing and construction noises had echoed south of Ipolysag throughout the evening as they prepared a makeshift ferry over the Ipoly at Homok. Damaged roads and bridges had to be repaired or constructed anew; new approach routes scouted through the mountains; fuel and ammunition brought forward and delivered; and artillery and mortars laid in on their designated targets. Delays in moving into its assembly areas on the eastern edge of the Börszeny Mountains and German actions would force the attack by the 30th Guards Mechanized Brigade, under Colonel M. V. Shutov, to be delayed until the morning of the following day; this delay would actually work to Volkov's benefit, as will be seen.

Surprisingly, the first blow was struck that day by *Div.Gr. Rintelen*. At 6.20am, a German artillery observer team atop Mt. Kámar on the *Divisions-Gruppe*'s right flank spotted a column of over 200 enemy horse-drawn vehicles moving northeast from Waitzen along the road between the towns of Borsosberény and Diósjeno, 4 kilometers away. Though at nearly the maximum range for the supporting 105mm howitzer battery, the observation team immediately called in artillery fire on the lucrative target. Target effects were immediate. The column, most likely hauling supplies for Soviet troops fighting in the Ipoly valley, scattered after losing numerous soldiers, wagons, and horses. This drew an immediate response—within an hour after the fire mission concluded, an estimated two or three Soviet rifle companies from the 30th Guards Mechanized Brigade attacked and pushed the Germans off Hill 662, until they were finally able to re-establish the *HKL* along Hill 446 a kilometer to the west.[8] The destruction of the Soviet supply column was to prove to be *Div. Gr. Rintelen*'s only good news of the day.

At roughly the same time that *Div.Gr. Rintelen*'s artillery was savaging the supply column, the 2nd Motorized Infantry Battalion of the 31st Guards Mechanized Brigade began moving west on foot from its assembly area in the hills a few hundred meters north of Kinszky Manor. Avoiding detection, the battalion followed the eastern bank of Kinszky creek for several hundred meters before its veered north towards the destroyed Ipoly River railroad bridge west of Ipolysag, a mere 500 meters east of the German *Flak* batteries positioned in Pereszlény.

Having forded the river, the battalion, under the command of Maj. Kopaev, began moving stealthily to the northeast, then east, fording two streams to get into the rear of the German troops defending Ipolysag. Shortly afterwards, the brigade's 3rd Battalion departed, following the same route used by the 2nd Battalion. Before the sun had risen, both battalions had occupied the fork in the road north of Ipolysag and moved into assault positions west of Ipolysag. So far, they had not been spotted, nor had they met any resistance.[9] From their new position, the two battalions were able to observe and hear any activity in the town. The sounds of departing wheeled and tracked vehicles from Zischler's battalion would have already dwindled in the distance. It was now deathly quiet.

Meanwhile, the sappers of the 31st Guards Mechanized Brigade had put the finishing touches to their makeshift bridge at Ipolyhidvég, making it strong enough to support tanks. The 83rd Guards Tank Regiment of the 18th Guards Mechanized Brigade, which had been sitting idle for the past three days, crossed the bridge at dawn to the north bank and rushed to rejoin the two motorized infantry battalions that had crossed the day before. With one battalion left behind on Hill 151 to block any counterattack from the Kelénye area, Col. Ovcharov prepared to attack Ipolysag from the east. At this point, the *Luftwaffe* once again made an unexpected appearance, several ground attack aircraft bombing and strafing the bridge at Ipolyhidvég after the tank regiment had already crossed. Having damaged the bridge, the German aircraft departed as quickly as they had arrived. Soviet sappers immediately began repair efforts and by noon the bridge was back in operation.[10] His brigade now assembled, Ovcharov waited for the signal to attack in conjunction with Col. Seleznev's brigade.

At the headquarters of *Div.Gr. Rintelen* in Vámosmikola, the first indications that the Red Army was moving forward were conveyed in a report received at 8am from *K.Gr. Grosse* that stated up to two enemy infantry companies were present in force at Kinszky Manor; in response, *Oberstltn.* Grosse ordered the machine-pistol platoon from the Hungarian *Pz.Rgt. 3* to once again retake the manor. Two hours later, Grosse reported that the enemy had attempted three separate probing attacks along the *HKL* 5 kilometers east of Kémence, which were all repulsed by the Hungarian *IV. Btl./Mot.Inf.Rgt. 3*.[11] So far, the two Dirlewanger battalions deployed east of Bernecebaráti had escaped notice, although the unofficial leadership of the politicals were planning a mass defection at the first suitable opportunity.

The first real indication that a general assault had begun was a report from Dirlewanger's command post stating that an attack against *K.Gr. Ruhsam's* position atop Hill 227 had been underway since 7.30am. After briefly penetrating the German line between Hills 227 and 245, Ruhsam led a counterattack that restored his *Kampfgruppe's* positions. Shortly afterwards, *Ostubaf.* Buchmann directed *Ostuf.* Meyer's *I. Btl./SS-St.Rgt. 1*, occupying a defensive line 4 kilometers east of Kistur, to carry out a supporting attack to secure Ruhsam's left flank. This Meyer did, and by noon that day his battalion had successfully pushed its line forward to the next terrain feature, the mountain encompassing Hills 283–277 that had been occupied by *1. Kp./Bau-Pio.Btl. 144* the previous day. With his troops in place on Mt. Magas and Mt. Somos, Meyer had outflanked the Soviet troops attempting to push *K.Gr. Ruhsam* out of its position. Thus emplaced, Meyer established contact with Polack's neighboring battalion in Kelénye with foot patrols, the first time Polack had physical contact with other troops from his regiment.

The attack against *K.Gr. Ruhsam* was merely the opening move of Volkov's attack. It may have been just a diversion, but whether or not intended as such, it did tie up Ruhsam's forces and drew Meyer's *I. Bataillon* towards the east and away from Ipolysag. Mount Magas could be retaken; but the prime objective of the IX Guards Mechanized Corps' attack had to be taken that day. It began with a deliberate attack that began at noon against Ipolysag by two infantry battalions of the 31st Guards Mechanized Brigade from the northwest. Heavy mortars and the full weight of the corps' self-propelled artillery fired in support. At the same time, at least one rifle battalion from the 18th Guards Mechanized Brigade and the 83rd Guards Tank Regiment attacked Ipolysag from the east.

It was all over in less than two hours. Secured by a mere 60 men of *SS-St.Rgt. 2*'s attached combat engineer platoon, they never stood a chance as the town was rapidly overwhelmed by two or three infantry battalions and a battalion's worth of M4A2 Shermans. Still, the *Pionierzug* attempted a defense, but after losing 24 men killed and wounded (including the platoon leader), the survivors fled towards Hill 227. The heavy machine guns and antitank weapons from *K.Gr. Ruhsam* being carried down the hill to augment the platoon in Ipolysag never made it that far. Attacked earlier that morning, Ruhsam had not yet had time to release the heavy weapons as instructed. Lacking any sort of communication means except runners, Ruhsam was unable to call for artillery or mortar fire to support the combat engineer platoon.

A few of the *SS-Pioniere* were captured, as well as several men from Ruhsam's *Kampfgruppe* who were caught between the town and Hill 227. Although a tiny number of Dirlewanger's troops had deserted by this point—nearly all from the *III. Btl./SS-St.Rgt. 2* in the Börzeny Mountains—this was the first time that a substantial number of his men had fought back and some, such as those in Ruhsam's *Kampfgruppe*, had acquitted themselves satisfactorily.

In the course of interrogating the few POWs they had taken from the Dirlewanger Brigade, Volkov and his staff came away with a very negative impression of their opponent. These unfortunates even merited a mention in the IX Guards Mechanized Corps war diary, which stated the following:

> One phenomenon that deserves attention should be noted here, since it characterizes in some way the state of the German army. The Dirlewanger Brigade operated against the Corps, manned by politically- and criminally-convicted conscripts from the Dachau Concentration Camp and others. There were people here who had been in prison for 10–11 years. A few individual commanders and officers in the brigade were *SS* men. In addition, there were two or three [regular] *SS* men …These prisoners are a vivid testimony to the quality of the "total" replenishment of the German army.[12]

How much this assessment affected the perspective of the Soviet commanders on the scene or at the headquarters of the 6th Guards Tank Army can only be surmised, but the presence of the Dirlewanger Brigade and its material condition would have provided a minor morale boost to the Soviet rank and file—after all, if Hitler's vaunted *Wehrmacht* was forced to resort to using such men in the front line, truly the end of the war could not be far off.

Of greater concern to Dirlewanger and Buchmann was the urgent need to retake Ipolysag, using whatever forces were available, before the enemy had time to fortify it. At 2pm on 14 December, the only units at hand were Meyer's *I. Bataillon* positioned east of the town, Ruhsam's small force on Hill 227, and Steinhauer's newly arrived *II. Btl./SS-St.Rgt. 1*, which began occupying an assembly area around noon several kilometers north of the town after marching from Kistompa. All three of these groups were ordered to immediately retake the town. The resulting counterattack, uncoordinated and without significant artillery support due to the lack of adequate communications equipment to direct their fire, did not get very far.

As bad as the loss of Ipolysag had been, and with Ruhsam's ability to hold his position on Hill 227 in doubt, Meyer realized that his battalion's right flank was vulnerable to envelopment. Soviet troops were also seen preparing to assault his position along the Mt. Magas–Mt. Somos ridgeline. Without consulting Buchmann, Meyer ordered his *I. Btl./SS-St.Rgt. 1* to pull back to its previous position, thus giving up the ground that he and his men had gained. Once again, the ability to observe Soviet troop movements from this commanding height had been lost, but perhaps this could be made good the following day.

Facing an opponent superior in numbers and backed up by at least 18 Soviet tanks as well as well-directed indirect fire, Buchmann's counterattack never stood much of a chance. Dirlewanger's command post later reported to *Div.Gr. Rintelen* that the counterattack had brought the Soviet advance north of Ipolysag to a halt, but there is no evidence to support this claim.[13] Dirlewanger's troops had pulled back before suffering an inordinate number of casualties, but they would soon try to regain the lost ground the following day. Buchmann, in his after-action report describing how Ipolysag was lost, merely stated that "The enemy thus hit the troops at a pronounced moment of weakness that could have been avoided if the relief-in-place had been carried out the next night," as was originally planned.[14]

The assault on Ipolysag was not the only Soviet action taking place north of the Ipoly River on 14 December. That same day, Volkov directed a reconnaissance in force be launched by the 18th Guards Mechanized Brigade towards Kelénye. Using the motorized infantry battalion that had been left behind to secure the brigade's right flank, this force pushed through Ipoly-Szecsenke and reached the southern outskirts of Kelénye before being forced to withdraw by elements of *Ustuf.* Polack's battalion positioned inside that town.

Bombarded by reports indicating enemy attacks from the south, east, and north, *Gen.Maj.* Rintelen's first full day in command of *Div.Gr. Rintelen* was not turning out to be a good one. His greatest concern was the reported deployment of large numbers of tanks by Volkov's corps. In his radio message to *A.Gr. Fretter-Pico* that evening, Rintelen wrote:

> *Division Rintelen* reports that with the available armor-piercing weapons [at its disposal], a breakthrough of stronger enemy tank forces cannot be prevented. The division has no heavy antitank guns at its disposal. The division requests the supply of an 88mm anti-aircraft battalion or anti-tank battalion in the Gyerk-Kistur area by the morning of 15 December 1944. If this is not possible, the division requests the deployment of the *3. Bttr./Flak-Abt. 181* in the Gyerk area.[15]

Actually, Rintelen was only partially correct in his assessment of available antitank assets. Although Zischler's *Panzergrenadier* battalion had taken their two heavy antitank guns with it when it pulled out of Ipolysag, *Div.Gr. Rintelen* still possessed nine 88mm *Flak* and two Hungarian 80mm antiaircraft guns. However, the 88s were directly controlled by the *Luftwaffe* and were not under Rintelen's command, hence his request that it be directly subordinated to him. There was little else available to stop tanks, except for hand-held weapons such as the *Panzerfaust* and *Panzerschreck*.

Antitank mines were not available apparently and the two German assault guns that had been operating under the control of the Hungarians had either been knocked out or were inoperational.

Josef Rintelen was fully aware of the significance of Ipolysag's loss and the consequences if it remained in the Red Army's hands. In his daily report submitted that evening, Rintelen stated his intentions for the following day—retake Ipolysag and carry out strong combat patrols along the entire front line. The news was not all bad, though. A number of Soviet troops had been killed while infiltrating through the woods surrounding the Kinszky Manor; the *HKL* in the Börszeny Mountains had held east of Kémence and Bernecebaráti; and Mt. Magas had been retaken and contact established along the far-left wing of his divisional group (he did not know at the time that Meyer had abandoned it). Most important of all, no Soviet tanks had penetrated beyond the Ipolysag Gap. While true, Rintelen and the leadership of *6. Armee/A.Gr. Fretter-Pico* must have known that the events of the day were only a prelude to what would probably happen over the next two or three days.

Rather than doing everything possible to buttress the defenses in the Ipolysag Gap as quickly as possible and assist *Div.Gr. Rintelen* with its mission of retaking Ipolysag, the staff of *6. Armee/A.Gr. Fretter-Pico* seemed to be more concerned with finger-pointing than anything else. Rather than expending their energy in helping Rintelen, the army chief of staff, *Gen.Maj.* Heinz Gaedke, and his *Führungsabteilung* seemed to focus instead on apportioning blame. And that blame disproportionately fell upon the leadership and troops of the Dirlewanger Brigade.

The exact time that the news of Ipolysag's fall reached the headquarters of *6. Armee/A.Gr. Fretter-Pico* cannot be determined precisely, but the army's staff *Ia* probably learned of it by mid-afternoon at the latest. Any report would have had to be relayed by Buchmann's command post to Dirlewanger's in Palást by runner or motorcycle dispatch rider, since Buchmann did not have any tactical radios. Nor had field telephone cable yet been laid, so Dirlewanger might have heard the sounds of heavy fighting before any message reached him. Whether he had himself driven to Kistur to speak to Buchmann is unknown, but he most likely remained where he was in Palást. Having received this information, probably from a series of hand-written messages, Dirlewanger would have then sorted out what was really going on. Once he had gained situational awareness, he would next have contacted *Div.Gr. Rintelen* using the radio set operated by his Hungarian liaison officer, who represented the *6. Armee Nachrichtenführer's* contribution to augmenting the brigade's communications ability.

General der Artillerie Fretter-Pico's personal thoughts about the loss of Ipolysag are not recorded, but he wasted no time in ordering another attempt to retake the town. After outlining a plan, he stated his intent that evening, informing *H.Gr. Süd* that for the following day he would both hold his current *HKL* and clear up the breakthroughs that had taken place that day. Specifically with regard to what

Div.Gr. Rintelen was to do, he informed the army group headquarters: "*Div.Gr. Rintelen* will conduct an attack to retake Ipolysag and thereby hinder any further enemy advances towards the west, in addition it will conduct attacks with limited objectives aimed towards pushing the *HKL* forwards in the Börszeny Mountains." This message was followed a few minutes later by a nearly identical one addressed to *Div.Gr. Rintelen* that directed it to carry out this mission, including additional details such as to "move the *HKL* forward in stages along the road running between Diósjeno, Kémence, and Kinszky Manor towards the northeastern edge of the mountains," a task that Rintelen had planned to do anyway.[16]

Whether or not Fretter-Pico harbored any doubts about the ability of Rintelen and Dirlewanger to master the situation, the reaction of *H.Gr. Süd*'s operations staff are a matter of record. In the daily report entered into the army group's war diary, written that evening several hours after the fall of Ipolysag, the significance of what had happened had finally begun to sink in. That evening, the army group's *Ia, Oberstltn.* Schäfer, wrote the following summary of the event that was the lead paragraph of the first page of the *Tagesmeldung* (daily report): "With the capture of Ipolysag, the enemy [has] reached the gateway to the Upper Hungarian Plain and thus the starting point for the expected concentrated breakthrough attempt of the 6th Guards Tank Army to the west." On the following page, the army group *Ia* or his deputy summarized the action that day as follows:

> In the *Div.Gr. Rintelen* sector: … The enemy, attacking from the southeast [this did not mention the attack from the north and west], took Ipolysag in the early afternoon, despite tough resistance from the town's garrison [60 men!], which had been weakened by the withdrawal of *II Btl./Pz.Gr.Rgt 26*. Since 4 p.m. a counterattack by *II. Btl./SS-Rgt. 1* of the Dirlewanger Brigade from the northwestern direction is in progress. Parts of *I. Btl./SS-Rgt. 1* of the Brigade simultaneously attacked Ipolysag from the east. Another portion of the Brigade attacked from the Felsötur–Palást area using its *I. Btl./* and *III. Btl./SS-Rgt. 1* that reached the *Margarethestellung* on the southeastern edge of Kelénye and the area southwest of it.[17]

Several pages later, in the analysis (*Erwägungen, Entschlüsse, und Befehle*; considerations, decisions, and orders) portion of the war diary entry concerning the day's events, *Oberstltn.* Schäfer recorded his own interpretation of *6. Armee/A.Gr. Fretter-Pico*'s performance that day. The first topic of discussion with that army's *Ia, Oberstltn.* Marcks, was its primary mission, that of executing Operation *Spätlese*, which was already behind schedule. But the main topic was the loss of Ipolysag that morning due to Volkov's surprise attack. In the exchange of views Schäfer entered into the official record, he wasted no time in ascribing blame for the disaster, even before Dirlewanger himself probably knew what had happened, never mind who or what lay at fault. In the war diary, Schäfer wrote:

> The cause of the sudden loss of the city is not yet completely clear, but it can already be said that the withdrawal was not in order. During the night, according to orders, the *II. Btl./Pz.Gr.Rgt 26* of the *24. Pz.Div.* was relieved by forces of the *SS* Dirlewanger Brigade in Ipolysag and returned

to [its own] division. The regimental commander of the *SS* Dirlewanger Brigade [Buchmann] apparently had not deployed an *SS* battalion for this purpose, but had left only a weak security force in place while he had his battalion secure the edge of the forest southeast of the village. The weak security force lost the place against [an attack by a] superior enemy. It is not yet clear whether the withdrawal was carried out so hastily on the orders of the battalion commander.

There were several inaccuracies present in this statement. First, it avoids mentioning who ordered Zischler's battalion to be withdrawn earlier than anticipated. This order could only have been issued by *A.Gr. Fretter-Pico* or *H.Gr. Süd*. Secondly, it states that the *SS* battalion that was supposed to secure the town was deployed at the edge of the forest southeast of the village; however, there is no forest southeast of the village, only the Ipoly River. Perhaps he was referring to Meyer's *I. Btl./SS-St.Rgt. 1*, which was holding ground northeast of the town, or *K.Gr. Ruhsam* atop Hill 227, also to the northeast. Both of these units were decisively engaged with the enemy that day and could not have come to the aid of the *Pionierzug* in Ipolysag without creating large gaps in the newly established *HKL* that could be easily exploited by an opportunistic enemy.

Lastly, Schäfer speculated that Zischler himself may have ordered the hasty withdrawal of his own battalion. Obviously, as mentioned earlier, the Dirlewanger Brigade had received an order from *Div.Gr. Rintelen* through the Hungarian liaison network that Zischler's battalion had to be withdrawn immediately. Rintelen himself had no cause to order this movement, since he was acutely aware of the shortage of the means required to carry out his orders to defend the area; the same reasoning applies to the leadership of *6. Armee/A.Gr. Fretter-Pico*, who also would not have wanted to give up a *Panzergrenadier* battalion so hastily. It could only have been *H.Gr. Süd*'s leadership that ordered this controversial movement in response to *8. Armee/A.Gr. Wöhler*'s urgent request to have it returned.

Oberstleutnant Schäfer then described the current situation and the outline of the plan to retake Ipolysag. The key component of the plan was the Dirlewanger Brigade, which would constitute the main body of the counterattacking force. Despite its losses so far, which were minimal, it was the strongest maneuver element that *Div.Gr. Rintelen* possessed; but there is no indication that Rintelen himself had an accurate understanding of what sort of unit he was actually relying upon to carry out the attack. Schäfer wrote:

> For the recapture of this key point on the northern wing of the army group, three battalions of the *SS* Dirlewanger Brigade have been deployed. The bridges over the Ipoly have been blown up [this was not strictly true]. [The area] southwest of Ipolysag is sealed off by our own *Flak*. Five battalions of the Dirlewanger Brigade are now deployed around Ipolysag.

Schäfer then described how the seizure of the town had changed the dynamic on the battlefield north of the Danube: "The loss of Ipolysag has created a completely new situation, since the enemy can now assemble his tanks there for a thrust into the Upper Hungarian Plain. It is necessary for the army group to place at least one more anti-aircraft battalion there." Schäfer suggested to Marcks that it should immediately move one of its heavy *Flak* batteries positioned elsewhere south of the Danube along the *Margarethestellung* to reinforce *Div. Gr. Rintelen*, but Marcks declared that he could not spare these guns at the moment, lest that *HKL* west of Budapest collapse.

In this interesting exchange, Schäfer wrote in the war diary that in his conversation he had emphasized the point to Marcks that *6. Armee/A. Gr. Fretter-Pico* must take this justifiable risk, since it had become essential to stop the enemy at Ipolysag, otherwise the "entire situation of *H. Gr. Süd* would change for the worse." As a result, *Gen.d.Art.* Fretter-Pico would be compelled to move more of his heavy *Flak* into the *Kampfraum* of *Div. Gr. Rintelen*. After he and his chief of staff, *Gen.Maj.* Grolman, had obtained *Gen. Obst.* Friessner's concurrence, Schäfer notified *Oberstltn.* von Buttlar of the *OKH Führungsabteilung* at 7.05pm and announced *H. Gr. Süd's* intention to retake the city tomorrow by massing all available forces there and using the *Luftwaffe*.[18]

He also submitted the army group's daily situation report to the *OKH* that would be reproduced almost verbatim in the *Tagesbericht* (daily report) of the *OKH* for that day, which described that day's events along the Ipoly River as follows:

> *Div. Gr. Rintelen* repulsed company-strength reconnaissance probes and sealed off enemy breakthroughs south of Ipolysag. In the early afternoon hours, the enemy, attacking from the southeast, was able to seize Ipolysag, despite tough resistance by our own units. Counterattacks from the east and northwest are now in progress.[19]

This was nearly an exact word-for-word repeat of what *H. Gr. Süd* has submitted, without any embellishment. This contrasts with the official *Bericht* (Communique) *des Oberkommando der Wehrmacht* for 14 December, which had been edited by the *OKW*'s propaganda department to make it sound as if the German Armed Forces had everything under control:

> The focal points of the heavy defensive battles in the east continue to be on the fronts in Hungary. On the northern and northeastern part of the arc around Budapest, German grenadiers and *SS* units crushed strong Soviet attacks. Between the Danube bend near Waitzen and the Matra Mountains, enemy pressure continues mainly in a northwesterly and northeasterly direction, but yesterday brought the Soviets only minor local successes.[20]

Admittedly, this information was already over 24 hours old; it would take another day or two before the true consequences of the loss of Ipolysag would be felt at the uppermost levels of the German high command.

Another significant event that evening was the army group's decision to attach the two northernmost battalions of the Dirlewanger Brigade to the *IV. Pz.Korps*, a move that was to occur the following day. These two battalions, Polack's *III. Btl./ SS-St.Rgt. 1* and Stegmann's *I. Btl./SS-St.Rgt. 2* under the control of the headquarters of *SS-St.Rgt. 1*, would be subordinated initially to the *24. Pz.Div.*[21] This, it can be assumed, was a further response to that division's concern about the security of its right flank and the need to maintain physical contact with the neighboring *Div. Gr. Rintelen* by controlling these two battalions, which in any case had only tenuous communications with their own brigade's command post and hence would be slow to respond to any developing situation in the Ipolysag area.

Despite the reverses suffered that afternoon, especially the unexpected loss of Ipolysag, by the end of the day the command and staff of *H. Gr. Süd* can be forgiven for thinking that *Div. Gr. Rintelen* would soon have the situation in hand. After all, the army group's collective brains trust must have reasoned that by skillful employment of his available units—especially the three battalions of the Dirlewanger Brigade augmented by *Feld-Ers. Btl. 357* of his own division, additional Hungarian antitank assets being sent by the *2. Pz. Div.*, and another German artillery battalion—*Gen. Maj.* Rintelen should have had sufficient forces to defeat the enemy and reoccupy the town.

On paper, the plan looked solid. But, paraphrasing the great Prussian military theorist Carl von Clausewitz, the enemy the Germans and Hungarians faced was not an inanimate object, but "a living one that reacts."[22] Or in modern parlance, "the enemy gets a vote." Whether the leadership of *H. Gr. Süd* realized it not, their plan had two fatal weaknesses—it had failed to augment *Div. Gr. Rintelen* with any armored fighting vehicles capable of meeting Soviet tanks on an equal basis (following the assumption that additional antitank guns would be sufficient), and had assumed that Soviet armor would not be able to operate in mountainous terrain. Both of these planning assumptions would soon prove to have been mistaken, creating an opportunity that would be exploited by the IX Guards Mechanized Corps to the fullest extent within the next 24 hours.

CHAPTER NINE

The Battle of Ipolysag, 15 December 1944

So far, the month of December 1944 in Hungary and Slovakia was shaping up to be one of the warmest and wettest on record. Heavy rainfall had in many places turned the Ipoly River and its tributaries into torrents, while overtopping its banks in others. Temperatures had continued to hover slightly above freezing in the valley, while in the mountains on either side sub-zero temperatures had become common. On the night of 14/15 December, a light snowfall was reported in the mountains. For the infantrymen, artillerymen, and pioneers of both sides occupying trenches or firing positions, life was miserable. Mud and dampness were a constant companion, and the inadvisability of lighting a warming fire near the front line made existence a trial of human endurance.

The skies had remained overcast during the middle of the month, and except for occasional and brief patches of sunny weather, German, Hungarian, and Soviet troops seemed to live in perpetual gloom. These were awful conditions in which to fight a major battle, but for both sides, war did not take a holiday in late 1944. Friday, 15 December was no exception—the high that day was forecasted to be only 44 degrees Fahrenheit (7 degrees Celsius), and it would be completely overcast. Off-road movement conditions were still considered to be "bad."

To Lt.Gen. of Tank Troops Volkov, the weather was just another factor to be taken into account when leading his corps—the most it could do was to keep the Red Air Force grounded. This was hardly something he had relied upon during the past week anyway, since most of the Soviet Fifth and Seventeenth Air Armies were busy elsewhere, primarily flying sorties in support of the Third Ukrainian Front in the fighting around Budapest. Conversely, the *Luftwaffe* had been uncommonly active against his forces, inflicting stinging attacks along the valley, in particular at Ipolyhidvég, Hont, and Homok. While inconvenient and occasionally frustrating, the German and Hungarian air attacks from 10–14 December had inflicted mere pinpricks and could generally be driven off by the gunners of the 388th Guards Antiaircraft Artillery Regiment. On 15 December, due to the weather, the hated "black crows" of the *Luftwaffe* would make no appearance at all in the skies over the Ipoly River valley.

What had affected the progress of Volkov's operations the most had been an insufficient amount of artillery support. His organic artillery regiments had only been brought back up to 50 percent of their authorized strength before 8 December. This, combined with the inherent limitations of the types of self-propelled artillery that he did have (Su-76Ms, Su-122s, and JSU-152s), which could not fully elevate to fire like their towed counterparts, meant that the accustomed weight of the artillery's firepower was not there, often when his troops needed it the most. Additionally, his forward elements had frequently outrun the maximum range of their accompanying artillery, forcing them to rely much more heavily on their medium and heavy mortar batteries, which lacked the range and hitting power of the larger-caliber shells. Fortunately for him, by 15 December, Volkov's artillery had caught up with the mechanized brigades and now occupied firing positions well within range of the German and Hungarian positions. Their opponents would soon notice the difference.

The IX Guards Mechanized Corps had been advancing methodically for the past week since it entered the Ipoly River valley. Despite the weakness of the enemy's defense, the terrain, foul weather, and *Luftwaffe* air interdiction had combined to slow its forward progress. On 14 December, the situation changed entirely for the better when the 18th Guards Mechanized Brigade took Ipolysag almost without a fight. Expecting heavy resistance from the *Panzergrenadier* battalion that had inflicted painful losses on 13 December, Col. Ovcharov had heavily weighted his attack the next day with a three-to-one advantage in tanks, artillery, and infantry to overcome what was expected to be a skilled defense. Instead, Ovcharov's troops encountered a 60-man security line of Dirlewanger's *Pioniere*, who were easily swept aside. The German counterattack that followed several hours later had been uncoordinated and was easily repulsed; Ovcharov would ensure that any repeated attempts to eject his men from Ipolysag would be met by a wall of fire.

In addition to the troops occupying Ipolysag and making it into a fortress, Lt.Gen. Volkov had sent two infantry battalions of Col. Seleznev's 31st Guards Mechanized Brigade in an envelopment movement around the town from the west. They remained in their new positions west of the town to prevent any attack from that direction. A bridge at Homok strong enough to allow the tanks of the 31st Guards Mechanized Brigade's 85th Guards Tank Regiment to cross the river had been built during the night of 14/15 December. In addition to enabling the tank regiment's crossing, which quickly took up an assembly area within Ipolysag, this field expedient bridge would allow further reinforcements and supplies for the 18th Guards Mechanized Brigade to cross the Ipoly.[1]

To the south, Seleznev's 3rd Motorized Infantry Battalion would continue to hold Kinszky Manor north of Bernecebaráti and defend Homok. Within Homok itself, the bulk of Lt.Col. B. I. Radko's 84th Guards Tank Regiment of the

30th Guards Mechanized Brigade moved into concealed attack positions. Should the opportunity present itself, this force was to continue pushing to the west and seize the key position of Pereszlény after eliminating the heavy *Flak* batteries emplaced there. South of Homok and to the left of Seleznev's brigade, the vanguard of Col. Shutov's 30th Guards Mechanized Brigade—with one tank company from Radko's regiment—had moved into position 5 kilometers east of Bernecebaráti and was prepared to advance through the mountains towards Kémence. Routes through the forest and mountains had been reconnoitered and marked by his pioneers to determine which ones were passable for tanks. These would soon present a nasty surprise for the men of the two battalions of the Dirlewanger Brigade emplaced there, evidence of Volkov's previous experience commanding a mountain division being put into action.

With the capture of Ipolysag, the IX Guards Mechanized Corps had officially crossed the international border of Hungary and entered the territory of pre-war Czechoslovakia. This seemingly minor accomplishment warranted the release of a communique by *Sovetskoye informatsionnoye byuro*, commonly known as *Sovinformburo* (the Soviet Information Agency), which announced to the world the occupation of the town and the beginning of the liberation of Slovakia by the U.S.S.R.[2] No one knew at the time that the complete liberation of Slovakia would require five more months of hard fighting and the loss of thousands of lives. But for the communist-led Slovakian government in exile, this marked an important milestone in their nation's history.

On the German and Hungarian side, the task laid before them for 15 December seemed straightforward enough. *Generalmajor* Rintelen's mission was to retake Ipolysag and defend his current positions in the mountains between Bernecebaráti and Kémence, while ensuring that he maintained contact with *K. Gr. Lehnert* west of Kismaros along the northern bank of the Danube. To retake Ipolysag and the terrain northeast of Bernecebaráti, Rintelen intended to use two-and-a-half battalions of the Dirlewanger Brigade north of the Ipoly River as his main effort. His secondary effort would be retaking the Kinszky Manor area, a task assigned to a mixed German-Hungarian battlegroup attacking from Bernecebaráti. Artillery support would be provided by a combination of German and Hungarian batteries, approximately 24 guns in all, ranging in size from 76.2mm to 105mm. Two Hungarian batteries of field howitzers would be firing in direct support of the two battalions carrying out the counterattack upon Ipolysag, since the brigade's two batteries of 105mm howitzers had not deployed.[3]

This counterattack on 15 December would be a repeat of the one carried out the day before that had failed to drive the enemy from Ipolysag. Rintelen would personally supervise the attack himself, although where he actually located his forward command post during the battle is still unknown.[4] Once again, this attack would be carried out in a concentric manner, with Steinhauer's *II. Btl./SS-St. Rgt. 1* attacking the town from the area west of Kistur, while the other battalion, Meyer's *I. Btl./SS-St. Rgt. 1*, covered Steinhauer's approach with fire from the area east of Kistur and the northeast of Ipolysag. When Meyer's troops had accomplished this task, they would push to the southeast to retake Mt. Magas and Mt. Somos in conjunction with *1. Kp./Bau-Pio.Btl. 144* and reoccupy the portion of the *Margarethestellung* between those two hills that they had abandoned the previous day. *Kampfgruppe Ruhsam*, with two companies from *II. Btl./SS-St.Rgt. 2* and half of the mixed battalion, would meanwhile remain in its current positions on Hill 227 and defend against any attacks from the southeast, while also supporting Steinhauer's attack with mortar fire.

Approximately 8 kilometers to the east, *Ustuf.* Polack's *III. Btl./SS-Rgt. 1* would continue pushing south and reoccupy all of the *Margarethestellung* between Kelénye and Ipoly-Födemes, while simultaneously linking up with Meyer's battalion on its right flank. The bulk of the antitank gun company from the mixed battalion would continue to block the narrow gap at Gyerk west of Ipolysag. The forces of *K.Gr. Grosse*, including the two SS battalions and the troops of the Hungarian *2. Pz.Div.*, would retake Kinszky Manor and continue to defend their current positions between Bernecebaráti and Kismaros. Once it arrived from its rest area in Neuhäusel that morning, *Feld-Ers.Btl. 357* (two companies with a combined *Kampfstärke* of 250 men) would become Rintelen's reserve force.

Having issued the orders considered sufficient to restore the situation in the Ipoly River valley, the commanders and staffs of *H.Gr. Süd* and *Armeegruppen Fretter-Pico* and *Wöhler* resumed their focus on what were perceived at the time to be the larger, more important battles then underway, including the one north of Szécsény in the *IV. Pz.Korps* sector, the battle on the outskirts of Budapest involving the *IX. SS-Geb. Korps*, and the continuing preparations for Operation *Spätlese*. The commanders of the army group and field armies could perhaps be forgiven for such apparent short-sightedness. Although the Ipolysag Gap was an operationally important terrain feature, and retaking it was paramount, the more immediate concerns of Friessner, Fretter-Pico, and Wöhler were to prevent the Second Ukrainian Front from rolling up *A.Gr. Wöhler*'s front in Slovakia. They were also focused on preventing the Second and Third Ukrainian Fronts from encircling Budapest.

Both *H.Gr. Süd* and *A.Gr. Fretter-Pico* were nearly ready to implement their plan to cut off and destroy the 4th Guards Army, the southern pincer movement of Malinovsky's Third Ukrainian Front south of Lake Balaton, beginning no later than 20 December, marking the second time the date had changed since 17 December. Operation *Spätlese* would involve no fewer than three newly arrived *panzer* divisions (the *3.*, *6.*, and *8. Pz.Div.*) to augment the two already fighting there (the *1.* and *23. Pz.Div.*), three newly equipped *Panzer V* Panther battalions, and one heavy tank battalion.

This force was deemed to be sufficient to annihilate Malinovsky's armored spearhead and his 4th Guards Army between Lakes Balaton and Velencze and re-establish the lines of the old *Margarethestellung* west of Budapest. It seems that the German leadership felt that once they had wiped out the threat south of the Danube, *A.Gr. Fretter-Pico* could redirect these same *panzer* divisions to do the same thing north of the river. In the meantime, Fretter-Pico and Friessner apparently believed that *Div.Gr. Rintelen* would be strong enough to retake Ipolysag and keep Kravchenko's tank army bottled up in the Ipoly River valley.

However, this time the first blows on 15 December were struck by the troops of the 30th Guards Mechanized Brigade, not *Div.Gr. Rintelen*. Infantry of this brigade, led by their commander, Col. Shutov, crossed the mountains during the early morning and launched an attack against Bernecebaráti from the east. A sign that something significant was about to happen was an obscure report early that morning by observers from *K.Gr. Grosse*, stating that Soviet pioneers were removing the antitank barrier erected west of the town of Nagyoroszi using antiaircraft searchlights for illumination.[5] Nagyoroszi lay at the eastern edge of the Börszeny Mountains 15 kilometers away from Kémence, which was also where Shutov had his brigade headquarters. The significance of that report appears to have eluded the *6.Armee/A.Gr. Fretter-Pico* watch officer on duty that morning and nothing more was mentioned about it.

The first indications that a large-scale Soviet attack had begun were reported at dawn when the area northeast of Bernecebaráti held by Ehlers's and Nitzkowski's *SS* battalions was blanketed by artillery fire (see Map 4). Nitzkowski's *III. Bataillon* had evidently been shuffled about and moved into the sector shortly beforehand from an adjacent portion of the main defense line at Csitari Puszta and was now positioned to the left of Ehlers's *II. Bataillon*. The enemy barrage had begun at an awkward time, with Nitzkowski's men still getting settled in. One eyewitness, the platoon leader from *Hstuf.* Harald Momm's *5. Kompanie* and one of the original members of the *Dirlewanger Einheit*, later remembered: "Not only had [these] men all been political prisoners, but the fact that they had only been soldiers for eight weeks raised a lot of doubts for me. Even if they tried, they were no match for the Russians!"

The situation rapidly deteriorated. The eyewitness continued describing the developing situation in his *II. Bataillon* area:

> Soon afterward, the Russian [*sic*] artillery fire increased, then it stopped, and suddenly we heard tanks starting up. The mood became uneasy. I didn't know how we were supposed to hold back the tanks, if it came to that. We didn't even have any [*Panzerfausts*]. The men became more and more unsettled, and I had no idea what I should do, other than urge calm. I walked around between the squads and observed the approach [of the tanks] which didn't lead directly towards us, but to the neighboring *III. Bataillon*. Since blood is thicker than water, I thought "Thank God they're not coming at us!" Suddenly, there was shooting in our area. I tried to make out what was happening there, because there were no Russians in sight yet. Then I saw it. A few men, and then more and more of them, began climbing out of the trenches and running forward through the shot-up barbed wire barriers. What was happening here? Again, there were shots and a few of the running men fell over.[6]

At the same time that this attack was beginning, 20 tanks (later confirmed to have been 22) of the 84th Guards Tank Regiment launched an attack along the highway from Homok to Bernecebaráti. The lead Shermans reached the blown-up bridge at the stream 1.5 kilometers northeast of the town and stopped. From here, they continued firing in support of the infantry attack against the town by a battalion from the 31st Guards Mechanized Brigade from the vantage point of their position on the opposite bank.

Meanwhile, a company-sized infantry force from the brigade advanced to the northwest towards Pereszlény, but was repulsed by the defending German troops positioned there. While engaging targets on the northern edge of Bernecebaráti, the tank battalion inadvertently exposed itself to flanking fire by the two batteries of 88mm *Flak* positioned along the high ground stretching from Pereszlény to the northwest outskirts of the former locality. After enduring accurate, withering fire that quickly destroyed eight (initially reported as five) of their number, the remaining tanks withdrew into Homok at 9.50am.[7] The Soviet infantry battalion, now without tank support and exposed to enemy fire, had no choice but to fall back to its previous positions in the hills around Kinszky Manor.

To the immediate south, things were going far better for the 30th Guards Mechanized Brigade. Here, the main body of Shutov's brigade began to carry out their assault against the line held by the two SS battalions of the Dirlewanger Brigade. By this point, Ehlers's and Nitzkowski's troops had been deployed in the mountains east of Bernecebaráti for five days and had received little logistical support. Dozens had deserted by this point, and the rest were freezing and demoralized. The objective of the Soviet attack that morning was the Dirlewanger battalion's defense line, a roughly U-shaped perimeter beginning at Görbe-Hagy in the northwest and running southeast for a kilometer to Hill 363, encompassing the settlement of Csitari-Puszta, the previous scene of heavy fighting and now defended by Ehlers's battalion. At Hill 363, the line bent to the west, where the Dirlewanger positions connected with those of a construction battalion from *K.Gr. Grosse.*

The assault was heralded by an increasingly heavy artillery barrage upon both SS battalions. As mentioned earlier, this had prompted a few men in the *II. Btl./ SS-St.Rgt. 2* on the right flank to begin fleeing towards the approaching Soviet troops. When a dozen or so tanks appeared, seemingly out of the forest where tanks were not supposed to be, chaos ensued. The anonymous *Oberscharführer* of the *5. Kompanie* continued:

> When I turned back around [after another platoon started deserting] I had a gun pointed in my chest and one of my men asked me "Are you coming or are you staying? We're going over to the Russians!" I said, "Hey, don't pull this crap! What are you doing?" He took my gun from me and said "Give thanks to your God and piss off!" Then the men from my platoon also climbed over the edge of the trench, threw their weapons and gear away after a few meters, and ran towards the Russian lines. I stared at the scene in stunned disbelief. I looked around.

The positions were practically empty. Two squad leaders looked as dumbfounded as I was. One [of them] was missing. Did he defect too?[8]

Afterwards, there was speculation that some of the Dirlewanger deserters who had gone over to the Red Army during the past several days had led the forward assault units through the forest and showed them the trails that could be navigated by tanks, though there is no direct evidence supporting this assertion. They had, however, certainly divulged this information when interrogated in the hours after their capture, according to survivors of the mass defection.[9]

At any rate, after being worked over by artillery and mortar fire, the appearance of a company's worth of Soviet tanks on the hilltop, along with hundreds of charging riflemen shouting "Urrah!" at the top of their lungs, was the final ingredient needed to make the disaster complete. Any remaining members of the battalions of Ehlers and Nitzkowski who had been entertaining thoughts about the wisdom of deserting to the enemy made their decisions on the spot—it was now or never. Dozens of men along the trench line, especially in the *III. Bataillon* sector, began throwing away their weapons and leaving their positions *en masse*. Squad leaders and platoon commanders who attempted to stop them were ignored, disarmed, or urged to come along with them. A few of the regular SS men who fired at the deserters were shot and killed by their own men. The anonymous NCO continued:

A few men who didn't want to go over to the Russians were still there too and looked at us quizzically. "Go look for weapons together," I ordered, and then I tried to sort out the situation. Then I went over to [company commander] Momm. He still didn't quite realize what had just happened. "*Rittmeister*" [Cavalry Captain], I said, "the company has defected and not just ours, but possibly the entire battalion!" "What did you say?" he screamed, and ran out of the command post. Just then, the enemy tanks had made it to the positions of our *III. Bataillon*, to our left. We saw the backs of the men running away. "Oh God," Momm said.[10]

The *III. Bataillon* had seemingly disappeared. Having the largest number of politicals within its ranks, it suffered the most defections of any other element of the Dirlewanger Brigade. The organized resistance cells of the "Antifascists in SS Uniform," led by a core of veteran communists like Richard Doering and Willy Fenger, they had finally carried out their carefully laid plans for staging a mass defection, hatched so many months before in the Sachsenhausen and Dachau *KL* and refined in the days after they had arrived in the Börszeny Mountains.

None of them fired their weapons at the approaching brown-clad figures while they waited for the artillery fire to pass over them. Then, the battalion's dramatic mass defection unfolded in front of the surprised Soviet troops and SS overseers. According to one of the participants in this act, the following took place in the *III. Bataillon* sector that morning:

Through our ranks resounded these anxious and joyful shouts: "The Russians are coming!" Despite the repeated order of the company commander to open fire on the attacking soldiers, we did not fire a single shot. Each of us comrades, lying under cover, slightly raised our heads and looked at one another. We no longer cared about the shouting of the company commander, who, in a rage, was running around the trench with a pistol in his hand, threatening to shoot each of us. Without giving any special sign or command, we all remained in our places. If one of our comrades nevertheless looked like he was going to flee to the rear, he was pulled to the ground by his comrades. The distance between us and the [Red Army] soldiers approaching in a firing line became closer and closer. Fortunately, the tanks had rolled past us on one side ... In order not to remain too long in this position, I straightened up along with some of my other comrades, threw away our weapons high in the air, and raised our hands. Several [Soviet] officers and soldiers approached us in loose formation. Their weapons were pointed threateningly at us ... But no shots were fired. Suddenly the tension in me was released, because all our other comrades had followed our example and had surrendered as well.[11]

Their leaders were powerless to stop them. Within minutes, most of the *9.* and *12. Kompanien* had run into the arms of the surprised Soviets. A few of defectors were shot down by *SS* machine-gun fire as they ran away, while others lay wounded in their trenches and foxholes and were unable to make a break for freedom. Disgraced *Hptm.* Paul Langelotz, the supposed "hero" of two days before, led his entire *10. Kompanie* from their positions and surrendered to their approaching "brethren." Of the two battalion commanders, Ehlers and Nitzkowski, nothing was seen nor heard—both had remained behind in Bernecebaráti at their battalion command posts and most likely only had a vague sense of the magnitude of the unfolding disaster based on what had been relayed via field telephones.

By 12.36pm, the two battalions from the 30th Guards Mechanized Brigade had rolled over the German trenches along the plateau and continued heading downhill towards the west, focused on their objective of Bernecebaráti, while the tank company remained atop the hill. The surviving company commanders of the *III. Bataillon* attempted to rally their men and block the onrushing advance, but it was a forlorn hope. Fortunately for the two companies of the *II. Battalion* (the *5.* and *6.*), they were not in the direct path of the tank attack and were positioned on the high ground around the Csitari-Puszta settlement. The anonymous *SS-Oberscharführer* added:

[Former *Oberst*] Momm ... ordered me to sort out how many men had deserted from our company. We had about 35 to 40 men left from over 150. To our left, we heard repeated shooting from the tanks. There was no resistance. Then came the order: "Move out!" We took all of the weapons we could find and carry, and pulled back. I was happy to finally get away from the line of fire. It had actually been completely irresponsible to bring a battalion with former prisoners into the *HKL*. It was pretty close to sabotage! We gathered in a small village behind the front and watched as the armored infantry of the Army rolled by ... to recapture the positions.[12]

The "armored infantry" that he referred to was the counterattack launched later that morning by the *Div. Gr. Rintelen* reserve force, *Feld-Ers. Btl. 357*, commanded by *Hptm.* Otto Hafner. Originally intended to be available to retake Ipolysag if needed, *Gen. Maj.* Rintelen had been forced to commit it instead to retake the eastern outskirts of Bernecebaráti, which was partially occupied later that morning by elements of the 30th Guards Mechanized Brigade after the two *SS* battalions had evaporated. Both Ehlers and Nitzkowski had been forced to hurriedly evacuate their battalion command posts from the town, along with the *Tross* from both battalions.

Initially, only 200 men were thought to have gone over to the enemy, but this figure was to grow much larger in the coming days. The first report of where they had gone arrived that evening from a German radio intercept of Red Army message traffic (known as an *Otto* report), which revealed that 160 German troops were taken prisoner earlier that day by the 30th Guards Mechanized Brigade. Though the report did not state from which unit they had defected, the *H.Gr. Süd Ib* (military intelligence) staff officer concluded that these were most likely from one or both of the *SS* battalions that had gone over to the enemy. A subsequent *Heinrich* report later that day (sent by an agent behind enemy lines) confirmed that they were from the *III. Btl./SS-St.Rgt. 2*, and that the number was 180 men, not 160.[13]

One of the survivors of the defection of the *II. Bataillon* who did not surrender but retreated with a few other of his fellow *SS* men, *Gren.* Franz M., wrote a letter about the time of the battle to his brother-in-law, a certain *Gren.* Hermann N., stating his impression of the politicals recently assigned to his company:

> I [had] just returned from surgery and found your letter of November 16th. Yes, we all must suffer in this war; My deepest condolences to you about the death of your wife. We just have to keep living until better times … We have the latest news: our Dirlewanger was awarded the Knight's Cross in October [actually the date was 30 September 1944]; there were no celebrations, operations are too difficult, and there was no time for it. The Slovaks are now openly in alliance with the Russians, and in every dirty village there is a nest of partisans. Forests and mountains in the Tatras have made partisans a mortal danger for us. We make short work of any prisoners we take … Now I am in a village near Ipolysag. Russians are very close. The reinforcements that we received are worthless, and it would be better if we had left them in the [concentration] camps. Twelve of them yesterday went over to the Russian side, all of them were old communists, it would be better if they were all hung on the gallows. But there are some true heroes here nonetheless. Well, the enemy artillery opens fire again, and I must return. Cordial greetings from your brother-in-law.[14]

It is not known whether "Franz" survived the battle or the ensuing fighting until his battalion was withdrawn, or until the end of the war for that matter, but his letter provides a window into what the "regular" *SS B-Schützen* thought of the concentration camp volunteers whom they felt they had been saddled with.

All thoughts of troop morale aside, with a nearly 2-kilometer-wide hole blasted in the German and Hungarian *HKL* east of Bernecebaráti, something had to be done quickly before the enemy broke out of the mountains and threatened the *Div.Gr. Rintelen* rear area. Quickly sizing up the situation after speaking to the remaining *SS* officers who had escaped (including Harald Momm), *Hptm.* Otto Hafner, a young and energetic commander who had already been awarded the Knight's Cross for a previous action, incorporated the survivors of the *SS* battalions into his force and launched his own counterattack, with the support of the available Hungarian armor, against the left flank of the attacking enemy brigade before it could set up a defense in the eastern outskirts of the town.

Hafner himself left us a description of his counterattack, which incorporated the remnants of the two SS battalions into his force.[15] After disembarking from the trucks that had brought them from Neuhäusel during the night, he quickly organized his troops and the SS and set off for his first objective, the eastern outskirts of Bernecebaráti, where some German troops were still holding out. The Hungarian armor support was not needed after all. Finding few or no enemy there, Hafner's next objective was the hill mass several hundred meters east of the town crowned by Hill 185. Hafner wrote:

> With the help of a cross-country guide [we moved eastwards] … none of us knew our way around … and into a side valley. This one led upwards, the landscape [was] like that in the foothills. Following a ridgeline, the attack would be led to the edge of a forest about one kilometer away. After the situation had been clarified using the map, I oriented the attacking companies on the terrain. I ordered scouts to the front and covering troops to the edge of the forest. The deployment went as quietly as possible. My plan of attack envisaged bypassing the steep slope in front of us, including the break in the forest where [our] heavy machine guns were to watch over this section, and support the main attack from the flanks. Infantry howitzers were sited on those sections of the forest which the infantry was to take.

Taking the first ridgeline without much fighting (evidently the troops of Shutov's 30th Guards Mechanized Brigade had already begun to pull back), he continued his attack towards the ridgeline recently vacated by Ehlers's and Nitzkowski's battalions stretching between Hills 241 and 363, including Csitari Puszta. He continued:

> The attack began … at first, [there was] little resistance, apparently only weak enemy outposts. It was my first battalion command and I felt the uneasiness not only in my stomach, but [it seemed] my heart was beating in my throat. Would it all work out? But everything went according to plan. The assault went forward quickly into the forest without much resistance.

After consolidating on their intermediate objective, Hafner continued pushing his troops forward into the heavily forested hills immediately south of Homok, moving beyond the ridge between Hills 241 and 363:

> [We moved down] several hundred meters of descending slope, all forested, then a little road above, again a slight ascent, only a little bit of undergrowth, but good visibility. Up to the small road and just above it everything went well. But then all at once the resistance became fierce and we had a hard time finding cover, digging in, or holding on at all. In the course of the morning, there were several times where we felt [very] uneasy. Two fierce counterattacks hit us and we clearly saw ourselves being driven out of our position.[16]

Fortunately for Hafner and his men, the Soviet tanks that had taken part in the attack that morning had not joined in the assault towards Bernecebaráti itself because there was no direct route into the lowlands from the plateau between Hills 241 and 363. Nor could they depress their guns low enough to engage any German counterattack coming from that direction. The tanks had apparently been withdrawn into Homok before this attack had begun, abandoning the high ground they had helped seize that morning. Their absence had assisted Hafner and his battalion to reoccupy Csitari-Puszta and the surrounding key terrain without having to fight very hard to retake it.

Their further advance towards Homok having been thwarted by the stout defense of the 30th Guards Mechanized Brigade, Hafner then ordered his *Kampfgruppe* to pull back to the ridgeline encompassing Csitari Puszta in the southeast and Kinszky Manor in the northwest, where he and his men would remain until 21 December. As for the remnant of Ehlers's and Nitzkowski's battalions (some 335 men in all out of nearly 1,000 who had been trucked in on 10 December), once they had been rounded up and accounted for, they would form two company-sized *Kampfgruppen* and would fight under *Hptm*. Hafner's command for the next 10 days.[17]

Another bright spot in that otherwise disastrous morning was the inability of Shutov's troops to fight their way through the blocking position erected by the reinforced *Pio.Btl. 666* in the Nagy Volgy valley 1 kilometer south of the SS position at Csitari-Puszta. After heavy fighting, the Soviet troops were pushed back from there as well as from Királyháza southeast of Kémence. In the war diary of the IX Guards Mechanized Corps for that evening, the failed attempt to seize Bernecebaráti and break out to the west between it and Pereszlény received only brief mention, just a single sentence stating: "However, this attack [ultimately] did not succeed, and soon 30th Guards Mechanized Brigade had to repel the counterattacks of the enemy, which almost continuously followed one after the other."[18]

Dramatic as this little battle had been, the decisive action of the day was only getting started 5 kilometers to the north. This was to be *Ostubaf*. Erich Buchmann's first experience in leading a regiment during a pitched battle. From his command post located in a house in the center of Kistur, a mere 2 kilometers north of the nearest Soviet positions, he was to directly command two-and-a-half battalions, coordinate with another, and be supported by the brigade's heavy mortar company, a light artillery battery, and two Hungarian 105mm howitzer batteries (see Map 5). The brigade's *Panzerjäger Kompanie*, less one platoon, was defending a blocking position within the gap at Gyerk, 4 kilometers northwest of Ipolysag.[19]

The night before the attack, Buchmann was notified that the rest of the mixed battalion, minus the heavy mortar company and antitank company, would be subordinated to him; this unit, now consisting of only two companies, had been split into two small *Kampfgruppen*. One would continue reinforcing *K.Gr. Ruhsam* on Hill 227 as extra infantrymen, while the other (the heavy machine-gun company) would form the regimental reserve in Kistur, with an on-order mission to support Steinhauer's battalion.

Immediately prior to launching his counterattack, Buchmann's antitank defenses were augmented by a single Hungarian towed 80mm *Flak*, to be followed by several lightly armored *Nimrod* 40mm self-propelled antiaircraft guns that Rintelen had requested the previous evening. The *Nimrods* would be nearly useless against tanks, but the powerful Bofors Model 28.39M 80mm *Flak* could kill any tank in the Soviet inventory. Since it could not move off-road, it had to be placed along the highway between Kistur and Közeptúr in an advantageous firing position. The *Nimrods*, which could be lethal when used against infantry in the open, were to be staged along with the regiment's reserve in Közeptúr with one gun platoon from the mixed battalion's *Panzerjäger Kompanie*. There would be no air support of any kind, although Rintelen had requested it; the foul weather simply would not allow it.

Major der Schutzpolizei Steinhauer's battalion of approximately 800 men would constitute the main effort of the attack. At the time the operation commenced, it was occupying a temporary position in the fields west of Kistur. The concept of maneuver involved a 2-kilometer-long movement to contact by his battalion from its attack position in a south-southeasterly direction across Boras Rét (known locally as Wine Meadow, an open field), towards the fork in the road 1 kilometer north of Ipolysag. This was believed to be in the enemy's possession (it was). Once his battalion had reached this location and occupied it, the battalion would continue its attack into the town proper.

A substantial portion of his battalion's avenue of approach included slogging across the waterlogged fields of Boras Rét. To his right, his movement was bounded by Krupina Patak (a creek), and on his left, at first the north–south highway leading to Palást, then Szölcz Creek. Both creeks were nearly overflowing their banks due to the constant rain. These terrain features would channel his attack, forcing his battalion to attack into an increasingly narrow piece of terrain before his companies entered the town's northern outskirts. Apparently, Steinhauer had received precious little information about the location of the enemy that he and his men would have to face. It is doubtful that he knew he might encounter flanking fire on his right by the elements of the 31st Guards Mechanized Brigade that had occupied the area the day before, or how many enemy tanks were positioned within the town.

Steinhauer's attack would be supported on his left by *Ostuf.* Herbert Meyer's *I. Btl./SS-Rgt. 1*, which also consisted of roughly 800 men augmented by the survivors of *1. Kp./Bau-Pio.Btl. 144*. His battalion had been positioned on the ridgeline east of Kistur stretching from just north of Hill 241 to Hill 291 for most of the past two days, except for the brief period occupying Mt. Magas and Somos on 14 December. Meyer's mission was twofold: first, he had to support the attack by *II. Btl./SS-Rgt. 1* with fire; second, once Steinhauer's force had reached a certain point, perhaps at the fork in the road (the records do not state exactly where), his battalion would change direction to advance southeast, wade across Berinesen Creek, assault Mt. Magas and Mt. Somos, and reoccupy the lines of the *Margarethestellung* vacated by *Kompanie Gaal* and *1. Kp./Bau-Pio.Btl. 144* two days before. Retaking these hills would once again enable German observation of most of the eastern Ipoly River valley.[20]

The lynchpin of the entire operation was maintaining possession of Hill 227 northeast of Ipolysag. *Hauptmann* Ruhsam and his men had held on to this key terrain despite the loss of Ipolysag the previous day and had been reinforced by the small *Kampfgruppe* from the mixed battalion that arrived during the early morning. In addition to his own *8. Kompanie* heavy weapons platoons (mortars, machine guns, and antitank rocket launchers), he also counted 30 remaining riflemen from the *7. Kompanie* of *Hstuf.* Ehlers's *II Bataillon*. Evidently, quite a few of them had become casualties or had defected to the enemy since being assigned to the position on 13 December. All told, he probably had somewhat less than 200 men at his disposal to hold a defensive position nearly a kilometer wide, stretching from Hill 227 to Hill 241, where it met the right flank of Meyer's battalion. For the counterattack, Ruhsam's mission was to hold his position on Hill 227 and support Steinhauer's attack with fire, using his heavy weapons.[21]

On paper, the plan probably would have been deemed sufficient, but there were some major flaws, not the least of which was that this would be the first truly comprehensive conventional attack planned and executed exclusively by the Dirlewanger Brigade. The hastily launched counterattack of the previous day had achieved little—it had been an uncoordinated, shambolic affair, centering on a battalion that had only arrived in the area a few hours before (Steinhauer's) and with little time to plan for artillery support. Having had at least 12 hours to prepare for the next attempt, Buchmann and his battalion commanders, aided by the skills of his talented *Ia Leiter*, former general staff officer but now *Gren.* Freiherr von Uckermann, they had probably done all they could do to prepare for it. Nevertheless, it would not be enough.

Two ingredients needed to guarantee success were lacking—the first was a good communications network necessary to pass messages back and forth with the battalions, with radios in the hands of artillery forward observers to pass target information and corrections to the supporting artillery batteries. With a battalion's worth of howitzers and field cannon available (approximately 12 barrels), as well as a heavy mortar company, it should have been enough firepower to effectively strike the Soviet troop concentration within Ipolysag. While flares could be used in a pinch to signal the need for certain prearranged fires, it was evident that his artillery forward observers had no way to directly call for fire without radios. That is, if there were artillery observer teams embedded with his battalions (there is no evidence in either case).

The battalions had finally been able to tie in their landline telephones to Buchmann's command post, but he himself had no direct telephone communication with Dirlewanger in Palást. Once Steinhauer and Meyer commenced their attack, he would lose contact with them completely until they could re-establish wire communication after taking their objectives. Buchmann's signal platoon, which included his own cable laying section, did not arrive until noon on 15 December, after the battle had already been underway for at least two hours, so he was not able to speak to Dirlewanger by telephone at any point during the fighting.

While Dirlewanger had a radio set in his own command post provided by the Hungarians, he had no means yet to directly contact Buchmann or anyone else in the valley, only Rintelen. Neither had his field telephone cables been laid in yet. With this arrangement, the only recourse Buchmann had to communicate with his commander and the supporting artillery was to rely on runners, mounted dispatch riders, or motorcycle messengers. This was sufficient for a World War I battlefield, but not for modern warfare as it was practiced in 1944.

The second flaw in the plan was that it was concocted with the barest amount of information about the enemy. Buchmann and Dirlewanger, as well as their underlings, obviously knew that Soviet troops had occupied Ipolysag. They already knew that there were a few tanks, and of course they were aware of enemy artillery, having been shelled by it the previous day. But they knew little more. Engine noises and construction sounds had been heard throughout the night. Whether Buchmann had ordered foot patrols to feel out the strength of the enemy, their activity, exact location, identity of the units engaged, and the type of equipment they possessed, could only be surmised. Essentially, Buchmann and his commanders were launching a major operation nearly blind. An experienced regimental commander would have done all of these things beforehand, but Buchmann was a novice promoted above his capabilities, and Steinhauer and Meyer were both former police officers, not infantrymen.

Again, the commander of *SS-St.Rgt. 2* had had nearly 12 hours to perform this basic task. Given how the battle progressed and the ultimate result, if his troops did carry out any foot patrols or armed reconnaissance, the information gained was either not passed up the chain of command, or if it was, it had been done so poorly. Should any German foot patrols have been engaged or wiped out prior to the battle, it would have been mentioned in Freiherr von Uckermann's post-operations report that he wrote on behalf of Buchmann. It would have made more sense to postpone the attack at least until the radio platoon arrived and telephone cable was laid, but the pressure being exerted by the commanders of *Div.Gr. Rintelen, 6. Armee/A.Gr. Fretter-Pico,* and *H.Gr. Süd* to retake Ipolysag was intense.

One remaining mystery is the location of *Gen.Maj.* Rintelen during the battle. He had been tasked to oversee the progress of the counterattack, but there is no mention of him appearing in either Buchmann's or Dirlewanger's after-action report. Most likely, he positioned himself at first in Pereszlény, which was located roughly in the center of the battlefields on the southern bank of the Ipoly, where the *Luftwaffe's* heavy *Flak* batteries were positioned. It was also the point where the commanders of *6. Armee/A.Gr. Fretter-Pico* and *H.Gr. Süd* had expected the enemy's main effort to be directed, so it would have been logical to position his forward command post there. Had he been with Buchmann in Kistur, there would have been little that he could have done, and he probably would have been killed, wounded, or captured. The die was cast and the players had no other choice but to perform the roles assigned them.

On the morning of 15 December, before the battle, *Gen.Obst.* Friessner decided to drive to the front lines on both sides of the Ipoly River to make a troop visit to the hot spots on his army group's left flank, including the command posts of *Div. Gr. Rintelen*, the Dirlewanger Brigade, and the *24. Pz.Div.* While he apparently trusted Rintelen and von Nostitz-Wallwitz, he had so far formed no opinion of Dirlewanger. Shortly after the battle had begun, Friessner visited Dirlewanger's command post in Palást at 12.45pm before moving on to meet with the commander of the neighboring *24. Pz.Div.* at his *Gefechtstand* in Zsély (Želovce), 42 kilometers away. What Friessner saw in Palást left him unimpressed; he found Dirlewanger, whom Friessner characterized as a "not very appealing adventurer type," sitting calmly behind his desk with a pet monkey on his shoulder.

When questioned about the current situation, Dirlewanger did not know where the front line was, nor was he aware of the status of Buchmann's operation.[22] According to Friessner, "The unit was, as suggested before, a wild bunch. One company, communists who were expected to prove themselves on the front, had just deserted to the enemy." Dirlewanger's Ia, *Stubaf.* Weisse, made a better impression, although it was clear to Friessner that Dirlewanger was out of his depth. When the infamous *SS* commander told Friessner that he was planning to move his command post back to a safer location (perhaps to Deménd, where his main headquarters lay), Friessner ordered him to stay put where he was and to see to his troops. He then went on his way to visit the *24. Pz.Div.* commander, who was fighting his own defensive battle north of Balassagyarmat a few dozen kilometers to the east.[23]

In comparison with Rintelen or Dirlewanger, Lt.Gen. Volkov had a very good idea of his enemy's order of battle and which units his troops were facing. The abortive German counterattack towards Ipolysag during the afternoon of the previous day had given him an idea of where any subsequent attack might originate. Due to the number of prisoners brought in during the past several days, he and his staff knew the locations of Dirlewanger's battalions north of the Ipoly River, their composition, and their relative strengths. He also must have suspected that any further attempt to punch through with his tanks at Pereszlény was doomed to fail, because the German antitank barrier was too strong to overcome without longer-ranging artillery or close air support. While the route through the mountains offered some promise, the valleys could easily be blocked to tanks and other motorized vehicles.

So even should his infantry break through and take Bernecebaráti and Kémence, they would not get very far unsupported. Therefore, his remaining options were the two avenues of approach north of the river—the one westward through the narrow gap at Gyerk via Ipolysag, and the other northward through Kistur to Palást. Taking Gyerk and pushing towards Kistompa would place his mechanized forces on the approaches to the Little Hungarian Plain; taking Palást would enable him to strike deep into southern Slovakia and threaten the right flank of *8. Armee/A.Gr. Wöhler* with a deep envelopment. Evidently, Volkov decided to do both. He knew that the V Guards Tank Corps was moving up from Waitzen on orders from the Sixth Guards Tank Army and would soon be available for employment. Off to his right flank, Cavalry-Mechanized Group Pliyev was carrying out powerful attacks against the overextended divisions of *Gen.d.Pz.Tr.* Ulrich Kleeman's *IV. Pz.Korps.*

Even while the morning's fighting in the Börszeny Mountains was still ongoing, Volkov's 18th and 31st Guards Mechanized Brigades were preparing to launch their own attack that afternoon. The 18th Guards Mechanized Brigade would strike north from Ipolysag, with Guards Maj. Grigory R. Nemchenko's 83rd Guards Tank Regiment in the lead, while the 31st Guards Mechanized Brigade, having moved its own 85th Guards Tank Regiment into Ipolysag during the night over the newly constructed bridge, would be available to reinforce the attack at Gyerk if needed. The large assemblage of troops in Ipolysag had not been spotted by any of *Div.Gr. Rintelen's* units, which were unable to observe enemy movement due to the inclement weather and the loss of the observation post on Mt. Magas the day before. All told, north of the Ipoly, Volkov's two brigades could bring as many as four motorized infantry battalions to bear and the better part of two tank regiments (approximately 60–70 tanks), guaranteeing overwhelming combat power anywhere he wished to apply it. However, for one of the few instances during this battle, the Germans struck first.

The exact time that Buchmann's attack began cannot be determined with certainty, though it had commenced while the morning's engagements south of the Ipoly between Pereszlény and Bernecebaráti were still in progress. It began with prearranged artillery barrages concentrated west of Dregelypalánk, Ipolysag, Hont, and Homok. Mentioned in Volkov's corps combat journal, these bombardments do not appear to have caused much damage, but inexplicably avoided the areas where Soviet troops were actually concentrated—that is, within these towns themselves. Having artillery forward observers equipped with radios might have helped avoid this error.

While these barrages were still impacting around but not within Ipolysag, Steinhauer's battalion launched its attack shortly after first light from the area between Hill 216 and Kistur. Presumably, Meyer's battalion began moving out with his troops at the same time, certainly by 10am at the latest. Off to the east, Polack's *III. Bataillon* began its own advance to the south. Little about his operations are known, but when his battalion did begin moving to the southwest there was no resistance, a sign that the IX Guards Mechanized Corps had not pushed its troops that far north. At first, Steinhauer's and Meyer's troops would have been undetected due to morning fog and perhaps a mid-morning snow flurry. However, troops from the 18th Guards Mechanized Brigade occupying the fork in the road 1 kilometer north of the town would have placed listening posts forward of their position and most likely would have been the first to detect and sound an alarm about the approaching enemy force.

Initially, the German assault force at first did not realize that anything was amiss; it was only when the *II. Bataillon* began to press its attack forward into Ipolysag across the open fields that its commander learned the size of the defending enemy force had been underestimated. As Steinhauer's leading platoons began to work their way towards the town's northern outskirts, they made contact with the enemy at the fork in the road. These Soviet troops withdrew into town rather than allow themselves to be overrun. To the Germans' surprise, their forward elements were soon pinned down by machine-gun fire from eight of Maj. Nemchenko's T-34s located among a row of houses on the northern edge of town. Bounded on both sides by streams and marshland, Steinhauer's battalion had no room to maneuver and was unable to call for supporting artillery fire. Steinhauer's troops could not advance, nor could they withdraw, all the while suffering losses to withering machine-gun fire from the T-34s. As a result, Steinhauer's attack had stalled by 12.45pm.

To the left of Steinhauer's battalion, the attack by Herbert Meyer's *I. Bataillon* initially made good progress against little to no opposition and had begun to ascend the slope of Mt. Magas. On Hill 227, *K.Gr. Ruhsam* sent a message via field telephone to Buchmann, reporting that they could hear tank engine noises south of their position, but otherwise it was calm. For about an hour, the attack by *II. Bataillon* was halted on the edge of Ipolysag due to the lack of forceful leadership by company commanders to urge their troops onward. While each company had brought a number of *Panzerfausts* along with them, they had not been trained how to use them, although the range to the enemy tanks was too far for them to be of use anyway (these antitank weapons had only been issued the day before and no training with them had been conducted).

Obersturmbannführer Buchmann, the regimental commander, remained behind in his headquarters in Kistur and could only rely on scant situation reports delivered by runners or motorcycle messengers. By default, this left leadership on the scene to his subordinates—Steinhauer, Ruhsam, and Meyer—none of whom were able to communicate directly with one another. Ongoing attempts to coordinate artillery support were similarly frustrated and gunners were unable to fire on prearranged targets for fear of hitting their own troops. Finally, Buchmann had managed to contact his three battalion commanders on the scene through couriers who relayed the message that the attack would be resumed at 1.30pm with the promised support of the four Hungarian *Nimrod* 40mm self-propelled antiaircraft guns that would move forward.

During this interlude, a single T-34 with mounted infantry, probably on a reconnaissance mission, drove through the German lines east of Ipolysag off

Steinhauer's left flank and went as far as Kistur, where it was finally fired upon by the regimental reserve, which at this point consisted solely of heavy machine guns and several 37mm antitank guns detached from the mixed battalion. After most of the Soviet infantry were shot off it, the solitary tank turned around and returned from whence it came. At the same time, *K.Gr. Ruhsam* reported that it had spotted as many as eight enemy tanks gathering several hundred meters south of its positions, but it lacked the means to call for artillery support to disperse them. These tanks were most likely from the 83rd Guards Tank Regiment. One kilometer to the east, Meyer's battalion had almost reached the summit of the ridgeline between Mt. Magas and Mt. Samos.

This momentary success was soon offset by a report from the *I. Bataillon* at 2.30pm that it had spotted the same eight T-34s with supporting infantry a kilometer off on their right flank, the Soviet tanks having suddenly appeared atop Hill 227. Evidently, this signified that Ruhsam and his battlegroup were being subjected to a concerted attack (see Map 6). Shortly afterwards, Meyer reported that he had observed Ruhsam's troops pulling back from the height in apparent panic with Soviet tanks in pursuit. It appears that his antitank rocket launchers had been of little use. To counteract this development, Buchmann, via telephone (evidently cables had been laid since his advance began), ordered the *I. Bataillon* commander to intercept Ruhsam's retreating troops, incorporate them into his own force, and counterattack to retake the hill. To do this, Meyer would have to divide his force—one portion to consolidate their gains on the mountaintop, and the other to intercept Ruhsam's troops and lead them in a counterattack to retake their own positions.[24]

Meyer called back to Buchmann's headquarters requesting supporting fire from the heavy mortar company to be laid on Mt. Magas, but since Buchmann had no direct telephone connection to the mortars, Meyer's request went unanswered. Earlier, Buchmann had also promised Meyer that he would be reinforced by two additional infantry companies after 6.30pm if they were needed, but since this force was supposed to come from *K.Gr. Ruhsam*, this request was impossible to fulfill, leaving Meyer no choice but to press his attack forward without the additional support.

This attack got nowhere, nor did his primary effort, for at the same time, just before Meyer's troops could take full possession of Mt. Magas, they were assaulted by a numerically superior enemy force that quickly drove them from the mountaintop (this attack probably came from the direction of Mt. Somos). Continuing onward, this counterattack by elements of the 18th Guards Mechanized Brigade charged down the mountainside and began to roll up the left flank of the *I. Bataillon*, forcing Meyer to withdraw in haste to the north before his battalion was cut off. While his unit managed to escape more or less intact, *K.Gr. Ruhsam* was cut to ribbons by the tank attack and its commander listed as missing in action.

While it was not as heavily filled with politicals as the *III. Bataillon of SS-St. Rgt. 2*, Ruhsam's *8. Kompanie* had been assigned its share while it was at Deviaky.

Their attempted defection to the Red Army did not turn out quite as well as it had for their comrades in the Börszeny Mountains. One of these men who survived the attack on Hill 227, Günther Wackernagel, recalled:

> [Defecting] alone seemed too dangerous to me. As a unified company or even as a platoon or group, I thought it would be safer and more effective. Therefore, I discussed this idea with reliable comrades in the company staff and in the individual platoons. We decided to stay in our positions during the next major attack and just lie there and let ourselves be overrun by the advancing Soviet soldiers ... At this section of the front all the "politicals" ... had to take up positions in the trenches that had been dug. The SS literally chased us into a barrage of artillery, grenade launchers, tanks and rocket launchers of the Soviet Army. A horrible mass death began among our comrades, with whom we had suffered and died under the terror of the fascists. They were devoured by the war's fury; they all died a senseless death.[25]

The remaining men of Ruhsam's *Kampfgruppe* who were not captured or killed on Hill 227 fled to the north, where they were eventually incorporated into Meyer's battalion, or northwest, where they joined Steinhauer's battalion or simply just kept running. This disaster had taken only minutes to unfold. Meanwhile, Dirlewanger and Weisse were briefing their army group commander at their command post in Palást and were unaware of what had just happened. They would soon find out.

The attempt to retake Ipolysag had clearly failed. Steinhauer's battalion was stuck, Ruhsam's destroyed—its commander probably dead—and Meyer's had barely been able to disengage in time before being completely overwhelmed. At least the *I. Bataillon* had been able to withdraw to its previous position, where its commander managed to get his men turned around and to face once more towards the enemy. Meanwhile, Polack's *III. Bataillon* had managed to make good progress and had occupied the remainder of the *Margarethestellung* southwest of Kelénye by the afternoon. Whether this counted as a success is debatable; to Polack's right, Meyer's battalion had pulled back on account of the Soviet counterattack at Mounts Magas and Samos that resulted in Polack's right flank becoming exposed and hence vulnerable to envelopment.

As bad as the situation was, especially with Ipolysag still firmly in Soviet hands, the situation became even more dire when 40 T-34s—nearly all of the 83rd Guards Tank Regiment—with clusters of *tankodesantniki* aboard, counterattacked Steinhauer's *II. Bataillon* at 2.35pm. Caught in the open north of Ipolysag by the onslaught of a tank battalion and at least two infantry battalions from the 18th Guards Mechanized Brigade, Steinhauer attempted to make a stand. This valiant gesture stood no chance of success whatsoever, even though some of his men were able to knock out two Soviet tanks with *Panzerfausts*. Facing annihilation, Steinhauer's battalion dissolved in panic as his men fled to the west and northwest as fast as their feet could carry them, while individual tanks shot them down with machine-gun fire or ran them over with their tracks. In an ironic twist of fate, the "Cruel Hunters" of the Dirlewanger Brigade had now become the hunted.

As eight T-34s pivoted west and advanced down the road towards the neighboring village of Gyerk, the remaining 32 tanks with infantry aboard continued driving north in the direction of the small village of Kistur. Positioned at its southern exit, the solitary Hungarian 80mm *Flak* opened fire at the lead tank and managed to get off three shots at close range but scored no hits, so poor was its crew's aim. In response, several T-34s returned fire, forcing the Hungarians to abandon their gun and flee for their lives. The four promised *Nimrod* self-propelled *Flak* vehicles had failed to make an appearance; but even if they had, they would have been quickly destroyed.

Guards Major Nemchenko's tank regiment continued moving on towards Buchmann's command post in Kistur. The first indication that the commander of *SS-St.Rgt. 2* received that his attack plan had gone awry came in the form of a telephone call at 2.50pm from Meyer, who had fallen back to his previous positions on Hill 245. Meyer reported to Buchmann that he could see enemy tanks approaching the regiment's command post. Shortly thereafter, the line to the *I. Bataillon* was cut.

Twenty minutes later, 32 T-34s with mounted infantry were on Buchmann's doorstep. He attempted to organize a defense of the village, but was unable to do so given the enemy's overwhelming superiority and the speed of their advance. He barely escaped capture when the building that he and his staff had been occupying was surrounded by several tanks that began to fire directly into the structure with machine guns and cannons. Like the rest of their troops, Buchmann and his acting *Adjutant*, Freiherr von Uckermann, were forced to retreat on foot to avoid being killed or captured. Evidently, Buchmann had recovered from his heart condition, as he seemed to have experienced no difficulty in fleeing the scene.

Leaving behind four tanks with infantry to mop up in Kistur, the 28 remaining T-34s of Maj. Nemchenko's regiment continued pushing north to Középtúr, the next town along the road. The southern approaches to it were protected by the four guns of the 76.2mm cannon battery and an antitank team armed with *Panzerfausts* emplaced behind an antitank barricade erected from bricks and stones. Despite the defenses, the battle for Középtúr was over in minutes. The Soviet armored force pinned down the antitank teams with machine-gun fire, preventing them from firing their *Panzerfausts* at the tanks, which at any rate were out of range.

The 76.2mm field cannon battery fired furiously at the tanks from a range of less than 500 meters using high-explosive shells, but these had little effect. Although his guns were capable of firing armor-piercing ammunition, the battery commander had been unable to procure any from the Hungarians. After expending all of his ammunition, he belatedly realized that his battery would soon be overrun. He ordered his gun crews to limber up and withdraw, but it was too late—his guns were quickly shot up by the tanks, although he and his men were able to escape with their horses.

At that point, any organized attempt by the Dirlewanger Brigade to defend Ipolysag became impossible. Shortly after Kistur fell, Középtúr was also in Soviet hands and the regiment's communications network knocked out. Not satisfied with what he had accomplished so far, Maj. Nemchenko ordered his tanks to continue pushing northward towards Palást after quickly disposing of *Ostuf.* Otto Rühs's heavy mortar company. Like the artillery battery, Rühs's troops were was also caught in the Red Army's crosshairs when they attempted to withdraw to a new firing position and were shot to bits, losing all six of their 120mm mortars.

Guards Major Nemchenko continued pushing northward along the highway, taking the village of Felsötur without a fight until calling a halt just short of the town of Palást, site of Dirlewanger's forward command post. With part of his brigade strung out after an 8-kilometer advance in a northerly direction, and another about to launch an attack towards Gyerk, Col. Ovcharov radioed Nemchenko and ordered him to halt for the time being, while in the meantime sending out scouts towards Palást to see what German forces were holding that town. The patrol soon radioed back to Nemchenko that the town was undefended and that no enemy troops were in sight.

This came about because at about the same time, Dirlewanger and Weisse heard—or were notified of—the advancing enemy tanks (perhaps by *Ostuf.* Rühs) and cleared out of their command post building in Palást in a hurry, without notifying anyone in their chain of command. The *Gefechtstand's* few signalers and its small security force hastily piled their equipment aboard several staff cars and trucks parked outside and retreated, barely avoiding Soviet reconnaissance patrols by only a few minutes. The brigade's commander reappeared several hours later at his *Hauptquartier* in Deménd, where Dirlewanger would re-establish control and attempt to lead his troops for the next several days. At some point during the next 24 hours, Buchmann and his staff company would also reappear in Deménd. With his regiment in tatters, he had very little left to command anyway.

Shortly after Dirlewanger and his crew abandoned Palást without a fight, *Gen. Obst.* Friessner, returning to his headquarters after visiting the commander of the *24. Pz.Div.*, re-entered the town to check back in at the brigade's command post to see if his earlier orders had been carried out. Surprised to see that Dirlewanger had evacuated the town despite orders to the contrary, Friessner and his aide-de-camp, *Oberltn.* van Rossum, encountered Soviet scouts instead and only just managed to escape capture.[26] Friessner was not pleased by this turn of events, to say the least, and it was not long before he realized that the loss of Palást would soon have massive implications.

Cut off from the rest of the regiment by Nemchenko's advance, *Ostuf.* Meyer and his *I. Bataillon* were forced to abandon their positions and withdraw to the northeast. After moving cross-country for nearly 5 kilometers, the battalion finally came to rest in the forest east of Palást, where it dug in again to await developments. Now without the means to contact Buchmann's headquarters, Meyer was also cut off from any supplies or means to evacuate his wounded. To his left, Polack's *III. Bataillon* had been forced to bend its right flank back to the edge of Ipoly-Födemes, where he maintained a tenuous link to Meyer. Both battalions would now have to draw support from their nearest neighbor from the *IV. Pz.Korps*, the *24. Pz.Div.*

West of Ipolysag, a remnant of Steinhauer's *II. Bataillon* and the brigade's *Panzerjäger Kompanie* attempted to block the Soviet force approaching Gyerk from Ipolysag and managed to keep at bay the vanguard of eight tanks and mounted infantry at 4.20pm. However, this desperate attempt to prevent them from breaking through the Ipolysag Gap failed an hour later when the enemy vanguard was reinforced by additional tanks and infantry, most likely from the 31st Guards Mechanized Brigade. To avoid being trapped once again, the survivors of the *II. Bataillon* fled in panic to Kistompa, where some of them were corraled and incorporated into a blocking position being rapidly organized by none other than former *Oberst*, now *Hstuf.* Momm.

With his own company dispersed and the remnant of both battalions organized into two battlegroups commanded by *Hstuf.* Ehlers at Bernecebaráti, *Hstuf.* Momm, the former Olympian horseman, was now at the disposal of *Div.Gr. Rintelen*. Rintelen had been on the move throughout the day, traveling from one hotspot to another in an effort to control a rapidly worsening situation. Rintelen had most likely learned of the unfolding disaster at Ipolysag shortly after 3pm and had started formulating a response. His timely decision to deploy *Hptm.* Hafner's battalion for the counterattack at Bernecebaráti had prevented a breakthrough at that location, but it was now unavailable to retrieve the situation at Ipolysag. Rintelen, grasping for a solution, must have spoken face-to-face with Momm at some point in mid-afternoon when he gave him the mission to take charge of the defense at Gyerk until reserves could be brought forward.

Hurrying to Gyerk that afternoon shortly after Steinhauer's force was routed at Ipolysag, Momm quickly learned that town had fallen and the defense in Gyerk was being routed. In the neighboring village of Kistompa 3 kilometers northwest of Gyerk, he managed to round up 27 stragglers from the Dirlewanger Brigade and take charge of them, along with three 37mm antitank guns and one 80mm mortar and their crews, who had evacuated the town before Soviet troops took it. With this meager force, Momm kept up a brisk fire on any enemy tanks attempting to seize the bridge over the Schemnitz (Selmec) River at Kistompa. Although the guns could inflict little damage to the tanks, Momm's troops slaughtered the escorting infantry riding upon them. After a brief exchange of fire, the T-34s returned to the safety of Gyerk until they could consolidate and try again with a deliberate attack.

By that point, the three battalions involved in the battle for Ipolysag had been reduced to ruins. The *II. Btl./SS-St.Rgt. 1* was scattered and no longer combat effective after suffering heavy losses. Ruhsam's *Kampfgruppe*, including a portion of the mixed battalion, was virtually wiped out, its commander dead. The remnants of both were later consolidated into a single 84-man company under Steinhauer's command, while Momm gathered other stragglers around him. The rest had fled to the rear and would be gradually rounded up during the next several days. The *I. Btl./SS-St.Rgt. 1* had suffered some losses, but was still combat capable, though cut off. The *III. Btl./SS-St.Rgt. 1* was relatively unscathed, since it had not participated in the fighting at all because it was too far away. Both the artillery battery and heavy mortar company had lost all of their weapons and equipment.

In addition to the losses suffered by the three battalions of *SS-St.Rgt. 1* and *K.Gr. Ruhsam* from *SS-St.Rgt. 2*, the two *SS* battalions from *SS-St.Rgt. 2* attached to *K.Gr. Grosse* had been dispersed; their remnants were rounded up and used to form two company-sized battlegroups after at least 200 of their men had defected to the Red Army early that morning. At least as many men were killed, wounded, or missing in action. Ipolysag was lost, as was Kistur, Közeptúr, Gyerk, Palást, Mt. Magas, and Mt. Somos. As a result of the Dirlewanger Brigade's defeat, the vanguard of the IX Guards Mechanized Corps was now poised to break out of the Ipolysag Gap with over 70 tanks still at its disposal, as well as three mechanized rifle brigades. His reserve, the 46th Guards Tank Brigade, had not yet even been committed to battle. The initiative now lay with Lt.Gen. Volkov, who could continue his attack against little if any resistance, should he wish.

Dirlewanger had exercised little if any influence on the fighting. Throughout the entire battle, he had sat in his command post in Palást, making only one recorded visit to the front lines to see for himself what was going on or to inspect the condition of his troops. Lacking any modern means of communication except one Hungarian radio (that could only communicate with Rintelen's headquarters) and with his brigade arrayed along a 12-kilometer-wide front, neither he nor Buchmann were able to employ their supporting arms to good effect. The two batteries of Hungarian 105mm howitzers could not bring their considerable firepower to bear after the initial barrages at a time when the infantry battalion needed it the most. Poor marksmanship by the crew of the Hungarian 80mm *Flak* at Közeptúr and the lack of armor-piercing ammunition for the brigade's light artillery battery had made a bad situation even worse. Although the troops of Steinhauer, Ruhsam, and Meyer had initially fought surprisingly well, even heroically in some instances, they were no match for two nearly full-strength Soviet mechanized brigades with two regiments of lethally effective T-34s and M4A2 Shermans.

Lacking any effective heavy antitank weapons except short-range *Panzerfausts* and *Panzerschreck* rocket launchers, they were nearly defenseless against such an armored juggernaut. With the knowledge that enemy tanks were already in Ipolysag as early as the afternoon of 14 December, the outcome of the battle should have been clearly foreseen before it even began. With the benefit of hindsight, it would have been more productive for the *SS* battalions around Ipolysag to defend their positions, rather than expend their limited strength on pointless frontal attacks that only left them exposed and vulnerable to a massive armored counterattack. But this was only the second act of the unfolding drama along the Ipoly River. More of the same was in the offing for the days to come.

The only saving grace that day was Volkov's decision not to continue his attack, which had been wildly successful so far, especially north of the Ipoly River. To understand the mystery of why he did not press on while he had the advantage, some factors need to be considered. One explanation could be that he had been ordered by Col.Gen. Kravchenko, his army commander, to consolidate the ground gained and be prepared to continue his attack within the next several days after he had been reinforced. After all, the V Guards Tank Corps was moving up the Ipoly River valley, but its exact direction of employment had not yet been decided.

Another explanation could be found in a statement recorded in the IX Guards Mechanized Corps' war diary. Although very successful at Ipolysag that day, things had not gone as well elsewhere. Colonels Shutov's and Seleznev's mechanized brigades had experienced the full effects of a powerful German antitank *Pakfront* at Pereszlény, where eight of their tanks were knocked out in as many minutes, and the furious counterattack by *Hptm.* Hafner's battalion at Bernecebaráti that drove their motorized infantry battalions back into the mountains. Armed with this knowledge, Lt.Gen. Volkov had good reason to be very wary of what the Germans would throw at him next.

In regards to these concerns, the following revealing war diary entry can be found for 16 December that reflects on the events from the day before: "It is obvious that in this area there is a large force of enemy tanks, infantry, and artillery." Apparently, Volkov believed that Hafner's force was the lead element of a much larger counterattack, although at the time there were no other reserves available, but of course Volkov did not know that. This situation would soon radically change.

Two days later, the IX Guards Mechanized Corps' war diary recorded an additional statement, a reflection of what *H.Gr. Süd* would soon decide to bring to bear against the corps:

> The size of these forces against us finally became clear later, after two or three days, when the enemy from the Vyškovce–Bernece area began a counterattack towards Homok by an envelopment, the purpose of which was to restore the situation in [Ipolysag] and cut off the corps from its communications.[27]

The genesis of these well-founded concerns was a direct consequence of Volkov's successes of 14–15 December. Thoroughly alarmed by the presence of a Soviet Guards Mechanized Corps on the doorstep of the upper Hungarian Plain, as well as the unexpected collapse of the Dirlewanger Brigade and fresh memories of his personal experience with its notorious commander in Palást, *Gen.Obst.* Friessner decided to pursue a much more powerful course of action that would have far-reaching implications for *H.Gr. Süd* and the course of the war in the Hungarian theater of operations.

CHAPTER TEN

Considerations, Decisions, and Orders, 16 December 1944

The news of the defeat at Ipolysag on 15 December soon had tremendous repercussions within the German high command in Hungary. The evening report submitted by *6. Armee/A.Gr. Fretter-Pico* to *H.Gr. Süd* led with the following dire summary:

> From the area of Ipolysag the enemy conducted attacks to the southwest, west and north. [North of the river] he used an additional number of tanks and advanced several kilometers to the west and north [of Ipolysag]. Tomorrow, the enemy will also try to gain space west of the narrows [at Gyerk] for his own rapid advance, and to this end will bring more forces through the gap. Therefore, increased continuation of his attacks is to be expected.[1]

In a similar vein, the events along the Ipolysag Gap were also the first items mentioned on the first page of *H.Gr. Süd*'s summarized daily report that evening, echoing Fretter-Pico's comments as well as mentioning for the first time the countermeasures that were already underway:

> The enemy advanced from the Ipolysag Gap with strong armored forces and was able to gain ground to the northwest and north. The movement of some of our own available forces has been initiated, with the aim of preventing an expansion of the breakthrough area.[2]

Not mentioned in either summary was the fact that the physical connection between *6. Armee/A.Gr. Fretter-Pico* and *8. Armee/A.Gr. Wöhler* had been severed when Soviet forces reached the southern outskirts of undefended Palást late that afternoon. While one of Dirlewanger's battalions was hunkered down in the forest east of Palást (Meyer's *I. Btl./SS-St.Rgt. 1*), it was cut off and out of contact with the left flank of *Div.Gr. Rintelen*. But at least Meyer's men had not run away in panic like so many others in Steinhauer's and Ruhsam's *Kampfgruppen* had, a mob that must have been at least several hundred men in size.

The fact that so many of the brigade's men had not stopped after escaping through the Ipolysag Gap, but had instead kept on running even after they reached the safety of German lines, had led to the establishment of an *Abfanglinie* (interception line) at 10.30pm west of Kistompa. A force of *Feldgendarmen* (military police) and *Wehrmachtstreifendienst* (special patrols led by dreaded *Feldjäger* and traffic regulation troops) was immediately established and led by a general officer, *Gen.Maj.* Enno von Roden, who was made responsible for rounding up the miscreants and returning them to the control of *Div.Gr. Rintelen*, where they would be reincorporated into their units.[3] The failure of the Dirlewanger Brigade and the role it played in this drama was not overlooked; its counterattack to retake Ipolysag and its ensuing crushing defeat was the lead item in that night's discussions between the commanders of *H.Gr. Süd* and *A.Gr. Fretter-Pico*, both of whom had quickly realized its ominous implications.

Aside from Dirlewanger's failure, the other major source of discontent with the battle was the completely disorganized and ineffective use of *Div.Gr. Rintelen's* artillery, which on paper had looked impressive (by then as many as 29 field cannon and howitzers). But its lack of responsiveness, poor targeting, and inability to communicate with the infantry was one of the factors that led to the failure of the counterattack to retake Ipolysag. Another factor was the lack of German armor to combat Volkov's tanks—the time for makeshift armor defenses was over, but this shortfall could not be as easily addressed. What was needed was *panzers*, and lots of them.

While the antitank barrier of *Luftwaffe* heavy *Flak* at Pereszlény had stopped the tank attack that morning, it was a static barrier and could not be used to support an offensive operation, except with indirect fire. A better solution was needed, but any help would have to come from outside. One of the items discussed that night was the fact that *Div.Gr. Rintelen* lacked an *Artillerie-Kommando* (*ARKO*, artillery command) of its own to coordinate and lead the artillery battle (the bulk of *Art.Rgt. 357*, including its headquarters, was still on Szentendre Island along the Danube). Nor did Rintelen have enough heavy antitank guns to do anything other than block the approaches leading out of Homok. Neither could he rely on *Hstuf.* Momm to keep a Soviet tank battalion at bay forever by using three antiquated small-caliber antitank guns.

As stated in the evening report, the greatest fear of the *H.Gr. Süd* leadership, having realized that the Dirlewanger Brigade's collapse had now opened the door to an advance along the Danube River basin towards Vienna, was that this could also lead to the loss of Budapest and the collapse of the front in Hungary, which would be even worse. The commanders and chiefs of staff of both *H.Gr. Süd* and *6. Armee/A.Gr. Fretter-Pico* were unanimous in believing that something had to be done quickly, even if it meant postponing Operation *Spätlese*. However, that evening, when Friessner proposed his idea to the *OKH Führungsabteilung* of diverting one or more *panzer* divisions earmarked for *Spätlese* to stop the IX Guards Mechanized Corps, both *Gen.Obst.* Heinz Guderian and Adolf Hitler vetoed his suggestion, in the continuing belief that achieving the goals of *Spätlese* was far more important.

In Friessner's mind, one thing had become crystal clear—a division headquarters was not going to be sufficient to orchestrate a coordinated response to Volkov's break-through. Achieving this goal required nothing less than a large-scale counterattack to seal off the area where the penetration had occurred. Although *Gen.Maj.* Rintelen had done everything he could and was not blamed for what had happened (surprisingly, neither was Dirlewanger), both Friessner and Fretter-Pico realized that the forces available to *Div.Gr. Rintelen* as well as its command-and-control apparatus were inadequate to handle the situation.[4] The ad-hoc, jury-rigged combination of such disparate units as the Dirlewanger Brigade, the Hungarian *2. Pz.Div.*, and *Pio.Rgt. Stab 36*, as well as a mix of artillery, engineer, and *Alarm* units, were no match for the experienced and well-balanced brigades of Volkov's IX Guards Mechanized Corps.

When queried that afternoon by Friessner's staff as to what they thought the defenses of the Ipolysag River valley needed in terms of units and capabilities for the future, Fretter-Pico's staff provided the following list of suggestions for his army group commander's consideration:

1. Deploy the Hungarian *Szent László Division* to Ipolysag from its current assembly area near Mór south of the Danube. But the *H.Gr. Süd* staff told us that they (i.e., the chief of staff and *Ia*) thought that this would be a waste of a unit, because it would not be able to break through against a tank-heavy enemy force; additionally, it was the only infantry division remaining in the army group's pool of units held in reserve for carrying out *Spätlese*.

2. or, [deploy the *Szent László Division*] and detach the *1.* and *23. Panzer Divisions* and have them both attack through a new position held by the *Szent László Division* at Ipolysag. This was ruled out because the Stuhlweissenburg Gap between Lakes Balaton and Velencze had to be held by German forces in view of the enemy's large-scale attack preparations then seen to be clearly underway. Also, the *Szent László* could not be spared (see Point 1 above). Additionally, both *Panzer* divisions were earmarked for Operation *Spätlese* and could not be released.

3. or, shift the *8. Pz.Div.* to the north of the Danube and use it to counterattack in order to restore the position at Ipolysag. Like Point 2 above, its absence also raised the danger of a breakthrough between Lakes Velencze and Balaton or one between Lake Velencze and Budapest. [After much discussion, Friessner concluded that this one was the most acceptable course of action.]

– or –

4. Combine the *Szent László* Division with one of the newly arriving *Pz.Kfw. V* "Panther" battalions under the leadership of the staff of the *13. Pz.Div.* or *Pz.Gr.Div.Feldherrnhalle*.

Friessner's staff deemed the last proposal to be a step too far, because in order to do this either division would have to be taken out of the Budapest bridgehead's eastern bank and Hitler had already expressly forbidden such a move, having declared Budapest to be a *Festung* (Fortress) on 1 December which categorically prohibited any troop withdrawals.[5]

Having done his analysis with his subordinate's staff, Friessner and his own chief of staff, *Gen.Lt.* von Grolman, concluded that what Fretter-Pico really needed was a corps headquarters *and* a panzer division, in addition to the forces that were already there. Before he could issue any orders, however, Friessner had to gain the permission of the *OKH* Chief of the General Staff. This had so far proven to be easier said than done, because any movement of significant forces had first to be approved by Guderian and then Hitler, who had the final say.

Friessner continued pleading for help from the *OKH* late into the evening of 15 December. Probably worn down by Friessner's persistence (perhaps also by his own focus on final preparations for supporting the upcoming Ardennes offensive), Guderian finally consented to allowing him to do two of the things that Friessner had proposed—immediately freeing up a corps headquarters to fight the battle and transferring a powerful, cohesive armored unit to carry out the necessary counterattack the following day. In concrete terms, Friessner proposed temporarily moving the headquarters of *LXXII. Armeekorps* and deploying the full-strength *8. Pz.Div.* to the Ipolysag area.

Once the counterattack had been carried out and German defenses in the Ipolysag Gap restored, Friessner suggested to Guderian that both the corps headquarters and the *panzer* division could be returned in time before Operation *Spätlese* commenced, five days hence. After some back and forth with Berlin that included securing Hitler's reluctant concurrence, Guderian finally agreed. Additionally, the remaining elements of the *357. Inf.Div.* along the Danube, *K.Gr. Thierfelder*—which amounted to an artillery *Abteilung* and a 273-man infantry *Kampfgruppe*—would be transferred from their positions north of Budapest and reunited under the division headquarters as soon as possible.

Armed with Guderian's (and Hitler's) permission, the *H.Gr. Süd* commander gave the green light for Fretter-Pico to order the deployment of the *LXXII. Armeekorps.* In the order, issued late in the evening on 15 December, the corps was to hand over its current area of operations and subordinate units to the neighboring *LVII. Pz.Korps,* cross the Danube at Esztergom, and become operational in its new command post at Vámosmikola no later than 10.00am the following day. Shortly after receiving his orders, and not wanting to waste any time, the corps commander, accompanied by his *Ia,* was driven from his headquarters at Alcsútdoboz, a few kilometers west of Budapest, to the command post of *Div.Gr. Rintelen* in Vámosmikola to survey the situation. The drive to the site of his new command post, 83 kilometers away, took at least two hours. By midnight, the commander of *LXXII. Armeekorps* was ready to take command, 10 hours earlier than the deadline.

In the same order, *K.Gr. Lehnert,* which had been subordinated to the *III. Pz.Korps* several days earlier, was once again placed under the control of the headquarters responsible for the unity of effort north of the Danube.[6] Lehnert had continued successfully blocking the highway west of Kismaros with his small battlegroup but would now be augmented by additional combat power, including the company from *M.G. Batallion Sachsen*, a light *Flak* battery, a light artillery section of two guns, and an engineer company. The resulting battlegroup would be retitled *K.Gr. Zirke* after its new commander, a certain *Hauptmann* Zirke from *Heeres-Pio.Btl. 751*, who had arrived to take control.

Once Zirke had taken over command of the defenses west of Kismaros, Lehnert and his *Panzerpionier* company from the *Feldherrnhalle* Division would be freed up for employment elsewhere as part of the *LXXII. Armeekorps'* reserve and would not rejoin the rest of his battalion in Budapest. Until the arrival of the *8. Pz.Div.*, the *LXXII. Armeekorps* would have to hold the line with makeshift units such as Zirke's, as well as the Hungarian *2. Pz.Div.* and *Div.Gr. Rintelen* for the next 24 hours. To bolster the strength of the Hungarian division, all of its remaining armored vehicles, whether operational or not, would be driven or towed from Esztergom to its assembly area north of the Danube and emplaced as static defenses.

The *LXXII. Armeekorps* commander was an experienced and hard-bitten officer and therefore the right man for the task. Fifty-two-year-old *Gen.Lt.* August Schmidt was a veteran of over three years of combat on the Eastern Front who had earned both the Knight's Cross and Oak Leaves to the Knight's Cross for his leadership. A native of the city of Fürth in Franconia, Schmidt had been appointed corps commander on 15 September 1944 after successfully leading the *10. Pz.Gren.Div.* in Ukraine, during the retreat through Bessarabia, and in defensive battles in the Carpathians. Along with his corps staff, Schmidt would be bringing along his corps signal battalion and, more importantly, *ARKO 472*, led by *Oberst* Harald-Christian Rose, who would assume the control and direction of all of the field artillery units deployed between the Danube and Palást, both German and Hungarian.

To add additional weight to the corps' firepower, one additional artillery battalion, a light *Flak* battalion, and two additional *Luftwaffe* heavy (88mm) *Flak* units—the Hungarian *lei.Art.Abt. 5 (mot.)*, *lei.Flak-Abt. 77*, *schw.Flak-Abt. 1/48*, and one additional heavy 88mm battalion of *Flak-Rgt. 24* from Esztergom—would be moved from their positions south of the Danube.[7] In addition to its traditional antiaircraft and antitank role, the *Luftwaffe's* 88mm guns could also be employed in the indirect fire role like regular artillery. To provide a staff to handle the burgeoning logistical and administrative requirements of these units and the other three existing artillery and two *Flak* battalion equivalents (11–12 firing batteries) that had been in the Ipolysag area for nearly a week, the staff of *schw.Art.Abt. 809* would accompany them as soon as they could be released from Budapest.

In addition to these reinforcements, during the same conversations that evening, the *H.Gr. Süd* chief of staff, *Gen.Lt.* Grolman, notified *6. Armee/A.Gr. Fretter-Pico* chief of staff *Gen.Maj.* Gaedke that the army group would be sending 25 *nagelneu* (brand-new) *Jgd.Pz. 38t Hetzers* to the Hungarian *2. Pz.Div.*[8] If this was to take place, it would represent a considerable addition to the incoming corps commander's armor strength. To get them into battle more quickly, these small but lethally effective tank destroyers would have to be manned by German crews, not Hungarian ones, because there was insufficient time to teach them to operate these vehicles. As events were to prove, not all of these *Hetzers* went to the Hungarian *2. Pz.Div.*, but were parceled out to several other formations to replace their own lost tank destroyers, such as *StuG.Kp. 1176*, which received 10 of them. Eight days later, this same company was attached to *Div.Gr. Rintelen*, where it remained until the end of the month.

The advance party of the *8. Pz.Div.* would begin moving as early as the afternoon of 16 December, but Guderian had levied one more caveat before agreeing to Friessner's proposal—it would have to leave most of its tanks behind, as well as its sole *SPW*-mounted *Panzergrenadier* battalion and its self-propelled armored artillery battalion. The *8. Pz.Div.* would not be able to pull out all at once, of course, but would have to withdraw incrementally to allow adjacent units to shuffle their forces left or right to gradually fill in the gap resulting from the departure of some the of the division's battalions still serving in the front line. The wheeled elements of the division would travel by road via the bridge over the Danube at Esztergom. The heavier tracked elements would be loaded on railroad flatcars at either Bicske or Stuhlweissenburg and offloaded upon arrival at the railhead at Ipoly-Székallos, 6.5 kilometers west of Kémence. The entire division, minus the armored elements that would remain behind as an emergency reserve, would not be completely assembled and ready to attack until 18 December.

The *8. Pz.Div.* was a battle-hardened division that had been in combat since the campaign in the West in 1940. It had repeatedly distinguished itself in combat, having fought in the East since June 1941 at Pleskau, Narva, Leningrad, Waldai Hills, Cholm, Smolensk, Briansk, Zhitomir, Tarnopol, Brody, Lemberg (Lviv), Dukla Pass in the Carpathians, and Slovakia. Its commander was the Knight's Cross awardee *Gen.Maj.* Gottfried Fröhlich, who had led the division for most of the past year. Battered during the withdrawal battles through the Carpathian Mountains and the eastern portion of Slovakia from August–October 1944, it underwent a partial reconstitution near Tarnow until the end of November while serving under the *17. Armee* in order for it to regain its offensive capability. Shipped to Hungary on 6 December, it took part in the *LXXII. Armeekorps'* abortive counterattack at Martonvasar west of Budapest two days later. When this was called off due to stiff Soviet resistance on 9 December, most of the division went into reserve, except for some of its *Panzergrenadier* battalions holding a quiet sector in the front lines, until it was called upon to begin moving north on 16 December.

Prior to its commitment north of the Danube, the *8. Pz.Div.* still had a significant amount of combat power. On 15 December, it fielded 24 operational *Pz.Kfw. V* Panthers from the attached *I. Abt./Pz.Rgt. 130*, eight *Pz.Kfw. IV*s, 14 *Jgd.Pz. IV* tank destroyers, and 11 heavy antitank guns. The following day, before it began moving north, its four *Panzergrenadier* battalions and reconnaissance battalion reported a total *Kampfstärke* of 2,100 men, a respectable amount at the time. Just as important, its artillery regiment had 45 operational field cannons and howitzers. Overall, its commander rated it as having a *Kampfwert* (combat potential) of Category II—able to carry out limited offensive operations and fully capable of any defensive mission.[9] However, as previously stated, a third of the division would have to remain behind at its old positions as a mobile reserve to prevent the breakout of any Soviet armor in the Lake Velencze area.

The decision to keep most of the division's armored elements behind, temporarily designated as *Panzergruppe Knoop* (*Pz.Gr. Knoop*, after its commander, *Oberstltn.* Waldemar Knoop), while the main body was being shipped north of the Danube was a very controversial one at the time.[10] In effect, this action would deprive *Gen. Maj.* Fröhlich of most of his armor as he prepared a counterattack that would be directed towards an enemy force much stronger in armor. Conversely, it would deprive *Pz.Gr. Knoop* of the supporting elements its commander needed to fight as a balanced team. The decision violated the basic tactical doctrine governing the employment of a *panzer* division, but the situation in the Budapest *Kampfraum* was so dire, and reserves so scarce, that Friessner felt he had no other option but to split up the division, carry out this mission quickly, and (hopefully) reassemble it in time for *Spätlese*.

Even without Guderian's agreement, Friessner would have known that he needed to keep enough troops and tanks on hand to carry out Operation *Spätlese*, its start date of 21 December now only five days away. Both Guderian and Hitler were now adamant that the counteroffensive be carried out; canceling it now was absolutely out of the question. Ironically, the idea of launching this counteroffensive had originally been Friessner's, but the risks that he was now taking undoubtedly must have weighed greatly on his mind. The bad weather was another factor influencing his decision—the steady rain and above-freezing temperatures would make any cross-country movement by tracked vehicles difficult. After the war, he recorded his thoughts on the matter in his account of the campaign in Hungary:

> We sensed the impending danger. To avert it to some extent, there was again nothing [I could] do but improvise. Thus the 8. *Pz.Div.* was quickly moved to the break-in area near Ipolysag with the order to regain the city, the key point [being] the gaps to the north and north-west, by attacking along with our own troops still present there [*Div.Gr. Rintelen*], to cut off the enemy force's forward elements and to make contact with the right wing of *A.Gr. Wöhler*. The OKH agreed with this measure, although the 8. *Pz.Div.* belonged to the *Panzer* group that was to carry out ... Operation *Spätlese*. The enemy did us the favor of not taking any action on the day the 8. *Pz.Div.* [approached] Ipolysag [since he was] putting his units in order.[11]

Regardless of Friessner's reservations, even without most of its armor (it would still bring along eight *Panzer IV* medium tanks, its two *Panzerjäger* companies, and 11 heavy antitank guns to Ipoly-Szákallos), the addition of *Gruppe Fröhlich* (*Gr.Fröhlich*)—as it would be designated—represented a considerable investment by

H.Gr. Süd towards restoring the situation at Ipolysag and sealing off the exit points from the valley.[12] Hopes seemed high that this would be sufficient to get the job done. For the first time in this battle, the defensive effort in the Ipoly River valley would be bolstered by a still-powerful and cohesive first-line German division and orchestrated by an experienced corps headquarters.

Besides sorting out how to plug the Ipolysag Gap and organizing a defense that could withstand further enemy advances, the leaders and chiefs of staff of *H.Gr. Süd*, *6. Armee/A.Gr. Fretter-Pico*, and *8. Armee/A.Gr. Wöhler* also discussed the matter of where the new boundary between the two field armies should lie and how to ensure that the connection between the two armies was maintained. Because all the participants in the conversation doubted that Dirlewanger's brigade had the strength to do this alone (the damage to the brigade was not yet appreciated, but there were now doubts about its reliability on account of the mass defection of the previous day), the *Ia* of *H.Gr. Süd*, *Obstlt.* Schäfer, proposed ordering the *24. Pz.Div.* to extend its right flank as far as the north–south railroad 10 kilometers west of Ipolysag, but excluded the requirement of retaking Ipolysag itself. This task would be the job of the *8. Pz.Div.* Any portion of the Dirlewanger Brigade east of the line drawn between Ipolysag and Palást would be automatically subordinated to the *24. Pz.Div.* (this was already in progress), while anything west of that line would remain under *Div.Gr. Rintelen.*

The *Ia* of *8. Armee/A.Gr. Wöhler*, *Oberst* Fritz Estor, protested, stating that this would be impossible to carry out because the *24. Pz.Div.* was decisively engaged in the battle for Szécsény and could not spare any forces to carry out such an assignment. Its forces were stretched too thin already. In sum, *H.Gr. Süd* would have to find another unit or provide additional forces if it wanted Wöhler to broaden his front lines. Regardless of the protestations by Wöhler's staff, the order outlining the new inter-army boundaries went out at 1.45am on 16 December to both *Armeegruppen*, stating:

> *Armeegruppe Wöhler* takes over with immediate effect the security of the area west of the previous dividing line with *A.Gr. Fretter-Pico* up to the line Ipolysag (excluded) to Szalatnya (included). The right to change the army boundaries is reserved by the *Heeresgruppe*. It is important [for *A.Gr. Wöhler*] to take over the command of our own forces [the battalions of the Dirlewanger Brigade] positioned east of the above-mentioned line, whose connection with its chain of command has been interrupted by the [Soviet] advance to the north, and to prevent an enemy advance to the north as far as possible.
>
> Signed, von Grolman, Chief of Staff, *H.Gr. Süd*.[13]

Since nothing else was available within his own army or *H.Gr. Süd* for that matter, *Gen.d.Art.* Fretter-Pico would have to be content for the moment with the deployment of the *8. Pz.Div.*, whether or not it brought any of its tanks, and assume the risk of having to temporarily get by with the barest minimum contact between the two armies. The same situation applied to Wöhler's army. The only saving grace of this situation was that the area in question occupied by the two battalions of the Dirlewanger Brigade holding the line east of Palást was even more mountainous than the terrain south of the Ipoly River and hence less suitable for the employment of armor.

Nevertheless, this meant that in practical terms, for the time being at least, until the *8. Pz.Div.* arrived, the *LXXII. Armeekorps* would have to make the most out of what it had—*Div.Gr. Rintelen* and the Hungarian *2. Pz.Div.* The remaining troops of the Dirlewanger Brigade would be divided between these two divisions, even if it meant that some of them would be under the direct control of Hungarians, something that *Ogruf.* Höfle had expressly forbidden. Force of circumstance had dictated otherwise. One result of this shuffling of command relationships was that the Hungarian commander, *Oberst* Zádor, would no longer be subordinated to Rintelen's headquarters, but would now fall directly under the control of *Gen.Lt.* Schmidt's *LXXII. Armeekorps.*

The mission of *LXXII Armeekorps* for 16 December would remain the same as it had been for *Div.Gr. Rintelen* in the wake of the failure of Dirlewanger's counterattack at Ipolysag on the afternoon of 15 December—block further enemy advances to the southwest and west using antiaircraft and antitank combat troops, including the intercepted and reassembled portions of the Dirlewanger Brigade. The enemy advance to the north via Palást was to be blocked by Dirlewanger's remaining troops (Meyer's *I. Btl.* and Polack's *III. Btl.* of SS-St.Rgt. *1*) that had been placed under the control of the *IV. Pz.Korps.* The importance of successfully carrying out this blocking mission was repeatedly stressed. Once the *8. Pz.Div.* had arrived, it would spearhead the *LXXII. Armeekorps'* counterattack to retake Ipolysag and block all of the exit points from the Ipoly River valley at Gyerk, Palást, and Pereszlény.

While all of these wheels were in motion at the higher levels of command, information about the actual condition of the various battalions of the Dirlewanger Brigade was scant at best. Despite the thrashing it had taken at the hands of Soviet troops on 15 December, few commanders or staff officers at army or army group level seemed to have understood what had actually happened and how badly it had been cut up. The main complaints about its performance centered around the defection of several hundred men of the *II.* and *III./SS-St.Rgt. 2* in the Börszeny Mountains, who by this point had all been labeled as communist sympathizers and the cause for most of the failure on 15 December. This concealed the fact that the most important defeat suffered that day had been north of the Ipoly, not in the mountains south of the river, but the two events were conflated in the minds of the staff officers of the higher headquarters.

Throughout the day, the realization slowly began to dawn upon the key leaders of *H.Gr. Süd* and *6. Armee/A.Gr. Fretter-Pico* that not only had the brigade performed poorly south of the Ipoly, but that the much larger portion north of the river had performed even worse. Not only had Buchmann's counterattack failed to throw the

18th Guards Mechanized Brigade out of Ipolysag, but many of his troops had fled in disarray when pressed by two enemy tank regiments and as many as four motorized rifle battalions. That the politicals in the *II*. and *III./SS-St.Rgt. 2* had changed sides seems to have come as no surprise—after all, Dirlewanger had warned them several days earlier about their unreliability.

But the troops in *SS-St.Rgt. 1* were mostly *SS* and *Wehrmacht B-Schützen*, men who had undergone formal military training and of whom many were decorated combat veterans. Some of these men must have hoped for eventual restoration of their previous rank after undergoing rehabilitation in combat. That the mass of them had fled in panic came as a great surprise to nearly everyone in their chain of command. German soldiers, even probationary or penal troops, were not supposed to run away from the enemy, even if they were outnumbered and outgunned. In accordance with long-established German military tradition, it would have been better for them had they fought and died where they stood.

The Dirlewanger Brigade was indeed in disarray. On the morning of 16 December, the situation was as follows: the two battalions south of the Ipoly, those of Ehlers and Nitzkowski, had been regrouped as two *Kampfgruppen* under Ehlers's command and placed under the control of the Hungarian *2. Pz.Div. Generalmajor* Rintelen had then directed that this *Kampfgruppe* be temporarily attached to *Hptm.* Hafner's *Kampfgruppe*, raising its combat strength to 450 men. Former *Oberstltn.* Nitzkowski, now without a battalion to command, was most likely ordered to return to Deménd and report to Dirlewanger. His subsequent fate is unknown, although having almost his entire battalion defect to the Red Army must not have looked good on his record.[14]

The two companies grouped together as *K.Gr. Ruhsam*, along with a small battlegroup from the mixed battalion, had been scattered after being overrun on Hill 227. An unknown though large proportion of its men had been killed or captured. The survivors had fled either to the north towards Palást or to the west towards Gyerk and Kistompa. *Obersturmbannführer* Buchmann had been forced to abandon his regimental command post in haste and flee for his life along with his *Stabskompanie* after a failed attempt at making a stand at Kistur. The cannon and mortar crews had mostly escaped with their lives, but all of their heavy weapons were lost to the tanks of the 83rd Guards Tank Regiment

Steinhauer's *II. Bataillon* had also been overrun by tanks and infantry north and west of Ipolysag, losing hundreds of men killed, wounded, and captured. After attempting to hold at Gyerk, he withdrew his remaining men at 5.30pm, supposedly "forming the battalion's rear guard" and marching them through Kistompa along with their remaining vehicles. However, the reality of their withdrawal gave the impression that it was anything but orderly. Only a portion of his men could be rounded up and formed into a small battlegroup led by Harald Momm at Kistompa, which managed to dissuade a Soviet attempt to cross the Schemnitz River bridge with a fusillade of small-caliber antitank gun fire.

After this brave show, Momm and his troops were soon subordinated directly to *Div.Gr. Rintelen*. Steinhauer's location after he withdrew was left unstated, but some of the men from his *II. Bataillon* continued running away until intercepted at *Maj.Gen.* von Roden's screen line. Some of his men even made it as far as the city of Pressburg before they were rounded up two weeks later by the *Feldgendarmes*. Eventually, Steinhauer had managed to assemble enough of his battalion and Ruhsam's surviving troops to form a 270-man battlegroup under the direct control of Dirlewanger's headquarters, all that was left of the 800-strong battalion he had started with three days before.

Obersturmführer Meyer's *I. Bataillon* had been roughly handled, but was still intact and under his control. However, after having retreated into the forest east of Palást and without communications, it was essentially out of the fight for the time being. *Untersturmführer* Polack's *III. Bataillon* had been relatively untouched and was still located between Kelénye and Ipoly-Födemes. While it was in communication with the *24. Pz.Div.*, it had none with Dirlewanger or Buchmann's regimental headquarters, although Polack could communicate with Meyer using runners. Off to the northeast and within Slovakia proper, *Ostuf.* Stegmann's *I. Btl./SS-St.Rgt. 2* was still occupying a blocking position north of Blauenstein under the control of the German Commander in Slovakia/*HSSPF-Slowakei*. It had not been engaged at all, but would soon be attached to the *24. Pz.Div.* and take part in fighting between Szécsény and Balassagyarmat.

Oberführer Dirlewanger had been compelled to move his command post to the town of Deménd against Friessner's direct order to remain in Palást, but apparently suffered no disciplinary action for his disobedience. After all, had he obeyed Friessner, he undoubtedly would have been killed or captured. At Deménd, he attempted to reorganize his brigade into a semblance of a military organization under the direct supervision of *Gen.Maj.* Rintelen. It was in dire need of it. Within the past three days, his brigade had lost nearly 50 per cent of its combat strength, and the battle was not yet over.

There were consequences of a sort, however; Dirlewanger was ordered to compose two after-action reports; one describing how the relief in place of Zischler's *II. Btl./Pz.Gr.Rgt. 26* on the night of 13/14 December had gone awry and another describing what had happened on 15 December to cause the failure of the counterattack to retake Ipolysag and the resulting breakthrough by Soviet armor. Both reports were written by the acting adjutant of Buchmann's *SS-St.Rgt. 2, Gren.* Freiherr von Uckermann.

These highly illuminating reports were sent the following day to both the *SS-HSSPF* in Slovakia and to the headquarters of *6. Armee/A.Gr. Fretter-Pico* and filed away. Both provided a wealth of information of what had happened and why, although neither of them touched upon events south of the Ipoly River where the two battalion from *SS-St.Rgt. 2* had fought. In his conclusion to the report, von Uckermann, with Dirlewanger's concurrence (since he signed it), listed the reasons for the enemy's surprising success as follows:

a. The Regiment [Buchmann's] lacked any effective antitank defense along a sector that was 12 kilometers wide. Most of the available *Panzerfausts* had been delivered the day before and training with this weapon had only taken place to a limited extent. Even the one Hungarian 80mm *Flak*, which would have been an effective antitank weapon, fired so poorly that it did not score a hit.

b. There were no [radio] communication links within the regiment. The personnel of the Regiment communications platoon were only newly assigned and completely untrained [the signal platoon with the badly needed radios did not arrive until the battle was already underway, far too late to be of use].

c. Large portions of the troops were prepared for a fight against enemy infantry troops. They were not prepared in any way for a fight against enemy tanks and some of them were in combat for the first time ever.

d. There was no reserve in the hands of the Regiment's commander to be able to stop enemy troops that had broken through or to fight the enemy infantry throughout the depth of the main battlefield. There was a lack of reserves during the battle, but [forming] a reserve was not possible due to the battle orders given.

e. There was a lack of sufficient artillery support.

f. The enemy was strongly superior to the Regiment in infantry and tanks. The 50 tanks and 8–10 infantry battalions [this was an exaggeration; the number was closer to three to four battalions] deployed on the enemy side could only be countered by the Regiment with two battalions weakened by hard fighting, sometimes lasting two days, heavy losses and preceded by marches lasting for days and were very exhausted; they also had insufficient equipment and armament, and were partly composed of personnel not suitable for the mission [referring to the recently assigned concentration camp prisoners].[15]

Much of these same points had already been noted by others higher up the chain of command, such as *Gen.Maj.* Rintelen, *Gen.Maj.* Gaedke, and *Gen.Lt.* von Grolman. But the report went on to discuss intangible factors that also influenced how the troops fought during the battle and why they performed the way they did:

> In total, probably three enemy tanks were destroyed on 15 December. The enemy also had suffered very considerable bloody losses especially in front of the *II. Battalion*, according to prisoner statements. The tactical command of the brigade was extremely difficult due to the special circumstances. The battalions were deployed individually from the movement and had been separated from their *Tross* and field kitchens for days on end due to their transport by motor vehicles [the company field kitchens and supply wagons were all horse-drawn]. The Brigade was at times spread over more than 100km in Slovakia without communication links. This in itself made it more difficult to give orders.

Freiherr von Uckermann also mentioned some of the issues involving the chain of command, and how the unauthorized dispersal of the brigade in violation of Himmler's orders affected its ability to perform its mission:

> In addition, various missions were assigned that affected the ongoing movements of the Brigade. Both the Hungarian 2. *Pz.Div.*, the commander of the *357. Inf.Div.*, and the commander of *Pio.Rgt.Stab 36* directly gave orders to individual battalions, which contradicted the orders given by the Brigade. Thus, for example, the commander of *Pio.Rgt.Stab 36* had agreed with the commander of *SS-St.Rgt. 2*, which had been laid down in a written order by *Pio.Rgt.Stab 36*, that the *III. Btl./SS-St.Rgt. 2* would move to the northern bank of the Ipoly during the night of 14–15 December 1944 and was supposed to have been deployed at Ipolysag. Without notifying the *SS-St.Rgt. 2* headquarters, the battalion remained [south of] the river ... under the command of *Pio.Rgt.Stab 36*.[16]

What is evident in the report, written by a formerly distinguished member of the German Army's vaunted General Staff, is that the manner in which the brigade was deployed and positioned, as well as the lack of suitable weapons, made its ability to carry out its mission as assigned questionable at best and the wisdom of deploying it in such a key position unwise. In conclusion, von Uckermann wrote: "Due to these difficult command relationships, the troops were put under considerable strain. Unnecessary marching movements, the misrouting of supplies and supply trains, as well as needlessly complicating the communication of orders were the result."

While Dirlewanger most likely had no business serving as a brigade commander in such a situation, even if provided sufficient communications equipment, he was by no means the only one at fault. It is true that it had been his idea to take in so many political prisoners and expand his regiment into an assault brigade capable of carrying out conventional missions. At some point, he must have oversold his brigade's capabilities, but the *Wehrmacht*'s chain of command in Hungary was just as much at fault. Its leaders had already expressed their reservations about the brigade and their preference for the *Pz.Feldausb.Div.Tatra*, which would most likely have carried out the defense of the Ipolysag Gap more successfully. *Generaloberst* Friessner should have demanded its deployment more forcefully. But that time was past; now was the time to shore up the defenses along the lines of the Schemnitz River before Volkov's mechanized corps got across it and leapt onwards towards the Hron River.

Of the front-line visits made by Dirlewanger in the immediate aftermath of the battle, only one eyewitness account remains, written by the same unnamed *Oberscharführer* who had been Harald Momm's deputy commander in the *5. Kompanie* of *SS-St.Rgt. 2*. Shortly after the disaster east of Bernecebaráti had occurred, where a large proportion of the *II.* and *III./SS-St.Rgt. 2* had defected to the Soviets, Dirlewanger arrived at the new command post of the consolidated battalion near Kémence to see for himself how his troops were doing. According to the eyewitness:

> Dirlewanger came with [Kurt] Weisse in the *Kübelwagen* and asked what had happened. He didn't blame those of us in charge, but he did rail against the Army generals who, in his

opinion, had intentionally precipitated the situation. He had the company commander give him a report on the troop levels and said, "At least the pigs are gone!" With that he expressed his dislike for the *KPD* and Social Democrats. He ordered us to gather the rest and to march to the area around Banská Štiavnica–Karpfen. Then he drove on again with Weisse. In total, our *II. Bataillon* still had the strength of a company. The *III. Bataillon* was about the same. Around 600 former prisoners had deserted to the Red Army.[17]

With the brigade now split into three different elements (Ehlers's *Kampfgruppe* with the Hungarian *2. Pz.Div.*, Steinhauer's and Momm's with *Div.Gr. Rintelen*, and the rest attached to the *24. Pz.Div.*), any sort of centralized command by Dirlewanger was impossible. In essence, he was a commander without troops, able only to exercise control of what had accumulated in Deménd—his and Buchmann's staffs, the *Tross* of several battalions, the small battlegroups of Steinhauer and Momm, stragglers, and the wounded. Even then, the remnant of his brigade was not yet out of danger. Its commitment in the Ipolysag River walley was not at an end, for some of its troops were to continue fighting there for two more weeks.

Although the brigades of the Soviet IX Guards Mechanized Corps dedicated most of 16 December towards making incremental advances and preparing defensive positions, the tempo of operations on both sides that day were markedly slower. Most of the action consisted of limited German and Hungarian counterattacks that had been ordered the previous evening to push Soviet troops off key terrain features and shore up their own defenses, as well as designating the Schemnitz River as the new antitank barrier incorporating the *Flak* battalions scheduled to arrive soon.[18] The incoming German command, the *LXXII. Armeekorps.* headquarters, mostly wanted to keep things from falling completely apart until the *8. Pz.Div.* arrived and a full-scale counterattack could be launched to retake the positions lost the previous day. The additional *Flak*, antitank, and artillery assets being brought up from the Budapest front lines would also be arriving later that day or the next to bolster the planned attack with more firepower.

Simply because the tempo of operations had slowed somewhat did not mean that there was no fighting that day. South of the Ipoly in the Hungarian *2. Pz.Div.* defensive sector, a German-Hungarian counterattack was launched against the Kinszky Manor at 7.30am and succeeded in temporarily reoccupying it after ejecting the defenders, who soon returned with a larger force and retook it a few hours later. During the previous evening, troops from the 31st Guards Mechanized Brigade had succeeded in infiltrating the southwestern portion of Pereszlény, threatening the *Flak* batteries emplaced there. At 9am, two companies of Soviet infantry launched an attack towards the southwest from their positions near Pereszlény in an attempt to roll up the entire *Pakfront* erected between Hills 151 and 158, but German reserves were able to successfully ward off this attack. Yet another counterattack at 10am returned Kinszky Manor to German-Hungarian possession.

A large concentration of Soviet troops was observed at 7.30am assembling near Csitari Puszta atop Hill 309, another large group at noon along the Nagy Volgy valley southeast of Bernecebaráti, and a battalion-sized group at 12.30pm in the area west of Homok. All of these troop concentrations were repeatedly assailed by German and Hungarian artillery fire, effectively disrupting their efforts to carry out any attacks. The artillery command deduced that these concentrations were intended as a precursor to a renewed enemy attempt to take Bernecebaráti, which was averted for the time being. South of the Nagy Volgy valley at 3pm, Soviet troops assaulted and seized fortifications erected on Hill 455 2 kilometers south of Istvan-Hegy (Hill 386). Hill 455 was the highest point still held by German and Hungarian forces in the Börzseny Mountains, but the cost of retaking it was considered too great for the benefits thus gained and the effort was abandoned for the time being.

Oberst Zádor's biggest concern at that moment was the lack of reserves to continue the defense of his extended front line extending from Kismaros on the Danube to Pereszlény, a distance of over 30 kilometers. On 16 December, in addition to 500 of his own remaining men, his division had been augmented by four German-led *Kampfgruppen* with a total of 1,364 men, including approximately 257 survivors of the two SS battalions incorporated into *Hptm.* Hafner's battlegroup. This still was not enough. Zádor had recently been sent 1,900 untrained Hungarian recruits across the Danube. These were intended to reconstitute the *IV.* and *VI. Bataillonen* of his division's *Inf.Rgt. 3 (mot.)*, but they were not yet prepared for combat and were to be held back in the rear until they were deemed ready.[19]

In regards to heavy weapons, the Hungarian *2. Pz.Div.* reported two operational German *Pz.Kfw. IV* medium tanks, one *Sturmgeschütz*, two heavy antitank guns, and four of its own 80mm heavy *Flak* guns. The *Luftwaffe*'s *Flak* batteries forming the *Pakfront* erected between Bernecebaráti and Pereszlény reported separately through *Luftwaffe* channels, but over a dozen 88mm *Flak* guns were now in position. Zádor's headquarters also reported the total loss during the past 24 hours of six *Nimrod* self-propelled *Flak* and two 80mm *Flak*. Undoubtedly, most of these losses occurred as part of the attempt to retake Ipolysag the day before. His division reported that it still fielded five light artillery batteries with a total of 19 operational howitzers.

North of the Ipoly, *Div.Gr. Rintelen* was still trying to sort out the situation and reorganize its limited resources to best delay any further Soviet attempts to break through. Fortunately, most of enemy's activity that day was dedicated towards heavily shelling known or suspected German positions and carrying out reconnaissance probes. All that Rintelen had to work with were two small *Kampfgruppen* of Dirlewanger's troops, including 130 men now led by Harald Momm and 140 of Steinhauer's, two *Luftwaffe* 88mm *Flak* batteries, three 37mm antitank guns, and five 20mm light *Flak* from the brigade's *gemischte Bataillon*. With this, Rintelen was expected to hold back one, perhaps two Soviet mechanized brigades supported by at least 50 tanks.

Rintelen reported to the headquarters of the *LXXII. Armeekorps* that the enemy initiated a strong reconnaissance in force at 10am with two assault groups, each consisting of five to six tanks and two to three companies of mounted infantry, from Kistompa towards Deménd and northwards towards the town of Szalatnya, following the course of the Schemnitz River. *Hauptsturmführer* Momm and his troops holding the blocking position a few hundred meters northwest of Kistompa were forced to displace towards the northwest to avoid being overrun. Their attempt to complete the destruction of the bridge at Kistoma before they retreated was only partially successful.

After the war, a villager who observed the fighting for the bridge near Kistompa on 16 December left the following personal account:

> The Hungarian soldiers [guarding] the wooden bridge that was mined for demolition were told that the SS would take over the bridge and then blow it up. The Hungarian soldiers then left … the two SS soldiers [guarding the bridge] saw two tanks approaching the bridge around 6pm. Relieved, they approached the tanks … too late, they realized that they were Soviet tanks—and paid for their mistake with their lives. The [other] German soldiers stationed on the outskirts of the village then shot at the tanks and the attacking soldiers, but [Soviet] superiority prevailed … The IX Guards Mechanized Corps of the Red Army, coming from Gyerk, entered Kistompa with a tank group … Several houses in the village were destroyed, many inhabitants of Kistompa were] killed. In the end, the SS troops in the village were defeated. Soviet soldiers were also killed in the fighting. Their bodies [were] taken away the next morning, but those of the dead SS men were not … About ten dead [German] soldiers lay next to the ditch for weeks without being buried … The next day, the Red Army occupied the neighboring towns of Szalatnya and Gyerk, as well as the northern district town of Leva, today's Levice.[20]

Forty-five minutes after the bridge was taken, a reconnaissance probe from the 31st Guards Mechanized Brigade pushed through the village of Felsöszemeréd (Horné Semerovce) and into the *Rautenwald* (a forest 1 kilometer west of that locality), a mere 4 kilometers east of Dirlewanger's *Hauptquartier* in Deménd. This Soviet patrol was stopped and forced to turn around before it reached Deménd when one of Momm's *B-Schützen* knocked out the lead tank with a *Panzerfaust*.

After that, things quietened down somewhat, although Momm's troops reported small groups of tanks and troops driving back and forth between Kistompa, Szalatnya, and Egeg (Hokovce) that afternoon. Egeg was on the border of Slovakia, and presumably within *Ogruf*. Höfle's area of responsibility, though luckily for him (he had positioned only a thin screen line of security troops), the only reported activity by the Red Army was the questioning of local civilians by dismounted tank crews, who then turned around and returned to Szalatnya after learning about local road conditions. Although the town of Palást was not within Rintelen's defense sector, he passed along a report by one of Dirlewanger's men that the brigade's command post had been chased out of the town the day before by four Soviet tanks. Rintelen did not know whether they were still there and had no means to find out; that would have to be done by the neighboring *24. Pz.Div.*

The biggest surprise that Rintelen experienced that day was the unexpected appearance of an *Ordonnanz-Offizier* (assistant operations officer) from the two isolated battalions from the Dirlewanger Brigade's *SS-St.Rgt. 1* located between Kelénye and the forest east of Palást. How he had made it that far alive through enemy-held territory was a wonder in itself. The unnamed *SS* officer (possibly from the regimental staff) reported that both *I.* and *III. Bataillonen* had been attacked at 12.00pm that day by strong enemy tank and infantry forces, an account that tallied with the war diary of the 18th Guards Mechanized Brigade which had been switched to that sector. In order to avoid being outflanked and overwhelmed, the officer said that both battalions had been compelled to withdraw into the woods north of the *Margarethestellung*, where they had dug in.

Instead of reporting the situation to their next higher headquarters, the *24. Pz.Div.*, the two Dirlewanger battalions learned that they were now under the control of *K.Gr. Schäfer*, a regiment-sized *Kampfgruppe* consisting of the bulk of *SS-Pz.Gren. Rgt. 40* from the *18. SS-Freiw.Pz.Gren.Div. Horst Wessel.* The *Horst Wessel*, which maintained a forward command post in Korpona, was scheduled for reconstitution and nearly all of it had been withdrawn to the Schemnitz (Banská Štiavnica) area in Slovakia, except for *Ostubaf.* Ernst Schäfer's battlegroup and several smaller attached groups from different units.[21] On 15 December, *Gen.d.Inf.* Wöhler had decided to move the *24. Pz.Div.* eastward and assign it the mission of defending against Cavalry-Mechanized Group Pliyev at Szécsény, an area better suited for the employment of armor, and have it trade places with Schäfer's *Kampfgruppe.*

Obersturmbannführer Schäfer's regiment, like the division itself, consisted chiefly of ethnic Germans from Hungary with a native German cadre and was severely understrength. Even though the division had not yet completed its formation, that had begun on 25 January 1944, it had been in nearly continuous action since 11 July, when it was committed to battle under *H.Gr. Nord-Ukraine.* By 16 December, the division was virtually *abgekämpft* (exhausted). On that date, the only element still in combat, *K.Gr. Schäfer*, consisted of two weak battalions (between 101 and 200 men), one exhausted battalion (100 men or less), four heavy *Pak* (75mm) guns, three *Sturmgeschütze*, two *Jgd.Pz. 38t Hetzers*, and one battery of artillery.

The *I.* and *III. Btl./SS-St.Rgt. 1*, nominally under the control of *SS-St.Rgt. 1* headquarters near Blauenstein, would now be responsible for defending Schäfer's right flank and maintaining contact with the left flank of *Div.Gr. Rintelen*. Initially, Schäfer reported directly to the *IV. Pz.Korps*, which was busily engaged in directly several battles, including those being fought at Szécsény and Balassagyarmat. Within a day or two, Schäfer and his troops would be subordinated to the *24. Pz.Div.* The critical hinge point was Palást, which remained unoccupied after the four Soviet tanks pulled out at some point early on the morning of 16 December. This key locality would have to be retaken in order to ensure the continuity of the front.

Throughout this entire period, the headquarters in Pressburg of the German Commander in Slovakia had been kept abreast of the situation involving the Dirlewanger Brigade by requiring it to submit daily status reports. Although it had been tactically subordinated to *H.Gr. Süd* since 13 December, *Ogruf.* Höfle was still required to monitor its administrative and logistical needs (other than fuel, food, and ammunition), as well as ensure the flow of replacement personnel and the evacuation and treatment of wounded. However, since these reports were submitted to his headquarters directly from Dirlewanger in Deménd, Höfle had to accept them at face value even though he was aware of Dirlewanger's penchant for prevarication and exaggeration. As he had not personally visited the latter's command post at any point during the battle, Höfle lacked the immediate knowledge about what had really happened.

For example, after the Dirlewanger Brigade had been defeated at the battle of Ipolysag, the brigade's evening report to Pressburg for 15 December merely stated "Brigade Dirlewanger, instructed to cooperate with *H.Gr. Süd*, continues to defend in the Ipolysag area."[22] Of course, this completely downplayed what had actually happened. The next evening report did not make things any clearer: "The enemy had not yet advanced any further than the current break-in area north of Ipolysag. In case of further continuation of the ongoing enemy attack, the deployment of motorized anti-armor units will be necessary."[23] Not only was this a gross understatement, but Dirlewanger's report made no mention of the heavy losses the brigade had suffered that day nor how its decisive defeat had made the already precarious position of German-Hungarian forces north of the Ipoly River even worse.

Thus, Höfle and his staff were kept in the dark about the true state of affairs and would not become aware how bad the situation actually was until Soviet forces had penetrated into southern Slovakia and directly threatened his fiefdom. As events were soon to prove, at that point he would be called upon to provide even more forces to shore up the crumbling front. If Höfle wanted to know the truth, he would have to contact *A.Gr. Süd* or *6. Armee/A.Gr. Fretter-Pico* directly, but even had he done so, there would have been very little he could have done about it on 16 December. His reckoning with Dirlewanger would have to wait until after the brigade had returned to the control of the German Commander in Slovakia at the end of the month.

As the fighting tapered off that afternoon, the Germans and Hungarians defending the Ipoly River valley had reasons to be grateful. Not only had the IX Guards Mechanized Corps not pushed aggressively to capitalize on its gains of the previous day, but its brigades had been thwarted at several points by counterattacks carried out by the Hungarian *2. Pz.Div.*, as well as the resistance of *K.Gr. Momm* east of Deménd. Help was on the way too, in the form of the vaunted *8. Pz.Div.* In addition, the *LXXII. Armeekorps.* would be reinforced by additional units being transferred from the Budapest Front that evening or the next morning to reinforce *K.Gr. Lehnert* standing firm west of Kismaros. The new *ARKO* that accompanied *Gen.Lt.* Schmidt's corps was getting established and would soon begin controlling the artillery fight on 17 December. Although snow had begun to fall and the temperatures at night had dropped to below freezing, the low cloud cover had also affected the Red Air Force, compelling it to ground its reconnaissance and tactical aircraft. It would thus remain unaware of the German-Hungarian counterattack until it was already underway.

Of course, the biggest development of all was the impending deployment of the *8. Pz.Div.* Moving such a large unit of over 10,000 men and hundreds of vehicles on such short notice would require a great deal of effort and would take more than 24 hours to accomplish. The most important aspect of the impending operation involved developing a plan to carry it out; this was done with utmost speed by the staffs of *H.Gr. Süd* and *6. Armee/A.Gr. Fretter-Pico*, in cooperation with plans officers from *LXXII. Armeekorps* and the *8. Pz.Div.* The order, which was issued by the *Führungsabteilung* of *H.Gr. Süd* to *6. Armee/A.Gr. Fretter-Pico* at 00.15am on 17 December, read as follows:

1. To seal off the enemy breach at Ipolysag, *8. Pz.Div.* (initially without *panzer* regiment) is to be moved at an accelerated pace to the area southwest of Ipolysag.

2. Mission: The enemy forces that have advanced to the west and northwest are to be cut off by attacking to regain Ipolysag Gap as the key point there. Once this is accomplished, then a cohesive front is to be built up on both sides of the gap in connection with the right wing of *A.Gr. Wöhler*. The important thing is to attack as quickly as possible and in a united manner before the enemy has succeeded in extending his previous success.

3. The division's *panzer* regiment is to be left between Lake Velencze and the Danube as an intervention reserve for the time being. [It must] be prepared for the possibility of a rapid withdrawal of this regiment. If the regiment is needed, the request and the reason for its transfer is to be addressed to the *Heeresgruppe*.

4. The task of the forces on the right wing of *A.Gr. Wöhler* is to support the attack of the *8. Pz.Div.* by advancing southwestward from the area northeast of Ipolysag in close liaison with *A.Gr. Fretter-Pico*.

5. In view of Operation *Spätlese*, the *8. Pz.Div.* must be disengaged as soon as the objectives of the attack have been achieved. For the occupation of the newly reestablished front, long-range observation forces (such as Hungarians, *Sicherungs* [security] units, etc.) must be made available in advance.

6. *Sicherungs-Bataillon 407* will be transferred to *A.Gr. Fretter-Pico* beginning on 18 December 1944 by motor transport to Leva, and two artillery batteries from *153. Feldausb.Div.* by land march to Vámosmikola.

7. Your concept of operations to carry out the mission is to be reported.

Signed, Friessner

The *8. Pz.Div.* would begin moving north across the Danube during the early hours the following day. Upon arrival, it would immediately be subordinated to the headquarters of *LXXII. Armeekorps*. The *8. Pz.Div.* had previously served under *Gen.Lt.* Schmidt's corps, therefore the transition would be relatively seamless because the staffs of the units already knew each other and understood how the other operated. A great deal of hope had been invested by all concerned in the success of the impending operation—now it would be the turn of the IX Guards Mechanized Corps to feel the pressure. Whether or not this would prove to be the case remained to be seen.

At this point, it might be worth asking what became of the hundreds of Dirlewanger's politicals who had defected to the Red Army between 12 and 28 December? In their postwar accounts, many of these men admitted that they had believed that their "comrades in the struggle" against fascism would welcome them with open arms, allowing them to join their ranks and fight their former tormentors. Nothing could have been further from the truth. Rather than being greeted as compatriots, their "liberators" treated them as they would any other German captives. Although German intelligence reports from the period are replete with accounts of men in German uniforms guiding Soviet troops into battle, few if any of these instances can be traced back to former members of the Dirlewanger Brigade.[24] Indeed, Soviet troops were very suspicious of their captives, especially since they had surrendered while wearing *SS* uniforms.

One of the defectors who expressed his disappointment with how events quickly turned against them was Franz Pfaffenhäuser, a former member of the Austrian Communist Party and the *III. Btl./SS-St.Rgt. 2*, who wrote in 1948:

> After a long interrogation [our captors] realized [what our motivations were] and a Russian tank colonel solemnly promised not to treat us as prisoners of war, but to take us into political or military action against Hitler. This promise was not kept despite our constant protests through all 10 prisoner of war camps we came through. There were always new promises, which were never kept, while our situation worsened in every respect.[25]

While in the prisoner of war camps, many of the defectors were harshly questioned and condemned as cowards or opportunists for not rising up in the concentration camps against their oppressors. "Why did you wait until now to defect?" was one of the most frequently asked questions. "Why did you join the SS if you hated it so much?" and so forth. The defectors' argument that it would not have changed things did not hold water as a defense with their new captors, despite the fact that they would have been slaughtered if they had risen up against the SS guards, especially in the concentration camps.

While in the Soviet prisoner of war camps, many of the Social Democrats and German Communist Party members grew disillusioned with this treatment, though some did everything they could to ingratiate themselves with their new masters. But at least they had survived the battle of Ipolysag, while many of their comrades had not. After the war and their repatriation from the Soviet Union, many of the survivors who had remained faithful to their ideology would be appointed to serve in influential positions in the new *Deutsche Demokratische Republik* (German Democratic Republic, East Germany) that was established in 1949.[26]

Some would write memoirs extolling the virtue of the "Anti-Fascists in SS Uniform" who had endured years of privation in both German and Soviet prison camps. Not all of the returnees remained active behind the Iron Curtain though. One *SPD* member who did not defect at Ipolysag, 43-year-old *Gren.* Philip Mees, surrendered to the Red Army on 1 May 1945. After repatriation from a Soviet prison camp, he resumed his prewar political activity in his home town of Kaiserslautern in West Germany, where he served on the city council from 1946–66 while remaining active as a union representative.[27]

How much their defection, capture, and interrogation had influenced the fighting in the Börszeny Mountains after 15 December can only be surmised. Soviet intelligence officers from the IX Guards Mechanized Corps would have gleaned from them some useful information about location, size, and activity of the German and Hungarian units holding the defense line between Bernecebaráti and Kémence. The defectors would have also provided the names of their commanders and what weapons their units were equipped with. Certainly, in the days that followed, Lt.Gen. Volkov's mechanized brigades would attempt to follow up with well-aimed attacks that would eventually break the back of the German and Hungarian defenses both north and south of the Ipoly. And that was exactly what he was planning during the lull between 15 and 17 December.

CHAPTER ELEVEN

The *8. Panzer-Division* Counterattacks, 17–19 December 1944

In contrast to the previous evening, the night of 16/17 December passed uneventfully. The temperature had sunk below freezing both in the lowlands and in the mountains, and sporadic snow showers continued to dust the landscape. Heavy cloud cover once again obscured the sun and rendered aerial reconnaissance problematic. Despite the onset of freezing weather, the ground had still not completely frozen in the valley, posing challenges to offroad wheeled vehicle movement. As it grew lighter, combat activity increased somewhat, though in comparison to the day before, most of the action that occurred was local in nature. What fighting there was took place during the day, consisting primarily of German and Hungarian attempts to ward off aggressive Soviet reconnaissance probes on the left and right flanks in the *LXXII. Armeekorps* sector.

By this point, most of the wheeled elements of the *8. Pz.Div.* had arrived at the division's assembly area in Ipoly-Szákallos, a mere 12 kilometers from the front lines. The few tracked elements had either arrived or were arriving during the early hours, with the exception of the two tank destroyer companies from the division's *Pz.Jäg. Abt. 43*. These two companies, with a mix of 14 operational *Jgd.Pz.Kfw. IV/70*s and *Jgd.Pz. 38t Hetzers*, were experiencing difficulties at the railhead in Bicske, where it was discovered that the flat cars were of the wrong type and would not bear the weight of these armored vehicles. It would take almost two days to sort out the mismatch. In the meantime, the division would have to do without the bulk of what few armored vehicles it had been allowed to bring north of the Danube for the counterattack (see Map 7).

A partial solution was found on 17 December when nine fully operational *Pz.Kfw. IV* tanks fresh from the factory and originally earmarked for issue to the *Honvéd* were found in the *Panzerstutzpunkt* (armor support base) of *H.Gr. Süd* at Tótmegyer, 45 kilometers west of the Hron River. These *panzers* had arrived by rail from Germany on 11 December as part of the *OKH Waffenamt* (Ordnance Department) monthly allocation of replacement vehicles for the Eastern Front. Crews from the *10. Schwadron/Pz.Rgt. 24* of the *24. Pz.Div.*, awaiting delivery of their own new tanks at the *Panzerstutzpunkt*, were ordered to commandeer them and drive to Ipoly-Székallos, where they would be temporarily attached to the *8. Pz.Div.* for the upcoming operation. These, combined with the eight *Pz.Kfw. IVs* the division was allowed to move north, would theoretically provide an adequate amount of armor support until the arrival of the 14 tank destroyers.[1]

At the front that day, even though relatively quiet by German standards, soldiers from both sides continued fighting and killing one another. However, reports were beginning to arrive at *Gen.Lt.* Schmidt's headquarters in Vámosmikola describing signs of enemy reinforcements being moved forward along the northern bank of the Danube. For example, on the *LXXII. Armeekorps'* right flank, the newly activated *K.Gr. Zirke*, positioned 2 kilometers west of Kismaros, repelled an advancing enemy force and brought in a number of prisoners from the 53rd Rifle Division, including some from the attached 63rd Penal Company. Twelve kilometers to the northeast, newly arrived Soviet artillery and multiple rocket launchers were spotted moving into position near the village of Nográd, but they were out of range of German guns.[2]

Five kilometers north of Kismaros, troops from the Hungarian *2. Pz.Div.* reported that they had observed an enemy force in the strength of two rifle battalions moving into the town of Szokolya. Shortly afterwards, a company-strong body of enemy troops began advancing in a westerly direction from the town, but this force was repulsed after several of its men were taken prisoner, establishing the presence of the 6th Guards Airborne Division. On the hills 6 kilometers east of Kémence, several enemy attacks were repulsed by elements of *K.Gr. Grosse*, which included troops from *K.Gr. Hafner* and Ehlers's *SS* battlegroup. However, the heights south of Csitari-Puszta, which were retaken in the morning by Ehlers's troops, were lost again that afternoon after three repeated counterattacks by a battalion-sized unit from the 30th Guards Mechanized Brigade. In addition, the 30th Guards Mechanized Brigade carried out battalion-sized attacks on Kinszky Manor supported by artillery, anti-tank guns, and tank fire.[3]

The Soviet attack, intended to once again regain this key position, fell short after being pummeled by the fire of German and Hungarian artillery and antiaircraft guns. Afterwards, 40 enemy dead were counted littering the fields around the farmstead. According to Hungarian reports, 30 enemy tanks from the 30th Guards Mechanized Brigade were spotted bedded down in the Homok area, which would be a key objective of the upcoming attack by the *8. Pz.Div.* Fortunately, none of these tanks conducted any sort of operation that day, but remained stationary. Five kilometers north of Bernecebaráti, a large number of enemy troops, most likely from the 31st Guards Mechanized Brigade, had assembled in the southeastern outskirts of Pereszlény.

In front of *Div.Gr. Rintelen*, the blocking position set up east of Deménd by *Hstuf.* Harald Momm continued to hold out against enemy probing attacks of up to company strength. Two kilometers south of Momm's position, troops from

Steinhauer's small *SS* battlegroup reported a concentration of enemy forces forming in the area surrounding the village of Alsószemeréd, which was promptly shelled by German artillery fire. To the north at the far-left flank of *LXXII. Armeekorps*, reconnaissance troops from *Div.Gr. Rintelen* reported at 5.10pm that they had spotted five enemy tanks moving between the town of Egeg and the approaches to the town of Gyügy (Dudince). This report indicated that Soviet reconnaissance forces had crossed the Slovakian border, where at that particular moment there was nothing to stop them except lightly armed security troops belonging to the German Commander in Slovakia. Upon being notified, the now-alarmed *Ogruf.* Höfle alerted some of his *SS* units, armed with hand-held antitank weapons, to begin deploying to that section of the border between Slovakia and Hungary before the IX Guards Mechanized Corps could secure a foothold.

In composing his estimate of the enemy's future intentions, *Gen.Lt.* Schmidt demonstrated that he had quickly acquired a level of local situational awareness that would guide his actions during the next several days. Drawing upon the knowledge derived by his own corps' *Ic* as well as military intelligence provided by the *6. Armee/A.Gr. Fretter-Pico* and *H.Gr. Süd* staffs, Schmidt deduced that the Red Army would continue to carry on attacks on the right flank of the corps, while along the rest of the *LXXII. Armeekorps*' front line it would continue its aggressive attempts to feel out German and Hungarian defensive positions using armed reconnaissance. In this, he got it partially correct; but he had no idea of the scale of what was headed his way, since German intelligence assets (air, ground, and electronic) had been unable to penetrate the thick cloud cover in the airspace over the battlefield. Nor had German intelligence been able to gain access to the Soviet tactical command network beyond front level or higher on the ground. For that, Schmidt would soon learn their intentions by bitter experience.

In the meantime, the mass of the *8. Pz.Div.* (without its armored elements) had arrived and was making final preparations to attack towards the Ipolysag Gap beginning on the night of 17/18 December. In his own *KTB* daily report composed that evening, *Gen.Lt.* Schmidt expressed his personal thoughts:

> Due to the non-arrival of the division's *Panzerjäger Abteilung*, which is to be brought in express transport from Bicske but will probably not arrive before the afternoon of 18 December, the enterprise is substantially impaired … On the other hand, we succeeded in establishing radio communication with the *24. Pz.Div.* headquarters, located in Csáb [Čebovce] … which will support the attack of the *8. Pz.Div.* from the northeast by attacking from the Kelénye area to the southwest. The coming days will decide whether it will be possible to cut off the enemy from his rear communications in the dangerous narrows of Ipolysag and to destroy the parts we will have trapped. [I] will first go to the command post of *K.Gr. Grosse* in Kémence and [then] to that of the *8. Pz.Div.* [in Ipoly-Szákallos].[4]

As the events of the day played out as described above, the *LXXII. Armeekorps* issued the operations order for its counterattack at 3.45pm to its three divisions—the

8. Pz.Div. (referred to as *Gr. Fröhlich*), the Hungarian *2. Pz.Div.*, and *Div.Gr. Rintelen.* It was short and succinct, an indication that the high standard of German staff planning techniques and procedures had not declined appreciably despite the hurried nature of this operation. The scheme of maneuver was described in the order as follows:

1. The assembly area for *Gr. Fröhlich* will be the area northeast of Bernecebaráti. Once the preparations in the assembly have been completed, it will commence its surprise attack during the night of 17–18 December without artillery preparation.

2. The initial objectives are the localities of Hont and Ipolysag. The advance of the first echelon will consist of two [*Panzergrenadier*] battalions, of which one will orient on Ipolysag. The second echelon, consisting of [*Gr. Fröhlich's*] third battalion, has the mission of attacking the [enemy's] antitank gun barrier [*Pakfront*] west of Ipolysag from the rear, thereby clearing the way for the penetration by the armored and motorized elements [of the division].

3. After regrouping, the advance will continue until Dregelypalánk and Ipolyhidvég have been taken, then a [defensive] barrier will be erected along the narrows facing towards the east … that will be defended by the *Pz.Jäg. Abt.* of the *8. Pz.Div.* In addition, the armored portion [of the attacking force] will advance from Ipolysag into the rear of the enemy force located to the northwest; [*Gr. Fröhlich*] will then erect an antitank barrier in Ipolysag using [the *Luftwaffe's*] heavy antiaircraft guns.[5]

4. Simultaneously, *Div.Gr. Rintelen* [including the Dirlewanger Brigade] will attack to tie up enemy forces to its front and depending on the effect of the attack by the *8. Pz.Div.*, will push [its front line] forward towards the area along the Schemnitz River.

5. Priority of Fires: Artillery and mortar units will support the attack [by *Gr. Fröhlich*] with concentrated fire.

6. Other units [*K.Gr. Grosse, K.Gr. Hafner*, Hungarian *2. Pz.Div.*, etc.] located in or on either side of the *8. Pz.Div.* zone of attack will be subordinated to the division in order to facilitate its advance [and to protect its flanks].

At the bottom of this order, *Gen.Lt.* Schmidt appended his own comments on the copy that was sent to Fretter-Pico's headquarters, stating: "This plan of attack is based on detailed terrain reconnaissance carried out by the commander of the *8. Pz.Div.* utilizing the knowledge of troops previously deployed in this sector that has been analyzed in detail by the *8. Pz.Div.* and incorporated within this order."[6] The order also listed additional specific tasks assigned to each of his subordinate units, as well as the requirement for them to evacuate civilians still residing in the combat zone and to keep all movement routes clear of unnecessary traffic.

Immediately prior to the attack, the three separate elements of the Dirlewanger Brigade were deployed as follows—in the south, as part of *K.Gr. Hafner*, the two understrength battalions of *SS-St.Rgt.* 2 would attack northeast towards Homok and presumably towards Hont (or Ipolysag) once Homok was taken; in *Div.Gr. Rintelen*'s area, Momm's and Steinhauer's *Kampfgruppen* would continue to block the approaches to Deménd and distract or tie down elements of the 31st Guards Mechanized Brigade while the *8. Pz.Div.* attacked towards Ipolysag; approximately 605 (the total reported *Kampfstärke*) of Dirlewanger's remaining men between Deménd and Kémence would take part directly or indirectly in the counterattack that day.

Lastly, Meyer's *I.* and Polack's *III. Btl./SS-St.Rgt. 1*, now operating under the control of *K.Gr Schäfer* of the *18. SS-Freiw.Pz.Gr.Div.*, would protect that division's right flank and attempt to ascertain the size of the enemy force holding Palást. As stated in the previous chapter, Dirlewanger himself would only have control of Steinhauer's small battlegroup. There are no other records indicating his activity during this period; possibly he had entrusted the tactical leadership to *Ostubaf.* Buchmann, who in any case had not demonstrated any sterling leadership qualities thus far. As for *Hstuf.* Harald Momm and his small force, they would continue operating directly under *Gen.Maj.* Rintelen's command.

All told, the initial phase of the attack by the *LXXII. Armeekorps* would consist of three *Panzergrenadier* battalions supported by the Hungarian *2. Pz.Div.*, *K.Gr. Grosse*, and *Div.Gr. Rintelen*. Artillery fire support would be provided by at least 47 guns of 105mm or larger, including 18 howitzers from the *8. Pz.Div.*'s artillery regiment and two 210mm M 19/L31 *Mörser* (actually a heavy howitzer) from *Heeres-schw.Art. Abt. 736*. In addition to the 10 heavy antitank guns already in position (including four from *Pz.Jäg.Abt. 357*), the *8. Pz.Div.* would bring along 14 of its own, as well as the 17 *Pz.Kfw. IV*s (including the nine of *10. Schw./Pz.Rgt. 24*) to augment the two tanks operated by the Hungarians.[7] On paper at least, this must have appeared to be an imposing amount of firepower.

Had *Gen.Lt.* Schmidt and his staff known what was in store for them, what optimism they possessed would have quickly evaporated. The relative quiet of 16 and 17 December was merely a sign that the Red Army was taking a brief operational pause, despite the fact that the IX Guards Mechanized Corps and other units of the 6th Guards Tank Army continued to aggressively pursue armed reconnaissance nearly everywhere. One reason for this was the need to keep the Germans and Hungarians off-balance; another was to secure more advantageous positions for future operations. At that moment, *H.Gr. Süd*'s greatest worry was not a deep penetration of the Ipolysag Gap (the thinking at the time seemed to be that the *8. Pz.Div.* counterattack would be sufficient to take care of that), but that the Soviet tanks spotted moving northward towards Egeg and Palást heralded a much more dangerous advance towards the large town of Karpfen and the possible envelopment of the right flank of *8. Armee/A. Gr. Wöhler.*

While the Second and Third Ukrainian Fronts were still developing a follow-on plan to their enormously successful drive on Budapest and the less successful assault into eastern Slovakia, their leaders were not blind to the opportunities that had arisen in the wake of the first phase of their offensive. The leading army of Tolbukhin's Third Ukrainian Front, the 4th Guards Army, had crossed the Danube south of Budapest and was pressing against the German-Hungarian *Margarethestellung* between Lake Balaton and Budapest from the east and southeast. If left unchecked, this army could breach this defense line and partially envelop the city from the south. Although Budapest was not the primary objective of the Soviet Union's offensive plans for the autumn of 1944 (seizing the approaches to Berlin in the *H. Gr. Mitte* area were), the *Stavka* had recognized the symbolic importance of the city and believed that its fall would hasten the collapse of the German-Hungarian alliance.

Thus, the outcome of the battle of Ipolysag on 15 December had created numerous possibilities. Not only did it offer the prospect of a rapid advance towards Vienna (which eventually was discarded as impractical at the moment), it also opened up the possibility of enveloping the right wing of Wöhler's *Armeegruppe* by a rapid thrust to the north aimed towards Karpfen, Altsohl (Zvoleń), and Neusohl, which is exactly what *Gen. Obst.* Friessner feared the most. This course of action was also considered by the Soviet leadership, but it was downgraded to the status of a supporting attack due to the difficulties inherent in fighting through the rugged terrain of southeastern Slovakia. But controlling the Ipolysag Gap also posed a tantalizing possibility—rather than attempting to force a crossing over the wide Hron River via a direct assault, it could be more easily overcome by an indirect approach towards the north followed by a crossing of the Hron, where German defenses seemed to be virtually non-existent. Then, an attacking force could execute a left turn, approach Esztergom from the north by moving parallel to the eastern bank of the Hron, and envelope Schmidt's entire *LXXII. Armeekorps* north of the Danube.

Once it had reached the northern bank of the Danube, such a force could launch a river crossing operation in the vicinity of Esztergom and continue pushing to the south with the aim of linking up with a complementary attack originating from the area controlled by the 4th Guards Army west of Budapest. With this, the Hungarian capital city would be completely encircled and four German and at least two Hungarian divisions trapped within it. Both attacks—the one in the north by the 6th Guards Tank Army and that in the south by the 4th Guards Army—could be supported by attacks along both banks of the Danube, neither of which up to that point had been aggressively pursued. That would soon change very quickly once the full weight of the 7th Guards Army was directed against Kismaros and the area immediately north of it.

German intelligence had actually already observed indications that rifle divisions of the newly arrived XXV Guards Rifle Corps were beginning to show up in that area between Diósjeno and Kismaros, as mentioned earlier. Along the southern bank of the Danube adjacent to the 7th Guards Army, a supporting attack by a mobile corps from the 4th Guards Army could secure the victory, but this line of approach was not being considered at the time. What the commander of the Second Ukrainian Front, Marshal Malinovsky, was considering, and what actually occurred, was to move Volkov's IX Guards Mechanized Corps north of the Ipoly to prepare for a sweeping assault to the north and northwest, to be joined by the V Guards Tank Corps with 89 operational T-34 tanks and self-propelled guns as soon as the situation permitted. At that moment, Volkov's corps still possessed 107 operational armored fighting vehicles, most of which were M-4A2 Shermans.[8]

The sector south of the Ipoly, including the Börszeny Mountains, would become the responsibility of the 7th Guards Army and its two corps—the XXVII and XXV Guards Rifle Corps, each with three divisions, with another in reserve. From north to south, these two corps would field the following divisions—in the XXVII Guards Rifle Corps, the 303rd Rifle Division would attack between Hidveg-Puszta and Hont, the 141st Rifle Division would attack between Nagyoroszi (Hill 662) and Diósjeno, and the 36th Guards Rifle Division would concentrate within Hont and defend that locality; on its left, the XXV Guards Rifle Corps would attack between Diósjeno and Kiralyret with the 6th Guards Airborne Division, the 409th Rifle Division between Szokolya-Hill 480 and Kóspallag-Hill 361, and the 53rd Rifle Division in the direction of Kismaros-Kismaros West. Altogether, the two corps of the 7th Guards Army would deploy seven divisions (including the 227th Rifle Division in reserve at Balassagyarmat), with over 60,000 men. In addition, the 7th Guards Army was supported by the 27th Independent Guards Tank Brigade, initially with 17 operational armored fighting vehicles (out of 57 assigned).[9]

How much Lt.Gen. Volkov knew of the details of this larger plan cannot be determined. Suffice to say, he had his own orders to carry out. Besides having already instructed his troops to perform the aforementioned reconnaissance, Volkov spent the period of 16–17 December consolidating and reorganizing his four brigades, bringing up supplies, and moving his artillery to positions closer to the front lines. He reported that his troops repelled several company-sized German and Hungarian counterattacks in the Börszeny Mountains east of Bernecebaráti that day, while carrying out some of his own to regain positions or to seize new ones, not all of which succeeded. Overall, the signs pointed to some sort of larger German counterattack in the offing, as was their enemy's *modus operandi.*

Volkov's three mechanized brigades dedicated as much time as possible to improving their defensive positions and preparing to ward off this anticipated attack. The 46th Guards Tank Brigade, positioned in and around Ipolysag, awaited orders that would either send its tanks to the north or northwest. Whatever the case, it was nearly at full strength, having seen very little fighting for the past five days. In the war diary entry of the IX Guards Mechanized Corps for 17 December, Volkov's operations officer, echoing his commander's thoughts, wrote:

> In a word, in front of the corps' units, there were weak groupings of enemy forces … at first glance, there appeared to be a wide possibility of an advance in the northern direction [by our troops], however, a sober assessment of the situation said otherwise. [Additionally], the left flank of the corps was unsecured. The actions of the 30th Guards Mechanized Brigade in the direction of Bernecebaráti had not brought success, but they did reveal that in the area of Bernecebaráti and Ipolyvisk [Vyškovce], the enemy was concentrating a significant amount of tanks and infantry. It is clear that the enemy intended to hold the area of Bernecebaráti in order to concentrate groups of its own forces and to organize a strike towards Ipolysag, i.e., in the rear of our troops from the [IX Guards Mechanized Corps] that were advancing towards the Palást, Szalatnya, Krinta, and Ipolysag areas. Further events showed that the assessment of the situation, made by the staff of the corps, was correct.[10]

What Volkov apparently was not privy to was the concept of operations of the neighboring 7th Guards Army, operating on his left flank. The fact that he did not know this was not unusual; Red Army corps and division commanders were usually only told what they needed to know. But as the XXV Guards Rifle Corps of that army moved westward along the northern bank of the Danube, opportunities for cooperation would soon appear. The approach of this corps, heralded by the Germans' detection of the presence of the 53rd Guards Rifle Division and 6th Guards Airborne Division, would soon exert tremendous pressure on the right flank of the *LXXII. Armeekorps* that would force *Gen.Lt.* Schmidt to send additional troops to that location. Interestingly, the final entry in Schmidt's *Tagesmeldung* for *LXXII. Armeekorps* for 17 December included a glowing report about the performance of duty on 15 December by *Hstuf.* Harald Momm submitted by *Gen.Maj.* Rintelen. The report, an indication of the good will that Rintelen must have felt for Dirlewanger's reluctant subordinate, stated:

> On 15 December 1944, *SS-Hstuf.* Momm of the *SS*-Brigade Dirlewanger, after the enemy tank breakthrough from Ipolysag to Palást and Kistompa, gathered 27 stragglers from his brigade with three light antitank guns and one medium grenade launcher, and overcame the appearance of panic and built up a defensive front one kilometer west of Kistompa. By concentrated fire, he made it difficult for the Russians to restore the partially destroyed bridge east of Kistompa, prevented the advance of enemy forces to the west, and enabled the further strengthening of the blocking position. This was of decisive importance for shutting down [the enemy's] western movement beyond the area of the breakthrough … *SS-Hstuf.* Momm was the only leader I found when I arrived in the Deménd breakthrough area who, by his independent and energetic decision, built up the defensive front in the Deménd section.[11]

It is not known whether Rintelen was driven by sympathy for a highly respected and former senior officer of the *Wehrmacht* who had been brought low for making statements critical of the regime, or by his admiration of Momm's sterling leadership qualities. Perhaps he insisted upon inserting this citation in the official record as a means to contrast Momm's performance of duty with that of Dirlewanger's *SS* officers, many of whom had joined in the general rout after the Soviet tank attack at Ipolysag two days before.[12]

Rintelen would go to great lengths to keep Momm within his unit, even after the Dirlewanger Brigade was pulled out on 19 December. But this was not to be the last deed of valor credited to Harald Momm during this battle; more was to follow. Whether or not he was aware of the praise that was being heaped upon him, Momm was still a convicted probationary soldier and Rintelen's accolades probably would not have impressed him or Dirlewanger. As things stood, Momm could only focus on his leadership duties and on preparing the men he had gathered around him for the next inevitable approach of enemy tanks. Like Dirlewanger's troops, the men of the *LXXII. Armeekorps* were most likely equally ignorant of Soviet intentions, but it probably would not have mattered to them anyway. Motivated by a sense of duty as much as by a fatal stoicism typical of this late stage of the war, thousands of German and Hungarian troops quietly moved into their attack positions during the evening of 17 December.

A great deal was riding on the outcome of this attack by the *8. Pz.Div.* The consensus among the German leaders was that a powerful thrust through the mountains on the right in a supporting attack aimed towards Homok, while the main effort on the left went through the gap between Bernecebaráti and Pereszlény, would be sufficient to retake Ipolysag and re-establish a solid defense line. The plan looked good on paper and it was thought that in a day or two—or three at the most—the situation would be cleared up and *Gen.Maj.* Fröhlich's division would be able to recross the Danube and return in time to play its designated role in *Spätlese*. It would not turn out that way.

After all of the preparations had been made and the troops given a brief opportunity to rest, *Gr. Fröhlich's* attack commenced at 6.30am on 18 December without the customary artillery barrage on known or suspected enemy positions. Most of the initial action took place in the forest north and northeast of Bernecebaráti. This fight was primarily an infantry battle, and Fröhlich's *Panzergrenadiere* experienced as much difficulty fighting their way through the forest as the two Dirlewanger battalions had nearly a week before.

At first, the advance by *Pz.Gren.Rgt. 28* and *98* proceeded satisfactorily against light resistance, and their objectives of Homok and Parassa-Puszta seemed nearly within their grasp. However, they found prepared defensive positions and an enemy that only grudgingly gave up ground. Losses began to mount, especially within the *II. Btl./Pz.Gren.Rgt. 28*, forcing the three leading battalions to call upon the artillery to support the advance before it stalled completely. This was a battle more suited for mountain troops, not mechanized troops accustomed to being supported by vehicle-mounted heavy weapons.

Kampfgruppe Hafner, operating in support of the main attack, was committed shortly thereafter to maintain the advance's momentum. Under Hafner's control was his own *Feld.Ers.Btl. 357* with 360 men as well as the remnants of *II.* and *III. Btl./ SS-St.Rgt. 2* under Ewald Ehlers. At this moment, Ehlers had 256 men under his command, a sign that he had rounded up a few more stragglers since both battalions had disintegrated on 15 December. According to Hafner after the war, this battalion performed very well and carried out its assigned duties as ordered. He remembered them as "magnificent guys, that's for sure. You could rely on them, at least that was my impression. I had [a] good experience with them." He was surprised that most of its leaders seemed to be demoted *Wehrmacht* officers, who wore no badges of rank and were addressed simply as "*Kompanie-Chef*" or "*Zugführer*."[13]

On the far left of the advance, the remnant of the *III. Btl./SS-St.Rgt. 2*, forming a *Kampfgruppe* of only 81 men, covered the left flank of *II. Btl./Pz.Gren.Rgt. 28*. It was under the nominal control of Hafner, but on this occasion was temporarily tactically subordinated to *Pz.Gren.Rgt. 28*. The name of the commander of this reconstituted "battalion" remains unknown, although it may have been former *Oberstltn.* Stockhaus, the commander of the battalion's heavy weapons company, which had the lowest number of politicals within its ranks and the highest number of former soldiers. This small *Kampfgruppe*'s mission was to advance beyond the Kinszky Manor and occupy the height immediately overlooking the fork in the road 1 kilometer southwest of Homok, while covering the left flank of the neighboring unit.

Next to it and on the left, *II. Btl./Pz.Gren.Rgt. 28* would conduct an attack in a northerly direction. Once it had reached the highway at the bottom of the hill southwest of Homok, this battalion would change the direction of its movement to the northwest in order to get behind Soviet defenses at Pereszlény. By 3.30pm, all three of the *Panzergrenadier* battalions (*I.* and *II./Pz.Gren.Rgt. 28* and *II./Pz.Gren. Rgt. 98*) and *K.Gr. Hafner* (including most of Ehlers's *Kampfgruppe*) finally broke through after heavy fighting and reached the highway running 500 meters southwest and south of Homok. Following a short period needed to reorganize after fighting their way past Hills 284 and 225, two of the battalions and *K.Gr. Hafner* continued their advance towards Homok and Parassa Puszta, while the third battalion began its turning movement on the left towards Pereszlény. The two battalions on the right and *K.Gr. Hafner* were immediately involved in heavy fighting and subjected to well-aimed enemy artillery and mortar fire. Evidently, the troops of the 30th Guards Mechanized Brigade had no intention of giving up Homok without a fight. At that point, the German attack stalled.

As the infantry worked their way slowly through the Soviet defensive network south of Homok, the armored elements of *Gr. Fröhlich* composing its *Panzergruppe* waited impatiently in their assault positions less than a kilometer southwest of Bernecebaráti. Consisting of the division's armored reconnaissance battalion (*Pz.Aufkl.Abt. 8*) and 17 tanks of *II. Abt./Pz.Rgt. 10* and *10. Schw./Pz.Rgt. 24*, its attack could not commence until the latter unit had returned from a deception operation it had been ordered to carry out during the previous evening. This operation, which does not seem to have had any impact on Soviet dispositions, consisted of having the *10. Schwadron* move to the Deménd area during the night, where its vehicles drove around making a lot of noise and wasting precious fuel in an attempt to create the impression that a large amount of German armor was concentrating in the area. Its mission accomplished, the company returned and rejoined the rest of the *Panzergruppe* by noon.

The *Panzergruppe* launched its own attack towards Homok at 2.40pm. It began well, as the tanks and armored cars successfully fought their way through the Soviet *Pakfront* that had been erected between the highway and the railroad line southwest of Homok. The attack stalled when the leading vehicles discovered that the bridge over the creek 1 kilometer southwest of Homok had been demolished and both banks mined; boggy ground on either side and high water ruled out any attempt to bypass it. After waiting until it grew dark, *Panzer-Pioniere* from *Pz.Rgt. 10* cleared the mines and made field expedient repairs to the bridge, allowing the advance to continue. After proceeding less than 500 meters beyond this point, the *Panzergruppe* halted for the night. While this was occurring, to the left of the *Panzergruppe* two battalions from *K.Gr. Grosse—Feld-Strafgef. Btl. 18* and *Bau-Pio.Btl. 144*—pushed out towards Pereszlény to widen the shoulders of the breakthrough. One company, ordered to carry out a reconnaissance into the village itself, met with enemy fire that forced it to turn around and rejoin its battalion.

On the far left of *Gr. Fröhlich*, a *Schwadron* (a company-sized unit) from *Pz.Aufkl.Abt. 8*, tasked with establishing contact with *Div.Gr. Rintelen*, advanced beyond Ipolyvisk and made good progress until it encountered enemy antitank guns occupying a position 2 kilometers north of the village on Hill 156. Faced with this obstacle and lacking any means to eliminate it, the *Schwadron* went to ground and submitted a report. A few kilometers to its north in the *Div.Gr. Rintelen* sector, fighting had intensified. At 7.00am, six T-34s, two battalions of Soviet infantry, and a pioneer company advanced from Kistompa towards Deménd, but after the leading tank was destroyed by a direct hit from an 88mm *Flak* operating alongside Harald Momm's little battlegroup, the Soviet force from the 31st Guards Mechanized Brigade was brought to a halt. For some German troops, this short but sharp action was apparently more than their nerves could withstand.

During this engagement, many of the remaining *SS B-Schützen* under the command of Momm and Steinhauer had panicked upon seeing the approach of the large enemy force and began to retreat towards the town. Observing Dirlewanger's men as they streamed towards the village, Rintelen stepped outside his command post, drew his pistol, and in a loud voice ordered them to return to the front line or he would personally shoot them. Aided by several officers who forcefully laid hands on some of the panic-stricken troops, Rintelen succeeded in restoring their composure and personally led them back towards the front line. Thankfully, the enemy had not observed the rout, and Rintelen, Momm, and other officers were able to re-establish a new blocking position a mere kilometer east of the town.

By 10am, Soviet troops began making moves to envelop the new German line, but well-directed fire from antitank guns, heavy *Flak*, mortars, and self-propelled 20mm antiaircraft guns prevented these attempts from making any progress. Notified of Rintelen's situation, *Gen.Lt.* Schmidt sent a portion of his reserve, *3. Kp./Pz.Pio.Kp.(gep.) FHH* commanded by *Oblt.* Lehnert, to lend a hand. Lehnert's force of combat engineers, who had been released from attachment to *K.Gr. Zirke* the previous evening, arrived later that afternoon after driving along a circuitous route through Szob, Ipolyszalka, Ipoly Szákallos, Százd, and Deménd. Although he had not brought a large number of troops with him, Lehnert's company of less than 100 men would provide additional firepower and mobility in the form of his *SPWs*.

Generalmajor Fröhlich, who had moved his forward command post to Kémence, summarized the progress of his attack in his evening report that day:

> [The] enemy defended tenaciously and doggedly and, in order to prevent us from cutting off his armored spearhead [in Homok] from its rearward connection, will bring in considerable reinforcements during the night. Particularly disadvantageous for our own attack were the deeply dug-in enemy antitank guns as well as the enemy tanks within populated areas and at the edge of the forest, against which our own infantry can attack only with artillery support.

Despite having only limited success that day, both *Gen.Lt.* Schmidt and Fröhlich appeared confident that the following day would bring more success after the attacking battalions had regrouped that evening. There were other bright spots to dwell upon—the corps' artillery had performed superbly that day, firing 660 rounds at various targets within the *Gr. Fröhlich* zone of attack and proving itself to be responsive to the needs of the ground assault, unlike the situation that existed on 15 December when the Dirlewanger Brigade had attempted to retake Ipolysag. Freshly provisioned and with more support on the way, the advance would then resume after midnight.

One aspect of the operation on 18 December is notable for its absence, or more accurately, its ineffectiveness—the supporting attack by the *24. Pz.Div.* from the Kelénye area that was supposed to be aimed to the southwest towards Ipolysag. Since the bulk of the *24. Pz.Div.* at that moment was tied up in heavy fighting between Szécsény and Balassagyarmat and could spare nothing of its own, the commander of the *IV. Pz.Korps* instructed the division to order the attached *K.Gr. Schäfer* to carry out the attack instead. In turn, this overcommitted battlegroup ordered the two battalions from the Dirlewanger Brigade (*I.* and *III. Btl./SS-St.Rgt. 1*) under its control to carry out this attack. How much artillery or armor support that Meyer's and Polack's battalions could expect was not mentioned, but it must not have been much.

Nevertheless, the two *SS* infantry battalions attacked from their positions in the forest northeast of Palást, and with the temporary assistance of two assault guns succeeded in occupying the town after driving out the defenders from the 18th Guards Mechanized Brigade. Shortly afterwards, a tank-supported Soviet counterattack retook Palást and forced the two Dirlewanger battalions to retreat to their original starting line. This little action provided no relief whatsoever to *Gr. Fröhlich's* attack. Suffice to say, the *IV. Pz.Korps* commander did not follow the intent of his supporting mission—assigning a motley force of *SS B-Schützen* and two assault guns to carry out such an important aspect of the plan did not auger well for the overall German *Schwerpunkt* for that day.

The leader of the IX Guards Mechanized Corps saw things unfold that day in more or less the same way as his opponents saw it. Although the two accounts of the fighting differ in some respects, especially when considering the numbers of troops and tanks committed to battle and enemy losses, there is no doubt that Volkov's corps was hard-pressed at times. In the corps' war diary, the operations officer somewhat colorfully wrote:

> At 9.00am on 18 December, the enemy went on the offensive with a large force against the 30th Guards Mechanized Brigade. Up to 2,000 soldiers and officers of the 2nd SS Assault Brigade reappeared in the attack on that part of front, [as well as the] *357. Infanterie-Division* ... The enemy offensive was conducted in three directions:[14] from Kémence, through the mountains towards Homok, to the crossing over the Ipoly river to Ipolysag; from Bernecebaráti to [the] northeast along the highway towards Homok; and from Ipolyvisk to the east in the direction of Homok ... The enemy succeeded in pushing the infantry of 30th Guards Mechanized Brigade away from Bernecebaráti by two to three kilometers, and successfully passed through the mountains and reached the railway station at Homok along the highway. There was a real threat of him seizing the station at Homok and encircling the 30th Guards Mechanized Brigade. The brigade command post, led by its brigade commander Colonel Shutov, was set up inside the station at Homok. A heavy unequal battle began that lasted six to seven hours.

There was evidently no shortage of bravery and personal initiative among the brigade's ranks. Led by an experienced and daring commander, the Soviet defenders refused to budge in the face of furious German attacks, as the war diary continued:

> The [troops] of the 30th Guards Mechanized Brigade, inspired by their heroic commander, fought like lions, and prevented the enemy from occupying the station. At 5.00pm, the enemy launched a second attack. The entire staff of the brigade headquarters, starting with the brigade commander and ending with the headquarters orderlies with weapons in their hands, repelled the enemy's attack. The continuous roar of explosions filled the air, and the valley of the Ipoly River was filled with smoke and soot as thick as fog ... The antitank regiment of the 202nd Guards Artillery Brigade and the corps' antiaircraft regiment blasted the enemy infantry with direct fire. The Germans, like madmen, continued advancing despite their heavy losses. But they did not know that their attack was being repulsed by Guards Colonel Shutov, a tortured and battle-hardened old warrior and Stalingrad survivor, whom the troops and officers loved like a father. Colonel Shutov did not retreat a step ... As the second attack of the Germans that day was repulsed, the slopes of the heights were blanketed by the corpses of the "Hitlerites."

At 5.30pm, 18 enemy tanks began to attack from Bernecebaráti along the highway to Homok. The artillerymen of 301st Guards Antitank Artillery Regiment and the tankers of the 84th Guards Tank Regiment courageously confronted the enemy. After losing four tanks, the enemy retreated to Bernecebaráti. By evening, the fighting had died down, but the counterattacks followed one after another.[15]

One thing had become clear to the German commanders after fighting concluded for that day: retaking Ipolysag and trapping the bulk of the IX Guards Mechanized Corps would be a lot more difficult that they had first thought. Besides having to continue the attack and achieve his objectives, *Gen.Lt.* Schmidt also had to worry about the corps' Danube front, where things were not going well at all. In the south of the *LXXII. Armeekorps*' sector, in comparison with the partially successful attack by the *8. Pz.Div.*, the Hungarian *2. Pz.Div.* was having an altogether more difficult time. At the same moment that Fröhlich's troops were pushing forward with their attack, *Oberst* Zádor's mixed German-Hungarian force was being subjected to a series of attacks all along his front, pointing to the introduction of additional enemy forces. In his report that evening, Zádor's German liaison team pinpointed several locations where fighting was heaviest and where the integrity of the *LXXII. Armeeekorps*' front line was quickly being compromised. The commander of the German liaison team, *D.V.K. 149, Maj.* von Gossla, wrote:

> The enemy's attacks yesterday afternoon against our positions on Klóki Hegy (Hill 307) were repulsed. At 8.30am today, an enemy attack in regimental strength centered on Csömole Völgy from Klóki Hegy and Királykö pushed back our *2. Aufkl.Abt.* towards the direction of Kóspallag. In spite of the last of our reserves being thrown into the fight, enemy troops from the 53rd Guards Rifle Division managed to reach the eastern edge of Kóspallag at 3.15pm, forcing us back towards the high ground on both sides of the Márianosztra–Kóspallag road (0.5 kilometers southwest of Kóspallag), where our troops then dug in. As of nightfall, there was still house-to-house fighting underway in Kóspallag. On the far right of our division's flank, at 9.00am Soviet troops attacked the positions of *K.Gr. Zirke* from the direction of Kismaros-West–János Domb (atop Hill 162), which, under the heavy enemy pressure, was forced to pull back to a line running from Hill 104 [less than 100 meters north of the Danube] to Hill 125.

At the time of the *Tagesmeldung*'s submission, Zádor's staff reported that enemy pressure all along the line was continuing and the course of the new *Hauptkampflinie* could not yet be determined. Zádor also informed *Gen.Lt.* Schmidt that he had committed all of his remaining reserves and that unless some of his units were released from positions they were holding in the mountains to the north, he did not believe that his division could bring the enemy to a halt with the forces available. Kóspallag was the key to the integrity of his defenses. If his forces could not retake this town, Zádor believed that the entire defensive endeavor in the south would be compromised. In closing, he stated that his division, including German troops in *K.Gr. Zirke*, had suffered heavy losses, the scale of which his staff could not yet determine.

Unfortunately, *Gen.Lt.* Schmidt could not spare any reinforcements at that moment from units holding the mountainous area between Kémence and Kóspallag. As part of the operations plan for the counterattack, Schmidt had ordered each of the battalions holding positions blocking the peaks and valleys in the Börzseny Mountains to detach one infantry company and send it to *K.Gr. Grosse* as reinforcements and to form a reserve near Kémence. Thus, *Pio.Btle. 112* and *666*, as well as the Hungarian *IV./Inf.Rgt. 3*, all of which were already understrength, had to pull one-third of their strength out of the line and have them march to their assembly area between Kémence and Bernecebaráti. In addition, all of *Bau-Pio.Btl. 144* had already been pulled out and moved to the far-left flank near Pereszlény, as previously described.

This transfer of forces from the mountain front to the Bernecebaráti area was soon to create adverse consequences for both *Gen.Lt.* Schmidt's attack and Zádor's attempt to hold his ground. During the morning, the German-Hungarian line of blocking positions running west of Kóspallag in the south to a point 3 kilometers northwest of Diósjeno was attacked by a strong battalion-sized enemy force that had attempted to infiltrate its position. Another enemy force successfully broke through a German-held security line 2 kilometers west of Mt. Kámar (Hill 662), forcing them to pull back to another terrain feature located a kilometer further west.

This last report was disconcerting. Up to this point in the campaign, this area of the Börzseny Mountains had not been the recipient of much attention from Volkov's corps and had been successfully held by *Pio.Btle. 112*, *144*, and *666* of *K.Gr. Grosse* that had been occupying the area since 9 December. Volkov had earlier ceded control of this area to the XXVII Guards Rifle Corps of the 7th Guards Army. Interestingly, Volkov's request for additional infantry support from the neighboring corps' 303rd Rifle Division were rebuffed; evidently this unit was earmarked for another mission in the south. At Schmidt's headquarters, the fact that the enemy was pursuing another course of action in the mountains north of the Hungarian *2. Pz.Div.* was a development that he had not anticipated; how much so would become evident within the next 24 hours.

The last event of the day occurred after *Div.Gr. Rintelen* had already submitted its own *Tagesmeldung* for 18 December. East of Deménd, Momm's *Kampfgruppe* had already brought a strong enemy force to a halt after knocking out one tank earlier during the day. However, this was not the end of the attempt by the 31st Guards Mechanized Brigade to reach the town and the bridge over Bur Creek on the town's west side, which the Soviets needed in order to continue their probes to the north and northwest. After sunset, Col. Seleznev's troops made another attempt to break through and this time they succeeded. Infiltrating through the countryside on either side of the town, Seleznev's two rifle battalions quickly overwhelmed the German defenders' right flank, putting them once again to flight, and seized the town by a *coup de main*. The staffs of *Div.Gr. Rintelen* and the Dirlewanger Brigade, which were already in the process of abandoning the town, were barely able to escape in time before it fell. Had it not been for *Oblt.* Lehnert's *Panzerpionier* company, which formed the rear guard, the situation would have been much worse.

Before withdrawing over the creek, German troops blew up the bridge over the Bur at 5.10pm, thus denying the enemy force its immediate objective. Providentially, *Div.Gr.* Rintelen was able to evacuate all of its antitank guns and the *Luftwaffe* heavy *Flak* by 4.30pm before the bridge went up in a cloud of smoke. Thanks to the energetic efforts of *Hstuf.* Momm, *Oblt.* Lehnert, and others, the rescued guns were quickly emplaced in three strong antitank blocking positions established north, south, and west of Deménd. *Division Gruppe Rintelen* and the Dirlewanger Brigade command posts were forced to displace rearward by 7 kilometers to the town of Hontfüzesgyarmat (Hontianska Vrbica), where both were re-established, safely out of range of all but the enemy's heaviest artillery. They would not remain at that location for very long.

The few remaining German infantrymen of the Dirlewanger Brigade (now reduced to approximately 120 men) were used to protect these guns, but establishing a new defense line was out of the question because there were simply not enough men. Part of the reason was due to the poor conduct of the men of the Dirlewanger Brigade—many of them had once again simply fled in the face of the Soviet night attack. This led Rintelen to conclude in a later report that evening that this unit no longer possessed any meaningful combat value (specifically, its men "lacked the will to fight"), with the exception of Momm and the few trustworthy men they had assembled around their battle standards. Dirlewanger's actions during this action are not known; perhaps he had already departed the scene by this point.

This incident prompted the corps commander to pen his own assessment of the brigade. Late that evening, Schmidt, echoing Rintelen, composed a memorandum to *6. Armee/A.Gr. Fretter-Pico*, using the defection of the *10. Kp./SS-St.Rgt. 2* (which had gone over to the Soviets on 15 December) as a point of departure:

> This incident makes it clear that the SS probationary units [employed here] can no longer be considered to be of any combat value. I have ordered that machine guns be set up behind these deployed SS units in order to open fire immediately on any who attempt to desert. However, even this measure can be expected to have only a limited effect in the mountainous forest terrain. In addition, these units will once again be instructed about *Sippenhaft* in order to combat the signs of any desertion.

At the bottom of this memorandum, *Gen.Lt.* Schmidt added: "In the same way [as with the *10. Kompanie*], the lack of the will to fight and actual desertion has also occurred in the SS [Dirlewanger] units subordinated to *Gruppe Rintelen*. General Rintelen stated that there was a real danger that the officers leading these units would be shot in the back."[16]

It is not known whether this memorandum was ever circulated to *8. Armee/A.Gr. Wöhler*, which still had control of the three other Dirlewanger battalions positioned in the neighboring *IV. Pz.Korps* area of operations. Two of them, the *I.* and *III. Btl./SS-St.Rgt. 1*, were attached at the moment to *K.Gr. Schäfer* of the *18. SS-Freiw. Pz.Gren.Div.*, where discipline was presumably stricter. Within *K.Gr. Hafner*, the two battalion battlegroups of *II.* and *III. Btl./SS-St.Rgt. 2* had also performed admirably, at least according to Hafner in a postwar interview. Whether he followed this order and positioned machine gunners behind these two units to prevent them from going over to the enemy is unknown, but both battalions had ample opportunities to defect if they had wished to do so. That they chose to stay is an indication that they believed that there was still something worth fighting for, if for no other reasons than their own rehabilitation or sense of honor.

Just as the defection of 15 December had become a topic of conversation within the headquarters of *H.Gr. Süd*, the poor performance of Dirlewanger's troops at Deménd was also highlighted in the official records on the evening of 18 December. The officer serving as the army group diarist wrote:

> The 1st General Staff Officer of *A.Gr. Fretter-Pico* reported that large parts of the Dirlewanger SS Brigade cannot be relied upon. He was told that some of the convicts and prisoners of conscience [the politicals] in the brigade had killed their leaders and that others had defected. *SS-Oberführer* Dirlewanger had nevertheless collected up some of his forces east of Deménd in order to repel the attacking enemy east of the town by constructing an anti-tank barrier.[17]

What is noteworthy in this statement is that Dirlewanger was given credit for Harald Momm's own delaying actions, when in fact there was no evidence whatsoever that he had been anywhere near the front lines that day, much less having heroically led his men in battle, although in the past he had shown no such reluctance. Momm's actions were specifically mentioned in the opening portion of the daily report that evening, with the diarist writing: "In Deménd, the stubbornly defending *K.Gr. Momm* was forced back to the [eastern] edge of [the town] … but he will hold."[18] Although *H.Gr. Süd, LXXII. Armeekorps*, and *Div.Gr. Rintelen* could not free Momm from his probation in the Dirlewanger Brigade, at least it seemed that they were making an honest attempt to hasten his rehabilitation.

In any case, neither *H.Gr. Süd* nor *6. Armee/A.Gr. Fretter-Pico* had much time to consider the tribulations of Momm's platoon-sized unit, which at the moment was of secondary importance in such a large battle. The general belief in both headquarters seemed to be that the counterattack by the *8. Pz.Div.* was still making good headway and going according to plan, though not as quickly as had been hoped. Much more attention was being paid at that moment to events taking place on the far-left flank of *8. Armee/A.Gr. Wöhler* as well as final preparations for Operation *Spätlese*, scheduled to take place in only two days under the control of the *III. Pz.Korps*. At that moment, bad weather and off-road movement conditions, in addition to ammunition and fuel shortfalls, seemed to mitigate in favor of postponing the counteroffensive until conditions were more favorable.

An ominous warning sign that began to capture the attention of the staffs of both army and army group headquarters during the afternoon of 18 December was the increasing amount of artillery fire being placed that day on the front lines of the *LVII. Pz.Korps*, which had taken over the sector recently vacated by *LXXII. Armeekorps*. This fire, focused on the Kapolnas Nyek and Baracska area at the eastern tip of Lake Velencze, bore the characteristics of a preparatory barrage conducted immediately prior to a Soviet offensive operation. This was unexpected, but an immediate counterattack by the Hungarian *1. Husaren-Division* seemed to put things right. Whether this event heralded something more consequential could only be surmised at the time. The intelligence staff believed that the 4th Guards Army had detected the departure of Fröhlich's *panzer* division and were merely taking advantage of a momentary weakness, but the commander of the *LVII. Pz.Korps*, *Gen.d.Pz.Tr.* Friedrich Kirschner, was not so certain.[19]

The German Commander in Slovakia was not left out of the discussion. A staff officer from *Ogruf.* Höfle's headquarters contacted Friessner's staff and notified the operations section that Soviet forces had been detected along the Slovakian border moving in a northwesterly direction between Palást and Egeg, and that small elements of the *Horst Wessel* Division had already been engaged in fighting delaying actions (whether Meyer's or Polack's battalions were involved was not mentioned). In addition, Höfle's staff in Bratislava reported that it had begun moving a Ukrainian battalion from the *14. Waffen-Gren.Div. der SS (Galizien Nr. 1)*, then undergoing reorganization, via wheeled transport to the threatened area, as well as another unspecified *SS* unit, two strong companies from a regiment of the *Heer*, and a regimental staff.[20]

This Ukrainian battalion, later identified as *K.Gr. Dern*, arrived in the vicinity of Leva at 9pm. Organized as a battlegroup, it was formed around *Ostubaf.* Karl Wildner's *III. Btl./Waffen-Gren.Rgt. 29* and included an artillery battery, an engineer company, and an antitank company from the division. It was intended to reinforce *Div.Gr. Rintelen*, which had sent an orderly officer to guide it to its positions that evening.[21] However, this did not come to pass, because the next time this unit appeared in the records several days later, it was located 15 kilometers northeast of Leva in the vicinity of the town of Bátovce under the operational control of the *18. SS-Freiw.Pz.Gren.Div.* battlegroup from the *IV. Pz.Korps*. This same Ukrainian battalion was later involved in heavy fighting as it helped to successfully block Soviet advances towards Schemnitz.[22] As events were soon to prove, *Div.Gr. Rintelen* could have put this battalion to better use at a location where its presence would have made a material difference.

One last point of interest occurred that evening before *Gr. Fröhlich*'s attack resumed after midnight. This was the decision by the commander of *6. Armee/A. Gr. Fretter-Pico* to add additional responsibilities to the *LXXII. Armeekorps*; in this case, *Gen.Lt.* Schmidt was to assume responsibility on 19 December for defending the western bank of the Danube north of Budapest from the Hungarian *VIII. Armeekorps*. This defensive sector encompassed Szentendre Island and extended as far west as the southern bank of the river at Esztergom. Why Schmidt was saddled with this additional headache at this critical moment was not explained—it appears that the Hungarian corps' mission was to focus strictly on the rear area immediately west of the garrison in Budapest. Suffice to say, *Gen.Lt.* Schmidt already had enough on his hands to deal with and this added responsibility only increased his burden.

To defend this rather lengthy piece of real estate, that included not only the south bank of the river but also supporting any friendly unit operating along the northern bank, Schmidt would assume control of *K.Gr. Thierfelder*, a rather small battlegroup consisting of the 273 men comprising the remnant of *Gren.Rgt. 945* of the *357. Inf.Div.* and two Hungarian infantry battalions, for a total of 843 men, five antitank guns, a few mortars, and two artillery pieces to cover over 46 kilometers of riverbank.[23] In addition, Thierfelder was instructed to cooperate with the Danube Flotilla, a motley assortment of German and Hungarian river gunboats that were armed with a total of eight cannon, including several 80mm antiaircraft guns. With this miniscule force, *Maj.* Georg Thierfelder, nominally commander of *Gren.Rgt. 945*, was supposed to observe the movements of the enemy on the opposite bank of the Danube and ward off any enemy landing attempts or reconnaissance parties.

Unlike the previous two evenings, fighting continued throughout the night, as both sides sought to gain advantageous positions for the morning's operations. Most noteworthy that day was the employment of a much greater amount of artillery, especially by the Soviet side. This was a sign that an infantry army (in this case, the approaching 7th Guards Army), which had a much greater complement of field artillery than a mechanized corps, had made its presence known. With more guns and a steady supply of ammunition, the volume of shelling increased significantly on both sides.

German and Soviet units frequently found themselves pinned down by heavy shelling, and instead of being able to continue their advance were forced to stop and dig in to avoid unnecessary casualties. The presence of *Oberst* Rose's *ARKO 472* was making a big difference in the effectiveness of *Gen.Lt.* Schmidt's artillery arm. German and Hungarian artillery, by the evening amounting to 50 field pieces and eight guns aboard Danube Flotilla gunboats, fired over 2,000 rounds that day alone at Soviet targets, with shells ranging in size from 75mm to 210mm heavy mortars.[24]

As it grew light enough to see, *Gr. Fröhlich* resumed its attack aimed at Homok and Ipolysag, while *Div.Gr. Rintelen* on the left and the Hungarian *2. Pz.Div.* on the right endeavored to protect its flanks. The operation began with artillery barrages directed against Soviet positions inside Homok and on the northern rim of the Börzeny Mountains. The two *Panzergrenadier* battalions (*I. Btl./Pz.Gren.Rgt. 28* and *II. Btl./Pz.Gren.Rgt. 98*) of the *8. Pz.Div.*, which the previous day had reached the railroad line on the southern edge of Homok, continued their attempt to seize

Homok station, joined by *K.Gr. Hafner* and the 180 men remaining in Ehlers's *II. Btl./SS-St.Rgt. 2*. After gaining some ground, they were thrown back into the forest south of Homok by an enemy counterattack supported by tanks, as a result suffering heavy losses.

The division's *Panzergruppe*, after artillery had worked over enemy positions west of Homok, launched its own attack at 2pm. The late start was necessary because the division's armored reconnaissance battalion (*Pz.Aufkl.Abt. 8*) needed time to reorganize and regroup its companies that morning after operating continuously for the past 24 hours at several different locations. Additionally, one of the tank destroyer companies from *Pz.Jäg.Abt. 43*, with five operational *Jgd.Pz. IV*s, had finally arrived from Bicske, adding more combat power to the assault. To provide more badly needed infantry support for the impending attack, *I. Btl./Pz.Gren. Rgt. 28* was moved from the center, where it was having no luck breaking into Homok, and then subordinated to the *Panzergruppe*, where it would hopefully enjoy more success. For the first time in days, the *Luftwaffe* also made a strong appearance, flying 186 sorties against enemy ground targets between Pereszlény and Dregelypalánk during the day and night, claiming 37 vehicles destroyed or damaged, including three tanks.[25]

To the left of the *Panzergruppe*, the *II. Btl./Pz.Gren.Rgt. 28* had begun its own attack to retake all of Pereszlény earlier that morning before sunrise. After penetrating the Soviet main defensive line undetected, the battalion approached the village from the east and caught the defending unit from the 31st Guards Mechanized Brigade completely by surprise. After a short but sharp fight, Pereszlény was back in German hands. Then, the *Panzergrenadiere* quickly organized an all-round defense of the village in anticipation of a Soviet counterattack. From their new position, the men of the *II. Bataillon* were able to observe the main attack of the day unfold less than a kilometer away towards the east along the highway connecting Kémence to Homok.

The main attack by the *Panzergruppe* made some initial progress during the first hour, approaching to within a few hundred meters of the western outskirts of Homok. Shortly thereafter, the two leading armored fighting vehicles—a *Pz.Kfw. IV* and a *Jagdpanzer IV*—were knocked out by a number of concealed antitank guns and tanks along the railroad line on the left and on the right in the wood line. Many others were hit but remained operational. Clearly, the Soviet troops defending Homok were prepared to withstand any assault and had dug fortified positions for their troops, tanks, and antitank weapons. Any chance of *Gr. Fröhlich* making rapid gains that day quickly evaporated in the heavy and sustained enemy fire.

During the fighting, the *Panzergruppe* knocked out four Soviet tanks, but this achievement was overshadowed when a report (possibly from a *Luftwaffe* reconnaissance aircraft) was received that stated 18 enemy tanks, most likely M4A2 Shermans, had been spotted in Homok. Halted by the intense defensive fire emanating from the horseshoe-shaped defensive line west and southwest of Homok, and its *Panzergrenadiere* pinned down by the combined defensive fire of the enemy, the *Panzergruppe* withdrew late that afternoon before it had suffered debilitating losses. That evening, Fröhlich reported that "the enemy probably considers his defensive barrier west of Homok to be absolutely secure and therefore has continued the movement [of his troops] to the north and northwest even during our own attacks against Homok."[26]

Meanwhile, throughout the day, the concentration of enemy tanks and troops in the Ipolysag area continued to increase in size. A large number of tanks had been observed moving into Ipolysag itself, though the actual size of the unit could not be determined. In the village of Gyerk, seven enemy tanks were detected. To add to the burgeoning number of tanks being reported seemingly everywhere, the number of armored fighting vehicles spotted in Homok had risen from 18 to 50 by the late afternoon. What these sightings indicated could be guessed at with some degree of certainty—the implications were that these were signs of impending attack by the IX Guards Mechanized Corps, if not the entire 6th Guards Tank Army. After all, the northward movement of large numbers of Soviet tanks and other armored fighting vehicles had been reported taking place between Budapest and Balassagyarmat for the past week. If the reports of increasing numbers of enemy tanks behind the front lines were true, then one of *Gen.Obst.* Friessner's most important questions might soon be answered—where was the V Guards Tank Corps?

In the evening report, the *LXXII. Armeekorps* recorded that in the *Div.Gr. Rintelen* sector, no fighting had taken place; but that was only half true. While direct ground combat did not take place that day, both sides exchanged artillery and mortar fire, with *ARKO 472* recording *Div.Gr. Rintelen* having fired 250 rounds of artillery ammunition alone. Targets included countering Soviet sapper attempts to replace the destroyed bridge over Bur Creek in Deménd, German artillery and direct fire from a *Luftwaffe* 88mm *Flak* battery ensuring that their work came to naught. Perhaps in retaliation, Soviet fire soon afterwards blanketed the German position atop Hill 210 overlooking Deménd with a deadly barrage, inflicting a considerable number of casualties among the troops occupying the hill and destroying materiel, most likely artillery or *Flak* pieces. Many of the casualties among the troops could have been avoided if the combatants had entrenching tools to dig in with; this probably refers to some of the rounded-up Dirlewanger men who had fled the previous day and thrown away some (or all) of their equipment.

Six enemy tanks were observed within Deménd itself, as well as a number of others moving along the front lines north and south of the village, apparently reconnoitering German positions and routes that could be used to bypass them. By this point, Steinhauer's *Kampfgruppe* had been reduced to only 84 men, while *Oberltn.* Lehnert had just 35. The status of Momm's little battlegroup was not given. Were it not for the 14 heavy (88mm) and 12 light *Flak* cannon (20–37mm) as well as 10 light and heavy howitzers, *Div.Gr. Rintelen* probably would not have been able to hold that day. All that Rintelen could do by this point was to hold on with what he had, and try to reinforce his defensive barrier as best he could. The arrival of at least one SS battalion from Slovakia was anticipated within the next 24 hours; should this occur, *Gen.Maj.* Rintelen informed *Gen.Lt.* Schmidt that he believed he could stitch together a continuous front line once more. Events would soon demonstrate that this was a wildly optimistic statement.

Kampfgruppe Thierfelder, on the south bank of the Danube, reported that its observation posts on Szentendre Island had spotted heavy enemy traffic of both motorized and horse-drawn vehicles moving through the town of Waitzen throughout the day, headed in a northerly direction. Otherwise, there was no significant combat activity to report. In *Maj.* Thierfelder's sector, the width of the Danube River along most of its course was beyond the maximum effective range of his weapons except his artillery and heavy mortars. Even with such a small number of guns, Thierfelder's artillery contingent maintained a brisk bombardment of the opposite shoreline throughout the day, destroying or scattering several enemy vehicles. With the exception of the narrows at Visegrád and the ferry site at Dömös, where the width of the river shrank to a mere 500 meters, the most that his infantry could do was to observe and report Soviet movements.

Along the northern bank of the Danube and in the southern hills of the Börszeny Mountains, the 53rd Guards Rifle Division continued its attacks on a broad front spearheaded by infantry units in overwhelming strength. To the west of Kismaros, the enemy broke through Hungarian and German defenses with a regiment-sized attack, smashed a Hungarian company that was preparing to carry out a counterattack, and reached the northern edge of the village of Zebegény in the strength of about two battalions (500–1,000 men). The heavily outnumbered *K.Gr. Zirke* was forced to set up an all-around defense in the riverside town of Nagymaros directly opposite the ferry landing at Visegrád.

On the eastern edge of Szob, a security line was established by *Ausbildungs-Einheiten* (training units) of the Hungarian *2. Pz.Div.* West of Kóspallag, a battalion-sized enemy attack was repulsed. North of Kóspallag, a Soviet unit of unknown strength easily broke through the thin Hungarian screening line, captured an entire Hungarian infantry company at a farmstead 4 kilometers southeast of the large town of Nagybörzsöny by bypassing it on both sides, and advanced to a point only 1.5 kilometers southwest of Nagybörzsöny. This set off alarm bells at the *LXXII. Armeekorps* headquarters, raising as it did the specter of the entire corps being cut off north of the Danube.

To address this critical situation, a portion of the *2. Pz.Aufkl.Abt.* of the Hungarian *2. Pz.Div.* was moved to that location, followed later that afternoon by a *Kampfgruppe* formed around *Pz.Aufkl.Abt. 8* of the *8. Pz.Div.* This battalion, commanded by

Hptm. Georg Amsel, was redirected from its offensive role with the *Panzergruppe* near Homok, and in cooperation with the Hungarians was able to establish a security line along the southeastern edge of Nagybörzsöny that evening. In the mountains north of Kismaros, a succession of company-sized Soviet attacks was reported northwest of Diósjeno, most likely carried out by the 6th Guards Airborne Division. These were all repulsed by elements of *K.Gr. Grosse* with the aid of artillery support.

In comparison to the detailed German reports for the day, the entries in the war diary of the IX Guards Mechanized Corps were short and succinct. Most of the corps and its brigades were focused on repelling the major German and Hungarian counterattack that was underway, while the 46th Guards Tank Brigade prepared to conduct offensive operations. The keeper of the corps' war diary, Lt.Col. Sobolev, wrote about the successful defense of Homok against the efforts of *Gr. Fröhlich*:

> There was heavy fighting all day on 19 December 1944 … to help 30th Guards Mechanized Brigade, the corps commander sent a tank battalion from the 46th Guards Tank Brigade, which by this time had concentrated in the dol. Turovce [Kistur] area. The tanks of the 46th Guards Tank Brigade struck at the [forward units] of the Germans and eased the situation of the 30th Guards Mechanized Brigade … At 4.00pm the 36th Rifle Division finally arrived in Homok. At 4.30pm, it took an active part in repelling the enemy's counterattack. Artillery of the [30th Guards Mechanized] Brigade and the 301st Guards Antitank Artillery Regiment destroyed six enemy tanks [and] the enemy attack failed. With the arrival of the 36th Guards Rifle Division, the positions of 30th Guards Mechanized Brigade were made much stronger.[27]

The forces of the *LXXII. Armeekorps* had indeed met with stiff opposition that day, especially Fröhlich's *8. Pz.Div.*, as borne out by its report of enemy losses. On that day, the corps claimed the destruction of nine Soviet tanks (four by men using infantry weapons), eight heavy antitank guns, various light vehicles and weapons, and estimated 470 enemy soldiers killed in action. In return, the *Panzergruppe* of the *8. Pz.Div.* had been reduced to only three operational *Pz.Kfw. IVs*, one *Jgd. Pz. IV*, nine *Jgd.Pz. 38 Hetzers*, and 14 heavy antitank guns.[28] According to Soviet figures, four German tanks were destroyed on 18 December, with six more on the following day, meaning a total of 10 had been lost so far in the battle, nearly half of what the Germans had started with. Apparently, several other *panzers* were rendered non-operational. With losses such as these, the hopes of a quick German victory in the Ipolysag Gap were fading fast.

Interestingly, the commander of *6. Armee/A.Gr. Fretter-Pico* was disappointed with the performance of the *8. Pz.Div.*, as evidenced by *Gr. Fröhlich's* failure to capture Homok. To express his concern and desire to see an improvement in the division's efficiency, Fretter-Pico authored a letter of admonition to *Gen.Maj.* Fröhlich that was not delivered until two days later. It stated:

> In the last several days, [your] division has demonstrated insufficient activity in the defense and lacked aggressiveness in battle. [You have] reported that it has been constantly surrounded by

the enemy and pushed out of its positions, instead of it surrounding the enemy and throwing him back. Even if there are units in the division's area [under your control] that are not part of the division, this is no reason to give way. These units are to be reinforced with your own troops. I expect the division to do its utmost to fulfil the task set for it with an indomitable will to fight and a dogged determination to win.[29]

General der Artillerie Fretter-Pico does not mention in his letter the specific incident that triggered this admonishment, but perhaps *Gen.Maj.* Fröhlich had earlier pinned the blame for whatever failure that occurred on one of the units under his control that were not part of his division.

At this particular moment, the only major "outside" unit under his division's control was *K.Gr. Grosse*, composed of several *Bau-Pioniere* battalions, *K.Gr. Hafner*, and the remnant of the two battalions from *SS-St.Rgt. 2*. It is worth pondering whether Fretter-Pico was referring to a *Versagen* (failure) on the part of Dirlewanger's troops for his division's inability to successfully complete its mission, but what really happened will never be known, as intriguing as this incident was. It is worthwhile noting, however, that the three *Panzergrenadier* battalions fighting under Fröhlich's control had suffered over 50 percent losses during the first three days of their commitment in the Börzseny Mountains, so if *Gr. Fröhlich* had failed in its task to take Homok, the blame should not have been placed upon any of his men or attached units.[30]

Meanwhile, the commander and staff of *6. Armee/A.Gr. Fretter-Pico* were quick to realize the implications of what had taken place on 19 December in the *LXXII. Armeekorps* area of operations. That evening, in summing up the situation north of the Danube after receiving *Gen.Lt.* Schmidt's report, *Oberstltn.* Marcks, the *Ia* of *6. Armee/A.Gr. Fretter-Pico*, wrote:

> North of the great Danube bend, the enemy attacked in a broad front to the west with his infantry units. He was able to throw back our defenses in several places and reach the western edge of the [Börzseny] mountains. Tomorrow [the enemy] will continue his attacks in the same direction as before and will try to establish and block the south–north road between Szob and Kémence with his leading elements.[31]

In addition to Fretter-Pico and his staff, the army group commander and his key staff were also struck by the fact that the attempt to plug the Ipolysag Gap with one reduced *panzer* division and two other burnt-out divisions was not going to suffice. Adding to this realization, which they shared with *Gen.Lt.* Schmidt, was the fear that unless something was done very quickly to stop the Soviet infantry from advancing along the northern bank of the Danube, all of the *LXXII. Armeekorps* might soon be cut off from the rest of *6. Armee/A.Gr. Fretter-Pico* and destroyed piecemeal. Not only would this compromise the entire front line of the army group and open the way for an advance towards Vienna, but Operation *Spätlese* could not then be carried out.

Just as ominous were reports from *Luftwaffe* reconnaissance aircraft that large numbers of enemy tanks and troops had been spotted that day in and around the Ipolysag area, including the area between Kistompa and Deménd. These reports indicated that the 6th Guards Tank Army was indeed positioning itself to launch an attack towards the northwest and north—seizing a bridgehead at Deménd itself would signify their intent to reach the Hron River and secure a crossing. If they followed this course of action, then the Soviets could pursue either of two often discussed options—cross the Hron and push towards Vienna (not considered very probable), or cross the Hron, turn south, and race for the Danube, where they would effectively cut off the *LXXII. Armeekorps* and seize a bridgehead over the Danube. This was considered the most dangerous course of action that the Second Ukrainian Front would most likely follow.

In the portion of the *H.Gr. Süd KTB* dedicated to analysis of likely enemy intentions and possible German counteractions, *Gen.Lt.* von Grolman, the army group chief of staff, wrote:

> Thus the major enemy attack from the Ipolysag Gap seems imminent. It can be countered only by blocking the roads leading out of the gap to the southwest, west and northwest in time [before he] attacks. The enemy's ... armored forces depend on [these roads]. Another prerequisite for the successful defense against a breakthrough at Ipolysag is to throw back the enemy infantry advancing through the Börszeny Mountains north of the Danube, in order to safeguard our own major supply routes from the south bank of the Danube via Esztergom against the threat against our flanks emanating from the mountains.[32]

Becoming aware of the enemy's intentions was one thing, but what to do about them was an entirely different matter. One thing had become clear though: the *LXXII. Armeekorps*, with three weak divisions, was not going to be enough to keep the 6th Guards Tank Army confined within the narrow space of the Ipoly River valley. The enemy's movements heralded a deadly threat that had to be eliminated quickly; this in turn demanded a response that was equally quick and deadly.

After conferring with his staff, *Gen.Obst.* Friessner notified *OKH* and briefed *Gen. Obst.* Guderian on the situation, stressing the need for immediate action. Surprisingly (although he had been kept continuously updated on the status of the attack by *LXXII. Armeekorps*), Guderian agreed. After further consultation with Friessner and his staff, *OKH* directed *H.Gr. Süd* to eliminate the threat north of the Danube first, and then to carry out *Spätlese* once that had been completed.[33] To carry out this mission, *6. Armee/A.Gr. Fretter-Pico* would send the newly arrived *3. Pz.Div.* and *6. Pz.Div.* north of the Danube without their armored components (the same as had been done with the *8. Pz.Div.*), join with the *8. Pz.Div.*, and have all three divisions continue the effort to block the Ipolysag Gap and destroy the enemy's armored forces under the control of a *Panzerkorps* headquarters. This *Panzerkorps* headquarters would also assume control of *Div.Gr. Rintelen*, including any remaining troops from the Dirlewanger Brigade.

To fulfill this role, Friessner selected the *LVII. Pz.Korps*, which would be transferred north of the Danube from its current defensive sector west of Budapest. It would assemble its forces west of Ipolysag and attack along the northern bank of the Ipoly River in a northeasterly direction, while the *LXXII. Armeekorps* would be responsible for the mountainous sector south of the Ipoly as far as the northern bank of the Danube. The armored elements of the two newly reconstituted divisions would be left behind in their current area southwest of Budapest to protect against any attack by the 4th Guards Army north or south of Lakes Velencze and Balaton, the same as had been done with the *8. Pz.Div.* armor. The neighboring *8. Armee/A.Gr. Wöhler* was ordered once again to carry out a supporting attack towards Ipolysag in a southwest direction with a regiment-size *Kampfgruppe* from the *24. Pz.Div.*

It would take two or three days to get the two *panzer* divisions into position before they could attack; in the meantime, the *LXXII. Armeekorps* would have to be reinforced to withstand the growing strength of the enemy's attacks long enough until help arrived. Towards this end, the rest of *Heeres-Pio.Btl. 751*, the remaining companies of *M.G. Btl. Sachsen*, another heavy mortar battery, and the Hungarian *II. Btl./Fallschirm.* (Parachute)-*Regiment 1* would be shifted from the Budapest bridgehead to the area north of the Danube, beginning that very evening. Additionally, the newly reconstituted elite Hungarian infantry division, the *Szent László* with four infantry battalions, would also begin moving immediately across the Danube to reinforce the *LXXII. Armeekorps*.

And what was the status of the Dirlewanger Brigade at this moment? One of its units, *K.Gr. Ehlers* (*II. Btl./SS-St.Rgt. 2*), was still operating under the control of *K.Gr. Hafner*, as was *III. Btl./SS-St.Rgt. 2*, which had rejoined its sister battalion at some point during the day. *Kampfgruppe Hafner* had been shifted over to the left of the two *Panzergrenadier* regiments and was now on the edge of the forest paralleling the road between Bernecebaráti and Homok. In his diary entry for 19 December, Otto Hafner wrote:

> I have moved my command post from the forest into the open, initially to the edge of the forest. Thus I have my "forest battalion" [his own *Feld-Ers.Btl. 357*] under control on the right and on the left around the open area the two battalions of the *SS* Dirlewanger Division [*sic*], which now also belong to me. Positioned in the open behind us are the tanks [from *8. Pz.Div.*], that is a reassurance also for the men. However, the Russians did manage to get out of the woods near Ipolysag, which means that this situation [is essentially unchanged from] before we were thrown in as infantry. But here we only have to secure from the south towards the north, [while] the Russians are trying to advance further to the west and north, possibly turning back to the south if the situation is favorable. For strong counterattacks, to prevent their exit from the Ipolysag Gap, our forces are probably not [strong] enough.[34]

Kampfgruppe Steinhauer was still fighting under the control of *Div.Gr. Rintelen*, as was Harald Momm's platoon. However, *H.Gr. Süd* issued an order that evening, signed by Friessner himself, directing that the Dirlewanger Brigade, except for elements fighting under *K.Gr. Grosse* with Hafner's battlegroup, would be entirely transferred to the control of the *IV. Pz.Korps* on 20 December. This included the brigade headquarters, the headquarters of Buchmann's *SS-St.Rgt. 2*, and everything else associated with the brigade. There was another exception. The day prior, *Gen. Lt.* Schmidt had already decided that if Dirlewanger and his brigade were to go to *8. Armee* and the *IV. Pz.Korps*, Harald Momm and the platoon he had gathered around him would temporarily remain with *Div.Gr. Rintelen*.[35]

The *I.* and *III. Btl./SS-St.Rgt. 1* (Meyer's and Polack's, respectively) were still fighting in the Palást area, attached to *K.Gr. Schäfer* of the *18. Freiw.SS-Pz.Gren.Div.*, which itself still operated under the control of the *24. Pz.Div.* The whereabouts of *I. Btl./SS-St.Rgt. 2* was unknown, although evidence indicates that it had been attached to the *24. Pz.Div.* and was fighting at Oroszd (Mahora) near Balassagyarmat.[36] The brigade headquarters would be re-established in Schemnitz, the same location as that of the *18. SS-Freiw.Pz.Gren.Div.* Most of the brigade's *Tross* would take up quarters in the town as well. The location of the headquarters of its two regiments is unknown, although by this point in the battle they had no troops under their direct control to order about anyway. By 19 December, the brigade had been reduced to a total *Kampfstärke* of between 850 and 1,050 men operating under three different commands, with few remaining heavy weapons and no artillery. It was a spent force.

Ironically, the threat of Soviet incursion into southeastern Slovakia had finally alerted the German Commander in Slovakia to the extreme danger looming ahead. In addition to promising to send two SS battalions to reinforce *Div.Gr. Rintelen* (of which neither had arrived by midnight on 19 December), he had sent a number of small *Alarm-Einheiten* (emergency units) from the *182. Reserve-Division* (*Res.Div.*) to construct roadblocks and provide early warning upon the approach of the enemy. On 19 December, this division's antitank platoon, while manning a roadblock near the Slovakian town of Gyügy (Dudince) less than 2 kilometers north of Egeg, knocked out four Soviet tanks and prevented the rest of the column from penetrating further, with *Luftwaffe-Inf.Btl. 81* providing infantry support.[37]

By this point, a battle that had begun as a relatively low-level affair, with the Dirlewanger Brigade serving as its most powerful German combat element, had ballooned into a large-scale operation that would soon involve two German corps with a total of four German and two Hungarian divisions. Initially facing a Soviet force consisting of one mechanized corps, the Germans and Hungarians soon realized that their opponent's effort had correspondingly mushroomed into an operation involving the better part of two Guards armies and one Cavalry-Mechanized Group of the Second Ukrainian Front. Rather than being initially seen as a minor sideshow, by 20 December the battle of Ipolysag would metamorphose into the most important battle being fought by *H.Gr. Süd* until the encirclement of Budapest five days later.

CHAPTER TWELVE

Reinforcing Failure, 20–28 December 1944

Although *Gen.Obst.* Friessner had made the decision to send a *panzer* corps north of the Danube to throw back the Soviet advance, several important things needed to be done before that could happen. The first in order of priority was an interim measure to reinforce the *LXXII. Armeekorps* with enough troops to ensure that it could continue to hold out long enough until the *LVII. Pz.Korps* arrived, otherwise any planned counterattack was moot. The next was to craft an operations plan that would guide the actions of all of the units involved. Lastly, *6. Armee/A.Gr. Fretter-Pico* had to get the two *panzer* divisions there in time to carry out the attack—both the *3.* and *6. Pz.Div.* had only recently arrived in the Hungarian theater of operations to take part in Operation *Spätlese* and portions of both divisions were still arriving by rail in the Veszprem area.

The reinforcement of *LXXII. Armeekorps* had been ordered the previous day and the troops involved had already begun moving to their new destination before midnight on 19 December. The operations plan for the counterattack by *LVII. Pz.Korps* had been drafted by the staff of *6. Armee/A.Gr. Fretter-Pico*, whose members had spent several hours working on it before launching it into the ether via teletype. It echoed and expanded upon a portion of the order that was issued by the *OKH's Gen.d.Pz. Tr.* Wenck before midnight on the same day. This *OKH* order directed *6. Armee/A. Gr. Fretter-Pico*, relayed via *H.Gr. Süd*, to perform the following task:

> The *3.* and *6. Panzer-Divisionen*, without their *Panther* battalions, are to be deployed immediately and in a unified fashion against the enemy's breakthrough attempt looming north of Budapest. It is important to quickly strike the enemy forces located in the area around Ipolysag decisively and to regain the general line [running from] Waitzen (Vac) to the Ipolysag Gap (center of gravity). *H.Gr. Süd* will take all measures to ensure that after this task is accomplished, the *3.*, *6.*, and *8. Panzer-Divisionen* will be immediately disengaged and made available for the execution of Operation *Spätlese*.[1]

Of course, this was rather broad guidance—the details of how to carry out this operation were left up to the organizations responsible for executing them. The order issued by *6. Armee/A.Gr. Fretter-Pico* (there does not seem to have been a corresponding order issued by *H.Gr. Süd*) was distributed to all the units involved during the early hours of 20 December. Its preamble was simple and stated the following:

1. With the arrival of the *LVII. Pz.Korps* in the Ipolysag sector (preliminary command post at Vámosmikola), the following division of command responsibilities in the previous sector held by the *LXXII. A.K.* will come immediately into force:
   a. The *LXXII. A.K.* will assume responsibility on the right [wing] with the subordinated *8. Pz.Div.*, Hungarian *2. Pz.Div.*, Hungarian *Szent László* Division, and the other German forces deployed in the Börszeny Mountains;
   b. The *LVII. Pz.Korps* will assume responsibility on the left with the subordinated *3.* and *6. Pz.Div.*, and *Div.Gr. Rintelen*;

The preliminaries out of the way, the individual tasks assigned to each corps were as follows:

2. *LXXII. A.K.* mission (until arrival of the *LVII. Pz.Korps*): To prevent further enemy advance through the Börszeny Mountains, especially on the Esztergom–Vámosmikola road, with the forces currently available. The enemy is to be thrown back into the mountains using the *Szent László* Division and the *Margarethestellung* is to be retaken. The *8. Pz.Div.* will transition to the defense in its current positions. The SS Companies Kaimer and Koch [from the *18. Freiw.SS-Pz.Gren.Div.*] located at Egeg and eastwards are to be brought in and placed under the command of *Div.Gr. Rintelen*.

3. *LVII. Pz.Korps* mission: The corps will attack at the earliest possible moment with *3.* and *6. Panzer Divisions* from the line Szete [Setich]–Százd [Sazdice] with a reinforced left wing via Kistompa and Felsötur towards the heights south of Palást, in order to turn [south] from here against Ipolysag to open the gap. The attack is to be supported by the artillery of the *8. Pz.Div.*; tanks, assault guns, and antitank guns of that [same] division are to be made available for this purpose. *Div.Gr. Rintelen* is to be charged with covering the northwest flank of the two *panzer* divisions.[2]

In concluding the order, *Gen.d.Art.* Fretter-Pico wrote: "The *LXXII. A.K.* will tie up the enemy by fire and by reconnaissance in force conducted by the *8. Pz.Div.*, which will be held in readiness to enter Ipolysag from the south via Homok when the attack by the *LVII. Pz.K.* has succeeded." This guidance was clear enough—whether there was sufficient time to carry it out or whether the forces allocated to this counterattack were strong enough had yet to be seen (perhaps an element of wishful thinking was involved in the crafting of this plan).

In turn, although no longer the main effort, *Gen.Lt.* Schmidt and his corps still had an important role to play. As was his habit, on the evening of 19 December Schmidt dictated a daily *LXXII. Armeekorps* order for 20 December detailing the situation, mission, concept of operations, tasks for individual major subordinate commands, fire support, and coordinating measures. The order read as follows:

1. **Situation.** The enemy continues to attack using the 53rd Rifle Division and the 6th Guards Airborne Division through the Börszeny Mountains and has reached the line Zebegény–Kóspallag and has made penetrations in the area to the north as far as the western exits of the mountains near Letkes and Nagy-Börszeny. In front of the corps' center, the enemy has also been strengthened considerably by bringing up and concentrating his armored forces. The attack by *Gr. Fröhlich* therefore was brought to a halt in front of Homok and Ipolysag, but has been able to prevent further advance of the enemy to the west and northwest.

2. **Mission.** *LXXII. A.K.* attacks to push the enemy back into the mountains in front of the Hungarian *2. Pz.Div.* and defends the positions gained so far with *Gr. Fröhlich* [in the center] and *Div.Gr. Rintelen* [on the left].

3. **Tasks for Individual Units:**
   a. *Gruppe Thierfelder* continues its current mission and additionally takes over security of the Danube from the northern end of Szentendre Island to Szob. [security of Szentendre Island itself became the responsibility of the *IX. SS-Geb.Korps*].
   b. **The Hungarian *2. Pz.Div.*** will be continuously reinforced by the following reinforcements: second half of *Heeres-Pio.Btl. 751*, the Hungarian *II. Btl./Fallschirm-Rgt. 1*, main body of *M.G. Bataillon Sachsen*, heavy *Mörser Batterie 8./959*, and two light howitzer batteries [from *Art.Rgt. 357*]. In addition, it will also receive the Hungarian division *Szent László* (4 battalions). With these forces, any further advance of the enemy to the west must first be prevented at all costs and with the use of the most severe means. Then, in a counterattack, the enemy is to be thrown back into the mountains. The latter is decisive for offensive operations in the coming days [the attack by the *LVII. Pz.Korps*].
   c. *8. Pz.Div.* holds its current position and attacks to throw the enemy who has advanced to Nagybörzsöny back into the mountains with as strong a force as possible. [This will] require the withdrawal of strong reserves [from elsewhere].
   d. *Div.Gr. Rintelen* mission remains unchanged; defend its current position.
   e. **Reconnaissance:** By active reconnaissance deep into the enemy-held areas—especially also on secondary routes—the enemy movements are to be monitored in order to take timely countermeasures.

4. **Artillery.**
   a. **Hungarian 2. Pz.Div.:** The *2. Art.Abt.(mot.)*—reinforced by *2. Bttr./6. Art.Abt.*—will immediately be returned to division control ... it is to prepare for the addition of two horse-drawn batteries from the *357. Inf. Div.* coming from Budapest. Mission: reinforced artillery will support defense in the division's southern defensive sector.
   b. **8. Pz.Div.:** *Pz.Art.Rgt. 80* reinforced by *2. Bttr./Art.Rgt. 736 (Mörser)* will support the division's defense.
   c. **Div.Gr. Rintelen:** Artillery support as before. The division will prepare to receive two batteries from *Feld-Ausb.Art.Rgt. 453* [*153. Feldausb. Div.*]. Once they arrive, be prepared to detach the Hungarian *5. Art. Abt.* Mission: continue defense as before.
5. The newly approaching reinforcements make it possible to pull out combat engineers [the bulk of *K.Gr. Grosse*] to carry out barrier construction. By drawing on the civilian population without exception—under the command of sappers—the barricades along and behind the entire corps front are to be continuously strengthened and completed.
6. *Korps-Nachr.Abt. 472:* Maintains telephone and radio communications as before.
7. **Corps command post:** Bela

Signed, Schmidt[3]

In summation, the key points of this order stressed defending current positions against an attack in the south by two enemy divisions, throwing them back, and reinforcement by the Hungarian *Szent László* Division. One shortcoming of the order, though not known at the time, was that it greatly underestimated the size of the enemy force headed its way. Nevertheless, the *LXXII. Armeekorps* would continue doing its best to carry out this mission for the next several days, with the *Szent László* Division playing an increasingly major role. Within the next two days, the *8. Pz.Div.* would be detached from Schmidt's corps and added to the arriving *LVII. Pz.Korps*, bringing *K.Gr. Hafner* along with it (see Map 8).

Meanwhile, the contribution by the Dirlewanger Brigade, though small by this point, was still relevant, adding as it did to the combat strength of *K.Gr. Hafner*, which at this time was still attached to the *8. Pz.Div. Hauptmann* Hafner's battlegroup, with a combat strength of 511 men, had finally been detached from *K.Gr. Grosse* and now consisted of three battalions—the remnant of his own *Feld-Ers.Btl. 357* and *II.* and *III. Btl./SS-St.Rgt. 2.* Decimated after a week of heavy fighting, desertions, and defections, the two combined *SS* battalions had dwindled to a company-sized battlegroup with a *Kampfstärke* of only 180 men by the morning of 20 December. Nevertheless, according to Hafner at least, it continued performing satisfactorily.

At some point after this date, former *Maj.d.Schu.Po.* Franz Falter, now holding the rank of a lowly *Grenadier*, took command of *II. Btl./SS-St.Rgt. 2*, replacing Ewald Ehlers, whom Dirlewanger had chosen to be the new commander of the regiment.[4] Included in this shuffling of senior leaders, *Ostubaf.* Buchmann would hand over his regiment and take command of *SS-St.Rgt. 1*, at that time fighting under the control of the *IV. Pz.Korps.* Although neither Ehlers nor Buchmann had performed their duties with much distinction, Dirlewanger had few other officers with the right qualifications to choose from, except former senior officers of the *Wehrmacht* such as Harald Momm and Freiherr von Uckermann, but that would have been going too far for Heinrich Himmler to countenance.

Dirlewanger seemed to have a penchant for recruiting former officers of the *Polizei*, such as Meyer, Steinhauer, Polack and others. Franz Falter was no exception. He had been demoted in rank because of his failure to follow orders during a battle against Tito's partisans in Podrac, Croatia, on 24 April 1944 while serving as a commander of a Croatian volunteer *Polizei* battalion. After being demoted, he served several months of incarceration at Dachau and was then assigned to the Dirlewanger Brigade on 23 September 1944. He was first assigned as a company commander in *II. Btl./SS-St.Rgt. 2* for rehabilitative purposes shortly before the brigade's commitment to the fighting at Ipolysag. Since then, he had been fighting in the Börszeny Mountains, most likely as commander of the *6. Kompanie* alongside Harald Momm's *5. Kompanie.*[5]

Besides Ehlers's (now Falter's) *Kampfgruppe*, composed of what was left of *II.* and *III. Btl./SS-St.Rgt. 2*, there was still a remnant fighting with *Div.Gr. Rintelen* under Steinhauer, but the division commander had little use for him or his troops, except for the platoon that Momm had gathered around him. By midnight on 19 December, even Steinhauer's troops along with Dirlewanger and his headquarters had departed for Schemnitz, with the exception of Momm's little group. Rintelen pinned his hopes for defending his sector upon the return of some of his men released from the Budapest garrison as well as the two *Waffen-SS* battalions that had been promised by Hermann Höfle (eventually all he received were two companies). As for the other three of Dirlewanger's battalions serving within the *IV. Pz.Korps*, they were heavily involved in fighting between Palást and Szécsény—two with *K.Gr. Schäfer* of the *18. SS-Freiw.Pz.Gren.Div.* and the other with *24. Pz.Div.*

By this point in the battle, the nonessential headquarters troops and the *Tross* from the companies, battalions, and regiments—i.e., the non-combat elements of the Dirlewanger Brigade—were no longer needed and were in the process of being withdrawn. The German Commander in Slovakia had designated the town of Schemnitz as the Dirlewanger Brigade's new assembly area, located 52 kilometers away from the headquarters of *Div.Gr. Rintelen*. For those units still fighting in the Börszeny Mountains, Schemnitz was even farther away, necessitating a march of over 80 kilometers, but that moment was nearly a week away. Until that point, they would continue fighting as part of *K.Gr. Hafner*.

Although the headquarters of the *LVII. Pz.Korps* and the *3.* and *6. Pz.Divs.* had already begun moving before midnight on 19 December into their forward assembly areas prior to launching their counterattack, there was still plenty of combat action in the *LXXII. Armeekorps* sector the next day. The Red Army was not simply going to wait for its opponent to become stronger, of course, and carried on with its own attacks before the Germans and Hungarians could mount their own. During the evening, there was little activity by the units of the *LXXII. Armeekorps*, the *8. Pz.Div.* being the only exception. *Gruppe Fröhlich* used the darkness that evening to conceal its regrouping as it prepared to carry out a deliberate defense west and southwest of Homok, with the exception of *K.Gr. Amsel*, formed from the division's *Pz.Aufkl. Abt. 8.* This battalion's mission was to retake the key town of Nagybörzsöny in the south the next morning, which had been occupied by two companies of Soviet infantry earlier that evening.

The past two days' fighting had also significantly diminished the amount of armored fighting vehicles available to the *LXXII. Armeekorps*. On the morning of 20 December, the *8. Pz.Div.* reported having only one operational *Jagd.Pz. IV* and nine *Jgd.Pz. 38t Hetzers*. All of its *Pz.Kfw. IV*s, as well as those of *10. Schw./Pz.Rgt. 24*, were non-operational, though the maintenance crews were working hard to get some of them back into the fray with functioning radios and main armament. The *357. Inf.Div.*, aka *Div.Gr. Rintelen*, also began its last full day as part of the *LXXII. Armeekorps* (or so its commander thought). It still fielded 14 operational *Luftwaffe* 88mm *Flak* cannon and one heavy antitank gun. The Hungarian *2. Pz.Div.* had only three operational *Nimrod* self-propelled 40mm *Flak* and two heavy antitank guns. It was not much to hold back the advancing 7th Guards Army, with over 60,000 men and an independent tank brigade.

The last day of the battle of Ipolysag wherein the Dirlewanger Brigade played an active role began shortly after sunrise, when the two Soviet Guards armies continued their attacks along the entire front of the *LXXII. Armeekorps*. South of the Danube, *K.Gr. Thierfelder* used its meager artillery and mortars to disrupt the visible movement of enemy forces along the northern bank highway in a bid to relieve the pressure being exerted upon the Hungarian *2. Pz.Div.* and to gain time for the approaching *Szent László* Division. During the day, Thierfelder's troops observed 20 Soviet self-propelled guns, 10 multiple rocket launchers, 10 tanks, and 200 trucks driving northwest towards Kismaros during the afternoon, but they were unable to inflict any significant damage or slow them down.

In the sector defended by the Hungarian *2. Pz.Div.*, the westward advancing enemy force was intercepted by leading elements of the newly arriving *Szent László* Division. Around Szob, the fighting continued throughout the day and into the night to prevent this *Schwerpunkt* from falling into enemy hands. North of Szob, the key heights east of the village of Letkes, which had fallen to Soviet troops the evening before, were recaptured by Hungarian paratroopers in a daring daytime counterattack. *Panzer-Pioniere Bataillon 59* of the *8. Pz.Div.*, sent to reinforce the Hungarian *2. Pz.Div.*, repulsed a battalion-sized enemy attack originating from the village of Ipolytölgyes to the east. Fighting around the critically important town of Nagybörzsöny raged throughout the day, as *K.Gr. Amsel* sought to regain control of this key locality and force the enemy back into the mountains.

The bulk of the *8. Pz.Div.* was also involved throughout the day in heavy fighting as it sought to prevent enemy infantry in superior numbers from breaking out through the Ipolysag Gap and its positions in the forest-covered mountains south of Homok. However, the division was unable to inflict any substantial damage on Soviet troops and tanks massing on the northern bank of the Ipoly. Despite intermittent German attempts to interrupt their movement by artillery fire, elements of the IX Guards Mechanized Corps were able to pass through the area with impunity, using the river to protect the left flank of its advancing column from any German attempt to intercept its movements. Undisturbed, Volkov's troops drove through the villages of Gyerk and Kistompa towards the northwest with a large number of motorized vehicles, including at least 80 tanks with *tankodesantniki* aboard.

Besides the concentration of Soviet troops on the right flank of the *LXXII. Armeekorps* adjacent to the Danube, the other flashpoint that day occurred on the corps' far left flank, where *Div.Gr. Rintelen* was defending at Hontfüzesgyarmat. Fighting relatively alone and unsupported, Rintelen's small force was attacked at 9am by a far superior enemy shock troop consisting of 36 tanks from the V Guards Tank Corps with mounted infantry aboard via the road leading westward from Hontfüzesgyarmat.[6] Two of the enemy's tanks were destroyed by the attached 88mm *Flak*, although two of Rintelen's own guns were destroyed in exchange. During the hasty withdrawal, a battery of three 105mm howitzers from the Hungarian *Art.Abt. 5* was overrun and captured intact at 3pm.[7] The approaching enemy force compelled Rintelen to relocate his command post to the village of Garam-Szt. György on the east bank of the Hron River.

Generalmajor Rintelen reported that after a failed attempts to storm the village from the north and south, the enemy commander on the scene had decided not to attempt to dislodge his small force by costly and time-consuming house-to-house fighting, but had instead chosen to bypass Garam-Szt. György entirely by going around to the north. At 2.30pm, 17 T-34s with *tankodesantniki* aboard reached the eastern outskirts of Leva, a small city a few kilometers south of the Slovak border. There was nothing there to stop them; the *Kampfgruppe* from the *14. Waffen-Gren. Div. der SS (Galizien Nr. 1)* that was supposed to establish defensive positions east of Leva on the evening of 18 December had vanished, only to reappear during the late afternoon two days later manning positions in Slovakia, 15 kilometers to the northeast.

Leaving a small force behind to mop up in Leva, which had been completely occupied by 3.20pm, the main body of the Soviet column proceeded towards the west, where it attempted to seize a crossing over the Hron River at Nagykalna (Kálnica) against light resistance. When three T-34s attempted to cross the bridge at 4.30pm, the highway span was blown up by German *Sprengtruppen* (demolition troops), although the adjacent railroad bridge was left standing; only *H.Gr. Süd* could approve of its demolition. During the next 24 hours, both Generals Rintelen and Schmidt argued back and forth with *6. Armee/A.Gr. Fretter-Pico* and *H.Gr. Süd* headquarters begging for permission to blow this bridge, but were overruled each time.

The only German forces remaining on the eastern bank of the northern Hron at this point were in a small bridgehead at Nagykalna and an equally small one downstream at Garam-Szt. György, both maintained by *Div.Gr. Rintelen*. On account of the danger, *Gen.Maj.* Rintelen's forward command post had already been relocated yet again to Graramveszele on the river's western bank before the Soviet spearhead took Leva.[8] Most of Rintelen's artillery and the *Luftwaffe*'s heavy *Flak* had been sent over the river to safety a few hours earlier. Fortunately for the Germans, the V Guards Tank Corps did not attempt to take the neighboring railroad bridge 6 kilometers downstream at Alsóvarád (Tekovský Hrádok) that was undefended at that moment. They would soon attempt to correct this oversight.

After reviewing the day's fighting within the *LXXII. Armeekorps* defensive sector, *Gen.Lt.* Schmidt was left with the impression that Marshal Malinovsky's objective was to reach and occupy the transportation hub of Parkany in the south, opposite the city of Esztergom, using the infantry divisions of Col.Gen. Shumilov's 7th Guards Army, while advancing in the north with the tanks of Col.Gen. Kravchenko's 6th Guards Tank Army, using the IX Guards Mechanized Corps and the V Guards Tank Corps, with the intent of gaining bridgeheads over the upper Hron River near Leva and Garam Szt. György. Seizing Parkany would cut off Schmidt's corps in the south and deny it a secure crossing point to the opposite bank; a bridgehead over the Hron in the vicinity of Leva would allow Soviet mechanized forces to strike southward and completely trap both the *LXXII. Armeekorps* and the *LVII. Pz.Korps* between the Hron and Ipoly rivers. If this were to happen, the result would be a disaster.

But after three days of fighting, *Gen.Lt.* Schmidt must have realized that his attempt to shore up the defenses in the Ipoly River valley had failed completely, just as those of *Gen.Maj.* Rintelen and *Oberst* Zádor had during the past eight days. Not only was the Ipolysag Gap still open to enemy movement in nearly every direction they chose, but the defenses in the Börszeny Mountains had been pierced in several locations and the Hungarian *2. Pz.Div.* was on the verge of collapse. However, with any luck, the *LVII. Pz.Korps* would arrive as scheduled in time to prevent these worse-case scenarios from becoming reality. With three *panzer* divisions attacking abreast, surely no enemy force could withstand the power of such an assault.

From the perspective of Lt.Gen. Volkov, the situation was developing very favorably indeed. Not only had his corps blunted the attempt by the *8. Pz.Div.* to retake Ipolysag, but the weakness of both enemy divisions on its flanks (*Div.Gr. Rintelen* and the Hungarian *2. Pz.Div.*) had been easily exploited. On the evening of 20 December, his corps' diarist wrote:

> The 36th Rifle Division had fully arrived and began to relieve the 30th Guards Mechanized Brigade from its area of operations south of the Ipoly on 20 December. The 36th Rifle Division did not achieve any significant success in breaking out into the area west of Homok, but did manage to push back the [*8. Pz.Div.*] by two to three kilometers and was able to restore the front line to where it was when the 30th Guards Mechanized Brigade made its greatest advance. Thus, the German threat in the Homok–Bernecebaráti area has been neutralized. The bridgehead to the southwest of [Homok] was firmly secured and most importantly, the left flank of the corps was securely protected [by the incoming XXVII Guards Rifle Corps]. The corps was then given the opportunity to pursue actions in another direction. [In a related development,] the 30th Guards Mechanized Brigade was [able to cross] to the north bank of the Ipeľ [Ipoly] River and rejoin the rest of the corps.[9]

Volkov would need this brigade for the upcoming operation, which had been designated Operation *Leviskaya* (after the corps' objective of Leva) and would also involve the newly committed V Guards Tank Corps, infantry divisions of the XXVII Guards Rifle Corps, and elements of Cavalry-Mechanized Group Pliyev.

According to the order he had been given by the commander of 6th Guards Tank Army, General of Tank Troops Kravchenko, the units of Volkov's corps began their attack at 10am on 20 December. It had actually started its mission of taking bridgeheads over the Hron River northwest of Ipolysag earlier than that, as related above. To reach its objective, his corps would advance through the municipalities of Tegzesborfő and Kálnaborfő (Dolne- and Horne-Brhlovce, respectively), Horhi (Horša), then swing to the west to seize the town of Talmach (Tlmače) and carry out crossings over the Hron northwest of Leva. Acting to the left of Volkov's corps, the V Guards Tank Corps had the mission of taking the city of Leva itself and the railroad bridge west of that city at Nagykalna, as mentioned previously.

Lieutenant General Volkov decided to advance along two axes. The first axis, on the right, would be directed in a northerly direction through Felsötur, Szalatnya, and Egeg, moving through Slovakia in the vicinity of Apátmarót (Opatove), Hontnadas (Nadošany), and Zemberovce. These forces would then establish positions protecting his corps' right flank against any attacks emanating from the *IV. Pz.Korps* or by troops of the German Commander in Slovakia. On the left, the second axis would follow the direction of Krinta, Potok, Hévmagyarád (Madarovce), Szántó (Santov), Csánk (Cankov), and Hontvarsany (Varshany), bypassing Leva on the left, before making a westward turn towards Kis-Kereskény (Mal. Krskany), Horša, and Tlmacé. Leading along the first axis would be the combat echelon of the 18th Guards Mechanized Brigade and in the second echelon the 46th Guards Tank Brigade. On the second axis on the left, the 31st Guards Mechanized Brigade would take the lead, while the battered 30th Guards Mechanized Brigade would serve as the commander's corps reserve.

Following this avenue of advance, Volkov's corps would attack through the defensive sector held by *Div. Gr. Rintelen* and into the area defended by troops from both the German Commander in Slovakia and the *IV. Pz. Korps*. If successful, his attack would have the added benefit of once again severing the connection between the 6. and 8. *Armee*. As his corps advanced, its former area of operations between Homok and Palást would become the responsibility of the Cavalry-Mechanized Group Pliyev, which would occupy the area and establish defensive positions designed to thwart an attack by German armor through Gyerk towards Ipolysag.

While Volkov's troops managed to reach the Hron River at Tlmacé on 21 December, they did not attempt a crossing. Instead, during the course of his advance he had been instructed to make a turning movement towards the south once he reached the river. At first, the troops of Volkov's first axis on the right met little resistance and Szalatnya was occupied without a fight. After crossing into Slovakia, however, the advance guard of 25 tanks from the 18th Guards Mechanized Brigade was stymied at the fork in the road 1 kilometer north of Egeg, where it was confronted by elements of the *18. Freiw.SS-Pz.Gren.Div.* equipped with antitank guns and reinforced by several armored fighting vehicles from the *24. Pz. Div.*[10]

During this engagement, as many as 10 Soviet tanks from the 83rd Guards Tank Regiment were knocked out, including several immobilized by a minefield. Scouts reported that they had spotted a further 11–12 German tanks and self-propelled guns in Apátmarót, but in reality, their opponent had one or two assault guns at the most. For suffering such heavy losses for so little gain, the commander of the 18th Guards Mechanized Brigade was reprimanded by the corps commander for his recklessness.[11] After withdrawing his tanks, the brigade commander ordered his motorized rifle battalions to the front of the column to lead the advance. To avoid being tied up any further, Volkov ordered the brigade commander to bypass Apátmarót to the south via a turning movement to the west and advance through Korbazi-Puszta (Korbos) instead, finally reaching the upper Hron River north of Leva by late afternoon just as the *LVII. Pz. Korps* was launching its own attack 20 kilometers to the southeast.

The biggest obstacle to the advance by the IX Guards Mechanized Corps had been a tremendous traffic jam that occurred on the night of 20/21 December, when the advancing columns of the 46th Guards Tank Brigade and the 18th Guards Mechanized Brigade became so entangled with one another along the limited road network that Volkov had to order a halt to straighten things out. As it soon proved, the only way to get the advance moving again was to turn the 46th Guards Tank Brigade around and change its direction of attack so that it would move independently a few kilometers south of the 18th Guards Mechanized Brigade, on the route via Szalatnya,

Kistompa, and Deménd, then turn north towards Santov (Szántó), through Bori, and finally reaching its objective at Borfö (Brhlovce). This detour began at approximately 10pm and continued throughout the evening and into the next morning. Thanks to his quick thinking, Volkov was able to get his corps moving again and adhering to the schedule dictated to him by his army commander.

With this new offensive underway, the direct involvement of Lt.Gen. Volkov's IX Guards Mechanized Corps' in the battle of Ipolysag came to an end. After fighting a series of successful engagements for the past 10 days against three separate German and Hungarian divisions, his troops had not only held on to their gains, but in the process had virtually destroyed the Dirlewanger Brigade, killing or capturing more than 1,500 of its men and wounding hundreds more. Capitalizing on the enemy's weaknesses as well as using the terrain to its advantage (especially when it went against Red Army tactical doctrine and employed tanks in the Börszeny Mountains), the IX Guards Mechanized Corps had successfully managed to completely unhinge its opponent's defenses in the Ipolysag Gap and had set the conditions for the successful advance along the entire upper Hron River that began the following day, despite the impending counterattack by the *LVII. Pz.Korps*.

The participation of General Volkov's IX Guards Mechanized Corps during the operation was not yet over; during the next phase, it, along with the V Guards Tank Corps, would be ordered to execute a wide turning movement to the south and attack abreast between the Hron and Ipoly Rivers from 22–26 December 1944 with the goal of trapping both German corps by pinning them against the Danube. Its positions northeast of Leva and in the Ipolysag area would be taken over by the three corps of Cavalry-Mechanized Group Pliyev.

Another significant development that day, spurred on by the danger of the approaching IX Guards Mechanized Corps, was the decision by the Commander of German Forces in Slovakia to deploy additional forces to protect the bridges across the upper Hron River in the vicinity of Nagykalna and Leva. The only sizeable unit remaining in *Ogruf.* Höfle's area of operations with sufficient mobility and heavy weapons to respond to this threat was ironically none other than *Pz.Feldausb.Div. Tatra*, which had been prevented from deploying to the Ipolysag area 10 days earlier by Höfle himself, who wanted to use it to block the Waag valley approach to his headquarters in Pressburg, as well as by *OKH* efforts in the person of *Gen.d.Pz.Tr.* Wenck, who wanted to safeguard its ability to train troops. By 20 December, the time had finally come for it to be cast into the inferno.

On the evening of 20 December, *Pz.Feldausb.Div. Tatra* was alerted and instructed to form a battalion-sized battlegroup to be ready to deploy as early as the following morning. Its mission was to defend along the west bank of the Hron River between Kozárove in the north and Nagykalna in the south, a frontal width of 16 kilometers. Along that particular stretch of the river, the only means available to cross was the bridge at Nagykalna (blown up by engineers on 20 December) or by the use of ferries. Initially, *K.Gr. Tatra* was intended to defend the area east of Leva after *K.Gr. Dern* from the *14. Waffen-Gren.Div. der SS* (*Galizien Nr. 1*) was shifted to the northeast (while failing to notify *K.Gr. Rintelen* of its departure), but the IX Guards Mechanized Corps had arrived there before it did, leaving a defense west of the river as the only option. Tactically, the battlegroup would be subordinated to the *182. Res.Div.*, not to *Div.Gr. Rintelen* (which would have made more sense).[12]

The battlegroup was commanded by *Maj.* Heinrich Hauptmann, a veteran of the Eastern Front and recipient of the Knight's Cross. It was formed from instructors and mobile troops who had completed training with *Pz.Gren.Ers.u.Ausb.Btl. 10* and consisted of four companies, two of which were *Panzergrenadiere* and two of heavy weapons for a total of 595 men. For such a small *Kampfgruppe*, it packed quite a punch. Besides infantry small arms, it was equipped with one medium and two heavy mortars, 64 machine guns, eight antitank rifles, three 88mm *Panzerschreck*, four 75mm light infantry howitzers, and four 75mm Pak 40 antitank guns. In addition to 95 soft-skinned vehicles and 11 *SPWs*, *K.Gr Tatra* also brought along two *Sturmgeschütze* with 75mm guns and two self-propelled antitank guns (one 75mm and the other 76.2mm) from the attached *Pz.Jäger.Ers.u.Ausb.Abt. 8*.[13]

One wonders how much of a difference it would have made had the decision been taken to deploy this *Kampfgruppe* along with the Dirlewanger Brigade, as *H.Gr. Süd* had originally requested on 10 December. *Major* Hauptmann's *Kampfgruppe* could certainly have carried out a more thorough and timely relief of *Rittmeister* Zischler's *II. Btl./Pz.Gren.Rgt. 26* than Dirlewanger's footsore engineer platoon, and would have provided Dirlewanger with a much more powerful and mobile unit to defend Ipolysag. Although speculation, it is not unreasonable to argue that had *K.Gr. Tatra* been deployed on 13 December, it would have been sufficient to temporarily block the advance of the 18th Guards Mechanized Brigade and might have given Dirlewanger and Buchmann the time needed to set up a more organized defense of the Ipolysag Gap. It could have made all the difference.

The last day that *K.Gr. Ehlers* took part in the fighting for the Ipolysag Gap was 21 December. By this point, aside from Harald Momm's small battlegroup still with *Div.Gr. Rintelen*, now positioned somewhere along the upper Hron, the battalion—now led by Franz Falter—was the only element of the Dirlewanger Brigade remaining south of the Ipoly. *Kampfgruppe Ehlers* was still subordinated to Otto Hafner's battlegroup, occupying defensive positions between Pereszlény and the mountains northeast of Bernecebaráti. This was also the same day that *K.Gr. Grosse*, based on *Pio.Rgt.Stab 36*, was disbanded. The various *Bau-Pionier* battalions, which had been fighting in the mountains almost without pause for the past two weeks, were slowly withdrawn from 21/22 December and given a brief period of rest, being replaced by the elite Hungarian troops of the *Szent László* Division.

Hafner and his troops (including Falter's) were directed to detach from the *8. Pz.Div.* on 21 December and return to *Div.Gr. Rintelen*, where his *Feld-Ers.Btl.*

357 would tentatively be assigned a defensive position along the western bank of the Hron. On that same day, *Div.Gr. Rintelen* reverted to its former designation, *357. Inf.Div.*, since nearly all of its remaining elements that had been scattered to the four winds since its defeat at Hatvan on 5 December had been reassembled.[14] Still woefully understrength, the division would soon undergo a lengthy period of reconstitution in order to regain its full combat capability. But since at that moment it was still lacking in infantry, and because *K.Gr. Ehlers* had acquitted itself in an acceptable manner (unlike *K.Gr. Steinhauer*), *Gen.Maj.* Rintelen decided to keep employing it.

Despite the changes in *K.Gr. Ehlers*'s assignment and the associated movements to its new defensive positions along the Hron, 21 December proved to be a day of heavy fighting for everyone else in the *LXXII. Armeekorps*. Indeed, it was a minor miracle that Falter's remaining men were not drawn into actions that might have prevented them from departing their former positions. As it was, that day was one that nearly saw *Gen.Lt.* Schmidt's corps cut off, except for a single bridge across the Hron River at Garam Kovesd, and pinned against the Danube. Most of the burden was borne by the Hungarian *2. Pz.Div.*, which was cut to ribbons that day, and by the aggressive actions of the *Szent László* Division. Even the *357. Inf.Div.*, which was due to be subordinated to the incoming *LVII. Pz.Korps* later that same day, saw its share of heavy combat as it fought to prevent the 6th Guards Tank Army's V Guards Tank Corps from seizing existing bridges intact that would allow its troops to establish firm bridgeheads on the western bank of the Hron.

In his evening situation report, *Gen.Lt.* Schmidt tersely reported the events that had occurred that day in his corps' defensive sector. Unless one was there on the spot, an observer from today's perspective would have no idea of the dramatic fashion in which events unfolded that day, as the *LXXII. Armeekorps* slowly buckled. Had not elements of the newly arriving *LVII. Pz.Korps* been diverted to Schmidt's area of operations to help hold the line, the outcome of the fighting on 21 December would have been much, much worse for the Germans and Hungarians.

Schmidt's report began by stating: "The enemy continued its attacks in front of the entire corps defensive line today. In the southern part of the Börszeny Mountains, for the first time [our troops encountered] overwhelming enemy artillery fire and large numbers of tanks." That was just the beginning. Along the southern bank of the Danube, *K.Gr. Thierfelder* reported increased enemy artillery and mortar fire directed against the northern part of Dunabogdány, the town of Visegrád, and the village of Dömös, the site of the ferry to the northern bank of the Danube. Surprisingly, there were no attempts by enemy troops to cross the Danube.

Throughout the day of 21 December, fierce fighting took place at what were now referred to as the Szob–Ipolydamásd bridgeheads, an indication that there were no longer any German or Hungarian troops east of the Ipoly River except at these two locations. Several Soviet attacks in company strength were carried out against these two bridgeheads, but even after heavy artillery preparatory fire and with the aid of tank support, these failed to dislodge the defenders. Knight's Cross awardee *Hptm.* Müller, the commander of *M.G. Bataillon Sachsen*, destroyed one tank himself with a *Panzerfaust* and set fire to another. Although they successfully held these two bridgeheads, German and Hungarian losses that day amounted to 30 percent of the remaining fighting strength of the Hungarian *2. Pz.Div.*

The situation was much more dire a few kilometers to the north, necessitating the premature commitment of elements of the *Szent László* Division to prevent things from getting out of hand. Enemy infantry from the XXV Guards Rifle Corps had broken through from the east and northeast of Ipolydamásd, with the leading elements advancing to the northwest along the Ipolydamásd–Letkes road. By this move, they raised the possibility of the loss of the town of Letkes and establishing a bridgehead on the western bank of the Ipoly River, a mere kilometer away from the headquarters of the Hungarian *2. Pz.Div.* in Ipolyszalka. Something had to be done immediately.

To avert this danger, the newly arrived *Luftwaffe-Schützen* (Air Force Infantry) *Regiment* of the *Szent László* Division disembarked from the trucks that had just brought them to Letkes and immediately launched a counterattack towards the southeast. Fighting against a tenaciously defending enemy, the Hungarians crushed the Soviet spearhead and forced the remainder to retreat a kilometer as far as the hamlet of Liliom-Puszta. Shortly thereafter, a portion of the *Luftwaffe-Schützen Regiment* continued its attack, reaching the farmstead of Lelédhidi-Puszta 2 kilometers away by 6.10pm, while another battalion held the heights east of Letkes against a superior enemy force.

Red Army infantry continued pouring out from the southwest corner of the Börszeny Mountains in large numbers, with the apparent goal of reaching the Ipoly and carrying out an assault river crossing that would split the *LXXII. Armeekorps* in half. To successfully carry out this scheme, the XXV Guards Rifle Corps needed the town of Ipolytölgyes to be taken as quickly as possible. Ipolytölgyes, located between the town of Ipolyszalka and Nagybörzsöny, sat on the eastern bank of the Ipoly and featured a wood line that extended from the western edge of the mountains nearly into the center of town, providing an ideally concealed avenue of approach for enemy infantry. Recognizing the danger, *Gen.Lt.* Schmidt dispatched the last remaining reserve of *LXXII. Armeekorps*, the recently arrived *Pz.Aufkl.Abt. 3* of the *3. Pz.Div.* Arriving in Letkes that afternoon, the heavily armed battalion linked up with a battalion of Hungarian paratroopers and drove north along the Letkes–Ipolytölgyes road, where the extemporized *Kampfgruppe* attacked enemy troops who had advanced as far south as the road west of Davidrévi Puszta and drove them back into the mountains.

Although detached from *Gen.Lt.* Schmidt's corps later that day, *Gr. Fröhlich* and *Div.Gr. Rintelen* experienced their share of heavy fighting, with the exception of *K.Gr. Hafner*, which saw very little action at all. On 21 December, the *Panzergrenadier* battalion from the *8. Pz.Div.* defending Pereszlény was forced to abandon the town after it came under heavy attack. Attempts by company- and battalion-sized units of the 36th Guards Rifle Division to seize the villages of Ipolyvisk, Szete, and Százd—which traced the designated line of departure for the *LVII. Pz.Korps* counterattack scheduled to begin that afternoon—were thwarted after heavy fighting.

In the *Div.Gr. Rintelen* sector, it was reported that Soviet troops had established a small bridgehead over the Hron at Saró (Sarovce), a village 2 kilometers south of Garam-Szt. György, although a counterattack managed to throw them back across the river. Throughout the day, Rintelen strove to establish outposts along the entire length of the upper Hron. With the welcome addition of *Pz.Aufkl.Abt. 6* of the *6. Pz.Div.* to his order of battle, his troops soon had the 14-kilometer-long portion of the river under continuous observation from Nagykalna to Garam-Szt. György, where *Div.Gr. Rintelen* managed to hang on to its two small bridgeheads on the eastern bank of the Hron. By nightfall of 21 December, *Gen.Maj.* Rintelen had moved his division command post to a central location, the large town of Nagy Salló (Tekovské Lužany), a mere 6 kilometers from the destroyed bridge at Šerovce.

The fighting that day had been especially costly, particularly for the Hungarians. After the heavy fighting of the last several days and that of 21 December, the Hungarian *2. Pz.Div.* had essentially ceased to exist. The combat strength of the Hungarian infantry units under its command had been reduced due to losses to only 150 soldiers (out of over 3,000 authorized), all that was left of the *IV. Btl./Inf. Rgt.(mot.) 3* and its *2. Pz.Aufkl.Abt.*. The three attached German units numbered only 400 men, including *K.Gr. Zirke* which reported a *Kampfstärke* of a mere 70 men. Were it not for the timely intervention of the *Szent László* Division, it is likely that the XXV Guards Rifle Corps would have crossed the Ipoly in strength and threatened the survival of the *LXXII. Armeekorps*. In addition to the rapidly increasing strength of the enemy's ground forces, the Red Air Force had become active again, with *Gen.Lt.* Schmidt reporting "Lively enemy air activity on the *HKL* and in the corps' rear area."

Based on what had been reported to him that day, Schmidt concluded that within the next 24 hours, the Soviets would attempt to overcome the Szob bridgehead, cross the Ipoly River, and penetrate into the woods west of Szob in order to attack other elements of *LXXII. Armeekorps* defending between Szob and Ipolyszalka. After that, he predicted that his opponent would carry out an enveloping maneuver that would trap most of the German and Hungarian units east of the Ipoly. Following this, he assumed that elements of the XXV Guards Rifle Corps, supported by tanks, would attempt to penetrate his defenses as far as the mouth of the Hron River opposite Esztergom. Should they succeed in doing so, it would convert a slow-rolling disaster into a catastrophe of epic proportions.

Of course, *Gen.Lt.* Schmidt would do everything within his power to prevent this from taking place. To hold the Szob bridgehead and establish a firm connection between Ipolydamásd and Letkes, he would continue the counterattack that had begun late that afternoon after the arrival of the remaining parts of the *Szent László* Division. Once the situation around Szob had been stabilized, he planned to make a comprehensive attack to the northeast to destroy the enemy who had emerged from the forest between Letkes and Nagybörzsöny. It had become a race against time to see which side would achieve its goals first. However, time was not on the side of the *LXXII. Armeekorps,* which was outnumbered by at least five to one. Even the attachment of two additional German combat engineer battalions and an artillery battalion the following day would not be sufficient to redress these odds.

Although it was officially supposed to subordinate itself to the *LVII. Pz.Korps* by 1pm on 21 December, the *8. Pz.Div.* found itself in the unenviable position of having to report to both corps at the same time; on the ground it remained temporarily under the control of *Gen.Lt.* Schmidt. The official explanation given by *6. Armee/A. Gr. Fretter-Pico* was that the *8. Pz.Div.* needed to remain in its current position and be tactically subordinated to *LXXII. Armeekorps* for at least another day in order to ensure the continuity of the physical connection between Schmidt's and Kirschner's neighboring corps until the *LVII. Pz.Korps* had begun its attack. Keeping the *8. Pz.Div.* in place southwest of Ipolysag would ensure that no enemy breakthrough would occur due to a lack of understanding of the boundaries between the two corps.

As the fighting intensified for both sides on 21 December, many of the men in *K.Gr. Hafner* and the attached *SS* battlegroup must have wondered whether they would be drawn into the fray before they could be relieved. Fortunately for them, their defensive sector remained quiet, while fighting involving adjacent units raged on both flanks. At 5.40pm, the *LXXII. Armeekorps* informed the commander of *Div.Gr. Rintelen* that *K.Gr. Hafner* would remain for the time being in its present positions west of Bernecebaráti and continue operating under the command of the *8. Pz.Div.* This order naturally applied to *K.Gr. Ehlers* as well. Some three hours earlier, *Gen.Maj.* Rintelen himself received the order at 2.22pm instructing him that effective immediately, the *357. Inf.Div.* was attached to the *LVII. Pz.Korps.* This order did not apply to *K.Gr. Hafner.*

On account of the arrival of the two additional *panzer* divisions, the *8. Pz.Div.* was forced to shuffle units along its front line to make room for them. On 20 December, *Hptm.* Hafner had been ordered to shift his *Kampfgruppe* several kilometers to the west somewhere in the vicinity of the village of Tesa (Tésa), only a kilometer east of the great bend in the Ipoly River. The exact location of his new area of operations is not known; Hafner's own diary is not precise. Hafner only describes his headquarters as being in a market town that lay alongside a good road network that facilitated movement up and down the river, as well as the shipment of supplies to the front lines.

Three *SS* officers pose in front of the *SS Hospital* in Minsk, April or May 1944. Flanked by two *SS* medical officers, former *Major der Schutzpolizei* Herbert Meyer, now reduced in rank to a mere *SS-Grenadier* but still serving in a leadership position as a battalion commander, stands in the center. Prominent on his right collar tab is the crossed rifles and hand grenade insignia of *Sonderkommando Dirlewanger*. (Ida Köhler Collection, via Krigsbilder.net))

The motorcycle reconnaissance platoon of *Sonderbataillon Dirlewanger*, Belarus, 1943. Their special crossed rifles collar insignia is clearly visible on four of these men. The *SS-Oberscharführer* on the far left has an Italian-made Beretta 9mm submachine gun slung around his neck, while the soldier behind him carries a captured French MAS 38 7.65mm submachine gun, designated as the MP 722(f) by the Germans. (Charles Trang)

Gruppe (squad) from *Sonderregiment Dirlewanger* during the suppression of the Warsaw Uprising, August 1944. During this battle, most of its troops consisted of men from various *Wehrmacht* punishment institutions or convicts recruited from concentration camps. The special *Sonderkommando* insignia on the collar of the soldier standing in the foreground is clearly visible. (French MacLean)

Two members of *Sonderregiment Dirlewanger*, including one soldier on the right equipped with a flamethrower fighting in Warsaw, August 1944. The soldier on the left without any rank insignia is evidently a degraded German Army officer or NCO, judging by the lack of collar insignia and two stripes on the lower left sleeve of his jacket, marking him as a platoon leader. (Soroya Kuklińska)

Squad or Platoon Leader from *Sonderregiment Dirlewanger* (third from left) outside of the Brühl Palace, Warsaw, early August 1944. On his left breast pocket he wears the *Bandenkampfabzeichen* (Anti-Partisan Badge), awarded for repeated engagements against so-called bandits. The *StuG III* assault gun in the background is most likely from *Sturmgeschütz-Ersatz-Abteilung 200*, which was briefly attached to *Kampfgruppe Dirlewanger* during this period. (B. Uhsemann Foto Archive)

Recent *Wehrmacht-Heer* probationary transfer to *Sonderregiment Dirlewanger* in Warsaw, August 1944. Festooned with a belt of ammunition for his squad's MG-42 and a *Nebelkerzen* (smoke pot) Model Nb.K. 39b, his German Army insignia has been replaced by ordinary blank *SS* collar insignia. (Stephen Andrew)

Two decorated veteran members of *Sondereinheit Dirlewanger*, both probably rehabilitated poachers, pose for a photograph, 1943 or 1944. (Soroya Kuklińska)

Group of tired and bedraggled soldiers from the *357. Inf.Div./Div.Gr. Rintelen* a few kilometers west of Vámosmikola, late December 1944. Shortly after the battle of Ipolysag, the entire division underwent a two-week period of reconstitution to restore it to its full capability. (Erich Craciun)

Photograph taken on 30 October 1944 in Neusohl (Banská Bystrica) depicting award ceremony wherein *SS-Obergruppenführer* Hans Höfle received a high award from the State President of Slovakia, Dr. Jozef Tiso, as a token of thanks from the people of his country for suppressing the Slovak Uprising. Of the two officers standing between them in the background, on the right is *SS-Oberführer* Wilhelm Trabandt, Commander of the *18. SS-Freiw.Pz.Gren.Div. Horst Wessel*, while on the left is *Generalmajor* Hans-Ulrich Back, acting Commander of *Pz.Div. Tatra*. (SS-Kriegsberichter H. Ahrens, Nr. 138/7a, courtesy of Andrew Found)

In the center of the photograph, a dejected member of the Dirlewanger Brigade sits in an American POW enclosure along with dozens of other *Waffen-SS* troops after escaping to safety across the Elbe River at Tangermünde 8 or 9 May 1945. His Dirlewanger collar insignia can be plainly seen here. He also wears the Iron Cross, First Class as well as the Close Combat Clasp and Infantry Assault Badge. (Richard Deveau-Maxwell and Peter DeForest, via Black Guard Research)

An example of the special collar insignia approved on 1 April 1943 for exclusive wear by *SS* troops assigned to *Sonderkommando Dirlewanger* until 1945. Unlike the *SS* "lightning bolts," this insignia consisted of silver woven cross rifles surmounting a hand grenade. Former members of the *Wehrmacht* serving out their punishment in the brigade as well as political prisoners recruited from the concentration camps were not permitted to wear this insignia unless they had been deemed "fully rehabilitated" and accepted as members of the *SS*. (Author's collection)

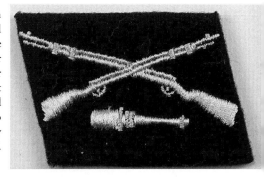

SS-Grenadier August Kaufeld, seen here wearing a concentration camp uniform while being held as a political prisoner at the Auschwitz KL, who was among one of 770 others who "volunteered" for the Dirlewanger Brigade in November 1944. Born on 16 October 1904 in Hanau, it is unknown whether he survived the battle of Ipolysag by defecting to the Red Army. (Archiv des Staatlichen Museums Auschwitz-Birkenau, D-Au I-III/3a, shown in Klausch, 583)

"Battle for the southern border of Slovakia." These images appeared in the Slovak *Nový Svet* (New World) magazine on 13 January 1945 and are the only known images of the Dirlewanger Brigade fighting in the Ipolysag area. The article states: "In this report, we bring you some photos from the front section on the southern border of Slovakia, where Hungarian-German troops are in heavy fighting with the Soviets. Our pictures show Hungarian-German units ready for a counterattack." The eight photographs were taken between 15 and 20 December 1944 by *Kriegsberichter* Heinz Bröker, who was assigned to the staff of the German Commander in Slovakia. Most of these men wear a mixture of Army and *SS* clothing and equipment. (courtesy of Vladimir Krajčovič). The original captions read as follows:

A. "In the front lines ready to attack" (a squad of *SS-Bewährung Schützen*, wearing a mix of Army and *SS* cold weather clothing, observe enemy movement to their direct front).

B. "Light machine gun crew ready to fire" (note the Czech 7.92mm ZB vz. 26 machine gun in use).

C. "A few more seconds and the artillery will fire a devastating fire on the enemy" (Hungarian troops operating German-provided 105mm Model 18 light field howitzers).

D. Same caption as above, but this image depicts a captured Czech 37mm KPUV antitank gun manned by some of Dirlewanger's soldiers.

E. "Anti-tank weapons are also on standby" (Hungarian soldier with a *Panzerfaust*, unit unknown).

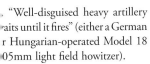 "Well-disguised heavy artillery aits until it fires" (either a German r Hungarian-operated Model 18 05mm light field howitzer).

G. "The tension in their faces revea[l] that this is a difficult moment" (soldi[er] on the right wears *SS* camouflage clothing with a German Army be[lt] buckle; in these photographs, ver[y] few of Dirlewanger's soldiers are see[n] to be wearing steel helmets).

H. "Reserves are also on standby" (rather bedraggled-looking soldiers with a variety of clothing and equipment await orders to move forward).

In his diary, Hafner provides a bleak description of the open terrain that he and his men, including *K.Gr. Ehlers*, were to defend, writing on 22 December:

> I move about the positions both during the day and at night, as far as the open terrain allowed. The [terrain here] is slightly undulated, [my] town lies in a hollow, from which the ground rises steadily northward towards a plateau in the far distance. The last houses and barns are nestled in these folds [in the terrain], then I walk across the open area towards the widely spaced, small fighting positions every hundred or so meters apart [stated as 500–700 meters away from town], in which the men (always two together) have more or less nestled with very little comfort, but somewhat covered against shelling and shell splinters. Visibility is unobstructed; the fields are without trees or bushes, making [this area] basically good tank terrain. I visit the battalions' command posts and, wherever possible, company command posts at night, including men in the forward positions. I am on my feet most of the time, and try to sleep in between.[15]

At this point in December, the weather was described as "clear, cold and dry, with good visibility, roadways passable for all types of wheeled vehicles," meaning that the ground had frozen hard. By this point, *K.Gr. Ehlers* had been living and fighting in the open air since 11 December, with little opportunity for rest behind the front lines. Without adequate winter clothing and on short rations, the *B-Schützen* and their *SS* leaders alike would have been cold, filthy, hungry, and lousy—literally. Living in a hole in the ground with little overhead cover and unable to move about during the daylight hours due to enemy snipers, the only reprieve the Dirlewanger troops got was in the form of less intense artillery fire than what they had grown accustomed to in the Börszeny Mountains.

Hauptmann Hafner's battalion surgeon, *Stabsartz* Dr. Felix Mlčzoch from Vienna, became acquainted with some of Dirlewanger's medical personnel during this period in their new positions along the Ipoly River. Doctor Mlčzoch, who became good friends with Otto Hafner after the war, remembered some of these men:

> In my medical clearing station, there was a doctor from Vienna, a Party member and therefore not convicted of a crime, but who had been caught performing an [illegal] abortion and came to perform his probation [in the Dirlewanger Brigade] wearing a doctor's uniform and civilian clothes [he is most likely describing Dr. Med. Hugo Erbguth]. I also remember a pharmacist from Munich, who wore a Gold [Nazi] Party Badge, [who was] a friend of the police president in secondary school, with whom he had a card game every week. During such a game, having become drunk, he expressed doubts about the final victory (in autumn 1944!). He was picked up early the next morning with a visiting card [from his classmate], stating "Forgive me, but I had to [turn you in]."[16]

From 21–28 December, *K.Gr. Ehlers*—renamed *K.Gr. Falter* by 25 December—continued serving under the control of *K.Gr. Hafner* along the Ipoly River defense line. During this period, Falter and his men were not involved in heavy fighting, except for occasional skirmishes with Soviet scouts attempting to infiltrate German positions. Artillery was a far greater danger. On Christmas Day, Falter presented Hafner with a hand-drawn Christmas card made by one of his troops depicting a small girl carrying a miniature Christmas tree (see Figure 1), inscribed "In the

Figure 1: 1944 Christmas Card presented to *Hauptmann* Otto Hafner by *Major der Schutzpolizei* Franz Falter on behalf of his *Kampfgruppe* (Klausch, p. 265).

name of all of the member of the *SS-Sturmbrigade Dirlewanger* serving under your command, I would like to wish the *Kampfgruppe* Commander and everyone in your *Kampfgruppe* Merry Christmas and continued soldier's luck!"[17]

Hauptmann Hafner did everything he could during this period to improve the morale if not the living conditions of his soldiers, both regular army and *SS*. On Christmas Eve, Falter and his surgeon Dr. Mlčzoch made multiple trips to the front line in the night carrying rucksacks full of baked goods and *Frontkämpferpäckchen* and delivered them to individual fighting positions directly on the front line, sometimes having to crawl to avoid being spotted by the enemy. Returning to his command post before dawn, Hafner collapsed on his bunk and slept for the rest of Christmas Day.[18]

While the *8. Pz.Div.* and *K.Gr. Hafner* continued to defend the front line 8 kilometers southwest of Ipolysag on 21 December, the *3.* and *6. Panzer Divisionen* continued their movement across the Danube and into their assembly areas for their impending attack, which was set to begin at 4pm that day. The start time was then changed to 6pm. Throughout this period, Generals Friessner and Fretter-Pico continued assembling their forces for Operation *Spätlese* south of the Danube, even as the weather and terrain conditions continued to delay final preparations. Amazingly, *6. Armee/A.Gr. Fretter-Pico* was about to simultaneously conduct two major multi-corps operations on two different axes, with a large river separating the two, as well as a major defensive battle at Budapest. It would soon prove to be more than a single field army headquarters could manage.

Operation *Spätlese*'s second start date of 20 December had already passed as continuing heavy rain showers and thawing conditions turned the Hungarian roads on either side of Lakes Velencze and Balaton into rivers of mud. These conditions made any kind of movement in armored vehicles, not to mention trucks and cars, extremely difficult. In justification of his decision to delay the attack by yet another day, Friessner wrote afterwards that "sending the designated armored formations into an immediate attack in the mud could not be justified; it was crucial to wait for the frost in order to be able to operate away from only paved roads."[19] Friessner was correct, although his leaders in Berlin did not see things the same way.

What Friessner really wanted was to postpone the offensive even longer until the ground froze sufficiently, but this could take another week. By 20 December, however, Guderian and Hitler had finally lost all patience and demanded that *H.Gr. Süd* begin its offensive the next day. The Panther *and SPW*-mounted armored infantry battalions from the *3.*, *6.*, and *8. Panzer Divisionen* had initially been formed into a battlegroup led by *Gen.Maj.* Ewald Kraeber, who lacked every means of command and control. This did not bode well for offensive success. Despite the weather, by 21 December all the forces had been assembled for the offensive to begin, whether they were ready or not. The missing lorry-mounted *Panzergrenadier*, *Pioniere*, and artillery components of these three divisions had been replaced by a conglomeration of troops, including Hungarian reserve units, troops from the *153. Feldausb.Div.*, and other bits and pieces of units scraped together at the last moment. The artillery and its coordinating headquarters had also been improvised.

Constituted as such, the forces marshaled for Operation *Spätlese* were even weaker than they appeared on paper. These last-minute additions would soon prove their overwhelming inadequacy as substitutes for what each of the three *panzer* divisions would have provided. Indeed, *panzer* divisions were designed to function as a unified whole using proven tactical doctrine. The absence of the balanced capability of these three *panzer* divisions practically doomed *Spätlese* before it had even begun. Lacking sufficient *Panzergrenadiere*, combat engineers, and their customary mobile artillery support, these division's *panzer* battalions would have difficulty overcoming the 4th Guards Army's echeloned defensive line erected between Lakes Balaton and Velencze.

As previously related, the main bodies of the three *panzer* divisions originally earmarked for *Spätlese* had already been or were being transferred north of the Danube to carry out the counterattack to regain control of the Ipoly River valley. However, without the armored elements that had been left behind to carry out Operation *Spätlese*, most of the inherent combat power of these three divisions had been left behind as well.[20] Although on paper the LVII. *Pz.Korps* appeared to be a powerful force, in reality all three *panzer* divisions in terms of capability were merely motorized infantry brigades with minimal armor support.

To make things worse for *Gen.d.Pz.Tr.* Kirschner's impending attack, not all of these divisions' battalions had arrived in time before their attack was due to start. Regardless, the attack would be carried forth anyway, even though many key supporting elements were lacking; they would simply have to join in the attack once they arrived. This shortcoming, especially the lack of armored fighting vehicles, would become painfully evident when the *LVII. Pz.Korps* and neighboring *LXXII. Armeekorps* faced over 200 tanks of the 6th Guards Tank Army.

Meanwhile, south of the Danube, the *panzer* regiments and the heavy tank battalion (with nearly 235 operational *panzers* in all), arrayed under *Gen.d.Pz. Tr.* Hermann Breith's *III. Pz.Korps*, attempted to follow the *Spätlese* plan against Tolbukhin's forces on 21 and 22 December, but their attacks met with little success.[21] Churning through the mud, the *panzers* used up massive amount of scarce fuel as they attempted to maneuver against their nimbler foot-bound opponent. The employment of these tank regiments and the separate *Pz.Kfw. VI Königstiger* (King Tiger) battalion proved to be a difficult challenge for Breith to command or control, since their accustomed division headquarters had been sent north of the Danube along with most of their signal battalions.

The last-minute creation of *Div.Gr. Pape* on 21 December, an attempt to use the division commander and staff of *Pz.Gr.Div. FHH* to control the three *Kampfgruppen* formed from the three *panzer* divisions transferred north of the Danube, came too late to make much difference. Its commander, *Gen.Maj.* Günther Pape, who had been pulled out of Budapest for this mission, had little time to get to know his subordinate commanders, draft an operations plan, or coordinate with supporting elements, such as artillery or combat engineers. Without adequate infantry support or mine-clearing capability, the 10 tank battalions of *III. Pz.Korps* quickly fell prey to Soviet minefields, tank hunting teams, and antitank guns. After failing to take much ground and suffering the loss of dozens of his precious *panzers*, *Gen.d.Pz.Tr.* Breith was finally forced to withdraw his armor behind the safety of the *Margarethestellung*. After nearly three weeks of preparations, Operation *Spätlese* came to an inglorious end by the evening of 22 December.

That same day, *Gen.Obst.* Friessner took the opportunity to request permission to withdraw the troops of the *IX. SS-Geb.Korps* from Fretter-Pico's *6. Armee* positioned in Pest on the eastern bank of the Danube, a move that he believed would free up badly needed infantry and armor but would also result in the abandonment of half of Budapest. This Hitler categorically refused to consider, believing it important to hold the eastern side of the city for political reasons. Budapest would continue to be held at all costs.[22] By this point, both Hitler and Guderian had lost patience with Friessner and Fretter-Pico, leaders they judged to be too cautious and lacking the kind of fighting spirit they felt the extreme situation required.

Consequently, on the night of 22 December, Friessner and Fretter-Pico were notified by the Operations Branch of *OKH* that they would both be relieved of their commands within the next 24 hours. The new commander of *H.Gr. Süd* would henceforth be *Gen.d.Inf.* Otto Wöhler, formerly commander of *8. Armee*, while Fretter-Pico, commander of *6. Armee*, would be replaced on 24 December by *Gen.d.Pz.Tr.* Hermann Balck, who would be brought over from the Western Front where he had been commanding *H.Gr. G.* At least Wöhler was familiar with the situation, having commanded *8. Armee* since August 1943, so his elevation to command the army group would be relatively seamless. Balck, on the other hand, had been fighting on the Western Front for the past three months and although he was an Eastern Front veteran, he would need to quickly orient himself in regards to his new *Kampfraum*.[23]

While the Germans dithered and changed commanders, Malinovsky and Tolbukhin relentlessly pushed forward. Though neither of these men possessed the strategic or operational talents of other more gifted Soviet commanders such as Zhukov, Konev, or Rokossovsky, they were good at following orders from the *Stavka* and were certainly up to the challenge of commanding army groups in a region of limited operational scope such as Hungary. Wherever the Germans displayed weakness, they exploited it; where their enemy showed strength, they went around it or crushed him with overwhelming firepower.

Before the *Spätlese* counteroffensive had even concluded, the Third Ukrainian Front began its own counteroffensive with a vengeance. On 22 December, 4th Guards Army attacked with overwhelming force north and south of Lake Velencze and took the cities of Bicske and Stuhlweissenburg against negligible resistance, thereby severing the last of the paved highways leading to Budapest. Now the only way in or out of the city was via a circuitous route that ran through the Pilis Mountains north of the city, consisting of a series of unpaved, winding, narrow roads covered with ice and snow. German forces defending the area along the southern banks of the Danube, chiefly *K.Gr. Thierfelder* and some Hungarian units, began withdrawing rapidly towards Esztergom before they were trapped.

Although *Spätlese* had achieved none of its goals and had thrown away a number of Friessner's carefully hoarded *panzers*, the aborted offensive had at least limited the scope of the Third Ukrainian Front's counteroffensive due to excessive caution on the part of Marshal Tolbukhin. Providentially for the Germans and Hungarians, Tolbukhin had evidently decided not to risk converting his front's penetration into a deep attack with so many *panzers* lurking about, but instead chose to conduct a shallow envelopment of Budapest from the west, which would seal the fate of the city's defenders in any case. While continuing to fix in place the last gasps of Operation *Spätlese*, on 25 December Tolbukhin ordered the commander of the 4th Guards Army, General of the Army G. F. Zakharov, to send the XVIII Tank Corps to the north in a bold drive towards Esztergom, a risky move considering German resistance, the mountainous terrain, and the condition of the snow-bound roads.

For a similar reason as Tolbukhin's, Malinovsky decided to limit the advance of his forces to the east bank of the Hron River, though he would continue his efforts to encircle as much as possible of the escaping German and Hungarian forces between Nagykalna and Esztergom and establish several bridgeheads on the river's west bank. Although his 6th Guards Tank and 7th Guards Armies had failed to trap his opponent's divisions, which managed to conduct an orderly retreat across the Hron and the Danube, Malinovsky and his armies had still managed to cut off Budapest in the north and establish a bridgehead across the lower Hron at Parkany (Štúrovo). On 26 December, his troops shook hands with those of the XVIII Tank Corps of the Third Ukrainian Front, which had taken Esztergom the same day. Only two days earlier, the retreating Germans had blown up the Maria Valeria Bridge connecting Esztergom on the southern bank with Parkany to the north, making good their escape. Any movement between the two fronts would now have to be conducted via ferry until a temporary bridge was constructed.[24]

While heavy fighting was taking place to their north and south, *K.Gr. Hafner* and the attached troops from *SS-St.Rgt. 2* continued defending their static positions southwest of Ipolysag, unaware of the major events taking place around them. It seemed to them as if the war had passed them by. On 26 December, Otto Hafner wrote in his diary: "Everything remained surprisingly quiet. No enemy contact. Had we become a sideshow, or did the Russians think they would be able to capture us later anyway, after they had advanced far enough, turned southwards and surrounded us?" But front-line rumors and hints from staff officers from the *8. Pz.Div.* had aroused his suspicions, which were confirmed the following day when he wrote: "Rumors and suspicions are confirmed, the Russians have [advanced] far beyond us. I got orders to prepare the infantry to load onto trucks. As part of the *Panzergruppe* [of the *8. Pz.Div.*] we were to be transported westward. It seems urgent and the distance [we were to travel] was apparently not small."

On Thursday 28 December, to his surprise, the promised trucks actually arrived. Leaving behind a temporary screening force to cover his *Kampfgruppe*'s departure, all of the infantry companies, including the SS troops attached to *K.Gr. Falter*, pulled out of their fighting positions and boarded the columns of trucks awaiting them on a wide road behind the village. Once the troops were aboard, the truck column immediately departed, destination unknown. Hafner left a graphic depiction of what followed:

> Supposedly they [the trucks] are going towards the Hron [River]. Everything rolls on undisturbed. My staff stayed on until the last parts [of the battlegroup] were loaded. The long column of our vehicles moved along a dusty trail for hours now … Empty and still, everything was eerily quiet. Along broad, rutted paths and paved roads, we wound our way along like a long worm, up sloping hillsides, down again into valleys, over waves and crests with wide vistas, while [maintaining] large distances between vehicles. Occasionally a short break, then onwards. We were not entirely comfortable in this absolute silence. It was as if we were only goods being transported, even I had no responsibility; the convoy was led by one of our own officers. No sign of the enemy, no friendly troops, no tanks of our own, the silence was almost eerie.[25]

After driving all night through the empty landscape, the next morning very little had changed. Around noon, Hafner and his troops began hearing artillery fire, a sign that they were approaching their destination. He learned later that the *Panzergruppe* of the *8. Pz.Div.* had been moving along the flanks of the truck column for the entire time as a protective screen. After a long descent, the Hron River and the temporary bridge they were to cross finally hove into view, as well as the dust clouds indicating that the area was being shelled at that very moment (the crossing site was most likely Garam-Szt. György). Hafner continued:

> A short drive further, then we dismounted. On foot, in very loosely organized groups, we made for the bridge. Then we had to hurry and cross it to get to the western bank ... It took some time until everyone was rounded up again, but we were quickly intercepted and directed towards the road [that ran] along the shore towards the north. Some of my companies that arrived before I did had already been assigned to positions along the Hron ... I promptly was assigned a fairly wide sector several kilometers north of our crossing. This meant I had to set up my command post in a house along the road ... the sporadic artillery strikes didn't bother us and of course I immediately moved forward to visit my companies to see how they were doing. The terrain was not very favorable [for defense], the river was wide, perhaps 25 to 30 meters, gently flowing and deep, but the banks were overgrown with trees and bushes, which basically made it hard to see the other side and difficult to cross, especially at night. The sector was wide, too wide for my weak companies [to defend]. During the day, it could be secured with machine-gun fire, but at night, scouting parties [had to be conducted] between the individual fighting positions, which acted as observation and listening posts ... they tried to identify, disrupt, and provide early warning should the Russians [*sic*] move against us. It was also a matter of luck, too, because 30 meters could be crossed quickly by boat in the dark, so I had to be ready to send off a patrol [to intercept them]. So, everyone had to be very careful.[26]

Hauptmann Hafner and his troops had finally made it home to their *357. Inf.Div.*, which had been holding this sector along the Hron for the past week. He and his men would remain in this position for the next two weeks as part of a larger battlegroup led by *Maj.* Erich Brocksch, the acting commander of *Gren.Rgt. 944.*[27]

This was also to be the last combat action the troops of the Dirlewanger Brigade experienced while remaining with *AOK 6/A.Gr. Balck*. They were not to stay along the Hron River for much longer. Two days earlier, *Gen.Maj.* Gaedke, Balck's new chief of staff, had sent out a message inquiring as to their whereabouts. He evidently believed that Falter and his remaining men were still with the Hungarian *2. Pz.Div.* It took nearly a day for the chief of staff of *Gen.Lt.* Schmidt's *LXXII. Armeekorps* to finally respond, answering that he did not know where they were, but that they were not with the Hungarians.

Shortly afterwards, Falter and his men were finally determined to be fighting with *K.Gr. Hafner* of the *357. Inf.Div.*, where they had been all along. The standing orders from *H.Gr. Süd* that had directed the rest of the Dirlewanger Brigade to be withdrawn finally caught up with them at some point during the night of 29/30 December. The next morning, *AOK 6/A.Gr. Balck* reported to *H.Gr. Süd* that this last remaining group of the Dirlewanger Brigade had finally departed the army's *Kampfraum* and were on their way on foot to rejoin the rest of their unit. The number of men accompanying *Maj.d.Schu.Po.* Falter totaled 237, including his and Harald Momm's small group.

While this minor drama played out, *Gen.d.Inf.* Wöhler, newly installed as the *Oberbefehlshaber* of *H.Gr. Süd*, had telephoned Guderian at *OKH* and briefed him on the deteriorating situation along the Danube, particularly regarding what was to be done with Budapest. Wöhler requested that he be given the authority to order the city's garrison to evacuate the eastern bank of the Danube and move into the inner defensive ring on the west bank of the Danube, which comprised the Buda portion of the city. This was ironically the same position that Friessner had advocated and was one of the factors that had led to his abrupt dismissal.[28] Surprisingly, Guderian did not reject his request outright, but informed him that he would pass it on to Hitler, who upon being notified of the *H.Gr. Süd* commander's request, characteristically refused to consider any mention of a withdrawal.[29] Hitler had designated Budapest a *Festung* on 1 December, and as such it would be defended to the last man and the last round of ammunition.[30]

As previously stated, tanks from the XVIII Tank Corps reached Esztergom on 26 December, cutting off the last escape route from the capital. Although on paper the defending German-Hungarian force appeared strong (with one *panzer*, one *panzergrenadier*, two *Waffen-SS* cavalry, and two-and-a-half Hungarian divisions), there was insufficient food, fuel, and ammunition for the 70,000-man garrison led by *Ogruf.* Karl Pfeffer-Wildenbruch, the commander of the *IX. SS-Geb.Korps*. Short of nearly everything, *Festung Budapest* was hardly in any shape to withstand a long siege, nor did it have the means to break out on its own. As for the city's population of nearly 800,000 men, women, and children, no food or fuel had been stockpiled for them at all, other than what they had managed to hoard on their own. To rescue the city and its garrison, a relief operation would have to be launched immediately. The only consolation, if there was one, was that an elite *SS panzer* corps was being hurriedly brought down from Poland at that very moment to lead the relief effort.[31]

Although the *panzer* divisions of the *LVII. Pz.Korps* (minus their tanks) were finally able to halt Kravchenko's force north of the Danube, it was not until Soviet tanks had reached the Hron River, 30 kilometers west of Ipolysag, and had fanned out along the river's eastern bank north and south of Nagykalna. The *LXXII. Armeekorps* was also unable to stop Col.Gen. Shumilov's 7th Guards Army, as his divisions forced the remnants of Schmidt's two Hungarian divisions to withdraw to the western bank of the Ipoly River and then towards the Hron River, where the *Szent László* Division was pinned against the northern shore of the Danube and nearly destroyed in the process. Shumilov's XXV Guards Rifle Corps then established a bridgehead at Parkany on the west bank of the Hron that repelled every German attempt to destroy it. *Kampfgruppe Zirke*, with 129 survivors, was only narrowly able to escape destruction after becoming surrounded at Nagymaros by crossing the Danube at Dömös with the aid of two river ferries operated by *Pionier-Landungs-Bataillon 771*.[32]

During the course of its withdrawal to the Hron, many of the subordinate elements of *Gen.Lt.* Schmidt's corps were virtually destroyed, including most of the Hungarian *2. Panzer* and *Szent László* Divisions. The attached German elements, especially those mobile units from the *3. Pz.Div.* and *8. Pz.Div.* (including *K.Gr. Hafner*), were able to successfully extricate themselves from enemy contact and withdraw across the Hron. Nevertheless, Schmidt's corps had been reduced so much in size by 27 December that it no longer had any troops left to command; the corps and its remaining units were thus attached to the *LVII. Pz.Korps.* Once this had been carried out by the following morning, Schmidt, his corps headquarters, and remaining corps troops were relieved and became available for employment elsewhere.

The entire effort by *6. Armee*/*A.Gr. Fretter-Pico*/*A.Gr. Balck* from 21–28 December to carry out a large-scale counterattack to regain the Ipolysag Gap and defend the Börzeny Mountains had failed completely. It had not all been in vain, however. In the process, the 6th Guards Tank Army had lost so much of its armor (the Germans claimed to have destroyed or damaged 149 enemy tanks out of 200 by 27 December), that its attack had run out of steam. In its own after-action report, the IX Guards Mechanized Corps admitted losing 68 tanks of all types plus 875 men killed and wounded.[33] Infantry losses within the 7th Guards Army had been so great that all that Malinovsky's weakened Second Ukrainian Front could do by 28 December was to consolidate control of the eastern bank of the Hron and hold the Parkany bridgehead and the northern bank of the Danube from Esztergom to Szentendre Island.[34]

Except for at Parkany, efforts by Soviet troops to seize river crossings and establish bridgeheads on the western bank of the Hron were repeatedly thwarted by counterattacks from the *357. Inf.Div.* and *3.* and *6. Pz.Div.* Thus weakened, the Second Ukrainian Front was no longer a threat to Vienna or Bratislava, allaying one of *Gen.Obst.* Friessner's greatest fears expressed on 10 December. But Friessner's other great fear, the encirclement of Budapest, had come to pass. For the next four weeks, beginning on 1 January 1945, the focus of most of *H.Gr. Süd*'s efforts would be directed towards the city's relief; three large-scale attempts would be made to rescue its garrison but all of them would ultimately fail. Finally, after a 48-day siege, the city fell to the forces of the Third Ukrainian Front on 11 February, after the garrison had attempted a last-minute breakout. In the ensuing disaster, all but 600–700 German and Hungarian troops reached the safety of their own lines west of the capital, while nearly everyone else was killed or captured. Six entire German and Hungarian divisions and a corps headquarters had been struck from the map.

In retrospect, it would have been far better for the *LVII. Pz.Korps* to have set up a coherent defense line between the Hron and Ipoly Rivers rather than carry out a large-scale counterattack with insufficient forces, especially since they lacked the offensive weight that their *panzers* could have provided. Although the towns of Gyerk, Kistompa, Pereszlény, and Palást changed hands several times between 22 and 27 December, there was no chance that Kirschner's troops could retake Ipolysag or encircle the numerically greater Soviet forces concentrated in the area. To make the chances of success even more elusive, the supporting attack by the *IV. Pz.Korps* had failed to materialize because of the advanced state of exhaustion of its own divisions. In the end, rather than cutting off and destroying the V Guards Tank Corps and IX Guards Mechanized Corps, the *LVII. Pz.Korps* and *LXXII. Armeekorps* found themselves nearly surrounded and escaped destruction only by the narrowest of margins.

General der Panzertruppe Kirschner soon realized that the further he tried to advance to the northeast with the ultimate goal of taking Ipolysag, the deeper his corps would be drawn into the noose being prepared for it. Finally, after over a week of heavy fighting, both sides lay exhausted, while the focus of the fighting shifted south of the Danube, where the relief effort of Budapest, Operation *Konrad*, would begin on 1 January 1945 (see Map 9). By the end of the year, the German and Hungarian front lines north of the Danube had finally become dormant after three weeks of heavy fighting. They would not change substantially until 10 January 1945, when the Second Ukrainian Front would once again be strong enough to launch another offensive. But by then, the Dirlewanger Brigade was long gone.

CHAPTER THIRTEEN

The Dirlewanger Brigade Departs Hungary, 29 December 1944–5 January 1945

The Dirlewanger Brigade, consisting primarily of its remaining elements subordinated to the *IV. Pz.Korps*, continued fighting until the end of the month. During this period, there was very little reference to its actions in the official records of *H.Gr. Süd* except for occasional brief mentions in its war diary.[1] By 21 December, the three battalions nominally under Dirlewanger's administrative control but not his tactical control were attached to the *18. SS-Freiw.Pz.Gren.Div.* and the *24. Pz.Div.*, with the *I.* and *III. Btl./SS-St.Rgt. 1* going to the former and *I. Btl./SS-St.Rgt. 2* to the latter. Dirlewanger's own primary activities as brigade commander would have been limited to providing replacements (if any) and evacuating casualties, approving promotions or demotions, and issuing award citations, while the divisions to which these battalions were subordinated provided everything else, especially food, fuel, ammunition, and initial casualty treatment.

These three battalions represented a substantial portion of the infantry remaining available to these two divisions, both of which were severely understrength having suffered heavy losses since their retreat after the battle of Hatvan nearly three weeks earlier. Since that battle, both divisions had been fighting continuously to prevent the Second Ukrainian Front from penetrating into southern Slovakia. On 23 December, the combined strength of the two Dirlewanger battalions fighting with the *Horst Wessel* Division amounted to a *Mittelstark* (medium-strong) battalion (approximately 301–400 men), while the one attached to *K.Gr. Schenz* of the *24. Pz.Div.* was of approximately equal strength.[2] As such, *IV. Pz.Korps* could not do without either of them at that moment.

The *I.* and *III. Btl./SS-St.Rgt. 1* were holding defensive positions in the forests north and northeast of Palást. While operating in this area, both took part in numerous attacks and counterattacks to regain or maintain possession of that key town as well as re-establish their old positions in the *Margarethestellung*. During fierce fighting against troops of the XXVII Guards Rifle Corps and Cavalry-Mechanized Group Pliyev, Palást changed hands at least three times during the week of 21–27 December. Little is known about the activities of *I. Btl./SS-St.Rgt. 2*, attached to

K.Gr. Schenz of the *24. Pz.Div.* During the same period, this battalion took part in defensive battles and counterattacks in the vicinity of Balassagyarmat and Szécsény, both of which finally fell to the Soviets at the end of the month after nearly three weeks of seesaw fighting.

During this period, these three battalions served more or less reliably. On 22 December, one Dirlewanger *Kampfgruppe* attached to the *18. SS-Freiw.Pz.Gren. Div.* was mentioned favorably in the *Kriegstagebuch* of *H.Gr. Süd* for retaking the high ground east of Szalatnya (the *KTB* does not specify whether it was Meyer's or Polack's), while the other was cited for carrying out a successful surprise attack that succeeded in retaking Palást. This achievement enabled a larger *Kampfgruppe* from the *24. Pz.Div.*—consisting of attached elements of the *18. SS-Freiw.Pz.Gren.Div.*, 10 *panzers* from *Pz.Rgt. 24*, and one of the two battalions from *SS-St.Rgt. 1*—to reoccupy the town.

Palást was then used as a jump-off point for this battlegroup's attack towards the south planned for the following day to coincide with the attack by Kirschner's *LVII. Pz.Korps.*[3] This particular attack, carried out on the morning of 23 December, succeeded in occupying the area southeast of Palást which Herbert Meyer's battalion had been forced to abandon on 15 December in the wake of its defeat during the battle of Ipolysag. While the *Kampfgruppe* from *24. Pz.Div.* was thus engaged, a counterattack that same day by the 303rd Rifle Division succeeded in retaking the village of Szalatnya 3 kilometers southwest of Palást. In response, the *24. Pz.Div.* had to delay its own operation in order to deal with this new threat with another counterattack of its own.

It was here in Szalatnya where the only documented war crime of the *Dirlewanger Einheit* while fighting on Hungarian territory took place.[4] When the village was reoccupied during the afternoon of 23 December after the German counterattack had driven back the Soviets, the Dirlewanger battalion (either the *I.* or *III. Btl./ SS-St.Rgt. 1*) discovered that some wagons from its baggage train that had been left behind earlier that day had been plundered by Soviet troops as well as by the local civilian population. One of the officers in charge (perhaps Meyer or Polack) had demanded to know who the culprits were. The village residents, no doubt wishing to avoid German retribution, identified the looters as members of the village's small Roma population. As a retaliatory measure, the troops from the *SS Sturmbrigade* rounded up and forced 56 of these unfortunates inside the house of a Koloman Fizik, shot them dead, and then burned it down around them. After the war, a Slovak tribunal interviewed eyewitnesses, but no one in the Dirlewanger Brigade was ever brought to justice for this crime.[5]

On 24 December, the first mention appeared in the official records of the participation of the headquarters of *SS-St.Rgt. 1* in the fighting, with a line in the *H.Gr. Süd* war diary stating that it had been subordinated to the *24. Pz.Div.* on that date.[6] The record did not mention which battalions the regiment was composed of, nor who was its commander, but it undoubtedly served in some sort of tactical command role over one or more of the three remaining battalions fighting along the Slovakian-Hungarian border. It is possible that *Ostubaf.* Buchmann had already taken command of this regiment after handing over his former *SS-St.Rgt. 2* to *Stubaf.* Ehlers. This formal mention in *H.Gr. Süd's* war diary may have been connected to the standing order issued over 10 days previously stating that Dirlewanger's troops were to be deployed in the front line as a unified whole under its own officers. Despite this measure, desertions continued, albeit at a much lower rate, perhaps a sign that the brigade's formal chain of command had begun to reassert itself.

For those surviving elements not in combat that had been withdrawn earlier to the brigade's assembly area between Karpfen and Nemce, Christmas 1944 was a bleak one. Quartered in barns, sheds, private homes, and anything else that had a roof on it, the survivors did their best to keep warm while celebrating a meagre holiday meal. One veteran who had made it back alive from Hungary was the unnamed *Oberscharführer* who had been Harald Momm's second in command, who left a brief eyewitness account of how he and his comrades attempted to celebrate the season:

> Christmas 1944 was the saddest I've ever had. Even in prison [before the war] we had a big Christmas tree and the prison authorities organized something resembling a party. The rest of our company celebrated Christmas sitting in a Slovakian house in a gloomy mood. Unlike previous years, there were no little presents, no cake, and no nice roast. A few pine branches lay on the table, a few Hindenburg lamps burned, and each of us scrounged what we had out of our haversacks. We didn't feel like singing. I shouted, "But we're still alive guys." Later I visited my pal Willi, who was serving in the *7. Kompanie.* He saw me and said, "Everything's gone to hell. Those damned Communist pigs. If I ever see one of them again, I'll shoot him dead!" Willi had a room with another fellow soldier in the home of a Slovakian family, and the three of us sat in the darkness with a tallow candle. The father of the family knocked on the door and brought us something to eat and drink. He spoke passable German and said, "Next year Christmas peace!" and we answered, "Yeah, hopefully!"[7]

Earlier in his account, he mentioned that shortly after they had moved into their new quarters he and some of the other survivors had been repeatedly questioned by the dreaded *SD* and even by Dirlewanger himself regarding the mass desertions in the *II.* and *III. Bataillone* of *SS-St.Rgt. 2* on 15 December and who had been the ringleaders. Luckily for him and his comrades, none of them were charged with anything and the matter was later dropped.

On 26 December, the *Diktat* concerning the splitting up of Dirlewanger units among different commands was repeated once again via an order emanating directly from *H.Gr. Süd* to *AOK 6/A.Gr. Balck* which stated once again: "For reasons owing to the special composition of the *SS-Brigade Dirlewanger*, any dispersion of these units is prohibited by the *Reichsführer-SS*."[8] This order also instructed *AOK 6/A.Gr. Balck* to direct the *LVII. Pz.Korps* to immediately begin pulling out any remaining elements of the Dirlewanger Brigade still serving on the front line under its command (including all troops still fighting with *K.Gr. Hafner* of the *357. Inf.Div.*) and send them on their way to the small town of Nemce, 10 kilometers southwest of the city of Karpfen, where they would once again revert to their brigade's control. Units were to report compliance with the order in the following day's *Tagesmeldung*.

Meanwhile, fighting on the Slovak border continued unabated. On 27 December, three Soviet rifle divisions supported by tanks made a renewed push to retake Palást and Szalatnya. During the heavy see-saw fighting that took place in the town's vicinity, the commander of *III. Btl./SS-St.Rgt. 1*, *Untersturmführer* Siegfried Polack, was declared missing in action near Palást, probably killed, and was therefore considered "rehabilitated." As such, he was reinstated to his old prewar *SS* rank of *Sturmbannführer* and posthumously back in the good graces of Heinrich Himmler, although this must have been small comfort to his widow and two young children. To this day, his body has not been recovered, though his name and personal data have been recorded in the memorial book at the German military cemetery in Budaörs.[9]

Even by this point, the continuing commitment of the Dirlewanger Brigade was still eliciting controversy. Apparently, Wöhler's message of 26 December pertaining to the 23 December ban from Himmler on mixing Dirlewanger troops with those from other units was still not being obeyed as thoroughly as he (or Himmler) liked. Wöhler relayed yet another telex from Himmler on 28 December specifically intended for *Gen.d.Pz.Tr.* Ullrich Kleeman, the new commander of *8. Armee* (which was no longer an *Armeegruppe* since all its Hungarian troops had been transferred elsewhere), stating:

> In another telex, the *Reichsführer-SS* has urged the strongest possible caution against the mixing of units of the Dirlewanger Brigade with other units. Contrary to the orders given by the *Heeresgruppe*, parts of the Dirlewanger Brigade are still split up with other units, without the brigade commander being given the necessary possibilities for the development and supervision of the members of this special brigade. I now hold the Commander-in-Chief [of the *8. Armee*] personally responsible for ensuring that all parts of the Dirlewanger Brigade are immediately withdrawn from the front and marched to the Nemce assembly area ... Renewed deployment of the Dirlewanger Brigade by the *8. Armee* is to take place only after approval by the German Commander in Slovakia. Execution of the order is to be reported to the *Heeresgruppe*.[10]

General der Panzertruppe Balck had already made clear his opinion of the Dirlewanger Brigade; he wanted no part of it. Balck held a longstanding animosity against the *Waffen-SS*, as did *Gen.Maj.* Gaedke, his chief of staff, and the presence of this penal formation within his area of operations filled him with distaste, to say the least (on 31 December, Balck told Wöhler that he was absolutely firm in his conviction that "this *SS* unit" must be removed from the front line).[11] He had already issued two orders on 27 December to the commander of the *LXXII. Armeekorps* to investigate whether there were any vestiges of this unit remaining within its ranks, and if there were, *Gen.Lt.* Schmidt was to remove them immediately and send them on their way to Nemce.[12]

Although this order applied equally to the *8. Armee*, due to the situation on the ground between Szécsény and Balassagyarmat and the aforementioned shortage of infantry in the *IV. Pz. Korps* sector, *Gen.d.Pz. Tr.* Kleemann could not yet release the three battalions still operating within his *Kampfraum*. However, on 29 December, Kleemann probably had new reasons to second-guess his decision to keep them when one of the Dirlewanger battalions broke and ran when overwhelmed by a superior enemy force while fighting near the town of Celovce (Čeľovce), a few kilometers south of Mt. Macko (Hill 521).[13] This battalion's collapse and resulting gap in the front lines forced the *24. Pz. Div.* to stop its own attack aimed at regaining control of Iploynyék and launch a counterattack in a different direction to restore the German positions near Celovce instead.

This minor disaster prompted yet another mention in the war diary of *H. Gr. Süd* of the need to deploy any Dirlewanger troops under their own chain of command:

> Due to the failure of parts of the SS Brigade Dirlewanger at Macko Mountain, at 10.00am the Chief of the [*Heeresgruppe*] General Staff once again pointed out to the *8. Armee* the *Heeresgruppe*'s order to reunite the brigade under its commander and not to break it up again. The brigade, consisting of convicts and probationary solders, can only be relied upon if it fights under the supervision of its commanders who are familiar with their people. The interspersing of parts of the brigade among other units is pointless.[14]

The circumstances and sequence of events that led to this failure were left unstated, as well as which battalion was involved and under which element of either the *18. SS-Freiw.Pz. Gren. Div.* or *24. Pz. Div.* it was attached. Whether Dirlewanger himself was present on the scene is highly unlikely; by this point he was in all likelihood back at the brigade's assembly point in Nemce.

While technically *SS-St.Rgt. 1* was in charge of the three battalions operating within the *IV. Pz. Korps* area of operations, it appears that it was not involved in this incident either, since the battalion concerned seems to have been operating directly under the control of either the *18. SS-Freiw.Pz. Gren. Div.* or the *24. Pz. Div.* Whatever the truth, this sorry incident resulted in the removal of all remaining elements of the brigade from the front line, beginning the next day. On 31 December, the *8. Armee* reported that the last battalion in its area of operations had been withdrawn from the front line and transported to the Karpfen area (probably meaning Nemce). Although the remnants of the two battalions operating along the upper Hron under the *357. Inf. Div.* had been withdrawn from the front lines by *Gen.d.Pz. Tr.* Balck's orders on 29 December, these troops did not begin their journey from the Nagykalna area to Nemce until 31 December.

This body of troops (*II.* and *III. Btl./SS-St.Rgt. 2*), under the command of former *Maj.d.Schu.Po.* Falter, were unaware that their march destination of Nemce had changed while they were still *en route*. Due to Soviet advances that had taken place after they had departed, Nemce was no longer safe. Instead, Falter reported that they had been rerouted to their former assembly area in Priewitz (Prievidza), where the brigade had been directed to reassemble after evacuating Nemce. Even then, Falter reported two days later via a local *Wehrmacht* radio transmission station in Slovakia that his march route had been changed once more. Due to strong Slovak partisan activity in the forest north of Golden-Morawetz through which he and his men would have to pass, on 2 January 1945 they were sent on a circuitous route that led them from Golden-Morawetz southwestward through Neutra before turning northeastwards following the Nitra valley towards Priewitz, a marching distance of over 120 kilometers.[15] Finally, Falter and his 236 troops arrived at their destination in Priewitz by 5 January 1945 without incident, though exhausted and footsore.

The last element of the Dirlewanger Brigade to depart the battle area appears to have been *I. Btl./SS-St.Rgt. 2*, which had been attached to *K.Gr. Schenz* of the *24. Pz.Div.* On 30 December, the division reported this battalion as having a *durchschnitt* (average) combat strength, defined as a *Kampfstärke* of between 201 and 300 men, signifying that it still retained a level of combat potential.[16] By 31 December, even this battalion and any remaining elements of the brigade still serving with the *IV. Pz.Korps* had been withdrawn from the front line and were reported to be assembling in Karpfen. On 3 January 1945, *8. Armee* officially announced that the Dirlewanger Brigade had begun moving *in toto* to its former base in Priewitz, thus officially ending its commitment with the *IV. Pz.Korps* and the Hungarian-Slovakian theater of war.[17]

Whether by rail, truck, or on foot, the war diary of the German Commander in Slovakia reported that the entire brigade had assembled at its base in the Priewitz-Deviaky area by 5 January 1945. Notable in this diary mention was the number of men who had returned. On that date, the Dirlewanger Brigade reported an *Iststärke* as follows: 1,056 men in *SS-St.Rgt. 1*, 1,151 men in *SS-St.Rgt. 2*, and 282 men in *SS-Art.Abt. Dirlewanger*, a total of 2,489 men.[18] These figures do not include other brigade elements, such as the supply company, mixed battalion, brigade headquarters company, and so forth. Neither do they include the number of men in hospital. The report concluded with a mention that more stragglers were to be expected, but did not state whether any of these numbers included personnel newly assigned to the brigade. Since the brigade's total strength as of 1 December 1944 was estimated by *Hstuf.* Bruno Wille to have been approximately 6,500, the number of men killed, wounded, and declared missing (or deserted) was probably half that number, perhaps as high as 3,000 men.

In essence, the Dirlewanger Brigade had been destroyed as an effective fighting force. Not only had the majority of two battalions deserted *en masse* to the Red Army on 15 December at Ipolysag, but the troops who did remain suffered heavy casualties due to a number of causes, including artillery and mortar fire, tank attacks, and frequent infantry clashes. Undoubtedly, a number of men were evacuated to field hospitals in the rear area due to illnesses resulting from living outdoors in a winter environment, such as pneumonia, frostbite, influenza, and other cold weather injuries. Poor diet and insufficient winter clothing was another factor to consider in the overall performance of the individual *B-Schützen* or *Straffäligen*.

In terms of equipment, the brigade had lost an entire artillery battery, its heavy mortar company, most of its antitank guns, nearly all of its other infantry heavy weapons, and other essential equipment such as radios, field telephones, tentage, wagons, horses, and motor vehicles. In short, it had been wrecked as much by incompetence, carelessness, and bad luck as by enemy action. Another factor contributing to its destruction was the low level of individual and collective training within its squads, platoons, companies, and battalions. Most of the new recruits from the concentration camps who were assigned in November 1944, including many so-called politicals, received hardly any training at all, rendering them nearly useless on the battlefield, even had they been willing to fight.

In terms of leadership, many of its officers were rejects from other *SS* or *Polizei* units due to incompetence, unsuitability, or criminality such as Erich Buchmann, Ewald Ehlers, and Kurt Weisse. The fact that the brigade had fought at all (and sometimes it did so effectively) was probably due to the large number of former officers of the *Heer* who had been condemned for a disciplinary offense or had spoken out against the regime. This also applied to former NCOs who had found themselves facing the same Hobson's choice: Dirlewanger or death. These men had been assigned to the brigade to perform their penance instead of suffering execution, where they could at least in theory redeem themselves. Some accepted *SS* ranks, while most were content to serve without rank at all, with the exception of bands of silver tress on their lower left sleeves. Counted among this number of former officers were Freiherr von Uckermann, Harald Momm, and Paul Ruhsam. Without them, the brigade's defeat at Ipolysag on 15 December would have been far worse with even greater negative consequences.

In addition to Siegfried Polack, the Dirlewanger Brigade lost several other formerly high-ranking *SS* and Nazi Party officials during the battle, regardless of whether they had served in leadership positions or as humble *Grenadiere*. Former *Sicherheitsdienst* officer and the highest-ranking *SD* officer in Paris, *Ostubaf.* Kurt Neifeind, was killed in action at Ipolysag on 15 December; in what capacity he was serving, whether as a rifleman or intelligence officer, is still unknown. *Obersturmführer* Wilhelm Stegmann, the former high-ranking *SA* officer and commander of *I. Btl./ SS-St.Rgt. 2*, had been listed as missing in action at some point between 15 and 31 December while carrying out a leader's reconnaissance, and presumed dead.[19] In addition to these two, former *SD Hstuf.* Josef Grohmann, who fought as a company commander at Ipolysag, is also believed to have fallen during the battle, although his remains were never recovered.[20]

Ironically, while the Dirlewanger Brigade was still fighting in the Ipoly River valley and after the disaster at Ipolysag, an order was issued by the *SS-FHA* (i.e, by *Ogruf.*

Jüttner's office) on 19 December that formalized the new composition and structure of the brigade, including the issuing of pertinent and up-to-date tables of organization and equipment. These documents would govern the organizational aspects of the unit and its structure, the types of weapons and vehicles authorized, as well as the full list of all of the weapons, equipment, and ammunition required to be carried into combat.[21] Naturally, while engaged in combat it was impossible for Dirlewanger to implement these directives, so this task had to wait until his brigade had been reassembled at Priewitz.

The new organizational structure formalized elements of the old one, required the elimination of other non-authorized elements, and authorized the creation of new elements that had previously been extemporized *auf der Kommandoweg* (on the commander's authority). It also issued formal organized structures based on similar or identical German Army *KStNs* for platoons, companies, battalions, and regiments. Most of these new *KStNs* were based on what had been created exclusively for the *Volks-Grenadier* divisions that had been activated during September and October 1944. In essence, the new *SS-Sturmbrigade Dirlewanger* would be transformed into a miniature *Volks-Grenadier* Division (*Volks-Gr.Div.*) with only two grenadier regiments instead of three, and only one artillery battalion instead of four. All of the other battalion-sized "division troops" elements of a *Volks-Gr.Div.*, such as engineer battalion, *Füsilier* battalion, and so forth, would be reduced to company-sized units.[22] All told, the newly reorganized brigade had an authorized *Sollstärke* of approximately 5,452 men.

Like those in a *Volks-Grenadier Division*, each regiment would consist of only two grenadier battalions, not three, so this would require that Dirlewanger disband the *III. Bataillone* of each of his two regiments. The *III. Btl./SS-St.Rgt. 2* had virtually disbanded itself anyway when most of its troops went over to the Red Army. At least this measure would reduce the pressure for Dirlewanger to find competent leadership for his grenadier companies, now that he had two less battalions to worry about. Each regiment would also (finally) receive its two dedicated heavy weapons companies, which were lacking in the previous makeshift structure. The addition of an infantry howitzer company and antitank company would finally give regimental commanders the wherewithal to support their own battalions without having to rely exclusively upon a makeshift mixed battalion, as had been the case at Ipolysag.

The number of administrative, logistical, and medical support troops would be greatly increased in the new structure, enabling the brigade to more effectively and efficiently provide the battalions with the food, ammunition, fuel, and medical services that would allow them to be far more self-sufficient than in the past. A new veterinary company was added, in recognition of the fact that the new brigade would be even more reliant on horses than it had been before. Even so, the motor vehicle park would receive a larger allocation of trucks and automobiles. Most of the new weapons and equipment would be of German manufacture, replacing the obsolete or ineffective foreign-made weapons that it had been forced to use since the *Sonderkommando*'s inception. Surprisingly, the new brigade structure did not include an antitank company and no armored vehicles were authorized at all, a sign that the title of "assault brigade" was nothing more than an honorific.[23]

For most of January 1945, the brigade spent its time in Priewitz reorganizing to conform to the newly authorized structure. New personnel from the *Wehrmacht* and *SS* prisons, as well as the usual sort of civilian *Straffälige* from concentration camps, continued to fill its ranks. New weapons and equipment arrived, new clothing was issued, and a training program was reinstituted. No more political prisoners from the *KL* system were accepted (except for the few remaining in the ranks who had not defected), a sign that even Berger and Dirlewanger had learned their lesson. New leaders had to be found to replace the many who had been lost at Ipolysag and afterwards. The personnel made available after the disbandment of the *gemischte Bataillon* would be used to form the cadre for the regimental heavy weapons companies.

The Dirlewanger Brigade's first readiness report while it was still undergoing reorganization was sent to the *SS-FHA Organisations-Abteilung* on 3 January 1945. This report, required by the order issued on 19 December, was used to measure the strength of the unit and the status of its conversion to the new structure. While portions of the report are missing, such as the number of personnel assigned, it does provide a snapshot of the scale of its losses while fighting at Ipolysag.[24] According to the chart (see Figure 2), the two battalions of *SS-St.Rgt. 1* reported their manpower strength as 69 and 56 percent respectively after the disbandment of one of its battalions, while the two of *SS-St.Rgt. 2* reported having 43 and 70 percent of their authorized personnel. All four grenadier battalions reported that between 22 and 46 percent of their troops (varying by battalion) were fresh replacements who had arrived in Priewitz while the brigade was still fighting in Hungary. The heavy mortar company was disbanded and its personnel parceled out to the grenadier regiments' heavy weapons companies. There were no personnel yet assigned to the new *Füsilier* and *Pionier* companies, which would have to be formed from scratch.

At least *Artillerie-Abteilung Dirlewanger* was in relatively good shape; it had lost only its light 75mm cannon battery at Ipolysag as the other two medium batteries had not deployed to the *Kampfraum* at all due to the lack of necessary equipment. In regards to small arms, there were still not enough on hand to equip all of its troops; in the status report of 3 January, the brigade reported having 2,018 rifles, 162 sniper rifles (rifles with telescopic sights), and 209 machine pistols. It still had four heavy (120mm) Soviet mortars of its own, five 37mm antitank guns of Czech manufacture, and four Soviet submachine guns.[25] New or reconditioned weapons would have to be issued by the *Heeres-Waffenamt* to make up for these shortfalls.

Throughout late December and into mid-January 1945, Dirlewanger was involved in various intrigues against Hermann Höfle, who still served as the *HSSPF-Slowakei*

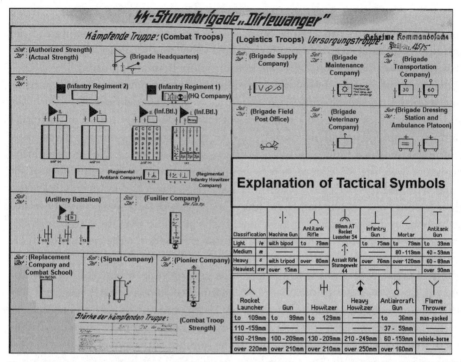

Figure 2: Organizational Diagram detailing the authorized structure of the Dirlewanger Brigade approved on 19 December 1944 by Amt II of the Organizations-Abteilung Ia/II (Organizational Department) of the *SS-Führungshauptamt* (NARA, Records Group T-175, Microfilm Roll 141, Image 0079).

when not acting as the German commander in that country. To cover up his brigade's failure on the battlefield, Dirlewanger, aided by Gottlob Berger, instituted a campaign to shift the blame for all of its shortcomings at Ipolysag onto the alleged lack of support by Höfle. Dirlewanger had written a letter to Hermann Fegelein during the last week of December blaming his brigade's destruction on Höfle. Himmler, who had received a copy of the letter from Fegelein, still harbored animosity towards Höfle dating back to the Slovak Uprising, and thus took Dirlewanger's side. This in turn generated a heated exchange of letters between Himmler and Höfle. In his first letter to Höfle dated 30 December 1944, an incensed Himmler wrote:

> With this letter I warn you for the last time before I relieve you of command. You are as disobedient a subordinate as you are weak in enforcing the orders given to you. I want to show you four cases [the first three unrelated cases are omitted]: You did not support the Dirlewanger Brigade in its formation, but as a disobedient subordinate, and contrary to the orders given by me clearly and unambiguously, you allowed the brigade to be torn into four parts and placed under the command of four different commanders. You have thus shown me that you have as little psychological understanding for the difficulty of this formation as any general of the *Wehrmacht*, from whom of course I cannot demand an explanation.[26]

Himmler also complained about Höfle's chief of staff, *Ostubaf.* Hans Greiner, who until September 1944 had been an *Oberstleutnant* in the *Heer.* Serving as one of the most senior of the few military professionals on the staff of the German Commander in Slovakia, Greiner was Höfle's chief advisor whose expertise contributed substantially to the successful suppression of the Slovak Uprising. Himmler believed that Greiner had far too much influence over his commander, stating:

> I have the impression that you are complete putty in the hands of your staff. I want you to tell me briefly and in writing—without any apology or explanation—whether you are now willing to obey my words and to pay more attention to orders from me, than to the instructions of your staff or to the instructions of the local army authorities. If you are not in a position to make this declaration, I await your request to be relieved, since I must then assume that in terms of health you are not up to the demands of your position. I think you can judge for yourself how much I regret having to write you this letter.[27]

Obergruppenführer Höfle, not one to take this false accusation lying down, ordered an investigation into the situation in Dirlewanger's artillery battalion. The investigative officer concluded that the *Artillerie Abteilung*, which had requested the necessary artillery firing tables, had indeed received them, but had remained behind at full strength in its quarters in Priewitz and was not deployed at Ipolysag at all. The light battery from the battalion, which was deployed (and destroyed) at Ipolysag, did have all the technical aids at its disposal. Höfle declared at his war crimes trial in 1946:

> When in the course of this situation [the battle of Ipolysag] that Dirlewanger's troops (probably through his own fault) completely failed, Dirlewanger thought that he had to safeguard himself against future reproaches from the *Heer* by the fact that behind my back, perhaps at Berger's instigation, he had [his] agents report to *SS-Gruppenführer* Fegelein that I was to blame for this development because I had refused a timely request by [Dirlewanger's] artillery section … or rather, because I had refused to help the artillery. [Dirlewanger claimed that] I was late in handing over the artillery firing tables that were necessary for [the artillery's] deployment in combat. Hence, it is said, the enemy shot up our units without the artillery being able to fire even once.[28]

Höfle formulated a response to Himmler on 6 January 1945 that disputed all of these accusations and included his own after-action report about the brigade's performance during the battle of Ipolysag and the weeks it spent fighting in Hungary. He began his cover letter by stating that he was responsible for every decision made during the past several weeks, thereby shielding Greiner from any repercussions from Himmler:

> *Reichsführer!* After I learned that Dirlewanger had handed over a report on the deployment of his brigade in the Ipolysag area directly to Fegelein, and that this report contains some one-sided representations, and that this report has been submitted to you, *Reichsführer*, I consider it my duty to send you an unsolicited report describing how the operations of the brigade went. I must report that all orders and orders given to the brigade by my chief of the general staff, *SS-Ostubaf.* Greiner, have been issued on my behalf and that I am fully responsible for them.[29]

Höfle then went into detail in the attached after-action report describing how the situation had developed where he had no choice but to deploy the Dirlewanger Brigade and to subordinate portions of it to *H.Gr. Süd*, in direct contravention of Himmler's instructions that he not do so:

> If, as a result of an impending breakthrough, *H.Gr. Süd* independently subordinated parts of the brigade, which were standing by immediately behind the front on the southern border of Slovakia, without informing me beforehand, that was undoubtedly absurd ... In the course of this conversation, General Wenck pointed out that the *Führer* himself had marked the importance of the narrows at Ipolysag with a black line on his map during the briefing ... This order confirmed the correctness of my decision, which [I had] already begun to carry out. The Dirlewanger Brigade was the most readily available [unit] for this assignment and was also my only unit that had any considerable artillery and heavy mortars.[30]

At this point, Höfle began to embellish his explanation in an attempt to justify his decision not to deploy *Division Tatra* to Ipolysag:

> *Kampfgruppe Tatra*, on the other hand ... had no artillery and little heavy infantry weapons at its disposal [this was not strictly true]. In addition, I could only entrust the immediate protection of the Waag valley, which represents the backbone of Slovakia and does not pose a major obstacle to an enemy approaching from the south or southeast, to another unit, albeit a weaker one. I therefore did not interrupt the express transport of *K.Gr. Tatra* [to the Waag valley] ... and ordered, among other things, the immediate onward march of the Dirlewanger Brigade, which was already causing considerable difficulties in Slovakia, and assigned the bulk of its troops to the border section between Hron and Stararieka—north of Balassagyarmat—as a security force and arranged the expedited transport of two [Dirlewanger] battalions to Ipolysag.

He then described how he had originally intended to follow Himmler's expressed orders to keep the brigade together and had instructed Dirlewanger to brief the chief of staff of *H.Gr. Süd* on the peculiarities of its commitment:

> It was clear to me that the combat value of the brigade only allowed this deployment to the front for a short time and that a unified brigade deployment to the front without the use of battle-hardened troops was out of the question because of its inadequate command and control apparatus. I therefore gave the order to send two reinforced battalions to Ipolysag along with the artillery battalion and the heavy mortar company ... and that *Oberführer* Dirlewanger was personally to inform the chief of staff of *H.Gr. Süd* by providing documentation about the special conditions [pertaining to] the brigade and to point out the resulting difficulties [if these were not taken into account]. The last order was given personally and verbally by [*SS-Ostubaf.* Greiner] on 10 December 1944, with the [order that it was a] special task of the Brigade Commander [Dirlewanger] to set up his command post near the command post of the staff [charged with] tactically leading his two reinforced battalions [Buchmann's *SS-St.Rgt. 2*] and to supervise from [that location] the consideration of the special needs [logistics, administration, etc.] of the otherwise tactically subordinated parts of his brigade.[31]

He thereafter went into detail describing the circumstances that led to the brigade being split up and placed under separate commands, the subject which drew Himmler's greatest ire:

At that time and in the ensuing hours, there was never any talk of the brigade being subordinated to *H.Gr. Süd*. The *Ia* of the army group was informed about *Oberführer* Dirlewanger's mission by *SS-Ostubaf.* Greiner by telephone. As late as 10 December 1944, the leading battalion, and on 11 December 1944, the mass of the brigade (except for the two battalions deployed furthest to the east) reached the ordered destinations … On the night from 12 to 13 December 1944 the enemy pressure northeastward of Ipolysag increased so much that an encirclement of the defensive barrier east of Ipolysag was to be expected. Therefore, at midnight [on 13 December] the army group committed the two battalions standing ready at the [Slovak-Hungarian] border at Szántó and Dudince and shortly after the two remaining battalions of the brigade into the area of Ipolysag and only informed [*SS-Ogruf.* Höfle] about these measures 10 hours later. At my request, the army group promised to detach these battalions after the situation had been resolved, and I agreed to this based on the current situation … After a further six hours passed, a call from Dirlewanger confirmed that the *Heeresgruppe* had taken independent measures. My chief of staff could only reply to him that this had been done without the prior approval of [*SS-Ogruf.* Höfle] and that the early release I had requested had been assured. Therefore, [I] was not able to deploy the *SS*-Brigade Dirlewanger as a unified whole due to the development of the situation.[32]

Obergruppenführer Höfle stated that at that particular moment in time, this was the only correct decision that he could have made, since *H.Gr. Süd* had no other forces available between 13 and 15 December that could have relieved the Dirlewanger Brigade, even if *Gen.Obst.* Friessner had wished it. Höfle attempted to provide Himmler a further explanation of his actions by describing the context in which they occurred:

The [adverse] development of the situation even made it necessary to deploy additional forces in the front line of the army group under my command to secure the rear area [the *182. Res. Div., K.Gr. Tatra*, the *14. Waffen-Gren.Div. der SS*, and other units]. [I] constantly demanded that the Dirlewanger Brigade be detached from the front, [a request that] was finally satisfied on 28 December 1944, after the situation had calmed down somewhat and after *Gen.d.Inf.* Wöhler took command [of *H.Gr. Süd*]. The Brigade is now assembled in the Priewitz-Novaky area and, in addition to carrying out some security tasks, has the task of reconstituting its battalions.[33]

In typical fashion, Himmler disregarded his subordinate's explanation entirely, apparently placing more faith in Dirlewanger's account than that of Höfle. Responding to his letter of 6 January, Himmler wrote on 14 January:

I had already sent you a sharply worded letter on 30 December 1944, which stated things as I saw them in absolute clarity. In keeping with my habit, I left this letter lying around for many days until I decided to write you another personal letter … I must repeat it to you: I have the impression that you are absolutely putty in the hands of your staff and that you are thereby more prone to obey them rather than myself. I will give you some examples: I had clearly ordered that the Dirlewanger Brigade may only be deployed in unison. You simply threw this order to the wind. Your statement of 6 January 1945 bears the stamp of a guilty conscience. On page 2 you declare "that a closed front deployment of the brigade without the support of battle-hardened troops was out of the question because of the insufficient command apparatus," while on page 3 you state that "the German commander in Slovakia did not have the possibility of deploying the brigade in this situation," i.e., two completely different versions. In reality, the following is clear: I had placed the Dirlewanger Brigade and the Ukrainian Division in your area so that they can be deployed there and, of course, to secure their own quarters. You know the conditions of the Dirlewanger Brigade yourself. To tear apart this bunch of convicts and criminals with their thin leadership framework [would] make them worthless. Even if you, like many *Wehrmacht* generals, have no understanding for such things [as] troop psychology, I could [at least] have expected you to obey me.[34]

Having called into question Höfle's willingness and ability to follow orders, and his loyalty to the SS, Himmler then attempted to encourage him in typically condescending terms, rather than relieve him of his duties outright, and shifted the blame once again towards his staff:

[I]n contrast to our normal relationship you have been disobedient towards me. Explanation of this can only be attributed to a form of weakness, which I had not previously recognized, and in a subservience and dependence on your colleagues and staff that I frankly find questionable. I can only ask you to finally become hard and finally understand that you are in command and that your chief of staff and his colleagues are not the brain that makes your decisions. Recognize the fundamental rule with which we were both raised, namely obedience, even if those around you try to influence you ... Had I known that this command, with which I have entrusted you, and which you accepted so reluctantly, would be such a burden to your spirit, I would never have transferred you, saving both you and me this sorrow. For the last time I express the hope that things will be different in 1945 and that the mistakes of 1944 will be avoided and not repeated.[35]

Himmler let the matter rest there. He did not remove Höfle from command, a command which he exercised until the 8 May 1945 capitulation. Perhaps this was due to Himmler's appointment to another field command, yet another assignment for which he was not qualified, that of *H.Gr. Weichsel* (Army Group Vistula) on 24 January. He was to lead this army group to near ruin for the next two months, until he was finally replaced at Guderian's urging on 20 March by the far more competent *Gen. Obst.* Gotthard Heinrici.

Nevertheless, Höfle had little time to dwell on this injustice, being preoccupied in keeping the Red Army out of Slovakia and ensuring that the units stationed in his domain, including the Dirlewanger Brigade, the *14. Waffen-Gren.Div. der SS*, and *Pz.Feldausb.Div. Tatra*, were receiving everything they needed to continue operating or while undergoing reconstitution. The Dirlewanger Brigade itself spent most of January 1945 being rebuilt and re-equipped. Replacements from *Wehrmacht* and SS penal institutions continued to flow into its replacement company in Cracow, as well as convicts from the *KL* system, except of course political prisoners. Dirlewanger had at least learned his lesson there.

Back in the relative safety and security of its old base area in Priewitz and Novaky, many of the brigade's "old hands" reverted to their previous ways and were blamed for an increase in petty theft, extortion, and other criminalities. The *Oberscharführer* who had been Harald Momm's second in command was elevated to command of the *5. Kompanie*, while Momm was made commander of the *II. Btl./SS-St.Rgt.2* (what became of Franz Falter is not known), and Ewald Ehlers was confirmed as the commander of the regiment. *Obersturmbannführer* Buchmann, of course, had already moved over to command *SS-St.Rgt.1* to enable Ehlers to succeed him. The anonymous NCO left the following account of that period:

> [We were] housed in private quarters and barns, and without any operations scheduled, we spent the turn of the year in Slovakia. At least it was a bit quieter for us … in early January we received 300 new replacement prisoners from Cracow. Around 35 of them came to my company, which was now 75 strong. I had the new guys line up and told them "You may have heard that a large number of prisoners deserted to the Russians a week ago [*sic*]. If there is anyone among you who is planning to do the same, then I will shoot you myself. Do you understand?"[36]

He had a great deal of work to do—not only did he have to teach these new men the basic skills to make them effective in battle and to increase their chances of survival, but he also had to keep an eye on them for signs of unrest or rumors of escape attempts. He continued:

> Training was then resumed with the new men. Marching and shooting theory, and now also training with the *Panzerfaust*. For that there was an NCO with two men and about 15 *Panzerfäuste*. Until then, I had only shot [one] twice in Warsaw. They explained the [firing] procedure … After around an hour of training on a somewhat remote field, we fired [them]. The target was a tree that stood about 40 meters away. From the 15 shots fired, only one hit the tree, three landed close by, some scattered wide, and four or five didn't explode at all … Anyway, my shot landed about two meters from the tree and I was satisfied enough. But the men ridiculed this *Wunderwaffe* (wonder weapon) ever since, which was quite understandable.[37]

That was all the antitank weapons training that this particular company received, but it was probably typical. By the end of the month, the brigade's reorganization had been completed, but in the meantime, the Red Army's Vistula-Oder Operation had begun on 12 January, with its goal being nothing less than the Oder River and the complete destruction of *H.Gr. Mitte*, including the occupation of East Prussia, Pomerania, and Silesia. After nearly four months in Slovakia, the Dirlewanger Brigade was to be given another mission.

CHAPTER FOURTEEN

The Dirlewanger Brigade Meets its Fate, 15 February–8 May 1945

While the German armies under Himmler's command in *H.Gr Weichsel* and in *G.F.M.* Ferdinand Schörner's *H.Gr. Mitte* were being forced to withdraw towards the Oder River by the overwhelming power of the Red Army's last great winter offensive, reinforcements were urgently needed, as dozens of divisions and even army corps were chewed up, some never to be heard of again. Everything was needed to plug the enormous gap yawning between the army groups—even units of uneven reliability or readiness, such as the Dirlewanger Brigade, were urgently required. Dozens of newly raised formations were being assembled and hurriedly rushed to the area east of the Oder River to help stem the tide.

On 2 February 1945, the bulk of the Dirlewanger Brigade was ordered to entrain for the *Oderfront*. After passing through Dresden, the trains carrying the brigade were unloaded in the the Guben area, which had been selected as its new assembly point. By 12 February, its assembly was complete and without further ado it was committed to battle two days later as part of *Gen.d.Pz.Tr.* Sigfrid Heinrici's *XL. Pz.Korps*, which was operating under the control of the *4. Pz.Armee*. It was immediately involved in heavy fighting against Soviet forces in the vicinity of the towns of Sommerfeld, Christianstadt, and Naumburg.[1] On 15 February, during the course of a counterattack to reoccupy Sommerfeld, Oskar Dirlewanger was seriously wounded in action, his 12th and most severe injury, which would sideline him for the remainder of the war.

Dirlewanger was replaced by *Brig.Fhr.* Fritz Schmedes, who had been assigned to the brigade a few days before Dirlewanger's injury to serve as his "Tactical Commander," even though Schmedes outranked him. This was to be only a temporary assignment, lasting only as long as it took for Dirlewanger to recuperate from his wounds, but as events were soon to prove, Schmedes was the last commander of the *Dirlewanger Einheit* and the only commander of the soon-to-be retitled Dirlewanger Division. He had previously served as the commander of the *4. SS-Polizei-Pz.Gren. Div.* until relieved of command by Himmler on 27 November 1944 for disobeying a *Führerbefehl* while leading that division in Hungary.[2] Sidelined in the *Waffen-SS*

Führerreserve for over two months, the highly decorated former police officer must have had some misgivings when he learned that his next assignment was to assume temporary command of a division of convicts. Still, he led it as best he could for the next two-and-a-half months.

On 14 February, the *SS-FHA* decreed that the Dirlewanger Brigade be upgraded in strength to that of a full division, with three grenadier regiments, an artillery regiment, and full-sized division troops, including engineer, antitank, *Füsilier*, and signal battalions. Once carried through, this would bring it up to its authorized strength of 10,500 men, the same size as the new *Grenadier-Division 45* structure then being brought into effect by the German Army.[3] It would be named the *36. Waffen-Grenadier Division der SS Dirlewanger*, since it was still technically equivalent to non-Germanic *SS* divisions and not considered a fully fledged unit of the *Waffen-SS*. Despite this elevation in status, it would continue to fill its ranks with *B-Schützen* and *Straffälige* until the end of the war.

Since there were not enough of these men to form a new regiment and populate all of the newly ordered divisional battalions, Himmler (through Jüttner's office) decreed that the shortages be made up by attaching a number of newly raised units from the *Ersatzheer* (the Replacement or Home Army) that were available at that moment. The order declaring its upgrade even specified these units by name: the third regiment would be created by attaching *Grenadier-Regiment 1244* (composed of army officer cadets, *Volkssturm*, and convalescent soldiers), the lack of a *Pionier* battalion addressed by adding *Heeres-Pio.Brig. 687*, two companies from *Pz.Jag.Abt. 681* would form the antitank battalion, and the newly raised *Pz.Abt. Stahnsdorf 1*, equipped with two companies of 14 assault guns each and one mixed *panzer* company, would round out the division.[4] These units retained their *Heer* designations, and from all available evidence, were not inducted into the *Waffen-SS*.

Had this reorganization been carried through to fruition, the *36. Waffen-Gren. Div.d.SS Dirlewanger* would for the first time have had everything it needed to perform as a balanced, all arms team—with one exception: it would not be augmented by any *Artillerie* units from the Heer; either this was an oversight, or more likely, there were simply too few remaining in the *Wehrmacht's* order of battle to provide them. It would have to make do with the same battalion that was activated in November 1944—the now-renumbered three-battery *SS-Art.Abt. 36*. Each of its two existing regiments (*SS-St.Rgt. 1* and *2*) would be renumbered and redesignated as *SS-Waffen-Gren.Rgter. 72* and *73*, respectively. However, it seems likely that the division and its new *Heer* attachments did not all fight together as a whole—whether due to force of circumstances or bureaucratic intervention, it is no longer possible to determine why.

There was another issue resulting from its expansion that was never made good—the lack of sufficiently trained and experienced officers and NCOs to lead its platoons, companies, and battalions, especially junior lieutenants. With the supply of imprisoned officers of the *Heer* incarcerated in the wake of the 20 July assassination plot having been apparently exhausted, Berger and Dirlewanger had to look elsewhere. Since every newly commissioned *Wehrmacht* officer was being assigned to units of the *Heer* to replace those lost in battle or to form new divisions, the *SS-Hauptamt* had to look inward to source officers from its own ranks. It found them in the form of the newly begun class of officer cadets from the *SS-Junkerschule* in Braunschweig. Several dozen of them (approximately 60) came from a group of 150 that had first been assigned to serve as part of *K.Gr. Schneider*. This *Kampfgruppe* had been briefly attached to the *1. Fallschirm-Pz.Div. Hermann Göring* for several weeks and would soon be redirected to the Dirlewanger Division on 10 March, where they were used to fill many of the vacant leadership positions in its grenadier companies.[5]

The degree to which the division fully attained its authorized *Sollstärke* in both men and equipment may never be known; suffice to say, once committed to the front line at Guben, it was almost continually involved in combat operations until its destruction at the end of April. From about 18 February until 15 April, it was engaged in positional warfare along the Oder Front, primarily in the area between the cities of Guben and Crossen.[6] The available records indicate that it fought in an acceptable manner and was not plagued by mass desertions as it had been in Hungary two months earlier, although desertions and executions continued, albeit at a lower scale.

The Third Reich's overall military situation became increasingly dire during the last several months of the war. Final victory was clearly no longer even a possibility. Morale among all of the elements of the *Wehrmacht* had begun to plummet as more and more soldiers began to realize that Germany was about to suffer complete and utter defeat. However, within the *Waffen-SS*, a surprisingly large number of its troops continued to fight with the same fanatical devotion that they had become famous for. Surrender for them was out of the question. In the Dirlewanger Division, it was announced that should anyone attempt to desert their position at this critical moment, *SS* officers and NCOs were to shoot to kill; if they were caught, they would suffer summary execution without trial.[7]

On 16 April, the Red Army's final great offensive of the war, the Berlin Operation, began with a massive bombardment along the Seelow Heights on the western bank of the Oder, a mere 68 kilometers east of the Brandenburg Gate. Two days later, the German front line collapsed and the Red Army's race towards Berlin began in earnest. The Dirlewanger Division, now referred to as *K.Gr. 36. SS-Division* on situation maps, continued to fight defensive battles in the Guben area, but by 20 April had begun to withdraw towards the northwest along with the rest of the *XL. Pz.Korps*. Sandwiched between the *342.* and *214. Inf.Div.* of the *Heer*, the Dirlewanger Division held the new front line for three days until forced to withdraw again on 23 April towards a switch line in the Neu-Zauche area. This temporary defensive line held firm until 26 April, when the division and its neighboring units were forced to pull back yet again to the Märkisch-Buchholz area.[8] *Oberführer* Schmedes led the division competently, attempting to hold it together as an effective fighting force while resisting the overwhelming pressure being exerted upon it by troops of Marshal Konev's First Ukrainian Front.

By 28 April, Schmedes and his troops had found themselves trapped along with most of *Gen.d.Inf.* Theodor Busse's *9. Armee* in the southeastern part of what soon became known as the *Halbekessel* (Halbe Pocket). Here, *K.Gr. 36. SS-Division* was forcibly split into at least two separate groups as German command and control collapsed, to be replaced by complete chaos. Some of Schmedes's troops managed to escape through the bottleneck at Halbe, but most were trapped. Hundreds of his men were killed and wounded, or later declared missing in action. Seeking to spare the lives of as many of his men as possible, Schmedes surrendered the remnants of the division to the Red Army on 29 April.[9]

How many of his men became prisoners at this point is unknown; what is known is that there was no general massacre of Dirlewanger prisoners, as has been reported in various tabloid and popular historical media. However, a few remnants, no more than several hundred men under the command of *Stubaf.* Kurt Weisse, managed to escaped the trap at Halbe and link up with *Gen.d.Pz.Tr.* Wenck's approaching *12. Armee*, now operating strictly as a relief force intent on rescuing as many soldiers from Busse's army and fleeing civilians as possible and not the relief of Berlin as was originally intended. These lucky few from Schmedes's division were able to reach the Elbe during Wenck's withdrawal. Many crossed the river over the partially destroyed bridge at Tangermünde on 3 May. Like all of the other *SS* troops surrendering during that period, surviving Dirlewanger members were shunted into various holding pens while they awaited their fate. Many of them shed their insignia to avoid possible retribution from their Soviet or Allied guards. In the West, most of these men were consigned to Allied prisoner of war camps under "automatic arrest" from which they were released between 1947–1948. Thus ended the nearly five-year history of the *Dirlewanger Einheit*.

According to some accounts, over 1,000 survivors surrendered at Halbe. How many surrendered to the Western Allies after escaping from the *Kessel* is unknown, although it was probably in the low hundreds. What is known is that 634 former prisoners were released by the Soviet Union by 1955, according to the German Red Cross tracing service, and that many others died while in captivity.[10] Some 750 men of the brigade and division are still listed as missing in action.

According to Klausch, many of those who returned after the war had been among the large group that had defected to the Red Army during the battle of Ipolysag. Some of these men from the group of politicals ended up working for the new East German government in various capacities, a visible sign that their loyalty to the *KPD* had finally been rewarded. Surprisingly, in the immediate postwar years most of the former members held in Western POW camps were not prosecuted because the deeds of the *Dirlewanger Einheit* were mostly unknown there. After undergoing de-Nazification and re-education in Western Allies-operated POW camps, by 1948 nearly all of them were released back into West German society to resume their lives.

Efforts by their victims in the Soviet Union, Poland, and Slovakia to locate, arrest, and put them on trial were hampered during the Cold War, although the U.S.S.R. tried and executed a number of Russian and Ukrainian *Hiwis* who had fought under Dirlewanger's command in Belarus.[11] Between 1948 and 1950, Czechoslovakia tried a number of former members of the brigade for crimes committed during the suppression of the Slovak Uprising, though nearly all of them were junior enlisted men. At least eight of them were found guilty and sentenced to prison terms varying in length from eight to 30 years. Some were acquitted due to lack of evidence. Of these men, who had all been released from Soviet POW camps to stand trial in Czechoslovakia, most retracted their statements made in the U.S.S.R. because they said that they had been written under duress. By 1955, most of them were granted amnesty and expelled from Czechoslovakia.[12]

The West German government on at least two occasions used the Ludwigsburg special criminal court to carry out investigations of the unit's war crimes, one in the early 1960s and the other in the mid-1970s. Although both sets of investigations brought forth several dozen suspects and a great amount of witness testimony, when eventually brought to trial, none of the former members of Dirlewanger's unit who had been accused were found guilty of any crimes, much less served time in prison for them.

More is known about the fate of the leaders. *Standartenführer* Erich Buchmann (promoted on 30 January 1945), former commander of *SS-St.Rgt. 1/SS-Gren.Rgt. 72*, escaped over the Elbe via Luckenwalde. He died on 5 July 1972 at his home in Düsseldorf and was never brought to trial. *Sturmbannführer* Ewald Ehlers (also promoted on 30 January 1945), former commander of *SS-St.Rgt. 2/SS-Gren.Rgt. 73* was not so lucky. During the fighting in the Halbe Pocket, he was severely wounded and lost an arm, according to Harald Momm, who was commanding the *II. Bataillon* in the regiment at the time. He apparently died of his wounds on 28 April 1945 and was buried in the German War Grave cemetery in Märkisch-Buchholz, where his remains still lie today. Some accounts have him being hung and disemboweled by his own troops, but these should be dismissed due to Momm's eyewitness testimony, which should be considered authoritative.[13]

Hauptsturmführer Fritz Missmahl, former high-ranking member of the *NSDAP* and a member of the *Dirlewanger Einheit* since September 1943, having served alternately as a *Kompanie-Chef*, *Bataillons-Führer*, brigade *IIb*, and commander of the *Artillerie-Abteilung*, was part of the large group that surrendered on 28 April. Apparently wounded at some point during the battle, he reportedly died from his wounds while in hospital at Trebbin on 30 May 1945, over a month later. There is also speculation that he was murdered by his Red Army captors once his true identity was revealed; whatever the truth, he lies interred at the German War Graves cemetery in Trebbin, southwest of Berlin. Ironically, Gottlob Berger had continued his efforts to clear Missmahl's name and to have his *KL* record expunged as late as 20 February 1945.

Commander of the *I. Bataillon* of *SS-St.Rgt. 1/SS-Gren.Rgt. 72*, former *Hptm.d.Schu.Po.* Herbert Meyer was one of the lucky few who escaped both captivity and war crimes tribunals after the war. The man who grieved about the loss of so many of his men in Warsaw in a conversation with Dr. Escher on 8 August 1944 was also the same man whose troops murdered hundreds, if not thousands, of Polish civilians while fighting their way to the Brühl Palace. Continuing in command of his battalion until the war's end, he evidently escaped with the group led by Kurt Weisse, successfully crossed the Elbe, and faded into the background of the postwar era. During postwar eyewitness testimony in a Bremen court for former comrade Johannes Hempel, Meyer stated that at one point he had been the acting commander of *Freiw.SS-Gren.Rgt. 72* near the war's end. His efforts to be reinstated in the German police were denied. He died on 19 November 1956 in Eltville (Rheingau) when he fell from a ladder and broke his neck while replacing a lightbulb in his home.[14]

Sturmbannführer Josef Steinhauer disappeared from the record before the end of the war, being declared missing in action and presumed killed near the village of Forst near Guben on 1 February 1945 when the brigade was in the process of moving to the front line. Steinhauer, the former police officer whose *II. Btl./Sonder-Rgt. Dirlewanger* was also responsible for the deaths of hundreds if not thousands of innocent civilians during the Warsaw Uprising, was another old-timer of Dirlewanger's gang, who had been fighting alongside the formation when it was still a battalion-sized unit while he commanded *Pol.-Art.Abt. 56*. A loyal subordinate, he proved an underperformer as a battalion commander while in combat at Ipolysag. His remains have still not been found. He was replaced as battalion commander by *Ostuf.* Fritz Zill, who may have been a cashiered officer from the *Heer* before being assigned to the brigade.

Hauptsturmführer and former *Oberst* Harald Momm was captured by the Red Army on 30 April 1945 and spent the next five years at hard labor working in the coal mines of the Caucasus. Surviving on 640 grams of coarse bread along with three bowls of thin *Graupensuppe* (barley soup) per day, Momm's health was ruined. Were it not for the commandant of one of the camps where Momm was incarcerated named Sandmaradze, Momm would not have survived. The Soviet officer, who knew of Momm's reputation as an Olympic showjumper, wanted him to care for his horse Olena. Momm credited this gesture as giving him a reason to live and sustaining him until his release on 3 January 1950.

Upon his return home to West Germany, Momm's former rank was restored after he had cleared his name. He soon found work as the *Chef d'Equipe* of the West German showjumping team in 1951 after the nation was again allowed to take part in international equestrian competitions. He retired in 1956 after the German equestrian team won the gold medal at the Stockholm Summer Olympics that year. After a long and eventful life, Harald Momm died at his home in Munich on 6 February 1979.[15]

Obersturmführer Helmut Lewandowski, after serving as Dirlewanger's *O1*, was given command of the brigade's new *Füsilier-Kompanie*, which served as its elite reconnaissance unit. He disappeared after the war and may have been part of the group that escaped with Kurt Weisse. Other survivors included *Stubaf.* Ernst Heidelberg and *Ostuf.* Franz Schmuckerschlag. Another survivor was *Maj.d.Schu. Po.* Franz Falter, who was classified as a Nazi "follower" in 1947 by the Darmstadt tribunal. As a result, his request for reinstatement with the police was denied the following year and he officially retired in 1949. Nothing further is known of his fate, but it appears that he was never brought up on charges by the Ludwigsburg criminal court investigating war crimes during the early 1960s, so he may have died before then.

Others who were not as fortunate included former division *Adjutant, Hstuf.* Julian Scherner, who had previously served as an *Oberführer* in Cracow before being tried and found guilty of embezzlement and corruption. Reduced in rank, the bespectacled and portly Scherner, described as an affable and well-liked officer, was killed on 28 April 1945, aged 50, during the breakout from the Halbe Pocket. He is buried in the German War Graves cemetery in Märkisch-Buchholz. Joining him in death was *Gren.* (and former *Oberst*) Walther Freiherr von Uckermann, who had continued to serve as the *Adjutant* of *SS-St.Rgt. 1/SS-Gren.Rgt. 72* until he was killed in action at some point between 19 and 24 April 1945. He lies buried in the German War Graves cemetery in Forst/Lausitz-Eulo, with his former rank reinstated.[16]

Another one of the big ones who got away was *Ostubaf.* Kurt Weisse (promoted to that rank in January 1945), who successfully led a large group of approximately 400 men from the division that escaped from the Halbe Pocket through the forest between Trebbin and Rieben. *Untersturmführer* Paul Zimmermann, who had commanded the replacement company in Cracow and was one of the few remaining "old timers" of the *Dirlewanger Einheit*, accompanied Weisse during this escape attempt, but was soon captured by the Red Army in the ensuing chaos. Zimmermann died on 22 November 1945 in a Soviet POW camp in Gajsin, Ukraine. Weisse, however, made good his escape and made it to safety across the Elbe. After that, his trail becomes more difficult to discern, with many contradictory elements.

One account holds that Weisse slipped away in the confusion from the remnant of the unit during the breakout and changed into the uniform of an ordinary *Wehrmacht* corporal. Thus attired, he is believed to have blended in with regular soldiers seeking to cross the Elbe and surrender to the Americans. As a result, according to this version, Weisse ended up in British captivity, from which escaped on 5 March 1946.[17] Afterwards, he allegedly evaded detection and supposedly lived the rest of his life under an assumed name somewhere in Baden-Württemberg. Investigators from the Ludwigsburg court in the 1970s established that he had crossed into the American zone and spent time in the camps at Bad Aibling and Dachau, but disappeared after that.[18]

There are also accounts that state he moved to South America in the 1950s, while others aver that he was seen in the East German state of Thuringia. Yet another version claims that he died during the breakout or was murdered by his own men and his body never recovered. An intriguing version attests that he worked for the U.S. Army's Counterintelligence Corps (CIC) after the war as an expert on antiguerrilla warfare, while a related account states that after working for the CIC, he found employment with the Gehlen Organization, the forerunner of the modern-day *Bundesnachrichtendienst* (the German Federal Intelligence Service).[19] Regardless of which version is correct, it seems most likely that Weisse escaped justice; whether he continued his pre-war criminal activities can only be surmised.

After surrendering what was left of the division near the city of Sagan on 28 (or 29, depending on the source) April 1945, *Brig.Fhr.* Fritz Schmedes—along with some members of his staff (but not Kurt Weisse)—were taken into Soviet captivity. He had only been affiliated with the *Dirlewanger Einheit* for less than three months and had by all accounts led it competently during that period. Surprisingly, he was not charged with any war crimes and was discharged shortly thereafter due to ill health. He died from natural causes on 7 February 1952 at his home in Springe-Deister, a small town a few kilometers southwest of Hanover. Unlike most *Waffen-SS* division commanders, Schmedes was never awarded the Knight's Cross, although he had been nominated for the award on 18 October 1944 by *Gen.d.Pz.Tr.* Kirschner of the *LVII. Pz.Korps* for his leadership of the *4. SS-Pol.Pz.Gren.Div.* while under his command during the fighting east of Budapest. Instead of approving the award, Himmler quashed it in connection with his relief of Schmedes on 27 November 1944 for disobeying orders which the latter had thought to be nonsensical.[20]

In contrast, *Ogruf.* Hermann Höfle, the *HSSPF-Slowakei* and German Commander in Slovakia, did not fare so well. After the front in southeastern Slovakia cooled down by the end of December 1944, Höfle was able to devote his attention to his normal security-related and force-generation tasks. He continued doing so even after forced to relocate his headquarters to Prague after Pressburg fell to advancing Soviet troops on 4 April 1945. He was arrested by U.S. Army troops in the village of Wildbad near Kreuth in Upper Bavaria and then shipped to an internment camp for high-ranking former Nazi officials near Frankfurt. From there, he was moved to the court prison in Nürnberg, and finally to the POW camp for senior SS officers in Dachau. Shortly thereafter, he was extradited to Czechoslovakia, where he was on the country's "most-wanted" list. On 3 December 1947, Höfle was tried by a Czech court in Bratislava together with the former German Minister to Slovakia, *SA-Ogruf.* Hanns Ludin, for his actions as *HSSPF-Slowakei* in suppressing the Slovak Uprising and crimes against humanity. He was executed by hanging six days later after his appeal was denied.[21]

Dirlewanger's friend and chief sponsor, *Ogruf.* Gottlob Berger, who in the meantime had been appointed as the *Führer's* military plenipotentiary for Bavaria, was apprehended near Berchtesgaden by French troops on 8 May 1945. After a short stay in a British POW cage in London, he was transferred to Germany in August 1945 to stand trial at Nuremberg and Dachau for war crimes, the use of forced labor, and crimes against humanity, one of 12 defendants in the Wilhelmstrasse Trial. On 13 April 1949, Berger was found guilty on three charges and sentenced to 25 years in prison. One of the crimes he was charged with was his sponsorship of Dirlewanger and his unit, and he was subsequently found responsible for its "persecution, enslavement, and murder" of local civilian populations as well as the forced conscription of foreigners into the *Waffen-SS.*

His sentence was reduced to 10 years in 1951, and after an appeal for clemency he was released from the Landsberg Prison for senior Nazi war criminals on 15 December that same year, having served less than half of his sentence. Incredibly, due to the persistent efforts of the Bosch Company, Berger—the self-styled Duke of Swabia and one of Heinrich Himmler's most loyal lieutenants—was declared "Denazified" by the German State of Lower Saxony on 30 March 1952. With his civil rights thus restored, he was quickly hired by a curtain rail factory in Böblingen, followed by work at a local newspaper. He retired in 1964 and died unrepentant at his home near Stuttgart on 5 January 1975 at the age of 79.[22]

Doctor Oskar Dirlewanger himself was never brought forth to appear at a formal tribunal to answer for his long list of crimes. After being wounded at Guben on 15 February 1945 and a lengthy stay in hospital, he roamed about the part of Germany not yet occupied by the Allies while convalescing and finally came to ground in southwest Württemberg. Having earlier donned civilian clothes, he sought to escape notice and thus avoid arrest and trial. Rounded up in a French Army dragnet seeking former Nazis in disguise, he was taken prisoner near Althausen in early June 1945 and placed under guard in a hop-drying barn along with some former Nazi Party members.

Apparently denounced to his captors by some newly liberated Polish concentration camp inmates who had recognized him from the period when the *Dirlewanger Einheit* had guarded Jewish slave laborers in Poland during 1941, he was beaten to death by his guards on 6 or 7 June 1945 and buried in a cheap pinewood coffin.[23] The hunter had indeed become the hunted. Although he had escaped a trial for his war crimes, his death sentence by the hands of his enemies was just as final as anything a tribunal would have handed out.

However, after the war, rumors persisted that Dirlewanger had escaped and made his way to South America or to Cairo, where he reportedly was employed by the Egyptian Army as an advisor or a house guest of the pro-Nazi Grand Mufti of Jerusalem in 1952. Other accounts claim that he was working in Syria instead. In the postwar chaos that was Germany under Allied occupation, his death at Altshausen at the hands of his captors was either not reported or overlooked. After all, in 1945, Nazi manhunts were focused on far bigger game such as Göring, Himmler, Bormann, or Kaltenbrunner, not small fry like Dirlewanger. Neither the Soviet Union nor Poland had forgotten about him, however, and both countries accused the Western Allies of a coverup or worse, alleging that the former head of the "Black Hunters" was employed by them in an intelligence capacity.[24]

To quell the rumors and put the matter to rest once and for all, West German federal judges ordered his remains to be exhumed and an investigation carried out to rule once and for all whether it was him in the shallow grave in Altshausen and not someone else. After some preliminaries, a Thaddeus Hund, the grave digger who buried him in the cheap coffin after Dirlewanger's murder in June 1945, was the same man who supervised the two penitentiary inmates (in an ironic twist) who dug him up again on 19 November 1960.

After examining the skeletal remains and dental records, the examining physician from the Institute of Judicial Medicine in Freiburg concluded on 2 December 1960 that the body that had been placed in the grave was indeed that of Dr. Oskar Dirlewanger.[25] At first, the remains were not reburied, but placed in storage where they later disappeared. Rumors still abound positing that his remains were reburied in the cemetery in Altshausen under an "*Unbekannt*" (unknown) grave marker, and while this is an intriguing possibility, it may be nothing more than mere speculation. Regardless, the notorious leader of the "Black Hunters" was no more, having been transformed into terrifying myth and evil legend.

CHAPTER FIFTEEN

Conclusion

The initial phase of the battle for Hungary, which began on 28 September 1944 when the first Soviet troops launched their advance through the passes in the Carpathians, and ended on 26 December 1944 with the encirclement of Budapest, was for Germany a long list of withdrawals, attacks, counterattacks, holding actions, and defeats.[1] Despite occasional short-lived victories, such as the battle of Debrecen (known in Germany as the *Panzerschlacht in der Puszta*), there were never enough tanks, troops, or artillery to stem the onrushing tide in the form of Malinovsky and Tolbukhin's armies. The destruction of 18 veteran infantry divisions of the *6.* and *8. Armeen* in the collapse of *H.Gr. Süd* in Romania during the withdrawal battles of August and September that year had meant that the burden of defending eastern Hungary would fall upon the shoulders of the Royal Hungarian Army, never a powerful force to begin with, and the overworked fire brigades of the *Panzertruppen*.

The beginning of the downward spiral of the Hungarian campaign can be directly traced to the loss of so many German infantry divisions in such a short period, which simply could not be replaced. Infantry has always been best suited for holding ground, compared to *panzer* divisions, which were designed to carry out deep attacks to disrupt and disable the enemy's command and control network. Thus constituted, *panzer* divisions were inherently unsuited for holding ground, lacking sufficient infantry of their own as well as the staying power to remain in static positions very long without sacrificing their offensive capability. Yet by 10 December 1944, most of the German divisions within *6. Armee/A. Gr. Fretter-Pico* defending central Hungary and the approaches to Budapest were mobile divisions, including the *1., 13., 23.,* and *24. Pz.Div.*, the *18. SS-Horst Wessel* and *60. Pz.Gren.Div. FHH*, and the *8.* and *22. SS-Kavallerie Divisionen*. There were only four German infantry divisions—the *46., 76.,* and *357. Inf.Div.*, and the *153. Feldausb.Div.*, the last not really a combat division at all.

Heeresgruppe Süd attempted to make up for the shortfall in ground troops by attaching the *Honvéd's* own *3. Armee* and as many as six Hungarian divisions to Fretter-Pico's army, but most of these were poor substitutes, with perhaps the exception of the *1. Husaren-Division*. In the case of the *8. Armee/A.Gr. Wöhler*, the situation was exactly the opposite—it was composed mostly of infantry divisions (a total of eight), with only one or two mobile divisions assigned at the most. However, Wöhler's army was defending along the Matra mountain chain in eastern Slovakia, where *panzer* divisions were completely unsuited except under certain circumstances. Only when one takes into account this shortage of German infantry and the important role they played, is it possible to understand the urgency that drove *H.Gr. Süd* and *6. Armee/A.Gr. Fretter-Pico* to accept the offer of the Dirlewanger Brigade by the German Commander in Slovakia.

With this in mind, the impending encirclement of Budapest by the end of December 1944 could have been confidently predicted by any member of *Gen.Obst.* Friessner's staff, as well as by Friessner himself. Friessner, however, had originally believed that a successful defense of the western bank of the Danube, including the Buda portion of the city could have been attempted, had Pest on the eastern bank been evacuated in a timely manner. This was not done, primarily because of Hitler's order of 1 December declaring the city a Fortress.

With this *Führerbefehl*, the city's fate was sealed. Seeking to defend everything while giving up nothing, while at the same time refusing to consider reinforcing *H.Gr. Süd* with the infantry it needed to carry out his orders, Hitler effectively tied the hands of his army group commander and handed the initiative to the enemy, making their job of "liberating" Hungary easier. With all of this in mind, Budapest would have fallen in any case. Yet the question bears repeating: was the Dirlewanger Brigade responsible? Along with the subsidiary question: did its defeat at the battle of Ipolysag hasten this process, or have any impact at all?

At the army group and army level, subordinate commanders and staff officers blamed the Dirlewanger Brigade for the city's encirclement. In one sense, they were correct; had the brigade been better handled during the battle of Ipolysag, it may well have resulted in a successful holding action and Operation *Spätlese* might have gone forward as originally scheduled with all of *6. Armee/A.Gr. Fretter-Pico's* five *panzer* divisions, including the three that were eventually sent across the Danube, beginning with the first one (*8. Pz.Div.*) on 17 December. Then, if the offensive had been successful (and that is a big if), Budapest might have been relieved and the *Margarethestellung* between the city and the eastern shore of Lake Velencze might have been re-established. But in its efforts to economize in order to concentrate its forces for *Spätlese*, *H.Gr. Süd* made a fatal error that set off a chain of events that, once begun, could not be reversed.

Heeresgruppe Süd's first error was to accept the Dirlewanger Brigade in the first place. Clearly, the brigade's performance during the battle of Ipolysag proves that point. It was simply insufficiently equipped, trained, and officered to be effective in a conventional battle. The lack of effective antitank weapons was another shortcoming, but probably would not have decided the outcome of the battle even had its battalions been equipped properly. There was also the issue of the reliability of a substantial number of its newly assigned soldiers, especially the 770 politicals assigned in November who had already decided to desert at the first practical opportunity.

In their defense, neither *H.Gr. Süd* nor the *6. Armee/A.Gr. Fretter-Pico* had a true understanding of the brigade's readiness or composition, part of the blame for which must rest with *Ogruf.* Höfle and his staff. Perhaps in their eagerness to divest themselves of Dirlewanger and his troublesome troops, they may have withheld information that would have influenced the outcome. To his credit, Dirlewanger warned Friessner's and Fretter-Pico's staffs on 10 December that he "could not fight communists with communists," but his words of caution were apparently not taken seriously.

The next error was the refusal of Höfle to part with all or part of *Pz.Feldausb.Div. Tatra*, ostensibly because he needed it to guard the approaches to Bratislava and, with *Gen.d.Pz.Tr.* Wenck's urging, enable it to continue training *panzer* troops. That this was patently false and misleading was illustrated on 21 December when a powerful *Kampfgruppe* formed from this same division was deployed to the reaches of the upper Hron to defend against Soviet attempts to cross the river. Only the combat-capable portion of the division was sent; the remainder remained in the Waag valley and continued with their training mission, while simultaneously protecting Bratislava. Had *Gen.Obst.* Friessner lobbied more strenuously for the release of all or part of *Pz.Feldausb.Div.Tatra* from the German Commander in Slovakia, it might have prevented the 6th Guards Tank Army from breaking through the Ipolysag Gap—at the very least, *K.Gr. Tatra* would have been able to relieve the *II. Btl./Pz.Gren.Rgt. 26* from the *24. Pz.Div.* on 14 December, and not the troops from the Dirlewanger Brigade, exhausted after a long march.

The bungled relief in place of the battalion from the *24. Pz.Div.* was another inflection point that contributed to the disaster on 15 December. Had it remained in its positions in Ipolysag for 12 more hours, as originally intended, it could have continued its successful defense of the town while enabling Steinhauer's *II. Btl./SS-St. Rgt. 1* to systematically conduct a relief in place and to become "set" in its defenses long enough to prepare itself against an attack. The premature relief of Zischler's *Panzergrenadier* battalion by a *Pionier* platoon from the Dirlewanger Brigade was not preordained, but was ordered by *6. Armee/A.Gr. Fretter-Pico* at the urging of the commander of the *IV. Pz.Korps.*

Despite the protests of those on the ground, *II. Btl./Pz.Gren.Rgt. 26* was pulled out at least six hours before Steinhauer's troops had arrived. Sending a platoon was the best that *Ostubaf.* Buchmann could do; everything else was already in the line and in contact with the enemy, or shortly would be. That the staffs of Friessner and Fretter-Pico blamed the Dirlewanger Brigade for the loss of Ipolysag during the morning of 14 December does not hold up to scrutiny, merely appearing to have been an effort to shift the blame for the loss away from them and onto the shoulders of the notorious Dirlewanger and his disreputable troops.

Once battle had been joined on 15 December, there was very little that could have been done to retake the town and re-exert control of the Ipoly River valley. The Dirlewanger Brigade was simply not strong enough to do that while holding back attacks by two tank-heavy Soviet mechanized brigades. That Steinhauer's battalion might flee the field in disarray could not have been predicted, but *Gen. Maj.* Rintelen's lack of reserves contributed to the loss. His one strong reserve force, *Hptm.* Hafner's battalion, which had been intended to shore up the situation in Ipolysag, was diverted while still *en route* to prevent the 31st Guards Mechanized Brigade from breaking out from the Börszeny Mountains at Bernecebaráti after Ehlers's and Nitzkowski's battalions had dissolved. While Hafner was successful in his mission, his battalion was consequently tied down in positional warfare and not available for anything else.

In this regard, the Dirlewanger Brigade was indeed culpable; had the two battalions been able to hold their positions, Otto Hafner may well have been able to continue marching towards Ipolysag and might have made a difference in the fighting there, or at least may have been able to reinforce the defense of Gyerk and prevent the spearhead of the 31st Guards Mechanized Brigade from breaking out through the Ipolysag Gap. Failing that, his battalion could have reinforced Harald Momm's tiny battlegroup defending the river crossing at Kistompa. All of these possibilities fall within the realm of conjecture, but they do give an indication of what could have been done to successfully defend the positions on both sides of the Ipoly River valley. That the two *SS* battalions in the Börszeny Mountains dissolved when they did could not have been predicted with any degree of certainty, at least not by Rintelen, but Dirlewanger's suspicions should at least have given his chain of command food for thought and might have prompted *Gen.d.Art.* Fretter-Pico's staff to develop contingency plans for this worst-case scenario.

The next domino to fall after the Dirlewanger Brigade's defeat on 15 December was the decision made by *H.Gr. Süd* to send the *LXXII. Armeekorps* and the *8. Pz.Div.* north of the Danube (on 16 and 17 December respectively) to carry out a counterattack to retake Ipolysag and re-establish a strong defensive position between the Danube and the Ipoly Rivers. Not only did this remove one of the *panzer* divisions envisaged to play a role in Operation *Spätlese*, but in the process it split the division into two parts—one armored and the other not. The risk that this entailed seems to have been downplayed in the assumption that it would carry out its mission and return in the nick of time to play its designated role in *Spätlese*.

In this particular case, it would have made more sense to send the entire division because its future opponent was a tank-heavy Soviet mechanized corps, something that *H.Gr. Süd* and *6. Armee/A.Gr. Fretter-Pico* had confirmed by 16 December. Despite the hopes by the commanders and staffs concerned that *Gr. Fröhlich* would be sufficiently strong to accomplish the objective, by 19 December its counterattack had failed to make much headway against an enemy force occupying prepared defensive positions with a large reserve of tanks standing by in case the Germans managed to break through to Ipolysag.

The last domino that fell, sealing the fate of Budapest, was Friessner's decision on the evening of 19 December to send another corps headquarters and two more *panzer* divisions north of the Danube to launch a larger and more comprehensive attack to retake Ipolysag and reestablish a front line. Not only were these two divisions split up and forced to leave their armor behind, like the *8. Pz.Div.* had done, but the amount of time spent in assembling them for their attack on 22 December gave the 6th Guards Tank Army's commander three days to pursue offensive plans of his own. These plans, featuring the envelopment of German and Hungarian forces between the northern bank of the Danube and the upper Hron River, were already well underway by the time that the *LVII. Pz.Korps* began its attack. At the same time, Operation *Spätlese*, having been postponed at least twice, got off to a fitful start. Lacking sufficient infantry and unable to make much headway through the mud in the face of determined Soviet resistance, *Spätlese* culminated prematurely without *Korpsgruppe Breith* having accomplished much, except the loss of many of its carefully hoarded *panzers*.

With Operation *Spätlese* a failure, the *6. Armee/A.Gr. Fretter-Pico* was poorly postured to offer effective resistance to the massive counterattack launched by the 4th Guards Army. Despite having many operational tanks on hand, the lack of their accustomed divisional headquarters, *Panzergrenadiere*, and supporting arms meant the three *ad hoc Panzergruppen* formed from the divisions deployed north of the Danube were hard-pressed to hold their ground and were forced to give up the key cities of Stuhlweissenburg and Bicske. As *Korpsgruppe Breith* was forced to withdraw to avoid encirclement, the 4th Guards Army was free to complete the envelopment of Budapest from the south; the complimentary counterattack along the northern bank of the Danube by the 7th Guards Army completed the envelopment of the city from the north when it linked up with the XVIII Tank Corps of the 4th Guards Army at Esztergom on 26 December.

In summation, none of the German and Hungarian offensive and defensive plans carried out between the Ipoly River valley and Lakes Balaton and Velencze between 11 and 26 December enjoyed any meaningful success. The fact that the bulk of three *panzer* divisions were able to escape across the Hron in time to avoid entrapment was a minor tactical miracle in itself. The reasons why the Germans and Hungarians failed to achieve any of their goals have already been touched upon, and it could be said that the encirclement of Budapest resulted from a number of cumulative factors.

The first factor was the powerful offensives being carried out skillfully by the Second and Third Ukrainian Fronts. By launching simultaneous attacks along the Ipoly River valley, the northern bank of the Danube, against Budapest itself, and south of the city on the western bank of the Danube, the Red Army posed so many threats that *H.Gr. Süd* could not effectively react to them all at once. His forces spread thin, and reliant on the unsteady *Honvéd* for much of his infantry support, *Gen.Obst.* Friessner had to prioritize which of these threats to address with his dwindling number of troops.

Hovering above all of Friessner's decisions was the requirement to carry out Operation *Spätlese*. Although the counteroffensive had originally been his own idea, Hitler seized upon it as a way to restore Germany's fortunes on the Hungarian Front at a minimum cost. As the weather worsened and supply issues came to the fore, Friessner began to doubt and then second-guess his decision to launch it. His own postwar memoir clearly illustrates his regret about having suggested the idea for the entire enterprise. Certainly, by 22 December, when it was finally launched, *Spätlese* no longer made any operational sense; it would have been far better to use some of the assembled armored divisions in a defensive role, poised behind the front lines west of Lake Velencze to carry out the kind of slashing counterattacks that *panzer* divisions were famous for. One or two others north of the Danube, with their full complement of armor, would have been sufficient to slow if not completely stop Lt.Gen. Volkov's IX Guards Mechanized Corps. But none of these actions would have been enough to prevent the loss of Budapest. The most that Friessner's army group could have done was to delay, not prevent, the inevitable.

It is clear that the Dirlewanger Brigade played an important role in the loss of Budapest, but was not solely responsible. It can be said that the brigade was the unfortunate recipient of a number of high-level decisions that resulted in the disruption of its organizational integrity. It was placed in an untenable position where it was tasked to carry out a mission for which it was not trained, equipped, or led to do. Its failure should have been foreseen, but the state of desperation at the army group and field army levels for infantry—any kind of infantry—was so great that the *Dirlewanger Einheit* was fated to be thrust into the Ipoly River valley to fight a battle that it could not win, and as a result was ground to bits in less than a week. Its destruction was inevitable and no amount of blame-shifting could obscure that reality.

Unaccountably, Himmler decided to retain Dirlewanger in command, despite the fact that Berger's favorite henchman had clearly demonstrated that he was unfit for brigade, much less division, command. Himmler's loyalty to his subordinates and his insistence on keeping in place some that were demonstrably unfit for command—such as Berger and Dirlewanger—was one of his many character flaws. The question is worth asking though: could Dirlewanger's style of hands-on leadership have made a difference?

After considering these factors, the conclusion must be probably not—even with the best of intentions and application of skillful, savvy leadership, Dirlewanger simply did not have the command-and-control apparatus needed to succeed on the conventional battlefield of 1944, especially with his brigade dispersed over such a wide distance. Without adequate radio, teletype, or field telephone networks and equipment, there is very little he could have done to make much of a difference, except by making occasional visits to the front lines. These factors do not, however, excuse his decision to passively sit in his command post in Palást while his troops were fighting for their lives.

To be fair, *Gen.Maj.* Rintelen may not have done much better in the same situation. However, Rintelen did move throughout the area during the afternoon of 15 December (though the location of his forward command post can only be surmised) and his area of operations was much larger. There is evidence that Rintelen was sufficiently aware of the gravity of the situation at Bernecebaráti on 15 December and acted appropriately when he directed *Hptm.* Hafner's freshly arriving battalion to launch the counterattack that forced the enemy to withdraw into the mountains. He also was aware of the deteriorating situation at Gyerk, as evidenced by his decision to dispatch Harald Momm to that location to take charge of events. There are no recorded instances of Dirlewanger practicing the same sort of hands-on leadership at Ipolysag.

Although the battle of Ipolysag was clearly a defeat for the Dirlewanger Brigade, for which its commander was partially responsible, it was not strictly the fault of the individual men of the brigade. Many of them had fought as well as they could, with the exception of the 500 or so politicals who had defected rather than fight.[2] The brigade's individual equipment was antiquated, insufficient, and inadequate. Some battalions fought with rifles that used ammunition of different caliber that were not interchangeable. The variety of foreign arms employed by the brigade and the differing ammunition they required would have been enough to make any supply officer pull his hair out.

The only truly modern weapons they employed, the *Panzerfaust* and *Panzerschreck*, were issued only a day before they marched to Hungary and in insufficient numbers; they thus had little or no opportunity to learn how to use them. Inadequately clothed, fed, and conditioned for living in the open air during winter in combat conditions, in retrospect it is amazing that Dirlewanger's troops performed as well as they did, especially those fighting in the Börszeny Mountains. After experiencing five days of this, one can only wonder why every single man in Ehlers's and Nitzkowski's battalions *did not* go over to the enemy.

After recovering from the debacle, the brigade was soon reorganized and upgraded to a division under a new commander. In Guben and along the Vistula River, *Brig. Fhr.* Schmedes's troops fought more or less reliably, even at times heroically, but the *36. Waffen-Gren.Div.d.SS Dirlewanger* never attained the same elite status enjoyed by the "classic" all-German divisions of the *Waffen-SS* like the *Leibstandarte, Das Reich,* and *Totenkopf.* The idea of using probationary troops, convicts, and political prisoners under the command of officers barely qualified to lead them had been conclusively proven to be a horrible but predictable mistake. While perhaps suitable for combatting insurgents behind the lines in their own bloody and inhumane way, such irregular units as the *Dirlewanger Einheit* proved themselves to be completely unsuited for modern warfare and therefore must be consigned to the ash heap of history alongside other such formations as Baron von Trenck's Pandurs and perhaps the convict soldiers of the Wagner Group, an experiment never to be repeated again.

Endnotes

Introduction

1. For detailed origins of *Sonderkommando Dirlewanger*, refer to Colonel (Ret.) French MacLean's *The Cruel Hunters* (Atglen, PA: Schiffer Military History, 1998), 12–16.
2. Correspondence with noted Polish researcher Mr. Hubert Kuberski, 16 April 2022.
3. The responsibility for combating the partisans in Eastern Europe and occupied areas of the Soviet Union was assigned to the *SS* according to a *Führerbefehl* (*Führer* Directive) 46, "General Directions for the intensified fight against banditry in the East," dated 18 August 1942. This authority did not extend to the *Kampfraum* (operational area or combat zone), which was the responsibility of the *Wehrmacht*. This arrangement had been codified in an agreement signed by Himmler and the chief of staff of the *Oberkommando der Wehrmacht*, as announced in an *SS* order dated 28 July 1942.
4. George Tessin, *Verbände und Truppen der deutschen Wehrmacht und Waffen-SS 1939–1945*, Vol. 13 (Osnabrück: Biblio Verlag, 1976), 200. This unit was initially raised as a brigade on 6 October 1942 before being expanded into a division.
5. Refer to "Trenck's Pandurs" (https://en.wikipedia.org/wiki/Trenck%27s_Pandurs), a thoroughly researched entry found in Wikipedia, the free encyclopedia, accessed 1 July 2022. For more information, refer to Horst Voigt's *Die verlor'nen Haufen: Sondertruppen zur Frontbewährung im 2. Weltkrieg* (Munich: Schild-Verlag, 1998).
6. https://en.wikipedia.org/wiki/Wagner_Group#cite_note-Goal-245, accessed 17 October 2022.
7. Helene Cooper, "Heavy Losses Leave Russia Short of Its Goal, U.S. Officials Say," *New York Times*, accessed 11 August 2022.
8. For more information, go to https://www.germandocsinrussia.org, Fund 500, Inventory 12493, Cases 70 and 88–90, and Fund 500, Inventory 12472, Case 380.
9. For more information about the former *WASt*, refer to the US Holocaust Memorial Museum website at https://www.ushmm.org/online/hsv/source_view.php?SourceId=33348.
10. TsAMO, Journal of Military Operations of the IX Guards Mechanized Corps during the Budapest Offensive Operation, by Lieutenant Colonel Sobolev, 1–31 December 1944. (Fund 3443, Inventory 1, File 77, beginning with Frame 170, Memory of the People, https://pamyat-naroda.ru/documents/view/?id=134588529, accessed 7 March 2022).

Chapter 1

1. Hugh Trevor-Roper, *Hitler's Secret Conversations, 1941–1944* (New York: Signet Books, 1953), xi. Referred to hereafter as *Hitler's Table Talk*.
2. *Hitler's Table Talk*, 94.
3. *Ibid.*, 640.

4. International Military Tribunal, *Trials of War Criminals Before the Nuremberg Military Tribunals, Volume XIII: The Ministries Case* (Washington, D.C.: U.S. Government Printing Office, 1952), ·534–45. Referred to hereafter as *Berger Nuremberg Testimony*. Incidentally, it is not known whether this particular Old Party member was ever inducted into the *Dirlewanger Einheit*.

5. *Ibid.*

6. *Hitler's Table Talk*, 640.

7. French MacLean, *The Cruel Hunters: SS-Sonderkommando Dirlewanger, Hitler's Most Notorious Anti-Partisan Unit* (Atglen, PA: Schiffer Military History, 1998), 42.

8. Bundesarchiv-Militärarchiv (BA-MA), Freiburg. Manuscript, SS-Brigade "Dirlewanger," accessed 7 March 2022, found at https://balsi.de/Weltkrieg/Einheiten/Waffen-SS/SS-Infanterie-Einheiten/SS-Brigaden/SS-Brigade-Dirlewanger.htm. Hereafter referred to as BA-MA Official History.

9. MacLean, 42. Frieser later become president of the infamous People's Court that judged the 20 July 1944 conspirators and sentenced them to death after humiliating them in a show trial.

10. Berger Nuremberg Testimony, 534–45

11. Letter, *SS-Hauptamt-Ergänzungsamt* to *Sondereinheit Dirlewanger*, dated 1 December 1941.

12. Lexikon der Wehrmacht, *SS-Sonderkommando "Dirlewanger,"* found at https://www.lexikon-der-wehrmacht.de/Gliederungen/InfanteriebrigadenSS/Gliederung.htm, accessed 10 September 2020.

13. BA-MA Official History.

14. Hellmuth Auerbach, *Vierteljahrshefte für Zeitgeschichte*, "Die Einheit Dirlewanger," Vol. 10, 3. (Munich: Institut für Zeitgeschichte, 1962), 1.

15. Rolf Michaelis, *Die SS-Sturmbrigade Dirlewanger vom Warschauer Aufstand bis zum Kessel von Halbe* (Berlin: Michaelis-Verlag, 2003), 7.

16. Details concerning Dirlewanger's wartime service in the *Kaiserheer* and his criminal record can be found in his *SS* Officer's File at the Berlin Document Center (BDC) under File NS 19/1207.

17. For a very good description of Dirlewanger's career leading up to his command of his eponymous unit, refer to French MacLean's *The Cruel Hunters*, 21–42.

18. Exactly which unit the two served in together during World War I and when is not clear. Their records indicate that near or shortly after the war's end, both were assigned to the Württemberg *51. Landwehr-Infanterie Brigade*; Dirlewanger to *Inf.Rgt. 123*, and Berger to *Inf.Rgt. 124*. Both may have taken part in postwar veterans' reunions or early Nazi Party rallies. In either case, they seem to have become acquainted with one another during the early 1920s and formed a bond of friendship that persisted until the fall of the Third Reich.

19. Gottlob Berger *SS* Officers File, courtesy of John P. Moore's *Führerliste der Waffen-SS* (Portland, OR: J. P. Moore Publishing, 2003).

20. Letter of recommendation from *Oberst* Ritter von Thoma, dated 20 November 1939.

21. MacLean, 40–41.

22. Dirlewanger had first joined the Nazi Party in 1926 during the *Kampfzeit* (time of struggle) with a low Party Number of 13566; when reinstated in 1940, he was issued a new number (1098716) and a new membership date. Letter, Oskar Dirlewanger to *NSDAP* Party Chancellery Munich, 6 December 1943.

23. To this day, it is not clear why Himmler hesitated to bring Dirlewanger into the *Waffen-SS*. Perhaps it was due to Dirlewanger's well-known criminal record and history of heavy drinking and womanizing. Or it could have been that Himmler did not want to taint the reputation of his elite hand-picked corps with someone of Dirlewanger's proven lack of moral character. At any rate, experienced leaders and instructors were scarce in the prewar *SS*, and it would have been difficult to exclude someone with Dirlewanger's combat record from the war effort.

24. Before the war, service in the *Allgemeine-SS* did not count as fulfilling one's military service obligation and members were frequently called to active duty in the *Wehrmacht*, while retaining membership in the *SS*. Once the war began, members were increasingly activated to perform full-time duty with units and headquarters of the *Waffen-SS, Reichssicherhauptamt,* and other *SS* administrative organizations. Surprisingly, an individual could hold different ranks in both the *Allgemeine-SS* and the *Waffen-SS.*

25. *Kommandoamt der Waffen-SS,* IIb/Az.: 18d/28.8.40 to *Ersatz-Bataillon SS-"Germania,"* Betr: Versetzung von SS-Unterführern zum Sonder-Kommando Dr. Dirlewanger, dated 28 August 1940 (BA-MA, RS 3-36/10, Frame 0326).

26. At one point or another over the next four years, the unit was to be unofficially referred to as the *Sondereinheit, Einheit Dirlewanger, Einsatz-Bataillon Dirlewanger,* and *Polizei-Bataillon Dirlewanger* even after it had received its formal designation from the *SS-FHA.*

27. Landwehr asserts that these men were "mostly non-poacher criminals who just volunteered to get out of the concentration camp," but there has been no evidence in the official records to support this yet. See Richard Landwehr in *Siegrunen* magazine's "The Evolution of the 36. Waffen-Grenadier Division der SS," No. 43, (Bennington, VT: Weapons and Warfare Press, 2014), 4. Referred to hereafter as Landwehr.

28. Bundesarchiv Official History.

29. *Ibid.*

30. MacLean, 60–61.

31. *Ibid.,* 64.

32. Message, *SS-Führungshauptamt* to *Sonderkommando Dirlewanger* via *HSSPF-Lublin,* dated 27 January 1942 (BA-MA, RS 3-36-11-b-0350).

33. BA-MA Official History.

34. MacLean, 65.

35. The new definition was spelled out in *Verordnungsblatt* (Bulletin) *der Waffen-SS,* Volume 3 No. 17, 1 September 1942 (Berlin: SS-Führungshauptamt, 1942).

36. Dieter Pohl, *Die Herrschaft der Wehrmacht: Deutsche Militärbesatzung und einheimische Bevölkerung in der Sowjetunion 1941–1944* (Munich: Oldenburg Wissenschaftsverlag GmbH, 2009), 293.

37. Christian Ingrao, *The SS-Dirlewanger Brigade: The History of the Black Hunters* (New York: Skyhorse Publishing, 2013), 50.

38. MacLean, 145.

39. Landwehr, 6.

40. Landwehr, 6, and Michaelis, *Die SS-Sturmbrigade Dirlewanger,* 45–48.

41. Bundesarchiv official history.

42. *SS-FHA* Berlin-Wilmersdorf, Ia Org.Abt., Amt II, Nr. II/5868/43 geheim., dated 10 August 1943, Betr: *SS-Sonderkommando Dirlewanger.*

43. *Der Armeefeldpostmeister-Ost,* Ia Nr. 2941, Bfb.Nr. 409/44 geheim, Betr: Feldpostnummern, addressed to *Dienststelle Feldpostnummer 00512 (Sonderkommando Dirlewanger),* dated 31 March 1944.

44. Letter from Adjutant, *SS Regiment Dirlewanger* addressed to *I. Batterie der Polizei-Abteilung Weissruthenien,* dated 26 June 1944. Initially attached to the *Sonderbataillon* on 30 April 1943, this unit had originally been designated *1. Batterie/Schutzmannschafts-Artillerie-Abteilung 56.*

45. Landwehr, 5. Also see Letter, VS-Tagebuch Nr. 3795/42 (Geheim) *Gruf.* Gottlob Berger to Dr. Oskar Dirlewanger, Subject: *Sonderkommando Dr. Dirlewanger,* dated 3 October 1942.

46. BA-MA Official History.

47. Aktenvermerk, *SS-Obersturmbannführer Dr. Dirlewanger*, Betr: Rücksprache mit *SS-Brigadeführer Klücke* am heutigen Tage, Berlin, 8 June 1943 (BA-MA, RS 3-36 10, 0178).

48. Bärbel Holtz, *Die Protokolle des Preußischen Staatsministeriums* (Hildesheim: Olms-Weidmann, 2001), 645, and Letter, *Gauleiter* Karl Florian to *Reichsführer-SS* Heinrich Himmler, 24 July 1942. Florian had written a personal appeal to Heinrich Himmler, requesting that Missmahl's life be spared and that he be allowed to "atone" for his crime through service at the Front.

49. Letter, *Reichsführer-SS* to *Sonderkommando Dirlewanger*, 1 December 1941 (BA-MA RS 3-36/10, image 0258).

50. Herbert Meyer *Personalakte*, Bundesarchiv File PERS 6/69565, BA-MA, Freiburg i.Breisgau. This file, maintained by his local *Wehrbezirkkommando* (Local Defense District Command) in Wiesbaden, covers the period from March 1941 to August 1943, focusing on Meyer's investigation, trial, and subsequent punishment.

51. Letter, *Reichsführer-SS* an das *SS-FHA*, Betr.: Kragenspiegel für *Sonderkommando "Dirlewanger,"* Personalstab RF-SS, Tagebuch Nr. 35/109/43, dated 26 January 1944, and *Verordnungsblat der Waffen-SS*, Verzeichnis Nr. 121, Kragenspiegel für *Sonderkommando "Dirlewanger,"* 4. Jahrgang Nr. 7, 1 April 1943 (Berlin: *SS-FHA*, Berlin-Wilmersdorf, 1943).

52. Rolf Michaelis (ed.), *The SS-Sonderkommando "Dirlewanger"—A Memoir* (Atglen, PA: Schiffer Military History, 2013), 26. Referred to hereafter as Michaelis Dirlewanger Memoir.

53. Auerbach, 259–60, and Befehl, Feld-Kommandostelle *Reichsführer-SS* RF/m. 35/26144 geheim, 20 Feb. 1944; Betrifft: Gerichtsbarkeit beim *Einsatz-Batl. "Dirlewanger."*

54. *Vierteljahrshefte für Zeitgeschichte*, "*Reichsführer-SS* Himmler auf der Gauleitertagung am 3. August 1944 in Posen," Vol. 1, 4 (Munich: Institut für Zeitgeschichte, 1953), 378.

55. Letter, *Reichsführer-SS* Himmler to *Gruf.* von Gottberg, *HSSPF Russland-Mitte*, dated 18 February 1944.

56. *Entwurf* (Draft Proposal) by *Ogruf.* Berger to Himmler, 22 March 1944.

57. Schreiben des SS-Richters beim *Reichsführer-SS* und *Chef der Deutschen Polizei* an das *Hauptamt SS-Gericht* vom 6 June 1944 (quoted in Michaelis, *Die Sturmbrigade Dirlewanger*, 14).

58. Hans-Peter Klausch, *Antifaschisten in SS-Uniform: Schicksal und Widerstand der Deutschen Politischen KZ-Häftlinge, Zuchthaus- und Werhmachtgefangenen in der SS-Sonderformation Dirlewanger* (Papenburg, Edition Temmen, 1993), 90.

59. *Ibid.*, 91. The concentration camp contributions were as follows: Sachsenhausen, 287; Auschwitz, 182; Buchenwald, 200–300. By this point, nearly all of the positions in the regiment were filled by native Germans.

60. Michaelis, *Die SS-Sturmbrigade Dirlewanger*, 6. Many of the departed Russians and Ukrainians were eventually sent either to Bronislav Kaminski's "Russian Liberation Army" (RONA) brigade, other SS anti-partisan formations, or used to form various Ukrainian SS units, respectively.

61. Message, *K.Gr. von Gottberg Ia* an *Sonderbataillon Dirlewanger*, Betr: Herauslösung der Russenkompanie des *SS-Sonderbataillon Dirlewanger*, dated 21 November 1943.

62. German Cross in Gold Award Nomination for *Ostubaf.* Oskar Dirlewanger, 9 August 1943, 7, courtesy of John P. Moore's *Führerliste der Waffen-SS*.

63. *Ibid.*

64. Klausch, 97.

65. Fernschreiben des *SS-Hauptamtes* SSD SHAS 8970 20/7 2030 (aufgenommen 24.7., 09.00, weitergeleitet durch AOK 4, Ia 3485/44 am 24.7.44, 18.45 Uhr) an *Ogruf. und General der Polizei* von Gottberg, Geheim VS Tgb.Nr. 421/44 geh., Adjutantur Tgb.Nr. 1928/44 geh.

66. An *SS-Hauptamt*, Amtsgruppe D, Berlin–Grunewald, Betr: "Anwerbung von Turkestanern," NARA, Records Group T-354, Roll 161, image 3806827.

67. *Chefs des SS-Hauptamtes*, VS-Tgb.Nr. 1945/44 geh. Amt AI (1a) – 442/44 geheim. Betreffend: "Aufstellung einer schweren Kompanie (mot)," dated 27 March 1944.

68. BA-MA N756, Nachlass Wolfgang Vopersal, *SS-Kraftfahrstaffel* (*Fronthilfe DRP*), 16 Seiten, Kopien im Besitz des Verfassers, 14.

69. Michaelis, *Die SS-Sturmbrigade Dirlewanger*, 26.

70. Fernschreiben des *SS-Hauptamtes* SSD SHAS 8970 20/7 2030 (intercepted 24.7. at 09.00), weitergeleitet durch *AOK 4*, Ia 3485/44 am 24.7.44, 18.45 Uhr. The initial order was issued earlier that same day, as shown by a message intercepted by ULTRA at 5.50am on 3 August 1944 that stated: "By order of the *Reichsführer-SS*, all orders given so far concerning the transfer of the unit are invalid. Unit immediately accelerates to the area northwest of Kutno to be used against revolt in Warsaw."

71. Hanns von Krannhals, *Der Warschauer Aufstand 1944* (Frankfurt: Bernhard und Graefe Verlag, 1964), 359, and Michaelis, *Die SS-Sturmbrigade Dirlewanger*, 24, TgbNr. 3579/44 geh. v. 5.8.1944.

72. It is not known how many of the replacements who arrived in July remained behind at Lyck with the *Ersatz-Kompanie* to continue with their training.

73. Flensburg Interrogation files, including the Ludwigsburg Dossier on the *Sonderregiment Dirlewanger*, "Bisheriges Ermittlungsergebnis über das *Sonderkommando Dirlewanger*," September 1963, 42–44. Referred to hereafter as the Ludwigsburg Dossier.

74. Erich von dem Bach, Personal Diary as *Chef der Bandenkampfverbände, Polizeitruppen und Schulen*, entry dated 4 August 1944 (Bundesarchiv, File R 020/000045b, Folio 1–117).

75. Bericht Erich von dem Bach über den Warschaer Aufstand (verfasst Februar 1947) "Die Kampfstärke der Brigade Dirlewanger am 8 August 1944." (KTB AOK 9 BuMi, H-12-§/9, Bl. 923 583), reproduced in Hanns von Krannhals, *Der Warschauer Aufstand 1944*, 239–40.

76. Ingrao, 38–39. Incidentally, Himmler had to give a direct order to Dirlewanger to fly to Warsaw and lead his regiment. Dirlewanger, so involved in conducting his own personal affairs that he had begun to neglect his normal duties, had repeatedly ignored orders from the *SS-FHA* to return to his unit.

77. Michaelis, *Die SS-Sturmbrigade Dirlewanger*, 30. Using Michaelis's numbers, subtracting the 40 survivors of *K.Gr. Meyer* from the total reported strength of 120 men, the regiment's other battlegroup, *K.Gr. Steinhauer*, had been reduced in strength to approximately 80 men.

78. The casualty count of *Korpsgruppe von dem Bach* by 13 September had risen to 591 killed in action (including 20 officers) and 3,969 wounded. This did not include casualties suffered by the other major combat elements fighting against the Warsaw Uprising, such as *K.Gr. Stahel*. The Uprising was to continue for 19 more days, while the number of German casualties would continue to mount (*Korps von dem Bach* Tagesmeldung 8:40 p.m. 13 September 1944).

79. *Sonderregiment Dirlewanger*, Ia, Funkspruch Nr. 57, Spruch Nr. 206, *Kommandant Warschau* an *Gruppe Litzmannstadt* (*K.Gr Reinefarth*), dated 7.15pm, 14 August 1944.

80. Ingrao, 39. One of the most gruesome atrocities committed during this period was the "massacre of the orphans," carried out in the Wola district of Warsaw on 5 and 6 August 1944, wherein some men from the *Dirlewanger Einheit*, *Ordnungspolizei*, and *Sicherheitsdienst* murdered as many as 500 orphans at the Orthodox Orphanage at 149 Wolska Street using rifle butts and bayonets. Despite claims to the contrary, the *I. Bataillon* under Herbert Meyer could not have perpetrated this atrocity, since he and his men were fighting to clear a path towards the Brühl Palace and had no time to stop to carry out such widespread killings. However, other elements of the *Sonderregiment* were present and undoubtedly participated, such as select personnel from the regimental headquarters.

81. Heinz Guderian, *Panzer Leader* (Cambridge, MA: Da Capo Press, 1996), 356.

82. Jost W. Schneider, *Their Honor was Loyalty! An Illustrated and Documentary History of the Knight's Cross Holders of the Waffen-SS and Police 1940–1945* (San Jose, CA: R. James Bender Publishing, 1977), 73–74.

83. Knight's Cross Award Nomination for *Oberführer* Oskar Dirlewanger, 10 September 1944, courtesy of John P. Moore's *Führerliste der Waffen-SS*, 8.

84. Michaelis, *Die SS-Sturmbrigade Dirlewanger*, 45.

85. *Das Schwarze Korps*, "*SS-Oberführer* Oskar Dirlewanger Verleihung des Ritterkreuzes," Berlin, 16 November 1944.

Chapter 2

1. Oskar Dirlewanger actually received the award on 16 October 1944 in Cracow, from Hans Frank, the Governor-General of the occupied Polish territories. It was presented in a reception hall of the Wawel Royal Castle where Frank had established his headquarters in 1939 (Letter, Oskar Dirlewanger to *Hstuf.* Otto Günsche, Adjutanten des Führers, Cracow, 17 October 1944). In his choice of the words "higher places," he most likely was referring to Hans Jüttner, head of the *SS-FHA* and one of his loudest critics.

2. Ingrao, 38–39, and Ludwigsburg Dossier, 44. The combined strength of both *Kampfgruppen* on the evening of 8 August 1944 was only 120 men, as mentioned in Michaelis, *Die SS-Sturmbrigade Dirlewanger*, 30. On that same date (8 August), the *Sonderregiment* received between 400 and 500 *Wehrmacht* probationary troops from the military prison in Glatz, Silesia, which accounts for the higher number shown in the 8 August unit *Kampfstärke* report.

3. *Armeeoberkommando (AOK) 9*, Ia Kriegstagebuch (KTB) Anlage: Truppeneinteilung *K.Gr. Reinefarth*, 8 August 1944 and Anlage, Ia Kriegstagebuch *AOK 9* Kampfstärken vom 1 October 1944, dated 2 October, 3.

4. Ingrao, 39, and Richard Landwehr, "The Evolution of the 36. Waffen-Grenadier Division der SS," in *Siegrunen* Volume 42 (New York: Merriam Press, 1987), 7. Klausch believes that the *Sonderregiment* may have received as many as 4,300 replacements during this period, though it is difficult to discern whether they were all "used up" in combat or held back and used to form new battalions of the regiment (Klausch, 122–23).

5. Fernschreiben des *Chefs des Kommandostabs des Reichsführers-SS* an verschiedene SS-Dienststellen betreffend der Bereitstellung und Einsatz von 1,500 Häftlingen aus dem Strafvollzugslager Danzig-Matzkau beim *Regiment Dirlewanger*, dated 20 September 1944 (BA-MA ZSG 122/75, Annex D: Nürnberger Dokument No-4518) and Auerbach in "Die Einheit Dirlewanger," *Vierteljahrshefte für Zeitgeschichte*, 256. Whether these men came directly from Danzig-Matzkau or via the *SS-Bewährungs Abteilung* in Chlum near Prague can no longer be determined with certainty. According to noted author Stuart B. T. Emmett, the entire transfer of such a large number of troops seems in retrospect to have been hurriedly carried out and it is doubtful that any of them arrived in time to see combat in Warsaw.

6. MacLean 196, referencing Hans Krannhals, *Der Warschauer Aufstand*, 214–15. Krannhals estimated the number of casualties suffered by the regiment as 2,700 men, but the exact number will probably never be known. The regiment's *III. Bataillon*, then undergoing activation, may have participated very little in the suppression of the uprising until the latter stages, if at all. For information about the numbers and arrival dates of replacement personnel from the various *Wehrmacht* and SS punishment installations, refer to pages 26–28 of the Ludwigsburg Dossier.

7. Klausch, 122. This initial transfer explains how *K.Gr. Dirlewanger* was able to report a *Kampfstärke* of 881 men on 8 August 1944 after suffering such heavy losses during the previous three days.

8. *AOK 9, Ia KTB*, Meldungen und Befehle, Ia. Nr. 5737/44 Fernschreiben, Betr: Unterbringung der rückwärtigen Verbände im Raum Radom, dated 11am 9 October 1944.

9. *AOK 9, Ia KTB*, Meldungen und Befehle, Bewegungsbericht, dated 13 October 1944. This document indicated that the first of eight trains needed to move the brigade by 9 October had already been scheduled to load and depart Radom on the evening of 13 October 1944. The term *Kampfraum* describes the area of operations allocated to a field army commander, but does not include the *Ruckwärtiger Gebiet* (rear area) where administration and logistics units were concentrated.

10. *AOK 9, Ia KTB*, Meldungen und Befehle, Ia. Nr. 5738/44 Fernschreiben an *Luftflottenkommando 6, Kommandant Flughafenbereich Tamaszow*, und *Korpsgruppe von dem Bach*, dated 9 October 1945.

11. Hellmuth Auerbach, *Miscellanea, Festschrift fuer Helmut Krausnick zum 75. Geburtstag*, "Konzentrationslagerhäftlinge im Fronteinsatz," and Bundesarchiv RS 3-36 R23 (Stuttgart: Deutsche Verlags-Anstalt Stuttgart, 1980), 4.

12. Kamen Nevenkin, *Fire Brigades: The Panzer Divisions 1943–1945* (Winnipeg, Canada: J. J. Fedorowicz Publishing, Inc., 2008), 702.

13. Ironically, Höfle, who as a senior *SS* officer was most likely well aware of the unit's insidious reputation, initially did not want the *Sonderregiment* to be transferred to his fiefdom in Slovakia and tried to halt it, but Himmler insisted upon its use there and overruled him. Auerbach, *Miscellanea*, 4.

14. Wolfgang Venohr, *Aufstand in der Tatra: Der Kampf um die Slowakei 1939–1944* (Königstein, Germany: Athenäum Verlag, 1979), 316.

15. International Military Tribunal, *Ministries Case*, Vol. XIII. SS Memorandum 19 September 1944, Concerning the Termination of Berger's Position as German Commander in Slovakia and Himmler's Entrusting Berger with the Organization of the Home Guard in Germany, Document NO-2282, Prosecution Exhibit 1107, 369.

16. Ingrao, 41–42.

17. Landwehr, 8, and MacLean, 200.

18. MacLean, 200.

19. Landwehr, 8, and MacLean, 205.

20. *SS-FHA Amt II Org.Abt.Ia/II*, Tagebuch Nr. 3614/44 g.Kdos., Berlin-Wilmersdorf, 11 October 1944, Betreffend: Bezeichnung der Feldeinheiten der Waffen-SS, 3.

21. *SS-FHA Amt II Org.Abt.Ia/II*, Tagebuch Nr. 4213/44 g.Kdos., Berlin-Wilmersdorf, 13 November 1944, Betreffend: Bezeichnung der Feldeinheiten der Waffen-SS, 2.

22. On 13 November 1944, the *SS-FHA* officially designated the *Einheit Dirlewanger* as a brigade and as a unit of the *Waffen-SS*, though the formal *Etatisierung* (formally established with an associated budget) would not take effect until 19 December (source: *SS-FHA, Amt II Org.Abt. Ia/II*, Tagebuch Nr. 4213/44 g.Kdos., Betreff: Bezeichnung der Feldeinheiten der Waffen-SS, dated 13 November 1944, Landwehr, 8, and Georg Tessin, Vol. 14, 60).

23. The actual order directing the formal activation of the brigade under this new structure was issued on 19 December 1944, when the brigade was already fighting in Hungary (see note 18 above).

24. SS Judge Bruno Wille, quoted in Auerbach, *Die Dirlewanger Einheit*, 258, and Dr. Bruno Wille's Nuremberg War Crimes *Eidessattliche Erklärung* (sworn statement), 28 June 1946, 2.

25. Landwehr, p. 9.

26. Ingrao, 41.

27. Auerbach, *Die Dirlewanger Einheit*, 258.

28. Simply being drafted or forced to wear an *SS* uniform did not automatically make someone an *SS-Mann*; for that, a soldier had to apply for membership in what was still perceived, even in

1944, as an exclusive club. If accepted, the new member would be given an *SS* membership number and would have to pay annual dues. Early in the war, an *SS* member may have served in the *Wehrmacht* if he had been called up to fulfill his military obligation, while still remaining a member of the *SS* in good standing.

29. Auerbach, 256.
30. Klausch, 140–41, referring to Dirlewanger's letter dated 7 October 1944 addressed to Himmler, concerning the proposal of *Ostubaf.* Egon Zill on the recruitment of political prisoners for the Dirlewanger Brigade.
31. Memoranda, Dirlewanger to Himmler, 7 October 1944, and Himmler to Berger, 15 October 1944. Subject: Enlistment of Former Opponents of the Movement for the *SS-Sturmbrigade Dirlewanger* (Bundesarchiv File NS 3/401).
32. Auerbach, *Miscellanea*, 15–17.
33. Auerbach, *Die Dirlewanger Einheit*, 256.
34. Wille was sent for the express purpose of deciding which prisoners merited clemency.
35. Ingrao, 44.
36. Rudolf Weiss SSO File, courtesy of John P. Moore and Joachim Lilla, *Statisten in Uniform: Die Mitglieder des Reichstages 1933–1945* (Düsseldorf: Droste Verlag, 2004), 719.
37. Auerbach, *Die Dirlewanger Einheit*, 259.
38. *Ibid.*, 258; Landwehr, 9–10; and *Der Spiegel*, 4 April 1951, 28.
39. *Der Spiegel*, 4 April 1951, 27, and Landwehr, 9–10.
40. *Ibid.*, 4 April 1951, 31
41. Michaelis Dirlewanger Memoir, 72–73.
42. Less than a year later, this regiment would be renumbered as *SS-Pz.Gren.Rgt 6 Theodor Eicke.*
43. Stuart Emmett, *Der Strafvollzugslager der SS und Polizei: Himmler's Wartime Institutions for the Detention of Waffen-SS and Polizei Criminals* (London: Fonthill Media Ltd, 2017), 448–51.
44. *Ibid.*, 451.
45. *Ibid.*
46. Rolf Michaelis, *Die SS-Sturmbrigade Dirlewanger*, 68.
47. BA Ludwigsburg, Records Group B 162/16574, Der Oberstaatsanwalt, 2 Js. 700/61, Witness Statement of former member Walter Fentzahn, Flensburg, 23 November1961.
48. SSO Files of Ernst Heidelberg and Wolfgang Plaul (courtesy of John Moore); *Funkspruch* (radio message) from *Standartenführer* Dr. Dirlewanger to *Strafvollzugslager der SS- und Polizei Danzig-Matzkau*, dated 2 June 1944 (BA-MA RS 3-36/19).
49. Ludwigsburg Dossier, 37.
50. *Ibid.*, 38. Steinhauer, born on 30 September 1908 in Cologne, had joined the *Allgemeine-SS* on 11 May 1938. A policeman since 1931, he had served a brief tour of duty in the *Wehrmacht-Heer* as an *Unteroffizier* in *III. Btl./Inf.Rgt. 77* in 1936. Shortly after the war's outbreak in September 1939, he joined the *SS-Polizei Division* as a *Leutnant der Polizei*. On 18 December 1941, he was promoted to *Oberleutnant der Polizei*, stationed somewhere in the rear area of *Heeresgruppe Mitte*. On 9 November 1943, he was promoted to *Hauptmann der Polizei*, serving as commander of *1. Batterie/Schutzmannschafts-Art.Abt. 56*, which was attached to *Sonderbataillon Dirlewanger* (BA-MA: RS 3-36 1b, image 0068, and Steinhauer files R 936-II 976432 and 199904, and VBS 1069 R 19 ZB 3302).
51. Michaelis Dirlewanger Memoir, 72.
52. MacLean, 206–07.
53. *SS* Officer's file and court records for Wilhelm Stegmann, Bundesarchiv/Berlin Document Center, Files R 9361-I 52955, II 969994, and III 557959, and Joachim Lilla, Martin Döring and Andreas Schulz, *Statisten in Uniform, Die Mitglieder des Reichstags 1933–1945* (Droste Verlag, 2004).

54. According to a judicial review of his case carried out by the *SS* and Police Court XV in Breslau on 29 January 1943: "The preliminary proceedings in the criminal case against Hstuf. Ewald Ehlers are provisionally closed in accordance with § 47 of the War Criminal Procedure Code [concerning disciplinary sanctions for the offence] A final clarification of the charges against the accused can only be brought about by the personal testimony of his accuser, Hstuf. Arnold … This confrontation is not possible in view of the current situation at the Front. The provisional suspension of the preliminary proceedings therefore seemed appropriate in order to give the accused the opportunity to demonstrate his moral conduct by courageous service during his front-line deployment and therefore refute the accusations made against him."

55. MacLean, 195.

56. Ewald Ehlers SSO File, courtesy of John P. Moore and Karl Schneider, *Auswärts eingesetzt: Bremer Polizeibataillone und der Holocaust* (Essen: Klartext Verlag, 2011), 560–61.

57. Klausch, 189–90, and *Der Spiegel*, "Sie haben Etwas Gutzumachen," 14 Feb 1951, 30, and 11 April 1951, 18. However, his name is not among the list of *Luftwaffe* officers presented with that award.

58. Emmett, 479–80. The men interviewed by Klausch and the reporter from *Der Spiegel* may have been mistaken; another candidate is *Luftwaffe Hauptmann* Wolfram von Skotnicki, who was transferred to the *Waffen-SS* at the end of September 1944. Whether he was sent to the Dirlewanger Brigade as a *B-Schütze* must remain conjecture until more information comes to light.

59. Klausch, 189.

60. *Der Spiegel*, 11 April 1951, 18, and Klaush, 190. Apparently, Langelotz had been sentenced to serve a sentence at the Dachau *KL*, on suspicion of being involved in espionage, which could have meant anything under the strict laws of the Third Reich.

61. Klausch, 187–88.

62. *Ibid.*, 191.

63. *Ibid.*, 188–89.

64. Michaelis, *Die SS-Sturmbrigade Dirlewanger*, 70.

65. MacLean, 205–06, quoting Rolf Michaelis, *Die Grenadier Divisionen der Waffen-SS*, 184.

66. Auerbach, *Die Dirlewanger Einheit*, 259.

67. Dr. Fridolin M. von Senger und Etterlin, *Die 24. Panzer-Division, vormals 1. Kavallerie-Division 1939–1945* (Neckargemund: Kurt Vowinckel Verlag, 1962), 281.

Chapter 3

1. Ruth Ellen Gruber, "A Border as Crossroad for Culture," *The New York Times*, 18 November 2005 (New York: The New York Times Corporation, 2005).

2. Earl F. Ziemke, *Stalingrad to Berlin: The German Defeat in the East* (Washington, D.C.: U.S. Army Center of Military History, 2002), 369–70.

3. *Ibid.*, 356–58.

4. Wilhelm Hoettl, *The Secret Front: The Inside Story of Nazi Political Espionage* (London: Weidenfeld & Nicholson, 1953), 216–18.

5. A fascinating account of *Unternehmen Panzerfaust* is found in Eric Kern's postwar book, *Dance of Death*, published in 1948 as *Der Grosse Rauch* (The Great Frenzy). The penname of former *Ustuf.* Eric Kernmayr, who was serving under Otto Skorzeny's command for this operation, Kern was responsible for psychological operations, including the seizure of the radio station and preventing Hungarian Arrow Cross members from using the station for their own nefarious ends.

6. Karl-Heinz Frieser (ed. and contributing author), Klaus Schmider, Klaus Schönherr, Gerhard Schreiber, Krisztian Ungvary and Bernd Wegner, *Germany and the Second World War, Vol. VIII:*

The Eastern Front 1943–1944—The War in the East and on Neighboring Fronts (Oxford: Clarendon Press, 2017), 876.

7. Ziemke, 363–64.

8. This account from Friessner is from his history of the campaign, *Verratene Schlachten, die Tragödie der deutschen Wehrmacht in Rumänien* (Hamburg: Holsten Verlag, 1956), and also quoted in *Campaign: Fortress Budapest* by Warlord Games (Oxford, U.K.: Bloomsbury Publishing PLC, 2019).

9. Ziemke, 378–82.

10. The 1st Guards Cavalry-Mechanized Group, informally known as Cavalry-Mechanized Group Pliyev, was named after its commander, the dynamic Lieutenant General Issa A. Pliyev. Virtually the size of a field army, in December 1944 this mixed armor-cavalry unit consisted of the IV and VI Guards Cavalry Corps and the XVIII Mechanized Corps (Glantz, 1986 Art of War Symposium, 119).

11. Ziemke, 382–83.

12. *Ibid.*, 383.

13. Friessner's concern about the possibility of these two events occurring occupied a substantial portion of the nightly discussion at his headquarters between 8 and 10 December 1944, as detailed in the army's group war diary for the period.

14. For a brief and concise description of the development of the military situation up to 12 December 1944, refer to Ziemke, 380–83.

15. Study of the *H.Gr. Süd* war diary shows that between 7 and 9 December, the leadership of *H.Gr. Süd* and both of its *Armeegruppen* were deeply preoccupied about the developments north of the Danube and how to counter any Soviet move towards the Ipolysag Gap, especially after Malinovsky's troops took Waitzen.

16. *H.Gr. Süd, Ia KTB* Meldungen und Befehle, Ia. Nr. 13590/44 geheim, Fernschreiben 10.10am, 8 December 1944.

17. *H.Gr. Süd, Ia KTB*, Betr: Wochenmeldung, reports dated 9 and 16 December 1944, 4.

18. *H.Gr. Süd, Ia KTB*, Meldungen und Befehle, Wochenmeldung, 9 December 1944, 5.

19. On 27 November 1944, the *IV. Pz.Korps* was renamed *Pz.Korps Feldherrnhalle* but continued to be referred to by it former designation by *H.Gr. Süd* until early January 1945. *H.Gr. Süd*'s contemporary designation of the corps will be continued in use here.

20. von Senger und Etterlin, 280.

21. The figure of 175 men is stated in the after-action report written by Dirlewanger's staff after the battle. It contrasts with the number quoted in the *24. Pz.Div.* postwar history written 18 years later by former *panzer* general and division commander Fridolin von Senger und Etterlin, who states "60 men" on page 281 although he was leading a *panzer* corps in Italy at the time and in no position to make this observation. Since the number quoted by Dirlewanger was made only three days after the battle began, it is the more authoritative number which the author has chosen to use here rather that von Senger und Etterlin's.

22. *6. Armee/A.Gr. Fretter-Pico, Ia KTB* Meldungen und Befehle, 10 December 1944 (CAMO 500-12472-387).

23. Unit boundaries are drawn on maps, so there are usually no graphic control measures that can be seen by human eyes. Frequently, they coincide with physical boundaries such as rivers or highways. Detecting these non-physical boundaries is done through the monitoring of radio message traffic or through intelligence gained from the capture and interrogation of enemy troops by foot soldiers. Quite often these boundaries are found the hard way—by encountering an enemy's forward line of troops and being fired upon by them. Thus, a certain amount of stealth and daring is involved, a trait that the Red Army had developed to a high degree.

24. Leo W. G. Niehorster, *The Royal Hungarian Army, 1920–1945, Volume 1: Organization and History* (privately published, Leo W. G. Niehorster, 1998), 140–45. The American or British equivalent rank to Vezérörnagy was Brigadier General, which had no German Army equivalent. The closest *Wehrmacht* approximation would be the rank of *Generalmajor*.

25. *H.Gr. Süd, Ia KTB*, Betr. Wochenmeldung, report dated 9 December 1944, 2. Combat power ratings ran from Category I (fully combat ready) to V (non-combat ready).

26. *H.Gr. Süd, Ia KTB* Meldungen und Befehle, Tagesmeldung 8 December 1944, 5.

27. Norbert Számvéber, *Days of Battle: Armoured Operations North of the River Danube, Hungary 1944–45* (Solihull, U.K.: Helion and Company, 2013), 17.

28 *6. Armee/A.Gr. Fretter-Pico, Ia KTB* Morgenmeldung der Generalkommandos, dated 10 December 1944 (CAMO 500-12472-382/0097).

29 *Ibid.*

30 *6. Armee/A.Gr. Fretter-Pico, Ia KTB*, Radio Message from *D.V.K. 149* to *A.Gr. Fretter-Pico* dated 7.10pm 10 December 1944 (CAMO 500-12472-387-0013).

Chapter 4

1. The *Honvéd* was the shortened form of *Magyar Királyi Honvédség*, or the Royal Hungarian Army. The official German reference to it was the *Königlich Ungarische Armee*, which existed from 1922–45.

2. *H.Gr Süd, Ia KTB* entry dated 9 December 1944, 13. At that very moment, final troop movements were taking place into assembly areas in the Ardennes and Eifel forests in preparation for the *Wacht am Rhein* (Watch on the Rhine) counteroffensive; nearly all available German armored reinforcements had been rushed into position, leaving few reserves available for the Eastern Front. The Hungarian theater was lucky to have gained three *panzer* divisions for *Spätlese*, but infantry was needed just as much if not more than armor.

3. Hans Greiner, born on 17 October 1909 in Raitbach, was an *Oberstleutnant* of the *Heer* General Staff, and had been *kommandiert* (seconded) to the German Commander in Chief, Slovakia as its chief of staff with the equivalent SS rank of *Obersturmbannführer* due to the lack of qualified general staff officers in the *Waffen-SS*. Greiner was not a member of the SS. Assigned to Höfle's headquarters in Pressburg at the end of October 1944 while the battle against the Slovak Mutiny was ongoing, he had previously served as the *Ia* of the *93. Inf.Div.*, where he had been awarded the German Cross in Gold on 23 April 1944. His opinion of Dirlewanger and his brigade is unknown; however, as a senior officer of the *Wehrmacht* and graduate of the *Kriegsakademie*, it would not be unusual for him to hold the brigade and its commander in the lowest possible esteem. Heinrich Himmler, in a letter to Höfle in January 1945, stated that he believed that Greiner exercised far too much influence over Höfle's decisions.

4. *H.Gr. Süd, Ia KTB* entry dated 9 December 1944, 13–14.

5. According to the division's monthly status report for December 1944, its ration strength was 2,293 men. It also fielded 24 *Schützenpanzerwagen* (*SPW*, armored halftracks), eight heavy antitank guns (both 75mm and 76.2mm), eight 105mm howitzers, 10 mortars (including four 120mm pieces), and six *Nebelwerfer*. All in all, this amounted to considerably more firepower than the Dirlewanger Brigade possessed at the time (Anlage 6, *Panzer Feldausbildungs-Division Tatra*, Zustandmeldung an Aussenstelle d.Gen.Insp.d.Pz.Tr. Nr. 1/45, g.Kdos. von 1.1.1945, Stand 25.12.1944).

6. In the *H.Gr Süd, Ia KTB* entry for 10 December, von Grolman or his *Ia*, *Oberstleutnant* Schäfer, wrote that Höfle's insistence of withholding *Pz.Feldausb.Div. Tatra* was a mistake not justified by the actual situation. The Waag valley area east of Bratislava was 130 kilometers away from the

Ipoly River valley and not immediately threatened; *H.Gr. Süd* believed that Höfle could have easily deployed it to the Ipolysag area without incurring much risk.

7. *H.Gr Süd, Ia KTB* entry dated 9 December 1944, 14–15. In this instance, "very strong" probably referred to the number of personnel, not its actual capability. As already described in the previous chapter, the brigade's armaments were mostly obsolete. Greiner would have been in the position to know; as the chief of staff for Höfle, he would have seen the daily strength reports of the brigade and would have known perfectly well what its true capability was. In the author's opinion, Greiner's statement was a deliberate misrepresentation that concealed the actual state of affairs, told in order to expedite the removal of a unit that had become a thorn in the side of the German Commander in Chief, Slovakia/*HSSPF-Slowakei*.

8. *Ibid.*, 14.

9. *H.Gr. Süd, Ia KTB* entry dated 9 December 1944, 14–15. Dobogókó was less than 30 kilometers north of Budapest, and would soon be forced to move to a more secure location along the Austrian border at *Eszterháza* castle over 100 kilometers to the west.

10. *6. Armee/A.Gr. Fretter-Pico, Ia KTB* Morgenmeldung der Gen.Kdos, 4.35am 10 December 1944. *Ohrkrank* (Hearing Impaired or Deaf) battalions consisted of men who had sustained severe hearing loss during combat and had been grouped together to more easily administer. Like *Reserve-Bataillon (O) 284*, they were never intended to be used in the front line, but extraordinary circumstances (such as what happened on 10 December 1944) dictated that they be used in combat anyway.

11. *Ibid.*

12. *Ibid.*, 13.

13. *Der Deutsche Befehlshaber in der Slowakei, SS-Ogruf. und General der Waffen-SS und Polizei* Höfle, Schreiben, Tagebuch Nummer 376/45 geheim, dated 6 January 1945 (Reproduced in Klausch, 221–24).

14. Message to Heinrich Himmler from Hermann Höfle, *HSSPF-Slowakei* Tagebuch Nr. 376/45 (geheim) as of 6 January 1945.

15. Had Wenck known this, he probably would have changed his mind and requested the release of *Pz.Feldausb.Div. Tatra* instead. At the time, no one really knew how Dirlewanger's brigade would prove itself in battle, though Greiner and Höfle probably had a good idea.

16. *H.Gr. Süd, Ia KTB* entry dated 10 December 1944, 11.

17. Email message from Vladimír Krajčovič to the author, 28 February 2023, referencing newly discovered document in the Slovakian Military Historical Archive in Bratislava containing an account of thefts perpetrated by Stegmann's *I. Btl./SS-St.Rgt. 1* in the area of the village of Trenčianska Turná between 2 and 3 December 1944.

18. Letter, *Reichsführer-SS* to *Ogruf.* Hermann Höfle, dated 30 December 1944. In this letter, Himmler restated his original standing order that the Dirlewanger Brigade had to be kept together and not piecemealed out to different field commands of the *Heer*.

19. *H.Gr. Süd, Ia KTB*, entry dated 9 December 1944, 8.

Chapter 5

1. H. G. W. Davie, *History of Military Logistics Blog*, "Organization of Soviet Mechanized Corps," Part I, https://www.hgwdavie.com/blog/2018/7/12/soviet-mechanised-corps, 31 July 2018, accessed 5 June 2022.

2. *Ibid.*

3. TsAMO, Journal of Military Operations of the 6th Guards Tank Army, by Tank Major General Troops Shtromberg, Colonel Shklyaruk, and Guards Major Svyatkovsky, 1–31 October 1944. Fund 339, Inventory: 5179, File: 4, Sheet of the beginning of the document in the file: 208,

Memory of the People, https://pamyat-naroda.ru/documents/view/?id=154015847, accessed 10 June 2022, 41–42.

4. TsAMO, Journal of Military Operations of the IX Guards Mechanized Corps during the Budapest Offensive Operation, by Lieutenant Colonel Sobolev, 1–31 December 1944. Fund 3443, Inventory 1, File 77, beginning with Frame 170, Memory of the People, https://pamyat-naroda.ru/documents/view/?id=134588529, accessed 7 March 2022, 37.

5. *Ibid.*, 16–17.

6. *6. Armee/A.Gr. Fretter-Pico, Ia KTB*, Tagesmeldung von *Divisions-Verbindungskommando (D.V.K.) 149* for the *2. ung.Pz.Div.*, dated 5pm 10 December 1944 (CAMO 500 12472, 392, 101).

7. TsAMO, Journal of Military Operations of the IX Guards Mechanized Corps. According to the corps' daily combat journal for 10 December 1944, prisoners had already been identified from the *24. Pz.Div.*, *18. SS-Pz.Gr.Div.*, *357. Inf.Div.*, and the Hungarian *1.* and *2. Pz.Div.*

8. *Ibid.*, 17–18.

9. *6. Armee/A.Gr. Fretter-Pico, Ia KTB* Morgenmeldung dated 4.35am 10 December 1944.

10. *Ibid.*, 11–12. Incidentally, in the left-hand margin of the war diary recording Dirlewanger's comment, two large exclamation points were hand-written in pencil, an indication of the astonishment felt by someone on the *Ia* staff (probably *Gen.Maj.* von Grolman or *Oberstleutnant* Marcks himself) when he reviewed the entry.

11. Although expedient, this was an unusual arrangement. The battalion still remained as part of *8. Armee/A.Gr. Wöhler*, but local control was exercised by a unit belonging to *6. Armee/A.Gr. Fretter-Pico* for three more days.

12. Wilhelm Engelhardt, quoted in Klausch, 226.

13. The *Sippenhaft Befehl* (Family Arrest Order) was instituted by the Special 20 July Commission of the *SS-RSHA* in the wake of the failed 20 July assassination plot against Hitler. The order read as follows: "The *Führer* has ordered: Whoever falls into enemy hands who is not wounded or has not fought with his utmost until being overpowered, has betrayed his honor. The community of decent and brave soldiers rejects him. Thus, his relatives are liable for him. Any payment of wages or support to his relatives shall be forfeited. This must be announced immediately. The details are regulated by the chief of the *OKW* on behalf of the *Führer*. Signed, Keitel, *Generalfeldmarschall*."

14. As previously mentioned, on 27 November 1944, the *IV. Pz.Korps* was renamed as *Pz.Korps Feldherrnhalle* but continued to be referred to by it former designation by *H.Gr. Süd* until early January 1945.

15. A Dirlewanger Brigade operations order describing its deployment between 11 and 13 December has yet to be located; the brigade's actual movements have been inferred based upon the *H.Gr. Süd* operations order issued on 11 December as well as the eventual positions they occupied upon arrival. The order was probably developed by Dirlewanger, Weisse, and Lewandowski, with input from some of the other senior officers, including Buchmann, Missmahl, Meyer, and Steinhauer.

16. Klausch, 221–24.

17. *6. Armee/A.Gr. Fretter-Pico, Ia KTB* Meldungen und Befehle, Ia Nr. 6187/44: Message to Hungarian *2. Pz.Div.*, 10 December 1944 (CAMO 500-12472-387-0006).

18. Why they were directed there instead of to Ipolysag can probably be explained by the fact that *II. Btl./Pz.Gren.Rgt. 26* was thought to be sufficient to hold that town, therefore either the commander of the Hungarian *2. Pz.Div.* or the chief of staff of *6. Armee/A.Gr. Fretter-Pico* thought they could be better employed in the mountains, where they could strengthen the defenses, as well as to keep them out of the path of the most likely Soviet attack due to their already referenced political unreliability.

19. At that time, *Rittmeister* Zischler, in addition to his own battalion, also controlled an attached company from *Pio.Btl. 144* and a Hungarian unit, *Kompanie Gaal*. He intended to use these attachments to defend the hill mass stretching from Mt. Magas (Hill 283) through Mt. Samos

(Hill 323), and ending at Mt. Vereb (Hill 312), while he kept his own battalion within Ipolysag proper.

20. *6. Armee/A.Gr. Fretter Pico, Ia KTB*, Morgenmeldung der Korps dated 4.45am 12 December 1944.

21. Klausch, 232–33. Which *Waffen-SS* unit he is referring to is unknown, since the only *Waffen-SS* units in that area were his own battalion or the neighboring *II. Bataillon*. He could have been referring to members of the battalion headquarters, which would have included veterans of the brigade who were still loyal to Dirlewanger.

22. *Ibid.*, 233. The *Wehrmacht* troops were moved out shortly after the *III. Bataillon* arrived and took up positions to the right flank or south.

23. Although it can no longer be verified with certainty, these two assault guns most likely were from *Sturmgeschütz-Brigade 325*.

24. *H.Gr. Süd, Ia KTB*, entry dated 10 December 1944, 11.

25. *6. Armee/A.Gr. Fretter-Pico, Ia KTB* Tagesmeldung *D.V.K. 149* (Hungarian *2. Pz.Div.*), 5pm 10 December 1944, and TsAMO, Journal of Military Operations of the IX Guards Mechanized Corps, 10 December 1944. Interestingly, the 46th Guards Tank Brigade reported that it had lost two tanks to land mines and a further three to German artillery fire.

26. *Ibid.* The original bridge had been destroyed by the Germans as they retreated.

27. TsAMO, Journal of Military Operations of the IX Guards Mechanized Corps, 10 December 1944.

28. *6. Armee/A.Gr. Fretter-Pico, Ia KTB* Morgenmeldung der Korps, dated 4.20am 11 December 1944. The unit defending Ipolyhidvég has yet to be determined, but it was most likely a small *Kampfgruppe* from the *IV. Pz.Korps*.

29. David Glantz *et al.*, Proceedings, 1986 Art of War Symposium, *From the Vistula to the Oder: Soviet Offensive Operations—October 1944–March 1945* (Carlisle, PA: U.S. Army War College Center for Land Warfare, 1986), 175–77, and Soviet General Staff, *The Budapest Operation: An Operational-Strategic Study*, edited and translated by Richard W. Harrison (Solihull, U.K.: Helion & Company Ltd, 2017), p. 27.

30. *6. Armee/A.Gr. Fretter-Pico, Ia KTB* Tagesmeldung *D.V.K. 149*, dated 6.35pm 11 December 1944.

31. *6. Armee/A.Gr. Fretter-Pico, Ia KTB* Meldungen und Befehle, Funksprüche von *D.V.K. 149* an *6. Armee*, dated 2.05am 10 December 1944.

32. Michaelis Dirlewanger Memoir, 73.

33. Klausch, 229–30.

34. *H.Gr. Süd, Ia KTB* entry dated 10 December 1944, 11. In normal practice, a command's *Ia* would maintain and edit its war diary, including the initial drafts of reports. The chief of staff would check his work, and make remarks or recommend corrections or edits before it was sent to the commander for his final approval. Once approved, the *Ia* would then send a copy to the next level of command as well as the *OKH Führungsabteilung* in Berlin, while keeping the original copy in a binder.

35. Friessner, *Verratene Schlachten*, 5.

Chapter 6

1. Dmitriy Loza, *Commanding the Red Army's Sherman Tanks: The World War II Memoirs of Hero of the Soviet Union Dmitriy Loza* (Lincoln, Nebraska: University of Nebraska Press, 1996), 37.

2. *Ibid.*, 37–38.

3. Norbert Szamveber, *Days of Battle: Armoured Operations North of the River Danube, Hungary 1944–45* (Warwick, U.K.: Helion & Company, 2013), 13–14.

4. *Ibid.* In his original account, Loza describes the aircraft as Junkers *Ju-88s*, but he was clearly but understandably mistaken. Both aircraft have similar twin-engine layouts and tail features, but according to *Luftwaffe* records, only squadrons equipped with the Henschel *Hs 129* were operating in the Ipoly River valley that day.

5. *H.Gr. Süd, Ia KTB*, Tagesmeldung, entry dated 11 December 1944, 2 and 4. Incidentally, the *Luftwaffe* admitted losing four of its aircraft that day in the *H.Gr. Süd Kampfraum*, in exchange for claiming 14 Red Air Force aircraft and 22 tanks destroyed.

6. *6. Armee/A.Gr. Fretter-Pico, Ia KTB* Meldungen und Befehle, Fernschreiben Ia Nr. 6237/44 geheim, dated 4.30am 12 December 1944.

7. *Ibid.*

8. During the panicked withdrawal from Hont, half of the Hungarian *IV. Btl./Inf.Rgt. 3* used the opportunity to desert to the Red Army, while a further 50 men (including 10 officers) were apprehended by Hungarian *Gendarmes* in the rear area while attempting to desert. *6. Armee/A. Gr. Fretter-Pico, Ia KTB* Funkspruch von *D.V.K. 149*, dated 10.42am 12 December 1944.

9. The standard Hungarian Steyr-Mannlicher M1895 rifle (and their light machine guns) fired the 8x56mmR cartridge, which is not interchangeable with the standard German Mauser 7.92mm round. This meant that German rifles and light machine guns could not fire the Hungarian round of ammunition, and vice versa.

10. *H.Gr. Süd, Ia KTB* dated 11 December 1944, 14–15.

11. *H.Gr. Süd, Ia KTB* Fernschreiben Ia. Nr. 4782/44 g.Kdos, dated 3.15pm 11 December 1944. In actuality, both of these battalions had already been removed from their regiment's control.

12. As will be shown, when these two battalions arrived, they were first subordinated to *K.Gr. Grosse* in the mountains east of Bernecebaráti, instead of to Buchmann, whose own headquarters would not arrive until 12 December. In the meantime, they would have to draw their logistical support from somewhere, so Grosse's *Pio.Rgt.Stab 36* would naturally have been given the responsibility, as was standard operating procedure.

13. This formalized the unofficial command relationship that had been put in place the day before; local control of Zischler's battalion had now become official by its attachment to the Hungarian *2. Pz.Div*. Once he had established his regimental command post, Buchmann would be given tactical control of Zischler's battalion for two days.

14. Klausch, 228, quoting *Der deutsche Befehlshaber in der Slowakei*, Fernschreiben 376/45 geheim dated 6 January 1945. How Dirlewanger was to accomplish this was not mentioned; the only means at his disposal to inspect the *II.* and *III.Btl./SS-St.Rgt. 2* was to drive there in person.

15. Again, because a copy of the Dirlewanger Brigade's operations order has not been found as of this writing, most of the key points stated here were deduced by careful study of the two after-action reports written after the battle—the first signed by Dirlewanger and the other by Freiherr von Uckermann of Buchmann's *SS-St.Rgt. 2*. Together, both documents provide a relatively clear description of where the brigade was deployed and how Dirlewanger intended to fight the battle.

16. Several hundred men would remain behind in Slovakia at the brigade's old billets in the Deviaky–Laskár–Mošovce area to form the *Nachkommando* (rear echelon), including logistics and administrative personnel, as well as incoming recruits, prisoners, convalescing wounded, or men recovering from non-battle injuries.

17. *6. Armee/A.Gr. Fretter-Pico, Ia KTB* Morgenmeldung der Korps, dated 4.45am 12 December 1944, 1. The number of officers stated in the *Kampfstärke* only includes SS officers who were not on probationary status; the other officers from the *SS* and *Heer* who had been demoted to enlisted rank but were still leading platoons and companies were not included in that number.

18. *6. Armee/A.Gr. Fretter-Pico, Ia KTB* Tagesmeldung der Korps, dated 12 December 1944, 2, and Szamveber, 14. Soviet records do not make it clear which type of Hungarian armored fighting

vehicles were destroyed during this action, but these were most likely *Toldi IIa* tanks. The *Nimrod* looked exactly like a tank, but lacked the armor and high-velocity cannon that would have made it an effective antiarmor weapon. No German armor was present during this action.

19. Klausch, 234.

20. *Ibid.*, 235.

21. *6. Armee/A. Gr. Fretter-Pico, Ia KTB* Meldungen, Funksprüche dated 11.10am 12 December 1944.

22. TsAMO, Journal of Military Operations of the IX Guards Mechanized Corps, 12 December 1944.

23. *6. Armee/A. Gr. Fretter-Pico, Ia KTB*, Tagesmeldung *D. V.K. 149* dated 5.45pm 12 December 1944.

24. TsAMO, Journal of Military Operations of the IX Guards Mechanized Corps, 12 December 1944. The Soviet records state that three "assault guns" were suppressed, but German records indicate that only two were deployed there; the other vehicle may have been of Hungarian origin.

25. German records do not specifically mention whether these were German or Hungarian armored fighting vehicles, nor which type. The two German assault guns dispatched earlier may have been involved in this action.

26. *6. Armee/A. Gr. Fretter-Pico, Ia KTB* Meldungen, Funkspruch von *D. V.K. 149*, dated 12.15pm 12 December 1944.

27. *6. Armee/A. Gr. Fretter-Pico, Ia KTB* Meldungen, Funkspruch von *D. V.K. 149*, dated 7.50pm 12 December 1944. What *Oberst* Zádor had in mind was the transfer of the *Szent László* Division, one of the few remaining elite and well-equipped divisions in the Honvéd. This division was also the only complete, combat capable division in *H. Gr. Süd*'s reserve. Zádor's request was denied.

28. *6. Armee/A. Gr. Fretter-Pico, Ia KTB* Meldungen und Befehle, Order Nr. 6266/44 dated 12 December 1944.

29. *H. Gr. Süd, Ia KTB*, Tagesmeldung, dated 12 December 1944, 13. Additionally, the German leadership was most likely concerned with Zádor's focus on the mission as well as his steadfastness. Only three days earlier, he had requested emergency leave to visit his mother, whom he said was "at the point of death" due to an illness. As the family's sole breadwinner, Zádor thought that his presence would help her obtain needed medical care. His request was denied. *6. Armee/A. Gr. Fretter-Pico* Funkspruch from *D. V.K. 149*, sent 1.30pm 9 December 1944.

30. *Ibid.*, 13–14.

31. Rintelen had been promoted to that rank on 1 August 1944.

32. *Korps-Gruppe Breith, Ia KTB* Tagesmeldung *Korpsgruppe Breith* an *A. Gr. Fretter-Pico*, dated 8.35pm 11 December 1944.

33. The remaining combat elements of the division that had not already been parceled out were grouped under the control of the headquarters of *Gren. Rgt. 945*, commanded by *Oberstltn.* Georg Theirfelder. This battlegroup, christened *K. Gr. Thierfelder*, continued the division's previous mission of securing Szentendre Island.

34. *6. Armee/A. Gr. Fretter-Pico, Ia KTB* Meldungen und Befehle, Order Nr. 6262/44 dated 12 December 1944.

35. *6. Armee/A. Gr. Fretter-Pico, Ia KTB* Morgenmeldung dated 13 December 1944, 1.

36. See "Die Überlaufodysee der 10. Kompanie und der Frontwechsel der Reste des III. Bataillon" in Klausch, 247–51.

37. The return of Langelotz's company even received a mention in the *6. Armee/A. Gr. Fretter-Pico's KTB*, which recorded that "*10. Kompanie* of the *SS-Sturm-Brig.* broke out of enemy encirclement and returned safely to its battalion" (*6. Armee/A. Gr. Fretter-Pico, Ia KTB*, Morgenmeldung der Generalkommandos, dated 6.20am 14 December 1944).

38. TsAMO, Journal of Military Operations of the IX Guards Mechanized Corps, 12 December 1944.

Chapter 7

1. On 12 December, *6. Armee/A.Gr. Fretter-Pico* ordered the Hungarian *2. Pz.Div.* to submit its proposed antitank defense plan, including a map overlay that depicted all of the primary and alternate antitank gun positions, no later than 16 December, but this plan was overcome by events before it could be implemented (*6. Armee/A.Gr. Fretter-Pico, Ia KTB* Meldungen und Befehle, Befehl Nr. 6271/44 geh., dated 1.20am 12 December 1944).

2. Funkspruch from *Oberführer* Dirlewanger via *D.V.K. 149* to *6. Armee/A.Gr. Fretter-Pico, Ia KTB*, dated 5.31pm 13 December 1944.

3. "Bericht über den feindlichen Panzereinbruch am 15.12.44 im Raum von Ipolysag," Ia, *SS-Sturm-Brigade Dirlewanger*, dated 17 December 1944.

4. *6. Armee/A.Gr. Fretter-Pico, Ia KTB* Meldungen und Befehle, Ia Befehl Nr. 1853/44 g.Kdos. dated 12 December 1944.

5. Tagesmeldung, ung. *2. Pz.Div.* an *6. Armee/A.Gr. Fretter-Pico*, dated 7.15pm 13 December 1944. In this same message, Zádor requested that Dirlewanger be named commander of "K.Gr. Nord," consisting of every unit positioned north of the Ipoly River. There is no record of this request ever being approved by *Gen.Maj.* Rintelen, since it was unnecessary.

6. "Bericht über die nach Übernahme des Abschnittes Ipolysag befohlene Ablösung des *II. Btl./Pz.Gr.Rgt 26* am 14.12.44," Adjutant, *SS-Sturm-Regiment 2*, 17 December 1944.

7. *6. Armee/A.Gr. Fretter-Pico, Ia KTB*, Tagesmeldung *D.V.K. 149*, dated 7.15pm 13 December 1944.

8. *Div.Gr. Rintelen, Ia KTB*, Tagesmeldung, dated 8.25pm 14 December 1944 (CAMO 500-12472-382-0177).

9. *6. Armee/A.Gr. Fretter-Pico, Ia KTB* Morgenmeldung der Gen.Kdos., dated 6.20am 14 December 1944.

10. *6. Armee/A.Gr. Fretter-Pico, Ia KTB* Tagesmeldung, Ia Nr. 6294/44, dated 13 December 1944, 2.

11. von Senger und Etterlin, 396.

12. *H.Gr. Süd, Ia KTB*, entry dated 13 December 1944, 4, and Tagesmeldung, *D.V.K. 149* Nr. 7 dated 7.15pm 13 December 1944.

13. "Bericht über die nach Übernahme des Abschnittes Ipolysag befohlene Ablösung des *II./Pz.Gr.Rgt 26* am 14.12.44." In his report, *Ostubaf.* Buchmann stated that the "Russians were behaving in a conspicuously loud manner, most like due to the issue of alcohol" (CAMO 500-12472-380-00084-0085).

14. TsAMO, Journal of Military Operations of the IX Guards Mechanized Corps, 13 December 1944.

15. Tagesmeldung, ung. *2. Pz.Div.* an *6. Armee/A.Gr. Fretter-Pico*, dated 7.15pm 13 December 1944.

16. *6. Armee/A.Gr. Fretter-Pico, Ia KTB* Meldungen und Befehle, Order Nr. 6262/44 dated 12 December 1944. Due to the confusion that ensued over the next several days, *Div.Gr. 357* was soon disbanded entirely and its troops (mostly Hungarians by this point) were parceled out among other units of the *IX. SS-Geb.Korps*. Thereafter, the terms *Div.Gr. Rintelen* and *Div.Gr. 357* were used interchangeably, both meaning the same tactical entity.

17. Rintelen biography located at https://www.lexikon-der-wehrmacht.de/Personenregister/R/RintelnJosef.htm, accessed on 15 October 2022. Additional biographical information provided by Stephen Craciun, the unofficial historian of the *357. Inf.Div.*, on 9 October 2022.

18. Efficiency Report of *Gen.Maj.* Josef Rintelen by *Gen.d.Pz.Tr.* Ulrich Kleemann dated 5 March 1945, approved by *Gen.d.Geb.Tr.* Hans Kreysing, Commander, *8. Armee* on 7 March 1945.

19. In addition to any stragglers or recovering wounded from the division who had been separated from their unit, the field replacement battalion would receive the 250 new replacements who were

allocated to the division on 10 December 1944 (*6. Armee/A. Gr. Fretter-Pico, Ia KTB*, Meldungen und Befehle, Order Nr. 4760/44, signed 1.30am 10 December 1944).

20. *LXXII. A.K., IIa/IIb* Tätigkeitsbericht für die Zeit vom 16.12. bis 31.12.1944, 3.

21. *LXXII. A.K., Ia KTB*, Notes of Conversation between Chief of Staff, *LXXII. A.K.* and *Ia* of *6. Armee/A.Gr. Fretter-Pico*, 1.30pm 19 December 1944.

22. After midnight on 14 December, *Div.Gr. Rintelen* began submitting its reports via its own signal battalion, and *D.V.K. 149* resumed its primary mission of serving as the liaison element for the Hungarian *2. Pz.Div.*, which now reported directly to Rintelen. *Div.Gr. Rintelen* would have maintained its own *KTB* but this document has been lost; however, its morning and daily summary reports, as well as messages sent or received by *6. Armee/A. Gr. Fretter-Pico*, still survive.

23. *6. Armee/A.Gr. Fretter-Pico, Ia KTB* Meldungen und Befehle, Funkspruch issued 7.43pm 13 December 1944 (CAMO 500-12472-387-0110).

Chapter 8

1. *6. Armee/A.Gr. Fretter-Pico, Ia KTB* Radio Message, Generalkommando *IV. Pz.K.* to *6. Armee/A. Gr. Fretter-Pico*, dated 10.20am 13 December 1944 (CAMO 500-12472-387-0137).

2. "*Bericht über die nach Übernahme des Abschnittes Ipolysag befohlene Ablösung des II./Pz. Gr.Rgt 26 am 14.12.44.*" This report, authored by former *Oberst* Freiherr von Uckermann acting as Buchmann's adjutant, is probably the most succinct and accurate account of what actually occurred between 13 and 15 December 1944.

3. Dirlewanger's signal team had to relay messages to the incoming *Div.Gr. Rintelen* through the Hungarian division (actually *D.V.K. 149*) because Rintelen's signal battalion would not become operational until 14 December 1944.

4. While in Buchmann's after-action report he states that this was "his" *Pionier* platoon, it was most likely part of the *Pionier* company from the mixed battalion that was attached to his regiment for this mission.

5. "*Bericht über die nach Übernahme des Abschnittes Ipolysag befohlene Ablösung des II./Pz.Gr.Rgt 26 am 14.12.44.*"

6. *Ibid.*

7. TsAMO, Journal of Military Operations of the IX Guards Mechanized Corps, 13 December 1944.

8. *6. Armee/A.Gr. Fretter-Pico, Ia KTB* Morgenmeldung der Gen.Kdos, 6.20am, 14 December 1944 (CAMO 500-12472-382-0176).

9. TsAMO, Journal of Military Operations of the IX Guards Mechanized Corps, 14 December 1944.

10. The *Luftwaffe's* after-action report for 14 December states that the bridge over the Ipoly at Hidveg was knocked out, 50 horse-drawn wagons and motor vehicles destroyed, and 17 enemy aircraft shot down (*H.Gr. Süd, Ia KTB* dated 14 December 1944); this conflicts with the Journal of Military Operations of the IX Guards Mechanized Corps entry for the same date, which stated that the bridge was attacked, but only damaged, not destroyed. Noteworthy was the fact that the *Luftwaffe* did not claim any Soviet tanks destroyed, evidence that the 83rd Guards Tank Regiment had escaped without serious loss.

11. *Div.Gr. Rintelen, Ia KTB*, Tagesmeldung 8.25pm 14 December 1944.

12. TsAMO, Journal of Military Operations of the IX Guards Mechanized Corps, 14 December 1944.

13. *6. Armee/A.Gr. Fretter-Pico, Ia KTB*, Morgenmeldung der *Div.Gr. Rintelen*, 5.15am 15 December 1944 (CAMO 500-12472-382-0194). One author has claimed that armored fighting vehicles

from the *24. Pz.Div.* were involved in this counterattack, but there is no documentary evidence to support this.

14. *"Bericht über die nach Übernahme des Abschnittes Ipolysag befohlene Ablösung des II./Pz.Gr.Rgt 26 am 14.12.44."*

15. *6. Armee/A.Gr. Fretter-Pico, Ia KTB* Meldung dated 7pm 14 December 1944 from *Div.Gr. Rintelen.* This *Luftwaffe Flak* battalion was equipped with 88mm cannons.

16. *6. Armee/A.Gr. Fretter-Pico, Ia KTB* Meldungen und Befehle, Order Nr. 6324/44 11.15pm 14 December 1944 and Order Nr. 6327/44 dated 14 December 1944.

17. *H.Gr. Süd, Ia KTB* Tagesmeldung, 14 December 1944, 1–2.

18. *Ibid.*, 7, 11–12.

19. Kurt Mehner (ed.), *Die Geheimentagesberichte der Deutschen Wehrmachtführung im Zweiten Weltkrieg 1939–1945, Volume 11: 1 September 1944–31 December 1944* (Osnabrück: Biblio Verlag, 1984), 289.

20. *Der Bericht des Oberkommando der Wehrmacht,* Thursday, 14 December 1944 (CAMO 500-12472-387-0156).

21. *H.Gr. Süd, Ia KTB,* Tagesmeldung, 14 December 1944, 7.

22. The excerpt from the exact quote by Clausewitz is "that war is not an exercise of the will directed at an inanimate object, as is the case with the mechanical arts, or at matter which is animate but passive and yielding, as is the case with the human mind and emotions in the fine arts. In war the will is directed at an animate object that reacts." Carl von Clausewitz, Michael Howard and Peter Paret (eds.), *On War* (Princeton: Princeton University Press, Revised Edition, 1989), 149.

Chapter 9

1. TsAMO, Journal of Military Operations of the IX Guards Mechanized Corps, 15 December 1944.

2. *Ibid.*

3. Vilém Prečan, *Slovenské Národné Povstanie: Dokumenty* (The Slovak National Uprising: A Documentation) (Bratislava: Vydavateľstvo Politickej Literatúry, 1965), 1058.

4. *Div.Gr. Rintelen,* Ia Tagesmeldung, dated 8.25pm 14 December 1944 (CAMO 500-12472-382-0177).

5. *6. Armee/A.Gr. Fretter-Pico, Ia KTB,* Morgenmeldung dated 15 December 1944.

6. Michaelis Dirlewanger Memoir, 73–74.

7. *H.Gr. Süd, Ia KTB,* Tagesmeldung 15 December 1944, 11.

8. *Ibid.,* 74.

9. Klausch, 274–77.

10. Michaelis Dirlewanger Memoir, 74.

11. Klausch, 258.

12. Michaelis Dirlewanger Memoir, 74.

13. *H.Gr. Süd, Ia KTB,* Tagesmeldung 15 December 1944, 2, and *6. Armee/A.Gr. Fretter-Pico, Ic KTB,* Tagesmeldung 15 December 1944.

14. Letter, Franz M. to Herman N., December 1944 (French MacLean's website, https://www.thefifthfield.com/published-books/ the-cruel-hunters/), accessed 3 January 2022. The last names were deleted in order to protect the families' privacy.

15. Horst Voigt, *Die verlor'nen Haufen, op. cit.,* Part VI, 432–34, as cited in Klausch, 503, note 137. Voigt had been one of the few *KL* inmates who had not defected to the Red Army earlier that day, but had been among those few who remained behind and had been conseqently incorporated into *K.Gr. Hafner.*

16. Otto Hafner, "Transdanubia Diary 1944–1945" (Munich: Unpublished private manuscript, 16 September 1979), 12–13.

17. *LXXII. A.K.*, *Ia KTB* Morgenmeldung unterstellter Einheiten, 18 December 1944.

18. TsAMO, Journal of Military Operations of the IX Guards Mechanized Corps, 15 December 1944.

19. Though the actual operations order for Buchmann's counterattack can no longer be found, the outline of the plan and the timeline are recounted step-by-step in the after-action report that Dirlewanger was directed to submit to the *HSSPF-Slowakei*, Hermann Höfle. This very detailed four-page report allows the researcher to trace the course of the attack, its failure, and the resulting Soviet attack that drove the Dirlewanger Brigade from the Ipolysag area. Though signed by Dirlewanger himself, it was actually written by Buchmann's *Ia Schreiber*, Freiherr von Uckermann. Hereafter referred to as Dirlewanger Report.

20. Dirlewanger Report, 2.

21. *Ibid.*, 2–3.

22. Again, telephone lines had not yet been laid between Buchmann's command post in Kistur, nor had the regiment's radio truck set up operations. Dirlewanger literally had no contact with Buchmann except for messengers.

23. Freissner, 190.

24. Dirlewanger Report, 3–4.

25. Klausch, 256.

26. Friessner, 190.

27. TsAMO, Journal of Military Operations of the IX Guards Mechanized Corps, 16 December 1944.

Chapter 10

1. *6. Armee/A.Gr. Fretter-Pico, Ia KTB*, entry dated 15 December 1944 (CAMO 500-12472-382-0188).

2. *H.Gr. Süd, Ia KTB*, Tagesmeldung, 15 December 1944, 1.

3. *Ibid.*, 14. The general officer in question was *Gen.Maj.* Enno von Roden, who was the *General z.b.V.* (for special tasks) on the staff of *H.Gr. Süd*. Known for his energetic zeal and ruthlessness, he was the last officer a deserter from the Dirlewanger Brigade would wish to meet.

4. Amazingly, despite his intense dislike of the *SS*, *Gen.Maj.* Gaedke, chief of staff of *6. Armee/A. Gr. Fretter-Pico*, remarked during the evening of 15 December: "We do not have any objections about the leadership of the northern battlegroup led by *SS-Oberführer* Dirlewanger, since he had no [telephone or radio] connections with the southern flank." *H.Gr. Süd, Ia KTB*, Tagesmeldung, 15 December 1944, 12.

5. The details were spelled out in an order from Hitler dated 1 December 1944, *Führerbefehl zur Verteidigung von Budapest*, sent through the headquarters of *H.Gr. Süd* under Friessner's signature. The order, citing *Führerbefehl* Nr. 11 dated 8 March 1944, *Kommandanten der festen Plätze und Kampfkommandanten*, enunciated specific duties and expectations of the fortress commander and its troops, including fighting "to the last man" if necessary.

6. *6. Armee/A.Gr. Fretter-Pico, Ia KTB*, Meldungen und Befehle, Betr: Neue Befehlsgliederung, Ia Nr. 1865/44, dated 15 December 1944 (CAMO 500-12472-387-0159).

7. *6. Armee/A.Gr. Fretter-Pico, Ia KTB*, Meldungen und Befehle, Betr: Div.Gr. Rintelen, Ia Nr. 6352/44, dated 15 December 1944 (CAMO 500-12472-387-0158).

8. *H.Gr. Süd, Ia KTB*, Tagesmeldung, 15 December 1944, 14.

9. *H.Gr. Süd, Ia KTB*, Anlagen, Panzer-, Sturmgeschütz- und Paklage, 15 December 1944; *6. Armee/A. Gr. Fretter-Pico, Ia KTB*, Kampfstärke 16 December 1944, 2 (CAMO 500-12472-387-0191);

and *H.Gr. Süd, Ia KTB* Betr: Wochenmeldungen an *O.K.H. Gen.St.d.H./Op.Abt.*, Stand vom 16 December 1944, 4.

10. *Kampfgruppe Knoop* would consist of the staff and staff company of *Pz.Rgt. 10, I. Abt./Pz.Lehr-Rgt. 130, I. Btl.(gep.)/Pz.Gren.Rgt. 98, I. Abt.(Sf)/Pz.Art.Rgt. 80*, one tank destroyer company of *Pz.Jäg. Abt. 43*, and *Pz.Pio.Btl. 53*'s sole *SPW*-equipped *Pionier Kompanie*.

11. Friessner, 190–191.

12. The arrival of the two tank destroyer companies would be significantly delayed due to issues in obtaining the proper rolling stock needed to transport heavier vehicles. They would arrive after the attack had begun and contributed very little, as will be seen.

13. *H.Gr. Süd*, Fernschreiben an A.Gr. Fretter-Pico, Ia Nr. 4844/44 gKdos. dated 1.45am 16 December 1944.

14. Accounts on Nitzkowski's subsequent fate differ; some postwar survivors who had defected during the battle claimed that he had been shot afterwards by Dirlewanger for treason, while others said that he had been reduced to prisoner status and returned to Buchenwald to serve out the remainder of his original sentence. In either case, he was never heard from again and there is no evidence disproving or proving either rumor. The German War Graves Commission lists a Gustav Nitzkowski (no rank given) born in 1898 having been declared missing in action on 1 January 1945. Perhaps Nitzkowski had defected as well to avoid execution?

15. *"Bericht über den feindlichen Panzereinbruch am 15.12.1944 im Raum von Ipolysag,"* 3–4.

16. Ibid. 4.

17. Michaelis Dirlewanger Memoir, 74. Most likely, Dirlewanger was referring to the consolidated supply trains and other men not engaged in the front line. The consolidated *Kampf-Bataillon* aka *K.Gr. Ehlers* remained in action with the Hungarian *2. Pz.Div.* for another week. The company commander referred to here was someone other than Harald Momm, who was fighting north of the Ipoly with his own small *Kampfgruppe*.

18. *6. Armee/A.Gr. Fretter-Pico, Ia KTB* Fernschreiben an H.Gr Süd, Ia Nr. 6351/44 gKdos, Betr: Absicht für 16.12.1944.

19. *6. Armee/A.Gr. Fretter-Pico, Ia KTB*, Kampfstärke 16 December 1944, 2 (CAMO 500-12472-387-0191).

20. Kai Althoetmar, *Feldpost: 23. Dezember 1944. Der Kampf um Ungarn. Eine Spurensuche* 8th Edition (Edition Zeitpunkte, ePubli, 9 November 2018).

21. The *18. SS-Freiw.Pz.Gren.Div. Horst Wessel* was an SS "volunteer" mechanized infantry division formed on 25 January 1944 in Zagreb, Croatia. It was composed primarily of ethnic Germans from Hungary and Romania, with German cadre from the disbanded *1. SS-Inf.Brig. (mot)*. Tessin: Vol. 4, 108.

22. *Deutsche Befehlshaber in der Slowakei, Ia KTB*, entry dated 15 December 1944.

23. *Ibid.*, entry dated 16 December 1944.

24. According to Klausch, only three members of the brigade who defected to the Red Army are known to have been kept on as collaborators; former *KL* inmate Anton Blatschek with an unnamed reconnaissance battalion of the 6th Guards Tank Army, and two (Richard Doering and Willi Fänger) on the staff of the Second Ukrainian Front as translators or "office help." The rest waited out the remainder of the war in a number of different POW camps. Klausch, 272.

25. *Ibid.*

26. *Ibid.*, 276–82.

27. Arlene Röper, "Stolpersteine in Kaiserslautern" (Stumbling Stones in Kaiserslautern), Biography of Philipp Mees (Website of the Kaiserslautern Stumbling Stone Initiative, https://stolpersteine-kl. de/vorstellung/), accessed 28 March 2023.

Chapter 11

1. *6. Armee/A.Gr. Fretter-Pico, Ia KTB*, Panzer-, Pak- und Sturmgeschützlage, 18 December 1944, and *OKH Generalinspekteur der Panzertruppe, Abt. Org.*, Führer-Vorträge, Zuführung November 1944, Panzer IV.

2. *6. Armee/A.Gr. Fretter-Pico, Ic KTB* Tagesmeldung of 17 December 1944 (CAMO 500-12472-382-0226).

3. *LXXII. A.K., Ia KTB*, 1 July–31 December 1944, entry dated 17 December, images 248–52 (5 pages).

4. *Ibid.*, image 252. Schmidt had no reason to travel to the headquarters of the Hungarian division, since his and Zádor's were located in the same town.

5. The *Luftwaffe's* contribution to the ground battle would be the 88mm guns of the reinforced *II. Abt./Flak-Rgt. 24* and *I. Abt./Flak-Rgt. 48*.

6. *LXXII. A.K., Ia KTB*, Fernschreiben an *A.Gr Fretter-Pico*, Betr: Beabsichtigte Angriffsführung bei *LXXII. A.K.*, Ia Nr. 2882/44 geh., signed *Oberst* i.G. Möller (Corps Chief of Staff), dated 3.45pm 17 December 1944.

7. *LXXII. A.K., Ia KTB*, Morgenmeldung unterstellten Einheiten dated 18 December 1944, and *6. Armee/A.Gr. Fretter-Pico, Ia KTB*, Ia Wochenmeldung an H.Gr. Süd, 16 December 1944.

8. Budapestskaya Operaciya, contemporary summary of the Second Ukrainian Front about the operations around Budapest, 123 (source: Szamveber, *Days of Battle*, 123).

9. 7th Guards Army, War Diary evening report dated 18 December 1944 (source: Szamveber, *Days of Battle*, 32).

10. War Diary, IX Guards Mechanized Corps, Part II, 16–31 December, entry dated 17 December 1944, 1–2. Incidentally, Krinta was an ancient crypt roughly 500 meters west of Felsőszemeréd atop Hill 219, a key height overlooking the valley of the Schemnitz River and the approaches to Deménd.

11. *LXXII. A.K., Ia KTB*, Tagesmeldung an *A.Gr. Fretter-Pico*, Nachmeldung *K.Gr. Rintelen*, dated 17 December 1944.

12. To be fair, none of the three battalion commanders who took part in the failed attempt to recapture Ipolysag on 15 December were professional soldiers; two were career *Polizei* officers (Meyer and Steinhauer) and one (Polack) had been an *NSDAP* politician. Only Paul Ruhsam had been qualified to lead a battalion but he was missing in action after the fighting for Hill 227 and most likely dead.

13. Otto Hafner, "Transdanubisches Tagebuch, Briefe und Erinnerungen," 19 December 1944, 13–14.

14. War Diary, IX Guards Mechanized Corps from 16–31 December 1944, entry dated 18 December 1944, 3–4. Of course, not all of the 2,000 men of the Dirlewanger Brigade took part in the fighting, only the two battlegroups comprising 335 men fighting as part of *K.Gr. Hafner*.

15. Ibid, entry dated 18 December 1944, 3–4.

16. *LXXII. A.K., Ia KTB*, Fernschreiben an *6. Armee/A.Gr. Fretter-Pico* Nr. 2887/44 geheim, Betr: Überlaufen von Teilen *10. Kp./SS-St.Rgt. 2*, dated 18 December 1944.

17. *H.Gr. Süd, Ia KTB*, entry dated 18 December 1944, 10.

18. *Ibid.*, 3.

19. *Ibid.*, 2, 7–8.

20. *Ibid.*, 11, and German Commander in Slovakia, *Ia KTB* Tagemeldung entry dated 18 December 1944. The division, which had originally been titled Galizien, was primarily composed of Ukrainians fighting on the German side to liberate their homeland. It had been sent to Höfle's area to reconstitute following its near-annihilation during the battle of the Brody Pocket.

21. *LXXII. A.K., Ia KTB*, KTB Notizen, entry dated 9pm 18 December 1944.

22. Mike Melnyk, *The History of the Galician Division of the Waffen-SS, Vol. 2: Stalin's Nemesis* (London: Fonthill Media Ltd, 2016), 121–22.

23. *6. Armee/A.Gr. Fretter-Pico, Ia KTB*, Tagesmeldung dated 18 December 1944, 2 (CAMO 500-12472-382-0244), and *A.Gr. Fretter-Pico, Ia KTB*, Panzer-, Pak-, und Sturmgeschützlage, 18 December 1944.

24. *LXXII. Armee Korps, Ia KTB*, Tagesmeldung unterstellten Einheiten, 19 December 1944, 2.

25. *6. Armee/A.Gr. Fretter-Pico, Ia KTB*, Luftwaffe Flieger *Verbindungsoffizier* (VOL) Luftlage, 19 December 1944 (CAMO 500-12472-382-0278), 1.

26. *Ibid.*, 3.

27. War Diary, IX Guards Mechanized Corps from 16–31 December 1944, entry dated 19 December, 3–4.

28. *LXXII. Armee Korps, Ia KTB*, Tagesmeldung unterstellten Einheiten, 19 December 1944, 3.

29. *6. Armee/A.Gr. Fretter-Pico, Ia KTB* Fernschreiben an *8. Pz.Div.*, Ia Nr. 6543/44 geheim, dated 21 December 1944 (CAMO 500-12472-387-0317).

30. *LXXII. A.K., Ia KTB*, Morgenmeldung unterstellter Einheiten vom 20.12.1944, 1.

31. *H.Gr. Süd, Ia KTB*, entry dated 19 December 1944, 1.

32. *Ibid.*, 7–8.

33. It is interesting to speculate whether Guderian and Friessner had both come to the realization that carrying out Operation *Spätlese* at this time would be pointless

34. Otto Hafner, "Transdanubian Diary," entry dated 19 December 1944, 14–15.

35. *6. Armee/A.Gr. Fretter-Pico, Ia KTB* Meldungen, Ia Nr. 4895/44 gKdos., Fernschreiben von *H.Gr. Süd* an *A.Gr. Fretter-Pico*, 9.30pm 19 December 1944, 3 (CAMO 500-12472-387-0271), and *LXXII. A.K., Ia KTB* Notizen, 6.40pm 18 December 1944.

36. *LXXII. A.K., Ia KTB*, Tagesmeldung an *A.Gr. Fretter-Pico* dated 17 December 1944.

37. *Deutsche Befehlshaber in der Slowakei, Ia KTB*, Abendmeldung 20 December 1944.

Chapter 12

1. *H.Gr. Süd, Ia KTB* Meldungen, Fernschreiben *OKH Generalstab des Heeres, Führungsabteilung/ Operationsabteilung an Heeresgruppe Süd*, Nr. 440 727/44, dated 19 December 1944, 1–2.

2. *6. Armee/A.Gr. Fretter-Pico, Ia KTB*, Anlagen 16–31 December, Order Ia Nr. 6464/44 geheim dated 20 December 1944.

3. *LXXII. A.K., Ia KTB*, Korpsbefehl für die Kampfführung am 20.12.1944, Ia Nr. 2896/44 geheim, dated 19 December 1944, 1–2.

4. By this point Ehlers had most likely been recalled by Dirlewanger to assume command of *SS-St. Rgt. 2* and had departed the area, leaving Falter in command.

5. Bundesarchiv, Berlin Document Center, police service record of *Major der Schutzpolizei* Franz Falter.

6. Rintelen did not yet know that these tanks were from the V Guards Tank Corps.

7. Szamveber, *Days of Battle*, 43.

8. *LXXII. A.K., Ia KTB*, Tagesmeldung 20 December 1944, 1.

9. War Diary, IX Guards Mechanized Corps covering the period from 16–31 December 1944, entry dated 20 December 1944, 4–5.

10. Most likely consisting of troops from *SS-Pz.Gren.Rgt. 40* with one or two *Sturmgeschütze* and one or two 75mm *Pak*. The missing *Kampfgruppe* from the *14. Waffen-Gren.Div. der SS* was also at that same location. The estimate of the enemy engaged by the 18th Guards Mechanized Brigade exaggerated the Germans' strength (source: Tieke, *Horst Wessel: Combat History of the 18th SS Panzer-Grenadier-Division*, 153–56).

11. War Diary, IX Guards Mechanized Corps covering the period from 16–31 December 1944, entry dated 20 December 1944, 5.

12. *Deutscher Befehlshaber in der Slowakei, Ia KTB*, Tagesmeldungen 19–21 December 1944. Interestingly, had *SS K.Gr. Dern* been deployed to the area east of Leva in a defensive posture on 18 December, it is doubtful whether the Soviets would have been able to take the city as quickly as they did.

13. Zustand *Pz.Feldausb.Div. Tatra*, 25.12.1944, Betr: Kriegsgliederung *Pz.Ers.u.Ausb.Div. Tatra*, 7. Anlage zu Aussenstellen Gen.Insp.d.Pz.Tr. Org.Abt. I/II 1/45 gKdos. 1 January 1945.

14. An exception was *Bataillon Wimmer*, whose 180 men continued to fight as part of *Gruppe Thierfelder*.

15. Hafner Diary, 13–14.

16. *Das Kriegsende*, Reminiscences of *Stabsartz* Dr. Mlčzoch, 3.

17. Klausch, 265.

18. Hafner Diary, 15–16. The *Frontkämpferpäckchen* was a special ration supplementary item that was issued to front-line troops only. Consisting of a small cardboard box containing cigarettes, vitamin biscuits, Zwieback (a type of rusk), sugar, fruit bars, instant coffee, and chocolate, they were a valuable and highly sought-after item popular with troops.

19. Friessner, 193.

20. In addition to the armored battlegroups formed from the *3., 6.*, and *8. Panzer Divisionen* constituting *Gruppe Pape*, Breith's *III. Pz.Korps* also controlled the *1.* and *23. Pz.Divn.*

21. Peter Gosztony, *Endkampf an der Donau 1944/45* (Vienna: Verlag Fritz Molden, 1969), 97–98, and Ungváry, 35–36. This figure (235) does not include 165 armored fighting vehicles that were non-operational.

22. Ziemke, 383–84.

23. *Ibid.*, 384–385.

24. The Maria Valeria Bridge was not rebuilt until 11 October 2001 in a joint effort by the governments of Hungary and Slovakia.

25. Hafner Diary, 16.

26. Ibid, 16–17.

27. *6. Armee/A.Gr. Fretter-Pico* Situation Map dated 23 December 1944, and Fernschreiben, *A.Gr. Fretter-Pico*, Ia/Id Nr. 6628/44 dated 23 December 1944 (CAMO 500-12472-408-0045).

28. When writing his memoirs after the war, Friessner noted that he believed both he and Fretter-Pico were relieved of command "Because they needed a scapegoat." Friessner's calls to Guderian and his chief of staff that day to inquire about the reasoning behind his dismissal were finally explained as a "spontaneous decision on the part of the Führer" in Perry Pierik's *Hungary 1944–1945: The Forgotten Tragedy* (Nieuwegein: Aspekt Publishing, 1996), 116.

29 Ziemke, 385–86.

30. The details were spelled out in an order from Hitler dated 1 December 1944, *Führerbefehl zur Verteidigung von Budapest*, sent through the headquarters of *H.Gr. Süd* under Friessner's signature. The order cited *Führerbefehl* Nr. 11 dated 8 March 1944, *Kommandanten der festen Plätze und Kampfkommandanten*.

31. This *Panzerkorps, Ogruf.* Otto Gille's *IV. SS-Pz.Korps*, would begin arriving during the last week of December and would start its relief attack, dubbed Operation *Konrad*, on 1 January. For more information, refer to Vol. 2 of the author's trilogy *From the Realm of the Dying Sun* from Casemate Publishing.

32. Lexikon der Wehrmacht, History of *Pionier-Landungs-Bataillon 771*, found at https://www. lexikon-der-wehrmacht.de/Gliederungen/PionierLandungsBataillone/PiLBatl771.htm, accessed 10 January 2023.

33. War Diary, IX Guards Mechanized Corps covering the period from 16–31 December 1944, 27.
34. *6. Armee/A.Gr. Balck, Ia KTB*, Tagesmeldung *LVII. Pz.K.*, dated 8.10pm 27 December 1944 (CAMO 500-12472-382-0419).

Chapter 13

1. Part of the reason for this lack of source material is that the operational records and war diaries of the *IV. Pz.Korps, 18. SS-Pz.Gren.Div., 24. Pz.Div.*, and Dirlewanger Brigade itself are missing, either destroyed at the war's end or still awaiting discovery in the Russian Military Archives. While the records of the *6. Armee* are extant, the fact that the brigade was subordinated to a different field army, whose own records are lacking, is a major contributing factor to this lack of knowledge. What is known about this period is briefly summarized in the daily war diary of *H.Gr. Süd*, particularly in the section dedicated to the daily events and activities of the *8. Armee*.
2. *H.Gr. Süd, 1a KTB*, Wochenmeldung, Stand von 23 December 1944, 3.
3. *H.Gr. Süd, Ia KTB*, Tagesmeldung for 22 December, 22.
4. Note: this area reverted to Czechoslovak (now Slovak) control after Treaty of Peace in 1947 that restored the boundaries to their prewar status.
5. Arne Mann and Zusza Kumanova, *Ma bisteren! (Do not forget!): The Genocide of Slavic Roma* (Accessed 6 January 2023 at https://www.romasintigenocide.eu/media/neutral/docs/ma-bisteren), 5, 8.
6. Note: The *18. SS-Pz.Gren.Div. Horst Wessel*, in reality only a *Kampfgruppe*, continued its attachment to the *24. Pz.Div.* for another week.
7. Michaelis Dirlewanger Memoir, 75.
8. *H.Gr. Süd, 1a KTB* Fernschreiben Nr. 14431/44 geheim, dated 1.30pm 26 December 1944.
9. Der Volksbund Deutsche Kriegsgräberfürsorge e. V. (German War Graves Commission), Grave search for Siegfried Polack, accessed 7 January 1944 at https://www.volksbund.de/en/erinnern-gedenken/gravesearch-online/detail/d47e322ea7fd390785359665011a9fcc.
10. *H.Gr. Süd, 1a KTB* Fernschreiben Nr. 14524/44 geheim, dated 8.45pm 28 December 1944; *Ogruf.* Höfle, the German Commander in Slovakia, had also issued his own similarly worded message on 27 December 1944.
11. Hermann Balck, *Order in Chaos*, 405, 421–22, and Fernschreiben, *Ia KTB, 6. Armee/A.Gr. Balck* to *H.Gr. Süd*, Betr.: *SS-Brigade Dirlewanger*, dated 31 December 1944.
12. *6. Armee/A.Gr. Balck, 1a KTB* Fernschreiben dated 3.05am 27 December 1944, and Fernschreiben Ia Nr. 6668/44 geheim, dated 27 December 1944.
13. *H.Gr. Süd, Ia KTB* entry dated 29 December 1944, 17.
14. *Ibid.*, 19.
15. *6. Armee/A.Gr. Balck, Ia KTB* Fernschreiben von Franz Falter, *Bataillon-Kommandeur an A.Gr. Balck* durch Fernschreibestelle Peter, dated 1pm 3 January 1945.
16. *H.Gr. Süd, Ia KTB* Wochenmeldung as of 30 December 1944, 3.
17. *H.Gr. Süd, Ia KTB* Tagesmeldung dated 3 January 1945, 6.
18. *Deutscher Befehlshaber in der Slowakei, Ia KTB*, Abendmeldung for 5 January 1945, dated 6 January 1945.
19. *Deutscher Roter Kreuz (DRK) Suchdienst*, Investigation concerning fate of Wilhelm Stegmann, 29 August 1975, and Dirlewanger Brigade File, BA-MA Nachlass Wolfgang Vopersal Records Grouping N756-204a, image P5010871.
20. Confirmed by visiting the *DRK Suchdienst* website search tool, accessed 5 January 2021, and the German War Graves Association website, accessed 22 March 2022.
21. *SS-FHA Abt. II Org.Abt. Ia/II*, Betr: Neugliederung *SS-Sturm-Brigade Dirlewanger*, Berlin-Wilmersdorf, 19 December 1944.

22. SS-FHA, Abt. II Org.Abt. Ia/II, Tagebuch Nr. 4897/44 g.Kdos., Betr.: Neugliederung SS-Sturm-Brigade Dirlewanger, dated 19 December 1944, seven pages. This document included a detailed list of which KStNs were authorized in order for it to meet the target goal end-strength or Sollstärke.

23. No dedicated Panzerjäger company was ever authorized; however, when it was expanded into a division in March 1945, a German Army antitank battalion was intended to be assigned but there is no evidence that it arrived before the war ended.

24. SS-Sturm-Brigade Dirlewanger, KTB, schematischer Kriegsgliederung, dated 3 January 1945, 1.

25. Ibid., 2.

26. Letter, RF-SS Heinrich Himmler to Ogruf. Hermann Höfle, Berlin, 30 December 1944, 1.

27. Ibid., 2.

28. Vilém Prečan, Sworn Statement Protocol, written with Hermann Höfle at the National Court in Bratislava, describing Höfle's activities in Slovakia, 1 August 1946, from Slovenské Narodné Povstanie: Dokumenty (The Slovak National Uprising: A Documentation) (Bratislava: Vydavateľtvo Politikej Literatúry, 1965), 1098.

29. Letter, Ogruf. Hermann Höfle to RF-SS Heinrich Himmler, Pressburg, 6 January 1945, 1.

30. Ibid., 2–3.

31. Ibid., 3–4.

32. Ibid., 4.

33. Ibid., 5.

34. Letter, RF-SS Heinrich Himmler to Ogruf. Hermann Höfle, Feld-Kommandostelle, Persönlicher Stab RF-SS Schreibgutverwaltung, 14 January 1945, 1–2.

35. Ibid., 3–4.

36. Michaelis Dirlewanger Memoir, 76.

37. Ibid., 76–77.

Chapter 14

1. MacLean, The Cruel Hunters, 215.

2. Ibid., 216.

3. Blitzsendung, SS-Führungshauptamt Org.Abt. am H.Gr Mitte, OKH Gen.St. Org./Op. Abt. III, Nr. 2645/45 geheim, dated 11.00pm 14 February 1945, and SS-FHA Amt II Org.Abt. Ia/II, Tagebuch Nr. 1283/45 g.Kdos, Betr.: Zusammenfassung SS-Sturmbrigade Dirlewanger und zugeteilte Heeresteile zur 36. Waffen-Gren.Div. d. SS, dated 20 February 1945.

4. Evidence indicates that Pio.Brig. 687, or at least a portion of it, was integrated into the division, as born out by several entries in a Soldbuch (Paybook) of former Ltn. Kurt Damisch, a soldier who was awarded the Iron Cross, Second Class by Schmedes on 10 March 1945.

5. Klausch, 302, and Roland Pfeiffer, "Der 20. Kriegs-Junker-Lehrgang Braunschweig bis 15.06.1945," unpublished 32-page manuscript, 31 July 2017. Also see Blitzsendung dated 14 February 1945 above (note 3) which directed the release of these officer cadets from the Hermann Göring Division.

6. MacLean, 221.

7. Landwehr in Siegrunen, Volume 57, 29, and MacLean, 221.

8. Landwehr, Siegrunen, Volume 42,13.

9. MacLean, 222–23.

10. Ingrao, 170–71. Ingrao (173) estimates that between the time the brigade arrived in Guben on 12 February and the surrender of the Dirlewanger Division on 29 April 1945, approximately 5,300 of its members were either killed or captured by the Red Army. The remainder either escaped captivity or were taken prisoner by the Western Allies.

11. Dmitry Zhukov and Ivan Kovtun, *Partisan Hunters: The Dirlewanger Brigade* (Moscow: Veche Publishing, 2018), 409–10.
12. Email from Vladimír Krajčovič, dated 29 March 2023.
13. Bayerisches Landeskriminalamt, IIIa/SK Tagebuch Nr. 489/62. Vernehmungsniederschrift (Witness Testimony) der *Oberst a.D.* Harald Momm, 28 May 1962 (five pages).
14. Death Certificate for Herbert Meyer, Town of Eltville am Rhein, West Germany, dated 19 November 1956.
15. Harald Momm, *Pferde, Reiter und Trophäen* (Munich: Copress-Verlag, 1957), 207–08.
16. Both Scherner and von Uckermann's dates of death and grave locations are documented by the German War Graves Commission.
17. Klausch, 314. Another source was found on the website War Thunder Online, an individual contributor who goes by the screen name KleineME 109. Apparently, he had a close relative who was a member of the brigade, who also supports this version. See article "Odyssey of the Gruppe Weisse" (accessed 18 January 2022 at https://live.warthunder.com/post/693225/en/).
18. Soraya Kuklińska, *Oskar Dirlewanger: SS-Sonderkommando "Dirlewanger"* (Warsaw: Instytut Pamięci Narodowej, 2021), 451.
19. Helge Lehmann, "The CIA's Gehlen Organization as a Refuge for Hitler's Secret Police," 3, from *Die Todesnacht in Stammheim – Eine Untersuchung.* The Gehlen group was controlled completely by the U.S. Army from 1945 until 1948. It was then taken over and controlled directly by the Central Intelligence Agency until 1955/56, when the group was taken over by the Federal Government of Germany and renamed the *Bundesnachrichtendienst* (BND) or State Intelligence Service. Whether the CIC, CIA, or Gehlen knew of Weisse's sordid past is unknown, but it would be rather surprising if they did not. Accessed 18 January 2023 at http://www.tbrnews.org/Archives/a072.htm. See also Heinz Duthel, *Global Secret and Intelligence Services: Hidden Systems that Deliver Unforgettable Customer Service* (Norderstedt, Germany: Books on Demand, 2014), 350.
20. Mark Yerger, *Waffen-SS Commanders: The Army, Corps, and Divisional Leaders of Legend*, Vol. 2 (Atglen, PA: Schiffer Military History, 1999), 196, 199; and Schmedes's *SS* Officer File from John Moore's *Führerliste.*
21. *SS* Officer file for Hermann Höfle provided by Mr. Michael Miller, 30 December 2021, and Venohr, 282–83.
22. Gerhard Reimpel, "Gottlob Berger, Ein Schwabengeneral der Tat," in *Die SS: Elite under dem Totenkopf: 30 Lebensläufe* by Smelser and Syring (Munich: Ferdinand Schoningh, 2000), 45–57.
23. Hubert Kuberski has written an extensively researched monograph about the death of Dirlewanger and the identity and motivations of the perpetrators. For anyone interested in exploring this subject in greater detail, the author recommends "The Finale of a War Criminal's Existence: Mysteries Surrounding Oskar Dirlewanger's Death," published in Vol. 54 No. 4 of *Studia z Dziejów Rosji i Europy Środkowo-Wschodniej* (Studies in the History of Russia and Central and Eastern Europe), 3 January 2020, https://orcid.org/0000-0003-0450-2537, accessed 21 December 2020.
24. MacLean, 249–50.
25. *Ibid.*, 252–54.

Chapter 15

1. Before the war had ended, Department B of the *OKH Chef der Heeresarchiv* (Chief of Army Archives) had officially proposed five chronological phases of the Hungarian campaign, designations which were confirmed by the modern-day Bundesarchiv-Militärarchiv. Within this rubric, the fighting described within this book falls within two periods encompassing operations

conducted between October 1944 and March 1945: "Battles between the Theiss and Donau Rivers" (29 October to 18 December 1944) and "Battles between Lake Balaton and the Danube" (19 December 1944 to 5 March 1945). Tessin, Volume 3, 7–8.

2. The number 500 comes from Klausch, based on interviews he conducted with a number of survivors of the *II.* and *III. Btl./SS-St.Rgt. 2* who deserted between 12 and 30 December 1944. He further estimated that of the original 770 men, approximately 200 were either killed or wounded, leaving only 70–80 men who elected to remain with their units, either due to lack of opportunity or a change of heart (Klausch, 263).

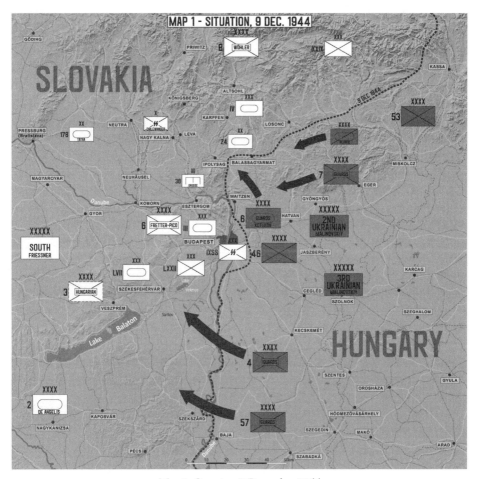

Map 1: Situation 9 December 1944

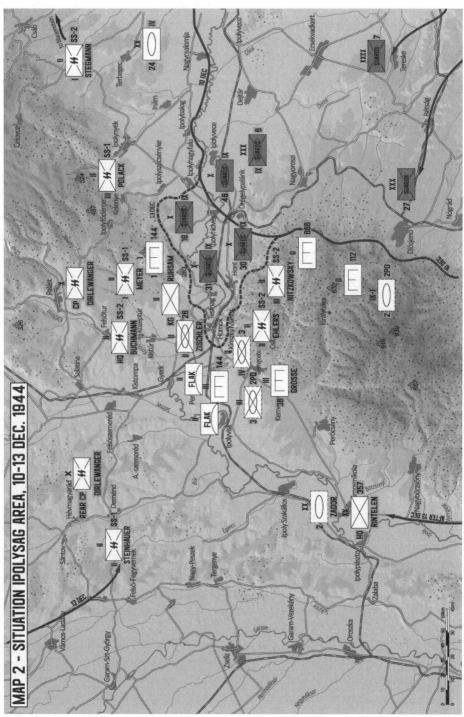

Map 2: Situation Ipolysag Area 10–13 December 1944

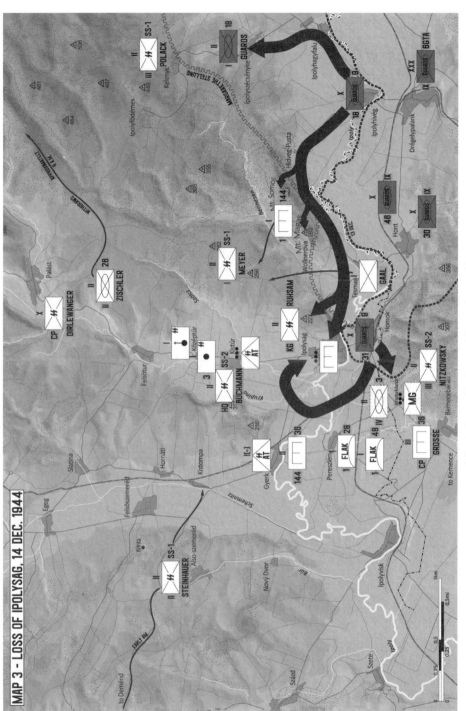

Map 3: Loss of Ipolysag 14 December 1944

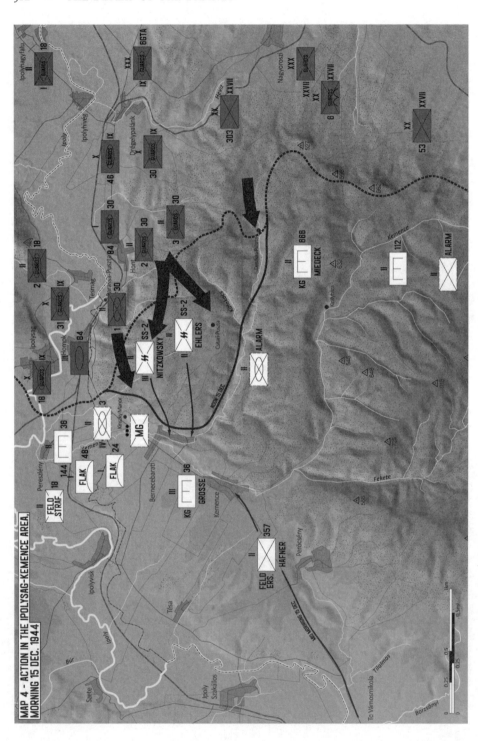

Map 4: Action in the Ipolysag-Kémence area 15 December 1944

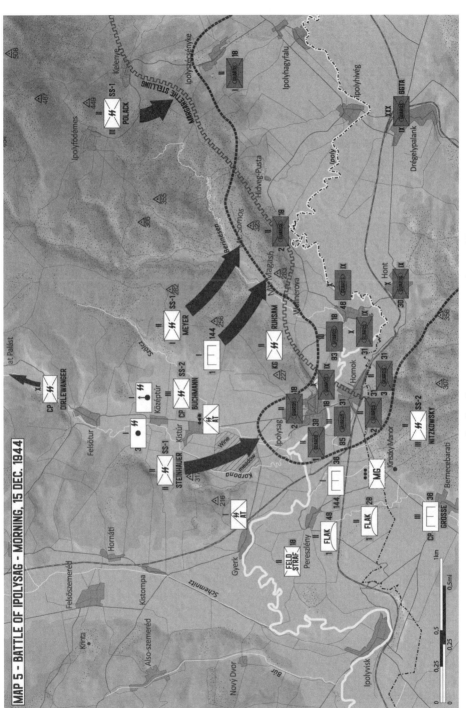

Map 5: Battle of Ipolysag, morning 15 December 1944

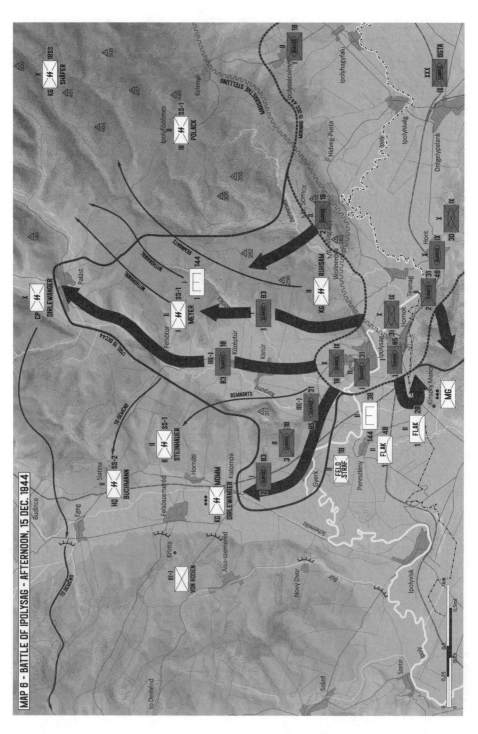

Map 6: Battle of Ipolysag, afternoon 15 December 1944

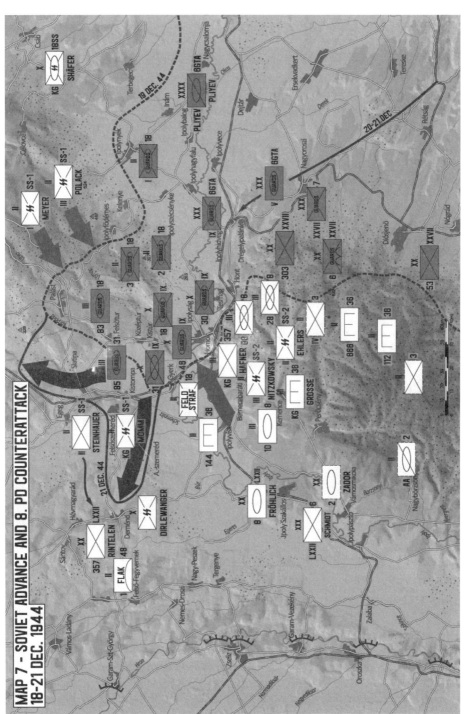

Map 7: Soviet Advance and 8 *Pz. Div.* Counterattack 18–21 December 1944

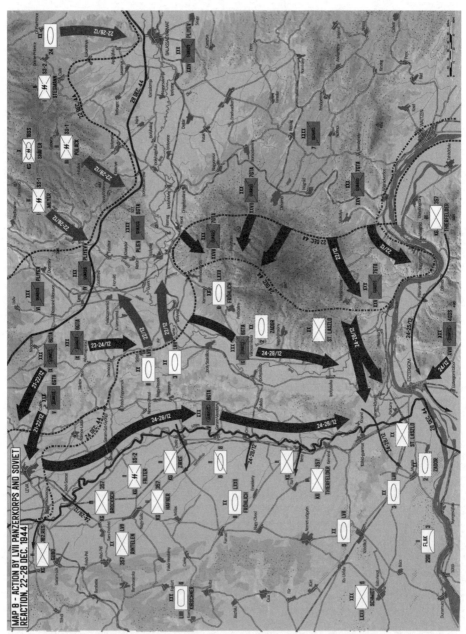

Map 8: Action by *LVII. Panzerkorps and Soviet Reactions, 22–28 December 1944*

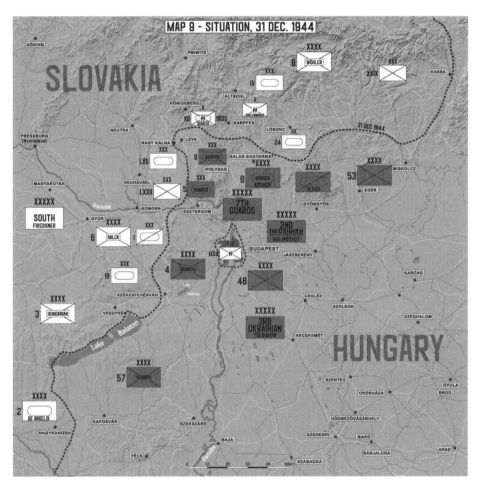

Map 9: Situation 31 December 1944

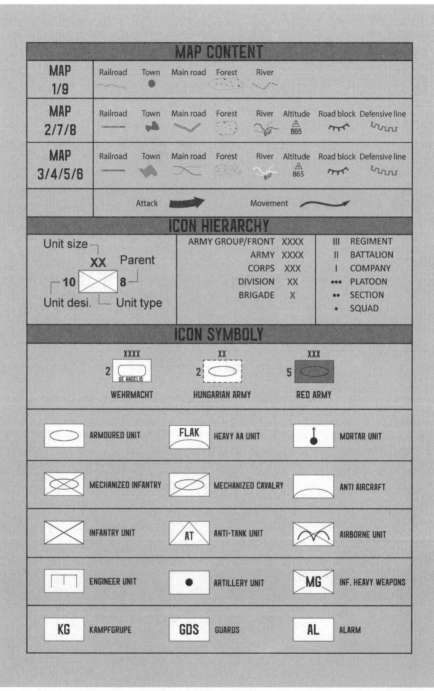

APPENDIX A

Command and Staff

2. SS-Sturmbrigade Dirlewanger

Late October – late December 1944

Kommandeur (commander): *SS-Oberführer* Dr. Oskar Dirlewanger

> *Ia* (operations officer): *SS-Stubaf.* Kurt Weisse
> *O1* (assistant operations officer): *SS-Ostuf.* Helmut Lewandowski
> *Ib* (supply officer): *SS-Hstuf.* Fritz Missmahl; replaced by *SS-Hstuf.* Hans
> Bünger
> *Ic* (intelligence officer): unknown
> *IIa Adjutant* (personnel officer): *SS-Ostuf.* Franz Bauser; replaced by *SS-Hstuf.*
> Julian Scherner
> *III* (staff judge advocate): *SS-Hstuf.* Dr. Bruno Wille (temporary assignment)
> *IVa* (*Stabsintendant*/supply officer): *SS-Ostuf.* Otto Gast, *SS-Ostuf.* Hans
> Schäftlmeier
> *IVb* (chief medical officer): *Stabsarzt* Dr. Heinz Hartlieb
> *IVc* (veterinarian): *SS-Ostuf.* Dr. Friedrich Turek

SS-St.Rgt. 1: command filled temporarily by *SS-Stubaf.* Josef Steinhauer, then
Kurt Weisse (before battle of Ipolysag); after Ipolysag, filled by *SS-Ostubaf.* Erich
Buchmann from *SS-St.Rgt. 2*.
> *I.   Btl*: *SS-Ostuf.* Herbert Meyer
> *II. Btl*: *Maj.d.Schu.Po.* Josef Steinhauer
> *III. Btl*: *SS-Ustuf.* Siegfried Pollack

SS-St.Rgt. 2: *SS-Ostubaf.* Erich Buchmann, then *SS-Stubaf.* Ewald Ehlers
> *I.   Btl*: *SS-Ostuf.* Wilhelm Stegmann
> *II. Btl*: *SS-Stubaf.* Ewald Ehlers, followed by temporary assignment of
> *Maj.d.Schu.Po.* Franz Falter, then *SS-Hstuf.* Harald Momm
> *III. Btl*: *Oberltn.* (former *Luftwaffe Oberstltn.*) Nitzkowski

Gemischte/Halb-Btl: *SS-Hstuf.* Ewald Ehlers, then *SS-Hstuf.* Walter Ehlers

SS-Artillerie-Abteilung Dirlewanger: *SS-Hstuf.* Willy Schneier (until November 1944); replaced by *SS-Hstuf.* Fritz Missmahl
1. *Batterie* (6 × 10.5cm *l.Inf.H.*):
2. *Bttr.* (6 × 10.5cm *l.Inf.H.*):
3. *Bttr.* (6 × 7.62cm *I.G. Pak 36r*):

SS-schwere Mörser (Heavy Mortar)-*Kompanie:* *SS-Ostuf.* Otto Rühs
SS-Nachrichten (Signal)-*Kompanie:* *SS-Ustuf.* Ludwig Bahrke
SS-Aufklärungs (Reconnaissance)-*Kompanie* (still forming): *SS-St.OJ* Paul Löffler
SS-Sanitäts (Medical)-*Kompanie:* *SS-Ostuf.* Werner Peiler
SS-Verwaltungs (Administrative/logistics)-*Kompanie:* *SS-Ustuf.* Hans Bünger
SS-Ersatz (Replacement)-*Kompanie:* *SS-Ostuf.* Paul Zimmermann
SS-Feldpost (Post office): *SS-Ostuf.* Walter Wiedemann

German and Hungarian Order of Battle

9–31 December 1944

6. Armee (AOK 6)/Armeegruppe Fretter-Pico: *Gen.d.Art.* Maximilian Fretter-Pico

LXXII. Armeekorps (after 16 December): *Gen.Lt.* August Schmidt
  ARKO 472
  Korps-Nachrichten Abteilung 472

> *Divisions-Gruppe Rintelen* (Staff of *357. Inf.Div.*): *Gen.Maj.* Josef Rintelen
>   *Feldersatz-Bataillon 357* (*Kampfgruppe Hafner*)
>   *Kampfgruppe Thierfelder*
>   *Kampfgruppe Wimmer*
>   *II. Abt./Art.Rgt. 357*
>   *1. Kp./Pz.Jag.Abt. 357*
>   *1. Kp./Pio.Btl. 357*
>   *1./2./Alarmkompanie*

> *Magyar Királyi 2. Páncéloshadosztály* (2nd Royal Hungarian Armored Division):
> *Oberst* vitez Zádor Endre
>   *IV. Bataillon, Infanterie-Regiment 3 (mot.)*
>   *3. Panzer-Regiment*
>   *2. Aufklärungs-Abteilung*
>   *2. Panzer-Pionier-Kompanie*
>   *3. Panzer-Pionier-Kompanie*
>   *2. Artillerie-Bataillon*
>   *6. Artillerie-Bataillon*
>   *52. Flugzeugabwehr (Flak) Abteilung (mot.)*

> *2. SS-Sturmbrigade Dirlewanger*
>   *SS-Sturmregiment 1 (I.–III. Btl.)*
>   *SS-Sturmregiment 2 (I.–III. Btl.)*

Gemischte (Mixed) Bataillon
SS-Art.Abt. Dirlewanger (3. Batterie only)

Pionier-Regiment Stab 36 (Kampfgruppe Grosse)
    Heeres-Bau-Pionier-Bataillon 112
    Heeres-Bau-Pionier-Bataillon 144
    Heeres-Pionier-Bataillon 666 (Kampfgruppe Miedeck)
    Kampfgruppe Struchtenmayer
    Kampfgruppe Zirke
    Feld-Strafgefangen Abteilung 18
    Reserve-Infanterie-Bataillon (Ohrkrank) 284

8. Panzer-Division/Gruppe Fröhlich: Gen.Maj. Gottfried Fröhlich
    Pz.Gren.Rgt. 28
    Pz.Gren.Rgt. 98 (minus I. Btl.)
    II. Abt./Pz.Rgt. 10
    10. Schwadron/Pz.Rgt. 24
    Pz.Art.Rgt. 80 (-)
    Pz.Jäg.Abt. 43 (-)
    Pz.Aufkl.Abt. 8
    Pz.Pio.Btl. 8

Division Szent László: Gen.Maj. Zoltán Szügyi
    1. Fallschirm-Regiment
    2. Infanterie-Regiment
    3. Luftwaffen-Regiment
    Artillerie-Regiment (Art.Btle. 1, 6, 9, and 76)
    Pionier Btl. Szent László
    Aufkl.Abt. Szent László

    Machinegewehr-Bataillon Sachsen
    2./schwere-Art.Abt. 736
    Mörser-Batterie 8./959
    Heeres-Pionier-Bataillon 751
    Heeres-Pionier-Battalion 52
    Panzer-Pionier Kompanie Feldherrnhalle (K.Gr. Lehnert)

LVII. Panzer-Korps: Gen.d.Pz.Tr. Friedrich Kirchner, after 21 December
    3. Pz.Div. (Gen.Lt. Wilhelm Phillip)
    6. Pz.Div. (Oberst Friedrich-Wilhelm Jürgens)
    8. Pz. Div. (after 21 December)

Luftwaffe Units
   II. Abt./Flak-Rgt. 24
   I. Abt./Flak-Rgt. 48
   Leichte Flak-Abteilung 77 and *91*
   3. Bttr./Flak-Rgt. 181

8. Armee (AOK 8)/Armeegruppe Wöhler: *Gen.d.Inf.* Otto Wöhler; after 25 December, *Gen.d.Pz.Tr.* Hans Kreysing

   IV. Panzer-Korps Feldherrnhalle: *Gen.d.Pz.Tr.* Ullrich Kleeman
      24. Pz.Div. (*Gen.Maj.* Gustav von Nostitz-Wallwitz)
      K.Gr. 4. SS-Polizei-Pz.Gren.Div. Polizei (*SS-Staf.* Walter Harzer)
      K.Gr. 18. SS-Freiw.Pz.Gren.Div. Horst Wessel: (*SS-Oberf.* Wilhelm Trabandt)
      SS-Sturm-Regiment 1 Dirlewanger (after 19 December)

Deutscher Befehlshaber in der Slowakei: *SS-Obergruppenführer* Hans Höfle
      14. Waffen-Grenadier Division der Waffen-SS (Galizien Nr. 1)
      182. Reserve-Division
      Panzer Feldausbildungs-Division Tatra

Second Belorussian Front Order of Battle

9–31 December 1944

6th Guards Tank Army: Col.Gen. of Tank Troops Andrey Kravchenko

IX Guards Mechanized Corps (107 tanks): Lt.Gen. of Tank Troops Mikhail V. Volkov

18th Guards Mechanized Brigade (Col. Alexander M. Ovcharov)
83rd Guards Tank Regiment (Maj. Nemchenko)
1st – 3rd Motorized Rifle Battalions
30th Guards Mechanized Brigade (Col. Mikhail V. Shutov)
84th Guards Tank Regiment (Lt.Col. B. I. Radko)
1st – 3rd Motorized Rifle Battalions
31st Guards Mechanized Brigade (Col. Kuzma F. Seleznev)
85th Guards Tank Regiment (Lt.Col. N. P. Belov)
1st – 3rd Motorized Rifle Battalions
46th Guards Tank Brigade (Lt.Col. Nikolay M. Mikhno)
1st Tank Battalion
2nd Tank Battalion
3rd Tank Battalion
Motorized Submachine gun Battalion
389th Guards Self-Propelled Artillery Regiment (Su-85s, Su-100s)
697th Self-Propelled Artillery Regiment (Su-76Ms)
388th Antiaircraft Artillery Regiment
301st Antitank Artillery Regiment
458th Mortar Regiment
14th Guards Motorcycle Battalion
385th Rocket Propelled Mortar Battalion (Maj. Kukushkin)
31st Sapper Battalion
70th Engineer Battalion

V Guards Tank Corps (89 tanks): Lt.Gen. of Tank Troops Mikhail I. Savelev
    20th Guards Tank Brigade
    21st Guards Tank Brigade
    22nd Guards Tank Brigade
    6th Guards Motorized Rifle Brigade
    390th Guards Self-Propelled Artillery Regiment
    301st Guards Antiaircraft Artillery Regiment

IV Guards Mechanized Corps (from 7th Guards Army after 23 December): Col.Gen. Vladimir I. Zhdanov

    36th Guards Tank Brigade
    14th Guards Mechanized Brigade
    15th Guards Mechanized Brigade

XXIII Tank Corps (from 7th Guards Army): Lt.Gen. of Tank Troops Aleksei O. Akhmanov
    3rd Tank Brigade
    39th Tank Brigade
    135th Tank Brigade
    56th Motorized Rifle Brigade

XXV Guards Rifle Corps (attached from 7th Guards Army): Lt.Gen. Safiulin G. Bekinovich

    6th Guards Airborne Division
    53rd Rifle Division
    409th Rifle Division

XXVII Guards Rifle Corps (attached from 7th Guards Army): Lt.Gen. Gennadi P. Korotkov
    36th Guards Rifle Division
    141st Rifle Division
    227th Rifle Division
    303rd Rifle Division

Army Troops

    51st Guards Self-Propelled Artillery Brigade
    208th Self-Propelled Artillery Brigade
    202nd Light Artillery Brigade

364th Self-Propelled Artillery Regiment
22nd Motorized Engineering Brigade
49th Guards Heavy Tank Regiment (21 JS-II heavy tanks)
57th Mortar Regiment
4th Guards Motorcycle Regiment

Cavalry-Mechanized Group Pliyev (Later retitled 1st Guards Cavalry Mechanized Group): Lt.Gen. Issa A. Pliyev
IV Guards Cavalry Corps
VI Guards Cavalry Corps
XXVII Guards Rifle Corps

Table of Rank Equivalents

Wehrmacht-Heer	Waffen-SS	Abbreviation	U.S. Equivalent
Generalfeldmarschall	N/A	*G.F.M.*	General of the Army
Generaloberst	*SS-Obergruppenführer und Generaloberst der Waffen-SS*	*Gen.Obst./Obstgruf.*	General
General der Infantrie, Kavalerie, etc.	*SS-Obergruppenführer und General der Waffen-SS*	*Gen.d.Inf./Ogruf.*	Lieutenant General
Generalleutnant	*SS-Gruppenführer und Generalleutnant der Waffen-SS*	*Gen.Lt./Gruf.*	Major General
Generalmajor	*SS-Brigadeführer und Generalmajor der Waffen-SS*	*Gen.Maj./Brig.Fhr.*	Brigadier General
Oberst	*SS-Oberführer*	*Oberfhr.*	Senior Colonel
Oberst	*SS-Standartenführer*	*Oberst/*Staf.	Colonel
Oberstleutnant	*SS-Obersturmbannführer*	*Oberstltn./Ostubaf.*	Lieutenant Colonel
Major	*SS-Sturmbannführer*	*Maj./Stubaf.*	Major
Hauptmann or *Rittmeister*	*SS-Hauptsturmführer*	*Hptm./Hstuf.*	Captain
Oberleutnant	*SS-Obersturmführer*	*Oberltn./Ostuf.*	First Lieutenant
Leutnant	*SS-Untersturmführer*	*Ltn./Ustuf.*	Second Lieutenant
Stabsfeldwebel	*SS-Sturmscharführer*	*Stabs Fw./*none	Sergeant Major
Oberfeldwebel	*SS-Hauptscharführer*	*Ofw./Hscha.*	Master Sergeant

Feldwebel	*SS-Oberscharführer*	*Fw./Oscha.*	Sergeant First Class
Unteroffizier	*SS-Unterscharführer*	*Uffz./Uscha.*	Staff Sergeant
Obergefreiter	*SS-Rottenführer*	*Ogefr./Rttf.*	Corporal/ Specialist
Gefreiter	*SS-Sturmann*	*Gef./Strm.*	Private First Class
Obergrenadier, Oberkanonier, etc.	*SS-Obergrenadier*, etc.	none	Private Second Class
Grenadier, Kanonier, Funker, etc.	*SS-Grenadier*, etc.	none	Private

Glossary

Abteilung (Abt.): Literally, detachment. A German unit of company size or greater, though normally of battalion size. Traditionally used to designate artillery, armor, or reconnaissance battalions.

Allgemeine-SS: The General *SS*, a Nazi organization led by Heinrich Himmler that encompassed ordinary part-time members of General *SS* regiments (*SS-Standarten*) and full-time members (normally officers) of non-combat *SS* units and headquarters.

Armeegruppe (A. Gr.): German field army with attached allied or co-belligerent units; not to be confused with army group (*Heeresgruppe*).

Armeekorps: German Infantry Corps.

Armee-Oberkommando (AOK): Field Army Headquarters.

Asoziale (Azos): "Asocials" were German citizens designated by Third Reich courts as drifters, vagabonds, pimps, and others who refused to work, as opposed to being career criminals (the *BVer*). Deemed slackers and social leeches, they were considered poor soldier material.

Aufklärungsabteilung (Aufkl.Abt.): Reconnaissance Battalion.

Batterie (Bttr.): Artillery or antiaircraft battery, usually consisting of two sections with two or three guns each.

Berufsverbrecher (BVer): Career criminal. Usually a repeat or habitual offender with a record of multiple arrests and periods of incarceration. A number of these men volunteered for the *Dirlewanger Einheit*.

Bewährungs-Bataillon: Probationary unit formed from men culled from *Wehrmacht* prisons who had committed minor offenses, such as theft, drunk on duty, absent without leave, dereliction of duty, etc. Considered *Wehrwürdig* (worthy of bearing arms), they were transferred to these battalions in order to redeem themselves and have their military ranks and privileges restored afterwards. Numbered in the 500-series, these battalions were often assigned particularly difficult tasks such as anti-partisan operations or assault operations. Trained and equipped as light infantry battalions, they were provided the best officer and non-commissioned officer leadership available and often acquitted themselves well in battle. Not to be confused with *Straf* (Penal) units.

Bewährungs-Schütze: A soldier assigned to a probationary unit, such as the Dirlewanger Brigade. Commonly referred to in official correspondence or conversation as *B-Schütze*.

Chef des Stabes (*Chef*): Chief of Staff.

Einheit: Unit.

Einsatzgruppe: Action group or task force formed to prosecute Hitler's war of annihilation against the Jewish population in occupied territories. Operating under the overall control of the *SS-Sicherheitshauptamt*, *SS-Einsatzgruppen* were brigade-sized organizations that consisted of *SS*, *Si.Po.*, *Waffen-SS*, and *Wehrmacht* troops, as well as local collaborators.

Ersatzheer: The Replacement, or Home Army, responsible for training replacements and sustaining the forces of the Field Army (*Feldheer*) fighting on the various fronts.

Fallschirmjäger: German for paratrooper.

Feldersatz-Bataillon (*Feld-Ers.Btl.*): Field Replacement Battalion, established in each German infantry, armored, airborne, mountain, or light infantry division to provide a pool of trained replacement personnel for the unit's battalions. Also included a division's field training cadre, who ran its *Kampfschule* (combat school). Often used during *in extremis* situations as the commander's reserve force to carry out emergency missions, such as mounting counterattacks.

Feldgendarme: German military policeman, employed for law enforcement as well as local security and traffic regulation. Distinguished by the silver metal gorget they wore around their neck on a chain as a symbol of their authority, they were sarcastically nicknamed *Kettenhund* or chained dog by ordinary soldiers.

Feld-Lazarette: Field hospital, usually located 30–40 kilometers behind the front line.

Fliegerabwehrkanonone (*Flak*): Any kind of German antiaircraft gun.

Freiwillige: Volunteer. In the *Waffen-SS*, by 1944 this had become somewhat of an elastic term, since many of its ethnic German "volunteers" living in occupied or allied territories such as Ukraine, Poland, Romania, Yugoslavia, and Hungary were involuntarily conscripted into the organization.

Führer: Leader, or officer(s) holding leadership position(s). Often designates an officer serving in a leadership position in a temporary capacity. Also the formal title of Adolf Hitler.

Füsilier-Bataillon (*Füs.Btl.*): Infantry battalion allocated to infantry or grenadier divisions in the place of disbanded or reconfigured *Aufklärungs* (reconnaissance) battalions. Each infantry division had one of these type units, which were considered the elite of the division and often used as a division's reserve force.

Gefechtstand: Command post of a battalion, regiment, division, corps, etc. Usually inhabited by the commander and his *Führungsstab* (operations and intelligence staffs) and communications specialists with appropriate radio, field telephone, and/ or teletype equipment. If positioned far forward, often referred to as *Vorgeschobener Gefechtstand.*

Granatenwerfer: "Grenade thrower," more commonly referred to as a mortar, firing a round ranging in size from 50mm to 120mm.

Hauptkampflinie (*HKL*): Main defense line, designating the boundary between friendly and enemy units.

Hauptquartier: Headquarters of a division, corps, field army, or army group, positioned anywhere between 20 and 200 kilometers behind the *HKL*, depending on the level of command. Normally, the logistics, administrative, and medical staffs were located therein, as opposed to the *Gefechtstand*, which was positioned forward near the *HKL*. Ensuring the day-to-day functioning of the *Hauptquartier* was the responsibility of the division, corps, army, or army group chief of staff.

Heer: German Army.

Heeresgruppe (*H.Gr.*): Army Group.

Hilfswilliger (*Hiwi*): "Volunteer helpers," Soviet prisoners of war who volunteered to serve in the *Wehrmacht* or *Waffen-SS* as auxiliaries employed in logistical or administrative capacities. In some instances, they were armed and fought alongside German forces.

Höherer SS- und Polizei-Führer (*HSSPF*): Senior *SS* and Police leader in a *Wehrkreis* in Germany or occupied territory; usually held the rank of *SS-Obergruppenführer* or *SS-Gruppenführer.*

Infanterie-Division (*Inf.Div.*, or *I.D.*): German Army infantry division.

Jagdpanzer (*Jgd.Pz.*): Tank destroyer, usually consisting of a large-caliber antitank gun mounted on a tank chassis. These lightly-armored turretless vehicles were used to defend against enemy tanks.

Kampfgruppe (*K.Gr.*): A temporary mission-focused organization, which may range in size from a company to a division plus attached troops, normally identified by its commander's name.

Kampfraum: Combat area or combat zone.

Kampfstärke: Front-line combat power, expressed in terms of the number of fighting troops in battalions (infantry, reconnaissance, or pioneers) manning front-line positions or available for combat. In practice, this term did not include troops manning heavy weapons, such as antitank guns, light Flak, or infantry howitzers.

Kompanie (*Kp.*): Company-sized unit, usually consisting of 100–200 men, commanded by a *Hauptmann* or *Hauptsturmführer.*

Kompaniechef: Officially selected commander of a company-sized infantry unit; in field artillery, the title of a battery commander was *Batteriechef.*

Kompanieführer: Acting commander of a company-sized unit who has not yet been officially selected as a *Kompaniechef.*

Kommandeur: Officially selected commander of battalion-size units and above.

Konzentrationslager (KL): Concentration Camp (also referred to as *KZ*).

Kraftfahrzeug (Kfz.): Any German motor vehicle, except armor.

Kriegsmarine: German Navy.

Kriegsstärkenachweisung (KStN.): Wartime strength establishment of a unit, similar to a U.S. Army Table of Organization and Equipment (TO&E), that lists the number of personnel authorized for that unit by grade and position and the number of weapons, vehicles, and other items of equipment necessary for the unit's accomplishment of its primary mission.

Kriegstageguch (KTB): Daily war diary or combat journal, normally maintained at the battalion level and above by a qualified staff officer or NCO, that records the significant events of the day. At division level and above, each staff element maintained its own dedicated *KTB*, including the *Ia* (Operations), *Ib* (Logistics), and *Ic* (Intelligence).

Kriminalpolizei (KriPo): Branch of security police in charge of the suppression of crime.

Kübelwagen: Bucket car, slang term for Volkswagen equivalent of U.S. Jeep.

Landeschützen-Bataillon (Ldsch.Btl.): German local defense battalion, formed from older reservists. Often used for local security duties in the occupied regions.

Luftflotte: Air Fleet, *Luftwaffe* administrative headquarters similar in function to an army headquarters, or *Armee-Oberkommando (AOK)*.

Luftwaffe: German Air Force.

Maschinepistole (M.Pi.): German submachine gun (usually firing 9mm cartridges) designed for use by assault troops.

Matrose: German for sailor or member of the *Kriegsmarine.*

Nebelwerfer: "Smoke Launcher" or mobile rocket launcher firing high-explosive projectiles ranging in in size from 150mm to 320mm.

Ordnungspolizei (OrPo): Uniformed police in occupied countries; usually served under the *HSSPF* in occupied territories and in Germany after 1943.

Pakfront: German term for an integrated antitank barrier consisting of several antitank companies or battalions comprised of dozens of mutually supporting heavy antitank guns. Initially a Soviet tactic, the Germans imitated it as best they could but lacked sufficient guns to practice it except for isolated instances. German tanks crews feared these more than enemy tanks.

Panzerabwehrkanone (Pak): Antitank gun.

Panzerfaust: A recoilless antitank grenade launcher designed to be used against armor at ranges from 25–100 meters. It consisted of a steel launching tube, which contained a percussion-fired propellant charge, and a hollow-charge antitank grenade mounted at the end. Could penetrate up to 6 inches of rolled steel plate.

Panzergrenadier (*Pz. Gren.*): Armored or mechanized infantryman.

Panzergruppe: Armored Group, could range in size from battalion to field army, but within a *panzer* division, they were usually composed of one tank battalion (usually the one equipped with *Pz. V* Panthers), the division's sole armored *Panzergrenadier* battalion, and the division's sole self-propelled artillery battalion, along with supporting logistical elements.

Panzerjäger (*Pz. Jäg.*): Tank hunter or antitank troops, trained to operate *Panzerabwehrkanonen*.

Panzerkampfwagen (*Pz. Kfw.*): Armored fighting vehicle (AFV), or tank, simply called "*panzer*" by the Germans.

Panzerkorps (*Pz. Korps*): German tank corps headquarters, capable of controlling two to four tank, armored infantry, or infantry divisions as well as various corps troops, such as artillery, engineer, antiaircraft, and antitank battalions or regiments.

Pionier: Engineer, including construction troops, combat engineers, road maintenance troops, etc.

Polizei-Bataillon: Main mobile units of the uniformed police in occupied territories from 1939 that became part of *Polizei-Regimenter* after 1942.

Raketenpanzerbüchse: A rocket-propelled antitank launcher, better known as the *Panzerschreck* ("Tank Terror"). Its 8.8cm rocket with a range of approximately 100 meters was extremely effective against all types of Allied armor.

Ritterkreuz: Knight's Cross of the Iron Cross. The *Ritterkreuz* was the highest class of the Iron Cross and the most prized of the German World War II military decorations. There were three grades of the award: *Ritterkreuz*, *Ritterkreuz mit Eichenlaub* (with Oak Leaves), and *Ritterkreuz mit Eichenlaub und Schwerten* (with Oak Leaves and Swords).

RONA: *Russkaya Osvoboditelnaya Narodnaya Armiya*, or Russian National Liberation Army, also known as the *Waffen-Sturm-Brigade der SS RONA*, was created by former Soviet citizen Bronislav Kaminski and fought under *SS* control as an anti-partisan unit.

Schützenpanzerwagen (*SPW*): Armored Personnel Carrier, typically of the type *Sd.Kfz. 250* and *251*.

Schutzpolizei (*Schu.Po.*): Protection police force of the Order Police with state or municipal status serving in police precincts, traffic control, or public security in mobile units.

Schwere Panzerabteilung: Heavy tank battalion, usually equipped with *Pz.Kfw. VI* Tiger tanks.

Schwimmwagen: Amphibious version of the Volkswagen.

Sicherheitsdienst (SD): Security Service of the *SS*; charged with combating espionage.

Sicherheitspolizei (Si.Po.): Security Police, usually worked in conjunction with the *SD.*

Sondereinheit: Special Unit, often used as an early title of Dirlewanger's command.

Sonderkommando: Special Command, another early title of Dirlewanger's unit.

Sonderregiment: Special Regiment, the official title of Dirlewanger's unit when it was upgraded to regimental status in the spring of 1944.

Sonderkraftfahrzeuge (Sd.Kfz.): Special purpose vehicle, such as halftracks, prime movers, or recovery vehicles.

SS-Führungshauptamt (SS-FHA): SS Operations Main Office, responsible for arming, educating, equipping, and training the *Waffen-SS.* It was administered throughout the war by *SS-Obergruppenführer* Hans Jüttner.

SS-Hauptamt (SS-HA): SS Main Office, responsible for administration of all *SS* sub-organizations, including recruiting and retention of personnel for the *Waffen-SS.* It was administered from 1943 on by Himmler's deputy, *SS-Obergruppenführer* Gottlob Berger.

Strafbataillon: Punishment or penal battalion, usually numbered in the 999-series, that consisted of men who had been charged with non-capital offenses and been sent to one of these units to serve out their term of punishment, usually near the front lines and in conditions that were considered extremely hazardous. Survivors were usually restored to their previous ranks or posted to a *Bewährungsbataillon* (see above) for further rehabilitation.

Straffällige: Convict or prison inmate.

Strafvollzugslager: Himmler's purpose-built wartime institutions for the detention and rehabilitation of *Waffen-SS* and *Polizei* criminals, such as the ones at Danzig-Matzkau or Chlum near Prague. In addition to these two disciplinary units, there was also an *SS Arbeits-*(Labor) *Bataillon* in Bobruisk. Discipline in these facilities was often very strict, making the life of a *B-Schütze* in the Dirlewanger unit appear favorable in comparison, thus inducing voluntary transfers.

Sturmabteilungen (SA): The Brown Shirts, or paramilitary arm of the Nazi Party, which propelled Hitler to power. Its influence was severely reduced when it attempted to compete with the *SS* after the so-called Night of the Long Knives, when its top leaders were summarily executed on Hitler's orders.

Sturmbrigade: Assault brigade, normally considered an elite force equipped with a larger than usual amount of automatic and heavy weapons. Although designated as a *Sturmbrigade,* the Dirlewanger Brigade was not equipped nor trained as such.

Sturmgeschütz (*StuG*): Armored assault gun specifically built to provide close-in infantry support using its 7.5cm or 10.5cm howitzer. Normally built on a *Pz.Kfw. III* or *IV* chassis, they were at a disadvantage when fighting tanks in open terrain due to their lack of a rotating turret, but were formidable when employed in built-up areas or as a tank destroyer firing from hidden positions.

Tankist: Russian military slang for tank crewmen or *Tankodesantniki*, meaning infantrymen who rode into battle holding on to special rails welded to a tank's turrets. Usually suffered heavy casualties in battle.

Tross: The "trains" where a unit's logistical and administrative units were located, from company to regimental level. In infantry units, the vehicles in the *Tross* usually consisted of horse-drawn supply wagons. Occasionally, a few trucks also complemented the *Tross* that were often used to haul ammunition supplies.

Unterführer: Non-commissioned officers (NCOs), holding the rank beginning with *Unteroffizier* or *SS-Unterscharführer* and ranging up to the ranks of *Hauptfeldwebel* or *SS-Hauptscharführer*. Frequently filled leadership positions at the platoon and company level when officers were not available.

Waffen-SS: Combat units of the *SS*.

Wehrkreis: Defense District, geographically designated areas in Germany and occupied areas of Europe that were designed to serve as the *Ersatzheer*'s (Home Army) base for the generation and constitution of forces for the *Feldheer* (Field Army), as well as to serve as the headquarters for controlling the various local security forces and POW camps in the zone of the interior.

Wehrmacht: The German Armed Forces, which included the *Heer*, *Luftwaffe*, and *Kriegsmarine*. Technically, the *Waffen-SS* was not a part of the *Wehrmacht*.

Wehrmachtbefehlshaber: Commander of the German Armed Forces in a geographic area; technically, had control over all three branches of the *Wehrmacht* but not the *Waffen-SS*. Occasionally, the role of *Befehlshaber* was combined with that of the *HSSPF* for an occupied area or country. In which case, he was usually titled "*Deutscher Befehlshaber in der* _____" (name of country or occupied area).

Wilddieb/Wilderer: Poacher, or someone who hunts wild game without a license or permission to hunt. A *Wildschütze* was a poacher who hunted wild game with a rifle.

Zug: Train or infantry/engineer/*Füsilier* platoon usually consisting of 25–50 men and commanded by a lieutenant or senior NCO.

Bibliography

Publications and Articles

Althoetmar, Kai. *Feldpost: 23. Dezember 1944. Der Kampf um Ungarn. Eine Spurensuche*, 8th Edition. Edition Zeitpunkte, ePubli, 9 November 2018.

Auerbach, Hellmuth. "Die Einheit Dirlewanger." In *Vierteljahrshefte für Zeitgeschichte*, 10, 3. 250–65. Munich: Institut für Zeitgeschichte, 1962.

Auerbach, Hellmuth. *Miscellanea, Festschrift für Helmut Krausnick zum 75. Geburtstag* "Konzentrationslagerhäftlinge im Fronteinsatz." Bundesarchiv RS 3-36 R23. Stuttgart: Deutsche Verlags-Anstalt Stuttgart, 1980.

Balck, Hermann. *Order in Chaos: The Memoirs of General of Panzer Troops Hermann Balck.* Lexington, KY: University Press of Kentucky, 2015.

Berthold, Will. *Death's Head Brigade.* London: Sphere Books Ltd, 1980. Originally published in 1960 as *Brigade Dirlewanger* by Lingen Verlag, Cologne.

Blood, Philip W. *Hitler's Bandit Hunters: The SS and the Nazi Occupation of Europe.* Dulles, Virginia: Potomac Books, Inc., 2006.

Center for Land Warfare, U.S. Army War College. *1986 Art of War Symposium.* "From the Vistula to the Oder: Soviet Offensive Operations—October 1944 – March 1945, A Transcript of Proceedings." Carlisle, PA: U.S. Army War College, 1986.

Connor, Albert Z. and Robert G. Poirier. *The Red Army Order of Battle in the Great Patriotic War.* Novato, CA: Presidio Press, 1985.

Cooper, Helene. "Heavy Losses Leave Russia Short of Its Goal, U.S. Officials Say." *The New York Times*, retrieved 11 August 2022.

Davie, H. G. W. *History of Military Logistics*, "Soviet Mechanized Corps Organization." 31 July 2018, accessed 8 June 2022. https://www.hgwdavie.com/blog/2018/7/12/soviet-mechanised-corps.

Duthel, Heinz. *Global Secret and Intelligence Services: Hidden Systems that Deliver Unforgettable Customer Service.* Norderstedt, Germany: Books on Demand, 2014.

Emmett, Stuart B. T. *Strafvollzugslager der SS und Polizei: Himmler's Wartime Institutions for the Detention of Waffe-SS and Polizei Criminals.* Croydon, U.K.: Fonthill Media Ltd, 2017.

Frieser, Karl-Heinz (editor and contributing author), Klaus Schmider, Klaus Schönherr, Gerhard Schreiber, Krisztian Ungvary, and Bernd Wegner. *Germany and the Second World War, Vol. VIII: The Eastern Front 1943–1944—The War in the East and on Neighboring Fronts.* Oxford: Clarendon Press, 2017.

Friessner, Johannes. *Verratene Schlachten, die Tragödie der deutschen Wehrmacht in Rumänien.* Hamburg: Holsten-Verlag, 1956.

Glantz, David, *et al.*, Proceedings, 1986 Art of War Symposium, *From the Vistula to the Oder: Soviet Offensive Operations—October 1944 – March 1945.* Carlisle, PA: U.S. Army War College Center for Land Warfare, 1986.

Gosztony, Peter. *Endkampf an der Donau 1944/45.* Vienna: Verlag Fritz Molden, 1969.

Gruber, Ruth Ellen. "A Border as Crossroad for Culture." *The New York Times*, 18 November 2005. New York: The New York Times Corporation.

Guderian, Heinz. *Panzer Leader*. Cambridge, MA: Da Capo Press, 1996.

Hoettl, Wilhelm. *The Secret Front: The Inside Story of Nazi Political Espionage*. London: Weidenfeld & Nicholson, 1953.

Höhne, Heinz. *The Order of the Death's Head: The Story of Hitler's SS*. New York: Ballantine Books, 1971.

Holtz, Bärbel. *Die Protokolle des Preußischen Staatsministeriums*. Hildesheim, Germany: Olms-Weidmann, 2001.

Ingrao, Christian. *The Dirlewanger Brigade: The History of the Black Hunters*. New York: Skyhorse Publishing, 2011.

Jerome, Georges and Phillip Nix. *The Uniformed Police Forces of the Third Reich 1933–1945*. Solna, Sweden: Leandoer & Ekholm Fölag, 2006.

Kern, Erich. *Dance of Death*. London: Collins Clear-Type Press, 1951.

Kern, Erich. *Die Letzte Schlacht: Ungarn 1944–45*. Göttingen, Germany: Verlag K. W. Schütz, 1960.

Klausch, Hans-Peter. *Antifaschisten in SS-Uniform. Schicksal und Widerstand der deutschen politischen KZ-Häftlingen, Zuchthaus- und Wehrmachtsgefangenen in der SS-Sonderformation Dirlewanger*. Bremen: Edition Temmen, 1993.

Kovtun, Ivan and Dmitry Zhukov. *Partisan Hunters: The Dirlewanger Brigade*. Moscow: Veche Publishing, 2018. 409–10.

Krannhals, Hanns von. *Der Warschauer Aufstand 1944*. Frankfurt: Bernhard und Graefe Verlag, 1964.

Kuberski, Hubert. "The Finale of a War Criminal's Existence: Mysteries Surrounding Oskar Dirlewanger's Death." *Studia z Dziejów Rosji i Europy Środkowo-Wschodniej*, LIV, 4. Warsaw: Instytut Historii PAN, 2019.

Kuklińska, Soraya. *Oskar Dirlewanger: SS-Sonderkommando "Dirlewanger."* Warsaw: Instytut Pamięci Narodowej, 2021.

Landwehr, Richard. "The Evolution of the 36. Waffen-Grenadier Division der SS." *Siegrunen*, No. 42, 1987. New York: Merriam Press.

Lilla, Joachim. *Statisten in Uniform: Die Mitglieder des Reichstages 1933–1945*. Düsseldorf: Droste Verlag, 2004.

Logusz, Michael O. *Galicia Division: The Waffen-SS 14th Grenadier Division 1943–1945*. Atglen, PA: Schiffer Military History, 1997.

Lombardi, Andrea. *Cacciatori Di Uomini: L'SS-Sonderkommando "Dirlewanger," la più spietata unità antipartigiana di Hitler*. Genova, Italy: Associazione Culturale, 2018.

Loza, Dmitriy. *Commanding the Red Army's Sherman Tanks: The World War II Memoirs of Hero of the Soviet Union Dmitriy Loza*. Lincoln, NE: University of Nebraska Press, 1996.

MacLean, French L. *The Cruel Hunters: SS-Sonderkommando Dirlewanger, Hitler's most notorious anti-partisan unit*. Atglen, PA: Schiffer Military History, 1998.

Megargee, Geoffrey P., Martin Dean, and Mel Hecker, eds. *The United States Holocaust Memorial Museum Encyclopedia of Camps and Ghettos, 1933–1945 Volume II: Ghettos in German-Occupied Eastern Europe, Parts A and B*. Bloomington, IN: Indiana University Press, 2012.

Mehner, Kurt. *Die geheimen Tagesberichter der Deutschen Wehrmachtsführung im Zweiten Weltkrieg 1939–1945*, Band 11 1. September 1944 – 31. Dezember 1944. Osnabrück: Biblio Verlag, 1984.

Mehner, Kurt. *Die Deutsche Wehrmacht 1939–1945: Führung und Truppe*. Norderstedt, Germany: Militär-Verlag Klaus D. Patzwall, 1993.

Mehner, Kurt. *Die Waffen-SS und Polizei 1939–1945: Vol. 3, Führung und Truppe*. Norderstedt, Germany: Militär-Verlag Klaus D. Patzwall, 1995.

Melnyk, Michael. *The History of the Galician Division of the Waffen-SS, Vol. 2: Stalin's Nemesis*. London: Fonthill Media Ltd, 2016.

Michaelis, Rolf. *Das SS-Sonderkommando Dirlewange: Vom Warschauer Aufstand bis zum Kessel von Halbe.* Berlin: Dörfler Verlag, 2003.

Michaelis, Rolf. *The SS-Sonderkommando "Dirlewanger:" A Memoir.* Atglen, PA: Schiffer Military History, 2013.

Mitcham, Samuel W. *The German Defeat in the East, 1944–45.* Mechanicsburg, PA: Stackpole Books, 2001.

Momm, Harald. *Pferde Reiter und Trophäen.* Munich: Copress-Verlag Hoffmann & Hass, 1957.

Moore, John P. *Führerliste der Waffen-SS,* Parts 1–4. Portland, OR: J. P. Moore Publishing, 2003.

Nevenkin, Kamen. *Fire Brigades: The Panzer Divisions 1943–1945.* Winnipeg, Canada: J. J. Fedorowicz Publishing, Inc., 2008.

Niehorster, Leo W. G. *The Royal Hungarian Army, 1920–1945, Volume 1: Organization and History.* Privately published, Leo W. G. Niehorster, 1998.

Pfeiffer, Roland. "Zur Geschichte der SS-Einheit Dirlewanger 1940-45." (Unpublished Manuscript, 24 September 2020. 174 pp.).

Pohl, Dieter. *Die Herrschaft der Wehrmacht: Deutsche Militärbesatzung und einheimische Bevölkerung in der Sowjetunion 1941–1944.* Munich: Oldenbourg Wissenschaftsverlag GmbH, 2009.

Prečan, Vilém. *Slovenské Národné Povstanie: Dokumenty* (The Slovak National Uprising: Documents). Bratislava: Vydavateľstvo Politickej Literatúry, 1965.

Reimpel, Gerhard. "Gottlob Berger, Ein Schwabengeneral der Tat" 45–59. In *Die SS: Elite unter dem Totenkopf: 30 Lebensläufe* by Ronald Smelser and Enrico Syring. Munich: Ferdinand Schoningh, 2000.

Reitlinger, Gerald. *The SS: Alibi of a Nation 1922–1945.* New York: The Viking Press, 1957.

Samo, Friede. *Oskar Dirlewanger und Gottlob Berger: Eine Täterfreundschaft am Rande.* Central Office of the State Justice Administrations for the Investigation of National Socialist Crimes, 11 November 2020. Accessed at https://www.fv-zentale-stelle.de on 11 September 2022.

Schneider, Jost W. *Their Honor was Loyalty! An Illustrated and Documentary History of the Knight's Cross Holders of the Waffen-SS and Police 1940–1945.* San Jose, CA: R. James Bender Publishing, 1977.

Schneider, Karl. *Auswärts eingesetzt: Bremer Polizeibataillone und der Holocaust.* Essen, Germany: Klartext Verlag, 2011.

von Senger und Etterlin, Dr. Fridolin M. *Die 24. Panzer-Division, vormals 1. Kavallerie-Division 1939–1945.* Neckargemund, Germany: Kurt Vowinckel Verlag, 1962).

"Sie haben etwas gutzumachen: Ein Tatsachenbericht von Eisatz der Strafsoldaten." *Der Spiegel,* Issues 05, 14–18. Hamburg: Spiegel Verlag, 1951.

Soviet General Staff. *The Budapest Operation: An Operational-Strategic Study.* Edited and translated by Richard W. Harrison. Solihull, U.K.: Helion & Company Ltd, 2017).

Stein, George H. *The Waffen SS: Hitler's Elite Guard at War, 1939–45.* Ithaca, NY: Cornell University Press, 1984.

Számvéber, Norbert. *Days of Battle: Armoured Operations North of the River Danube, Hungary 1944–45.* Solihull, U.K.: Helion and Company, 2013.

Tessin, Georg. *Verbände und Truppen der deutschen Wehrmacht und der Waffen-SS im Zweiten Weltkrieg 1939–1945,* Band 5, *Die Landstreitkräfte 31-70* and Band 14, *Die Landstreitkräfte: Namensverbände,* 2. Auflage. Bissendorf, Germany: Biblio-Verlag, 1976.

Tieke, Wilhelm and Friedrich Rebstock. *Horst Wessel: The Combat History of the 18. SS-Panzer-Grenadier-Division.* Winnipeg, Canada: J. J. Fedorowicz Books, 2015.

Trevor-Roper, H. R. *Hitler's Secret Conversations 1941–1944.* New York: Signet Books, 1961.

Venohr, Wolfgang. *Aufstand in der Tatra: Der Kampf um die Slowakei 1939–1944.* Königstein, Germany: Athenäum Verlag, 1979.

Voigt, Horst. *Die verlor'nen Haufen: Sondertruppen zur Frontbewährung im 2. Weltkrieg: Ein Beitrag zu ihrer Geschichte.* Munich: Schild-Verlag, 2010.

Wachsmann, Nilolaus. *KL: A History of the Nazi Concentration Camps.* New York: Farrar, Straus and Giroux, 2015.

Westermann, Edward B. *Hitler's Police Battalions: Enforcing Racial War in the East.* Lawrence, KS: University Press of Kansas, 2005.

Yerger, Mark. *Waffen-SS Commanders: The Army, Corps, and Divisional Leaders of Legend*, Vol. 2. Atglen, PA: Schiffer Military History, 1999.

Ziemke, Earl F. *Stalingrad to Berlin: The German Defeat in the East.* Washington, D.C.: U.S. Army Center of Military History, 1966.

Diaries and Letters

Buchhorn, Ernst. Member, *SS-Sonderkommando Dirlewanger.* Letter to Sister Maria, 11 July 1944.

Dobrak, Erich. Member, *11. Kompanie, SS-Sturmbrigade Dirlewanger.* Letter, 6 November 1944.

Haake, Günther. Member, *357. Inf.Div.* "Der Abwehrkampf der 6./AR 357 an der Ostfront 1944/45." Privately published manuscript, 1970.

Hafner, Otto. "Transdanubisches Tagebuch, Briefe und Erinnerungen, 1944–1945." Gemünd, Austria: Unpublished private manuscript, 16 September 1979.

Karbe, Jürgen. Member, *357. Inf.Div.* Tagebuch des Ia – Generalstabsoffizier, 1944–45.

Karow, Wolfgang. Member, 357. Inf.Div., Berlin-Lichterfelde. Letter, 22 March 1958.

M., Franz. Member, *II. Btl./SS-Sonderkommando Dirlewanger.* Letter to Hermann N., 13 December 1944.

Malina, Eugen. Member, *357. Inf.Div.* Various letters and diary entries from a staff officer in the *357. Inf.Div.* Unknown location: unpublished private papers, undated.

Mlčzoch, Dr. Felix. Member, *K.Gr. Hafner.* "Das Kriegsende." Vienna: unpublished private manuscript, undated.

Official Correspondence and Records

von dem Bach, Erich, Chef der Bandenkampfverbände, Polizeitruppen und Schulen, Tagebuch 1941–1945. Bundesarchiv: R 020/000045b Folio 1–117.

Bayerisches Landeskriminalamt, IIIa/SK Tagebuch Nr. 489/62. Vernehmungsniederschrift der Oberst a.D. Harald Momm, 28 May 1962 (5 pages).

Bundesarchiv Koblenz. Zentrale Stelle der Landesjustizverwaltung Ludwigsburg AR-Z 302 AR 509/70, Band III Bl. 714: Tatort: Weiss-Russland. Abgegeben am 22 February 1971.

Bundesarchiv Koblenz. Zentrale Stelle der Landesjustizverwaltung Ludwigsburg, B-162/19830, Bisheriges Ermittlungsergebnis über das Sonderkommando "Dirlewanger," 19 September 1963.

Bundesarchiv-Militärarchiv, Freiburg. Official BA-MA History of the Dirlewanger Brigade, accessed on 11 June 2021 at https://balsi.de/Weltkrieg/Einheiten/Waffen-SS/SS-Infanterie-Einheiten/SS-Brigaden/SS-Brigade-Dirlewanger.htm.

Bundesarchiv-Militärarchiv, Freiburg. Extensive collections of original unit documents on the activities of the Dirlewanger Sondereinheit from January 1942 to June 1944, found in the following file folders: RS 3-36/1a; RS 3-36/1b; RS 3-36/2; RS 3-36/3; RS 3-36/4; RS 3-36/5; RS 3-36/6; RS 3-36/7; RS 3-36/8; RS 3-36/9; RS 3-36/10; RS 3-36/11a; RS 3-36/11b; RS 3-36/12; RS 3-36/13; RS 3-36/14; RS 3-36/15; RS 3-36/16; RS 3-36/17; RS 3-36/18; RS 3-36/19; RS 3-36/20; RS 3-36/21; RS 3-36/22; RS 3-36/23; and RS 70-38.

Dirlewanger, SS-Oberführer Oskar. "Bericht über den feindlichen Panzereinbruch am 15.12.1944 in Raum von Ipolysag." Brig.Gef.St., dated 17 December 1944. CAMO 500-12472-380, pp. 0086–0089.

German-Russian Project to Digitize German Documents in Archives of the Russian Federation (*Deutsch-Russisch Projekt zur Digitalisierung Deutscher Dokumente in Archiven der Russischen Föderation*): Accessed at GermandocsinRussia.org in Stock 500, Finding Aid 12472 (1st through 10th Armies) Files 382 - 408 (AOK 6/Armeegruppe Fretter-Pico).

Höfle, Hermann, SS-Obergruppenführer und General der Waffen-SS und Polizei. Tagebuch, der Deutsche Befehlshaber in der Slowakei, Tagebuch Nr. 376/45 geheim, Betr: Brigade Dirlewanger, dated 6 January 1945.

International Military Tribunal, IMT Nuremberg Archives H-919. Testimony of Hans Jüttner to the International Military Tribunal, 23 May 1946.

International Military Tribunal, *Trials of War Criminals before the Nuremberg Military Tribunals under Control Council Law No. 10*, "The Ministries Case," Testimony of the Accused, Vol. 13. (Washington, D.C.: U.S. Government Printing Office, 1949), 508–51.

International Military Tribunal, *Trials of War Criminals before the Nuremberg Military Tribunals under Control Council Law No. 10*, "The Ministries Case," Closing Statements, Vol. 14. (Washington, D.C.: U.S. Government Printing Office, 1949), 531–32, 541–46.

Kriegstagebuch, Heeresgruppe Süd (H.Gr. Süd), Abteilung Ia, 1–15 and 16–31 December 1944.

Kriegstagebuch, Heeresgruppe Süd, Abteilung Ia Meldungen und Befehle, 1–31 December 1944.

Kriegstagebuch, Höherer SS und Polizeiführer (HSSPF) Slowakei, 1–31 December 1944.

Kriegstagebuch, Armeeoberkommando (AOK) 6/Armeegruppe Fretter-Pico, Abteilung Ia Meldungen und Befehle, 11–25 December 1944.

Kriegstagebuch, Armeeoberkommando (AOK) 6/Armeegruppe Balck, Abteilung Ia Meldungen und Befehle, 26–31 December 1944.

Kriegstagebuch, Armeeoberkommando (AOK) 6/Armeegruppe Fretter-Pico, Abteilung Ia, 11–19 December 1944.

Kriegstagebuch, LXXII. Armee-Korps, Abteilung Ia, 1–31 December 1944.

Kriegstagebuch, LXXII. Armee-Korps, Abteilung Ia, Meldungen und Befehle, Abt. Ia/III Nr. 283744 geheim, Betr: Überlaufen von Teilen 10./SS-Sturm-Rgt. 2, dated 18 December 1944.

Kriminalpolizei Stade K424, Vernehmungsniederschrift Gustav Brusberg, 18 December 1975.

Landgericht Bremen, Anm. 378 Vernehmungsniederschrift von Karl Schneider, S. 125, vom 18 February 1952 Az.: OH 2024/50 (E).

Oberstaatsanwalt Flensburg, 2 Js 700/61, Vernehmungsniederschrift Peter Gossens, 5 May 1963 and 20 May 1976.

Slovak State Archive, Bratislava. Ministry of the Interior of the Slovak Republic, District Peoples' Court, Case Number 170/1948, Interrogation of Rudolf Bretschneider, ex-member of the Dirlewanger Brigade, Bratislava 12 June 1948 (92 pp.).

Slovak State Archive, Bratislava. Ministry of the Interior of the Slovak Republic, District Peoples' Court, Case Number 164/1948, Interrogation of Rudolf Hossinger, ex-member of the Dirlewanger Brigade, Bratislava 28 June 1948 (123 pp.).

Slovak State Archive, Bratislava. Ministry of the Interior of the Slovak Republic, District Peoples' Court, Case Number 162/1948, Interrogation of Konrad Kristmann, ex-member of the Dirlewanger Brigade, Bratislava 16 February 1946 (176 pp.).

Slovak State Archive, Bratislava. Ministry of the Interior of the Slovak Republic, District Peoples' Court, Case Number 161/1948, Interrogation of Erich Kühn, ex-member of the Dirlewanger Brigade, Bratislava 28 June 1948 (125 pp.).

Slovak State Archive, Bratislava. Ministry of the Interior of the Slovak Republic, District Peoples' Court, Case Number 169/1948, Interrogation of Hans Römer, ex-member of the Dirlewanger Brigade, Bratislava 28 June 1948 (82 pp.).

ТАНКОВЫЙ ФРОНТ 1939–1945 (Tank Front 1939–1945). Order of Battle of the 9th Guards Tank Corps and subordinate units. http://tankfront.ru/ussr/mk/gvmk09.html, accessed 20 August 2022.

TsAMO (Central Archives of the Ministry of Defense of the Russian Federation). Journal of Military Operations of the IX Guards Mechanized Corps during the Budapest Offensive Operation, by Lieutenant Colonel Sobolev, 1–31 December 1944. Fund: 3443, Inventory 1, File 77, beginning with Frame 170, Memory of the People, https://pamyat-naroda.ru/documents/view/?id=134588529, accessed 7 March 2022.

TsAMO (Central Archives of the Ministry of Defense of the Russian Federation), Journal of Military Operations of the 6th Guards Tank Army, by Tank Major General Troops Shtromberg, Colonel Shklyaruk, and Guards Major Svyatkovsky, 1–31 October 1944. Fund: 339, Inventory: 5179, File: 4, Sheet of the beginning of the document in the file: 208, Memory of the People, https://pamyat-naroda.ru/documents/view/?id=154015847, accessed 10 June 2022.

Uckermann, Oberst i.G. Paul. "Bericht über die nach Übernahme des Abschnittes Ipolysag befohlene Ablösung des II. Btl./Pz.Gren.Rgt. 26 am 14.12.44," 2. Sturmregiment/SS-Sturmbrig. Dirlewanger, dated 17 December 1944. CAMO 500-12472-380, 0084–0085.

U.S. National Archives and Records Administration (NARA), College Park, Maryland: National Archives Microcopy Series T-175 concerning records of the Reichsführer-SS, SS-Führungshauptamt and SS-Hauptamt including the Dirlewanger Brigade (Rolls 140, 141, 178, 179, and 225) and Series T-354 combat units of the Waffen-SS including the Dirlewanger Brigade (Rolls 648 and 651).

Index

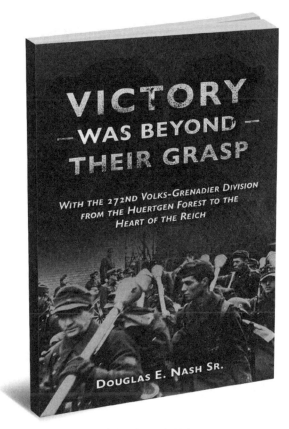

9781636240541

"Nash illustrates clearly the late 1944 situation of the German Army in the west in ways not always considered… To be sure, the book does assume that the reader is familiar with the 1944 campaign in the west. Even the novice, however, would profit from Nash's knowledge of the German Army, its men and equipment at that stage of the war. Thus, for both students of the German Army in World War II as well as those interested in the late 1944 campaign, this is a must-read."—*The NYMAS Review*

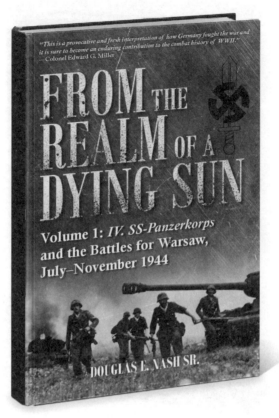

9781612006352

"This book is definitely written for grognards, with a level of detail and trivia that would make David Glantz, the dean of Eastern Front operational history, proud."—*New York Journal of Books*

"The book is eminently readable and, unlike a myriad of other books that focus on units, never seems to get mired in writing mud but moves along briskly. Overall the volume is well-illustrated, and the reader will sense this is a well-researched book. Critically the book is well-steeped in doctrinal materials from both sides of the hill in a deft manner."—*ARMOR Magazine*

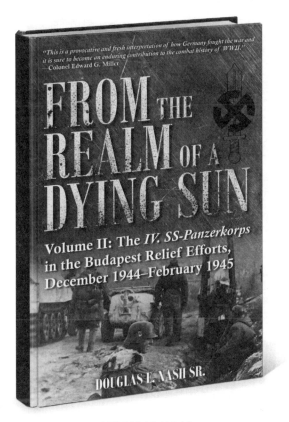

9781636240541

"Through its focus upon providing a detailed study of an often overlooked chapter of the war on the Russian Front, volume two of *From the Realm of a Dying Sun* will likely stand as one of the foremost accounts of the Budapest relief operation for years to come. Concurrently, the series will also likely prove to be the definitive history of the IV. SS-Panzer Corps. It is recommended for both the dedicated military historian and general readers alike."
—Michigan War Studies Review

"The scholarship that went into these books is impeccable, with the author deftly weaving primary and secondary sources to form an excellent and thought provoking picture of this period in the Second World War."
—Globe at War

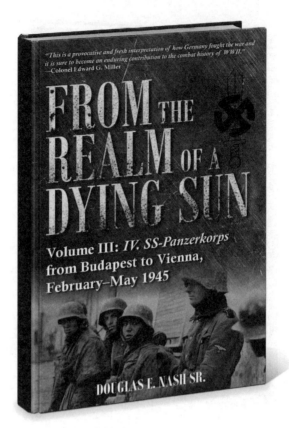

9781636240541

"For anyone with the slightest interest in the Eastern Front, this concluding volume of the trilogy of IV SS Panzer-korps is simply a must-read. Nash has done yeoman's work in marshaling sources for this period of the war when records and record-keeping went into an abeyance, from the Lake Balaton Offensive to keeping the Hungarian oil fields."—*ARMOR Magazine*

"Doug Nash has written not just one classic, but three works that stand on their own. His ability to provide academic and professional expertise to the story of the IV SS Panzer Corps is reflected in these accounts of fighting for three of Europe's great capital cities: Warsaw, Budapest, and Vienna. Previous western accounts of World War II overlooked these inclusive events from July 1944 through May 1945. Nash graphically brings this to life with words and images with a model of the operational account."—*Charles D. Melson, Chief Historian, Retired, U.S. Marine Corps University, author of* **Kleinkrieg**